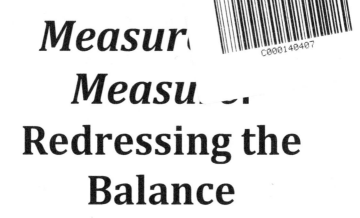

Measure for Measure. Redressing the Balance

A Critical Reappraisal of Shakespeare's Play

by

P. S. Miller

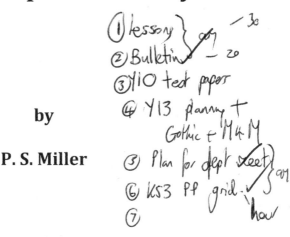

For Carol and Kate

whose love and support have been unstinting

Dr Paul Miller was educated at Barnsley Holgate Grammar School and at Keble College, Oxford, where he was Holroyd Scholar in English. He was Head of English for many years at Worth School, West Sussex, and at Stowe School, Buckingham. He has taught at the Queen's University of Belfast and at Exeter University. He had also given lectures on his doctoral research at Bristol, Buckingham, Liverpool, and Oxford Universities. He retired from teaching in 2015.

Table of Contents

Preface

Shakespeare's *Measure for Measure* has proved an unusually controversial play since its earliest recorded performance in 1604. It has provoked extreme and conflicting views, not merely because of the fluctuations of contemporary tastes, but also because the overall interpretation of the play, and the moral status of many of its characters, are by no means self-evident. Even its literary merit was disputed in the same century in which it appeared when, during the Restoration, it was dismissed as poorly written and dramatically unappealing. Such opinions were reflected in late-seventeenth-century stage-productions that treated the play as a repository of situations, characters, and lines that could be freely adapted, better to comply with contemporary tastes. In the centuries that followed, the textual cruces, the morally questionable characters, and the ethical conundrums encountered in *Measure for Measure* led to sometimes drastic editing of the play in performance, which did little to sway critical opinion in favour of what Shakespeare might actually have written. The reputation of *Measure for Measure* suffered particularly in the Victorian era, which was intolerant of any text that savoured of immorality. Critics were battling over mutually exclusive readings long before the Twentieth Century, when entrenched positions were dug more deeply. In recent years, political interpretations, some influenced by modern critical theory, have challenged more conservative perceptions of the play among theatregoers and readers. All well and good— provided that a critic or director, striving for innovation, does not perversely demand of *Measure for Measure* (as Angelo does of Isabella), 'Fit thy consent to my sharp appetite' (II, iv, 160).

In his widely-praised study of *Shakespeare's Language* (London and New York: Penguin, 2000), Frank Kermode expressed misgivings about these 'prevailing modes of Shakespeare criticism' (p. ix). He deplored the 'recurring need to find something different to say', evident when critics focus on 'topics that happen to interest the writer more than Shakespeare's words' (p. viii). From the outset, therefore, Kermode proposed to address his work to

> a non-professional audience with an interest in Shakespeare that has not, I believe, been well served by modern critics, who on the whole seem to have little time for his language.
>
> [p. vii]

By taking its direction from Kermode's injunction to concentrate on Shakespeare's language for the benefit of the general reader, this book seeks to redress any critical imbalance in *Measure for Measure* studies by arbitrating between extreme and mutually contradictory opinions. The commentary has been shaped by thorough, impartial, textual analysis, offering possibilities and alternatives without pursuing one predetermined overview. It may make reference to aspects of recent critical theory, but does not treat evidence so selectively as to crush or otherwise to distort it into a single politically-correct mould. The purpose is to offer analysis that is 'measured' (that is, both moderate and carefully gauged), out of respect for Shakespeare's chosen title.

This book's proposed readership, like Kermode's, is not an academic *coterie*, but rather those willing to approach *Measure for Measure* with an open mind, exploring afresh the subtleties and challenges of the text. It is, nevertheless, well-nigh impossible to write a single analytical sentence about *Measure for Measure* without courting controversy, so violently does it polarise critical opinion. I do not, therefore, expect readers consistently to agree with me about vital aspects of the play. Often, our own critical reactions to a text become clear to us when we encounter another's opinions, only to recognise how strongly we differ. For some readers, this may be the principal value of this book. Those seeking to stimulate, to inform, or to develop their responses to the play should, nevertheless, welcome a non-partisan reading that thoroughly explores language, character, and context.

Accessibility is a prime objective of this study. Each chapter is divided into sections, with subheadings to facilitate navigation and to identify contexts. All chapters may be treated as free-standing essays, in that they may be read independently, without reference to the book as a whole. Nevertheless, in the order presented, they offer a comprehensive investigation of *Measure for Measure*. Although this plan has inevitably led to a certain degree of overlap between chapters, duplication has been avoided wherever possible.

By exploring radical human emotions, thoughts, motives, and behaviour, *Measure for Measure* encourages and rewards close critical examination. In response, this study scrutinizes all the speaking-roles in the play: each of the three protagonists—the Duke, Angelo, and Isabella—is allocated an individual chapter, while all the remaining characters are considered in chapters variously devoted to marriage ('The Lovers'), lawlessness ('The Underworld'), and authority ('Church and State'). For some, this aspect of the book may seem a reversion to the kind of character-analysis rejected by many modern critics. Robert N. Watson, however, offers a sturdy defence of the approach in his Introduction to the Arden Edition (Third Series) of *Measure for Measure* (London and New York: Bloomsbury, 2020):

> A talent that distinguished Shakespeare . . . was the psychological verisimilitude of his dramaturgy: his ability to create the illusion of full depth and individuality in his characters. . . . Watching the ways in which these psyches react and interact in moments of social crisis is a main part of the fascination and education Shakespeare's plays provide. . . . [I]t therefore seems valid to study the implied personalities of the play's characters, based on the text and on performance history. . . . Prominent critics have dismissed character analysis by saying that dramatic characters are really only a few black-and-white markings on a page; but it is hard to imagine what analysis of drama would in fact be feasible if scholars took that point to heart. [Pp. 56–7]

Granted, stage-creations cannot be discussed as if they were 'real' human beings, but must be recognised as dramatic constructs. Speculation would therefore be vain about what they might be feeling or thinking at a particular moment, or about what unseen circumstances might have motivated their actions. The putative emotions, thoughts, motives, and behaviour of characters—when unsupported by explicit textual evidence—must be attributed either to the audience's assumptions or to textual implications, rather than to any undocumented life that Shakespeare's dramatic creations might have beyond the text. In avoiding this pitfall, phrasing to suggest inference rather than certitude is necessary, although the result can sometimes seem verbose.

In his 1930 'Preface' to *Shakespeare's Problem Comedies* (London: Macmillan, 1931; repr. Harmondsworth: Penguin, 1969), William Witherle Lawrence included a significant proviso:

> The bibliography of Shakespeare is now so large that it is impossible to give credit for every borrowed idea, or to be sure that ideas which one thinks original may not lurk somewhere in print. [p. 12]

If the size of the Shakespeare bibliography was so formidable in 1930 that identifying derivative ideas and acknowledging borrowings was then a challenge, how much greater must the problem be now, after ninety years of further scholarship, especially with the proliferation since then of courses in English Literature in universities world-wide! Additionally, as this book was completed during coronavirus lockdown, it was not always possible for me to pursue references as scrupulously as I should have wished. I hope that any scholars who feel that my work derives unacknowledged ideas from them will console themselves with the recognition that imitation is the sincerest form of flattery. Your assistance, gratefully received, has enriched my appreciation of Shakespeare's achievements in *Measure for Measure*.

My ambition in undertaking this book was to increase the reader's enjoyment and understanding of a Shakespearian play that, for centuries, was seriously underrated. The result is the book that I might have wished to support my own reading when first I encountered *Measure for Measure* as a student.

Bredon
Worcestershire
July, 2020

Abbreviations

For the purposes of convenience and concision, references to the following important sources are abbreviated in the manner indicated.

Abbreviation	Full title
Braunmuller and Watson	A. R. Braunmuller and Robert N. Watson, eds., *Measure for Measure*: The Arden Shakespeare, Third Series (London and New York: Bloomsbury, 2020)
CUP	Cambridge University Press
ELH	*English Literary History* (periodical)
Geckle	George L. Geckle, ed., *Measure for Measure: Shakespeare: The Critical Tradition,* vol. 6 (London and New York: Athlone, 2001)
Kamps and Raber	Ivo Kamps and Karen Raber, eds., *William Shakespeare: Measure for Measure: Texts and Contexts* (Boston and New York: Bedford/St. Martin's, 2004)
Lever	J. W. Lever, ed., *Measure for Measure*: The Arden Shakespeare, Second Series (London and New York: Bloomsbury, 1965; repr. 2015)
OED	*Oxford English Dictionary* @ oed.com
OUP	Oxford University Press
PMLA	*Publications of the Modern Language Association* (periodical)
RES	*Review of English Studies* (periodical)
RSC	Royal Shakespeare Company, Stratford-upon-Avon
SS	*Shakespeare Survey* (periodical)

A Note on Major Sources

Quotations from *Measure for Measure* derive from the text printed by J. W. Lever in his Arden Edition, Second Series (London and New York: Bloomsbury, 1965; repr. 2015), itself closely based on the 1623 text of the First Folio of Shakespeare's plays. This text has been preferred to that of the recently-published Arden Edition, Third Series, edited by A. R. Braunmuller and Robert N. Watson (London and New York: Bloomsbury, 2020) for two reasons. First and foremost, the later Arden Edition was not available until I had completed this book in draft form; and second because, as Braunmuller concedes, 'This edition follows a practice of enquiring textual conservatism, sometimes in the face of editorial tradition' (p. 374). Some of the key readings discussed in my text (e.g. 'jades' or 'steeds', rather than ''weedes', at I, iii, 20) derive from the editorial tradition, and hence are the variants most frequently encountered in performance.

Generally, this study does not consider variant textual readings, which may be found in the footnotes of Lever's scholarly edition. Neither does it offer comprehensive comparison and analysis of sources and analogues: these are extensively presented and discussed both in Lever's edition and in the richly-furnished edition of Ivo Kamps and Karen Raber (*Measure for Measure: Texts and Contexts* [Boston and New York: Bedford/St. Martin's, 2004]).

Quotations from other plays and poems attributed to Shakespeare derive from Peter Alexander's edition of *The Complete Works* (London and Glasgow: Collins, 1951; repr. 1978).

References to influential historical opinions on the play and its characters, unless otherwise indicated in footnotes, may be found in George L. Geckle, ed., *Measure for Measure: Shakespeare: The Critical Tradition*, vol. 6 (London and New York: Athlone, 2001).

Biblical quotations derive from the Geneva Bible, the version best known to Shakespeare. The 1599 edition may be retrieved from https://www.biblegateway.com/versions/1599-Geneva-Bible-GNV/.

A Note on Authorship

We cannot confidently attribute every word of *Measure for Measure*, as presented in the First Folio of 1623, to Shakespeare. The playwright Thomas Middleton, the scribe Ralph Crane, certain players among the King's Men, or the compositor(s) responsible for setting the text, may have emended—or corrupted—Shakespeare's play before its publication.

A. R. Braunmuller, in the Third Series Arden Edition of *Measure for Measure*, acknowledges the possibility that Middleton (Shakespeare's associate and collaborator, and probably his successor as chief playwright to the King's Men) was responsible for one section of one early scene in the play. Braunmuller is hesitant, however, to attribute the authorship of any further passages to Middleton:

> Though evidence for Middleton's putative authorship of 1.2.1–78 is impressively wide-reaching, much of it is circumstantial, and his presence beyond this scene, and perhaps 4.1.7–23 and 4.3.1–19, remains conjectural. . . . Middleton's presence in the play should still be seen as an intriguing hypothesis rather than a fully proven attribution.
>
> [pp. 371–2]

There is a scholarly consensus that Ralph Crane, employed as a scribe by Shakespeare's players, provided the text of *Measure for Measure* as set in the First Folio. Braunmuller concludes (p. 367) that Crane is likely to have copied the text, not from Shakespeare's foul papers, but from the playbook of the King's Men, which would have been open to revisions, perhaps by hands other than Shakespeare's. As the text of *Measure for Measure* first appeared in print nearly twenty years after the play's first recorded performance, there was ample opportunity for such emendation and interpolation. However, we cannot at present be certain of the nature, extent, or authorship of any assumed alterations.

Because of these uncertainties, and for the sake of brevity and convenience, whenever reference is made to 'Shakespeare' in this study, that name is intended to encompass any playwright(s), scribe(s), actor(s), or compositor(s) who may have altered, added to, or subtracted from Shakespeare's text before its appearance in the First Folio, from which all editions of the play ultimately derive.

Chapter 1

Opening Perspectives

Measure for Measure is neither the most famous nor the most popular of Shakespeare's plays among modern audiences and readers; but it has strong recommendations as a quintessential play for today. Although it explores contentious issues that affected Church and state at the beginning of the reign of James I, the extent to which it continues to hold up a mirror to society in the second decade of the Twenty-First Century is remarkable. *Measure for Measure* suffered (at best) neglect and (at worst) denigration for over three hundred years of its history; but the issues that it considers are both timeless and trenchant: for example, the corruptive influence of both power and lust, especially when they coexist in one person; the tension between individual integrity and familial obligations; the suffering that results from gender inequality, both in personal relationships and in wider society; the question of whether marriage is validated by voluntary mutual commitment rather than by social obligation or religious ritual; and the prerequisite of forgiveness in healing personal divisions. In addition, themes associated specifically with forensic issues include the disturbing divergence between the law and justice, the challenges of tempering justice with mercy, the extent to which the law should seek to enforce standards of personal (including sexual) morality, and the injustices faced by victims of abuse seeking redress from a prejudiced, sceptical, or wilfully ignorant society. All these issues, important enough to Shakespeare and his contemporaries to provide the thematic foundations of *Measure for Measure*, have sustained their relevance or acquired still greater relevance with the passage of time.

Why, then, has *Measure for Measure* not been performed or read more frequently over the centuries? A major reason is that this play, although consistently absorbing, is not an easy play to watch or to study. It makes considerable demands on audiences and readers, who cannot simply sit back to be entertained by the play as they might be by some of Shakespeare's more readily accessible 'happy comedies'. Especially in Act II, *Measure for Measure* becomes a play of ideas that requires sustained intellectual engagement from the viewer or reader. The morally complex political and social issues that the play presents are uncomfortable to contemplate because, rather than seeking refuge in facile solutions, *Measure for Measure* generally tends to perplex us with issues that we might expect to be resolved, but which are not.[1] In short, this is an intelligent play that requires an intelligent response.

Well before the end of the century in which it was written, however, *Measure for Measure* began attracting adverse criticism. In 1672, John Dryden complained that the play (together with *The Winter's Tale* and *Love's Labour's Lost*) is 'so meanly written, that the comedy neither caused your mirth, nor the serious part your concernment.'[2] Such a damning judgement demands a response. Some of the early writing in *Measure for Measure* ranks with the very best of Shakespeare's tragedies in its poetic exploration of challenging political and moral issues. The climaxes in the first half of the play—the extraordinary cerebral (and, in some productions, physical) tussle between Isabella and Angelo towards the end of Act II, and the powerfully emotional exchanges in the prison between Claudio and his sister early in Act III—have a dramatic

---

[1] Although it could be argued that marriage is presented in the final scene as a panacea, some more recent productions have, quite legitimately, challenged that interpretation by presenting Isabella as rejecting the Duke's concluding offers of marriage. See Chapter 8, 'Performances in More Recent Years', especially pp. 539–542.

[2] 'Dramatic Poetry of the Last Age', quoted by C. K. Stead, ed., *Shakespeare*: Measure for Measure: *A Casebook* (London: Macmillan, 1971), p. 12.

intensity comparable with the very best of Shakespeare's writing. The second half of the play, although more contrived and improbable than the first, enjoys the ingenious convolutions of plot and the concluding multiple marriages (four in total—not surpassed elsewhere) encountered in Shakespeare's most successful comedies. Furthermore, the concluding scene of *Measure for Measure* satisfies that enduring passion for courtroom drama in which complications and vagaries maintain suspense until the very end. The range of characters in the play (nobility, clergy, and commons) is unusually wide and varied, corresponding to the range of settings, from court to prison, from convent to brothel. There is much here to enjoy, to admire, and—especially—to ponder.

Plot Outline

Those familiar with *Measure for Measure* may safely ignore the summary that follows. An initial synopsis should, nevertheless, be helpful to those uncertain of the play's major characters and events, or to those wishing to refresh their memories.

In the first half of the *Measure for Measure*, Vincentio, the Duke of Vienna, departs mysteriously from his court, deputing Angelo, a man renowned for asceticism and stringency, as governor in his place. Although Vincentio's ostensible reason for appointing Angelo may be to correct the licentious conduct that is rife in Viennese society, it emerges that the Duke is also testing his new deputy, whom he expects to be corrupted by power.

Angelo proves a puritanical character, preoccupied with regulating human sexual activity. He sentences to death a noble youth named Claudio for impregnating Julietta,[3] Claudio's

---

[3] Throughout this study, the name Julietta (as used by Claudio for his betrothed when first he names her at I, ii, 135) is preferred to 'Juliet', the name by which she is more frequently known in the play. This is simply to avoid any confusion that might arise between her and the

betrothed. Claudio's sister, a novice nun named Isabella, is persuaded by Lucio, Claudio's dissolute friend, to petition Angelo to repeal the death-sentence on her brother. Isabella's virtuous conduct and speech, however, inflame Angelo with unprecedented sexual desire. He demands her virginity as the price of repeal for her brother. When informed of Angelo's proposed bargain, Claudio pleads with Isabella to save him by complying. Outraged, she refuses.

The Duke, in disguise as Friar Lodowick, has been observing these events. In the second half of the play, he informs Isabella about Mariana, Angelo's former betrothed, whom Angelo cruelly rejected but who still mourns for his love. The disguised Duke persuades Isabella to involve Mariana in the 'bed-trick': to save Claudio's life, Mariana will take Isabella's place at Angelo's nocturnal tryst, Angelo remaining unaware of the deception. Meanwhile, in encounters with Lucio, the disguised Duke hears himself slandered as sexually promiscuous, drunken, foolish, and ignorant.

His desires satisfied, Angelo breaks his oath to pardon Claudio and instead demands the prisoner's head. In response, the Duke devises the 'head-trick' to deceive Angelo by substituting the head of a dead pirate who (fortuitously) closely resembles Claudio. Vincentio then proclaims his return to Vienna to reassume authority in the state, inviting any with grievances about Angelo's government to present their petitions. While retaining his disguise as a friar, he instructs Mariana and Isabella how they should accuse Angelo.

In the final scene, Vincentio reappears before the people in his ducal guise. Having heard Isabella and Mariana present equivocal accounts that they were instructed to employ in evidence against Angelo, the Duke pretends to disbelieve the accusers, appointing Angelo to judge his own case. The Duke

---

more famous Juliet from Shakespeare's earlier tragedy involving young lovers.

then departs to reassume his disguise as a friar, returning publicly to condemn the administration of justice in Vienna.

Once the pseudo-friar has cast off his garb to reveal his true identity as the Duke, he passes sentence on Angelo. As Claudio has been saved by the Duke from execution, and as Isabella has preserved her virginity, Angelo's potentially greatest crimes were never committed. The Duke can therefore exercise clemency on Angelo as part of a more general amnesty that also involves Claudio and (to a substantial extent) Lucio. The play ends in multiple marriages, performed or anticipated: Angelo and Mariana; Claudio and Julietta; and Lucio and Kate Keepdown (the woman whom he has admitted impregnating); with the Duke proposing matrimony to Isabella.

The first half of the *Measure for Measure*, although summarised here in two paragraphs, is the most profound and intriguing part of the play. It is the dramatic context in which the painful political and ethical conundrums, and the complex psychology of the characters (particularly Isabella, Angelo, and Claudio), are explored in the greatest depth. In these respects, it belongs in the tradition of Shakespeare's tragedies. In the second half of the play, (from III, i, 150), we move into the territory of the comedies: under the general direction of the enigmatic Duke, narrative development and plot-resolutions (involving multiple unforeseen twists) predominate. Shakespeare, nevertheless, skilfully maintains the audience's interest in the 'tragic' protagonists during this lengthy coda, with further startling but convincing insights into the characters of both Angelo and Isabella.

Structure and Form[4]

Shakespeare habitually provides clear indications of the overriding thematic issues of a play early in its opening scene.

---

[4] Problems concerning the treatment of time in the play are discussed in detail by Lever, pp. xiv–xvii and xxii–xxiii. See also Appendix 1 of this study, pp. 567–576.

Measure for Measure is no exception. Before a dozen lines have been spoken, Shakespeare has sketched out his structural plan. The play will seek

> Of government the properties to unfold. [I, i, 3]

Furthermore, if the members of an audience are to judge the characters and events of this play with any confidence, then they (like Escalus, the learned lord addressed here by Vincentio) will need to be conversant with

> The nature of our people,
> Our city's institutions, and the terms
> For common justice. . . . [I, i, 9–11]

In developing these lines subsequently, Shakespeare provides his audience with a thorough dramatic induction: Act I demonstrates the range of the 'people' and 'institutions' of Vienna, while Act II illustrates 'the terms / For common justice' in investigating the workings of secular and religious authority in the state.

Shakespeare presents the whole gamut of Viennese society in the first Act of *Measure for Measure*. The audience is introduced to the sophistication of the ducal court in scene i, only to be transported abruptly in scene ii to the underworld of Vienna's backstreets and brothels. Having explored, by this bold juxtaposition, the extremes of secular life in the city, the play then discovers Vienna's spiritual life by visiting religious institutions in consecutive scenes: a friary in scene iii, and a nunnery in scene iv.

In this opening Act, as elsewhere in this play, structure—involving the sequencing of themes, events, and settings, for dramatic purposes—closely determines the form of the language. The versatility of Shakespeare's dialogue and its appropriateness to context are everywhere apparent, from the earnest and often sophisticated poetry of the noble characters—in verse ranging from the authoritative to the penitent—to the coarser prose of the comic underclasses.[5] This contrast is underlined towards the end of the second scene, in the exchanges between the nobly-born Claudio, who speaks in refined, philosophical poetry, and the dissolute Lucio, who responds in jocular, flippant prose:

> *Cla.*   So every scope by the immoderate use
> Turns to restraint. Our natures do pursue,
> Like rats that ravin down their proper bane,
> A thirsty evil; and when we drink, we die.
>   *Lucio.*   If I could speak so wisely under an arrest, I
> would send for certain of my creditors. [I, ii, 119–24]

The only profane intrusion into the sacred world of scenes iii and iv occurs when Lucio petitions Isabella in the nunnery—but, as if to show his deference for his surroundings, he speaks entirely in verse in that context (as he sometimes does during court-proceedings in II, ii and V, i)):

> I would not, though 'tis my familiar sin,
> With maids to seem the lapwing, and to jest
> Tongue far from heart, play with all virgins so.
> I hold you as a thing enskied and sainted
> By your renouncement, an immortal spirit,
> And to be talk'd with in sincerity,
> As with a saint. [I, iv, 31–7]

Although Lucio's tone in these lines might be ironic—and Isabella's immediate response (at line 38) suggests that she believes no less—the sophisticated language in which he expresses himself suggests a man who is self-consciously

---

[5] The dialogue of *Measure for Measure*, as in other plays by Shakespeare and his contemporaries, is frequently conducted in blank verse: unrhymed iambic pentameters. In this play, rhyming couplets occur intermittently; for example, as gnomic utterances, and to denote the end of scenes (e.g. I, iii, 53–4). The versification of the Duke's asides in Acts III and IV, which varies considerably, is discussed in Chapter 2, 'The Duke's Monologues', pp. 87–96.

adapting his diction, imagery, and general expression to match the solemnity of the environment in which he finds himself.

Act II, the intellectual core of *Measure for Measure*, is one of Shakespeare's greatest dramatic achievements. It scrutinises the complex issues of law, authority, and morality that are central to the play. The scene shifts between the purlieus of the ducal court (II, i; II, ii; and II, iv) and the interior of Vienna's prison (II, iii). The three court-scenes consider the appropriate secular response to illicit sexual activity, while the prison-scene offers the corresponding religious judgement on fornication and illegitimate conception.

The great debate between 'Mortality and mercy in Vienna' (I, i, 44) is introduced at the very opening of Act II, scene i, Angelo arguing for inflexible severity in enforcing the law, while Escalus pleads the cause of pragmatic leniency. For the duration of the Act, Angelo remains the sole spokesperson for unerring stringency in administering Vienna's statutes. Inevitably, however, his moral authority—and therefore the audience's respect for his doctrine—decreases as his corruption increases. The corresponding strict dogmatism of the Church is voiced by the Duke, in his disguise as Friar Lodowick, when he confesses Julietta in scene iii. Responsibility for arguing the case for mercy, on the other hand, passes from Escalus (scene i) to the Provost (scene ii) and thence to Isabella (scenes ii and iv) as the Act progresses. With his pragmatic philosophising in scene i, even Pompey, a member of the underclasses, offers earthy support for the principle of what Lucio will later call 'lenity to lechery' (III, ii, 94).

The dialogue of this second Act is predominantly conducted in skilfully modulated verse, the only major excursion into prose occurring after line forty of the first scene. Angelo's sententious (and latterly smug) verse with which the Act begins contrasts with Escalus's more moderate, diplomatic tone until the intrusion of three comic characters from the Viennese underworld: Elbow, Pompey, and Froth. Their clumsy speech seemingly infects the language of the two magistrates, as all then bluster and banter in prose:

> *Elbow.* . . . I am the poor Duke's constable. . . . and do bring in here before your good honour two notorious benefactors.
> *Ang.*   Benefactors? Well, what benefactors are they? Are they not malefactors?
> *Elbow.* If it please your honour, I know not well what they are. But precise villains they are, that I am sure of, and void of all profanation in the world, that good Christians ought to have.
> *Esc. [to Angelo]* This comes off well. Here's a wise officer.
> *Ang.*   Go to. What quality are they of? Elbow is your name? Why dost thou not speak, Elbow?
> *Pom.*   He cannot, sir: he's out at elbow.
> *Ang.*   What are you, sir?
> *Elbow.* He, sir? A tapster, sir; parcel bawd. . . .
> [II, i, 47–62]

Verse returns only when Angelo, as if attempting to recover his dignity, takes his peevish leave, pre-judging the case and relinquishing authority to Escalus, who acknowledges in respectful verse:

> *Ang.*   This will last out a night in Russia
> When nights are longest there. I'll take my leave,
> And leave you to the hearing of the cause;
> Hoping you'll find good cause to whip them all.
> *Esc.*   I think no less: good morrow to your lordship.
> [II, i, 133–7]

Facetious prose then prevails for nearly 140 lines, during which the law appears powerless to arbitrate between the accusations and counterclaims of the three comic characters. We even encounter a section where roles are apparently reversed, where the language of Pompey the pimp, in

9

challenging the legislation against sexual activity, seems more judicious and authoritative than that of Escalus the magistrate:

> *Pom.* Does your worship mean to geld and splay all the youth of the city?
> *Esc.* No, Pompey.
> *Pom.* Truly sir, in my poor opinion, they will to't then. If your worship will take order for the drabs and the knaves, you need not fear the bawds.
> *Esc.* There is pretty orders beginning, I can tell you. It is but heading and hanging.
> *Pom.* If you head and hang all that offend that way but for ten year together, you'll be glad to give out a commission for more heads: if this law hold in Vienna ten year, I'll rent the fairest house in it after three pence a bay.
> [II, i, 227–39]

Pompey, emphasising how futile it is for the state to attempt control of youthful sexual activity, suggests that the law should confine itself to prosecuting only 'the drabs and the knaves', that is, prostitutes and their clients. When Escalus's response implies that the death-penalty is to be imposed on *all* sexual offenders, Pompey warns that the direct result will be a catastrophic decline of both Vienna's population and its economy within a decade. Escalus, as if recognising the validity of this shrewd prophecy, can do no more than to dismiss Pompey with a warning about the pimp's future conduct (at lines 241–8). It is only when all three comic characters (Froth, Pompey, and Elbow) have quit the stage that Escalus can recover his philosophical poise in a brief coda of contemplative verse that concludes,

> Mercy is not itself, that oft looks so;
> Pardon is still the nurse of second woe.
> But yet, poor Claudio! There is no remedy. [II, i, 280–2].

Based on this evidence, the obvious supposition would be that Shakespeare reserves blank verse for the serious passages, allowing prose to dominate the comic exchanges. A more subtle inference might be that, in reducing the refined language of justice to the coarser vernacular, Shakespeare represents the susceptibility of sophistication to corruption, foreshadowing linguistically what he presents dramatically with the fall of Angelo in the later scenes of Act II.

As the representatives of licentiousness and anarchy remain in the wings for the remainder of Act II (with the exception of Lucio who appears in scene ii), the dialogue of scenes ii–iv is delivered almost exclusively in verse. Angelo and Isabella conduct their exchanges entirely in strongly rhetorical poetry, with two or three extra-metrical interjections from Lucio being arguably the only non-verse components of scene ii. Scene iv is particularly skilfully constructed, with two painful soliloquies (Angelo's at the beginning of the scene and Isabella's at the end) enclosing the dialogue in which Angelo gradually reveals to Isabella his lecherous intentions. Paradoxically, tension is accentuated because unruly passions, often threatening to break into violent actions, are restrained within the formality of the blank verse:

> *Ang.*   Be that you are,
> That is, a woman; if you be more, you're none.
> If you be one—as you are well express'd
> By all external warrants—show it now,
> By putting on the destin'd livery.
>   *Isab.*   I have no tongue but one; gentle my lord,
> Let me entreat you speak the former language.
>   *Ang.*   Plainly conceive, I love you.
>   *Isab.*   My brother did love Juliet,
> And you tell me that he shall die for't.
>   *Ang.*   He shall not, Isabel, if you give me love.
>   *Isab.*   I know your virtue hath a licence in't,
> Which seems a little fouler than it is,
> To pluck on others.
>   *Ang.*   Believe me, on mine honour,
> My words express my purpose.
>   *Isab.*   Ha? Little honour, to be much believ'd,
> And most pernicious purpose! Seeming, seeming!

I will proclaim thee, Angelo, look for't.
Sign me a present pardon for my brother,
Or with an outstretch'd throat I'll tell the world aloud
What man thou art. [II, iv, 133–53]

Here, Angelo's initial address to Isabella appears brusque, his imperatives demanding that she should submit to him because it is the 'destin'd livery' (line 137) of women to comply with men's sexual demands. When entreated to revert to his 'former language', however, he strikes the pose of the courtly lover (lines 140, 143, and 146–7), expressing his passion in gentler, more dignified terms such as 'love' and 'honour'. Isabella's language moves in the opposite direction: initially, she is shocked but respectful as she pleads with Angelo to relinquish his coarse, intimidating tone (lines 138–9); but rapidly her moral outrage overtakes her and she becomes threateningly aggressive, condemning Angelo roundly, threatening him with public exposure, challenging his authority by adopting the imperative mood, and addressing him with the demeaning pronouns 'thou' and 'thee' (rather than the respectful 'you').

Angelo responds in kind, his apparent frustration with this inversion of power and authority recalling his exasperation at Pompey's insolence in an earlier context (II, i, 133–6). His passion degenerates into verbal—and perhaps even physical— violence, as he enforces his sexual blackmail. This aggression is immediately apparent when Angelo, although continuing to speak in verse, imitates Isabella by changing his mode of address from the more formal 'you' and 'your' to the more peremptory 'thee' and 'thy', while beginning several consecutive main clauses abruptly, with formidable imperatives,:

Who will believe thee, Isabel? . . .
Fit thy consent to my sharp appetite;
Lay by all nicety and prolixious blushes
That banish what they sue for. Redeem thy brother
By yielding up thy body to my will;
Or else he must not only die the death,

But thy unkindness shall his death draw out
To ling'ring sufferance. Answer me tomorrow. . . .
[II, iv, 153 and 160–6]

This development in the language of his verse vividly and abruptly transforms Angelo from would-be courtly lover into bullying tyrant.

The whole of Act III is set in—or in the immediate vicinity of—the prison.[6] The First Folio prints Act III as a single scene of about 550 lines, although J. W. Lever, in his Arden edition of the play, proposes a division immediately after line 270.[7] At the heart of the Act is the most dramatically intense exchange in *Measure for Measure*: the agonising confrontation between brother and sister, when Claudio, in desperation, pleads for his life and Isabella, in horror, vilifies him as a base coward (III, i, 53–149). The Duke, a seemingly peripheral figure previously, especially during the high drama of Act II, now comes to the fore in his disguise as Friar Lodowick. Although Act III begins with Claudio being reconciled to death, it ends with hope of his reprieve, the Duke being the prime mover in both cases. Vincentio dominates the Act, observing disputes and arrests, offering moral commentary, and engaging in significant dialogue with other principal characters.

Act III is conducted entirely in verse until line 151, after which prose strongly predominates. Simultaneously, the dramatic balance tips abruptly: after exploring the realms of tragedy, we suddenly find ourselves in the provinces of comedy. The Duke's early exchanges with Claudio are conducted in philosophical poetry, but he reverts to prose after the first line of his re-entry, following the encounter between Claudio and Isabella. For the rest of the Act (except in his

---

[6] When it was first encountered in II, iii, Vienna's prison was the last of 'Our city's institutions' to be presented. The prison and its environs will now become the dominant setting in Acts III and IV.

[7] Braunmuller and Watson, in the latest Arden Edition, present Act III as a single scene of 538 lines.

gnomic asides), the Duke speaks in prose, although he is taken with brief fits of versification when condemning Pompey for bawdry (III, ii, 18–38) and when first addressing Escalus (III, ii, 211–14). Similarly, Isabella, who has spoken exclusively in verse until the re-entry of the disguised Duke, now adopts the language of prose. However, even when she and the disguised Duke speak in prose, they generally retain the dignity proper to their dramatic roles:

> *Duke.* . . . I do make myself believe that you may most uprighteously do a poor wronged lady a merited benefit; redeem your brother from the angry law; do no stain upon your own gracious person; and much please the absent Duke, if peradventure he shall ever return to have hearing of this business.
> *Isab.* Let me hear you speak farther. I have spirit to do anything that appears not foul in the truth of my spirit.
> *Duke.* Virtue is bold, and goodness never fearful. Have you not heard speak of Mariana, the sister of Frederick, the great soldier who miscarried at sea?
> *Isab.* I have heard of the lady, and good words went with her name. [III, i, 198–212]

The language here is restrained and respectful, a far cry from the intense passions of Isabella's verse-exchanges in her immediately preceding scenes, and further still from the malapropisms, prevarications, and innuendos that frequented the plebeians' prose in Act II scene i.

The prose-sections of Act III are as versatile tonally as Shakespeare's earlier poetry. For example, when Lucio and Escalus give accounts of the Duke's reputation, both speak in prose; but the former's egregious, abrasive slanders are diametrically opposed to the latter's gracious, measured commendations. Lucio represents the Duke as a dissolute lecher:

> Ere he would have hanged a man for the getting a hundred bastards, he would have paid for the nursing a thousand. He

14

had some feeling for the sport; he knew the service; and that instructed him to mercy. / . . . He would be drunk too, that let me inform you. / . . . A very superficial, ignorant, unweighing fellow— [III, ii, 113–37]

By contrast, Escalus regards Vincentio as the epitome of contemplative moderation:

One that, above all other strifes, contended especially to know himself. / . . . Rather rejoicing to see another merry, than merry at anything which professed to make him rejoice. A gentleman of all temperance. [III, ii, 226–31]

Both portraits, ostensibly of the Duke, reflect more plausibly on the speakers themselves: Lucio's insults are a reflection of his own dissolute life (and that of his associates in the Viennese underworld) rather than a credible indictment of Duke Vincentio;[8] while Escalus identifies virtues in the Duke that an audience might more readily recognise in Escalus himself. In these two examples, Shakespeare's prose is sharply divergent tonally, but performs a subtle structural function in establishing parallels between the two contexts.

The plot of Act IV is deliberately convoluted, as Shakespeare manages the dramatic transition between the 'bedtrick' and the 'head-trick', in preparation for the denouement of the play. As in the earlier Acts, figures from the Viennese underclasses flit here and there to comic effect, Pompey the pimp, Abhorson the executioner, Barnadine the murderer, and Lucio the fantastic being prominent in scenes ii and iii of the Act. Again, the figure of the disguised Duke dominates in all but two of the six scenes, the two exceptions (IV, iv, and IV, vi) totalling under fifty lines.

---

[8] Thus, Shakespeare's Duke of Albany observes how the sensibilities of the wicked are so corrupted by their own evil that they perceive virtue as vice: 'Wisdom and goodness to the vile seem vile; / Filths savour but themselves' [*King Lear*: IV, ii, 38–9].

Like its immediate predecessor, Act IV vacillates between verse and prose. Scene i, which introduces Mariana to the audience, is written almost entirely in dignified, lyrical verse, and even includes a song (the only one in the play) to represent Mariana's plight objectively. In the next two scenes, however, the language moves freely between prose and verse (usually, but not consistently, to reflect the seriousness of the encounter), as in the following exchanges involving the Provost, Pompey, Abhorson, and Claudio:

> *Prov.* Are you agreed?
> *Pom.* Sir, I will serve him; for I do find your hangman is a more penitent trade than your bawd; he doth oftener ask forgiveness.
> *Prov.* You, sirrah, provide your block and your axe tomorrow four o'clock.
> *Abhor.* Come on, bawd, I will instruct thee in my trade. Follow.
> *Pomp.* I do desire to learn, sir; and I hope, if you have occasion to use me for your own turn, you shall find me yare. For truly, sir, for your kindness I owe you a good turn.
> *Prov.* Call hither Barnadine and Claudio.
>   *Exeunt* [Abhorson *and* Pompey]
> Th'one has my pity; not a jot the other,
> Being a murderer, though he were my brother.
>
>   *Enter* Claudio
>
> Look, here's the warrant, Claudio, for thy death;
> 'Tis now dead midnight, and by eight tomorrow
> Thou must be made immortal. Where's Barnadine?
> *Clau.* As fast lock'd up in sleep as guiltless labour
> When it lies starkly in the traveller's bones.
>   [IV, ii, 46–65]

The similarity to Act II, scene i is noticeable: when comic characters are on stage, a figure of authority will speak in prose, but revert to verse on their departure. Here, no sooner have Abhorson and Pompey departed than the Provost, like Escalus in the earlier context, reflects in a gnomic rhyming couplet on the paradoxes of justice. He then addresses the noble Claudio in verse, the latter replying in lyrical poetry that is remarkably dignified, restrained, and selfless for one condemned to die in a few hours.

In an Act in which deception and lies are so prevalent, it is appropriate that scene iv should reintroduce Angelo, the arch deceiver and liar, who has been absent from the stage since Act II. When Angelo and Escalus are notified of Vincentio's imminent homecoming, their exchanges are conducted in prose—agitated questions on Angelo's part, to convey the effect of his guilty conscience (lines 4–9). Angelo reverts to verse, however, for the high seriousness of his third and final great soliloquy at the end of the scene (lines 18–32). Structurally, this scene mirrors the concluding lines of the opening scene of the play (I, i, 76–83). There, exchanges between Angelo and Escalus immediately followed the scene representing the Duke's departure; here, the scene representing the Duke's return (V, i) is immediately preceded by exchanges between Angelo and Escalus. This dramatic structure is redolent of a favourite linguistic device in *Measure for Measure*: antimetabole, the repetition of words in successive clauses, but with their order transposed, to achieve equilibrium.[9]

The concluding scenes of the Act (v and vi) are conducted in brisk, generally businesslike verse, to prepare the audience for the formal dignity that underpins the great final scene:

> *Duke.*   Go call at Flavius' house,
> And tell him where I stay. Give the like notice
> To Valencius, Rowland, and to Crassus,
> And bid them bring the trumpets to the gate:
> But send me Flavius first.

---

[9] E.g. the Duke's 'What's mine is yours, and what is yours is mine' (V, i, 534), or the Provost's description of Barnadine: 'Drunk many times a day, if not many days entirely drunk' (IV, ii, 147–8).

| *Friar Peter.* | It shall be speeded well. |
| | [*Exit* Friar.] |

Enter Varrius.

Duke. I thank thee, Varrius, Thou hast made good haste.
Come, we will walk. There's other of our friends
Will greet us here anon. My gentle Varrius!
Exeunt. [IV, v, 6–13]

This is verse stripped down to its most functional base. There is no imagery, and no memorable phrasing. Rather, it conveys necessary information in poetic measure, suggesting that the Duke (who, in his guise as Friar Lodowick, has spoken in prose for much of Acts III and IV) is in the process of speedily re-establishing his dignity and authority in the state. After all, poetry is principally the preserve of patricians in the play.

Act V resembles Act III in that it is one extended scene of over 500 lines in which the Duke dominates and passes judgement, both in his guise of Friar Lodowick and in propria persona. Verse is deployed almost exclusively, although Lucio sometimes speaks in prose. Accordingly, when disguised as Friar Lodowick, the Duke reverts to prose when speaking to Lucio, as do Angelo and Escalus when they intervene in this same context:

Lucio. Come hither, goodman Bald-pate, do you know me?
Duke. I remember you, sir, by the sound of your voice; I met you at the prison, in the absence of the Duke.
Lucio. O, did you so? And do you remember what you said of the Duke?
Duke. Most notedly, sir.
Lucio. Do you so, sir? And was the Duke a fleshmonger, a fool, and a coward, as you reported him to be?
Duke. You must, sir, change persons with me, ere you make that my report. You indeed spoke so of him, and much more, much worse.

Lucio. O, thou damnable fellow! Did I not pluck thee by the nose for thy speeches?
Duke. I protest, I love the Duke as I love myself.
Ang. Hark how the villain would close now, after his treasonable abuses!
Esc. Such a fellow is not to be talked withal. Away with him to prison! Where is the Provost? Away with him to prison! Lay bolts enough upon him: let him speak no more.

[V, i, 324–44]

Even the customarily restrained and dignified Escalus has lost his composure. Again, as in the slapstick trial conducted in Act II scene i, we see the tendency for the dignity of courtly verse to be corrupted into knockabout prose after exposure to dissolute members of the underworld. The result here is that, despite the prevailing seriousness of Act V, a more chaotic, comic tone is infused into these exchanges, perhaps to prepare the audience for the Duke's 'happy comedy' leniency towards Lucio as part of his final judgement.

This final Act presents the culmination of the sequence of tests conducted by the Duke: Isabella and Mariana prove virtuous and worthy of public acclaim, while Angelo and Lucio prove perfidious, being exposed to public humiliation. Escalus and the Duke himself are also tested by circumstances. Although their integrity is not compromised to the same extent as that of Angelo and Lucio, it might be argued that this series of tests proves the two women to be more estimable than any of the men. Towards the conclusion of the scene, the Duke introduces a general amnesty, not only for Claudio but even for Barnadine, a murderer. Lucio and Angelo must undergo marriage, be it as their penance or as their moral corrective. In the play's closing tableau, marriage, the great reconciler, unites Claudio and Julietta, Angelo and Mariana, Lucio and Mistress Kate Keep-down, and (perhaps) the Duke and Isabella.

Shakespeare's subtlety ensures that structure and form in *Measure for Measure* are closely interdependent and dramatically expressive. Once the physical divisions between court and underworld have been clearly established in the first two scenes, social divisions are blurred linguistically as the different classes intrude into each other's domains. For example, Lucio leaves the underworld to venture into both the nunnery and the court, where he can practise more sophisticated converse in contrast to his customary scurrility; the Duke and Isabella, both associated early in the play with dignity and piety, move freely between religious communities, the court, and the common prison, adapting converse and conduct accordingly; while Pompey successfully transforms himself from common pimp to cunning pleader before two magistrates at court, only to be relegated in prison to the baser functions and discourse of assistant executioner. Knaves prove capable of linguistic sophistication in the purlieus of the patricians, while nobles revert to demotic in encounters with the underworld. Audiences become aware that apparent quirks of tone and linguistic form—including transitions from verse to prose and back—suggest how social distinctions are eroded or otherwise transformed by dramatic context.

Sources of the Plot

Although Shakespeare's plot in *Measure for Measure* is 'original' when regarded in its entirety, it involves strands from a variety of sources in the popular tradition, the Judaeo-Christian tradition, and even the classical tradition. Shakespeare's originality lies in the way in which he adapts each strand and twists it with others to form the fabric of his plot.[10]

The Angelo/Isabella story—the indecent proposal to a woman desperate to save a family-relation from sentence of death—may be encountered in the Christian tradition twelve hundred years before Shakespeare wrote his play. An analogous

---

[10] Lever offers a detailed survey of such sources (pp. xxxv–lv and 151–200), which may be supplemented with reference to the generous selection of relevant extracts from sources and analogues offered by Kamps and Raber, pp. 117–353.

story is recorded by St. Augustine (354–430 AD) in his commentary on The Sermon on the Mount,[11] that same Biblical text from which Shakespeare derived the title of his play, *Measure for Measure*. In 1547, the narrative was given new currency in a letter written by Joseph Macarius, a Hungarian student. He recorded the alleged actions of a Spanish count who, as magistrate, was eager to take sexual advantage of a Milanese woman petitioning him to redeem her husband from sentence of death.[12] Macarius's account prompted a flurry of literary texts exploring imaginatively the quandary of the victim and the fate of the tyrant, including plays and prose-texts that proved particularly influential on Shakespeare: *Hecatommithi* (1565) and *Epitia* (1583) by Cinthio, and *Promos and Cassandra* (1578), *Heptameron* (1582) and *Aurelia* (1592) by George Whetstone.[13]

Shakespeare's masterstroke is to make the female victim a postulant to a religious order as well as a sibling to the condemned man: she is thus a 'sister' in both cases. As a nun pledges her chastity to Christ when she takes her solemn vows, Isabella cannot comply with the demands of the lascivious magistrate without jeopardising her religious vocation. Other victimised women in the tradition had concluded that the preservation of the life of a loved-one was of greater value than the loss of their chastity. Isabella famously (or notoriously, depending on your point of view), reaches the opposite conclusion:

> Then, Isabel live chaste, and brother, die:
> More than our brother is our chastity. [II, iv, 183–4]

In Thomas Lupton's English version (1581) of the tale, the magistrate became inflamed when the woman pledged that she

---

[11] *New Advent*, http://www.newadvent.org/fathers/16011.htm: Book I, Chapter 16, paragraph 50, accessed 18 July 2020.
[12] Lever, pp. 151–154, offers the Latin text and a translation of this letter.
[13] Lever, pp. 155–193, includes relevant extracts from these sources.

would willingly do anything to save her relation under sentence of death.[14] Shakespeare subtly adapts this device when Isabella calls the retreating Angelo back with the words, 'Hark, how I'll bribe you' (II, ii, 146). Regardless of whether Angelo's inarticulate response—'How! Bribe me?' (II, ii, 147)—is presented by an actor as outraged, incredulous, or breathlessly excited, an audience should perceive the possibility that Angelo might be incited to lascivious hopes by Isabella's offer, only to have those hopes tantalisingly frustrated when Isabella explains that her proposed bribe would be prayers for Angelo from the sisterhood of Saint Clare, rather than any sexual incentive.

Two further erotic elements of Shakespeare's plot find their origins in long-established narrative traditions. In the first tradition, tales abound of men deceived into a sexual relationship with one woman when believing themselves in the embraces of another; or, more specifically, brides substituted in the marital bed without the knowledge of husbands. For example, in the Judaeo-Christian tradition, Laban deceived Jacob by substituting his elder daughter, Leah, for his younger daughter, Rachel, on Jacob's wedding-night (Genesis 29: 21–5). Such stories are also encountered in the popular tradition of ballads and legends.[15] Shakespeare himself incorporated the device into *All's Well that Ends Well* when Helena takes the place of Diana in Bertram's bed.[16] Shakespeare deploys the convention for a second time here in *Measure for Measure,* with Mariana rather than Isabella accepting Angelo's embraces.[17] After Shakespeare's death, the motif would be

---

[14] The relevant extract is quoted by Lever, p. 195.

[15] William Witherle Lawrence notes two parallel situations occurring in ballads and one in the Tristram legend: *Shakespeare's Problem Comedies* (London: Macmillan, 1931; repr. Harmondsworth: Penguin, 1969), p. 211, n. 24.

[16] Shakespeare borrowed his basic plot, including the bed-trick, from Boccaccio's *Decameron* (the ninth story of the third day).

[17] A variation on this dramatic device may be detected in *Much Ado About Nothing*, when Don Pedro and Claudio are misled into believing that Borachio has successfully wooed Hero (rather than Margaret) on the night before Hero's wedding to Claudio.

repeated by his friend and collaborator, Thomas Middleton, in *The Changeling* (1622), when Diaphanta takes Beatrice-Joanna's place on the latter's wedding-night. Shakespeare's contemporaries would have accepted this narrative convention as a time-honoured means of resolving a sexual conundrum; it is unlikely that they would have been unduly surprised, shocked, or sceptical that Angelo could embrace Mariana while believing her to be Isabella—after all, there was biblical authority for the success of such a device.

The second narrative tradition entails a great man admiring the beauty and/or testing the virtue of a woman of humbler birth, after which he enjoys her favours, or rewards her by taking her as his wife. For example, the legend of King Cophetua's marriage to the beautiful beggar maid was well-known to Shakespeare: he refers to this folk-tale in four plays, including *Love's Labour's Lost* (IV, i, 65) and *Romeo and Juliet* (II, i, 14). The Clerk in Chaucer's *The Canterbury Tales* (composed during the 1390s) treated of similar material in his tale of the patience of the peasant-girl, Griselda, sorely tested by her noble husband, Marquis Walter. Shakespeare incorporates this romantic tradition into the ending of *Measure for Measure* when the Duke, having tested the full range of Isabella's virtues, offers to make her his bride.

A further strand of Shakespeare's plot stems from tales of rulers who move incognito among their people, canvassing opinions and noting abuses, often before returning to pass judgement. A classical pedigree was attached to this legend in the Sixteenth Century: the Roman Emperor, Alexander Severus, was reputed to have adopted this practice during his rule—at least, according to Sir Thomas Elyot in *The Image of Governaunce* (1541). King James I's grandfather, James V of Scotland, allegedly went in disguise to observe his people.[18] A dozen years before the first recorded performance of *Measure for Measure*, Barnabe Riche, in *The Adventures of Brusanus, Prince of Hungary*, recorded a story in which Leonarchus, King

---

[18] Braunmuller and Watson, p. 115.

23

of Epirus, disguised himself as a merchant to mingle with his people, eventually condemning a boastful courtier who (like the slanderous Lucio in *Measure for Measure*) falsely accused him of treasonable conversation. A further literary source likely to have influenced Shakespeare was Middleton's play, *The Phoenix*, performed before James I in February of 1604, just ten months before the first recorded performance of *Measure for Measure*. In *The Phoenix*, the eponymous prince grows in wisdom and understanding by passing in disguise among courtiers and commoners as a prelude to assuming the reins of government. Then there is John Marston's *The Malcontent* to consider, a play entered in the Stationers' Register on 5 July 1604 and subsequently acquired by Shakespeare's newly patronised King's Men as part of their repertoire. Malevole, the titular malcontent, turns out to be Altofronto, the disguised former Duke of Genoa, who returns to rail against corruption in the state before revealing his true identity and reclaiming his dukedom. Duke Vincentio's decision to disguise himself as a friar more freely to observe and censure Viennese society clearly draws on this popular narrative/dramatic tradition.

Finally, there is the literary convention of seemingly hopeless circumstances being resolved into a happy ending by the sudden and late intervention of a powerful and benign justice. In Greek drama, this was embodied in the deus ex machina, the god who descended to earth to restore order after discord.[19] In the Judaeo-Christian tradition, the Biblical story of the Judgement of Solomon (1 Kings 3: 16–28) occupies a prominent position, where an enigmatic ruling ultimately enabled Solomon wisely to determine the more loving mother for a disputed child. The role of Duke Vincentio may derive

---

[19] The clearest example in Shakespeare's work of his deployment of this classical device occurs in *Cymbeline*, when Posthumus Leonatus produces the 'label' left on his sleeping bosom by 'Great Jupiter' (V, v, 426–32). This message is interpreted by the Soothsayer as divine intervention to ensure enduring reconciliation after conflict: 'The fingers of the pow'rs above do tune / The harmony of this peace' (V, v, 464–5).

from this tradition, as he miraculously materialises in the final scene to expel tyranny from Vienna, restoring just, benevolent government by ingenious means.

Doctrinal influences on *Measure for Measure*—that is, social, political, or religious ideologies incorporated into the play, as opposed to narrative sources influencing the plot—will be considered, where appropriate, in later chapters. Suffice it to say for the present that it is a measure of Shakespeare's achievement that he embodied such a wide variety of narrative and doctrinal sources so relatively seamlessly and successfully into a single play. Although recognising certain narrative conventions, an audience viewing *Measure for Measure* should not feel subjected to a loosely-intertwined web of dramatic clichés, but rather should admire the complexity of a well-woven theatrical tapestry in which familiar situations are given fresh vitality and coherency by their incorporation into new contexts.

To what genre of drama, though, should this complex amalgam of sources be attributed? That is a question best reserved for the very end of this study, after all the relevant evidence has been sifted. Without much further consideration, however, we can reject any notion that *Measure for Measure* is a play for puritans.

The Sexual Imperative

The frankness—nay, outspokenness—of *Measure for Measure* on sexual matters was the principal reason for its suppression for so many years. The language can be extremely coarse, treating of subjects that for so long were unmentionable in polite society, such as fornication, rape, prostitution, and sexually-transmitted diseases. Just as disquieting to moralists was the fact that so many of the characters in the play seem powerless to resist the promptings of lust.

The plot of *Measure for Measure* hinges on Claudio's offence, which was too distasteful to be mentioned in some productions during the long but patchy stage-history of the play. Claudio is to be executed 'for getting Madam Julietta with child' (Mistress Overdone: I, ii, 66–7). Their sexual encounter, however, has been consensual rather than impulsive, 'most mutual entertainment' (I, ii, 143) within 'a true contract' (I, ii, 134) of handfasting. Claudio considers Julietta 'my wife' (I, ii, 136), but concedes that their banns have not been read and that their nuptials have yet to be confirmed by a church-ceremony (I, ii, 137–8). Under the statutes against fornication enforced by Angelo, Claudio will suffer capital punishment for this seemingly venial slip. His faithful and loving relationship with his betrothed contrasts sharply with the lustful impulsiveness of so many other men encountered in the play. Yet even Claudio must concede that he has been guilty of 'too much liberty' (I, ii, 117), which leads him to philosophize ruefully on the human condition:

> Our natures do pursue,
> Like rats that ravin down their proper bane,
> A thirsty evil; and when we drink, we die. [I, ii, 120–2]

Claudio here equates the urgent, self-destructive appetites of rats with humanity's inability to resist temptation, specifically the temptation of illicit sexual indulgence.

So it is that, in the Viennese underworld of *Measure for Measure*, prostitution is rife. Pompey the pimp names ten inmates of the Provost's prison with whom he is 'well acquainted' as a result of their previous association with Mistress Overdone's brothel, her 'house of profession' (IV, iii, 1–4). He adds that the prison also contains 'forty more, all great doers in our trade' (IV, iii, 18–19). By 'doers' (a customary euphemism from Pompey), he means fornicators who use the services of prostitutes. The close connection between brothels and the criminal classes is firmly established—although those 'doers' whose names are prefaced by the title 'Master' may have enjoyed a degree of respectability before their committal.[20]

It follows that 'gentlemen' in *Measure for Measure* are no more immune from the lure of lechery than common criminals, from whom they show little distinction. Lucio and his two gentleman-friends frequent Mistress Overdone's brothel, and joke about the consequences. Among this reckless triumvirate, the penalties of sexual excess—piles, baldness, oral infection, hollow bones, and sciatica (all presented as symptoms of syphilis)—are considered suitable subjects for banter (I, ii, 30–55). Lucio and the Second Gentleman even jest at the paradox that whoremasters, such as they are, pay serious money for serious infections:

> *Lucio.* I have purchased as many diseases under [Mistress Overdone's] roof as come to— . . . / . . .
> *2 Gent.* To three thousand dolours a year. [I, ii, 42–6].

According to the Second Gentleman's sardonic riposte, 'dolours' signifies both the price of whoremongering in 'dollars' (German: *Thaler*) and its cost in disease and suffering (French: *douleur*). Lucio and his friends show no inclination to desist from their dissolute lifestyles, even though they know full well of Angelo's 'proclamation' (I, ii, 73) condemning fornication and imposing dire penalties. Another young gentleman, Master Froth, must be warned away from Mistress Overdone's brothel with a grim prediction of particularly harsh penalties under the law (II, i, 200–8). The twin threats of severe infections and severe punishments nevertheless seem an inadequate deterrent to these ostensibly more respectable Viennese citizens.

---

[20] Pompey refers to six of the ten whom he names at IV, iii, 4–17 as 'Master', a title implying respectability. In addition, four are 'young' and one is 'wild', words suggesting that youthful impulsiveness rather than hardened criminality has driven them to offend.

Mistress Overdone is a victim both of her sexual appetite and of her trade: she has 'worn [her] eyes almost out in the service' (Pompey: I, ii, 102). According to Pompey, she has had nine husbands, 'Overdone by the last' (II, i, 199). 'Overdone' is not merely her marital name but also her predicament: she is sexually dissipated. Pompey will later add that 'she hath eaten up all her beef, and she is herself in the tub' (III, ii, 54–5).[21] He is insinuating that she has over-indulged her sexual appetite[22] and, having contracted venereal disease as a consequence, is now receiving the standard treatment: immersion in the sweating-tub (which resembled the casks in which beef was salted to preserve it).[23] According to Lucio, Mistress Overdone's fate is characteristic of those of her trade: the 'fresh' prostitute (young and pretty, but with insinuations of 'fresh meat') will ultimately develop into the aged, diseased brothel-keeper, 'powdered' with cosmetics, like beef salted in the tub (III, ii, 57).

Pompey's language is as dubious as his profession. When he is not exhausting the sexual connotations of the verb 'to do' and its related vocabulary,[24] his imagery, implicitly accompanied by crude gestures, can be grossly suggestive. A man arrested for fornication—possibly Claudio—has been guilty of 'Groping for trouts, in a peculiar river' (I, ii, 83), a line inviting an obscene

---

[21] Lever thinks this a mere joke, the logic extending no further (p. 85n.). Debilitation and disease, however, seem the all-too-likely consequences of Mistress Overdone's life.

[22] Lever is silent on the phrase 'eaten up all her beef', while Kamps and Raber gloss the phrase as 'run through all her prostitutes' (p. 70n.). Braunmuller and Watson (p. 276n.) concur with Kamps and Raber. But cf. Lucio's references to 'my dear morsel' (III, ii, 52), to the 'fresh whore' (III, ii, 57), and to eating 'mutton' (III, ii, 175). To Shakespeare's audience, meat-eating was a euphemism for sexual activity, as both involved satisfying an appetite for flesh. Hence, Lucio's association between eating and sexual intercourse at I, iv, 40 and III, ii, 97–9.

[23] Braunmuller and Watson (p. 276n.) refer to Pistol's 'powdering tub of infamy' (*Henry V*: II, i, 73).

[24] E.g. at I, ii, 80, II, i, 138–40, and IV, iii, 19.

hand-movement. When hauled before Escalus 'for being a bawd' (Elbow: III, ii, 63), Pompey reverts to irrelevance and prevarication to conceal his activities (II, i, 84–132), but hints at his profession by studding his language with innuendos supported by coarse gesticulation.[25] Pompey is the embodiment of foul-mouthed, physical comedy in the play.

Although, at one level, they are merely a pimp and a whoremaster, Pompey and Lucio are capable of astute philosophical reflection on the irresistibility of the sexual impulse. Unabashed by his arrest, Pompey engages the eminent jurist, Escalus, in debate on the subject. When Escalus warns that all illicit sexual activity will be prosecuted henceforward, Pompey quips that, as the young find it impossible to control sexual desire, neutering them will be the only means to ensure that they do not offend against the law (II, i, 225–30). When Escalus threatens 'heading and hanging' as the ultimate deterrent for fornication, Pompey sardonically predicts the collapse of both the population and the economy within a decade (II, i, 233–40): Vienna will lack citizens once so many, unable to resist the sexual imperative, have been executed.

To Lucio, sexual intercourse is as natural as eating, as the cycle of the seasons, or as the tillage of the land (I, iv, 40–4), as innocent as sport or a game (I, ii, 180–1), as blameless as a domestic chore (III, ii, 166), as functional as mere undressing (III, ii, 173). He is a self-confessed fornicator (I, ii, 41–8 and IV, iii, 167–72) effectively pleading the cause of 'lenity to lechery' (III, ii, 94). This is achieved by arguing how prevalent sexual transgression is throughout all generations and among all social ranks, because the sexual appetite is so closely associated with those other appetites—eating and drinking—necessary to sustain human life (III, ii, 97–9). The earthy pragmatism of

---

[25] These innuendos are pinpointed by Lever, p. 31 (note to lines 88–112), and p. 32 (notes to lines 93 and 115–21). A modern audience would need the assistance of obscene gestures to identify all these references as bawdy. See also the notes to this passage supplied by Braunmuller and Watson, pp. 201–2.

Lucio counterbalances the sophisticated moral theorising of the representatives of Church and state in the play.

All these contexts prepare us for the fates of the Duke and Angelo, both of whom think themselves proof against sexual desire. The Duke dismisses the possibility that he could be subject to erotic passion, insisting to Friar Thomas that he is beyond the age when love could sway him:

> No. Holy father, throw away that thought;
> Believe not that the dribbling dart of love
> Can pierce a complete bosom. Why I desire thee
> To give me secret harbour hath a purpose
> More grave and wrinkled than the aims and ends
> Of burning youth. [I, iii, 1–6]

Given how universal the sexual imperative is elsewhere in Vienna, we may feel that this speech smacks of complacency. The Duke is rashly denying that the arrows of Cupid, the God of Love, could ever strike him, as his breast is fully armoured ('complete') against such an assault. He expresses confidently that the passionate urges of 'burning youth' are excluded from his mature ('grave and wrinkled') political objectives. Nevertheless, those objectives achieved, he is apparently smitten with erotic desire in the concluding lines of the play. His two proposals of marriage to Isabella (at V, i, 488–91 and 531–4) could—at a stretch—be regarded as practical policy, an invitation for the chaste novice to unite her moral virtues with the Duke's political power, to redeem Vienna from its licentiousness; but, in the context of what has gone before in the play, the lines appear to be further evidence of amatory desire taking control of a man. Has 'the dribbling dart of love' at last pierced the Duke's 'complete bosom', or rather, has the successful restoration of his authority and popularity emboldened him to exploit an opportunity? Are his motives for proposing marriage laudable, or does he, like Angelo, find the acquisition of absolute power an irresistible aphrodisiac?

Angelo presents the most extreme illustration of the inability of so many men in *Measure for Measure* to withstand sexual temptation. Like the Duke, Angelo believes himself immune to lust, but he is much less tolerant than Vincentio of sexual desire in others, in that he is determined to punish, with the full force of the law, those sexual misdemeanours to which the Duke has given 'their permissive pass' (I, iii, 38). He is a 'man of stricture and firm abstinence' who 'scarce confesses / That his blood flows' (the Duke: I, iii, 12 and 51–2). Angelo is entirely inexperienced in controlling his (as opposed to others') sexual desire as he 'never feels / The wanton stings and motions of the sense' (Lucio: I, iv, 58–9). When erotic desire strikes him, with the virtuous Isabella as its object, Angelo has therefore prepared no defence, and he succumbs helplessly. His rational detachment is transformed into brutal lust as he flouts those very laws by which he was seeking to curb sexual promiscuity in Vienna. His first soliloquy (at II, ii, 162–87) reveals a radically-divided self: the ascetic justice cannot recognise himself in the hypocritical lecher. Like so many other men in Shakespeare's Vienna, his inability to regulate his own sexual desire threatens to destroy Angelo; but he is fortunate enough to avoid the customary penalties: mortal disease and capital punishment. When he is ultimately redeemed, it is not by his own willpower, but rather by the loving intervention of Mariana, a woman who 'crave[s] no other, nor no better man' (V, i, 424).

Mariana's case differs in important respects from those examined so far. Unlike those men impatient for sexual gratification, she has waited for five years (V, i, 216–17), with no expectation of ultimate fulfilment. She has remained faithful to the object of her desire, but has made no attempt to satisfy her longings until she is not merely authorised but even incited to do so by a (seeming) spiritual authority: the Duke, in his disguise as Friar Lodowick (IV, i, 66–7). Her fidelity has persisted, despite the cruelty of the man whom she loves, who has not only rejected her, but also falsely smeared her reputation (III, i, 208–30). When she at last has the opportunity to seek redress in the Duke's court, she pursues neither

31

recompense (V, i, 420–6) nor retribution (V, i, 437–9). Hers is a love unalloyed with baser instincts, an ideal against which an audience can 'measure' the lust and hypocrisy of other characters.

Although Claudio's betrothed, Julietta, 'Hath blister'd her report [and] is with child' (II, iii, 12), she is both penitent and patient (II, iii, 19–20). At a time when she is racked by labour-pains (as attested by the Provost at II, ii, 15–16), she meekly confesses to the disguised Duke, accepting a heavier burden of responsibility than Claudio's for their 'most offenceful act' (II, iii, 26). She bravely shoulders the burden of shame and imprisonment (II, iii, 35–6), until she becomes distraught at the news of Claudio's imminent execution, recognising that she has been spared merely because she is bearing their child (II, iii, 40–2). Like Mariana's, her fidelity and the purity of her love are sorely tested; and, like Mariana, she perseveres and is ultimately rewarded by marriage to the man who, she feared, would be 'a forfeit of the law' (II, ii, 71).

But what of Isabella, who seeks sanctuary with Sister Francisca and the Prioress of the convent of Saint Clare, in a place remote from the temptations of the flesh that afflict Vienna? Isabella guards her virginity with a fierce piety against the assaults of Angelo (II, iv, 30–186) and the entreaties of Claudio (III, i, 53–149). She is, nevertheless, acutely aware of the susceptibility of women to sexual impulsiveness (II, iv, 124–9), which may suggest a fear that her natural desires might betray her. In one much-discussed speech (II, iv, 100–4), she seems to equate a martyr's suffering with sexual ecstasy, subliminally conflating the two contemporary meanings of 'death': mortality, and orgasm.[26] She nevertheless never expresses any intention to form an amatory relationship, which makes problematic her open silences in response to the Duke's concluding proposals of marriage. Is Isabella entirely proof against the sexual imperative?

---

[26] Claudio, her brother, does the same at III, i, 82–4.

With the exception of Mistress Overdone, the women who speak in the play are less tainted by sexual corruption than the men. Unruly passion afflicts all social ranks of Viennese males, whose sexual impulsiveness is usually self-destructive. Women seem less motivated by desire than by deep affection, more subject to love than to lust. In this play, the sexual imperative compels most men towards their doom, regardless of their social rank; but the virtuous women prove better able to resist 'The wanton stings and motions of the sense' (I, iv, 59).

Soliloquy and Silence

Although dialogue is the foundation of Shakespearian drama, his later plays (and *Measure for Measure* in particular) abound in occasions when no words pass between characters, but the context encourages the audience to consider what thoughts and feelings might be affecting those who remain silent.[27] Sometimes, any limitation in dialogue is supplied by that quintessential device of the Elizabethan and Jacobean theatre, the soliloquy, whereby the audience overhears the thoughts and feelings of the speaker. Nowhere is this dramatic device more prominent than in *Hamlet*, in which the Prince speaks more lines of soliloquy than any other Shakespearian character, in addition to conducting many exchanges with Horatio when his friend acts as little more than a sounding-board for Hamlet's meditations. The effect of the soliloquy is usually to enable the audience to empathise with the dramatic character by witnessing his or her 'inner life'. Thus, audiences viewing *Hamlet* form an intimate sympathy for the Prince; those overhearing the thoughts of Richard III or Iago in *Othello*

---

[27] Frank Kermode observes in Shakespeare's plays 'an increasing interest in silence, . . . a general development away from rhetorical explicitness and towards a language that does not try to give everything away. . . . Much has come to depend on everything not being said, and this is essential to the later Shakespearian development of character. At such moments silence and speech are complementary.' [*Shakespeare's Language* (London: Penguin, 2001), pp. 10–12]

experience a conspiratorial thrill in sharing in the ruthless scheming of these stage-villains; while audiences in *Macbeth* are led to understand the agony of conscience that Macbeth endures and therefore to view him as a suffering fellow human being rather than merely as the 'dead butcher' condemned by Malcolm at the end of the tragedy. This third function of the soliloquy is fundamental to audience response to Angelo in *Measure for Measure*, another Shakespearian villain partially redeemed by evidence, revealed in soliloquy, of the workings of his conscience.

Soliloquy is used sparingly in *Measure for Measure*. Isabella has only one soliloquy, and Angelo has only three.[28] In Acts III–IV, the Duke offers a number of choric asides, commenting on central issues of the play, but it is doubtful whether these should be considered as soliloquies as they do not substantially reveal his 'inner life'. Numerous other characters are given asides, brief 'soliloquies' in which they express their thoughts on their circumstances, but not in sufficient detail fully to develop an audience's deeper appreciation of the complexity of their characters (e.g. Mistress Overdone at I, ii, 75–7, or Julietta at II, iii, 40–2). Such asides nevertheless resemble soliloquies as they convey information necessary for audiences better to comprehend thoughts, feelings, and dramatic situation.

Silence, by contrast, is employed with uncommon frequency in *Measure for Measure*, and its significance is often challenging to fathom. Like soliloquy, it usually occurs when a character is undergoing a crisis but, unlike soliloquy, it leaves that character's responses unspecified textually. There is, of course, the legal tradition to consider that silence indicates consent—*qui tacet consentire videtur*—but was this legalistic interpretation readily recognised by Shakespeare's audience, or

---

[28] As Angelo's second soliloquy (at the beginning of II, iv) is divided into two parts by a message from a servant (after line 17), it could be argued that he speaks four soliloquies in total. It seems more sensible, however, to regard II, iv, 1–30 as a single, interrupted soliloquy.

has it been by any audience since Jacobean times? It is therefore for the actor and director to determine how most plausibly to present the character's response to the crisis by looking to evidence elsewhere in the text. With no dialogue, stage-directions, or other textual clues provided in the immediate context, readers, audiences, and performers are invited by silence to ponder a range of possible interpretations.

Although such pregnant silences occur intermittently in the course of *Measure for Measure*, they are particularly prevalent in the final scene. For example, Claudio is reunited with his sister, Isabella (who believed him dead and whose last words to him were a cruel curse), but there is no indication of how joyous—or possibly painful—their reconciliation might be: neither character speaks again in the play. Claudio and Barnadine, both condemned to death by Angelo, do not speak at all in this final scene to indicate their gratitude (or indifference) towards the Duke for his clemency. Claudio is reunited with his true love, Julietta, but neither speaks. Similarly, Angelo remains almost entirely silent throughout the proceedings in which his fate is decided, and never expresses any change in his feelings towards Mariana, the woman whom he perfidiously rejected but whose love and devotion save his life. Most problematically of all, each of the Duke's two proposals of marriage to Isabella is met with silence. How these open (i.e. unresolved) silences are interpreted will determine the mood which prevails at the end of the performance: cheerful optimism; or profound disquiet.[29]

---

[29] A second Claudio, in an earlier Shakespearian comedy, declares that 'Silence is the perfectest herald of joy' (*Much Ado about Nothing*: II, i, 275). In a later comedy, *The Winter's Tale*, Paulina says to Leontes, 'I like your silence; it the more shows off / Your wonder' (V, iii, 21–2). If silence were interpreted on these lines at the end of *Measure for Measure*, then Claudio and Isabella would display unalloyed delight at their reunion, and Isabella would joyously accept the Duke's offer of marriage. Confidence in such a fairy-tale ending, however, is by no means secure.

Setting: What's in a Name?

Although the opening of the text in the First Folio, and incidental remarks in the course of the play, set the scene of *Measure for Measure* 'in Vienna' (e.g. I, i, 22), that location is problematical. The names of the (generally) patrician characters in the play, those who frequent court and convent, sound suspiciously Italian: among the males, Vincentio, Angelo, Claudio (often addressed with the Italianate title *Signior*), and Lucio; among the females, Isabella, Mariana, Julietta, and Francisca. In addition, the courtiers, as if they have stepped out of the pages of Shakespeare's copy of Plutarch's *Lives*, tend to have classical Roman names: Escalus, Flavius, Valencius, and Crassus (with Rowland—from Carolingian legend?—thrown in for good measure). Such names give some credence to the relatively recent scholarly opinion that Shakespeare originally set the play in Ferrara, and that this setting was changed to Vienna—possibly by Shakespeare's friend and collaborator, Thomas Middleton—not long before the publication of the First Folio in 1623.[30]

---

[30] For evidence that Middleton revised the play for the stage, see Gary Taylor and John Jowett, *Shakespeare Reshaped, 1606–1623* (Oxford: OUP, 1993), pp. 191–229. See also 'Shakespeare's Mediterranean *Measure for Measure*', in *Shakespeare and the Mediterranean: The Selected Proceedings of the International Shakespeare Association World Congress, Valencia, 2001*, edited by Tom Clayton, Susan Brock, and Vicente Forés (Newark: University of Delaware Press, 2004), pp. 243–269. Taylor and Jowett suggest that Middleton changed the setting of *Measure for Measure* from Italy to Vienna, possibly because Ferrara was already the setting of *The Phoenix* and Middleton wanted to avoid confusion between Shakespeare's play about a disguised ruler, and his own. Metrically, both 'Vienna' and 'Ferrara' are natural amphibrachs (weak/strong/weak), which would render seamless the substitution of the latter for the former location in Shakespeare's play whenever the name of the setting occurs in verse. Either setting would work in performance. Trish Thomas Henley reviews two parallel productions of *Measure for Measure* in Indianapolis in February–March 2013, one set in Ferrara and one in Vienna: '*Measure for Measure, Ferrara* and *Measure for Measure,*

Unlike his close colleague and theatrical rival, Ben Jonson, Shakespeare never unambiguously set a comedy in London, to reflect contemporary conditions and institutions.[31] Nevertheless, the underworld of the city of Vienna represented in *Measure for Measure* closely resembles the seamy side of Southwark, an area of London well-known to Shakespeare as the site of theatres such as the Rose, the Swan, and the Globe, as well as of numerous prisons, taverns, brothels, and gaming-houses. Significantly, although the more reputable characters in the play are distinguished by Italianate or Latin names, the characters who frequent the underworld and the prison of *Measure for Measure* have comic (sometimes vulgar) names of English origin: Froth, Abhorson, Overdone, and Bum (Pompey's surname) among the speaking-roles; together with the numerous offenders, mentioned by Pompey at the start of Act IV scene iii, whose names show strong affinities with the English morality-play tradition.

Then, at the interface between the criminal world and the prison, we encounter Elbow. He is Shakespeare's stock, blundering English constable rather than any putative member of a Viennese constabulary.[32] Elected by the parish, in the English fashion, Elbow performs his functions 'for some piece of money' (II, i, 267). His replacement will be chosen from a

---

Vienna (review)', *Shakespeare Bulletin* 31, no. 3 (Autumn 2013), pp. 499–505.

[31] Jonson's 'London' comedies include *Eastward Ho!* (1605, in collaboration with Chapman and Marston), *The Alchemist* (1610), *Bartholomew Fair* (1614) and *Every Man in his Humour* (the 1616 edition). All these plays post-date *Measure for Measure* in holding up a mirror to the very metropolis in which they were performed.

[32] Elbow's close kinship with Dogberry, the obtuse constable in *Much Ado about Nothing*, has frequently been identified in the critical tradition. Both are quintessentially English. According to John Aubrey (1626–97), Shakespeare based Dogberry on the 'humour' of a Buckinghamshire constable whom he met on his travels. The relevant passage from *Brief Lives* is quoted by Arthur R. Humphreys, ed., *Much Ado About Nothing* (London: Methuen, 1981), p. 21.

list of names submitted to the magistrate. (II, i, 269–70). These practices would be familiar to Shakespeare's audience as English, rather than continental, customs.

Much of the supporting evidence that Mistress Overdone's underworld would have been entirely familiar to Shakespeare's audience derives from the second scene of the play, which is set in (or in the vicinity of) her brothel.[33] Pompey's news that 'All houses in the suburbs . . . must be plucked down' (I, ii, 88–9) finds its parallel in King James I's measure, dated 16 September 1603, to curb the spread of the plague in London by demolishing 'houses of resort' in the suburbs—that is, in areas such as Southwark, immediately beyond London Bridge and therefore outside the limits of the city.[34] Similarly, Pompey's reference to the 'wise burgher' who 'put in' for morally dubious 'houses . . . in the city' (I, ii, 88–92) is a reminder that many prominent figures in Shakespeare's London—including at least one senior courtier, at least one bishop, and a number of theatrical entrepreneurs—owned property leased for the sex-trade.[35] Lever even suggests that Mistress Overdone's lament over her loss of trade (I, ii, 75–7) might all be closely related to the immediate circumstances prevailing in Shakespeare's contemporary society.[36] '[W]hat with the war' would have reminded his audience of the long conflict between England and Spain that began in 1585 and was waged intermittently until concluded by James I through the Treaty of London in

---

[33] Dominic Dromgoole's 2015 production for the Globe Theatre went further. Before the opening words of Act I, scene i, an interlude had been played in the pit, with Mistress Overdone and her retinue of whores, pimps, and clients mixing freely with the audience, some of the costumed characters retiring to the privacy of a 'house of resort' (here, a kind of overgrown Wendy-house) for extravagant sexual activity.

[34] Lever, pp. xxxii and 13.

[35] Jane Coles and Rex Gibson, ed., *Measure for Measure* (Cambridge: CUP, 1993), p. 29, n. 7. The identity and significance of some of these prominent figures is discussed in Chapter 6 of this study, pp. 356–359.

[36] Lever, p. xxxii.

August 1604, just a few months before the new monarch attended a performance of *Measure for Measure*. '[W]hat with the sweat' (i.e. fever) might link to the high incidence of syphilis in early-seventeenth-century society (to which *Measure for Measure* makes frequent reference), but is more likely to refer to the major outbreak of the plague in London in 1603 that killed over 30,000 of those living in the city,[37] and that closed the theatres until April 1604 because of the risk to public health. In a country in which 'every law day between twenty and thirty condemned men were hanged',[38] 'what with the gallows' might be particularly topical because of the fate of the conspirators in the Bye Plot against James I, who were tried at executed at Winchester in the last two months of 1603. Finally, 'what with poverty' might mirror the steep decline in trade in England's capital in 1603–4, the result of deaths from the plague and the flight of many more from the infected city.

One occupant of Vienna's prison, Ragozine, bears a name that is clearly not of English origin. It may suggest that he is a native of the Adriatic coastal area around Dubrovnik, which was known in Shakespeare's day as the *Respublica Ragusina*.[39] This victim of 'a cruel fever' was 'a most notorious pirate' (IV, iii, 69–70). Piracy was a topical issue to Shakespeare's audience. James I issued 'Proclamations . . . for the search and apprehension of certaine Pirates . . . [and] . . . to represse all Piracies' in response to Spain's demands under the Treaty of London of August 1604. Anglo-Dutch 'piracy' against Spanish vessels, especially treasure fleets from the New World, was a drain on the Spanish exchequer: hence Spain's demands of England to curb the activity as a pre-condition for the cessation of hostilities between the two nations. Piracy is, by definition, a

---

[37] Braunmuller and Watson, p. 8. The reference may even recall the sweating-sickness of 1551, although this mysterious Tudor plague had not recurred during Shakespeare's lifetime.

[38] Gamini Salgado, *The Elizabethan Underworld* (London: Dent, 1977; repr. Stroud: Alan Sutton, 1992), p. 11.

[39] https://en.wikipedia.org/wiki/Republic_of_Ragusa, accessed 18 July 2020.

seaborne offence (as Lucio indicates early in *Measure for Measure*: I, ii, 7–8). As England's large navy and numerous merchant-vessels had immediate access to the oceans of the world, it would be entirely plausible that a troublesome pirate might be festering in one of London's prisons, for example the Marshalsea in Southwark, a short walk from Shakespeare's Globe Theatre.[40] One would be considerably less likely to encounter a pirate in the vicinity of Vienna, several hundred kilometres from the nearest sea-coast.[41]

Despite the textual references to Vienna, the eclectic range of names encountered in the play suggests an indeterminate setting. For audiences then and now, however, so much of the incidental detail of *Measure for Measure* reflects early-seventeenth-century London society more closely than some exotic city in central Europe. It was therefore possible for director David Thacker, in his 1994 production for BBC Television, to make modern Britain a convincing location by removing all references to Vienna while adding nothing to the text.

Themes, Language, and Imagery[42]

The title of *Measure for Measure* ultimately derives from Christ's words in the Sermon on the Mount, where he warned of the dangers of earthly judgement:

1. Judge not, that ye be not judged.

---

[40] The Marshalsea was particularly associated with maritime offences: see Salgado, p. 184.

[41] Gary Taylor's suggestion that *Measure for Measure* was originally set in Ferrara, an Italian city relatively close to the Adriatic, may explain Shakespeare's choice of Ragozine's name.

[42] I do not discuss the centrality and associations of the word 'sense' in *Measure for Measure* as the task has already been undertaken admirably by William Empson in *The Structure of Complex Words* (London: Chatto and Windus, 1951). The relevant chapter is reprinted by Stead, pp. 187–212.

2. For with what judgment ye judge, ye shall be judged, and with what measure ye mete, it shall be measured unto you again. [Matthew 7: 1–2][43]

Here, the word 'measure' refers to the 'quantity or degree of something', suggesting that severity in judgement will be answered with severity, and leniency with leniency. Shakespeare expresses this biblical doctrine not merely in the general drift of the play but more specifically in the exchanges between the two magistrates at the opening of Act II. Escalus's warning (II, i, 4–16) tactfully expresses to his colleague the injunction expressed in Verse 1 of Matthew 7: judges should beware of incurring the same penalty under the law as those whom they condemn. Angelo's reply (II, i, 17–31) complacently accepts the future consequences for him of the second verse from the Gospel: he is content to be judged according to the severity with which he sentences offenders.

In response to this passage from Matthew 7, Shakespeare's language in *Measure for Measure* is frequently founded on comparisons that 'measure' the equivalence of pairings. Central to this formula are those images involving scales, balancing items of equal weight, and those related images involving coinage, which is exchangeable for a precise value. The former concept is at its most apparent when the Duke, passing sentence on Angelo, condemns his Deputy in words that justify the title of the play, confirming the equilibrium of the scales of justice. This speech by Vincentio also incorporates the word 'pays', linking the imagery of coinage apparent since the first scene with this rhetorical flourish at the very end of the play:

'An Angelo for Claudio; death for death.
Haste still pays haste, and leisure answers leisure;

---

[43] Kermode, p. 146, notes the similar injunction to be found in St. Paul's Epistle to the Romans 2: 1: ' Therefore thou art inexcusable, O man, whosoever thou art that condemnest: for in that thou condemnest another, thou condemnest thyself: for thou that condemnest, doest the same things.'

Like doth quit like; and Measure still for Measure.'

[V, i, 407–9]

Angelo had condemned Claudio to death for the very fault that he, Angelo, has subsequently committed. The Duke here claims to be recording what 'the law cries out / Most audible, even from his proper tongue' (V, i, 405–6); but, in deploying key diction from the Sermon on the Mount in this sentence on Angelo, the Duke is also echoing what Claudio calls 'The words of Heaven' (I, ii, 114) in both language and spirit. Vincentio's speech suggests that earthly and divine law are in complete accord in condemning Angelo.

Thus, 'measure' in the play signifies 'treatment' or, more specifically, 'sentence under the law'. When Claudio (according to the Duke *qua* friar) accepts that he has 'received no sinister measure from his judge' (III, ii, 236–37), the condemned man is acknowledging that his death-sentence under the statutes governing fornication is just. The play abounds in such 'measures' against offenders: Julietta, Pompey, Mistress Overdone, Lucio, and Barnadine— as well as Claudio and Angelo—all have corrective 'measures' imposed upon them. The whole of the final scene of the play comprises a series of 'measures' pronounced according to the deserts of the recipients. The scales of justice determine that the 'measure' (or 'judgement') that each ultimately receives from the Duke is appropriate to the 'measure' (or 'extent') of praise or blame that each deserves.

A 'measure' is therefore also a gauge, the means by which the scope of something is ascertained. In this sense, from the very beginning of the play, the Duke employs an ethical yardstick to 'measure' those whom he encounters. These tests culminate when the Duke investigates the moral 'measure' of all the characters who speak in the final scene, before undergoing a similar moral trial himself.[44]

---

[44] This second sense of 'measure' is more fully investigated in Chapter 2, 'The Return of the Duke', pp. 130–148.

42

According to a third sense of 'measure'—prevalent since the Middle Ages and therefore familiar to Shakespeare's audience (if less so to a modern audience)—'measure' means 'moderation'. *Measure for Measure* could therefore be regarded as a dramatic vindication of moderation in government generally and, more specifically, in judicial sentencing. The Duke's excessive leniency, to which he confesses to Friar Thomas in Act I, scene iii, contrasts sharply with Angelo's subsequent rigorous enforcement of the statutes; yet both indulgence and severity bring suffering and injustice. When the Duke returns in the final scene, his 'measure', that is, his moderation in dispensing justice, might be regarded as a temperate way of achieving equilibrium between merciless stringency and reckless clemency.

That the Duke should be regarded as the dramatic embodiment of 'measure' in the sense of 'moderation' might be justified by reference to the words of the wise old counsellor, Escalus. He characterises Duke Vincentio as 'A gentleman of all temperance' (III, ii, 231), praising his self-government and the restraint of his pleasures:

One that, above all other strifes, contended especially to know himself. . . . Rather rejoicing to see another merry, than merry at anything that professed to make him rejoice.
[III, ii, 226–30]

'Temperance' might readily be equated here with 'measure': Escalus's testimony to the Duke's composed disposition and to the priority that he gives to self-understanding presents him as the personification of moderation. The description also contrasts him sharply with Angelo, whose first soliloquy shows how little he knows himself, who gives his 'sensual race the rein' (II, iv, 159) in his assault on Isabella, and who abandons all temperance—both in his personal life and in his administration of the law—once he has succumbed to lust.

43

The title of the play, *Measure for Measure*, is also relevant to economic considerations. In ensuring that 'with what measure ye mete, it shall be measured unto you again', scales not only symbolise justice but also establish the value of the coinage of the realm according to the weight of precious metal that each coin contains. From the very first scene of *Measure for Measure*, images of coining are prominent. Coins bear the likeness of the head of state, guaranteeing the validity of the currency. Forgery and 'laundering and barbing' (dissolving or shaving precious metal from coins) are therefore offences against the monarch as well as against the economy, as they simultaneously debase the royal image and the currency. Such offences were punishable by death, which brings us neatly back to the scales of justice which determine sentence according to the seriousness of the offence.

In the first scene of the play, the Duke lectures Angelo on his duties as Deputy, developing a financial image (I, i, 36–40) by deploying the words 'lends', 'scruple' (that is, a tiny weight), 'thrifty', 'creditor' and 'use' (that is, financial interest). In response, Angelo expresses his doubts about his ability to occupy the Ducal position:

> Now, my good lord,
> Let there be some more test made of my metal,
> Before so noble and so great a figure
> Be stamp'd upon it. [I, i, 47–50]

Angelo doubts his own value: he fears that he may not be pure gold and will therefore be unworthy to bear the image of the head of state. He invites a test of his metal/mettle to establish whether he is worth the honour of governing in the Duke's absence—ironic, as the Duke will later (I, iii, 50–4) reveal that he is testing his new deputy by this very act of giving Angelo authority. Angelo will fail the test because his metal/mettle is alloyed with baser material, his impure desire. The 'measure' of his metal/mettle will be insufficient to counterpoise the weight of responsibility that he will bear in governing the state. When the Duke promises Isabella that she will see 'the corrupt deputy scaled' (III, i, 255–6), he is predicting that his deputy will be weighed in the balance of justice and (implicitly) found wanting.

Angelo returns to the imagery of the scales of justice and coinage in his exchanges with Isabella, who is attempting to save her brother from execution under the statutes against fornication:

> Ha? Fie, these filthy vices! It were as good
> To pardon him that hath from nature stolen
> A man already made, as to remit
> Their saucy sweetness that do coin heaven's image
> In stamps that are forbid. 'Tis all as easy
> Falsely to take away a life true made,
> As to put mettle in restrained means
> To make a false one. [II, iv, 42–9]

To justify the capital sentence that he has imposed upon Claudio, Angelo seeks to equate the sin of begetting illegitimate offspring (lines 45–6) with the sin of murder (lines 43–4). In Angelo's scales of justice, the two offences are equally culpable. When repeating his assertion, he uses the image of minting a false coin ('put[ting] mettle [/metal] in restrained means / To make a false one') to equate debasing the state's population by illicit procreation with debasing the state's coinage by forgery.[45] For Angelo, murder, coining, and

---

[45] Cf. *Cymbeline*, II, v, 2–6, where Posthumus, convinced that 'We are all bastards', talks of his conception as the time 'When I was stamp'd' and concludes, 'Some coiner with his tools / Made me a counterfeit.' Braunmuller and Watson point out (p. 243) a striking parallel in *Edward III* (a play attributed in part to Shakespeare), where the Countess, in admonishing the King, equates the mortal consequences of forgery with those of illegitimate begetting:

> He that doth clip or counterfeit your stamp,
> Shall die, my lord; and will your sacred self
> Commit high treason against the king of heaven
> To stamp his image in forbidden metal? [II, 421–4]

unlawful sexual reproduction weigh equally in the balance, all deserving the death-penalty.

But Shakespeare's language here is strikingly ironic in echoing Angelo's coining image in the very first scene (where he requested that 'some more test' should be 'made of [his] metal, / Before so noble and so great a figure / Be stamp'd upon it'). When, in these later exchanges with Isabella, Angelo equates illicit sexual activity with capital offences, his words recoil on himself as they are part of his strategy in the intended seduction of Isabella. A test, then, has been made of his 'metal/mettle', and he has failed it because of his desire 'to put mettle in restrained means', a phrase superficially concerned with minting but burdened with strong sexual connotations. He stands condemned to death under his own judgement, as he is contemplating a sin that he has weighed in the balance and determined to be of similar gravity to murder and forgery.

Angelo's very name links him to this imagery of coinage, in that an angel was a gold piece (introduced in England by Edward IV in 1465). In one of his gnomic asides, the Duke exclaims indignantly,

Twice treble shame on Angelo,
To weed my vice, and let his grow!
O, what may man within him hide,
Though angel on the outward side! [III, ii, 262–5]

Angelo is an 'angel on the outward side' in that he is superficially pious and just; but evil and hypocrisy 'within him hide'. Similarly, a coin may have the divine image of an angel stamped upon it, but that is no guarantee that it contains unalloyed precious metal. The Duke's words imply that Angelo has proved to be false currency, debasing the coinage of government.

Angelo's last words before his long absence from the stage (from the end of Act II until towards the end of Act IV) synthesize these images of the scales of justice and coinage.

46

Having boasted to Isabella that his reputation, ascetic life, testimony, and rank will 'your accusation overweigh' (II, iv, 154–6), he concludes: 'my false o'erweighs your true' (II, iv, 169). The antithesis presents a glaring perversion of justice: Angelo's lies carry more weight and authority than Isabella's truth. But there is also a monetary paradox. The validity of coinage might usually be established on the monetary scales because gold weighs more than base metals, but Angelo's 'false' coinage tips the balance against the truepenny, Isabella. Angelo is sneeringly confident that the 'gravity' (literally, 'weightiness': see II, iv, 9–10) in which he takes such pride will outweigh Isabella's truthful testimony, should the two be publicly counterpoised.

We should not set aside these references to coinage without noting the connection between the monetary imagery in the play and the theme of disfiguring the divine image, both the image of God and the image of God's deputy on Earth, the ruler of the state. As has already been established, Angelo closely associates the begetting of an illegitimate child—the defacing of God's image—with damaging the coinage that bears the image of the ruler (II, iv, 42–9). Undeniably, Angelo, who doubted from the outset whether his 'metal' was worthy to 'be stamp'd' with 'so noble and so great a figure' (I, i, 47–50), seriously impairs the image of the head of state by the offences that he commits while wielding power.

The blasphemy of illicit sexual reproduction and the crime of lese-majesty in disfiguring the image of God's viceroy are further associated dramatically and linguistically in the play through the figure of Lucio. Lucio the whoremaster is not only the begetter of an illegitimate child, corrupting God's image, but also one who defaces the Duke's image by uttering slanders against Vincentio (III, ii, 83–182 and IV, iii, 148–77). According to Lucio, the Duke was sexually promiscuous, fathering 'a thousand' bastards (III, ii, 113–17). In addition, Lucio alleges that Vincentio is unstable, drunken, foolish, and ignorant—seriously damaging accusations that Lucio speaks merely 'according to the trick' (V, i, 502–3) rather than from any foundation of hard evidence.

It might even be argued that Vincentio himself defaces the ducal image in donning his disguise as a friar: in Lucio's words, 'It was a mad, fantastical trick of him to steal from the state and usurp the beggary he was never born to' (III, ii, 89–90). The Duke's behaviour while in disguise—swearing false oaths, usurping the holy sacraments, deceiving and manipulating the vulnerable—scarcely does credit to his position as head of state. The ducal image is tarnished by malpractice just as surely as the coinage of the state would be debased by forgery, laundering, or barbing.

A further strain of imagery that Shakespeare deploys when exploring the 'properties of government' relates to animals. For example, both the Duke (I, iii, 22–3) and Lucio (I, iv, 62–4) envisage the negligent head of state as an inactive lion whose function should be to regulate the behaviour of other beasts by the fear that it inspires.[46] Most prominent among these animal images, however, are those related to horses, where the horse represents baser human instincts and corrupt desires in need of external regulation. For example, Claudio, in describing the early regime of Angelo, speculates on the new Deputy's possible motives for ruthless enforcement of the law:

> . . . whether that the body public be
> A horse whereon the governor doth ride,
> Who, newly in the seat, that it may know
> He can command, lets it straight feel the spur . . .
> I stagger in. . . . [I, ii, 148–54]

Angelo is here imagined as an imperious horseman, determined from the outset to prove his fitness to govern by imposing his

---

[46] The imagery probably derives from Aesop's popular fable of the sleeping lion and the mouse, possibly via Robert Henryson's *Morall Fabillis* (written in the 1480s), where the story was expanded to explore its relevance to government and the administration of justice.

will on the animal, that is, on the 'body public' and its bestial passions; hence, the arrest and severe sentencing of Claudio and his betrothed, Julietta, under previously neglected statutes that condemn fornication and unauthorised procreation. The Duke himself deploys a similar image when explaining to Friar Thomas the function of Vienna's laws:

> We have strict statutes and most biting laws,
> The needful bits and curbs to headstrong jades. . . .
>
> [I, iii, 19–20]

In these lines, stringent laws are the harness (the 'bits and curbs') by which the unruly populace (the 'headstrong jades', signifying 'wayward horses') are restrained. This pattern of imagery reaches its apotheosis when Angelo makes his assault on Isabella's virginity:

> And now I give my sensual race the rein. . . . [II, iv, 159]

Angelo's 'sensual race' is a stud of unruly horses being given free rein, as he allows his lascivious desires full liberty. Thus Angelo, who was previously described by Claudio as a horseman intent on regulating the baser instincts of the beast when he was newly in the saddle of state, now proves incapable of governing his own animalistic desires. This strain of equine imagery supports a central concept of *Measure for Measure*: that a ruler becomes a tyrant when indulging in the very offences for which he prosecutes others under the law. This is confirmed when the Duke, speaking of Angelo, remarks,

> . . . were he meal'd with that
> Which he corrects, then he were tyrannous. . . .
>
> [IV, ii, 81–2][47]

---

[47] Such hypocrisy in government seems to be the prevailing conception of tyranny in the Jacobean era. James I's speech to Parliament of 21 March 1610 defines a tyrant in closely comparable terms: 'And therefore a King governing in a settled Kingdome, leaves to be a King, and degenerates into a Tyrant, assoone as he leaves off

Having failed to control the 'headstrong jades' of his own desires, Angelo becomes a tyrant, and (according to contemporary political theory) a tyrant can justifiably be deposed—as Angelo is in the final scene.

A further pattern of language discernible in the text is that relating Angelo to the Devil and Hell. Angelo, the fallen angel, becomes a type of Lucifer, the 'Light Bearer', the trusted deputy once favoured by 'power divine' (V, i, 367) but now transformed into Satan, fallen from grace into sin and resident in Hell. Much of the infernal imagery directed against Angelo derives from the oppressed, indignant Isabella in her exchanges with her brother in the prison:

> There is a devilish mercy in the judge. . . . [III, i, 64]

> This outward-sainted deputy . . .
> . . . is yet a devil:
> His filth within being cast, he would appear
> A pond as deep as hell. [III, i, 88–93]

> O, 'tis the cunning livery of hell
> The damnedst body to invest and cover
> In precise guards! [III, i, 94–96]

Each of these extracts focuses on hypocrisy, deploring the divergence between the pious, judicious, external appearance of Angelo ('mercy', 'outward-sainted', 'cunning livery' and 'precise guards') and the concealed evil of his true identity ('devilish', 'devil', 'filth', 'hell', and 'damnedst body'). The Devil, commonly known as 'the father of lies' to Shakespeare's contemporaries, would generally be recognised as the author of all such hypocrisy. When the horrified Isabella is informed by the disguised Duke that Angelo has broken his oath and executed her brother, her opinion of Angelo's diabolical evil is

---

to rule according to his Lawes.' [*King James VI and I: Political Writings*, ed. Johann P Sommerville (Cambridge: CUP, 1995), p. 183]

forcibly confirmed: the Deputy is now 'most damned Angelo!' (IV, iii, 122). In his disguise as Friar Lodowick, the Duke also equates Angelo with the Devil when he confronts his deputy occupying the judgement seat:

> . . . let the devil
> Be sometime honour'd for his burning throne.
>
> [V, i, 290–1]

Once the Duke doffs his disguise to appear 'like power divine' (V, i, 367), the fallen angel has been cast down by the seemingly omniscient, omnipotent sovereign and must submit to judgement.

Angelo's conception of his own virtuous nature forbids him to recognize himself as a devil, although he recognizes the role of the devil in his downfall:

> O cunning enemy, that, to catch a saint,
> With saints dost bait thy hook! Most dangerous
> Is that temptation that doth goad us on
> To sin in loving virtue. [II, ii, 180–3]

The 'cunning enemy' to whom Angelo refers is Satan, who presents him with temptation in the saintly form of Isabella. Angelo speaks in the tradition of Marlowe's Doctor Faustus, who was tempted into mortal sin by the 'heavenly' form of Helen of Troy, even while recognising that such an apparition must have been deployed by a devil, one of the 'spirits as can lively resemble' the long-dead beauty (Dr. Faustus, IV, i, 50). An equation therefore arises, in which Isabella thinks that Angelo is an embodiment of the devil, while Angelo believes the same of Isabella, or at least that she is the means by which the devil achieves his ends. Angelo's words, presenting Isabella as the devil's agent, recall Hamlet's recognition that 'the devil hath power / T'assume a pleasing shape' (Hamlet: II, ii, 595–6). Angelo, though, is attempting to rationalise what is false within, to alleviate his guilt by transferring from himself to an external agent the responsibility for his fall from grace. His words are characteristic of those male attitudes in the play that seek to equate women with sin and temptation, according to the Judeo-Christian tradition of the fallen Eve. However, although *Measure for Measure* may refer to this belief on a number of occasions, it does not follow that the play endorses what would nowadays be regarded as an offensively sexist attitude.

Women and the Patriarchy

At the very beginning of Creation Theatre's 2008 production of *Measure for Measure* in Oxford, back-lighting presented the silhouettes of two men standing, each with a woman kneeling before him in apparently identical submissive postures. As the main stage-lighting rose, it gradually revealed that one of the pairings involved a friar blessing a nun, and the other comprised a male compelling a female to offer him sexual gratification orally. The tableau presented the Vienna of *Measure for Measure* as a patriarchy, a society where women are subservient to male authority from the nunnery to the brothel, and where men may use their dominance promiscuously, to virtuous or to vicious effect.

As implied by the Creation Theatre tableau, the women presented in the first half of *Measure for Measure* might indeed be regarded as falling into only two categories: saints and sinners. In Act I scene ii, the audience learns of the sex-trade in Mistress Overdone's 'house of resort' and witnesses the public humiliation of the pregnant Julietta, sentenced by Angelo under the statutes against fornication. Later, in Act II, scene ii, it is suggested that Constable Elbow's wife sought to cuckold her husband with Master Froth through the agency of Pompey the pimp. Counterpoising these early representations of fallen women is Act I, scene iv: in the convent of the Poor Clares, Francisca the nun converses with Isabella the novice about the rules of the order and—with reference to the benevolent regime of the Prioress—protection from potentially predatory males. The female roles comprise only these two extremes, saints and sinners, until a third, more 'measured' category of women is introduced into the play at the end of Act III scene i, with the first mention of the betrothed but abandoned Mariana.

The women in the play are generally subject to the judgement of males in positions of judicial authority.[48] Mistress Overdone is condemned by Escalus and the Provost. Evidence against Mistress Kate Keep-down (mother of Lucio's illegitimate child) and Constable Elbow's wife (who consorted with Master Froth in a brothel) is presented before Escalus. Julietta, Mariana, and Isabella are separately judged by both Angelo and the Duke, although the judgements of these two authority-figures prove quite distinct. In the world beyond the nunnery, male judgement prevails.

The Duke expresses a patriarchal view in the final scene of the play, where he acknowledges only three types of women:

> *Duke.*   What, are you married?
> *Mariana.* No, my lord.
> *Duke.* Are you a maid?
> *Mariana.* No, my lord.
> *Duke.* A widow, then?
> *Mariana.* Neither my lord.
> *Duke.* Why, you are nothing then: neither maid, widow, nor wife! [V, i, 172–9]

This formula presupposes that all women should be defined solely according to the *legitimate* stage that they have reached in their association with men: they are either virgin, married, or widowed. As the Duke has excluded from his consideration the *illegitimate* fourth category—an unmarried woman who has lost her virginity—Lucio jocularly corrects him:

> My lord, she may be a punk; for many of them are neither maid, widow nor wife. [V, i, 180–1]

---

[48] The exceptions are confined to the nunnery: the Prioress, who is mentioned in one speech but never appears on stage, and Francisca the nun, who appears solely in Act I, scene iv.

The definition and social status of Lucio's additional type of woman—the prostitute—is again determined by her association with men. A modern audience may find such definitions—both the Duke's ostensibly more reputable view and Lucio's characteristically degenerate view—uncomfortably sexist. As women are categorised *by* men according to their relationship *with* men, they would seem to have no independent identity, nor any right to define themselves.

Measure for Measure is, nevertheless, far from presenting women as simply the dutiful handmaids of men. Most obviously, in Isabella, Shakespeare creates a young woman who has sufficient courage, integrity, and intellect to confront the tyrannical patriarchy that she encounters in Vienna. Additionally, Mariana achieves her objective of securing her reputation and her happiness by challenging publicly both the influential man whom she loves and the ruler who appointed him to power. These two women ultimately prove both determined and resourceful, rather than merely dependent submissively on men for their identity and destiny.

Two of the less prominent women in the play, Julietta and Mistress Overdone, may evoke sympathy from the audience for their redeeming features. Although both fall victim to a patriarchal society that regulates their sexual activity with the punishment of imprisonment, both take responsibility for the consequences of sin and show compassion for others, despite their own miserable circumstances. Julietta bravely accepts the blame for her sexual relationship with Claudio and grieves, not for her imprisoned self, but for the fate of her partner who is to be executed for his offence. Mistress Overdone assumes the burden of nurturing Lucio's illegitimate child, even though she is not the mother. Julietta is variously described as 'Madam Julietta' (I, ii, 66–7), 'Madam Juliet' (I, ii, 107), 'the lady' (I, ii, 136), and 'a gentlewoman' (II, iii, 10), suggesting noble birth, while Mistress Overdone may qualify for the Duke's more legitimate title of 'widow' (as Pompey insists at II, i, 195); but both have been reduced, by lack of discrimination under

Viennese law, to the level of Lucio's derogatory fourth category of women—the punk, who is 'neither maid, widow, nor wife'. Julietta and Mistress Overdone nevertheless merit some regard from the audience for the compassion and benevolence that they both show during the privations that they suffer.

The Duke subjects three of these four women to trials of their virtue. Just as he imposed a test on Angelo in the very first scene (by deputing further powers upon him to reveal the extent of his corruptibility), so the Duke tests Julietta, Mariana, and Isabella as the play progresses. The audience is alerted to the prospect of such tests when the disguised Duke informs Claudio (falsely) that 'Angelo had never the purpose to corrupt [Isabella]; only he hath made an assay of her virtue, to practise his judgement with the disposition of natures' (III, i, 160–3). He similarly warns Isabella that, were she publicly to accuse Angelo of his attempt on her virtue, he would respond that 'he made trial of you only' (III, I, 195–6). Such trials and tests are entirely appropriate in a play entitled *Measure for Measure*, with its connotations of judgement tempered by moderation. Although Angelo fails his test, being exposed as a hypocritical tyrant, all three of the women emerge from their trials with their integrity affirmed. Julietta proves her penitence and her selfless devotion to her partner, Claudio, in her confessional scene with the Duke (II, iii). Mariana endures a public trial and seeming condemnation to win the man whom she loves, pleading for his repeal to the Duke and rejecting his alternative offer of great wealth 'to buy you a better husband' (V, i, 423). Lastly, Isabella endures the most demanding series of trials as, in turn, her patience, humility, obedience, compassion, and forgiveness are tested by the Duke in the latter half of the play, proof of her virtue leading to his two offers of marriage to her at the close of the final scene.

Reputation and Notoriety

Judgement of others, however, is not the preserve of the Duke, Angelo, Escalus, and the remaining (male) officers of the law; it is also present in the common voice, the means by which reputation is conveyed. As is the case with Shakespeare's contemporaneous play, *Othello*, reputation is a central concern of *Measure for Measure*. The first impressions imparted of dramatic characters—their initial appearance, words, and actions—are always highly influential on an audience. In *Measure for Measure*, however, many important characters are introduced to the audience *prior* to their first appearance on stage, by the reports that others give of them. Their reputations go before them as evidence of how they have been 'judged' by public opinion and therefore of how an audience might judge them.

Shakespeare offers pertinent perspectives on reputation in *Othello*, a play that was performed by the King's Men before James I in Whitehall on 1 November 1604, the month before the first recorded performance of *Measure for Measure* before the same monarch.[49] In that earlier production, the new King would have heard 'good name in man and woman' defined as 'the immediate jewel of their souls' (*Othello*: III, iii, 159–60): reputation is presented as an individual's most treasured possession. In *Othello*, however, reputation proves an unstable attribute, painstakingly acquired over a lifetime, and lost in a moment as the result of false report or rash indiscretion. Thus Cassio, dismissed from his military commission for drunkenness on duty, laments, 'O, I have lost my reputation! I have lost the immortal part of myself, and what remains is bestial' (*Othello*: II, iii, 254–6). Iago's pragmatic response, however, calls into question the validity of many reputations: 'Reputation is an idle and most false imposition; oft got without merit and lost without deserving' (*Othello*: II, iii, 261–3). A good reputation is thus subject to vagaries and open to question: it may be unjustly undermined, or it may not have been merited in the first place. These caveats should be borne in mind when

[49] Gamini Salgado, *Eyewitnesses of Shakespeare: First Hand Accounts of Performances 1590-1890* (New York: Harper and Row, 1975), pp. 23–24.

characters are first introduced by reputation in *Measure for Measure*.

The reputations of Claudio and Julietta are established prior to their first appearance on stage. Mistress Overdone, addressing the gentlemen who frequent her 'house of resort', boldly asserts that Claudio is 'worth five thousand of you all' (I, ii, 57). Her hyperbole (Claudio's first mention in the play) immediately establishes Claudio's esteem among the common people. When Mistress Overdone refers to him as '*Signior* Claudio' (I, ii, 59; italics added) and to his betrothed as '*Madam* Julietta' (I, ii, 66–7; italics added), she bestows upon each a distinguished title that she does not employ elsewhere and that expresses high regard for the two lovers. Reputation, though, can be fragile and deceptive. Mistress Overdone's brutally-phrased message that 'within these three days [Claudio's] head [is] to be chopped off' (I, ii, 62–3) shocks the audience that such a respected young man, convicted for illicit sexual activity, is to suffer imminent capital punishment. Sympathy for the plight of the two lovers is reinforced when their reputations are undermined by their humiliating exposure to public ridicule on their first entry, under fifty lines later. The dignity and restraint with which Claudio speaks of his trial and sentence suggest that he fully merits the compassionate esteem that so many characters in the play demonstrate towards him.

Claudio refers to the reputation of Isabella, his sister, when he begs Lucio to recruit her as his potential saviour. He praises her ability to persuade, anticipating her two great scenes in Act II by referring to her 'prone and speechless dialect / Such as move men' in conjunction with her 'prosperous art / When she will play with reason and discourse' (I, ii, 173–5). He also, in referring to her novitiate at the cloister, implies that she is religiously devout (I, ii, 167–8). Ironically, however, these very qualities that he praises in her will increase his anguish. She will indeed 'move' Angelo with her 'prone . . . dialect' when he is transformed by lust for her into a tyrant threatening to torture Claudio to death unless she should submit to his sexual demands. In addition, her piety will transform into moral

57

outrage against her brother when, in the prison, she condemns Claudio to suffer such an agonizing death.

What, though, of the bad rather than the good reputation? Mistress Overdone suffers as a result of her notoriety. The Provost's testimony that she is 'a bawd of eleven years' continuance' confirms Escalus's resolve to dispatch her to prison, ignoring her appeals and denying her any further hearing (III, ii, 190–200). Of all the disreputable characters in the play, however, it is Barnadine, the murderer, whose reputation seems most monstrous. Far more words are spoken about Barnadine than are spoken by him, and those that precede his first appearance are unerringly damning (IV, ii, 59–60 and 126–51). Pompey seems apprehensive of Barnadine's fearsome reputation when he refuses to enter Barnadine's cell to bring him to the block (IV, iii, 21–35). When Barnadine finally enters the stage, the expectation is that he will be as intimidating in appearance and as loathsome in manners as he is in reputation.[50]

The most significant reputation in *Measure for Measure*, however, is Angelo's. In the opening lines of the play, the Duke informs us that Escalus is more learned and experienced in affairs of state than any whom he can remember (I, i, 3–13); but it is upon Angelo that the Duke intends to bestow power in his absence, his decision implying that Angelo's abilities transcend even those of the Duke's most accomplished courtier. This appraisal of Angelo is (ambiguously) endorsed by Escalus: if anyone in Vienna should deserve promotion to such a distinguished position as deputy to the absent Duke, Angelo is

---

[50] However, as *Measure for Measure* elsewhere confirms Iago's premise that reputation 'is an idle and most false imposition, oft got without merit', a subtle dramatic point might be made were Barnadine's appearance to belie all previous reports of his character and behaviour. In seeking to amuse and to challenge the audience by defying expectation, a bold director might decide that such a mountainous reputation should give birth to a lounge-lizard, if not to a ridiculous mouse.

he (I, i, 22–4). Angelo's illustrious reputation in government is thus established before he first appears. Subsequently, Shakespeare allocates Angelo under sixty words before the Duke's departure (sufficient merely to extend Angelo's character sketch to include humility and obedience). The task of communicating Angelo's formidable professional achievements and renown has already been achieved by means of the testimony of other characters.

Early in the play, Claudio strongly suspects that Angelo's initial stringency—enforcing the law rigorously, including statutes that had long fallen into disuse—is an attempt to enhance his 'name', that is, his reputation (I, ii, 154–60). Angelo himself so firmly believes in his reputation for sobriety, wisdom, and rigid discipline that he cannot recognise himself when he encounters the first stirrings of his lust for Isabella: this confusion is apparent throughout his first soliloquy (II, ii, 163–87). In his second soliloquy, Angelo confesses that his 'gravity'—the image of dignified, 'weighty' solemnity—is the reputation that he most values and desires to present to the public (II, iv, 9–12). He is so confident of his good reputation in Vienna that he can boldly defy Isabella's threat to expose him as the lecherous tyrant into which he has degenerated (II, iv, 153–8). Isabella herself is obliged to acknowledge that Angelo's reputation is such that her just accusations against him, were she to utter them, would be dismissed: 'Did I tell this / Who would believe me?' (II, iv, 170–1). Those in elevated positions in the state habitually enjoy immunity from accusation because of their enhanced reputations.

Inextricably intertwined with the issue of Angelo's reputation is the reputation of his former betrothed, Mariana. When she is first named by the Duke, Isabella responds, 'I have heard of the lady, and good words went with her name' (III, i, 208–12). Although the two women have seemingly never met, Mariana's reputation for integrity is already well known to Isabella. Before Mariana ever appears on stage, the audience learns much from the Duke of her circumstances. Mariana's beauty and virtue are her only remaining dowry, as her wealth was lost at sea with her brother's shipwreck. Mariana's honour, however, has been unjustly tarnished: Angelo, seeking on the loss of her dowry to justify his breach of promise to marry her, has blackened her reputation, 'pretending in her discoveries of dishonour' (III, i, 226–7). As a result, Mariana has seemingly withdrawn from—or been ostracised by—society, retreating into the 'moated grange' (III, i, 265), a prisoner of her grief, her enduring love for Angelo, and her public disgrace at his hands.

Later, after Mariana's first appearance on stage, she risks further public humiliation by acceding to the 'bed trick' and then by confessing publicly that she 'ne'er was married', even though she is now 'no maid' (V, i, 185–6). The Duke enables her to purge her tarnished reputation by marrying her to Angelo as 'safeguard of [her] honour',

> . . . else imputation,
> For that he knew you, might reproach your life,
> And choke your good to come. [V, i, 417–20]

Angelo, having sullied Mariana's honour by his words and actions, must redeem her reputation through marriage.

It is therefore entirely appropriate that Angelo's ultimate punishment should be public humiliation and the entire loss of *his own* reputation. Such a loss to him should appear as traumatic as Cassio's loss of his reputation in *Othello*: Angelo loses what Cassio calls 'the immortal part' of himself, and appears to regard 'what remains' as 'bestial'. When Escalus expresses sorrow that Angelo's reputation as 'one so learned and so wise' has been betrayed by his 'heat of blood / And lack of temper'd judgement' (V, i, 468–471), Angelo responds that, for him, execution will be preferable to pardon:

> . . . I crave death more willingly than mercy;
> 'Tis my deserving, and I do entreat it. [V, i, 474–75]

These are Angelo's last words in the play, confirmation that death is a consummation devoutly to be wish'd when it provides release from public disgrace and loss of reputation.

Disguise, Deception, and Seeming

Just as Shakespeare investigates the dichotomy between appearance and reality through the presentation of reputation, so he furthers this investigation through his presentation of disguise, deception, and 'seeming' (that is, hypocrisy). Although the Duke is the chief practitioner of disguise and deception, and Angelo the most obvious example of 'seeming', these issues in *Measure for Measure* are multifaceted, affecting many other characters and situations.

For example, in response to the demands of propriety and then (more pressingly) the proclamation that all houses of resort in the suburbs are to be 'plucked down' (I, ii, 88–9), Mistress Overdone is obliged to disguise her brothel as a tavern (Pompey is named as her 'tapster' or bartender at I, ii, 104), a bath-house (II, i, 65), or an eating-house (II, i, 88–108). Pompey equivocates and prevaricates to disguise his true occupation as a pimp, so that Froth and he may 'seem' innocent when they face Elbow's charges before Escalus (II, i, 84–253). The Provost sends Angelo the head of Ragozine disguised as Claudio's, to thwart the Deputy's intention to execute Isabella's brother (IV, iii, 68–77 and V, i, 529–31). When the disguised Mariana takes Isabella's place in Angelo's bed, he is tricked into consummating his vow of marriage to the woman whom he deserted (III, i, 243–51 and V, i, 171–232). It is particularly appropriate that the arch-seemer, Angelo, should himself be deceived by the judicious 'seeming' of others. Disguise, deception, and 'seeming' form intricate patterns in this play.

Particularly prominent among the 'seemers' is Lucio. He appears to be a loyal associate—indeed, to Claudio, he is 'good friend Lucio' (I, ii, 182), and there is ample evidence to justify this assessment, in that he is consistently supportive both to Isabella and to her unfortunate brother. But others who trust

61

him are betrayed. Pompey refers to Lucio as 'a gentleman, and a friend of mine' (III, ii, 40–41), but he is deceived on both counts. Lucio refuses to bail him, and there is the implication, in Lucio's words, 'say I sent thee thither [i.e. to prison]' (III, ii, 61–2), that Lucio informed on Pompey to the state. Certainly, on her arrest and imprisonment, Mistress Overdone asserts that it is Lucio who has betrayed her: 'this is one Lucio's information against me' (III, ii, 192–3). Only an accomplished 'seemer' could betray the confidences of his close associates in this manner.

Lucio frequently resorts to lies and deception. He freely admits to Isabella that his seduction-technique involves insincerity and hypocrisy to impress young women:

> . . . 'tis my familiar sin,
> With maids to seem the lapwing, and to jest
> Tongue far from heart. . . . [I, iv, 31–3]

His boasts and slanders to the disguised Duke are of a rather different order. An audience may accept Lucio's admission to Isabella at face value—that he is indeed a deceitful seducer of impressionable girls—but that same audience is less likely to believe his claim that 'I was an inward' of the Duke (III, ii, 127), particularly as the Duke shows no signs of recognising any previous acquaintance between them. Lucio is clearly bragging, attempting to enhance his dubious social status by claiming that he was a courtier with intimate knowledge of the absent ruler. The audience should therefore be similarly sceptical about Lucio's estimations of the Duke: 'A very superficial, ignorant, unweighing fellow' (III, ii, 136) who 'had some feeling of the sport' of illicit sexual activity (III, ii, 115–16). If Lucio had no intimate acquaintance with the Duke, he had no opportunity to acquire evidence of such secret defects in Vincentio's character. Despite the inconsistencies of the Duke's behaviour as portrayed by Shakespeare, there is no verification elsewhere in the text of any of the flaws that Lucio attributes to Vincentio. Additionally, 'unweighing' proves ironic as a description of one who presides over the concluding judgement-scene in the play, balancing measure for measure in the scales of justice.

Lying, even under oath, is Lucio's obvious means of deception to avoid the consequences of his actions. He admits to the disguised Duke that

I was once before [Vincentio] for getting a wench with child. . . . Yes, marry, did I; but I was fain to forswear it.
[IV, iii, 167–70]

He is quick to lie, even when he thereby incriminates an innocent party: in the final scene of the play, he falsely maintains to the court that his own slanders against Vincentio were spoken by Friar Lodowick (V, i, 262–63 and 328–33). An audience will anticipate with relish the 'unhooding' of Lucio when he pulls down the Duke's cowl. Shakespeare counterpoints Lucio's nemesis with the more serious public revelation of Angelo's lies against his accusers, the two 'seemers' being exposed simultaneously when the Duke casts off his Franciscan attire. Deception—the Duke's disguise—has been used to expose deception—the 'false seeming' of Lucio and Angelo.

Although Lucio's 'seeming' may sometimes appear spontaneous and whimsical—'I spoke it but according to the trick' (V, i, 502–3)—Angelo's is consistently studied and devious. The former amuses us with his 'fantastical' behaviour; the latter horrifies us with his insidious evil. Angelo may seek to deceive everyone in the play with his outward show of sober authority, but he cannot deceive himself. His great soliloquies (particularly II, ii, 163–87 and II, iv, 1–23) suggest how dismayed the learned ascetic is to encounter the lecherous despot within. It does not appear that he has deliberately concealed his true character from himself: rather, like Lear, it would seem that 'he hath ever but slenderly known himself' (*King Lear*: I, i, 292–3).

He has not, however, deceived the Duke who, as early as the third scene of the play, predicted Angelo's ultimate exposure as a 'seemer' corrupted by power (I, iii, 53–4). Soon, Isabella will be confronted by the truth of Angelo's '[s]eeming, seeming!' (II, iv, 149) when he seeks to strike his indecent bargain with her. Angelo cunningly disguises his words, insinuating his meaning to maintain, for as long as necessary, the opportunity to retreat to an inviolable position of power and privilege. Finally, however, the brutal tyrant emerges as he threatens to torture Claudio to death should Isabella refuse to satisfy his sexual demands. Angelo compounds his offence against Isabella by relying on the 'seeming' virtue of his reputation and status to thwart any appeal that she might make against him (II, iv, 154–5). In the final scene of the play, to disguise his guilt, he publicly impugns the sanity of both Isabella and Mariana when they testify against him (V, i, 35 and 236). However, when the Duke expresses absolute confidence in his deputy and grants Angelo's petition to preside over his own trial (V, i, 238), it is the prelude to Vincentio's revelation of Angelo's guilt. Deception is again deployed to expose the deceiver.

This is merely one example of the numerous times that the Duke resorts to disguise, deception, and 'seeming' to achieve his ends. At the very beginning of the play, he deliberately misleads his entire court, which 'supposes me travell'd to Poland; / For so I have strew'd it in the common ear, / And so it is receiv'd' (I, iii, 14–16). His purpose is to test Angelo, a man on whom he lavishes apparently unstinted praise and supreme authority (I, i, 15–52), while disguising his suspicions that Angelo, the 'precise' puritan, is a 'seemer' whose 'purpose' will be corrupted by 'power' (I, iii, 50–4).

Better to observe Angelo's rule and the people whom it affects, the Duke proposes to disguise himself as a friar. Like Henry VIII seventy years before *Measure for Measure* was first performed, Vincentio usurps the authority of the Catholic Church for morally questionable purposes. In so doing, he will also usurp four of the seven sacraments of the Church: holy orders, penance, extreme unction, and matrimony. In his guise as Friar Lodowick, the Duke will insinuate his way into the prison, confess Julietta, reconcile Claudio to death, and eavesdrop on Isabella's private interview with her brother. While publicly seeming to support Angelo's measures against sexual offences, he will secretly labour to save Claudio from the sentence of death imposed by Angelo. While still disguised as a friar, he will persuade Isabella—a novice nun—deliberately to deceive his deputy: she will pledge to gratify Angelo's sexual desires, but another woman (Mariana) will take her place in Angelo's bed. In addition, the Duke will deceive both Angelo and Isabella into believing that Claudio has been executed. Each of these morally dubious activities raises the question of whether the end justifies the means—disguise, deception, and 'seeming'—that the Duke employs.

The Duke's deceptions span the entire play. Before the final judgement-scene, Vincentio (in the guise of Friar Lodowick) has instructed Mariana and Isabella in equivocation and 'indirect' speaking, the better to deceive Angelo. Appearing then in propria persona, the Duke pretends to believe that Angelo's conduct as Deputy has rendered him beyond suspicion. Vincentio's deception encourages Angelo's hubristic belief that his lies will triumph over the truths spoken by his accusers. Once Vincentio has revealed his dual identity as duke *and* friar, he seemingly feigns an intention to execute Angelo, not only to mortify his deputy but also to test the reactions of Mariana and Isabella. Similarly, the Duke seemingly feigns an intention to dismiss the Provost for beheading Claudio without a warrant, and to execute Lucio for his slanders, although he will remit his sentence on all three men. Finally, he reveals an intention that he has kept disguised throughout the play, even from the audience: he twice proposes marriage to Isabella.

In *Measure for Measure*, characters wishing to 'seem' other than they are practise 'deception' involving 'disguise'. Sometimes, they become 'substitutes' for others.[51] Substitutes

---

[51] Braunmuller and Watson (pp. 16–24) note the importance of the word 'substitute' and its derivatives in *Measure for Measure*, which

imitate the actions and appearance of those whom they emulate, appropriate clothing being a vital component. It was a mediaeval and renaissance commonplace that a ruler was God's substitute on earth, aspiring to God's magnificence and authority. In *Measure for Measure*, Angelo is Vincentio's substitute in Vienna. Vincentio has therefore 'dress'd him in our love' (I, i, 19) so that Angelo can perform 'my [i.e., the Duke's] part' (I, i, 41). The 1974 RSC production, directed by Keith Hack, offered striking visual confirmation of the close association between costume and role in *Measure for Measure*: in the final scene, the Duke literally stripped his Deputy of his great cloak of office before reassuming it himself. Authority was symbolised by a single, imposing garment. Whoever wore the garment, whether a duke or his substitute, wielded supreme power.[52]

The metatheatrical nature of the final scene is implied when Isabella reminds Mariana of her 'part' in accusing Angelo (IV, vi, 3), while Mariana subsequently pleads with Isabella to 'take my part' (V, i, 428). As Mariana has already played the 'part' of Isabella in ensuring the success of the bed-trick, each woman becomes a substitute for the other in time of need. In the RSC's 1998 production, directed by Michael Boyd, Mariana and Isabella literally changed clothes: Mariana thus 'became' Isabella for the tryst with Angelo, making the deception more plausible to the audience.[53]

Imagery of clothing used to conceal true identity is particularly significant in the language of Isabella and Angelo. Isabella addresses Angelo with a general condemnation of

---

uses the word more often than any other Shakespeare play—more than a quarter of the uses in the entire Shakespearian canon.

[52] Braunmuller and Watson (p. 133) reproduce a photograph of the final scene of this production, where the huge cloak dominates the entire image.

[53] As the title of Gottfried Keller's 1874 novella suggests, *Kleider machen Leute* (literally, 'clothes make people').

'man, proud man, / Dress'd in a little brief authority' (II, ii, 118–19) before her more specific condemnation of the Deputy:

O, 'tis the cunning livery of hell
The damnedst body to invest and cover
In precise guards. [III, i, 94–6]

The 'precise guards' are the puritanical trappings that clothe ('invest') Angelo, part of the clever costume ('cunning livery') that the Devil has provided to conceal the Deputy's evil. Angelo urges Isabella to acknowledge her femininity 'By putting on the destin'd livery' (II, iv, 137), as if it were preordained that any nun's austere garb should be discarded in acknowledgement of a woman's sexual subservience to men. When he turns his scrutiny on himself in his second soliloquy, Angelo recognises that his external appearance ('case') and dress ('habit') conceal his hypocrisy ('false seeming'), even from the more discerning:

O place, O form,
How often dost thou with thy case, thy habit,
Wrench awe from fools, and tie the wiser souls
To thy false seeming! [II, iv, 12–15]

As convincing clothing is indispensable to the hypocritical seemer, so it is to the Duke's substitute.

Angelo's remarks about disguise prepare us for the great final scene of the play, in which clothing, both literal and metaphorical, will be stripped away to produce successive moments of *anagnorisis*, those occasions of sudden and profound revelation encountered in classical tragedy. Mariana will lift her veil to reveal Angelo's betrothed; Vincentio will cast off his monastic garb to reveal the Duke; Barnadine and Claudio will be 'unmuffled' to reveal their miraculous survival; while Angelo and Lucio will be revealed as criminals, stripped of all moral disguise. The language in this final scene confirms that clothing conceals rather than reveals the truth, that wickedness cannot be readily identified until the clothing that disguises it is torn away. Lucio asserts that a monastic cowl does not necessarily signify a holy man (V, i, 261); while Isabella deplores 'the evil which is here wrapt up / In countenance' (V, i, 120–1). The two contexts are fused into a striking example of proleptic irony. Removal of Friar Lodowick's monastic cowl will reveal the Duke, at which point Angelo's 'evil', metaphorically 'wrapt up in countenance', will be disclosed.[54]

Actors undertake their roles by dressing in other people's clothes, assuming their mannerisms, and borrowing their speech. Disguise, deception, and seeming are therefore an indispensable component of all theatre. *Measure for Measure*, however, takes disguise, deception and seeming further: when so many actors play characters who conceal the truth about themselves, or who transform themselves into new roles in the course of the play, those frequent changes of appearance or identity assume a metatheatrical significance. Layers of dramatic meaning are uncovered in certain key words: 'play', 'part' and 'act'. Like any other drama, this is a *play* in which *players* assume the *parts* of characters; but some of those characters *play* both themselves and *parts* other than themselves. For five *Acts*, the *actors* portray those who perform immoral *acts* and those who enforce legislative *acts* against such offenders;[55] but those enforcing the legislative *acts* may be employing disguise, deception and 'seeming' to conceal their immoral *acts*.

In *Measure for Measure*, strands of disguise, deception, and 'seeming' are interwoven with other threads of the plot to establish a richly dramatic tapestry. Implicitly, the characters by whom—and the contexts in which—disguise, deception, and 'seeming' are deployed will determine whether specific words

---

[54] Isabella's line might even anticipate Barnadine's ultimate appearance, when the Duke at first cannot identify this 'evil'-doer because his 'countenance' is 'wrapt up'.
[55] Cf. 'His act did not o'ertake his bad intent' (IV, i, 449) and 'Condemn'd upon the act of fornication' (V, i, 73).

and actions are considered defensible or morally culpable. Angelo's hypocrisy, although rendered human and comprehensible in soliloquy, is consistently appalling. The deceptions practiced by the Provost and Mariana are entirely vindicated. Those prevarications in which Mistress Overdone and Pompey indulge could be condoned on the grounds of necessity, in keeping with Pompey's protests in defending his way of life: 'I am a poor fellow that would live' (II, i, 220). Definitive moral judgement of Lucio's deceptions and lies is more problematical: he betrays trusts and disseminates slanders but, as a 'fantastique', he may be redeemed somewhat by his wit, humour, and teeming imagination. And what of the deceptions practised by the Duke and Isabella? If their ends always justify their means, then they are exonerated; but there lingers the suspicion that both could be accused of culpable conduct, compromising moral principles for personal benefit.

Mercy and Forgiveness

At the end of the play, nevertheless, an audience is encouraged to pardon the Duke and Isabella, as the pre-eminence of mercy and forgiveness has been established. These two protagonists are themselves central to this process: the Duke offers a general amnesty to those who have offended against the law; and Isabella pleads specifically for Angelo's life while still believing him guilty of executing her brother in contravention of his oath to her. Angelo, so harsh in his administration of justice, must forgive Claudio and Julietta their offences, and pardon the Provost who deceived Angelo while disobeying his orders. In complying, Angelo may prove himself worthy of the mercy of the Duke—and the forgiveness of the audience. Implicitly, Isabella and Claudio must forgive each other for their harsh words in the prison, while the Duke must forgive the personal slanders of Lucio. Although darker interpretations are possible, what textual evidence there is suggests that the play concludes harmoniously, with mercy and forgiveness ending conflict and ensuring reconciliation.

The importance of mercy was established early in the play. In the very first scene, the Duke deputed power to Angelo with the words,

> Mortality and mercy in Vienna
> Live in thy tongue, and heart. [I, i, 44–5]

The Duke's phrasing carefully balances the two poles of the law: judgement must arbitrate between punishment ('mortality', which signifies the death-sentence) and pardon ('mercy', which may extend as far as forgiveness). The conjunction 'and' (line 44) suggests that these two extremes should be kept in careful balance: the 'tongue' may pronounce 'mortality' in imposing capital punishment, but the 'heart' should mollify the severity of that sentence by offering 'mercy'. The Duke's words suggest that he requires Angelo to preserve this balance between stringency and lenity in his administration of the scales of justice. In addition, his injunction to Angelo anticipates the Duke's own actions in the final scene, where he will condemn both Angelo and Lucio to death before commuting their sentence.

Act II, however, presents Angelo as heedless of this prescription from the Duke: Angelo's rule promotes 'mortality' and denies 'mercy'. Escalus's plea for clemency for Claudio (II, i, 6–16) falls on deaf ears as the puritanical Angelo cannot empathise with a man who has succumbed to sexual temptation. When Isabella attempts to remind Angelo that mercy is a more admirable attribute in a ruler than any material symbol of office (II, ii, 58–63), she receives a blunt rebuff: 'Pray you be gone' (II, ii, 67). Considerations of mercy are banished from Angelo's court. It is therefore necessary for Isabella to remind the Deputy of the Christian conception of mercy:

> Why, all the souls that were, were forfeit once,
> And He that might the vantage best have took
> Found out the remedy. How would you be,
> If He, which is the top of judgement, should
> But judge you as you are? O, think on that,

And mercy then will breathe within your lips,
Like man new made. [II, ii, 73–9]⁵⁶

Isabella's opening lines consider the fallen nature of humankind, whom God might justly have condemned to eternity in Hell for their sins; but God's mercy 'found out the remedy' in Christ's blood-sacrifice to redeem sinners. Her two concluding sentences (lines 75–9) recall Christ's words in the Sermon on the Mount (Matthew 7), from which *Measure for Measure* derives its title: Angelo is reminded that, if he hopes for mercy from God's Final Judgement, then he should be merciful to Claudio. Angelo, however, remains unmoved. When he eventually offers to repeal the sentence on Claudio, it will be in exchange for Isabella's sexual favours. Such a transaction treats mercy as a commodity to be bartered in exchange for carnal gratification, not as compassionate forbearance in imitation of God's grace.

Isabella herself shows little mercy towards Claudio in their encounter early in Act III: with her chastity threatened, she is as unwilling as Angelo to counterpoise justice with mercy, savagely condemning her brother to a cruel death and offering 'No word to save [him]' (III, i, 135–50). This is one of several respects in which Isabella is closely comparable with her antagonist, Angelo. In the first half of the play, neither recognises the imperatives of either love or life, as each is preoccupied with icy virtue. A thought-provoking modern definition of mercy—'the willingness to enter into the chaos of another'⁵⁷—raises the question of whether Angelo and Isabella, having no sympathy with such moral disorder, lack both the

---

⁵⁶ The whole of this context (II, ii, 58–79) invites close comparison with an earlier speech from a Shakespearian 'problem' comedy: Portia's address to Shylock in *The Merchant of Venice*: IV, i, 179–97.
⁵⁷ James F. Keenan, SJ, *Thinking Faith*, 4 December 2015, https://www.thinkingfaith.org/articles/scandal-mercy-excludes-no-one. Over the centuries, several prominent writers have been scandalized by the Duke's pardon for Angelo at the end of the play. Professor Keenan contends that mercy is scandalous precisely because it excludes no-one.

inclination and the capacity to empathise with what they perceive as disgusting human weakness. Ultimately, to merit forgiveness, both must learn how to forgive.

In the latter half of *Measure for Measure*, the Duke is the prime mover in ensuring that mercy ultimately prevails, although this objective is partly achieved through the agency of other characters. Ably assisted by the Provost—who has already pleaded for Claudio to Angelo (II, ii, 2–14)—the Duke successfully labours to save the condemned man from the Deputy's death-sentence. He also instructs the virtuous Mariana, first encountered in Act IV, who is instrumental in saving both Isabella and Angelo from their guilty condemnation of Claudio. Mariana, the embodiment of compassion, not only rescues Isabella from her loathsome compact with Angelo but also, admirably, proves able to forgive the man who has broken his oath to marry her and who, by dishonestly blackening her reputation, has condemned her to five years of ostracism and misery.

A viewer or reader cannot avoid assessing the moral status, the motives, and the behaviour of Shakespeare's characters in *Measure for Measure*. The play invites such a judgemental approach, as so many of the characters, while repeatedly passing judgement on other characters (and sometimes on themselves), are subject to the most testing circumstances. Not all emerge from their trials to their credit. The ascendancy of mercy and forgiveness in the final scene, however, confirms the Christian message implicit in the title, *Measure for Measure*: in echoing the wording of Christ's Sermon on the Mount, the play implicitly warns of the consequences of judging and condemning too harshly when all are fallible, requiring the ultimate mercy of God. The supreme accomplishment of mercy in *Measure for Measure* is that it can forgive an Angelo.

William Hazlitt, who published his thoughts on *Measure for Measure* in 1817, deserves the last word on the issue:

Shakespeare was in one sense the least moral of all writers; for morality (commonly so called) is made up of antipathies; and his talent consisted in sympathy with human nature, in all its shapes, degrees, depressions, and elevations. The object of the pedantic moralist is to find out the bad in everything: his was to shew that 'there is some soul of goodness in things evil'. . . . In one sense, Shakespeare was no moralist at all; in another, he was the greatest of all moralists.[58]

---

[58] *Characters of Shakespeare's Plays*: Measure for Measure, Project Gutenberg, 29 January 2011, http://www.gutenberg.org/cache/epub/5085/pg5085.html (partly quoted by Braunmuller and Watson, p. 86).

Chapter 2

The Duke

In *Measure for Measure*, Duke Vincentio is the dominant role, if only because he speaks more than 30% of the total lines, twice as many as his nearest rival (Isabella) in the play. He determines the development of the plot and the fate of the principal characters, while commenting authoritatively on political, moral, and philosophical issues that arise. His own moral character, however, is difficult to fathom. There are contradictions in the presentation of the Duke that cannot be explained away as the understandable inconsistencies of a 'realistic' character, or as plausible personal developments resulting from his experiences or from his changing circumstances. The Duke is fairly typical of the improbable protagonists often encountered in Shakespeare's romantic comedies—for example, the corresponding dukes in *As You Like It* (Duke Senior and Duke Frederick) and *Twelfth Night* (Duke Orsino)—but he inhabits the potentially tragic world of *Measure for Measure* less comfortably. Of the three major roles in *Measure for Measure*—Duke Vincentio, Angelo, and Isabella—the Duke proves the least tractable to consideration as a credibly 'human' character.

This may explain why it was proposed, in the last century, that the Duke is an embodiment of divinity rather than a realistic representation of humanity. In 1930, G. Wilson Knight attributed to Duke Vincentio an 'almost divine power of foreknowledge, and control, and wisdom'.[1] Ten years later, one of

---

[1] '*Measure for Measure* and the Gospels', in *Shakespeare*: Measure for Measure: *A Casebook*, ed. C. K. Stead, (London: Macmillan, 1971), p. 93. Stead (pp. 91–121) reprints the whole of this influential

the most influential English critics of the modern era, F. R. Leavis, endorsed this reading as 'the only adequate account', adding that the Duke is 'a kind of Providence directing the action from above'.[2] This interpretation, insisting that the Duke should be regarded as a moral and spiritual ideal, continued to hold sway in criticism during the 1940s.[3] It influenced stage-productions for more than twenty years: for example, at Stratford-upon-Avon, the Duke was presented as presiding 'like power divine' (V, i, 367) in William Bridges-Adams's production in 1931, and in subsequent productions by Frank McMullan (1946), Peter Brook (1950), and Anthony Quayle (1956).

A reaction was inevitable.[4] Once John Barton had directed his young Isabella to reject an aged Duke's advances in his 1970 production for the Royal Shakespeare Company, the tide had turned. Subsequent directors discovered a devious and sometimes downright disreputable side to the Duke, as the following random examples illustrate. When Charles Marowitz directed the play at the Open Space Theatre, London, in 1975, his Duke was a shameless political opportunist. At the New York Shakespeare Festival in 1983, Michael Rudman presented a Duke in the guise of a white imperialist. Simon McBurney's Duke at the National Theatre, London, in 2004 used electronic surveillance-systems to spy on a Vienna that resembled a

---

chapter from G. Wilson Knight, *The Wheel of Fire: Interpretations of Shakespearian Tragedy* (Cleveland and New York: Meridian, 1930).
[2] Stead, p. 18.
[3] For example, Roy W. Battenhouse believed that Vincentio resembles 'the Incarnate Lord' and is 'a sort of secret, omniscient, and omnipresent Providence' ('*Measure for Measure* and Christian Doctrine of the Atonement', *PMLA* 61, no. 4 [December 1946], pp. 1042 and 1047), while Elizabeth Marie Pope confirmed Vincentio's identification as 'an embodied Providence' ('The Renaissance Background of *Measure for Measure*', *SS* 2 [1949], p. 71).
[4] Braunmuller and Watson (pp. 63–64) refer to a number of twentieth-century literary critics who opposed the concept of the Duke's 'divine' image, including Clifford Leech, E. K. Chambers, William Empson, A. D. Nuttall, and Harry Berger Jr.

prison-camp or a torture-chamber; and when Josie Rourke directed the play at the Donmar Warehouse in 2018, her Duke was a manipulative sexist.[5]

Divergent interpretations of this problematical character have arisen because so many potentially conflicting elements encountered in the sources on which the plot of *Measure for Measure* is based find their dramatic expression in the Duke. For example, he embodies in one role at least three distinct figures encountered in a long narrative tradition comprising folk-tales and legends: the ruler who observes his people while moving incognito among them; the nobleman who seeks the hand of the virtuous woman of lower birth; and the judge who arbitrates shrewdly over a seemingly intractable case.[6] On investigation, Duke Vincentio may prove less a credible character than a composite dramatic device, whose actions and words, if observed too scrupulously, adversely affect the moral authority proper to his role as instigator, observer, and arbiter of others' actions in the play.

Vincentio, Machiavelli, and James I

Already a heavily-burdened dramatic construct, the Duke is also the medium through which Shakespeare embodies certain political doctrines of the new King, James I, and addresses the contentious issue of Machiavellian political philosophy.

The shadow of *The Prince* (1513–14), Niccolo Machiavelli's most famous—or rather most infamous—work, falls across *Measure for Measure* just as surely as it does across so many dramas of the Jacobean era. The realpolitik advocated

---

[5] These interpretations are discussed in greater detail in Chapter 8, 'Performances in More Recent Years', pp. 535–551.

[6] In the Judeo-Christian tradition, the story of the Judgement of Solomon from the First Book of Kings presents him as the archetypal wise judge; while, in the classical tradition, we encounter the deus ex machina who descends to restore order and happiness at the end of a Greek tragedy.

in Machiavelli's manual for efficient government was loathed and feared in Shakespeare's England. As early as 1589–90, Christopher Marlowe had presented Machiavelli on stage in the guise of 'Machevil', the dramatic induction to *The Jew of Malta* who relishes the villainy of the protagonist, Barabas. Only a year or two later, Shakespeare himself created the ultimate Machiavellian villain, whose declared aim was to 'set the murderous Machiavel to school' (3 *Henry VI*: III, ii, 193): this was Richard, Duke of Gloucester, the future Richard III, who lies, deceives, betrays, and murders to gain and retain the crown.[7] At the end of the Nineteenth Century, with the relatively limited resources then available, Edward Meyer counted 395 separate references to Machiavelli in Elizabethan literature alone,[8] suggesting the English preoccupation, in the years immediately before *Measure for Measure* was first performed, with what were perceived as Machiavelli's devilish doctrines.

The lines from Machiavelli's *The Prince* that concern us most in the context of *Measure for Measure*—indeed, the lines that most outraged Shakespeare's contemporaries—are found in chapter 17 of Machiavelli's advice to princes concerning effective government:

> From hence arises a dispute, whether it is better to be beloved or feared. I answer, a man would wish he might be the one and the other; but because hardly can they subsist both together, it is much safer to be feared than be loved, being that one of the two must needs fail. . . .[9]

---

[7] Machiavelli's Christian name may even have become contracted into 'Old Nick', synonymous with the devil. Although *OED* records no usage before 1643, the etymology linking the Devil to Machiavelli was attested by Samuel (*Hudibras*) Butler in the Seventeenth Century and by Lord Macaulay in the Nineteenth Century.

[8] *Machiavelli and the Elizabethan Drama* (Weimar: Litterarhistorische Forschungen, 1897).

[9] Quoted from Kamps and Raber, p.162.

The polarity suggested here between the beloved prince and the feared potentate is explored in Shakespeare's play in the presentation of the Duke and Angelo. Angelo's administration spreads fear in Vienna as he remorselessly seeks to regulate human sexual behaviour. Once he is discredited, however, the Duke can resume the business of good government to popular acclaim as the beloved ruler restored. In a play that proposes in its opening lines that its objective is 'of government the properties to unfold', this would seem to vindicate the popular opinion of Shakespeare's contemporaries in England: that Machiavelli was the Devil's advocate and that a good ruler should be loved rather than feared.

Such a simplistic interpretation of the text would confirm that the Duke, Vincentio, is the hero to be admired and the Deputy, Angelo, the villain to be abhorred, refuting Machiavelli's assertion that government inspiring fear is preferable to government inspiring love. *The Prince*, however, advocates that many morally dubious devices should be deployed by the successful ruler, including feigned piety, deception, lies, and swearing false oaths.[10] Such strategies, the refuge of the Machiavellian villain of popular Jacobean imagination, are more frequently the resort of the Duke than of Angelo. It is the Duke who disguises himself as a friar, who deceives his court about his intentions, who lies to Isabella about her brother's death, and who swears solemn (and false) oaths by the holy order to which he does not belong. Both Angelo and Vincentio, therefore, show symptoms of Machiavellianism. An important distinction, however, is that Angelo is publicly revealed to be a tyrant, whereas Vincentio, who deploys the tools of tyranny recommended by Machiavelli, appears virtuous to his subjects. As Machiavelli advocates this latter course to his prince—that is, that the successful prince should simply avoid being perceived as a tyrant by his people, even when resorting to the devices of tyranny—then Duke

---

[10] Kamps and Raber (pp. 132–134) discuss how these doctrines influenced Shakespeare's portrayal of Richard III.

Vincentio might, paradoxically, be considered a greater (and more successful) Machiavellian than his deputy, Angelo.[11]

We know of no performance of Meas*ure for Measure* earlier than that recorded in the Revels Accounts: it took place in the Banqueting Hall at Whitehall on 26 December 1604, before King James I. James's political works had been published frequently and read eagerly in England around the time of his accession on 24 March 1603, the day of Elizabeth I's death. Following the royal patent of 19 May 1603, Shakespeare's company, previously (since 1594) known as the Lord Chamberlain's Men, could now style themselves *The King's Men*. It would be inconceivable that Shakespeare, when writing a play so intimately concerned with the 'properties of government' for performance before the new King, would not have familiarised himself with at least the general tenets of James's political works to ensure that he gave no offence by challenging or contradicting the monarch who had so speedily granted royal patronage to Shakespeare's company.

The two works by James I with which we are here concerned are based on James's experience as King of Scotland prior to his accession to the English throne in 1603: *The True Law of Free Monarchies* (1598) and *Basilikon Doron* (1599).[12] In the former, James maintains that a monarch is above the law, asserting that, as he is the initiator of the law, he cannot be

---

[11] Braunmuller and Watson (p. 109) cite a context in *The Prince* (Book 6, 58–9) which would also suggest that Vincentio is created in the image of a devious Machiavellian. The story is of a duke who, having taken possession of Romagna, found that it had been weakly governed. He therefore installed a despot to reintroduce the rule of law ruthlessly. Afterwards, he held a court to exonerate himself and inculpate his deputy for any malpractice. The deputy was executed and his body left on display in Cesena, to chasten the people.

[12] The details quoted in this and the two paragraphs that follow derive from the extracts from James's writings discussed by Kamps and Raber, pp. 117–166.

subject to it.[13] He concedes, nevertheless, that a good king will abide by the law both in governing his subjects and in his own conduct, while insisting that a king may enforce, interpret, or mitigate laws according to his will. In such matters, he is answerable to no-one. By these criteria, Duke Vincentio in *Measure for Measure* might be entirely justified, first in having failed to enforce the 'strict statutes and most biting laws' (I, iii, 19) of Vienna, second in appointing Angelo temporarily to apply those laws more rigorously, and third in returning ultimately to re-establish his own, more moderate, regime. *The True Law of Free Monarchies* maintains that such a ruler should not be judged by lesser mortals as in any way culpable for his actions, either in tolerating unruly behaviour or in suppressing it stringently.

In *Basilikon Doron*, James's political treatise addressed to his son and heir, Henry, Duke of Rothesay, the King sharply contradicts Machiavelli's doctrine that a monarch should be feared rather than loved. He portrays the true monarch as a 'natural father and kindly master' to his people, one whose 'greatest surety' lies 'in having their hearts'. By contrast, he defines a tyrant as one who, 'counterfeiting the saint', will cause 'the ruins of the republic' by 'building his surety upon the people's misery'.[14] Arguably, Duke Vincentio's courting of public acclaim (when he scripts, directs, stage-manages, and takes the leading role in the final scene of *Measure for Measure*) illustrates his desire to appear as 'a natural father and kindly master' to his people, while Angelo, 'counterfeiting the saint', proves to have built 'his surety upon the people's misery'.

It has been proposed by certain editors and critics that Shakespeare created Duke Vincentio entirely in the image of

---

[13] James would have been acutely aware of how the authority of the monarchy had been undermined by the accusations of adultery, murder, and treason of which his mother, Mary, Queen of Scots, had been variously accused in Scotland and England.

[14] *Basilikon Doron* 20, quoted by Kamps and Raber, p. 132.

James I,[15] but it is safer to say that the Duke's attitudes, beliefs, and behaviour correspond with those of James I whenever Shakespeare finds it dramatically expedient. For example, James's distaste for crowds, frequently cited in modern editions, is likely to have influenced the presentation of Duke Vincentio early in *Measure for Measure*, specifically the Duke's words about not wishing to 'stage' himself to 'the people' (I, i, 67–70), or to 'haunt assemblies, / Where youth, and cost, witless bravery keeps' (I, iii, 9–10). There is, though, a metatheatrical device apparent here: first, the actor playing the Duke is literally staging himself to the people in a place where 'youth and cost, witless bravery keeps', as he is speaking the lines in a theatre.[16] In addition, the audience would have been aware, on at least one occasion (the first recorded performance in December, 1604), of the presence at the performance of the very monarch whose aversion receives reference in the Duke's speech. The Duke's opinion on crowds is repeated by Angelo who, in his second soliloquy, refers to how '[t]he general subject' cause 'offence' to a 'well-wished king' when they '[c]rowd to his presence' in 'obsequious fondness' (II, iv, 27–30). Evidence of James's distaste for crowded places derives from a contemporary treatise, *The Time Triumphant* (1604). This pamphlet records the King's strong displeasure at being accosted by a crowd when he (like Vincentio, seeking to pass among his people unrecognised) attempted to visit the Exchange incognito. Although *The Time Triumphant* was attributed to Gilbert Dugdale, who observed the incident at the Exchange, the credit for writing the tract was claimed by Robert Armin, one of Shakespeare's newly-promoted King's Men. It seems almost inevitable, then, that

---

[15] The evolution of this theory from its origin in the late Eighteenth Century is traced by Ernest Schanzer in *The Problem Plays of Shakespeare* (London: Routledge and Kegan Paul, 1963), pp. 123–126.

[16] As in Brechtian *Verfremdungseffekt*, the Duke's words disturb the willing suspension of disbelief at a theatrical performance by reminding the audience of the illusory nature of the drama, thereby encouraging a more rational, objective view of the issues being presented.

Shakespeare was fully aware of the King's aversion, which would explain why the Duke in *Measure for Measure* remarks, 'Nor do I think the man of safe discretion / That doth affect' the 'loud applause and *Aves* vehement' of 'the people' (I, i, 67–72). There is, however, an obvious inconsistency: although the Duke of the early scenes (like the scholarly James I) has 'ever lov'd the life removed' (I, iii, 8), on his return to Vienna at the end of the play, he becomes the ruler who delights in staging himself to the eyes of the people to win popular acclaim. Shakespeare thus endorses King James's wish to retain his distance from the common people while conveniently overlooking the issue when the dramatic context requires the converse.

Reputation, Rumour, and Rudolph II

The Duke's reputation in the play is established principally by three people: Lucio, Escalus, and Vincentio himself. Of these three characters, two give the Duke an unblemished (although, at times, contradictory) reputation; while the third (Lucio), who has most to say, presents a deeply flawed Vincentio.[17]

Escalus regards Vincentio as contemplative and introspective, seeking primarily 'to know himself', finding delight in others' enjoyment rather than seeking his own gratification, and practising moderation in all things (III, ii, 226–31). Escalus's portrait of the Duke is very much in keeping with the way in which Vincentio represents himself to Friar Thomas:

> . . . I have ever lov'd the life remov'd,
> And held in idle price to haunt assemblies. . . .
>
> [I, iii, 8–9]

---

[17] There is also a passing reference from Isabella to 'the good Duke' (III, i, 190), rather vague and generalised approval, but from the strictest of moral judges.

In addition, the Duke claims to be proof against sexual desire (I, iii, 1–3) as he possesses 'a purpose / More grave and wrinkled than the aims and ends / Of burning youth' (I, iii, 4–6).[18] When confronted by Lucio, he presents himself as sexually abstemious, maintaining that 'I have never heard the absent Duke much detected for women; he was not inclined that way' (III, ii, 118–19). These testimonies characterise the Duke as reserved and phlegmatic, an impression bolstered by Lucio's observation that Vincentio was a 'shy fellow' in his 'withdrawing' (III, ii, 127–9).

By contrast, when at bay and assailed by the allegations of Lucio, Vincentio (in disguise) claims the Duke to be 'a scholar, a statesman, and a soldier' (III, ii, 142). We have only his word for it! Although the Duke's language in the play is shot through with wise aphorisms, and although Vincentio's expressed preference for 'the life remov'd' (I, iii, 8) could imply a predilection for the scholarly pursuits of the cloister, there is no evidence elsewhere in the play of his success either as a statesman or as a soldier. Escalus's testimony and the Duke's words to Friar Thomas suggest a reclusive and possibly studious Duke rather than an active, outgoing head of state and military commander.

From the outset, Lucio represents Vincentio as irrational and untrustworthy. His words to Isabella, 'The Duke is *very strangely* gone from hence' (I, iv, 50; italics added), suggest puzzlement at—or even disapproval of—Vincentio's inscrutable actions. His further allegation—that the Duke on his departure 'Bore many gentlemen . . . / In hand' (that is, deceived them) because 'His giving out were of an infinite distance / From his true-meant design' (I, iv, 51–5)—might be accounted malicious slander on Lucio's part had the Duke himself not admitted to such a deception in the previous scene

---

[18] Like Angelo, however, the Duke will be tempted from abstinence by Isabella's 'prone and speechless dialect / Such as move men' (I, ii, 173–4).

(I, iii, 14–16). As the Duke has, indeed, used lies to disguise his intentions, Lucio's testimony here is well-founded.

Which brings us to Lucio's allegations against the Duke of gross sexual indulgence. Here, the immediate context of Lucio's remarks should not be disregarded. Apparently exasperated by the imminent threat to the life of Claudio, Lucio rails against the Duke's 'mad, fantastical trick' (III, ii, 89) to leave the state under the authority of Angelo, who has condemned Lucio's friend to death for fornication and illegitimate procreation. Seemingly carried away by his indignation at the injustice suffered by Claudio as a result of the Duke's dereliction of duty, Lucio presents the Duke as a man who not only condoned such sexual activity as that for which Claudio stands condemned, but also indulged in it himself:

> Would the Duke that is absent have done this? Ere he would have hanged a man for the getting a hundred bastards, he would have paid for the nursing a thousand. . . . Yes, your beggar of fifty; and his use was to put a ducat in her clack-dish. . . . [III, ii, 112–23]

The two allegations—fathering numerous illegitimate children and indulging in indiscriminate sexual activity—are suspect in that they mischievously distort apparently praiseworthy charitable activities into evidence of illicit sexual indulgence. As the play portrays the Duke as eager to avoid the public gaze (until the final scene, at least), it would be plausible for such a ruler to keep from public scrutiny his altruistic donations to abandoned children and to the poor. Here, an audience might conclude that confidentiality born of modesty is perverted by the distorting mirror of Lucio's 'fantastical' imagination into evidence of covert philandering. Once he has invented the offence, Lucio, seemingly by fanciful extrapolation, presents Vincentio as a seasoned lecher:

> He had some feeling of the sport; he knew the service. . . .
> The Duke yet would have dark deeds darkly answered: he would never bring them to light. . . . The Duke, I say to thee

again, would eat mutton on Fridays. He . . . would mouth
with a beggar though she smelt brown bread and garlic. . . .

[III, ii, 115–78]

Every one of these allegations accuses the Duke of promiscuity:
'the service' is clearly sexual activity, here portrayed as if it
were a facility provided by the state; 'dark deeds' suggests what
happens at night in the secrecy of the bed-chamber; to 'eat
mutton on Fridays' might, in a different context, be no more
than a literal reference to flouting the Catholic injunction to
abstain from eating meat on Fridays—but 'mutton' was slang
for a prostitute, implying that the Duke regularly defied a
different religious prohibition on fleshly indulgence; while the
allegation that he would 'mouth with a beggar' suggests that the
Duke was entirely indiscriminate in seeking sexual
gratification.[19]

To most audiences and critics, Lucio's allegations against
Vincentio—that he is 'mad' and sexually promiscuous—are
difficult to accept as credible. They are, however, surprisingly
similar to the rumours about the Emperor Rudolph II that were
circulating Europe at the time that *Measure for Measure* was
first staged. Rudolph was born in 1552 in Vienna, the city in
which *Measure for Measure* is set and from which Rudolph
governed from 1576 to 1583 (when he transferred his seat of
power to Prague). Afflicted by mental instability (both his
parents were grandchildren of Juana the Mad of Castile), he
would frequently withdraw entirely from public view. Although
Rudolph II never married, he is reputed to have been
indiscriminate in his sexual affairs—with both men and women.
Several women claimed to have been impregnated by him;
certainly, he fathered a number of illegitimate children by
Catherina Strada. A morbid indulgence in sexual activities may
well have contributed to Rudolph II's downfall, as sexual

---

[19] Lucio's words more accurately portray a different Duke, the 'royal
lecher' whom we encounter in Thomas Middleton's *The Revenger's
Tragedy* (I, i, 1), first performed in 1606, two years after *Measure for
Measure*.

allegations are likely to have been part of the whispering-campaign conducted by the Habsburg family and the Catholic Church that brought about his deposition in 1611.

Like Duke Vincentio, Rudolph 'ever lov'd the life remov'd' (I, iii, 8). He devoted his energies to the study of arts and science, commissioning many works, especially decorative objects and scientific instruments. Additionally, in 1604, the year of the first recorded performance of *Measure for Measure*, he faced revolt in Hungary, which perhaps prompted Lucio's references at the very beginning of the second scene in *Measure for Measure* to Vienna's incipient military campaign against Hungary.

It seems plausible, then, that the allegations about the secrecy, the irrationality, and the sexual excesses of Vincentio, 'the old fantastical duke of dark corners' (IV, iii, 156), might have been borrowed from these tales emanating from the Holy Roman Empire. According to Lucio, the Duke, 'a shy fellow', played a 'mad, fantastical trick' when he absented himself from affairs of state (III, ii, 127 and 89–90), the implication being that the Duke, like Rudolph II, is anti-social and mentally unstable, given to irrational whims. In addition, Lucio's allegation that Vincentio supported numerous bastards (implicitly, ones that he had fathered) and had 'some feeling of the sport' of fornication (III, ii, 112–16) creates a Vincentio very much in the image of the sexually promiscuous Rudolph II. Perhaps even the Duke's claim to be 'a scholar' (III, ii, 142) finds its origin in Rudolph, who was fluent in at least six languages as well as being a major patron of Renaissance arts and sciences.

Whose account is to be trusted—Lucio's or Vincentio's—with regard to the Duke's attitude to women in *Measure for Measure*? The Duke's proposal (proposition?) to Isabella at the end of the play invites consideration prior to any final decision on this matter. Lucio had regarded Vincentio as 'now past it' (III, ii, 176), but perhaps there is still heat in the blood of the 'grave and wrinkled' Duke (I, iii, 5) when, like Angelo, he finds the virtues of Isabella so alluring. Certainly, Vincentio's offer of marriage calls into question whether he is indeed proof against 'the dribbling dart of love' that he so confidently dismissed from consideration in his early conversation with Friar Thomas (I, iii, 1–3). It appears that Vincentio's efforts 'especially to know himself' (Escalus: III, ii, 226–7) have not met with much success in respect of his own amatory affairs (any more than they did in respect of his attitude to crowds). Ultimately, however, an audience is likely to conclude that Lucio's sexual allegations against the Duke would owe much more to the vivid imagination and personal indulgences of the former than to any lurid misdemeanours on the part of the latter.

The Duke's Monologues

The Duke's function as a dramatic device rather than as a psychologically convincing character may be illustrated by close reference to his 'soliloquies', which are probably more accurately described as choric monologues. These speeches by the Duke (all of which occur in Acts III and IV) are fundamentally different from Angelo's three soliloquies or Isabella's single soliloquy in that they throw no light on the speaker's deepest emotions or intimate thoughts. It is significant, for example, that an audience is not given the slightest indication in soliloquy of the Duke's amatory intentions towards Isabella: when he springs his proposal of marriage on her at the very end of the play, we as an audience are as surprised as she as a dramatic character should appear to be. The only context in which the Duke gives any substantial clues to his motives and feelings is in Act I scene iii, where the privacy of a conversation with Friar Thomas—most probably a confessional—gives him the opportunity for introspection. Friar Tomas is to the Duke what Horatio is to Hamlet: a sounding-board for the protagonist's thoughts. Elsewhere in *Measure for Measure*, however, there is little evidence in the Duke of the scrupulous self-examination of a Hamlet. Much of the Duke's 'inner life' remains a closed book as he defies the psychological scrutiny with which an audience may contemplate both Angelo and Isabella.

A few of the Duke's monologues might more properly be termed asides, but the majority have a choric function. Just as the Duke of Act V resembles the deus ex machina of Greek tragedy, so the Duke of Acts III and IV intermittently performs the function of the chorus of the Greek theatre, commenting on issues raised by the play and offering significant background information. Rather than revealing depths to his character, the Duke's monologues express generalised political philosophy, pass judgement on other characters, and map out future actions.

Between his re-entry in Act III scene i (at line 151) and the end of Act IV, most of the Duke's dialogue is in prose. The proverbial wisdom of the Duke's political philosophy is, however, consistently expressed in verse—just as the Greek chorus chanted its commentary on the action of the play in strophes. Further to distinguish between the Duke as chorus and the Duke when conversing with other characters, Shakespeare often incorporates rhyme into these ducal deliberations. For example, when informed by Elbow that Pompey the 'whoremonger' will be tried by Angelo, who 'cannot abide a whoremaster' (III, ii, 33–6), the Duke comments ruefully on the irony:

> That we were all, as some would seem to be,
> From our faults, as faults from seeming, free!
>
> [III, ii, 37–8]

His couplet (expressing the wish that all humanity could be as free from faults as 'some' appear to be, and that any faults committed should be undisguised and readily apparent) is a condemnation of the hypocrisy of the seemingly virtuous but secretly lascivious Angelo in passing judgement on a sexual offender.

When the Duke 'soliloquizes', his political philosophy is generalized rather than focused on his immediate personal circumstances. This is apparent after his first meeting in the play with Lucio: in disguise, he has heard himself represented as a lecher, a drunkard, and a fool by a man who claims to be 'an inward of his' (III, ii, 112–36). His response, when alone on stage, is curiously dispassionate, placidly judicious rather than passionately indignant:

> No might nor greatness in mortality
> Can censure 'scape. Back-wounding calumny
> The whitest virtue strikes. What king so strong
> Can tie the gall up in a slanderous tongue?
>
> [III, ii, 179–82]

Rather than expressing outrage or offering specific refutations to Lucio's allegations against him—which might convey the Duke's personal resentment and present him as more 'human' in his emotional responses—the speech comprises three brief, gnomic sentences, generalisations proposing that no ruler, however virtuous or powerful, can avoid slander. The form here is iambic pentameter couplets with liberal enjambment and irregular caesurae; however, when a further opportunity arises for the Duke to speak his thoughts at the end of the same scene, he changes to stilted trochaic tetrameters with lines heavily stopped at the end of each couplet—a form possibly in imitation of the wisdom of Cato's *Distichs*, popular since the Middle Ages. The Duke's subject is now the ideal ruler:

> He who the sword of heaven will bear
> Should be as holy as severe:
> Pattern in himself to know,
> Grace to stand, and virtue go:
> More nor less to others paying
> Than by self-offences weighing. [III, ii, 254–9]

There is no sense here that Vincentio has *learned* this doctrine from his observation of immediately-preceding events (witnessing the imprisonment of Mistress Overdone and hearing Escalus's praise of the absent Duke); rather, the Duke is stating a philosophical principle for the benefit of the audience—unfolding the properties of government to which he referred in his first full line in the play. Having offered to the audience a portrait of the ideal ruler, he can now consider the converse—that is, the corrupt official:

> Shame to him whose cruel striking
> Kills for faults of his own liking!
> Twice treble shame on Angelo,
> To weed my vice, and let his grow!
> O, what may man within him hide,
> Though angel on the outward side. [III, ii, 260–5]

The specific condemnation of Angelo's hypocrisy is embedded between two gnomic couplets, the first deploring the injustice of the magistrate who imposes capital punishment on others for offences in which he himself delights, and the last lamenting that an angelic appearance can be entirely deceptive. The language is 'impersonal' as it resembles the tone of a sermon or an oration rather than any spontaneous overflow of moral indignation on the Duke's part.

Vincentio's choric speech develops into what seems to be a consideration of the difficulty that the law faces in prosecuting the powerful (III, ii, 266–9). The meaning here is more difficult to follow;[20] but clearly, as the distich-form suggests, the Duke is sharing long-established wisdom with the audience, not expressing impulsive thoughts prompted by immediate circumstances. At the very end of the Third Act, he is inviting a dispassionate appraisal of preceding events in the play.

As in Act III, so in Act IV: the Duke takes opportunities when he is alone on stage to moralise in verse. When Isabella withdraws with Mariana to persuade her to undertake the bed-trick, the Duke returns to his political philosophy:

---

[20] There could be a couplet missing between lines 267 and 268, as is suggested by the fact that this is a four-line unit (a quatrain), whereas the rest of the speech falls into six-line units (sestets), each comprising three couplets.

O place and greatness! Millions of false eyes
Are stuck upon thee: volumes of report
Run with these false, and most contrarious quest
Upon thy doings: thousand escapes of wit
Make thee the father of their idle dream
And rack thee in their fancies. [IV, i, 60–5]

Certainly, the Duke needs a speech here to occupy the time required for Isabella to recruit Mariana to his plan; but his speech is insufficiently substantial to allow dramatically for such a protracted off-stage interview, and has no relevance at all to the context. At a time when he is seemingly preoccupied with ensuring the success of his device to foil Angelo's lascivious intent, it is puzzling that the Duke should revert to a subject on which he had already ruminated: the popular taste for lurid slanders about leaders of state.[21] Nevertheless, even if these lines are an interpolation belonging more properly elsewhere in the play, the Duke is undeniably behaving to type as the text stands: speaking sententiously while revealing little or nothing of his 'inner life' as a character.

---

[21] Concurring with a previous editor (Warburton), Lever (pp. xx-xxi and 99) believes that these lines were transplanted from the Duke's philosophical reflections following his first encounter with Lucio (Act III, scene ii, lines 179–82). However, although the two passages are similarly sinewy in caesurae and enjambment, and have the same theme of defamation of the ruler, this latter passage lacks the rhymes apparent in the two couplets that form the earlier speech, which may suggest that it does not belong in that context. The implication of the text as it stands is, nevertheless, difficult to justify dramatically: the Duke appears so preoccupied with Lucio's slanders that he digresses from the more pressing issues that Mariana and Isabella were dispatched to discuss. Gary Taylor and John Jowett (*Shakespeare Reshaped 1606-1623* [Oxford, 1993, rev. 2007], follow Alice Walker (*RES*, n.s., 34 [1983], 1–20) in proposing that the Duke's gnomic utterances at III, ii, 254–75 should replace IV, i, 60–65. Braunmuller and Watson confirm that 'This placing has been tested in more than one production and has been found doubly effective, in that it both affords adequate time for the offstage dialogue and keeps the topic of that unheard dialogue firmly in the minds of the audience' (p. 372).

Ironically, later, when the Provost receives a letter from Angelo concerning Claudio, the Duke bases his last piece of moral rhyming on a false premise. Here, Vincentio is no omniscient 'demi-god, Authority' (I, ii, 112); for once, the Duke's sententiousness seems intended to reveal the limitations of his perception, rather than the extent of his wisdom:

> This is his pardon, purchas'd by such sin
> For which the pardoner himself is in.
> Hence hath offence his quick celerity,
> When it is borne in high authority.
> When vice makes mercy, mercy's so extended
> That for the fault's love is the offender friended.[22]
>
> [IV, ii, 106–11]

Any interpretation of *Measure for Measure* which presents the Duke as a figure of divine omniscience and infallibility must be shaken to its foundations by these lines. The Duke is simply wrong in assuming, in his first couplet, that Angelo's letter will confirm Claudio's pardon when it contains the converse: a firm injunction to execute the prisoner. Vincentio's attempt to extrapolate from this initial misconception in the remaining two couplets of his aside serves to compound the error: in defiance of the Duke's theory that corrupt authority will speedily pardon its own faults in others, the Deputy's letter will demand immediate punishment for those sentenced for the very crimes that Angelo himself is committing. Were Claudio to be executed on Angelo's command, it would be for a sexual offence much less culpable than that which Angelo sought to enforce upon Isabella. In breaking his pledge to Isabella to pardon her brother, Angelo would be guilty of murder, the crime for which he condemns Barnadine to the block in the same 'private message' that the Provost is now reading. The

---

[22] Again, the influence of the form of Cato's moralising *Distichs* may be suspected, although here the couplets are pentameters rather than the tetrameters encountered earlier. The Duke's asides, although unerringly sententious, are at least metrically varied.

Duke's seemingly smug moralising completely misinterprets both the immediate circumstances and their ramifications.

Nevertheless, rather than customary soliloquies, all these asides are choric utterances with a strong didactic function. The Duke is teaching the audience political truisms by presenting ethical principles and indicating how far short of those ideals society falls in practice. He is unfolding the properties of government, in keeping with his first full line of the play—although, at times, he also seems 't'affect speech and discourse' which, in the very next line of the play, he expressed his intention to avoid!

The Duke's second choric function is to pass moral judgement on characters and their actions, as we have already seen in his lines specific to Angelo (III, ii, 262–3). This tendency is evident in the Duke's brief asides in Act III scene ii, when he observes the arrest of Pompey by Elbow. He communicates dismay and repulsion with the line, 'O heavens, what stuff is here!' (line 5). When Lucio intervenes to mock Pompey, the Duke again provides the audience with the appropriate moral response, possibly with suitable condemnatory gestures towards the two antagonists: 'Still thus, and thus: still worse!' (line 51). Similarly, when the unregenerate Barnadine refuses any ministrations to his spiritual needs prior to execution, the Duke comments, 'Unfit to live or die! O gravel heart' (IV, iii, 63). By contrast, having observed the assiduity of the Provost in the prison, the Duke offers a favourable moral judgement that quickly develops into a characteristically ducal gnomic couplet:

> This is a gentle provost; seldom when
> The steeled gaoler is the friend of men. [IV, ii, 84–8]

The Duke's dramatic function in these asides is clear and simple: he confirms to the audience the appropriate moral judgement on the character or characters whom he is observing.

The final function of the Duke's monologues is to explain circumstances, a metatheatrical device to prompt the audience not only to reflect on the present situation but also to anticipate possible outcomes. In its most simple form, this device is seen when the Duke interprets for the audience the knocking on the door of the prison:

> How now? What noise? That spirit's possess'd with haste
> That wounds th'unstinting postern with these strokes.
>
> [IV, ii, 86–7]

The purpose of the speech is to accelerate the dramatic pace of the scene and to create suspense, as the Duke's immediately-preceding conversation with the Provost has hinted that there is yet hope of some comfort for Claudio (IV, ii, 75). The audience's expectation that Angelo has reprieved Claudio in return for the satisfaction of his immoral desires will be dramatically refuted once Angelo's letter insisting on Claudio's execution is read aloud. The Duke's confident prediction, in a previous choric aside, that Claudio's life would be spared (IV, ii, 106–11) further intensifies the shock at the depth of Angelo's perfidy.

A more substantial example of this function of the Duke as a choric figure comes as he concludes his speech at the end of Act III by explaining to the audience his plan for Act IV:

> Craft against vice I must apply.
> With Angelo tonight shall lie
> His old betrothed, but despised:
> So disguise shall by th'disguised
> Pay with falsehood false exacting,
> And perform an old contracting. [III, ii, 270–5]

As with the character-portraits that he offers in his monologues and asides, moral judgements are to the fore in this speech. The Duke justifies his intrigues ('craft') as the necessary remedy for Angelo's lechery and treachery ('vice'). Furthermore, he predicts the consummation of the 'old contracting' between

Angelo and Mariana, vindicating her 'falsehood' in donning a 'disguised' appearance by contrasting it with Angelo's 'false' attempt to 'disguise' his betrayal of his vows to her. The title of the play, *Measure for Measure*, implicitly suggests that this is fair dealing on the part of the Duke and Mariana: it is legitimate to employ deception to thwart the arch-deceiver, Angelo.

Similarly, towards the end of Act IV, the Duke provides the audience with a clear synopsis of his proposals for the conclusion of the play:

> Now will I write letters to Angelo,
> The Provost, he shall bear them, whose contents
> Shall witness to him I am near at home;
> And that by great injunctions I am bound
> To enter publicly. Him I'll desire
> To meet me at the consecrated fount
> A league below the city; and from thence,
> By cold gradation and well-balanced form,
> We shall proceed with Angelo. [IV, iii, 92–100]

This is a simple statement of intent concerning Vincentio's public return to Vienna in propria persona, rather than any moral commentary. Some of the details (specifically the reference to the meeting at the sacred fountain outside the city) may not be borne out by subsequent events, but the important issue is that Angelo's conscience should be given time to anticipate the Duke's return before, by dispassionate steps ('cold gradation': line 99), the Duke passes judgement on his Deputy's crimes.

More controversial is the aside that follows almost immediately, where the Duke seeks to justify his intended behaviour towards Isabella:

> The tongue of Isabel. She's come to know
> If yet her brother's pardon be come hither;
> But I will keep her ignorant of her good,
> To make her heavenly comforts of despair

95

When it is least expected. [IV, iii, 106–10]

This speech would again seem to carry its own moral commentary with it. As the Duke is proposing to offer Isabella 'holy comforts' to save her from 'despair', an audience is conditioned morally to condone the Duke's as-yet-unspecified policy 'to keep her ignorant of her good'. That audience, however, may question how 'holy' the Duke's 'comforts' have been to Isabella as the details of his strategy emerge. The Duke deliberately lies to Isabella that her brother has been executed, not revealing Claudio's true condition until the very end of the play, when the Duke immediately takes advantage of Isabella's apparent emotional vulnerability to propose marriage to her. This aside from the Duke, in which he announces his intention to deceive Isabella, may ultimately be recognised as an attempt dramatically to justify the morally unjustifiable, to put a veneer of respectability on what would be, in a 'realistic' character, deplorable behaviour.[23] It is, nevertheless, sufficient evidence to remind us that a dramatic device such as the Duke cannot reasonably be judged by orthodox moral standards when he conflates in his person such a variety of disparate roles.

First Impressions of the Duke

So far, it has been proposed that the Duke is a dramatic construct, incorporating in one character three distinct figures from a variety of narrative traditions, performing the function of a Greek chorus in his monologues, and acknowledging in his words and behaviour the influence of King James I, Niccolo

---

[23] Shakespeare employs a similar device in *King Lear*, a play performed before James I exactly two years after the first recorded performance of *Measure for Measure*. There, Edgar seeks to justify his bizarre treatment of his blind father's suffering with the lines, 'Why I do trifle this with his despair / Is done to cure it' (IV, iii, 33–4), an argument by which the Duke might equally seek to excuse his brutal lie to Isabella. Later, however, Edgar must concede that it was a 'fault' to conceal his true identity from his father (V, iii, 192), an admission that the Duke never makes. See Braunmuller and Watson, p. 142.

Machiavelli, and possibly even the Holy Roman Emperor, Rudolph II. How, then, can this multifaceted dramatic construct be portrayed satisfactorily on stage? First impressions are vital, and must be predetermined by actor, director, and designer working in close conjunction. The presentation of the Duke at the opening of the first scene will profoundly affect the way in which the audience views him for the duration of the play—and, by extension, how the audience views the circumstances prevailing in the state that he governs.[24] Two BBC television-productions, the first shown in February 1979 (a full-text version directed by Desmond Davis) and the second televised in November 1994 (adapted and directed by David Thacker) give a clear indication of how sharply divergent possible interpretations may be.

Immediately, there is the issue of the Duke's age to address. Kenneth Colley's 1979 Duke retains much of his youthful vigour, whereas Tom Wilkinson's 1994 Duke seems somewhat declin'd into the vale of years. Lucio's reference to the 'old . . . Duke' (IV, iii, 156) should not be overlooked when considering this issue, even if the veracity of Lucio's words is frequently suspect. The word 'old' could be no more than a familiarity by which Lucio reasserts his intimacy with his 'old friend', or might simply be a way of referring to the 'former' Duke who preceded the current deputy, Angelo. Alternatively, it could have the major implication that the Duke should be presented as an old man.[25] Were the Duke indeed 'now past it',[26] he might

---

[24] For example, the RSC's 2019 production, directed by Gregory Doran, was set in fin de siècle Vienna. At the opening of the performance, Antony Byrne's Duke was waltzing with his court when he caught sight of himself in the reflective panels at the back of the stage. Apparently shocked by his own frivolity, he broke away from the carefree dancers and seemed to resolve spontaneously on his future course of action.

[25] As already noted, in an early conversation with Friar Thomas, the Duke attributes to himself 'a purpose / More grave and wrinkled' than that 'of burning youth' (I, iii, 4–6), which may imply that the Duke considers that he has left youthful desires and activities long behind and is already afflicted by the furrows of time.

present less of a sexual threat to Isabella, who is so fearful of the carnal 'vice that most I do abhor' (II, ii, 29). An old man's proposal of marriage to a young postulant, however, might seem to an audience a particularly disturbing conclusion to the play.[27]

In the 1979 production, Kenneth Colley's spruce, cheerful, confident Duke presides over a bustling, brightly-lit, Baroque court. He is first seen toying with a scientific instrument (apparently, an astrolabe—one of Rudolph II's favourite scientific instruments) to suggest his scholarship. He governs proceedings from a throne elevated on a dais, surmounted by an eagle crest, to suggest his transcendent status. He addresses Escalus face-to-face, with a benevolent hand on his chief courtier's shoulder, evidence of how comfortable he feels in authority. His words and actions are accompanied by laughter and applause from a multitude of courtiers who are fashionably-dressed (if rather decadently daubed in cosmetics), evidence that he is a respected and popular ruler of a flourishing state. Although the Duke's decision to absent himself (having deputed power to Angelo) inevitably creates a mystery, there is as yet no clear hint of crisis in Vienna. As he departs, however, the Duke casts a long and ominous glance over his shoulder at his rather foppish court: the gesture, suggesting suspicion and disapproval, produces a change of mood, foreshadowing his close, critical observation of his people in Acts II–IV. This Duke is clearly in control of events, even if his deeper purposes have yet to be revealed.

By contrast, Tom Wilkinson's 1994 Duke is presented in a closely-shuttered chamber, as if he fears the light: this is Lucio's 'duke of dark corners' (IV, iii, 156). Open books are strewn over the floor and on every horizontal surface, the

---

[26] Such is Lucio's offhand remark at III, ii, 176, suggesting that the Duke has become decrepit because of age, disease, or sexual over-indulgence.

[27] This issue is considered in Chapter 8, 'Performances in More Recent Years', especially pp. 539–543.

disorganisation hinting that this Duke is desperately but unsuccessfully looking for answers to the problems of government that he faces. Apparently demoralised and seeking refuge in alcohol, he sprawls, unkempt, on a sofa, clutching a glass, closely accompanied by a half-empty bottle of spirits. Before him, a giant screen projects multiple CCTV images of debauchery, violence, and crime, evidence of a crisis of immorality and lawlessness in the state. When he addresses Escalus in a subdued tone, he does not turn to face him, as if ashamed to make eye-contact. Only one other person is present in the room to witness his degradation, a female official (later reappearing as the anonymous Justice of Act II scene i) who is dispatched to summon Angelo. The design suggests gloom, isolation, and confusion, presenting a vision of a ruler who, in his lonely position of authority, has lost control of the state and now recognises how disastrous the consequences have become. This Duke, when he absents himself from court, is seeking refuge from responsibility.

In this latter production, Angelo's first action as Deputy will be to throw open the shutters to allow light to cascade into the chaos of the Duke's chamber. When next this room is shown, with Angelo seated at the Duke's desk (Act II, scene i), the clutter will have disappeared and order will have been restored. Such an interpretation fundamentally challenges the presentation of both the Duke and Angelo in the earlier BBC production. In that 1979 version, an able duke bequeaths a harmonious court and a stable state to a deputy who jeopardises both by his tyrannous misrule; whereas, in the 1994 production, a weak and ineffectual duke abandons a mismanaged state to the authority of the courtier who appears most capable of restoring law and order.

The Duke's only other appearance in Act I is in the third scene, when an audience's response will be confirmed by how the actor delivers to Friar Thomas the Duke's major speech about government which begins, 'We have strict statutes and most biting laws' (I, iii, 19). Kenneth Colley performs his speech with cheerful confidence, a kind of philosophical detachment, as he strolls around a sunlit cloister declaiming and gesturing expansively to the friar. Here is a Duke who feels no lingering guilt for the circumstances that have arisen in Vienna, and who is confident of his ability to rectify the situation. By contrast, Tom Wilkinson's Duke, racked with remorse, whispers the words in a darkened confessional, the camera close to his anguished face. This Duke is clearly dismayed by his mismanagement of the state and its dire consequences. Vincentio's admission that ''twas my fault to give the people scope' (I, iii, 35) gives particular plausibility to Wilkinson's performance, which presents the audience with a morally flawed Duke, one whose right to sit in judgement on others at the end of the play might be questioned. Although neither Kenneth Colley's nor Tom Wilkinson's presentation of the Duke is definitive, when the two televised BBC versions are compared, they illustrate how widely divergent is the range of potential interpretations of this problematical character and his circumstances.

The Problems of Act I

In the first Act of *Measure for Measure*, the audience is frequently perplexed by the Duke's actions and speeches. For example, in the opening scene, the words that he addresses to his courtiers, his decision to withdraw from the court, and his appointment of Angelo to rule in his absence all seem highly questionable.

First, there is the issue of Escalus, the senior courtier, to consider. It becomes apparent as early as line 18 that the Duke is proposing to absent himself from Vienna and to appoint a deputy in his place. This deputy will wield all the 'terror' and 'power' of the Duke's authority (I, i, 19–21). Escalus would be the obvious candidate for this promotion. The Duke's opening words declare that it would be vain affectation on his part to lecture Escalus on the properties of government because Escalus's 'science / Exceeds . . . the lists of all advice' that the Duke could offer (I, i, 5–6). Indeed, Escalus's understanding and experience of the diverse issues of government are recognised by the Duke as at least equal to 'any / That we remember' (I, i, 12–13). It would therefore seem most likely that, when he departs from Vienna, the Duke will bestow supreme authority on Escalus to rule in his absence. But he does not.

Instead, Vincentio imposes that power on Angelo. With curious inconsistency, the Duke *does* give a substantial lecture on moral and political responsibility to his new appointee (I, i, 26–40), anticipating the sententious choric speeches that he will offer to the audience in Acts III and IV. Among the biblical sources detectable in his speech are the Sermon on the Mount and the Parable of the Talents.[28] Vincentio is presenting himself in this early context as God's viceroy on Earth, expressing what Claudio will later call 'The words of heaven' (I, ii, 14).

The Duke greets Angelo with words that seem to present the Deputy as a man of exceptional talents and virtues, but the Duke's speeches and actions later in the play will indicate that he already has considerable evidence that Angelo lacks integrity. When, therefore, the Duke refers to the 'kind of character' in Angelo's life that 'to th'observer doth [his] history / Fully unfold' (I, i, 27–9), his words might be delivered in such a way as to hint that they are equivocations (as much of his language will be in the climactic final scene of the play). The suspicion would then arise that the 'character', far from being a testimony to Angelo's virtues, might record his mistreatment of Mariana, who could testify to Angelo's perfidy. Why, then, is the Duke neglecting the worthier candidate, Escalus, to promote the morally questionable candidate, Angelo? Why, indeed, is he departing from Vienna in the first place? Although answers to these questions are offered two scenes later (I, iii), those answers will create further conundrums.

The Duke's determination to quit Vienna without escort or support—'I'll privily away' (I, i, 67)—and to bestow the entirety of his power upon an untested subordinate may appear

---

[28] Lever, pp. 5–6n., and Braunmuller and Watson, p. 158n.

rash and politically irresponsible both to the characters on stage and to the audience. For example, when the Duke asks for Escalus's opinion on this decision to appoint Angelo as his deputy, Escalus's response is diplomatic but ambiguous:

> If any in Vienna be of worth
> To undergo such ample grace and honour,
> It is Lord Angelo. [I, i, 22–4]

The phrasing begs the question of whether any in Vienna *could indeed* be qualified to supply the Duke's absence, potentially an adverse criticism of the Duke's decision to relinquish power to a subordinate. Angelo himself invites 'some more test' (I, i, 48) of his abilities before power is delegated to him, which suggests that even the beneficiary fears that the Duke's decision may be overhasty. In addition, Angelo's exclamation, 'The heavens give safety to your purposes!' (I, i, 73), although seemingly no more than a tactful farewell, may imply fear of some danger to the Duke, who insists on travelling without escort. Thus, Shakespeare's text subtly suggests that both Escalus and Angelo may doubt whether the Duke is wise in deputing power and absenting himself from his secure position of responsibility in the state.

Reference has already been made to the inconsistency of the Duke's attitude to courting popularity. Of course, Vincentio's expressed wish to avoid public attention on his departure from court might relate to his desire to disguise his true intentions, not only in delegating full authority to Angelo but also in returning incognito to observe his city. That, however, would not explain why the Duke should call into question the 'discretion' of the man who seeks public acclaim (I, i, 71–2). The Duke of Act I scene i would seem to judge the Duke of Act V scene i to be of unsafe discretion! Why should Vincentio so fundamentally change his opinion on appearances in public during the course of the play? It could be postulated that Lucio's slander of the Duke in Acts III–IV might have persuaded a ruler of the need to present himself and his justice more publicly. This tentative hypothesis, however, is scarcely likely to occur to an audience and is never suggested by any of the Duke's frequent asides, rich as they are in moral and political philosophy. Rather, the Duke's attitudes appear to suit the immediate dramatic demands of the scene rather than to be part of a consistent or developing portrayal of character.

In the Duke's conference with Friar Thomas, a similar contradiction arises when Vincentio scorns the notion that 'the dribbling dart of love' could ever pierce his 'complete bosom' (I, iii, 1–2). In deriding the force of Cupid's arrow ('dribbling', perhaps with connotations of childishness as well as of feeble movement), he boasts hubristically that he is proof against any amatory assault. He seems to consider himself too mature in years to be concerned with juvenile, erotic relationships, dismissing the carnal 'aims and ends / Of burning youth' to prioritise a political 'purpose more grave and wrinkled' (I, iii, 3–5). In the final scene of *Measure for Measure*, however, the Duke will twice propose marriage to Isabella, having first engineered the circumstances in which she will find it most difficult to refuse his offer. His earlier disdain for love has, opportunely, been set aside or forgotten.

There is, though, a long-established narrative convention here: characters who sneer at love early in their story are most likely to succumb to love before the end of their tale. Such is the case with Troilus in Geoffrey Chaucer's long narrative poem, *Troilus and Criseyde* (completed in the 1380s), and also with Shakespeare's own creations, Benedick and Beatrice, in *Much Ado about Nothing* (1598–9). Similarly, in *Love's Labour's Lost* (1597), the King of Navarre and his three senior courtiers resolve to forego the company of women for three years, but they quickly capitulate when visited by the Princess of France and her ladies. In succumbing ultimately to Eros, the Duke is conforming to a literary convention, exemplifying the pattern of *hubris* against the God of Love leading to *nemesis* when erotic desire eventually prevails.

Further inconsistencies in the presentation of the Duke are apparent in this scene with Friar Thomas. In addressing his reasons for quitting the court and deputing Angelo in his place, Vincentio complicates rather than resolves the earlier conundrums. In addition to his assertion here that he disdains 'assemblies' of 'witless bravery' when he will welcome such an audience in the final scene, the Duke confesses or boasts to the Friar that he deliberately deceived his court and his people about his intentions in quitting Vienna:

And he [Angelo] supposes me travell'd to Poland;
For so I have strew'd it in the common ear,
And so it is receiv'd.[29] [I, iii, 14–16]

In this scene, the Duke reveals that he suspects Angelo of being a 'seemer' (I, iii, 54) and yet, by his own testimony here, Vincentio has played the seemer by deliberately misinforming others about his mission. This is one of many lies that he will tell deliberately to misguide other characters. Although an audience will generally tend to view Vincentio's apparently well-intentioned deceptions as of a different moral order from Angelo's vicious hypocrisy, the Duke's motives are not always patently benevolent, especially in the latter half of the play.

Although Vincentio seems oblivious to most of the contradictions in his position, the shortcomings of his government of Vienna are apparent even to him. In a speech that is a crux of *Measure for Measure*, he acknowledges that his indulgent (mis)management of the state has produced social turmoil:

We have strict statutes and most biting laws,
The needful bits and curbs to headstrong jades,
Which for these fourteen years we have let slip;

---

[29] The general confusion in Vienna about the Duke's motives for absenting himself is suggested by the contrast between this reference and Lucio's words at the start of I, ii. Lucio had believed the Duke to be on a political mission negotiating between 'the King of Hungary' and 'the other dukes'. See also III, ii, 85–6 for further rumours involving Russia and Rome as the Duke's putative destinations.

Even like an o'er-grown lion in a cave
That goes not out to prey. Now, as fond fathers,
Having bound up the threatening twigs of birch,
Only to stick it in their children's sight
For terror, not to use, in time the rod
Becomes more mock'd than fear'd: so our decrees,
Dead to infliction, to themselves are dead,
And Liberty plucks Justice by the nose,
The baby beats the nurse, and quite athwart
Goes all decorum. [I, iii, 19–31]

The language of these two sentences is complex, conflating animal and domestic imagery to emphasise the fatal consequences of neglecting the proper regulation of established social and judicial order. The statutes are envisaged as restraints, 'bits and curbs' to govern the animalistic behaviour of the 'headstrong jades', that is, society's 'unruly horses'. These wilful creatures have been 'let slip'; that is, the restraints have been removed from disorderly members of society and, as the statutes have not been enforced 'this fourteen years',[30] lawlessness has flourished. The description of the laws as 'biting' foreshadows the image of the 'o'er-grown lion' which should govern the other creatures by the fear that it inspires by its presence; but it has grown too cumbersome to emerge from its cave. The implication is that, because the Duke's unwieldy statute-book has fallen into lengthy abeyance, it no longer

---

[30] According to the Duke in this context, enforcement of certain strict laws has been neglected for fourteen years (I, iii, 21). According to Claudio two scenes earlier, 'nineteen zodiacs have gone round [i.e. nineteen years have elapsed], / And none of them been worn' (I, ii, 157–8). If the text is not corrupt (*xiv* and *xix* being easily confused), the discrepancy between the Duke's and Claudio's testimony could be explained variously: the Duke does not consider the rule of his predecessor when the laws first fell into abeyance, but only his own neglect of the laws; or Claudio, in his agitation, deliberately or inadvertently exaggerates. The most likely case, though, is that Shakespeare was characteristically negligent in his treatment of time in these two contexts. See Appendix 1, especially pp. 575–576, for further discussion of this issue.

inspires awe in the population of Vienna. Vincentio's rueful admissions associate him with the 'fond fathers' to whom he refers, authority figures who, through affection but equally through folly,[31] prepare 'threatening twigs of birch' but never apply them to correct their wayward children. Such instruments of punishment cease to inspire terror when they are never employed for their disciplinary purpose. Because of this neglect, the authority of the law has expired, offenders ('Liberty') defy the judiciary ('Justice'), and the natural hierarchy is entirely inverted ('The baby beats the nurse'). Overall, the Duke's speech makes clear that stringent laws are already in place to govern Vienna, but that anarchy now prevails because Vincentio himself has neglected to enforce those laws, as the Duke seems to admit in the final scene of the play while disguised as Friar Lodowick (V, i, 314–20). The 'permissive' behaviour of characters such as Lucio and Pompey during the play would seem to confirm that 'quite athwart / Goes all decorum' in Vienna, and that primary responsibility for such dire circumstances must rest with the Duke.

But the first three lines of this important confessional speech reward further consideration. The reading of the First folio at line 20, 'headstrong weedes', has generally been rejected by editors, as it produces a clumsy mixed metaphor: 'bits' and 'curbs' are used to restrain horses, not to suppress unwanted plants.[32] Imagery of unruly horses in this context would deliberately echo Claudio's words at I, ii, 148–51, where the 'body public' is envisaged as a horse in need of firm restraint. Here in Vincentio's speech, if the lawlessness of the populace is equated with equine waywardness (as in Claudio's image), 'headstrong steeds' might be hypothesized as the correct reading: 'steeds' and 'weedes' might easily be confused in

---

[31] 'Foolish' was the customary meaning of 'fond' to Shakespeare's contemporaries: e.g. 'I am a very foolish fond old man' (*King Lear*, IV, vii. 60). This meaning is retained in the modern dialect of, for example, certain parts of Yorkshire.

[32] Braunmuller and Watson nevertheless revert to the First Folio reading, 'weeds'.

transcription. Lever's edition of the text, however, favours 'headstrong jades', as a similar figure is encountered in the writings of two authors whose influence on Shakespeare is indisputable.[33] Either reading confirms that unruly citizens, envisaged as wilful horses, challenge the rule of law.

This brings us to a seemingly sterile but, nevertheless, important grammatical question: what is the referent of the relative pronoun 'Which' at the beginning of line 21? A modern audience may conclude that it refers to the 'strict statutes and most biting laws' that have been 'let slip', in the sense of negligently administered; but that is not the sense that Shakespeare's audience would have identified. To 'let slip' involved releasing the collar or noose from the neck of a restrained animal, as is the case in Mark Antony's famous exclamation, 'Cry 'Havoc!' and let slip the dogs of war' (*Julius Caesar*: III, i, 274).[34] The 'headstrong jades', rather than the 'strict statutes', have been 'let slip'.

Once this grammatical issue has been settled, its implications for the overall interpretation of the play become clearer. For fourteen years, the Duke has 'let slip' capital offenders, in that he has released the noose from the neck of many sentenced to be executed under the 'strict statutes and most biting laws' of Vienna. Although the Duke recognises that such leniency has increased social disorder, he will persist with his characteristic clemency at the end of the play. No fewer

---

[33] Lever, p. 20, notes that Marlowe, in *Tamburlaine the Great* Part 2 (c.1587), IV, iii, 12, writes of the 'headstrong jades' of King Aegeus; while George Whetstone, a particularly important source of plot, character, and language in *Measure for Measure*, writes in *A Mirour for Magestrates of Cyties* (London, 1584), sig. A4v–5, of how a criminal, like 'a Braynsicke Iade', needs 'a sharpe Bitte [to] bridle him'.

[34] Confirmation of the idiom may be found in the words of Queen Margaret to Queen Elizabeth in *Richard III*: 'Now thy proud neck bears half my burden'd yoke, / From which even here *I slip my weary head* / And leave the burden of it all on thee' (IV, iv, 111–13; italics added).

than four characters sentenced to death will be 'let slip' at the last moment: the noose will be removed from the necks of Claudio, Angelo, Barnadine, and Lucio in the final scene, each of whom stood under sentence of death according to the 'strict statutes'.[35] Despite his recognition of how 'all decorum' had previously gone 'quite athwart' because of his 'fond' administration, the Duke ultimately returns to his lenient ways.

After Vincentio's crucial confessional-speech, implicit criticism by Friar Thomas leads to further self-examination by the Duke. He must defend his recent decisions when Friar Thomas proposes that, had the Duke taken responsibility for re-imposing the full force of the laws in Vienna, it would have been more effective than similar action taken by Angelo, a mere deputy (I, iii, 31–34). The tone of the Duke's demurral, however, is debatable. Is it a confident refutation of Friar Thomas's words, or a hesitant attempt to disguise his own pusillanimity? Vincentio's initial justification is that he faces a political dilemma that is difficult to resolve. He explains that it would be a 'tyranny' for him now to punish misdeeds that he had previously seemed to condone by his inaction:

> Sith 'twas my fault to give the people scope,
> 'Twould be my tyranny to strike and gall them
> For what I bid them do: for we bid this be done,
> When evil deeds have their permissive pass,
> And not the punishment. [I, iii, 35–9]

In recognising that his 'fault' is greater than mere neglect of the statutes, he admits by rueful repetition (line 37) that he has

---

[35] King James I's last-minute reprieve offered to the Raleigh conspirators at Winchester in the winter of 1603–04 (a few months before the first recorded performance of *Measure for Measure*) might well have served as an example to Shakespeare of how a ruler might 'let slip' condemned men even as the noose was about their necks. See Lever, p. l, and Kamps and Raber, p. 136. Braunmuller and Watson (p. 114) add that, after Elizabeth's death, James had issued blanket pardons to offenders (excluding murderers and Jesuits) on his journey south from Scotland to London.

actively promoted crime by failing to punish offenders. Accordingly, he believes that, were he now to 'strike and gall' criminals, he would be guilty of tyranny for prosecuting crimes that previously he had implicitly encouraged. In relating tyranny closely to inconsistency and hypocrisy, Shakespeare is preparing the audience for the offences of Angelo when he severely punishes others for crimes that he himself commits. In context, however, the Duke's words suggest how he, Vincentio, has been weakened politically by his 'permissive' administration of the state.

There remains the suspicion that the Duke is rather more concerned with selfish motives than with social reform. In justifying his appointment of Angelo, Vincentio's words focus on the issue of preserving his (the Duke's) own reputation and popularity, rather than on the need to clean the Augean Stables of Vienna:

> Therefore, indeed, my father,
> I have on Angelo impos'd the office;
> Who may in th'ambush of my name strike home,
> And yet my nature never in the fight
> To do in slander. [I, iii, 39–44]

In short, Vincentio is happy for his authority to be used to rectify Vienna's social ills, provided that he is not personally associated with the inevitably unpopular reforms. These lines are symptomatic of Shakespeare's portrayal of the Duke throughout the remainder of the play: at the very moment when the audience might be ready to accept that Vincentio's intentions are moral, responsible, and altruistic, evidence tends to emerge that he is swayed by self-interest, for example, the concern for his public image shown here.

Vincentio's speeches to Friar Thomas—combining confessions of negligence with assertions of self-justification—also foreshadow his words as Friar Lodowick before Angelo, Escalus, and the people of Vienna at the end of the play:

> My business in this state
> Made me a looker-on here in Vienna,
> Where I have seen corruption boil and bubble
> Till it o'errun the stew: laws for all faults,
> But faults so countenanc'd that the strong statutes
> Stand like the forfeits in a barber's shop,
> As much in mock as mark. [V, i, 314–20]

This later speech, however, is not an admission but an accusation. The Duke *qua* friar is apparently indignant at the 'corruption' that he has observed: because 'faults' have been 'countenanc'd' in Vienna, the 'strong statutes' have been exposed to 'mock[ery]'. By his own earlier admission, however, this 'corruption' has resulted from Vincentio's neglect of the 'strict statutes and most biting laws' of Vienna (I, iii, 19–21). His speech before the people of Vienna in the final scene would therefore seem to be a further attempt to protect his own reputation at the expense of Angelo's, by making his deputy appear responsible for the lax administration from which Vienna has suffered. Angelo, however, far from endorsing the Duke's tolerant regime, has enforced the statutes much more strictly than his predecessor in government. To an attentive audience, the Duke's attempt to transfer the blame to save his own reputation may appear tawdry—comparable with Angelo's earlier attempt to preserve his reputation by undermining Mariana's.

Which brings us to consider an issue possibly more disturbing to Shakespeare's contemporaries than to a modern audience: the Duke intends to disguise himself as a friar (I, iii, 43–8). He expresses no intention permanently to join the order: were he to become a postulant, he would be obliged to swear an oath of chastity, which would preclude any proposal of marriage to Isabella in the final scene. A twenty-first-century viewer or reader might have some misgivings about the Duke practising such deception: after all, the Duke, who will condemn Angelo as a 'seemer' before the end of the scene, is here proposing to become a 'seemer' himself, by assuming a false identity. Members of a Jacobean audience might have been more disturbed by his specific choice of alias. Hypocritical friars had been *the* favourite target of satirists since the later Middle Ages.[36] Those of Shakespeare's contemporaries of Protestant conviction might have regarded Vincentio as tainted by his association with a religious order discredited and suppressed under King Henry VIII. Those who remained covertly loyal to Roman Catholicism might have felt disquiet about a layman, however noble, usurping the functions of the regular clergy.[37]

As Lucio will later observe,

It was a mad, fantastical trick of him to steal from the state and usurp the beggary he was never born to. [III, ii, 89–90].

---

[36] Ever since the great dispute over prerogatives between the friars and the secular masters in the University of Paris in the late Thirteenth Century, there had been a rich vein of anti-mendicant satire apparent in the literature of western Christendom. Jean de Meun in France, Giovanni Boccaccio in Italy, and Geoffrey Chaucer in England were prominent contributors to this tradition. For the prevalence of satire against the friars in England, see Penn W. Szittya, 'The Antifraternal Tradition in Middle English Literature', *Speculum* 52 (1977), pp. 287–313. See also my doctoral thesis, 'The Mediaeval Literary Theory of Satire and its Relevance to the Works of Gower, Langland, and Chaucer' (The Queen's University of Belfast, 1982), especially pp. 210–12.

[37] Furthermore, Braunmuller and Watson (p. 183n.) observe that George Chapman's comedy, *May Day*, includes lines declaring that disguising oneself as a friar 'is worn threadbare upon every stage, and so much villa[i]ny committed under that habit that 'tis grown as suspicious as the vilest' (II, i, 473-7). *May Day* may have been written in 1601–2 (that is, sufficient time before the first recorded performance of *Measure for Measure* to have influenced Shakespeare when writing his play). It is, nevertheless, possible that the reference in Chapman's play was included when it was revised in 1609, before its first publication in 1611. If so, then *Measure for Measure* may have been one of the plays that justified Chapman's quip, circumstantial evidence that the Duke, when disguised as Friar Lodowick, could be regarded by one of Shakespeare's contemporaries as embodying 'villa[i]ny committed under that habit'.

111

Although Lucio knows only that the Duke has stripped himself of the trappings of his wealth and privilege, 'beggary' is an ironically suitable word to choose concerning the Duke's transformation to a friar, a member of a mendicant order (that is, one that supported itself by begging). Lucio's adverse criticism of the Duke's behaviour warrants careful consideration, as it calls into question the Duke's integrity. Worse still, in the Duke's dealings with Mariana, Vincentio claims that he has not merely falsely assumed the sacrament of holy orders but also performed the sacrament of penance: 'I have confess'd her, and I know her virtue' (V, i, 524).[38] In the presence of Mariana, he assumes authority in interpreting the sacrament of marriage, insisting that her troth-plighting with Angelo entitles her to consummate the relationship without sin (IV, i, 71–5). In addition, we may detect that the Duke is usurping the sacrament of extreme unction in his ministrations to Claudio and Barnadine in the prison, immediately before their scheduled executions. None of these holy sacraments may be appropriated by a member of the laity, however powerful in the hierarchy of state. It is necessary for the purposes of the play for the Duke to pass, unidentified, among the people of Vienna, better to observe and understand their conduct; but to assume the appearance and functions of a Franciscan friar[39] is a highly questionable moral choice.

At the beginning and at the end of this scene (I, iii), the Duke examines the moral status of Angelo, the man whom he

---

[38] The friars themselves had battled with the secular clergy long and hard in the Thirteenth Century to obtain from the Pope the right to perform the sacrament of penance. It was certainly not permitted to delegate such spiritual responsibilities to laymen, however nobly born. Administration of the holy sacraments was the province of the clergy, not of the nobility or the commons, under the rigid hierarchy of the three estates.

[39] That Vincentio specifically assumes the guise of a Franciscan is confirmed by Elbow's words at III, ii, 39: 'His neck will come to your waist—a cord, sir.' Franciscan friars wore a distinguishing cord about their waists: hence their soubriquet: Cordeliers.

has placed in authority over his state. First, Vincentio characterises Angelo as 'A man of stricture and firm abstinence' (I, iii, 12), where the Deputy's capacity for self-denial would seem to endorse his suitability for his new role: political theory, deriving from Pythagoras via Plato, demands that he who would govern others should first learn to govern his own unruly passions. In terms of the Duke's description, Angelo appears to be such a 'well-governed and well-governing' man. When the Duke returns to his consideration of Angelo at the end of the scene, however, the tone of his remarks no longer seems complimentary:

> . . . Lord Angelo is precise;
> Stands at a guard with Envy; scarce confesses
> That his blood flows, or that his appetite
> Is more to bread than stone. Hence shall we see
> If power change purpose, what our seemers be.
>
> [I, iii, 50–4]

The word 'precise' has connotations of Puritanism, anathema to all those associated with the drama in Shakespeare's time because Puritans campaigned to close the theatres, which they regarded as dens of vice. The Duke is now presenting Angelo's abstemiousness in a much more unfavourable light than before. Angelo's hostility to those who challenge his authority (line 51) and his refusal to acknowledge his own natural needs (lines 51–3) seem particularly unattractive, a denial of his humanity. The reference to 'blood' should be equated with sexual passion, as frequently elsewhere in the works of Shakespeare and his contemporaries:[40] the Duke shrewdly suggests that Angelo has

---

[40] See, for example, Angelo's exclamation in his second soliloquy, 'Blood, thou are blood' (II, iv, 15), where he is forced to acknowledge that the same 'blood' that makes him human makes him susceptible to sexual desire. Cf. *Othello* (V, ii, 1ff.), where the Moor, in soliloquy, recognises that the 'cause' of his murderous intent is Desdemona's illicit sexual passion ('blood'); and John Webster, *The White Devil*, where the sexually corrupt Vittoria Corombona faces death with the words, 'O my greatest sin lay in my blood. / Now my blood pays for it.' [Christina Luckyj, ed., 2nd ed. (London: A & C Black, 1996), V,

sexual feelings that he is reluctant to acknowledge, thereby prefiguring Act II, in which Angelo will be made all too aware of his unruly desires. The concluding couplet (lines 53–4), however, is the most disturbing part of the portrait. The Duke apparently expects 'power' to 'change purpose', just as Lord Acton in the Nineteenth Century recognised that 'power tends to corrupt, and absolute power corrupts absolutely'. Clearly, unless anarchy is to prevail, someone must govern the state and therefore contend with the corruptive influence of supreme political power; but the penultimate word of the scene indicates that the Duke already regards Angelo as one of the 'seemers' whose hypocrisy will be revealed once they hold sway over others. Angelo, then, is expected to be corrupted by the power that has been bestowed on him. In addition, by reference to Angelo's 'blood', the Duke has implicitly predicted that his Deputy's corruption may take the form of submission to sexual temptation.

If the Duke expects Angelo to fail as his Deputy, why has the Duke bestowed such power on him? An audience might conclude that allowing the puritanical, repressive Angelo to discredit himself would encourage the people of Vienna to desire the return of their more indulgent Duke. Again, the Duke, who is so frequently the necessary moral arbiter in the play, has resorted to morally questionable means to obtain seemingly selfish ends.

The Friar in the Prison

When the Duke reappears in his guise as Friar Lodowick to address the issues created by Angelo's stringent application of the laws that Vincentio himself had previously neglected, he persistently uses dubious methods to achieve his objectives.

---

vi, 238–9.] Although 'My fault lay in my blood' is ambiguous, as it could refer either to sexual desire or to the 'blood ties' of family, the line is best interpreted as referring to both simultaneously: Vittoria's corrupt family blood, also exemplified in her pander-brother, Flamineo, has been the source of her illicit desires.

From the outset, the Duke appears an accomplished 'seemer', pretending not to know his own Provost (II, iii, 1), representing himself falsely as 'Bound by . . . my bless'd order' to visit the 'afflicted spirits' in the prison (II, iii, 3–5), and confessing Julietta, although he has no religious authority to do so (II, iii, 19–39).[41]

In the course of this confessional, the Duke expresses an opinion that a twenty-first-century audience will probably find distasteful. When Julietta admits that her 'most offenceful act / Was mutually committed', the Duke declares her sin 'of heavier kind' than Claudio's (II, iii, 26–8). Despite her honesty and penitence, the Duke's words present her as the seducer, in the Christian tradition of the fallen Eve tempting Adam.[42] A modern audience is likely to be uncomfortable with the Duke's dogma. It nevertheless appears that he has performed a charitable function in reconciling Julietta to her punishment: her words—'I do repent me as it is an evil, /And take the shame with joy' (II, iii, 35–6)—suggest that she has found peace of mind through his ministrations. This effect, however, is immediately destroyed with the Duke's parting remark:

Your partner, as I hear, must die tomorrow. . . .

[II, iii, 37]

By informing her in this offhand (perhaps even callous) manner of Claudio's imminent execution, the Duke renews her distress:

Must die to-morrow! O injurious love,

---

[41] II, iii is the only scene in the Act in which Angelo does not appear, his justice being illustrated in the previous two scenes and in the subsequent scene. Thus, Angelo's administration of justice is dramatically counterpointed by this one scene in which the Duke presides.

[42] There could be a bawdy or physiological dimension to the Duke's words: Julietta has been 'heavier . . . by the weight of a man' (*Much Ado About Nothing*, III, iv, 24), and she now bears the extra weight of her child—but such an innuendo would scarcely befit a putative friar confessing a penitent.

That respites me a life, whose very comfort
Is still a dying horror! [II, iii, 40–2]

As this is the only scene in which Julietta speaks, these are her last words in the play, her anguished exclamations suggesting that her 'afflicted spirit' has been far from comforted by Friar Lodowick's visit.

So it proves in the Duke's next encounter in the prison where, in addition to the prerogatives of holy orders and confession, he appears to usurp a third Catholic sacrament (the *viaticum*) in preparing Claudio for his death. There is, though, a strange anomaly in the Duke's words to Claudio and a surprising oversight by a putative friar: his lengthy speech beginning 'Be absolute for death' (III, i, 5–41) does not contain a single overtly Christian reference. Like the lady Philosophy, who appears to the condemned prisoner in Boethius's *The Consolation of Philosophy*, the Duke offers 'consolation' to Claudio without recourse to orthodox religious dogma.[43] His speech, based entirely on 'reason' (line 6), will contrast sharply with Claudio's implicit reply (III, i, 117–31), which derives from 'fear' (line 131). Both speeches contemplate the end of life, but the Duke's words, although unerringly logical, lack human empathy, while Claudio's terrified flight of fancy finds no refuge in philosophical rationality.

The Duke's objective in his lengthy speech is to recommend death by denigrating life. His initial proposal that 'death or life / Shall thereby be the sweeter' if Claudio is 'absolute for death' (lines 4–5)—that is, if he fatalistically accepts the inevitability of his imminent execution—sounds plausible enough

---

[43] Boethius's *De consolatione philosophiae*, written AD 523 by a Christian prisoner awaiting execution by Theodric the Ostrogoth, was widely influential, having been translated into the English vernacular by (among others) Alfred the Great, Geoffrey Chaucer, and Queen Elizabeth I. The more direct influences on the Duke's speech and Claudio's (implicit) reply at III, i, 117–31 are considered by Lever, pp. lxxxvii–lxxxviii, 66–69, and 73–74.

psychologically; but the unmitigated contempt for life expressed in the remainder of the Duke's speech, if fully accepted by Claudio, would destroy any joy that the prisoner might feel if pardoned. All human dignity and self-respect are stripped away in the Duke's speech, which is structured by means of rhetorical repetition: 'A breath thou art' (line 8); 'thou art death's fool' (line 11); 'Thou art not noble' (line 13); 'Thou'rt by no means valiant' (line 15); Thou art not thyself (line 19); 'Happy thou art not' (line 21); 'Thou art not certain' (line 23); 'If thou art rich, thou'rt poor' (line 25); 'Friends hast thou none' (line 29); 'Thou hast nor youth, nor age' (line 32). Each of these proposals is supported by evidence, rationally (but nihilistically) presented to support the Duke's initial advice to

> Reason thus with life:
> If I do lose thee, I do lose a thing
> That none but fools would keep. [III, i, 6–8]

For example, the Duke's contention that Claudio (or, rather, all humanity) is 'Death's fool' is justified by means of an ironic contradiction:

> ... him [i.e. Death] thou labour'st by thy flight to shun,
> And yet run'st toward him still.' [III, i, 12–13]

The choice of the two finite verbs contributes to the paradox: 'labour'st' suggests the immense effort expended and pain suffered in attempting to avoid death, contrasting with 'run'st', which suggests the easy rapidity with which humanity is always ('still') approaching death. Other justifications for *contemptus mundi* (contempt for worldly concerns) include reference to the human fear of 'soft and tender' grave-worms as proof of lack of valour (lines 15–17),[44] and allusion to the burden of wealth,

---

[44] Although the reference in Shakespeare's line to the 'fork / Of a poor worm' might suggest a poisonous snake, a grave-worm is more likely to be a universal symbol of death and its terrors. Grave-worms may have no fork, but Shakespeare's zoological knowledge of small

117

borne through life but lost at death, to justify the paradox that the rich are actually poor (lines 25–8).

The Duke's portrayal of old age towards the end of his speech is particularly disturbing. He maintains that even the affection and support of family are illusory, as children would greatly prefer an ailing parent to be dead rather than alive:

> Friend hast thou none;
> For thine own bowels which do call thee sire,
> The mere effusion of thy proper loins,
> Do curse the gout, serpigo, and the rheum
> For ending thee no sooner. [III, i, 28–32]

The reference to 'thine own bowels which do call thee sire' and the phrase 'the mere effusion of thy proper loins' are characteristic of biblical periphrases employed to define 'offspring'. The sense, then, is that these ungrateful children 'curse' diseases for not killing off their parent more promptly (implicitly, to allow the children to enjoy their inheritance all the sooner).[45] The Duke's reference to offspring eagerly anticipating the death of the parent seems particularly heartless when directed to Claudio, who is apparently to lose his life without ever seeing his new-born child. In addition, the Duke maintains that survival into old age would be no consolation, for

> . . . when thou art old and rich,
> Thou hast neither heat, affection, limb, nor beauty
> To make thy riches pleasant. [III, i, 36–8]

---

creatures was scarcely faultless (cf. *Antony and Cleopatra*, I, iii, 68–9). In any case, the 'fork' of a serpent is not poisonous: the fangs might be a more likely source of trepidation. M. R. Ridley, in his 1935 edition of *Measure for Measure*, suggests that the 'fork' is the penetration of the dead body by the worm.

[45] The Duke's words here anticipate Shakespeare's creation of the ungrateful and rapacious children, Goneril, Regan, and Edmund, in *King Lear*, first performed only two years after *Measure for Measure*.

Certainly, the Duke achieves his aim to make Claudio 'absolute for death', but such grim ruminations might instil in Claudio fear of—and loathing for—life, rather than any noble, valiant, or Christian resolution to face death unflinchingly.

In addition, if the members of an audience were to pause for consideration, they might recognise a certain perversity in reconciling to death a young man whose life the Duke has every intention of preserving (while keeping the condemned man ignorant of that intention). Vincentio could achieve his objective of saving Claudio from execution by 'rash remonstrance of [his] hidden power', as he later admits to Isabella (V, i, 390); but Claudio knows him as a friar rather than as the Duke and therefore harbours no such hope of reprieve. This is a double deception on the Duke's part, and characteristic of the way in which he toys with other characters' emotions for the remainder of the play. Again, if we were to consider the Duke as a credible character rather than as a dramatic device, we might recognize that Lord Acton's adage about the corruptive influence of power applies as much to Vincentio as to Angelo. We might also observe that, just as the Duke's consolatory meeting with Julietta ended in bitter anguish after apparent reconciliation to fate, so will this meeting with Julietta's betrothed, once Claudio has heard his sister's news. The question therefore arises: should an audience consider that the Duke's early interventions relieve the suffering of others, or rather that they increase their suffering? What is certain is that, in keeping with the Duke's function in the play, his interventions intensify the drama.

An audience might also harbour misgivings concerning the Duke's request to the Provost (III, i, 52) for the opportunity to eavesdrop on a private and intimate conversation between Claudio and his sister, Isabella, who has newly arrived in the prison. A benevolent intention might justify such dubious means, but the Duke, ignorant of Angelo's indecent proposal to Isabella, may appear to be motivated by morbid, unseemly curiosity. It is, nevertheless, dramatically expedient for the Duke to learn, by means of spying, both of the Deputy's corrupt action and of the nun's fierce chastity. As before, it may be ill-advised to examine the motives of the Duke too closely here, as dramatic devices defy moral analysis.

E. M. W. Tillyard insists that the Duke's re-entry at III, i, 152 is the hinge of the play.[46] This is the point where dramatic situation and language—both of which are rooted in the political realism and moral complexity of Shakespeare's great tragedies—transform into the fantasy and wishful outcomes encountered in Shakespeare's middle-period comedies. At the same time, predominantly poetic speech transforms into predominantly prosaic dialogue. This is the point when the Duke becomes fully active in his role of directing the events and circumstances of the play towards the happy conclusion and multiple marriages suitable for a Shakespearian comedy. But the principal means that the Duke uses to achieve his ends are even more dubious than before: deploying shameless lies and recruiting others to be complicit in his persistent deceptions.

The Duke tells Claudio that Angelo's attempted seduction of Isabella was the Deputy's test of her virtue, and that Angelo was delighted to be rejected by her (III, i, 160–5). An audience, having witnessed Angelo's indecent proposal to Isabella in Act II scene iv, knows this assertion to be entirely untrue. Then, the Duke claims that he can be sure of Angelo's intentions as he is Angelo's confessor (III, i, 165–6). He thereby avoids admitting that his information derives from eavesdropping on a private conversation. It is as inconceivable that Friar Lodowick could be Angelo's confessor as that Angelo was merely testing Isabella with his sexual advances.[47] Even were an attempt made

---

[46] *Shakespeare's Problem Plays* (London: Chatto and Windus, 1950; repr. Harmondsworth: Penguin, 1970), p. 131.

[47] Later, when introduced to Escalus as the friar who has 'advised [Claudio] for th'entertainment of death' (III, ii, 207), the Duke will indulge in an even more egregious fantasy about his status when he claims to be a papal emissary 'late come from the See / In special business from his Holiness' (III, ii, 213–14).

to justify this double deception of Claudio on the grounds that the Duke is consoling a distraught condemned man, the moral position would remain extremely dubious.

Similarly, the Duke equivocates with Isabella, claiming that 'fortune hath conveyed to [his] understanding' (III, i, 183–4) the obscene bargain that Angelo has proposed to her (rather than confessing that he deliberately spied on her conversation with her brother). Having informed Isabella of Mariana and her lamentable circumstances, he then encourages Isabella to practise deception herself, by lying to Angelo and by participating in the bed-trick, whereby a disguised Mariana, already betrothed to Angelo, will take Isabella's place in Angelo's bed. The astonishing ease with which Isabella is persuaded to undertake this deception is considered in Chapter 4 of this study; suffice it here to say that a scrupulous consideration might determine that, in seeking to expose Angelo as a 'seemer', the Duke is now, by 'seeming' in words and deeds, persuading others to act as 'seemers'. Hypocrisy and lies abound, not least in the Duke who, although directing the action towards a successful conclusion, persistently appears to be acting out of self-interest. An audience may come to sympathise with Lucio's view of Lodowick: 'a meddling friar; / I do not like the man' (V, i, 130–1).

The complex moral issues of the play receive a further jolt when the Duke encounters Pompey under arrest for pimping: the Duke lectures him on the 'filthy vice' [III, ii, 22] of bringing procreants together—sharply ironic as this was exactly what the Duke himself was arranging only moments before in stage-time, when planning the encounter between Mariana and Angelo. Similarly, in the exchanges with Lucio that follow, the Duke calls fornication 'too general a vice, and severity must cure it' (III, ii, 96), although he will spend the rest of the play labouring to ameliorate the severity of Angelo's judgement on such sexual misdemeanours. Later, when subjected to Lucio's allegations that the Duke was sexually indulgent, Vincentio's defence is that 'I never heard the absent Duke much detected for women; he was not inclined that way' (III, ii, 118-19); but his two proposals to Isabella in the final scene suggest that, like Angelo, Vincentio does not recognise his latent erotic desires until they are provoked by the presence of the novice nun. These contradictions in the Duke's position are so prominent that they invite consideration as a deliberate, metatheatrical device, inviting the audience to recognise the moral distinction between casual sexual commerce (as promoted by Pompey and Mistress Overdone), sexual compulsion (as attempted by Angelo), and sexual union after solemn handfasting. The play may even be conceding the need sternly to regulate promiscuous sexual activity, while showing tolerance to those in mutually loving relationships.

Although an audience is unlikely to accept at face value many of the slanders that the garrulous Lucio directs at the Duke in the context of this scene (III, ii, 83–178), two of Lucio's accusations deserve consideration as plausible judgements on the Duke's policies in government. First, Lucio identifies the Duke as sexually indulgent: 'He had some feeling of the sport; he knew the service' (lines 115–16). Significantly, 'service' is the very word that Pompey had used for brothels and the sex-industry in his ironic encomium to Mistress Overdone (I, ii, 102). Lucio's words to Friar Lodowick may even hint that, under the Duke, brothels had become an institution condoned by the state to supply a recognised public need.[48] Lucio further alleges that the Duke was 'A very superficial, ignorant, unweighing fellow' (line 136). The word 'unweighing' acquires particular prominence in a play entitled *Measure for Measure*: it may remind an audience that the Duke has misapplied the scales of justice, failing properly to weigh offences against penalties. Inevitably, those alert to such

---

[48] A 'riotously funny' production of the play directed by Robert Falls at the Goodman Theatre in Chicago went so far as to set an opening tableau in a brothel, with the Duke as an active sexual participant: Lawrence B. Johnson, '*Measure for Measure* (read laugh for laugh), Goodman's screamer would be hard to top', *Chicago on the aisle*, 21 March 2013, https://chicagoontheaisle.com/2013/03/21/review-of-shakespeares-measure-for-measure-at-goodman-theatre-directed-by-robert-falls/.

implications will hear in this context an echo of the Duke's admission to Friar Thomas that he had neglected the 'strict statutes and most biting laws' of Vienna, as a result of which 'quite athwart' went 'all decorum' under his rule (I, iii, 19–31). Lucio's apparently slanderous account of the Duke's government has at least *some* firm foundations.

Set against Lucio's adverse judgement of the Duke, we have Vincentio's self-justification speech and the testimony of the judicious Escalus. The Duke *qua* friar protests about himself,

Let him but be testimonied in his own bringings-forth, and he shall appear to the envious a scholar, a statesman, and a soldier. [III, ii, 140–2]

His boasts do not necessarily contradict the two accusations from Lucio isolated above: scholar, statesman, and soldier he may have been, but was he a lecher, negligent in his administration of the law? The matter is not immediately resolved. When prompted by Vincentio in disguise, however, Escalus characterises the Duke as

One that, above all other strifes, contended especially to know himself. . . . Rather rejoicing to see another merry, than merry at anything which professed to make him rejoice. A gentleman of all temperance. [III, ii, 226–31]

As Escalus has been presented as a judicious magistrate, an audience may accept this character-sketch as an accurate portrait of a restrained, contemplative, and benevolent ruler. This would refute Lucio's slanders that the Duke was a sexually promiscuous drunkard. Again, though, it does not address the issues of maladministration of the state and its consequences under the Duke's regime. A wise, self-possessed man does not necessarily make a decisive, efficient ruler. Furthermore, it is possible to interpret this exchange as presenting the Duke in a much less favourable light. When Friar Lodowick seeks Escalus's opinion of the Duke, it may be evidence of Vincentio's narcissism; while Escalus's diplomatic response may suggest, through the implications of the word 'contended', that the Duke *tried* to achieve self-knowledge, but was unsuccessful.[49]

In addition, Lucio's initial judgement on the Duke—'It was a mad, fantastical trick of him to steal from the state' (III, ii, 89–90)—has the ring of truth about it. Although, according to the dramatis personae included in the First Folio, it is Lucio (rather than the Duke) who is the 'fantastique', the Duke's various irrational, whimsical, or unjustifiable actions objectively deserve such a judgement. It may, nevertheless, seem surprising to find Shakespeare using the words of Lucio, the 'fantastique', to draw the audience's attention to these inconsistencies in the Duke's behaviour. This further metatheatrical technique encourages an audience to consider more objectively its responses to the Duke, and more clearly to recognise his inconsistencies: even by Lucio's fanciful standards, the Duke is 'fantastical'.

'Bed-Trick' and 'Head-Trick'

When the Duke takes stock of circumstances at the end of Act III, he defends his actions, past and to come, in the line, 'Craft against vice I must apply' (III, ii, 270). Again, however, we might pause to consider whether the means employed by the Duke can be morally justified by his ends.

For example, some troublesome issues will be raised by the Duke's words and deeds early in Act IV. When the Duke encounters Mariana at the moated grange, inconsistencies in his behaviour are again apparent. It may seem incongruous to an audience that, as a friar, he is praising Isabella's lies in setting up the 'bed-trick'—even more incongruous that he himself was instigator of the 'bed-trick' and persuaded Isabella to involve herself in the deception. Next, he authorises the consummation of Mariana's relationship with her former betrothed:

---

[49] This interpretation is suggested by Brownmuller and Watson, pp. 40–1.

Nor, gentle daughter, fear you not at all.
He is your husband on a pre-contract:
To bring you thus together 'tis no sin,
Sith that the justice of your title to him
Doth flourish the deceit. [IV, i, 71–5]

The Duke's encouragement to Mariana, though necessary dramatically, defies the terms of the 'drowsy and neglected act' (I, ii, 159) that Angelo inherited from Vincentio, under which Claudio stands condemned. The 'pre-contract' between Claudio and Julietta is in so many vital respects identical to that between Angelo and Mariana; yet the Duke urges Mariana to commit the very act that he repeatedly condemned as a 'sin' to Julietta (II, iii, 19–36). One woman has been convicted under the Duke's statutes for consummating her relationship, while another receives his blessing to consummate her well-nigh identical relationship.

When he returns to the prison to effect Claudio's release (IV, ii, 70ff.), the Duke's actions become still more problematical, as can be illustrated by taking two morally opposing views of his conduct. According to the negative view, the Duke's tendency towards intrigue and deception shown in this scene is incompatible with his role as a friar, let alone with his reputation as a virtuous ruler. Having been thwarted by Angelo, who has reneged on his pledge to pardon Claudio in exchange for sexual gratification, the Duke reverts to devious plotting. With the failure of the 'bed-trick', there follows the 'head-trick': Barnadine's head is to be substituted for Claudio's, to satisfy Angelo that the execution has indeed taken place. Again, the Duke is thwarted by circumstances: Barnadine, who in any case looks nothing like Claudio, escapes execution on the dubious pretext that he needs to sleep off a hangover. At the Duke's promptings, however, the Provost proposes an alternative. It is determined that Ragozine, who fortuitously *does* look like Claudio and who has conveniently died in the prison overnight, should be decapitated to provide the head necessary to satisfy Angelo that his order to execute

Claudio has been carried out. This labyrinthine passage of intrigue may be suspenseful and dramatically engaging for the audience, but it also could be seen to present the Duke as deviously manipulative, a Shakespearian 'vile politician'[50] who entangles the benevolent Provost in a dangerous conspiracy to conceal Claudio and to deceive Angelo.

A diametrically opposite view, likely to appeal to those who regard the Duke as a morality-play construct, would be that the Duke's compassion and piety are ultimately rewarded by divine intervention in these prison-scenes. Even though the death of Barnadine, a hardened criminal, might achieve the objective of saving Claudio's life, Vincentio refuses to execute him: it would be 'damnable' as Barnadine is 'unmeet for death' (IV, iii, 66–8). Here, the Duke is swayed by the same argument for mercy that Isabella unsuccessfully deployed when pleading to Angelo for postponement of her brother's execution (II, ii, 85–8): a condemned criminal must be prepared for the afterlife or the execution will kill soul as well as body, usurping God's function at the Last Judgement. Unlike Angelo, who was inflexible in his determination to achieve his objectives regardless of the state of Claudio's soul, the Duke tempers justice with mercy, postponing punishment for the drunken Barnadine, even though he may thereby frustrate his own plans to save Claudio's life. The Duke's actions illustrate Isabella's earlier words to Angelo that human justice should carefully reflect divine justice (II, ii, 73–9) in qualifying punishment with mercy. As if the event had occurred in direct response to the Duke's pious decision to spare Barnadine, the Provost immediately informs Vincentio of the death of Ragozine (IV, iii, 68–75), which the Duke identifies as a providence: 'O, 'tis an accident that heaven provides' (IV, iii, 76). It appears that divine intervention has resolved the Duke's dilemma, rewarding him for his refusal to execute Barnadine when

---

[50] The phrase is borrowed from Harry Hotspur's condemnation of the King in *Henry IV* Part 1 (I, iii, 241). In Shakespeare's works, the 'scurvy politician' (*King Lear*: IV, vi, 171) is always vilified as the scheming wheeler-dealer.

Barnadine was unprepared for death. This poses the question of whether the Duke's ploys to preserve Claudio's life—'bed-trick' and 'head-trick'—should be regarded as divinely sanctioned.

Frustratingly, the Duke's actions immediately following his exchanges with the Provost again call his moral status into question. The Duke seeks to justify his forthcoming hurtful lies to Isabella in an aside that prefixes their meeting:

> . . . I will keep her ignorant of her good,
> To make her heavenly comforts of despair
> When it is least expected. [IV, iii, 108–10]

Can this pretext, though, justify what he says next to Isabella, who is eagerly expecting news of Claudio's release?

> His head is off, and sent to Angelo. [IV, iii, 115]

Not only is this another lie, but it is also brutal in its terse, monosyllabic bluntness. Such trifling with bereavement cannot be so extenuated: it seems inconceivable that the 'heavenly comforts' of discovering ultimately that her brother has survived could offset the 'despair' endured by a sister deceived into believing him dead. For all the Duke's self-justification, his lie to Isabella here, although a convenient dramatic device, is unconvincing as a benevolent ploy. More than a cruel practical joke, it is part of the Duke's plan (or, rather, Shakespeare's dramatic design) to involve Isabella and various others in the great pageant of the final scene, where the Duke will emerge with his popularity and reputation among the common people restored—and perhaps with a new wife into the bargain. Isabella might appear more emotionally susceptible to his suit of marriage as a result of all the Duke's deceptions, especially those concerning the execution of her brother.

In return for her acquiescence with his plans to bring Angelo to justice, the Duke promises Isabella 'revenges', 'grace', and 'honour' (IV, iii, 135–6), but his qualifying oath—'trust not my holy order / If I pervert your course' (IV, iii, 147–8)—seems to be a metatheatrical device. It is a reminder that his 'holy order' is a fabrication, making an audience uncomfortably aware that his oath is invalidated by the very terms by which he swears it. Indeed, the oath follows yet another ducal lie: 'I am combined by a sacred vow, / And shall be absent' (IV, iii, 144–5). Far from being absent from the final scene, the Duke/friar will be present for all but eighteen of the 536 lines! These deceptions have dramatic justification but might strike an audience as morally obnoxious.

The stage-business during these exchanges sometimes involves the disguised Duke embracing Isabella, to comfort her. If so, then Lucio may witness this physical closeness on his entry at IV, iii, 148, and hear the Duke's oath not to 'pervert [Isabella's] course'. Such a scene would be ripe for misinterpretation by a man always alert to innuendo, and may explain why Lucio will later accuse Lodowick of being 'a meddling friar' (V, i, 130), perhaps with an obscene gesture or intonation to suggest suspected sexual activity.[51] Immediately afterwards, Lucio's derogatory reference to 'the old fantastical duke of dark corners' (IV, iii, 156) again hints at surreptitious (potentially erotic) encounters; but it is arguably justified. The Duke's interviews with Isabella and Mariana, in which he persuades them to agree to satisfy Angelo's sexual demands and then to equivocate about them publicly, confirm him as a 'keeper of secret assignations', the likely insinuation of Lucio's phrase 'of dark corners'.[52] Additionally, many of the Duke's courses of action have seemed whimsical, even perverse

---

[51] Braunmuller and Watson further suggest that the phrase 'sheep-biting' that Lucio applies to Friar Lodowick (V, i, 352) is used in the sense of 'whoremongering' (p. 347, n, citing Gordon Williams: *A Dictionary of Sexual Language and Imagery in Shakespearean and Stuart Literature*, 3 vols. (London and Atlantic Highlands, NJ: Athlone, 1994).

[52] This is the construction placed upon the phrase by Lever, p. 119n. Braunmuller and Watson (p. 318n.) gloss the phrase 'out-of-the-way places (for sexual assignations)'.

('fantastical'), as he has lurked in shadowy places, spying and manipulating, while disguising both his person and his intentions.

The Duke is presented as planning his public re-entry into Vienna meticulously. He expresses his intention to write to Angelo to meet him 'at the consecrated fount / A league below the city' (IV, iii, 96–7) as a prelude to bringing Angelo to justice 'By cold gradation and well-balanc'd form' (IV, iii, 99). These lines, however, create certain expectations that remain unfulfilled. The meeting with Angelo will take place at the city gates, with no further mention of any 'consecrated fount'. Furthermore, Angelo's prosecution will not be conducted by 'cold gradation', which suggests slow, dispassionate progress, nor by 'well-balanc'd form', which implies weighing issues conventionally in the scales of justice, but rather by a series of flamboyant pantomime tricks devised and executed by the Duke. Additionally, the Duke briefs Friar Peter, Flavius, Valencius, Rowland, Crassus, and Varrius, either by word of mouth or by letter, about his imminent return to public life (Act IV, scene v). The tenor of his instructions is unimportant; the dramatic function of the scene is to foreshadow the Duke's re-establishment of his supremacy in the state. Finally, at the very end of Act IV, we learn that Isabella (and, by implication, Mariana) has received from her friar specific instructions about what to do and what to say on the Duke's entry into the city. The overall impression conveyed to the audience is that the Duke will script, direct, stage-manage, and star in, the public spectacle of his own return to power.

As the Duke prepares for the final scene, his likely objectives on his return to public life will engage the audience's imagination. He will be expected to re-establish his authority in the state, to expose and condemn the perfidy of his deputy, and to redeem Claudio from execution. So much could have been predicted from the evidence of Acts III and IV. As the final scene evolves, however, the Duke will prove to have further, ulterior motives. The manner in which he reassumes power will seem intended to earn him the popular acclaim that he previously scorned (at I, i, 67–72). He will also seek to forestall any accusation that he was responsible for Vienna's misgovernment. Finally, when Isabella is at her most vulnerable, he will propose marriage to her. In each of these enterprises (with the possible exception of the last), he will achieve his objective—albeit by questionable means.

Although, dramatically, the Duke has been indispensable throughout the play, the presentation of the Duke's character has been inconsistent from the outset. The evidence presented so far confirms that the Duke is no more a credible character to be judged on the principles of plausible behaviour and stable morality than many other figures from the popular narrative tradition of folk-tale and legend. The problem is that, as E. M. W. Tillyard argued, *Measure for Measure* did not transform itself from incipient tragedy into romantic comedy until the re-entry of the Duke at III, i, 151. Before then, the moral, legal, and political complexities of the plot had been so convincingly conveyed that the expectation of realism and consistency in the presentation of characters had been created. Isabella and Angelo may have fulfilled that expectation—but not the Duke. No expectation has therefore been created that the Duke should show consistency of character in word or deed at the denouement of the play. At least he will prove consistent in his inconsistency!

The Return of the Duke

The Duke's words and deeds in Act V are a public performance (for the citizens of Vienna as well as for the theatrical audience), disguising his intentions until the very end. He presents himself in three distinct roles consecutively: the credulous revenant, feigning ignorance of abuses committed during his absence; the indignant moralist, condemning corruption in Vienna; and the omniscient judge, punishing offences to the full extent of the law—only to mitigate initial severity with ultimate mercy. These changes of persona enable him to complete the project begun at the start of the play: testing the integrity of the other major characters. His 'assay[s] of . . . virtue' (III, i, 161–2), which are concluded concurrently rather than consecutively, span the whole of Act V.[53] The Duke's trial of Angelo's character includes in its scope further tests of Isabella, Friar Peter, Mariana, Escalus, the Provost, and Lucio. All those who speak in the final scene are 'measured' against the Duke's moral yardstick—before the Duke himself is ultimately put to the test.

The conclusion of the test on Angelo, begun in the first scene of the play when the Duke bestowed supreme power on him, recommences immediately on Vincentio's re-entry into the city. The Duke's apparent confidence in his deputy encourages Angelo to persist in denying his guilt, even when justly accused. Vincentio greets Escalus and (especially) Angelo with gratitude and praise, offering 'Many and hearty thankings' for the 'goodness of your justice' and promising 'public thanks / Forerunning more requital' (V, i, 4–8). For the people of Vienna, the Duke's words are a reassurance of the continuity of stable government; for Escalus, they acknowledge his integrity and good offices; but for Angelo, they incite complacency. Again, however, the audience may note that the Duke is using deception—'seeming', the very offence for which he is prosecuting Angelo—to achieve his ends. In addition, as he did in the very first scene of the play, the Duke employs equivocation:

> . . . your desert speaks loud, and . . .
> . . . it deserves with characters of brass
> A forted residence 'gainst the tooth of time
> And razure of oblivion. [V, i, 10–14]

---

[53] Vincentio could be regarded as testing and judging many of the other characters in the play from his first encounter with them on stage: thus, Angelo's and Escalus's tests begin in the very first scene of Act I; the Provost's and Julietta's in Act II; Isabella's and Lucio's in Act III; and Mariana's and Friar Peter's in Act IV. All but one of these tests (Julietta's, conducted in its entirety in II, iii) are concluded in this final Act.

To Angelo, the words seem to promise enduring praise but, to an alert audience, the Duke's speech ominously threatens Angelo with his just 'desert' of public humiliation and perpetual shame. The metaphor is of a commemorative plaque: an unassailable structure ('forted residence'—perhaps with suggestions of a prison) of indelible letters ('characters of brass'—with subliminal hints at brazen behaviour) will record his true 'desert' for perpetuity.

Immediately, the Duke incorporates into Angelo's trial a further test: that of Isabella. When she charges Angelo with a series of offences (V, i, 21–105), an audience would attribute the misleading and equivocal elements in her account to her obedience to Friar Lodowick, the Duke's alter ego. Speaking in propria persona, however, the Duke chooses further to test her patience and fortitude while simultaneously augmenting Angelo's sense of invulnerability. He is initially condescending towards Isabella, dismissing her as deranged:

> Away with her. Poor soul,
> She speaks this in th'infirmity of sense. [V, i, 49–50]

After hearing the full scope of her testimony, he expresses scepticism with his ironic riposte, 'This is most likely!' (V, i, 106). Gradually increasing his hostility towards the witness, the Duke condemns Isabella emphatically when she insists on the truth of her deposition:

> By heaven, fond wretch, thou know'st not what thou speak'st,
> Or else thou art suborn'd against his honour
> In hateful practice. First, his integrity
> Stands without blemish; next, it imports no reason
> That with such vehemency he should pursue
> Faults proper to himself. If he had so offended,
> He would have weigh'd thy brother by himself,
> And not have cut him off. Someone hath set you on:
> Confess the truth, and say by whose advice
> Thou cam'st here to complain. [V, i, 108–17]

The Duke is compelling Isabella patiently to endure the public ordeal of hearing herself denounced by her ruler as foolish and contemptible, a 'fond wretch' guilty of being 'suborn'd' (corruptly induced) into a 'hateful practice' (malicious plot). He dismisses her accusations on the (already discredited) grounds that Angelo would not have executed her brother for a crime of which he himself was guilty.[54] By contrast, the Duke publishes Angelo as a man of 'honour' and 'integrity' whose record is 'without blemish'—inciting his deputy to complacency. Additionally, Vincentio allows Angelo the pretext that there is a conspiracy against him, a ploy repeated when the Duke orders Isabella's arrested for sedition:

> I know you'd fain be gone. An officer!
> To prison with her! Shall we thus permit
> A blasting and a scandalous breath to fall
> On him so near us? This needs must be a practice.
> [V, i, 123–6]

Vincentio has apparently confirmed his supreme confidence in the integrity of his Deputy, who has witnessed his accuser condemned and committed to prison as a participant in a broader intrigue. Throughout these exchanges, Angelo's silence[55] suggests that he is content falsely to be exonerated by the Duke whilst Isabella is unjustly persecuted. The Duke's strategy is 'measuring' the extent of Angelo's perfidy, while simultaneously 'measuring' the patience and steadfastness of Isabella, who cannot recognise the Duke as the same Friar Lodowick who incited and formulated her public accusations against Angelo.

---

[54] The Duke is here repeating the erroneous opinion that he expressed at IV, ii, 106–11, immediately prior to the revelation that Angelo *did* intend to execute Claudio for the same offence that he (Angelo) had committed.

[55] Lines 35–8, an early attempt to discredit Isabella as a witness, are his only utterance during these exchanges.

The interlude that follows (V, i, 139–64) illustrates that, even in the untruths that he supplies to his agents, the Duke is inconsistent and contradictory. Friar Peter's intervention, implicitly 'scripted' by the Duke beforehand, alleges that Angelo's prime accuser, Friar Lodowick, is absent because he is 'sick . . . / Of a strange fever' (V, i, 153–54), rather than 'combined by a sacred vow' (IV, iii, 144), as the Duke/friar had alleged to Isabella. Neither account is true, as Friar Lodowick is present on stage, in the person of the Duke. Vincentio appears deliberately to be sowing uncertainty, disguising his activities with contradictory rumours (as he did to veil his purpose when he withdrew from government). To the audience, the Duke's most plausible objective in staging this interlude involving Friar Peter is to increase Angelo's conviction that those who accuse the Deputy are powerless to hurt him. Angelo is further incited to compound his crimes when, after Isabella's temporary departure from stage, the Duke coaxes him to ridicule his accuser:

> Do you not smile at this, Lord Angelo?
> O heaven, the vanity of wretched fools! [V, i, 165–6]

Although Angelo again makes no verbal response, either of agreement or of demurral, his silence suggests that he is content for Isabella to stand publicly condemned for impeaching him.

While continuing to encourage complacency in Angelo by feigning absolute trust in him, Vincentio extends the test of patience and obedience to Mariana and her supporter, Friar Peter. Having heard Mariana's evidence (V, i, 170–232), the Duke even appoints Angelo as judge in his own case, urging him to 'punish them [his three accusers] to your height of pleasure' (line 239), as their guilt is presumed:

> Thou foolish friar, and thou pernicious woman,
> Compact with her that's gone; think'st thou thy oaths,
> Though they would swear down each particular saint,
> Were testimonies against his worth and credit
> That's seal'd in approbation? [V, i, 240–4]

In referring to the petitioners as 'foolish' (Friar Peter), 'pernicious' (Mariana) and 'her that's gone' (a dismissive reference to Isabella), the Duke feigns belief that the three are guilty of conspiracy ('Compact') while apparently confirming, with the words 'worth', 'credit', and 'seal'd in approbation', his confidence in Angelo's integrity. The Duke's test of Angelo 'measures' how much further into iniquity Angelo will decline if left to preside over the interrogation and sentencing of those who have testified justly against him.

The Duke, however, is indulging in what a modern audience might regard as entrapment, encouraging Angelo to compound his offences. This is the same method practised by Hecate and the Weird Women in corrupting Macbeth:

> . . . the strength of . . . illusion,
> Shall draw him on to his confusion.
> He shall spurn fate, scorn death, and bear
> His hopes 'bove wisdom, grace, and fear;
> And you all know security
> Is mortals' chiefest enemy. [*Macbeth*: III, v, 28–33]

'Security'—that is, a false sense of security, or 'complacency' as we should call it—is precisely what the Duke's words encourage in Angelo. As the witches in *Macbeth* are undoubtedly a malign influence, this parallel with their technique to corrupt their victim again calls into question the moral status of the Duke's actions.

When he reappears as Friar Lodowick, Vincentio rectifies the balance of the judicial scales. He condemns the obvious injustice not only of Angelo's appointment as judge in own trial but also of the court's summary dismissal of the testimonies of Angelo's accusers:

> The Duke's unjust
> Thus to retort your manifest appeal,
> And put your trial in the villain's mouth

135

Which here you come to accuse. [V, i, 298–301]

As Friar Lodowick, he now reverses the Duke's previous judgement, declaring that the evidence against Angelo is 'manifest'—that is, obviously truthful—and that the Deputy himself is the 'villain'. This indictment quickly develops into a general denunciation of misrule in Vienna:

> My business in this state
> Made me a looker-on here in Vienna,
> Where I have seen corruption boil and bubble
> Till it o'errun the stew: laws for all faults,
> But faults so countenanc'd that the strong statutes
> Stand like the forfeits in a barber's shop,
> As much in mock as mark. [V, i, 314–20]

This criticism, however, reflects the plight of Vienna at the beginning of the play, under the Duke's rule, rather than its current state under his deputy. Angelo's stringent government has sought to address the very issues that the friar condemns ('laws for all faults, / But faults . . . countenanced'). Furthermore, because 'stews' was the popular term for brothels, Friar Lodowick's reference to Vienna as a 'stew' (line 317) would seem specifically to allude to promiscuity, the lax sexual morality that the Duke failed to prosecute but that Angelo has rigorously suppressed in others (if not in himself) since his appointment as Deputy.

Why, then, should the Duke be so scathing about his own misrule (other than because, by this means, Shakespeare complicates and intensifies the dramatic effect of the final scene)? Two possible explanations suggest themselves. Coming so soon after Friar Lodowick's condemnation of Angelo as a 'villain' (line 300), the speech implies that full responsibility for the parlous condition of the state lies with the Deputy rather than with the Duke. Alternatively (or additionally), Friar Lodowick's denunciation of government in Vienna could be seen as part of Vincentio's ploy to test the extent of Escalus's loyalty to the Duke, compelling him to silence all criticism by declaring that 'to tax [the Duke] with injustice' (line 308) is '[s]lander to th'state' (V, i, 320), warranting dire punishment. There remains the suspicion, nevertheless, that Friar Lodowick's condemnation of corruption in Vienna is further evidence that inconsistencies in the language and actions of the Duke may have been conceded by Shakespeare primarily in the interests of spectacular dramatic impact.

There follows one of the most dramatically effective moments in the play: the unhooding of the Duke. Surprise, shock, delight, and anguish should erupt across the stage. The other two major 'unhooding' sequences in this final scene, involving Mariana and Claudio, are preludes to recognition and reconciliation;[56] but the Duke's literal unhooding is the immediate prelude to the metaphorical 'unhooding' of both Angelo and Lucio. It is therefore deliciously ironic that Angelo should authorise Lucio's assault on Friar Lodowick (line 348), which culminates when the friar's cowl is pulled off to reveal the Duke whose authority both have abused (line 353). Angelo and Lucio bring about their own *peripeteia*—that sudden reversal of fortune encountered in classical drama—as their own offences and falsehoods cannot remain hidden once they have stripped the Duke of his disguise.

Once revealed, the Duke assumes the role of the deus ex machina, the divinity who descended to restore order and to rectify injustices in Greek drama. He 'deposes' Angelo by demanding the judgement seat from him, addressing him in a new, contemptuous tone:

> Hast thou or word, or wit, or impudence,
> That yet can do thee office? [V, i, 361–2]

---

[56] The presentation of Barnadine on stage, prior to the Duke's merciful judgement on him, is less of a coup de théâtre than the other three 'unhoodings', as Barnadine's survival has been announced in advance (lines 463–5).

Angelo's reply elevates the Duke to divine status, attributing to him the omniscience of God displayed at the Last Judgement:

> O my dread lord,
> I should be guiltier than my guiltiness
> To think I can be undiscernible,
> When I perceive your Grace, like power divine,
> Hath looked upon my passes. [V, i, 365–8]

We therefore have two extreme and mutually exclusive views of the Duke's moral status expressed towards the end of the play. From Lucio's portrait of the 'old fantastical duke of dark corners' (IV, iii, 156), Vincentio appears irrational, unpredictable, prone to intrigue, and guilty of dubious deeds, an unworthy man who has presided over a dissolute state. By contrast, in Angelo's words here, the Duke is presented as all-knowing, endowed with 'power divine' to observe and judge his people. Shakespeare has conflated these incompatible elements into the dramatic construct that is the Duke. Many in an audience, engaged with ever-changing aspects of narrative, conflict, and suspense throughout the play, may accept whichever Duke is presented according to the particular context, and perhaps will not be too conscious of the inconsistencies of characterisation. Nevertheless, those inconsistencies persist.

If we, with Angelo, regard the Duke as 'like power divine', then his pronouncements at the end of the play will seem to us a kind of Last Judgement. Here, the sacrament of marriage receives particular emphasis, both as a reward and, paradoxically, as a penance, evident when the virtuous Mariana and the sinful Angelo are the first to undergo this judgement. Once they are married, though, the Duke apparently imposes a much harsher penalty on his deputy:

> 'An Angelo for Claudio; death for death.
> Haste still pays haste, and leisure answers leisure;
> Like doth quit like, and Measure still for Measure.'
> Then, Angelo, thy fault's thus manifested,

Which, though thou would'st deny, denies thee vantage.
We do condemn thee to the very block
Where Claudio stoop'd to death, and with like haste.

[V, i, 407–13]

Shakespeare's audience, however, should recognise that the
Duke is again equivocating, to chasten Angelo and the citizens
of Vienna with his 'remonstrance of . . . power' (V, i, 390).
Throughout the speech quoted above, the Duke has emphasized
that Angelo deserves exactly the same fate as Claudio, his
putative victim; hence, as the Duke has spared Claudio from
execution, he should also remit Angelo's death-sentence. In the
balanced, 'measured' world of this play, both the condemned
prisoner and the false judge are redeemable.

The Duke's equivocation at this point involves further
testing—not only of Angelo, but also of Mariana and Isabella.
Angelo's penitence and fortitude are being gauged: he has
already requested '[i]mmediate sentence' and 'sequent death'
without the formality of a trial. The Duke has apparently given
him the opportunity (through marriage to Mariana) to gain a
reprieve for his sins, but such a hope would now appear vain to
him. This creates an expectation that Angelo, like Claudio (in
his interview with Isabella), might desperately plead for his life.
Instead, like Julietta, Angelo is subjected by the Duke to a test
of his patience and deference for the law. He passes that test
when he 'crave[s] death more willingly than mercy' (line 474),
welcoming his opportunity to atone for his crimes.

Simultaneously, the Duke is testing whether Mariana's love
and fidelity are fickle or materialistic. 'To buy [her] a better
husband' (line 423), he offers her all of Angelo's possessions
that should otherwise, after Angelo's execution, revert to the
state. Unlike Angelo, when he rejected Mariana on the loss of
her dowry, she is not swayed by considerations of wealth: her
virtue is confirmed when she craves 'no other, nor no better
man' (line 424).

139

Finally (and especially), the Duke continues to test Isabella, to establish whether she has learned compassion and forgiveness since her cruel rejection of her brother in the prison. Mariana, having saved Isabella from the 'vice that most I do abhor' (II, ii, 29), pleads with Isabella to speak in extenuation of the crimes of Angelo. Angelo, however, is the very man who demanded Isabella's virginity and, she believes, broke his vow to spare her brother from sentence of death in return for sexual gratification. The Duke deliberately reminds Isabella of the death of her brother, feigning that he (the Duke) was thwarted in his attempts to save Claudio by the speed with which Angelo enforced the execution (V, i, 387–97). Isabella is thus seen by the audience to be drawn in contrary directions by the ties of gratitude to her redeemer, Mariana, and the urge for revenge on her tormentor, Angelo. She passes the Duke's test when she kneels and prays for mercy to be shown to Mariana's new husband. The Duke's strategy 'measures' the extent to which she can conduct herself in accordance with her own doctrine of mercy, articulated in her first exchanges with Angelo (II, ii, 58–79).

The Duke's 'rewards' to Isabella for passing his final test will be twofold: reunion with her brother, whose life has been preserved despite Vincentio's report that Claudio had been executed; and proposals of marriage from the Duke. Both these 'rewards', however, are problematical. The acrimony in the parting of Claudio and Isabella in Act III would temper with mortification any joy in their reunification. As for the Duke's two offers of marriage (at V, i, 488–90 and 531–4), Isabella's silence on both occasions is ambiguous. In more traditional performances, she tacitly communicates her grateful acceptance of the Duke's 'reward'. In recent years, however, there has been an increasing tendency to end the play with Isabella's demurral or outright rejection of Vincentio, a plausible tableau as the Duke appears shamelessly to be exploiting Isabella's emotional vulnerability.[57]

---

[57] The contrast appears clearly in the two BBC productions, the 1979 screening concluding with a triumphal procession led by the Duke and

It is no coincidence that the first offer of marriage immediately follows the unhooding of Claudio. Like some macabre magician or reality TV host, the Duke first convinces Isabella that her brother has been beheaded while unreconciled to her, and then stages the public spectacle of reuniting the siblings. In these circumstances, any loving sister would be overwhelmed by conflicting feelings—from amazement to shame, from joy to remorse. The Duke seeks to exploit this emotional turmoil:

> If he be like your brother, for his sake
> Is he pardon'd; and for your lovely sake
> Give me your hand and say you will be mine.
> He is my brother too. . . . [V, i, 488–91]

Silence may, in other contexts in the play, indicate consent, but does not appear to do so here. The Duke's next words, an integral part of the last line quoted above, suggest that he has received no favourable response from Isabella: '. . . but fitter time for that' (line 491). Isabella might register anything from bafflement to indignation at the Duke's suggestion, but she has spoken no word of response. The Duke's half-line implies the discomfiture of a wooer who has suddenly recognised the impropriety of his proposal.[58]

The tables have been turned by Isabella's silence. She has proved herself worthy of the Duke by exhibiting, in turn, the virtues of chastity, patience, humility, obedience, and compassion in response to his tests; but the Duke must now

---

Isabella, hand in hand, while the 1994 production ends with Isabella staring at the Duke in horror and refusing his approach. A fuller account of variations in the presentation of this finale in productions on stage and screen is offered in Chapter 8, 'Performances in More Recent Years', especially pp. 539–542.

[58] Braunmuller and Watson (pp. 46 and 52) note that Kemble, in his late-eighteenth-century production, cut the Duke's first proposal to make Isabella's silence less uncomfortable—as did Margaret Webster in her 1957 Old Vic production.

141

prove himself worthy of Isabella. He must show the mercy that Isabella had so extolled in her first interview with Angelo (II, ii, 58ff.). Then, Angelo had refused to temper justice with mercy, despite Isabella's pleading; but now the Duke offers mercy to all offenders. Having already begun with Barnadine (V, i, 477–83), the Duke grants Isabella's plea for mercy for Angelo (V, i, 492–5).

The Duke has morally tested other major characters before punishing or rewarding them according to their deserving. Shakespeare, however, reserves the ultimate test for the Duke himself. Although he declares, 'I find an apt remission in myself' (V, i, 496), the Duke must now consider sentence on Lucio. Lucio's offence is a personal one against the Duke, who has twice been obliged to endure Lucio's outrageous slanders (at III, ii, 83–178 and IV, iii, 156–164). The Duke addresses Lucio as 'one in place I cannot pardon' (V, i, 497): speaking ill of a prince is apparently an offence that eclipses even the murder committed by Barnadine and Angelo's hypocritical tyranny. Vincentio's policy of forgiveness and reconciliation might plausibly have been sorely tried by Lucio's attempt to attribute his own slanders to Friar Lodowick (the Duke's alias).[59] Then, there is the further issue to resolve of Mistress Kate Keep-down and her illegitimate child, responsibility for whom Lucio had boasted to the disguised Duke (at IV, iii, 167–72; cf. III, ii, 192–7). This self-incrimination provides the Duke with the opportunity to revenge himself on Lucio: his slanderer could be 'Condemn'd upon the act of fornication' (V, i, 73) under which Angelo had sentenced Claudio. There can therefore be no doubt that the Duke has the authority, the motive, and the legislation necessary to impose a capital sentence on Lucio for his offences—but such ruthlessness would invite comparison between the Duke and the corrupt Deputy, Angelo.

---

[59] In this respect, Lucio's role is the 'comic' counterpart to Angelo's 'tragic' one: both sought to discredit their just accusers before their persistent lies were 'unhooded' with the unhooding of the Duke.

The Duke's initial sentence on Lucio (as was the case with his sentence on Angelo) is severe:

> . . . he shall marry her. The nuptial finish'd,
> Let him be whipp'd and hang'd. [V, i, 510–11]

Lucio's atonement, it seems, is to be threefold, each stage of greater severity than the last: public humiliation, followed by corporal punishment, followed by capital punishment. Before long, however, the sentence is commuted, as the Duke again tempers justice with mercy:

> Upon mine honour, thou shalt marry her.
> Thy slanders I forgive, and therewithal
> Remit thy other forfeits. [V, i, 516–18]

In short, at the end of *Measure for Measure*, no-one will die by the law. Although Lucio must make reparation to the woman whom he wronged, the Duke imposes no penalty for Lucio's personal slanders.[60] Again, the audience should feel that the moral compass has moved in the Duke's favour, and that he is now more deserving of Isabella's virtues.

Further to establish publicly the pattern of his justice, the Duke has also performed an interlude with the Provost, seeming to dismiss him for failure to abide by legal protocol: 'For which I do discharge you of your office' (line 459). Once the Provost has brought Barnadine and Claudio before the assembly and revealed their identities, however, the Duke promises the Provost promotion, in keeping with the reinstatement of the

---

[60] It is therefore difficult to equate Vincentio with James I, who argued in *Basilikon Doron* that those who 'judge and speak rashly of princes' deserve a capital sentence because they are guilty of '*unpardonable* crimes' (italics added) to be ranked with 'murder . . . poisoning and false coin' (quoted by Kamps and Raber, p. 145). Surprisingly, in their edition (pp. 145–148), Kamps and Raber maintain that Lucio is nevertheless to be flogged as 'Slandering a prince deserves it'. The Duke's final sentence at V, i, 516–18 seems to have been disregarded.

Duke's benevolent government: 'We shall employ thee in a worthier place' (line 528). With the benefit of hindsight, the earlier remark whereby Vincentio removed the Provost from office seems a minor test of the Provost's fortitude and/or a characteristic ducal equivocation.

And so to other aspects of the Duke's final speech, which is also the final speech in the play. Mercy and grace abound. Claudio is encouraged to complete his nuptials with Julietta (line 522); happiness is bestowed on Mariana, and Angelo is encouraged to love her for her virtues (lines 523–34); Escalus is promised a greater reward for his justice than mere public acknowledgement (lines 525–6); the Provost's promotion is confirmed (lines 527–8); and Angelo is instructed to pardon the Provost for disobeying and deceiving him (lines 529–31).[61] All have been 'measured', their merits and demerits weighed in the balance.

Having thus resolved all the specific issues of justice and injustice raised in the play, the Duke can now return to Isabella and repeat his offer of marriage:

> Dear Isabel,
> I have a motion which imports your good;
> Whereto if you'll a willing ear incline,
> What's mine is yours, and what is yours is mine.
> [V, i, 531–4]

Circumstances have changed considerably since the Duke's first proposal, under fifty lines earlier. The Duke's more recent words and actions have suggested that he has virtues of justice and mercy worthy of those complementary virtues that Isabella has displayed in the series of tests that he imposed on her. Furthermore, where the Duke's previous proposal had emphasised what *he* would gain from marriage ('your lovely

---

[61] Curiously, Friar Peter, such an important functionary in the Duke's re-establishment of his rule in Vienna, receives neither thanks, praise, promise of reward, nor even acknowledgement in this final speech.

hand'; 'you will be mine'; 'he is my brother too'), the proposed contract now seems more balanced, with greater emphasis on what Isabella will achieve ('your good', 'what's mine is yours'). As the title of the play suggests, marriage involves measure for measure, each party bringing to the union a balance of material and spiritual riches.

Although Isabella is again silent, her silence here is more likely to signify assent, as the Duke's final couplet suggests:

So bring us to our palace, where we'll show
What's yet behind that's meet you all should know.
[V, i, 535–6]

The Duke's first word in this couplet, 'So', seems to confirm that his offer has been accepted. The concluding parade that he then proposes would be particularly visually satisfying for the audience. The Duke and Isabella, as a couple, might lead offstage a procession of the other couples: Angelo and Mariana, Claudio and Julietta, perhaps even Lucio and Mistress Kate Keep-down, with Escalus and the Provost as a pairing signifying righteous earthly judgement, and Friar Peter accompanying Barnadine to denote forthcoming divine judgement.[62]

The possibility, nevertheless, remains that Isabella's continued silence does *not* indicate consent to the Duke's proposal of marriage. From their first meeting, he has deceived her in his appearance and with his words. He has allowed her to suffer the anguish of believing her brother dead under her cruel curse in the prison (III, i, 135–49). He has instructed her to lie and to deceive others, both in her indecent bargain with Angelo and in her public accusations against the Deputy before the people of Vienna. Finally, he has sought to take advantage of her when she was most emotionally exposed. Isabella is a woman who has already suffered under the tyranny of a

---

[62] In general terms, this was the finale presented in the BBC's 1979 televised version, directed by Desmond Davis.

manipulative male—Angelo—who took advantage of her emotional vulnerability to proposition her for his own sexual advantage. When the Duke addresses her with the words, 'What's mine is yours, and what is yours is mine' (V, i, 534), is he proposing a sordid transaction of his material 'treasure' for what, elsewhere, Laertes calls a woman's 'chaste treasure' (*Hamlet*: I, iii, 31)?[63] In the circumstances, is Isabella likely to consider the Duke's offer any more favourably than she did Angelo's? Has she overcome her abhorrence of illicit sexual activity which, by extension, might suggest an abhorrence of any sexual activity? Why would she wish in these circumstances to compromise her determination expressed in her one soliloquy in the play: 'Then, Isabel live chaste' (II, iv, 183)? Besides, if a plausible reason for her retreat to a convent at the beginning of the play was to avoid the depraved society illustrated in Act I, why would she accept an offer of marriage from the man whose leniency then—by his own admission (I, iii, 35)—had caused that corruption, one whose conduct in this final scene suggests that indulgent rule, with all its propensity to cause 'decorum' to go 'quite athwart', is being reinstated in Vienna?

With the benefit of hindsight, an audience may ponder plausible motives for the Duke's actions since the start of the play. By his own admission, the Duke has been a lenient ruler who, having 'let slip' the 'headstrong jades' of Viennese society for many years by slackening the 'bits and curbs' of legal restraints, has brought about social disorder (I, iii, 19–31). He, like Angelo, is concerned for his reputation among the people (I, iii, 34–43), which has suffered because of his indulgent approach to government (a credible pretext for Lucio's slanders in Act III, scene ii and Act IV, scene iii). He appoints Angelo, a man whose integrity he believes to be questionable and whom he confidently foresees will be inflexible and oppressive in government, in the expectation that his deputy will be corrupted by power (I, iii, 50–4). The

---

[63] Angelo's earlier image justifies this interpretation when he proposes, 'You must lay down the treasures of your body' (II, iv, 96).

stringent regime that Angelo enforces alienates his fellows in government: the noble Escalus (II, i, 1–40), his colleague, the Justice (II, i, 277–82), and the Duke's jailor, the Provost (II, ii, 3–14 and IV, ii. 76). It also alienates the people of Vienna whom we encounter: Claudio (I, ii, 146–60), Pompey (II, i, 227–240), Isabella (II, ii, 107–42), Lucio (III, ii, 110–12 and 167–9) and, implicitly, Mistress Overdone on her arrest (III, ii, 184–200). When this unpopular deputy is ultimately revealed as profoundly corrupt, a chastened Vienna welcomes back its long-absent ruler, implicitly with new appreciation of the virtues of the Duke's leniency in government, and with recognition that flouting the law severely damages the state. As the Duke has vindicated his previously lenient rule by contrast with the rigours suffered in Vienna under Angelo, his pardon of all the malefactors at the end of the play resembles a pageant of self-justification, teaching his people how fortunate they should consider themselves to live under such a benevolent rule. An audience may view this denouement as the Duke's objective from the outset: to regain the love and obedience of his people—to win their 'loud applause and *Aves* vehement' (I, i, 70) at the expense of Angelo's reputation.

In the course of his observation of Vienna, the Duke has focused on Isabella as an embodiment of virtue. Despite his disdainful denial of the power of the 'dribbling dart of love' to affect him (I, iii, 1–3), he offers Isabella the opportunity to be his duchess at the end of the play. What might this action represent? As he is her lord in marriage, so he is lord to the people whom he governs: she is the embodiment of moral qualities that he might wish to promote in dissolute Vienna. Although chaste from the outset, she has developed patience, humility, obedience, compassion, and forgiveness under his tutelage. If, as Lucio twice implies, the Duke is an 'old' man who is 'now past it', it is even possible that Isabella might be able not merely to 'live chaste' but entirely to avoid the 'abhorred pollution'—sexual congress—that so frightens and disgusts her. When seen in this light, the ending of the play may convince the audience that Vienna, under the Duke's benevolent guidance, can acquire Isabella's virtues without further imposition of the inflexible rule of law practised by Angelo. Perhaps this is Shakespeare's implicit riposte to Machiavelli's political maxim that 'it is much safer to be feared than be loved, being that one of the two must needs fail.'[64] Shakespeare, through the presentation of the Duke, implicitly proposes that it is better for a state to be governed by a beloved prince (Vincentio) rather than by a feared tyrant (Angelo).

At her first meeting with Angelo, Isabella noted that the powerful are not subject to the same rules and restrictions that apply to lesser mortals:

> That in the captain's but a choleric word,
> Which in the soldier is flat blasphemy. [II, ii, 131–2]

The Duke's contradictory statements and morally dubious words and actions throughout the play may, however, seem too blatant to excuse as a prerogative of power. If a production favours emphasis on the Duke's imperfections, then Isabella's rejection of the Duke at the end of the play will seem fully appropriate. If, by contrast, a production represents the Duke as redeemed by his mercy, particularly towards Lucio, then Isabella's ultimate acceptance of his offer of marriage in the concluding lines will be justified to the audience. As for the extraordinary elaborations, the twists and turns of the final scene, although we may consider that they reflect poorly on the character and motives of the Duke who (through Shakespeare's choices as a dramatist) brought them about, we cannot but concede that the ending of *Measure for Measure* might be dramatically unsatisfying—even insipid—without them. Ultimately, for those who insist that *Measure for Measure* is a 'problem play', the Duke is a major embodiment of these problems in that he may leave audiences baffled as to the appropriate moral response to him. Those audiences should, nevertheless, remain fascinated by his machinations that have successfully sustained their dramatic engagement until the very end of the play.

---

[64] Kamps and Raber, p. 162, quoting *The Prince*, Chapter 17.

Vincentio's Apologia

With the benefit of hindsight, we may recognise a justification for many of the Duke's morally questionable words and actions in one of Vincentio's most opaque speeches. When Escalus enquires about 'news abroad i'th'world' (III, ii, 215), the reply of the disguised Duke begins in enigmatic fashion:

> . . . there is so great a fever on goodness that the dissolution of it must cure it.[65] [III, ii, 216–17]

The sense is in doubt because the referent of the neuter pronoun 'it', twice deployed at the end of the sentence, is unclear. The meaning is simple if the first 'it' refers to 'fever' and the second 'it' to 'goodness': the fever that afflicts goodness must be entirely vanquished to restore goodness to health.[66] But why would Friar Lodowick state the blindingly obvious? Any disease must be totally overcome to return the patient to full health. The context requires not a truism but rather a controversial statement: the Duke's emphatic 'so great' suggests that the raging fever that he describes requires a desperate remedy. If, on both occasions, the pronoun 'it' refers to 'goodness' then the Duke's words present us with a moral paradox: when goodness is seriously diseased, then that goodness must suffer 'dissolution' (literally, 'death') for goodness ultimately to be restored.[67] Such a reading might justify the Duke's actions from the opening scene to the final scene of the play.

---

[65] Braunmuller and Watson (p. 285n.) suggest that the Duke is disguising the fact that, as he has travelled no further than Vienna, he has no knowledge of 'news abroad i'th'world' and must revert to 'platitudes'.

[66] The silence of some recent editors (e.g. Jane Coles and Rex Gibson) may suggest that they accept this obvious meaning.

[67] 'The fever can only be 'cured' by the death of the patient (i.e. of goodness)' (Lever, p. 92n.) and 'only by dying can goodness be rid of the disease' (Kamps and Raber, p. 74n.).

149

Goodness in Vienna has become deeply infected, as the Duke twice declares, first to Friar Thomas (I, iii, 19–31) and second to the assembled people of the city (V, i, 314–19). Goodness must therefore suffer a drastic purgation before it can be cured of its disease.[68] The Duke, in his disguise as a Christian friar, takes it upon himself to eradicate the sexual 'fever' of otherwise virtuous characters by a process of mortification prior to restoring them to virtue. He brings the innocent Julietta close to despair by informing her that her lover is to be executed the following day (II, iii, 36–42), only to dispel her misery when he ultimately releases Claudio, reuniting the two lovers (V, i, 475–87). He quells all the noble Claudio's hope for (and love of) life in a lengthy speech expressing contempt for the world (III, i, 1–43); but then he restores Claudio to happiness by pardoning him and reuniting him with Julietta (V, i, 484–9). The Duke lies to the fiercely chaste Isabella that her brother is dead, causing her 'dissolution' into vengeful imprecations (IV, iii, 114–22), before he gradually remodels her virtue by means of a series of 'measures' in the concluding scenes. The patient, faithful Mariana, who has waited so long for the consummation of her love, experiences further 'dissolution' when she hears her newly-married husband sentenced to death by the Duke; but she is subsequently rewarded when the Duke repeals Angelo's sentence and blesses their union (V, i, 398–524). There remains to consider the case of Angelo himself, whose virtues of knowledge, wisdom, and abstinence were widely recognised in

---

[68] The concept is central to the Christian mystery, in that Christ, embodiment of 'goodness', died and was resurrected, bringing the promise of salvation to humankind, previously condemned to Hell for its sins. There followed a long theological tradition that the faithful should achieve salvation through mortification, in imitation of Christ's Passion and Resurrection. Before being reborn in Christ, the faithful, and converts (like Saint Paul) needed to be 'almost unmade' (the phrase derives from the opening stanza of 'The Wreck of the Deutschland' by Gerard Manley Hopkins). A parallel might also be drawn with the sacrament of baptism, where a figurative 'drowning' enables the faithful to emerge cleansed of sin.

Vienna,[69] but whose susceptibility to sexual corruption was revealed only when Vincentio bestowed absolute power on him. Angelo undergoes 'dissolution' through public humiliation and sentence of death, before being redeemed by the Duke's general amnesty and by the fidelity of a virtuous wife (V, i, 361–524).

Even the role of the Duke himself may be interpreted in the light of the words of his alias, Friar Lodowick, to Escalus. A frequently-encountered proverb in mediaeval and renaissance political theory is *si caput dolet, membra dolent* ('if the head is sick, then so are the limbs'), the sense being that a defect in the head of state will taint the rest of the body politic. Despite his (presumably) good intentions, Vincentio, as head of state, has been lax in his administration of the law (I, iii, 19ff.), causing moral degeneration among his people.[70] He must therefore suffer 'dissolution' by 'usurp[ing] the beggary he was never born to' (III, ii, 90) as a friar, before he can re-establish the rule of virtue on his return to government. When interpreted in this way, Friar Lodowick's sixteen words to Escalus (at III, ii, 216–17) have exceptionally broad ramifications.

The disguised Duke's enigmatic response to Escalus continues with a second sentence that is just as problematic as his first:

> Novelty is only in request, and it is as dangerous to be aged in any kind of course as it is virtuous to be constant in any undertaking. [III, ii, 217–20]

Although the overall meaning of the first five words is obscure, it can be conjectured from the context of what follows. The curious idiom seems to mean that the 'only' thing that is 'request[ed]' is 'novelty'—that is, people are always demanding change. It follows from the remainder of the Duke's

---

[69] For example, by Escalus at I, i, 23–5, by the Duke at I, iii, 12, and by Lucio at I, iv, 60–1.
[70] Vincentio resembles James I in *Basilikon Doron* by conceding that excessive leniency in his earlier rule was misguided.

sentence that, politically, it is 'dangerous' to persist in a 'course' of action even though, morally, it would be 'virtuous' to be 'constant'. The Duke's words form a critique of Vienna: he cannot follow the virtuous course of constancy because his people perpetually require 'novelty' which, if not supplied, will cause upheaval in the state.

When reappraised in the light of these lines, the Duke's enigmatic behaviour in Act I becomes more comprehensible and justifiable. Vincentio has persisted for 'fourteen years' with a policy of leniency in administering the law (as he concedes at I, iii, 19–23), which has encouraged his people to become morally lax (I, iii, 23–31). He therefore institutes 'novelty' by disappearing from the state and deputing to Angelo the power to 'strike home' against abuses (I, iii, 39–43). Once this 'glimpse of newness' (Claudio: I, ii, 147) has chastened Vienna, the Duke returns before Angelo's increasing corruption can infect the state more widely. In the final scene (V, i), the Duke stages the 'novelty' of an elaborate spectacle: a public trial in which one ruler (Angelo) is deposed, and another (Vincentio himself) is reinstated. As the people should be satisfied with this 'novelty', the Duke may expect the re-establishment of social order—at least until the fickle temperament of his people requires further change.[71] All benefit when the Duke, by catering for the public appetite for 'novelty', restores stable government at the end of the play.

It would be easy to disregard the disguised Duke's words to Escalus as conventional—and relatively insignificant—moral sententiousness on the evils of the world (in keeping with

---

[71] Like the ladies in Sir Thomas Wyatt's poem beginning 'They flee from me', the people of Vienna are 'Busily seeking . . . continual change' because they love to 'use newfangleness' (Ballade LXXX, lines 7 and 19). The Duke has learned that mutability (that favourite topic of Elizabethan and Jacobean literature: e.g. in Edmund Spenser's *Two Cantos of Mutabilitie*, appended since 1609 to the full text of *The Faerie Queene*) both threatens and secures long-term stability in Vienna. It threatens when it is an unsatisfied desire among the people; and it secures when that craving for change is gratified.

Vincentio's gnomic asides elsewhere in Acts III and IV). When carefully considered, however, Vincentio's two sentences explain his treatment of Julietta, Claudio, Isabella, Mariana, and Angelo, as well as his general conduct before his court and his people. If this reading is adopted (and I concede that the concision and obscurity of the Duke's language make it unlikely that an audience would recognise the potential significance of the speech), then Friar Lodowick's words to Escalus become a covert statement of intent, an apologia anticipating measures that the Duke will deploy to restore happiness and social order. His words may not *morally* vindicate his proposed actions, but they do explain, in keeping with the strain of Machiavellian realpolitik in his character, why he might deem such actions necessary. Ultimately, this speech promotes a more 'measured' assessment of the Duke: although we might still regard him as a dramatic construct comprising contradictory elements and motivated primarily by self-interest, we should recognise that his conduct is, nevertheless, conducive to the welfare of those whom he governs.

In retrospect, we might confirm that, of the three major characters in *Measure for Measure*—the Duke, Angelo, and Isabella—it is the Duke who most clearly shows his origins in the popular narrative tradition and who proves most inimical to plausible presentation. The most 'realistic' and credible part of the play—that is, the first half, up to the Duke's re-entry at III, i, 150—is the part in which he figures least prominently. It is, however, self-evident that his withdrawal from power and his appointment of a potentially corrupt deputy to enforce those laws that he has neglected are fundamental to the development of those early scenes. Latterly in the play, Vincentio emerges as more of a Machiavellian ruler than Angelo, for the Duke secretly uses the devices of lies, deception, and false oaths to win public acclaim and to re-establish his supremacy in government.

The Duke cannot entirely shake off the folk-tale garb of the monarch who moves incognito among his people before returning triumphantly to government, of the judge who resolves a seemingly intractable problem with a dazzling strategy, of the nobleman who tests and then weds the virtuous maid of lower social status. Although, in these guises, he would not appear out of place in the fanciful world of one of Shakespeare's 'happy comedies', he fits less comfortably into those parts of *Measure for Measure* that explore compelling political situations and intense moral dilemmas. It is, nevertheless, to the Duke that the audience will turn, throughout the play, for guidance on the development of the plot, for elucidation of the principles of good government, and for definitive judgements on the moral status of all other major characters.

Chapter 3

Angelo

Although Angelo speaks under an eighth of the total number of lines in *Measure for Measure*, he is one of Shakespeare's most prominent and memorable dramatic creations. Angelo resembles Macbeth not only in that his deeds are repugnant but also in that certain of his speeches, particularly those uttered in soliloquy, invite an audience to empathize with his circumstances. Indeed, we may feel as ambivalent about Angelo as about his intended victim, Isabella, especially during Acts II and III of the play. What is indisputable is that, towards the end of *Measure for Measure*, Angelo would believe himself to be exactly what Isabella accuses him of being: 'forsworn', 'a murderer', 'an adulterous thief', '[a]n hypocrite', and 'a virgin-violator' (V, i, 40–4). He even perseveres in wickedness after this public accusation, being prepared for his accusers to suffer severe penalties for their righteous testimonies against him. Only when the Duke throws off his disguise as Friar Lodowick (V, i, 353ff.) does Angelo finally capitulate by admitting his crimes and accepting his sentence. If an audience can feel stirrings of compassion for such a man, it is because, rather than being inveterately evil, he falls victim to his own limitations and to the corruptive influence of the absolute power that he is obliged to assume.

An audience's responses to Angelo are likely to go through at least four phases in the course of the play. Initially, there is every reason for an audience unfamiliar with subsequent evidence of his moral degeneracy to consider Angelo a man of exceptional integrity and ability, as he is chosen by the Duke to rule Vienna in Vincentio's absence. In addition, in the first scene, Angelo (although somewhat taciturn) appears dutiful, considerate, and modest in his speech, a man to inspire respect in an audience.

A transformation occurs, however, once he becomes 'proud man, / Dress'd in a little brief authority' (Isabella: II, ii, 118–19). Before Angelo reappears in the play in Act II, various characters testify to the coldly authoritarian regime that he establishes, his particular objective being to regulate human sexual activity. When we first encounter him in his new role as Deputy, in the first scene of Act II, he appears complacent, haughty, and insensitive. An audience, even when respecting his government, may feel least sympathy for him in this second phase, when he is presented as lacking humanity.

In the third phase, however, his 'humanity' is all too apparent. From late in Act II, scene ii until the middle of the final scene (V, i), an audience's responses to Angelo are likely to be highly volatile, ranging from compassion to revulsion. When Angelo is unable to control his desire for Isabella and veers towards rapacious tyranny, an audience may become more interested in him and, paradoxically, more sympathetic towards him—interested because he has slipped from perfection into recognisable human frailty, and sympathetic because Shakespeare reveals in soliloquy the tormented inner self beneath Angelo's dogmatic but devious exterior. Sympathy, however, all too frequently transforms into horror and revulsion, particularly when Angelo threatens to torture Claudio to death if Isabella should refuse to gratify his sexual demands, and also when, towards the end of the play, Angelo seems prepared for his accusers to suffer dire punishment for testifying truthfully against him.

The final Angelo is only lightly sketched in Shakespeare's text at the conclusion of the last scene, although the audience can feel little doubt that a man presented as particularly jealous of his reputation would find his ultimate punishment of exposure and humiliation a formidable torment. Once it is clear to Angelo that his crimes are known to the Duke, Angelo confesses, forgoes his right to a trial, and begs for immediate execution to escape his shame. Instead, the arguably more severe punishment of enduring public disgrace is imposed on him: Angelo will become what Shakespeare describes elsewhere as 'The fixed figure for the time of scorn / To point his slow unmoving finger at' (*Othello*, IV, ii, 55–6). Just as, in the first scene of the play, he acquiesced in silence to the Duke's command to take his commission, so Angelo now tacitly accepts his fate of being stripped in public, Dreyfus-like, of his rank and reputation. Similarly, he silently obeys the Duke's injunction that he should marry Mariana. As Angelo is ultimately a chastened sinner, fortunate to have been thwarted in his attempts to commit the worst of his intended crimes, an audience can understand the justification for repealing the capital sentence that his misdeeds would otherwise have warranted. As Angelo has been granted a wife as virtuous, faithful, and forgiving as Mariana, an audience may even regard him as redeemable.

The Puritan

In Catholic Vienna, the putative setting of *Measure for Measure*, it would be implausible to encounter a Puritan, a strict Protestant; but it might be possible to encounter a person with a puritanical disposition. Angelo is revealed in the course of *Measure for Measure* to be excessively pious but fundamentally hypocritical, qualities that were associated in the minds of Shakespeare's contemporaries with the Puritans. For example, Elizabeth I's Archbishop of Canterbury, John Whitgift, decried the posturing of Puritans, censuring them as sanctimonious and supercilious:

> The name Puritan is very aptly given to these men; not because they be pure . . . but because they think themselves to be *mundiores ceteris*, "more pure than others" . . . . they persuade themselves not only of such an outward perfection, but of such an inward purity also. . . .[1]

---

[1] *Defense of the Aunswere to the Admonition, Against the Replie of T.C.* (London: 1574), pp. 73–74.

Shakespeare's portrayal of Angelo exactly corresponds with this definition of the Puritan published fully thirty years before the first recorded performance of *Measure for Measure*—which was staged for a new king whose antipathy towards puritanism matched that of Archbishop Whitgift.[2] The very name of Vincentio's Deputy, Angelo, may suggest that he aspires to the superhuman, spiritual status of an angel. In the early scenes, Angelo is consistently presented as believing himself to be morally superior to the rest of humanity, proof against the vanities and temptations to which others succumb—yet succumb he quickly does.

The words 'Puritan' and 'puritanical' are never used to describe Angelo during the play.[3] Behaviour that might be described as puritanical is, nevertheless, closely associated with Angelo in the first Act of *Measure for Measure*: Claudio (I, ii, 111–60), Lucio (I, iv, 55–68), and the Duke (I, iii, 11–54) describe the stringently ascetic regime that Angelo requires of himself and others. In his exchanges with Friar Thomas, the Duke refers to his newly-appointed Deputy as 'precise', numbering him among the 'seemers' of Vienna (I, iii, 50 and 54). 'Precise' behaviour—that is, extreme punctiliousness in religious observance and morality—was closely associated with Puritans, who accordingly were sometimes called 'Precisians' from the mid-Sixteenth Century. The word 'precise' is (possibly) echoed later by both Isabella and Claudio when speaking of Angelo (III, i, 93 and 96).[4] In addition, 'seemers'—

---

[2] Braunmuller and Watson (p. 112) note that James I expressed his distaste for Puritans in *Basilicon Doron*, 27, where James advises his son to 'hate no man more then a proude Puritane.'

[3] Similarly, in *Antony and Cleopatra*, which followed about two years after *Measure for Measure*, Shakespeare portrayed a strongly puritanical streak in the mean-spirited Octavius Caesar, but avoided the word 'Puritan', which would have been as anachronistic in the context of ancient Rome as it is inappropriate in the context of renaissance Vienna.

[4] The Folio puzzlingly reads 'prenzie' in both these latter contexts, causing scholars (e.g. Tieck, Knight, and Lever) to speculate that the

the word came into use towards the end of the Sixteenth Century—are people guilty of pretence, that is, hypocrites. In Isabella's presence, the Duke echoes his earlier condemnation of his deputy when he refers to 'this well-*seeming* Angelo' (III, i, 223; italics added). Isabella, however, has already identified Angelo as a 'seemer': she accuses him of 'seeming' when he reveals his lustful intentions towards her (II, iv, 149). When Isabella subsequently refers to Angelo as 'This outward-sainted deputy' (III, i, 88), her words hint at the claims of Elizabethan and Jacobean Puritans to be 'visible saints' within a 'brotherhood of saints'.[5] This insistence on Angelo's puritanical character should therefore affect the way in which he is initially presented to the audience: for example, a customary suit of solemn black, in conjunction with a pious, fastidious manner, might contrast him strikingly with a flamboyant Viennese court in the opening scene.

Puritans were targets of contempt and derision in Elizabethan and Jacobean drama, predominantly because they were self-professed enemies of the stage, seeking the closure of the playhouses where, they believed, moral as well as physical diseases proliferated. Under three years before the date of the first recorded performance of *Measure for Measure*, Shakespeare had delighted his late-Elizabethan audience with the humiliation of the puritanical Malvolio in *Twelfth Night*. Like Malvolio, Angelo uses his authority to suppress the pleasures of others, pleasures that he condemns with strong moral distaste. Later in his lifetime, Shakespeare's friend, Ben Jonson, would present further hypocritical, mean-spirited Puritans on the stage: Tribulation Wholesome and Ananias in *The Alchemist* (1610), and Zeal-of-the-land Busy in

---

word in the Folio is a misreading for 'precise'. Plausible alternatives would be 'princely' (as authorised by the Second Folio) or 'priestly' (suggested in his edition by Hanmer in the Eighteenth Century). A rather more likely alternative is that 'prenzie' is Shakespeare's attempt to reproduce an old Italian word, *prenze* (i.e. 'a prince'), as used by Boccaccio.

[5] Braunmuller and Watson, p. 82.

Bartholomew Fair (1614). As is the case with all these other stage-Puritans, Angelo's hubris will lead to his nemesis. A paradigm of tragedy is thus introduced into plays that are all essentially comedies: the Puritan's pride will lead to a 'tragic' downfall, paradoxically to secure the happy ending required of the comic genre.

Take Thy Commission

In the first scene, however, Angelo is consistently presented to the audience as abounding in laudable qualities: modesty, obedience, wisdom, consideration for others, and skill in government. Unlike Macbeth, whose 'vaulting ambition' is revealed early in his portrayal and will prove his nemesis, Angelo shows no early signs of a craving for power—rather, the opposite: Angelo reluctantly has greatness thrust upon him by the Duke's sudden departure from Vienna.

Angelo's experience and ability in affairs of state are beyond question. Duke Vincentio, having praised Escalus's knowledge of 'The nature of our people, / Our city's institutions, and the terms / For common justice' (I, i, 9–11), nevertheless appoints Angelo as Escalus's superior, thereby suggesting Angelo's greater suitability for the senior post of Deputy during the Duke's absence. Clearly, then, Angelo's capabilities in government and law have already been approved. The Duke, in a speech reminiscent of the parable of the talents, lectures Angelo on the need to put such God-given virtues and abilities to best use (I, i, 26–40). The obvious sense of the Duke's words—certainly the one that the audience will immediately recognise—is that Angelo's abundance of merits should be deployed for the public good on his appointment to replace the absent Duke.

The opening lines of the Duke's speech are, however, ambiguous. With the benefit of hindsight, an attentive audience may identify the first clue that Angelo's earlier life has been less than perfect:

There is a kind of character in thy life
That to th'observer doth thy history
Fully unfold. [I, i, 27–9]

We shall later learn of the Duke's knowledge of Angelo's ignoble treatment of Mariana, Angelo's former betrothed. It is therefore possible, on reflection, to interpret the Duke's words here as equivocation: Angelo's 'history' is 'fully unfold[ed]' by the 'character' recording his materialistic rejection of Mariana and his cowardly attempt to justify his action by blackening her reputation. Evidence of this blemish on Angelo's history is not, however, apparent in this opening scene, and only those in an audience conversant with the second half of the play might immediately identify this ambiguity.

On his first entry, Angelo appears obedient, modest, and unambitious.[6] His first words in the play are a testimony to his dutiful nature, although some may detect a hint of sycophancy:

Always obedient to your grace's will,
I come to know your pleasure. [I, i, 25–6]

Although Macbeth is similarly dutiful before King Duncan, Shakespeare is careful to provide, in asides and soliloquies, plentiful indications of Macbeth's secret desire for kingship. No such evidence of ambition is encountered in the early presentation of Angelo in *Measure for Measure*. A possible interpretation would be that, unlike Macbeth, Angelo is betrayed less by a predisposition to evil and more by the corruptive influence of the absolute power that he reluctantly

---

[6] In Gregory Doran's 2019 production for the RSC, Sandy Grierson's Angelo appeared like an anxious and dutiful schoolboy summoned before the headmaster: his back was rigid, his shoulders were tensed, and he was tightly confined in a drab, shapeless suit. The clear implication was that this was a repressed character: like his jacket, he was severely buttoned-up. He did not unbutton (literally) until II, ii, 173, when he looked in the reflective panels at the back of the stage and recognised his sexual desire for Isabella with the line, 'What dost thou, or what art thou, Angelo?'

161

undertakes. Such an interpretation, however, might be challenged by reference to the revelations, later in the play, of Angelo's dishonest treatment of Mariana.

When he is offered the opportunity to rule Vienna in Duke Vincentio's absence, Angelo appears loath to accept the responsibility. Initially, the Duke presents the commission to Angelo as the opportunity for him to fulfil his potential—

> Hold, therefore, Angelo.
> In our remove, be thou at full ourself.
> Mortality and mercy in Vienna
> Live in thy tongue, and heart [I, i, 41–4]—

but Angelo remains silent, apparently making no move to accept the proffered document. The Duke must therefore offer the commission for a second time ('Take thy commission': line 47). Angelo's reply suggests not eagerness but rather reluctance to wield such formidable authority:

> Now, good my lord,
> Let there be some more test made of my metal,
> Before so noble and so great a figure
> Be stamp'd upon it. [I, i, 47–50]

His words, expressing his sense of unworthiness, are shot through with proleptic irony: two scenes later, it will emerge that the test of his worthiness that Angelo so earnestly requests here is in fact being conducted by the Duke through this very process of appointing Angelo as his deputy. The image that Angelo employs here, developing the Duke's subtle image of coining and currency-exchange (at I, i, 35–40), is also significant as a prime responsibility of a ruler was to safeguard the coinage that bore the imprint of his head. Angelo appears uncertain that he is of the necessary metal/mettle to carry the stamp of ruler. Future events will prove such self-doubts to be well-founded: Angelo will be weighed in the balance of the monetary/judicial scales and found to be false coin.

Even when he ultimately yields to the Duke's repeated requests, Angelo shows no eager appetite for political power, but rather assiduous concern for the Duke's welfare. It requires a third imperative from Vincentio ('therefore take your honours': line 52) before Angelo will accept the commission in tacit acquiescence. Angelo's primary concern, however, is the Duke's security rather than his own promotion:

> Yet give me leave, my lord,
> That we may bring you something on the way.
>
> [I, i, 60–1]

> The heavens give safety to your purposes! [I, i, 73]

It is only after the Duke's departure, and at the instigation of Escalus, that Angelo turns to the commission that he has been given:

> Let us withdraw together,
> And we may soon our satisfaction have
> Touching that point. [I, i, 81–3]

Angelo shows no immediate signs of relishing his new-found power or of seeking to establish Escalus's subordination under him: rather, Angelo speaks here of 'us', 'together', 'we', and 'our', suggesting that he regards his new position of regent as an opportunity for co-operation with his fellow-courtier in government, rather than as the occasion to exercise sole authority.

The general impression conveyed to an audience in this first scene was summarised in the Duke's speech at lines 29–39: that Angelo is one of those 'Spirits . . . finely touch'd', full of 'excellence' and 'virtues' that 'Heaven' will deploy to 'fine issues'. These opinions, however, will be undermined before Angelo next appears at the beginning of Act II, and totally negated by the end of that same Act. As Shakespeare observes in Sonnet 94,

. . . sweetest things turn sourest by their deeds;
Lilies that fester smell far worse than weeds.

[Lines 13–14]

The Fault and Glimpse of Newness

Although Angelo is absent in person from the rest of Act I, significant reference is made to him in the interim by the Provost, Claudio, the Duke, and Lucio. Initially, his conduct as Deputy is implicit in references to the arrest and sentencing of Claudio under the statutes condemning fornication, and to the related injunction to demolish the brothels in the suburbs of Vienna (I, ii, 56ff.). From the outset, it seems that Angelo's government is to be associated with the regulation of sexual conduct in Vienna. This is confirmed when Claudio asks why he is suffering public humiliation by being paraded through the streets. The Provost replies,

I do it not in evil disposition,
But from Lord Angelo by special charge. [I, ii, 109–10]

Clearly, Claudio is to be made an example by Angelo, to dissuade others from illicit sexual indulgence. It is significant, however, that the Provost associates the public humiliation of Claudio with 'evil disposition'—potentially the first adverse judgement of Angelo's conduct in the play.

Claudio himself, the first victim of Angelo's new regime, is ambivalent in his response to the Deputy. His reference to 'the demi-god, Authority' applying '[t]he words of heaven' (I, ii, 112–14) seems philosophically detached, but could be spoken sarcastically. Similarly, his exclamation about Angelo's application of the statute of fornication—'yet still 'tis just' (I, ii, 115)—seems to be a stoical acknowledgement of the rectitude of his sentence under Viennese law, but might be uttered as an incredulous question or as an ironic commendation, to imply that a gross injustice has been done. A subsequent speech from Claudio is more unambiguously pejorative in portraying Angelo

164

as a man unduly swayed by power and by concern for his reputation:

> And the new deputy now for the Duke—
> Whether it be the fault and glimpse of newness,
> Or whether that the body public be
> A horse whereon the governor doth ride,
> Who, newly in the seat, that it may know
> He can command, lets it straight feel the spur;
> Whether the tyranny be in his place,
> Or in his eminence that fills it up,
> I stagger in—but this new governor
> Awakes me all the enrolled penalties
> Which have, like unscour'd armour, hung by th'wall
> So long, that nineteen zodiacs have gone round,
> And none of them been worn; and for a name
> Now puts the drowsy and neglected act
> Freshly on me: 'tis surely for a name. [I, ii, 146–60]

Here, Angelo is the dominant figure in an equestrian tableau, newly-clad in the previously 'unscour'd armour' of neglected statutes, and proudly astride a 'horse' representative of the 'body public', to which he applies the 'spur' to compel obedience. Claudio's sense of injustice is clearly conveyed by his references to 'fault', 'tyranny', and 'for a name' (repeated): Angelo, corrupted by power, is indulging in what might be termed judicial posturing to establish, as soon as possible after his appointment, a reputation for rigorous authority amongst the people of Vienna.

Similarly, when the Duke characterises Angelo to Friar Thomas in the next scene, his remarks initially seem to compliment his Deputy; but ultimately they express profound misgivings about Angelo's character. Vincentio admits that, as he has neglected the 'strict statutes and most biting laws' of Vienna during his rule (I, iii, 18–20), he has 'impos'd' on Angelo the task of rectifying social order (I, iii, 40), because Angelo is

A man of stricture and firm abstinence. [I, iii, 12]

So far, so good: Angelo is presented as a man of abstemious character, well fitted to undertake the task of remedying Vienna's social ills. It was a mediaeval and renaissance commonplace (deriving ultimately from classical Greek philosophy) that the man appointed to govern others must first have learned to govern his own disorderly desires. Angelo apparently conforms to this prerequisite. The Duke's tone changes radically, however, at the end of the scene:

> Lord Angelo is precise;
> Stands at a guard with Envy; scarce confesses
> That his blood flows; or that his appetite
> Is more to bread than stone. Hence shall we see
> If power change purpose, what our seemers be.
>
> [I, iii, 50–4]

Here, Angelo's abstemiousness is presented as perverse, as if he would deny his human functions, specifically the movement of the blood and the need for sustenance. The references to 'bread' and 'stone' inevitably recall Christ's temptation in the wilderness (Matthew 4: 3–4), hinting that Angelo may be guilty of hubris in seeking to imitate Christ's resistance against the Devil. 'Blood' includes the specific renaissance meaning of 'sexual desire', Vincentio's words suggesting that Angelo is reluctant to admit that, as a man, he is susceptible to carnal craving. Furthermore, Angelo's manner appears defensive ('Stands at a guard with Envy'), implying that he is insecure and reacts with unnecessary hostility when his authority is challenged (as will be confirmed when the Provost tactfully questions the severity of Claudio's sentence at II, ii, 6–14). Worse, Angelo is said to be 'precise' and a 'seemer', words that portray him as a puritanical hypocrite. The Duke is therefore confirming what Claudio implied in his critical speech about Angelo: that the new Deputy's apparent severity towards Claudio and others is pretentious rather than scrupulous. Additionally, the final sentence of Vincentio's speech indicates that the Duke, from the outset, expects Angelo to be corrupted

166

by power. Angelo has been set up to fail, and will be tested to destruction.

The other character in Act I who expresses opinions about Angelo is Lucio, whose comments about the Deputy are disapproving but not necessarily condemnatory. When addressing Isabella in the nunnery, he describes Angelo as

> . . . a man whose blood
> Is very snow-broth; one who never feels
> The wanton stings and motions of the sense;
> But doth rebate and blunt his natural edge
> With profits of the mind, study and fast. [I, iv, 57–61]

Lucio's words may suggest antipathy towards Angelo, but antipathy based on personal preferences rather than on objective moral judgements. For the sensual Lucio, the cold-blooded Angelo is clearly alien but, other than the accusation that the Deputy lacks human warmth, Lucio's words seem to grant Angelo some grudging respect for his self-control and virtuous pursuits.

There is, then, a considerable discrepancy between the Angelo witnessed by the audience in Act I scene i, and the Angelo about whom we hear in Act I scenes ii–iv. The initial impression was of an able and respectful courtier free from the potentially corruptive influence of ambition. Later reports, however, have placed great emphasis on his ostentatious self-denial and undue harshness in administering the law, particularly legislation concerning human sexual activity. These less attractive qualities might have been assumed to have resulted from the corruptive influence of the exercise of his new powers, were it not for the Duke's testimony to Friar Peter in I, iii: the Duke's foreknowledge of these characteristics in Angelo suggests that his Deputy was ever thus.

The Voice of the Recorded Law

The reports that we have heard from the Provost, Claudio, the Duke, and Lucio prepare the audience for the Angelo whom we meet in the opening exchanges of the Second Act. Angelo's language has been transformed since his last appearance in the first scene of Act I; hesitancy, brevity, and humility have been replaced by decisiveness, expansiveness, and assertiveness. Now, he speaks with the voice of impersonal authority, deploying aphorisms and proverbial wisdom to insist that the letter of the law must be enforced without compromise:

> We must not make a scarecrow of the law,
> Setting it up to fear the birds of prey,
> And let it keep one shape till custom make it
> Their perch, and not their terror. [II, i, 1–4]

Angelo's metaphor vividly confirms an incontrovertible truth: if the law threatens but does not enforce, those who would prey on society will in time flout rather than fear the statutes.

Angelo shows no sense of his own moral vulnerability before his encounter with Isabella: rather, he appears hubristic. When Escalus questions whether Angelo might have succumbed to temptation had he found himself in Claudio's situation, Angelo's response, conspicuous for its proleptic irony, is supercilious:

> 'Tis one thing to be tempted, Escalus,
> Another thing to fall. I not deny
> The jury passing on the prisoner's life
> May in the sworn twelve have a thief, or two,
> Guiltier than him they try. What's open made to justice,
> That justice seizes. What knows the laws
> That thieves do pass on thieves? 'Tis very pregnant,
> The jewel that we find, we stoop and take 't,
> Because we see it; but what we do not see,
> We tread upon, and never think of it. [II, i, 17–26]

Here, Angelo makes no reference, direct or indirect, to the man whom he has condemned to death. The words are sententious, steeped in judicial theory, but refusing to address the extenuating circumstances in Claudio's case that Escalus has sought to draw to the Deputy's attention.

When he ultimately refers to Claudio, Angelo avoids naming the condemned man, just as he will later refuse to name Julietta when considering her circumstances (II, ii, 15–25). Implicitly, Angelo needs to maintain a disdainful distance from those whom he condemns:

> You may not so extenuate his offence
> For I have had such faults; but rather tell me,
> When I that censure him do so offend,
> Let mine own judgement pattern out my death,
> And nothing come in partial. Sir, he must die.
> [II, i, 27–31]

This is the impersonal voice of the law, a pronouncement ex cathedra, rather than an exchange between friends and colleagues such as we saw in the brief conversation between Escalus and Angelo at the end of Act I scene i. The implication is that Angelo has become more aloof and less compassionate—less considerate of others. There is also a convincing psychological dimension to Angelo's words: he is so smugly confident of his inviolable chastity that he is incapable of imagining circumstances in which he might be 'tempted' and 'fall' (lines 17–18). Accordingly, as he has prepared no means of defence, he will capitulate speedily and entirely when temptation does arise, in the form of Isabella. More obviously, when Angelo offends, he will stand condemned by his own words here.[7]

---

[7] Angelo himself acknowledges this interpretation with his last words in the play: '. . . I crave death more willingly than mercy; / *'Tis my deserving*, and I do entreat it' (V, i, 474–75; italics added).

When Angelo finally names Claudio, it is merely to confirm the schedule for the prisoner's execution:

> See that Claudio
> Be executed by nine tomorrow morning;
> Bring him his confessor, let him be prepar'd,
> For that's the utmost of his pilgrimage. [II, i, 33–6]

The language remains dispassionate, peremptory, and uncompromising. The modest courtier of the first scene of *Measure for Measure* has been transformed by supreme power into the most authoritarian of judges.

De Minimis Non Curat Praetor

As Shakespeare does not present the trial of Claudio on stage, speculation about how Angelo might have conducted himself as Claudio's judge would be futile. His sentence on Claudio—public humiliation, imprisonment, and execution—is, however, made clear during Act I, and the sentence of death repeated here at the beginning of Act II. Claudio is to lose his head because Vienna's statutes concerning fornication—or perhaps Angelo's interpretation of those statutes—do not recognise Claudio's 'true contract' of marriage (I, ii, 126) as legitimate. The issue was topical to Shakespeare's audience: many of his contemporaries regarded marriages *per verba de praesenti*, such as that between Claudio and Julietta, as entirely valid and honourable; but the statutes of the Canons of the Church of England were revised in 1604 to exclude marriages conducted without witnesses or parental consent. Thus, in the very year that *Measure for Measure* was performed before the new King, the legality of spousals similar to that between Claudio and Julietta was under close scrutiny.

Angelo's puritanical ideals may compel him to enforce the statutes against fornication, even in borderline cases such as Claudio's, but his patience and impartiality are tested to breaking-point when Elbow brings Pompey and Froth before the court for trial. Elbow is apparently accusing both of an offence under those same statutes against fornication—or rather, he is *attempting* to accuse both, but the limitations of his language and understanding (together with the artful filibustering of Pompey) obscure the case against the accused. Shakespeare uses the opportunity to contrast the urbane restraint of Escalus with the irritable aggression of Angelo. The latter's attitude is apparent in the short, sharp questions that he directs at Elbow and Pompey:

> How now sir, what's your name? And what's the matter? [II, i, 45–6]

> Benefactors? Well, what benefactors are they? Are they not malefactors? [II, i, 51–2]

Clearly, Angelo lacks Escalus's good humour. Accordingly, when Escalus comments on Elbow's incompetence with light-hearted irony, Angelo snubs the amiable remark with a dismissive 'Go to' and continues his blunt interrogation:

> What quality are they of? Elbow is your name? Why dost thou not speak, Elbow? [II, i, 58–9]

A plausible response to Angelo's question might be that Elbow is silent because he has been intimidated and perhaps humiliated by Angelo's brusque, humourless manner. In these circumstances, Angelo must defer to Escalus, allowing him to continue the questioning.

After a further seventy lines of prevarication, especially from Pompey, Angelo's exasperation breaks forth:

> This will last out a night in Russia
> When nights are longest there. I'll take my leave,
> And leave you to the hearing of the cause;
> Hoping you'll find good cause to whip them all.
> [II, i, 133–6]

Although Angelo is now deputing judgement of the case entirely to Escalus, he is doing so in the most imperious fashion, prejudging the verdict and suggesting the punishment before it has even been established whether an offence has been committed. This looks less like justice and more like dereliction of duty from an arrogant and impatient man who considers it beneath his dignity to sit in judgement on squalid cases involving petty characters.[8] In this manner, he leaves the case to the discretion of the more diplomatic Escalus, his senior in experience but his junior in authority.

The context invites the audience to compare how authority is wielded by Angelo and Escalus respectively. Escalus manages the hearing with commendable tact and restraint, dismissing the suspects with a warning and the incompetent constable with a diplomatic suggestion that he should find a suitable substitute to alleviate his burden of responsibility. The dialogue then refocuses on the conduct of the absent Angelo. A justice, who has been silent since the beginning of the scene, expresses an implicitly negative opinion of the absent Deputy:

Lord Angelo is severe. [II, i, 279]

Escalus, however, can recognise the justification for Angelo's intransigence:

It is but needful.
Mercy is not itself, that oft looks so;
Pardon is still the nurse of second woe. [II, i, 279–81]

Escalus proves as capable as Angelo of constructing gnomic utterances concerning the law. Here, he anticipates Angelo's words to Isabella (at II, ii, 100–5) in recognising that mercy transforms itself into dangerous indulgence if it is offered too frequently, and that excusing an offence once is always likely to encourage that offence to be committed again. In short, Escalus defends Angelo's severity in judgement, declaring that leniency

---

[8] Lever, however, disagrees (p. 33n.).

in the judge prompts laxity in the offender.[9] But, having acknowledged that 'Mercy' and 'Pardon' can be counterproductive, Escalus still shows sympathy for the offender who must suffer as a consequence of their denial:

> But yet, poor Claudio! [II, i, 282]

Here lies a clear distinction between Escalus and Angelo: both understand the importance of enforcing the letter of the law, but Escalus's judgement is tempered by compassion for the individual malefactor. The Duke, however, has chosen to empower the obdurate Angelo rather than the conscientious Escalus as his deputy, and so Angelo's judgement prevails.

Angelo in the Judgement Seat

This lack of human compassion in Angelo is confirmed moments later in performance. The opening of Act II scene ii finds Angelo rejecting a diplomatic appeal from the Provost for Claudio's life, and responding to the predicament of Julietta, Claudio's beloved, in a coldly impersonal manner.

When the Provost enquires whether Angelo has reconsidered his death-sentence on Claudio, Angelo's response is aggressively blunt, showing both his remorselessness toward the prisoner and his lack of appreciation of the Provost's good offices:

> Do you your office, or give up your place,
> And you shall be well spar'd. [II, ii, 13–14]

Angelo humiliates the Provost for daring, however tactfully, to question his decision to condemn Claudio. At the end of the play, however, the Duke will thank and reward the Provost for his conscientious actions to save Claudio (V, i, 527–8). The contrast between these two contexts serves to accentuate Angelo's harshness.

---

[9] Cf. the Duke's similar opinion at I, iii, 23–31.

His treatment of Julietta is as impersonal and ruthless as his treatment of Claudio. Angelo never speaks her name (as if it might sully his tongue), preferring to refer to her as 'the fornicatress' (line 23) when he concedes, grudgingly, that she should be provided with 'needful, but not lavish means' (line 24) during her labour. Clearly, he makes no distinction between the criminal ('fornicatress') and the crime, which will set him at odds with Isabella on her entry, who is eager for Angelo to regard Claudio as a human being to be redeemed from his offence:

> I have a brother is condemn'd to die;
> I do beseech you, let it be his fault,
> And not my brother. [II, ii, 34–6]

Angelo's response to Isabella's plea is coldly logical:

> Condemn the fault, and not the actor of it?
> Why, every fault's condemn'd ere it be done:
> Mine were the very cipher of a function
> To fine the faults, whose fine stands in record,
> And let go by the actor. [II, ii, 37–41]

In contrast to Angelo's earlier sharpness to the Provost, when he apparently felt his authority challenged, the language here is calm and fluent: the iambic pentameters are generally regular and end-stopped, allowing a measured and untroubled delivery. By this means, Shakespeare suggests that Angelo senses no threat to his authority from this young woman. His words are rational and incontrovertible: the law condemns faults before they are committed, and the judge condemns offenders after they are committed. There would be no need for judges or courts of law if the simple act of defining crimes in a statute-book were sufficient to eradicate those crimes from society. As before, when discussing the case of Claudio with Escalus, Angelo reverts to maxims and gnomic statements about the law, general principles that might help a judge to avoid consideration of the particular human circumstances of the case.

Angelo's complacency, however, will be challenged. With prompting from Lucio, Isabella continues to press the case for her brother's pardon and, as she comes to dominate the exchanges, Angelo's responses become more fragmentary:

I will not do't. [II, ii, 51]

Look what I will not, that I cannot do. [II, ii, 52]

He's sentenc'd, 'tis too late. [II, ii, 55]

Pray you be gone. [II, ii, 66]

Your brother is a forfeit of the law,
And you but waste your words. [II, ii, 71–72]

With Isabella's persistent challenges to his sentence on her brother, Angelo's growing impatience perhaps turns to anger as he rudely dismisses her at line 66, and then to exasperation as she refuses to be silent.

It is worth pausing at this point to ask whether Shakespeare gives any indication in Angelo's language as to when his attitude to Isabella begins to change. By the end of the scene, he will be expressing intense sexual desire for her. When should an actor suggest that the character whom he is portraying first experiences the stirrings of such passion?[10] Presumably, not at line 66,[11] when his impatience with her is comparable to his earlier offhand dismissal of the case involving Elbow's wife, Pompey, and Froth. Nor at lines 71–2, where his predominantly

---

[10] In the RSC's 2019 production, the critical moment was as late as Isabella's instruction, 'Go to your bosom,' (II, iv, 137) when Lucy Phelps's Isabella approached Sandy Grierson's Angelo to place her hand over his heart.

[11] Unless Angelo's words 'Pray you be gone are' an attempt to distance himself from temptation.

monosyllabic bluntness must surely be accompanied by a harshness of tone.

The phrasing of his next speech, however, is more conciliatory, and significantly contains the vocative '*fair* maid' (line 79; italics added), the flattering adjective hinting that he has now become aware of Isabella's physical attraction. This could suggest that the actor playing Angelo might, for the first time, have looked fixedly at Isabella during the immediately preceding speech in which she referred to the divine judgement that awaits all humanity, inviting Angelo to consider his own sins in that context (lines 72–9). Angelo has found himself confronted by a woman who appears his equal in piety and percipience, and who has the assurance, the intelligence, and the command of language to challenge his debating-skills. An audience may suspect that he sees, reflected in her, the very qualities that he might admire most in himself. Moreover, she is dressed in holy garb, suggestive of her purity, but is speaking of universal human sinfulness, suggestive of her potential corruptibility. Is this the point at which the fall of Angelo commences?

What is indisputable is that, unlike Escalus and the Provost before her, Isabella has vigorously persisted with her plea for Claudio's pardon, forcing Angelo to a fuller justification of his position by referring to the higher judgement of God. Angelo becomes more defensive, and begins to consider the human cost of enforcing the law:

> Be you content, fair maid;
> It is the law, not I, condemn your brother;
> Were he my kinsman, brother, or my son,
> It should be thus with him. He must die tomorrow.
>
> [II, ii, 79–82]

There is certainly a change here in Angelo's speech in both content and form. His language had previously focused predominantly on the impersonal law, whereas now the focus is entirely human: on the 'fair maid' before him, on her 'brother' the condemned man, and on the penalty to be faced by his own (entirely hypothetical) 'kinsman, brother, or my son'. The measured fluency of his earlier pronouncements on the law is here replaced by irregularities in caesurae and (at line 82) in metre. In this way, the form of Shakespeare's language suggests that Angelo is already faltering, as if stirred by the close physical proximity of Isabella.

It would seem, though, that he recovers his moral strength and inflexibility, for Isabella's ensuing plea for Claudio's execution to be postponed leads to two of Angelo's most confident speeches (lines 91–100 and 101–6), in which he returns to the task of defending the law in sententious remarks, while justifying punishment of offenders as the means of eradicating abuse to protect society. To justify his apparent recovery of dispassionate authority, the actor playing Angelo might turn away, or deliberately establish a greater physical distance between himself and the temptation embodied in Isabella.

Far from discouraging Isabella, Angelo's remoteness goads her into scrutinising his role as judge and accusing him of hubris: he is a typical 'pelting petty officer', an example of 'man, proud man / Dress'd in a little brief authority' usurping divine power. Except for one brief, confused question, Angelo is silent for over 35 lines during this tirade, although the actor playing Angelo must indicate by expression and gesture his fascination with Isabella's words, to justify Lucio's comment at line 126: 'He's coming: I perceiv't.' It should nevertheless be astonishing to an audience when Angelo admits, in an aside,

> She speaks, and 'tis such sense
> That my sense breeds with it. [II, ii, 142–3]

Here, Angelo is doing more than acknowledging the power of Isabella's argument, her 'sense': he is admitting, in the suggestive clause 'my sense breeds with it', that she has aroused his sensual desire.[12]

A Natural Guiltiness

How could it be that the ascetic Angelo should so suddenly become aware of the power of sexual craving in circumstances such as these? A reconsideration of the earlier parts of the scene will establish that Shakespeare has prepared the ground carefully, creating in Isabella a female replica of Angelo. Like Narcissus, Angelo has been confronted by a reflection of himself with which he has fallen in love—or rather, in lust. Isabella has condemned illicit sexual activity as the 'vice that most I do abhor / And most desire should meet the blow of justice' (II, ii, 29-30), words which entirely endorse Angelo's puritanical enforcement of the statutes against fornication. When addressing Angelo, Isabella has twice been accused by Lucio of being 'too cold' (II, ii, 45 and 56), precisely the accusation that Lucio levelled at Angelo when he represented him to Isabella as 'a man whose blood / Is very snow-broth' (I, iv, 57–8). Like Angelo, Isabella delights in sustained intellectual debate and, unlike Escalus and the Provost, refuses to defer to Angelo's superior authority. She shows the same steely resolution as Angelo, and the same conviction that her own judgement is unimpeachable.

Most importantly, Isabella has encouraged Angelo to search out his own sexual desires in the speech immediately preceding Angelo's guilty aside, where he first acknowledges his rising passion. In attempting to save Claudio, she seeks to make Angelo empathise with her brother, but inadvertently directs Angelo's sexual attention to herself:

---

[12] William Empson's *The Structure of Complex Words* (London: Chatto and Windus, 1951) includes an extensive discussion of the shifting meanings of 'sense' as deployed in *Measure for Measure*. Empson's analysis is reprinted as 'Sense in *Measure for Measure*' in *Shakespeare*: Measure for Measure: *A Casebook*, ed. C. K. Stead (London: Macmillan, 1971), pp. 187–212.

> Go to your bosom,
> Knock there, and ask your heart what it doth know
> That's like my brother's fault. If it confess
> A natural guiltiness, such as is his,
> Let it not sound a thought upon your tongue
> Against my brother's life. [II, ii, 137–42]

Isabella, in characterising forbidden sexual desire as 'a natural guiltiness', has encouraged Angelo to recognise that he himself (and, perhaps, even she) must have such darker passions. In standing before him as a novice nun, she has presented herself to him a possible object for illicit erotic desires.

In this context, it is tempting to speculate whether Lucio's words that encourage Isabella to persist in petitioning Angelo might have been scripted by Shakespeare as a subliminal incitement to sexual desire in the Deputy. Lucio's exclamations such as 'Give it not o'er so.—To him again' (II, ii, 43), 'You are too cold' (lines 45 and 56), 'Ay, touch him: there's the vein' (line 70), 'O, to him, to him, wench! . . . He's coming' (lines 125–6), and 'Art avis'd o' that? More on't' (line 133) echo the steamy language of the brothels that Lucio frequents. Although Angelo thinks himself proof against 'the strumpet / With all her double vigour, art and nature' (II, ii, 183–4), Lucio's language might represent Isabella to him as a sexual neophyte receiving instruction in how to stimulate the response of the client whom she is attending.

In a memorably theatrical moment, Shakespeare now increases the dramatic tension by tempting Angelo through the innocent words of Isabella:

> Hark, how I'll bribe you. . . . [II, ii, 146]

Angelo's response is well-nigh inarticulate:

> How! Bribe me? [II, ii, 147]

179

Of course, these words from Angelo could be delivered in a tone of moral outrage suitable for a respectable judge, jealous of his reputation and horrified by an attempt to corrupt him; but, as Angelo has already shown evidence that he is succumbing to sexual temptation and that his desire is focused on Isabella, the words might plausibly be uttered as a breathless, excited gasp, suggesting that Angelo desires Isabella to proposition him sexually. Once Isabella makes it clear that her 'bribe' will be no more than her prayers and those of her sisterhood, Angelo dismisses her abruptly from his presence:

Well: come to me tomorrow. [II, ii, 156]

His tone may be disappointed, but his words ensure not only Isabella's return but also a respite for himself. He needs the opportunity for self-examination as well as for planning his assault on Isabella's virtue.

The First Soliloquy

Angelo's sexual desire for Isabella is now incontrovertible—both to the audience and to himself. As Isabella departs, Angelo admits in an aside that he is on the 'way . . . to temptation' (II, ii, 159) and that his 'honour', the title by which she addresses him, is in jeopardy from her 'virtue' (line 162). Her intellectual perspicuity and moral absolutism, qualities that he so values in himself, are an irresistible allure for him.

There follows the first and greatest of Angelo's three soliloquies, a remarkable and psychologically convincing achievement in which his forensic methods are turned upon himself. For much of Act II, the audience has witnessed Angelo speaking in measured, fluent statements, particularly when expounding the law. By Isabella's departure, however, his speech has become broken: strong, irregular caesurae intrude frequently, the rhythm is erratic, and confident statements are transformed into hesitant questions. The law is forgotten as Angelo follows Isabella's instructions: 'Go to your bosom, /

Knock there' (II, ii, 137–38). What confronts him there initially baffles him:

> What's this? What's this? Is this her fault, or mine?
> The tempter, or the tempted, who sins most, ha?
>
> [II, ii, 163–4]

Angelo recognises that his desire for Isabella is sinful but, at first, he is confused because he needs to apportion blame for this sexual aberration, having previously thought himself incapable of harbouring lust within himself. After all, he has been 'A man of stricture and firm abstinence' who 'scarce confesses / That his blood flows; or that his appetite / Is more to bread than stone' (the Duke: I, iii, 12 and 51–3). He has used study and fasting to 'rebate and blunt . . . The wanton stings and motions of the sense' (Lucio: I, iv, 59–60). His incredulity is emphasised by the extra syllable in line 164, the incoherent exclamation 'ha?' suggesting the difficulty that he faces in acknowledging the truth of his condition.[13]

With amazement, and furthermore with a degree of honesty that an audience might respect, he is obliged to confess that the fault must lie with him alone:

> Not she; nor doth she tempt; but it is I
> That, lying by the violet in the sun,
> Do as the carrion does, not as the flower,
> Corrupt with virtuous season. [II, ii, 165–8]

---

[13] Braunmuller and Watson (p. 84) observe that Paul Rhys, playing Angelo in the 2004 National Theatre / Complicité production, addressed 'What's this? What's this?' to his erection, promptly wounding his arm with a razor in an attempt either to atone for his sin or to subdue the flesh. This stage-business is confirmed by Michael Billington, '*Measure for Measure*: National, London', *The Guardian*, 28 May 2004, https://www.theguardian.com/stage/2004/may/28/theatre1.

In fully exonerating Isabella, he recognises his own unqualified guilt in an image of startling intensity. The general significance of three central elements of the image—flower, carrion, and sun—is readily understood. The sun is rich in divine associations, disseminating light, warmth, and life. The violet is beautiful and fragrant, flourishing under the sun's benevolent influence. By contrast, the carrion is rotting meat that becomes fouler in the sun's heat. The complexity of the language, however, demands deeper analysis. In the image, the flower ('violet') and the dead flesh ('carrion') lie side by side. This juxtaposition recalls the interview that has just passed between Isabella (the violet) and Angelo (the carrion), while simultaneously looking forward to the sexual consummation that Angelo desires, when he will lie by Isabella. The sun is at one and the same time the eye of God, looking down on foul desires and sinful acts, and the divine love towards which Isabella, as a nun, aspires. It might even imply concurrently the heat of Angelo's lust or the enlightenment that Angelo achieves from his self-scrutiny. The verb 'corrupt' is simultaneously transitive and intransitive: Angelo, the rotting flesh, is becoming more corrupt in himself, but he is also guilty of corrupting what is close to him: the violet, Isabella. The implicit stench of rotting flesh contrasts sharply with the implicit perfume of the flower.[14] She has responded appropriately to the 'virtuous season', the heat and light of the summer sun, with growth and fragrance; he, perversely, has reacted by stinking, rotting, and contaminating. The 'virtuous season' of summer may prompt natural things to flourish, but virtue fails to 'season' (that is, to preserve, as with spices) corrupt flesh against its own degeneration. Angelo's self-disgust, and his antithetical admiration for Isabella, are strongly apparent in this complex but powerfully-compressed image.

Angelo's conception of Isabella's purity and delicacy, evident in the violet metaphor, leads him to contemplate one of the glaring paradoxes of his predicament: that a demure,

---

[14] Elsewhere, Shakespeare associates the violet with sweet fragrance, e.g. in Duke Orsino's opening speech in *Twelfth Night*, I, i, 6–7.

virtuous woman rather than a scheming temptress has provoked his illicit desire. Again, he expresses himself in questions, seemingly incredulous that such a situation could arise:

> Can it be
> That modesty may more betray our sense
> Than woman's lightness? Having waste ground enough,
> Shall we desire to raze the sanctuary
> And pitch our evils there? O fie, fie, fie! [II, ii 168–72]

Perhaps the reference to 'lightness' (wantonness) subliminally recalls the effect of the light of the sun on carrion, producing corruption. Certainly, the image of the sanctuary (temple) razed (obliterated) to build an edifice of evil (perhaps a brothel or, more probably, a privy) reminds us that Isabella, as a novice nun, has dedicated herself to Christ: to defile her would be not merely sinful but also blasphemous desecration. If, throughout her interview with Angelo, the actress playing Isabella has worn her nun's habit, that impression on the audience should be reinforced.[15] The metaphor of pitching 'evils' on the site previously occupied by the sanctuary might also have recalled to Shakespeare's audience (probably more familiar with the Bible than its modern equivalent) Solomon's construction of heathen temples on the sacred Mount of Olives to satisfy his concubines (2 Kings 23: 13), an abomination to the faithful. Like Solomon, Angelo, the wise judge, is being compelled by sexual desire to commit a mortal sin in defiance of his faith.

Of equal significance is the use of plural first-person pronouns in these lines. Angelo speaks of '*our* sense' being betrayed and asks, 'Shall *we* desire . . . to pitch *our* evils there?' (italics added). Here, he is surely *not* using the majestic plural (that is, the 'royal *we*') to refer to himself alone; rather, the

---

[15] Thus, Kate Nelligan was clad in pure white throughout the BBC's 1979 production, Juliet Aubrey was closely shorn and wore sack-cloth throughout the corresponding encounter in the BBC's 1994 production, while Mariah Gale wore a simple Franciscan garb with a rope around the waist throughout the 2015 production at the Globe.

lines suggest his recognition of what he previously refused to acknowledge: that he is a man amongst men, subject to human desires and temptations. The fervent exclamation with which the image concludes—'O fie, fie, fie!'—expresses the shame that he feels in recognising that he is morally no better than those whom he has condemned for indulging their sexual desires.

At the heart of the soliloquy, Angelo addresses himself as if he were the accused under interrogation in a court of law:

> What dost thou, or what art thou, Angelo? [II, ii, 173]

Angelo, the stern judge, does not recognise Angelo, the guilty sinner.[16] In his perplexity, he has become a 'divided self'. This is the same man who, at the beginning of the Act, was so blissfully confident that he was proof against 'the working of [his] own affections' and 'the resolute acting of [his] blood' (Escalus: II, i, 10–12) that he could blandly declare,

> When I . . . do so offend,
> Let mine own judgement pattern out my death,
> And nothing come in partial. [II, i, 28–30]

Now, he is struggling to control feelings with which he is entirely unfamiliar. The political aphorism that he who seeks to rule a state must first learn to govern his own unruly passions invites the audience, and the Deputy himself, to recognise that Angelo is now unfit to sit in judgement on others.

Angelo, the outraged judge, continues his interrogation by proposing that the very qualities that excite the illicit desires of

---

[16] In the RSC's 2019 production of the play, Sandy Grierson's Angelo, at this line, observed his reflection in the mirrors that formed the backdrop to the stage, as if seeing himself for the first time. This was the cue for him to relax his physical tension and to unbutton his constricting suit, razing the image of the sexually-repressed, inflexible Deputy that he had presented since the first scene.

Angelo, the guilty criminal, are the virtues of Isabella, the innocent novice:

> Does thou desire her foully for those things
> That make her good? [II, ii, 174–5]

In keeping with the notion of 'measure for measure', the phrasing is carefully balanced, with the antithetical 'foully' and 'good' clearly expressing the paradox that virtue has provoked vice. In addition, the fact that Angelo's words comprise a simple question, not a sophisticated statement, suggests his uncertainty, or even incredulity.

The exclamations that follow this interrogation of his own motives stand in stark contrast to Angelo's smug certitude at the beginning of Act II, when he was confident of his incorruptibility. Now, he recognises that his illicit desires, even though they have yet to lead to any wrongdoing, exonerate Claudio from blame for his crime of passion:

> O, let her brother live!
> Thieves for their robbery have authority,
> When judges steal themselves. [II, ii, 175–7]

This is a profound shift from his position when responding to Escalus at the beginning of Act II. There, he had suggested that both guilty defendant and corrupt judge should pay the same extreme penalty under the law if responsible for the same crime, rather than that the convict should be pardoned because of the corresponding guilt of the justice:

> You may not so extenuate his offence
> For I have had such faults; but rather tell me,
> When I that censure him do so offend,
> Let mine own judgement pattern out my death,
> And nothing come in partial. [II, i, 27–31]

Here in the soliloquy, the pattern of forensic questioning culminating in outraged exclamations continues as Angelo struggles to identify his emotions, intentions, and circumstances:

> What, do I love her,
> That I desire to hear her speak again?
> And feast upon her eyes? What is't I dream on?
> O cunning enemy, that, to catch a saint,
> With saints dost bait thy hook! [II, ii, 177–81]

Angelo makes no distinction here between love and lust. Perhaps Shakespeare is suggesting that, because of his inexperience of human emotions and desires, such a man could recognise no such distinction. The questions that Angelo asks of himself may seem to express an innocent wish to hear and see Isabella again, but the verbs 'desire' and 'feast' express his appetite in subliminally sensual language, while the final question 'What is't I dream on?' is no mere rhetorical gesture, as it hints at his sexual craving for Isabella, his 'dream' being physical consummation of his relationship with her.

At the end of this series of questions, in the exclamation that identifies the particular cunning of the Devil (the 'enemy'), Angelo reveals that he hubristically regards himself as a 'saint', in the Christian tradition of those ascetics who experienced temptation of the flesh.[17] In Angelo's case, he is ensnared by the lure of the saintly Isabella in whom he sees reflected the virtues that he so prizes in himself. Angelo's recognition that he has been ensnared by the Devil leads him to utter another of

---

[17] For example, Athanasius (296–373), in his life of St. Anthony (who is often identified as the earliest of the Christian monastic ascetics), records that the saint was troubled in his early life by the appearance of a devil in the form of a woman. When defeated, the devil identified himself as the spirit of lust. Accordingly, an object of sexual desire in the form of a naked woman sometimes appears in representations of the Temptation of St. Anthony in sixteenth-century art, e.g. in the depictions by Jan Wellens de Cock (Leiden/Antwerp: 1480–1527) and Cornelius Massys (Antwerp: 1510–62), where a bevy of seductive, naked women confront the praying saint.

those gnomic statements about morality with which he was so richly furnished at the start of Act II, before his 'fall':

> Most dangerous
> Is that temptation that doth goad us on
> To sin in loving virtue. [II, ii, 181–3]

It is worth pausing on these words to consider how central they are to Shakespeare's conception of his three protagonists in *Measure for Measure*. Their relevance to Angelo is clear: his sinful attraction to Isabella is based on his admiration for her virtues. Also, Isabella herself could be judged by Angelo's maxim: when her jealous regard for her chastity leads to her brutal condemnation of her brother in the prison-scene (III, i). In addition, the Duke's desire to rectify the injustices that he has witnessed in Vienna causes him, in the second half of the play, to resort to lying and deception on a grand scale to achieve his ends.

For Angelo, however, the notion that the resolute pursuit of virtue can lead to vice apparently comes as a revelation. He has never faced difficulty in repelling sexual temptation when it has appeared in overtly provocative form, but is now unable to resist the unintentional allure of a modest woman:

> Never could the strumpet
> With all her double vigour, art and nature,
> Once stir my temper: but this virtuous maid
> Subdues me quite. [II, ii, 183–6]

If, as the soliloquy suggests here and in its closing couplet, Angelo is portrayed as having never previously encountered the intensity of sexual desire, then it would be plausible to suppose that he would have developed no strategies for resisting such temptation. The words 'subdues me quite' are his confession that he considers himself powerless to resist Isabella, whereas the 'double vigour' of the 'strumpet' (her natural beauty, enhanced by cosmetics and provocative dress) could never defeat his self-control. He is so entirely overcome by his desire for Isabella that, unlike the Christian 'saints' with whom he identified himself earlier in the soliloquy, he knows that he will succumb to his lascivious desires. This recognition causes him ruefully to reflect on his previous scorn and incredulity when he observed others experiencing infatuation:

> Ever till now
> When men were fond, I smil'd, and wonder'd how.
>
> [II, ii, 186–7]

Angelo can no longer consider himself a saint, morally superior to other men: he has been forced by circumstances to acknowledge his human frailty and sinfulness. In so doing, however, he is likely to have elicited more sympathy from the audience than he did as the stern, inflexible judge who condemned Claudio. Angelo has uttered a heartfelt confession, witnessed by the members of the audience, who can now empathise with him more fully. His proposed offence, like Macbeth's as he contemplates the murder of Duncan (*Macbeth*, I, vii, 1–28), has been rendered comprehensible and 'human' through the medium of soliloquy.[18]

The Second Soliloquy

Shakespeare positions a brief scene involving the Duke and Julietta between the two great scenes in Act II involving Angelo and Isabella. Like Angelo, the Duke is a male authority figure, apparently sworn to celibacy, who is dealing with a

---

[18] Additionally, this concluding couplet confirms a disturbing association between the Duke and his deputy. The Duke has denied that 'the dribbling dart of love' could ever pierce his 'complete bosom' (I, iii, 2–3) and will insist that 'I have never heard the absent Duke much detected for women; he was not inclined that way' (III, ii, 118–19). Yet both the Duke and Angelo, having failed to recognise their susceptibility to women, will succumb to Isabella's allure. It would appear that each, like *King Lear,* 'hath ever but slenderly known himself' (*King Lear*: I, i, 293)—at least as far as erotic inclinations are concerned.

female supplicant;[19] but, unlike Angelo, he is not sexually corrupted by the proximity of the young woman. When Angelo re-appears on stage (at the beginning of Act II, scene iv), the audience is aware that he is a changed character. That change is apparent in the corruption of his language, which suggests a preoccupation with sensuality. It might also be reflected in a change of costume, as Angelo's former austere garb might be replaced by dress more appropriate to a would-be lover.[20]

Angelo's second soliloquy (interrupted by a brief exchange with a servant at lines 18–19) is no mere reiteration of the thoughts expressed in his previous soliloquy. Initially, this second glimpse into his 'inner life' is more contemplative than his previous speech: the tone is less agitated and the reflections more analytical, as Angelo has had time to reflect on his discoveries about himself. As before, the first half of this second soliloquy focuses on Angelo's preoccupation with Isabella; what is new is that he now identifies sensuality as negating the three things formerly most precious to him: his piety, his professionalism, and his reputation.

Angelo shows considerable perspicacity in identifying how these virtues that he most values in himself have been corrupted through his desire for Isabella. Having previously thought himself superior to the rest of humanity, proof against any immoral or illicit action, he is now fully aware of the power of unbridled sexual desire. Paradoxically, however, his previous moral rigour exposes his greatest moral weakness: he appears incapable of controlling or repressing sexual craving *because*

---

[19] Julietta implicitly requests guidance with the words 'I'll gladly learn' (II, iii, 23).

[20] Such was the case in the 1979 BBC production, in which Tim Pigott-Smith reappeared in a flowing robe and loose-fitting shirt, open at the neck. This replaced his former trim, sober doublet and ruff. By contrast, in the 2019 RSC production, Sandy Grierson temporarily adjusted his shapeless suit to reveal, around the top of his left leg, a bloody tourniquet used to suppress desire. He removed it before Isabella's approach, as if to give his 'sensual race the rein' (II, iv, 159).

he has never experienced it before. Instead of resisting Isabella's innocent allure, he totally capitulates by concluding that those who encounter such powerful temptations *must* succumb to them. His earlier smug maxim whereby "'Tis one thing to be tempted, Escalus, / Another thing to fall' (II, i, 17–18) is now confirmed as vain self-delusion. Deplorable as his capitulation may be, at least Angelo now appears honest in acknowledging to himself that he is corruptible.

First, he recognises that his sexual desire for Isabella invalidates his prayers:

> When I would pray and think, I think and pray
> To several subjects: Heaven hath my empty words,
> Whilst my invention, hearing not my tongue,
> Anchors on Isabel: Heaven in my mouth,
> As if I did but only chew his name,
> And in my heart the strong and swelling evil
> Of my conception. [II, iv, 1–7]

There is a veiled suggestion here that Angelo no longer feels in communion with his God: 'Heaven in my mouth / As if I did but only chew his name' suggests that the redemptive power of the Body and Blood of Christ, of which he would partake in the Eucharist, has been nullified because of the crime that he is contemplating. His mouth speaks holy words by rote, but his thoughts are elsewhere. Here, Angelo closely resembles Shakespeare's earlier creation, Claudius the King, yearning for redemption but unable to repent the murder of his brother:

> My words fly up, my thoughts remain below:
> Words without thoughts never to heaven go.
> [*Hamlet*: III, iii, 97–8]

Both men realise that pious prayers are invalidated by continued capitulation to illicit desires. Angelo's language, however, is the more sensual ('in my mouth as if I did but only chew'; 'strong and swelling evil of my conception'), appropriately reflecting his sexual preoccupations.

Secondly, Angelo is compelled to admit that the business of government no longer holds his attention or interest:

> The state whereon I studied
> Is, like a good thing being often read,
> Grown sere and tedious. . . . [II, iv, 7–9]

Angelo's professional discipline had previously kept desire in check; now, unbridled desire has overwhelmed his commitment to the business of government. Since his first encounter with Isabella, Angelo has been obliged to confront evidence of his own human fallibility: 'profits of the mind' and 'study and fast' (Lucio: I, iv, 61) are no longer sufficient to defend him from the temptations of the flesh.

Thirdly, his public image as a man of wisdom and integrity is now in jeopardy:

> . . . yea, my gravity,
> Wherein—let no man hear me—I take pride,
> Could I with boot change for an idle plume
> Which the air beats for vain. [II, iv, 9–12]

He now regards his precious reputation as worth less than an ostentatious fashion-accessory, a feather, driven by the wind hither and thither, and powerless to resist. The wind-blown feather clearly symbolizes vanity, but it also has darker, sexual connotations, because it is too light to resist the force that impels it. Angelo's 'gravity', literally the 'weightiness' of his public persona, is now as light as this feather, implicitly because the sexual impulse that is driving him irresistibly to sin is equated with 'levity'. 'Lightness' is licentiousness, as in Lucio's quip, 'women are light at midnight' (V, i, 278). Angelo had previously considered himself proof against the 'levity' of sexual temptation (II, ii, 183–87). He had levelled a false accusation against Mariana that 'her reputation was disvalu'd / In levity' (V, i, 220–21). Now, he has been forced to

191

acknowledge that his 'gravity' is no more weighty than the 'idle plume' and that, by implication, he is a helpless sinner.[21]

Angelo's loss of self-respect leads him to recognise the hypocrisy of authority figures whose grave appearance, commanding respect from all ranks of society, conceals inward corruption:

> O place, O form,
> How often dost thou with thy case, thy habit,
> Wrench awe from fools, and tie the wiser souls
> To thy false seeming! [II, iv, 12–15]

As before, Angelo is speaking sententiously, but now his former fluency is gone, the strong and irregular caesurae in each line suggesting the crisis of identity that he is suffering as he recognises himself as no more than a 'seemer' amongst impressionable dupes. An attentive audience will be reminded that the Duke's plan in promoting Angelo was to reveal 'If power change purpose, what our seemers be' (I, iii, 54). The revelation has now struck Angelo that he is such a seemer, corrupted by power. The man 'whose blood / Is very snow-broth' (Lucio: I, iv, 57–8) must now admit,

> Blood, thou art blood. [II, iv, 15]

This terse exclamation is Angelo's acknowledgement that the demands of sexual passion ('blood') cannot be denied, disguised, or resisted by any being made human by the 'blood' in his or her veins, that hereditary 'blood' bequeathed by the sexual act between mother and father.

---

[21] When, in his third and final soliloquy, Angelo talks of his authority bearing a 'credent bulk' (IV, iv, 24), he is echoing the reference to his 'gravity' here in this second soliloquy: his seeming 'weightiness' makes him valid coinage (in terms of the strain of imagery apparent since the opening speeches of the first scene). His 'lightness', however, would reveal him to be a counterfeit, as lecherous as the criminals whom he prosecutes. Such is the subtlety and complexity of Shakespeare's imagery.

There follows the much-disputed sentence,

Let's write good angel on the devil's horn—
'Tis not the devil's crest.   [II, iv, 16–17]

Certainly, the cryptic expression here creates a fruitful ambiguity. Is Isabella being represented as the devil in disguise, a seeming 'good angel' seeking to conceal what Angelo believes to be her diabolical purpose; or (more plausibly) is Angelo the devil, disguising his 'devil's horn', an oblique reference to his sexual arousal, beneath both his 'angelic' name as written on legal documents, and the 'angelic' trappings of authority that he wears in public? Perhaps the lines suggest both interpretations simultaneously, implying that Angelo's confusion between 'the tempter [and] the tempted' (see II, ii, 164) has yet to be resolved fully. Whichever interpretation is preferred, Angelo is questioning whether evil can ever transform itself into goodness by the mere outward show of piety.

These two lines nevertheless require closer scrutiny. Their sense is dependent on the immediately-preceding context, where Angelo meditated on the capacity of 'seeming' to deceive the gullible. The horn is the distinguishing feature of the devil. The gullible might be deceived if 'good angel' were written on the devil's horn. So much is readily apparent; but what precisely is the referent of the abbreviated 'it' in the compression ''Tis'? Lever, a scholarly and reliable editor, is well-supported in his contention that it is the phrase 'good angel'. The rest of the line might then mean that 'good angel' cannot be the devil's 'crest' or motto; that is, it cannot signify the devil. According to this interpretation, the attempted disguise is unsuccessful: the devil's evil nature, the distinguishing 'horn', remains apparent to the observer. The immediately-preceding context, however, suggests a different— and more convincing—interpretation, whereby ''Tis' should refer to 'the devil's horn'. The sense of what follows is then that, once 'good angel' has been written upon the horn, it is no longer readily identifiable (by the gullible, at least) as the sign or 'crest' of the devil. According to this interpretation, the disguise *is* successful in that it can still 'Wrench awe from fools, and tie the wiser souls / To [its] false seeming' (lines 14–15). This interpretation would justify why Angelo persists in his 'seeming' until the very end of the play: he is convinced that he can disguise 'the devil's horn', that is, his evil desire, under his appearance as a 'good angel', that is, under his facade as the noble ascetic, Angelo, whose name and reputation suggest that he should be valued as true coinage (a 'good angel'). Angelo is proposing to himself a strategy that he believes will successfully conceal his corruption.

Angelo seems startled by the knock at the door that concludes the first section of this soliloquy: 'How now! Who's there?' (line 17). Such a sudden, nervous exclamation would suggest a fear in Angelo that his meditation on 'the devil's horn' and 'the devil's crest' might indeed have summoned up a devil. It might even imply that Angelo regards Isabella as the Devil's agent, tempting him, throughout the remaining exchanges of this scene.

The news brought by the servant, that Isabella is awaiting audience with Angelo, leads to the second half of the soliloquy in which the emotional turmoil of Angelo's first soliloquy returns. Angelo is overwhelmed by excitement, his 'blood . . . muster[ing] to [his] heart' and 'dispossessing' all his other faculties of their capacities (lines 20–2). Again, the presentation of Angelo is entirely psychologically convincing: his heart, weakened as it races excitedly in anticipation of Isabella's appearance, robs him of his customary detached, professional manner. Perhaps less psychologically convincing are the two elaborate, related similes that follow, comparing Angelo's racing heart to the experience of 'one that swounds' and of a 'well-wish'd king' when they are mobbed by those who surround them (lines 24–30). The paired images may reflect Angelo's interest in public events and ironically foreshadow the great pageant in the final scene of *Measure for Measure*, when Angelo himself will be overwhelmed in the presence of a great assembly; but they look suspiciously like an acknowledgement of King James I's dislike of being mobbed by crowds.[22] James was, after all, in the audience for that first recorded performance of *Measure for Measure* at Whitehall Palace on 26 December, 1604, and might well have been gratified by such a reference. These two linked images, however, may seem an undramatic aberration to a modern audience, to whom James I's preoccupations are of little concern. There is therefore justification for cutting these lines (24–30) from a modern performance, as was done, for example, in the RSC's 2019 production.

Equivocation and Prevarication

Much of Act II scene iv is particularly demanding to present in the theatre. As there is little obvious stage-business or physical activity, the scene relies on language for its success, and the language can be challenging to fathom. Angelo's words have become like those of Adam and Eve after the Fall in Book IX of Milton's *Paradise Lost*: infected by sensuality. An actor must convey subtly to the audience the phases by which Angelo reveals his dishonourable intentions towards Isabella. The Deputy begins indirectly, by sly insinuation.

Angelo does not bluntly proposition Isabella at the start of their second interview; rather, he resorts to equivocation and prevarication. From the outset, however, his language is tainted with innuendo. When Isabella innocently asks to know his 'pleasure' (II, iv, 31), his muttered response puns on the sexual sense of the word, incorporating a further bawdy play on the verb 'know':

That you might know it, would much better please me,
Than to demand what 'tis. [II, iv, 32–3]

---

[22] This issue is discussed in Chapter 2, 'Vincentio, Machiavelli, and James I', pp. 80–82. Cf. pp. 102–103.

His meaning in this aside is that he would greatly prefer to enjoy her sexual favours without being forced to explain his desires verbally. Isabella should appear not to have heard the equivocation—or, at least, not to have understood its riddling expression. Angelo's refusal to speak openly might suggest a reluctance to incriminate himself, augmented by a strong sense of shame.

Angelo is tentatively exploring Isabella's responses, unwilling yet to reveal his gross intentions. Although the words 'Your brother cannot live' (line 33) initially appear to be an unambiguous confirmation of the death-sentence on Claudio, Angelo has thereby exerted extreme emotional pressure on Isabella while leaving himself room to exploit her distress. As she accepts his judgement and prepares to withdraw from his presence—which would defeat his lascivious objective—he intervenes to offer her a thread of hope to grasp:

Yet may he live a while; and, it may be,
As long as you or I; yet he must die. [II, iv, 35–6]

The words confirm Angelo's equivocation: Claudio must die, but Angelo has not yet specified *when*. Claudio's life must end in death as surely as Angelo's and Isabella's lives must, because all human beings 'cannot live' indefinitely. Is Shakespeare now representing Angelo as callously toying with Isabella's emotions, relishing the exercise of his power, or rather as frantically improvising when fearful of losing the delight of her presence? The lines could legitimately be performed to suggest either interpretation, although the latter would be more congruent with Angelo's uncertainty in the immediately-preceding soliloquies.

Angelo seeks to justify the sentence of death on Claudio in ambivalent language that subtly hints at his new awareness of the allure of sexual delight. Although he condemns fornication as one of 'these filthy vices!' that (according to him, at least) is as culpable as murder, he implicitly concedes that it tempts with its 'saucy sweetness' (lines 41–4), both words confirming the sensual pleasure to be found in gratifying an appetite. He also seeks to equate illicit sexual activity with the capital offence of forgery (lines 45–6) for, whereas the forger reproduces the monarch's image in creating an illicit coin, the fornicator reproduces God's image in creating an illegitimate child. In associating these two disparate activities, his language becomes heavily burdened with innuendo:

> [Those who] do coin heaven's image
> In stamps that are forbid . . .
> . . . put mettle in restrained means
> To make a false one. [II, iv, 45–9]

Although the language here is ostensibly concerned with forgery, the vigour of illicit copulation is conveyed in the expression 'coin heaven's image / In stamps', while the phrasing 'put mettle in restrained means' contains a covert reference to male penetration ('put mettle in') of a woman compelled to comply ('restrained means').

Angelo has the advantageous position: he knows both his own objective (Isabella's virginity) and hers (Claudio's reprieve). She remains ignorant of his intentions, and so can do no more than respond to whatever course Angelo determines for their verbal exchanges. Seizing the opportunity provided by Isabella's argument that— on Earth, at least—fornication is a lesser offence than killing (line 50), Angelo eagerly seeks to draw a further concession from her, that will enable him ultimately to reveal his immoral intent:

> Then I shall pose you quickly.
> Which had you rather, that the most just law
> Now took your brother's life; or, to redeem him,
> Give up your body to such sweet uncleanness
> As she that he hath stained? [II, iv, 51–5]

The oxymoron 'sweet uncleanness', as well as asserting the moral culpability of sexual licence, confirms Angelo's new awareness of its 'sweet' allure. Angelo seeks to compel Isabella into a seemingly hypothetical choice of such 'sweet uncleanness' as the lesser of two evils: succumbing to sexual enjoyment to save Claudio from death. Were she to make that concession, his task of persuading her to comply with his sexual desires might be so much easier.

Isabella, however, meets prevarication with evasion— 'I had rather give my body than my soul' (line 56)—which forces Angelo to shift his ground. His ploy, in response, is to suggest that there may be occasions when sins do not imperil the soul; namely, when we act under duress:

> . . . our compell'd sins
> Stand more for number than for accompt. [II, iv, 57–8]

Having established this premise, he can now argue that a sin might be transformed into a virtue if committed for a benevolent purpose:

> I—now the voice of the recorded law—
> Pronounce a sentence on your brother's life:
> Might there not be a charity in sin
> To save this brother's life? [II, iv, 61–4]

Were Isabella to accept this rationale, then Angelo might quickly encompass his desires by arguing that she would be performing a virtuous act by yielding her virginity to him in exchange for Claudio's life.

The dangers of Angelo's prevarication are made apparent by Isabella's responses, in which she—intentionally or innocently—ignores Angelo's lustful insinuations. Here, she prefers to believe that the sin which he is proposing must be either a sin on Angelo's part in pardoning a fornicator, or a sin on Isabella's part in pleading for her brother to be spared the penalty demanded by the law for his offence. Angelo, suspecting that Isabella may deliberately be misunderstanding him, becomes more impatient and accusatory:

> Nay, but hear me;
> Your sense pursues not mine: either you are ignorant,
> Or seem so, crafty; and that's not good. [II, iv, 73–5]

Here, the word 'sense' is employed by Angelo with an equivocal meaning (as it was in his aside at II, ii, 142 that first confirmed his illicit passion): it could mean 'understanding', or 'sexual desire', or both, simultaneously. Frustrated by Isabella's seeming misunderstanding of his intentions, Angelo will now be obliged to 'speak more gross' (II, iv, 82).

Now I Give My Sensual Race the Rein

As Angelo draws ever closer to his objective—to reveal to Isabella his sexual intentions towards her—his language evolves into that of the deceitful tempter, the Devil in the Garden of Eden.[23] In a single convoluted sentence of considerable length, Angelo weaves his serpentine way towards a simple, concluding, four-word question to Isabella:

> Admit no other way to save his life—
> As I subscribe not that, nor any other,
> But in the loss of question—that you, his sister,
> Finding yourself desir'd of such a person
> Whose credit with the judge, or own great place,
> Could fetch your brother from the manacles
> Of the all-binding law; and that there were
> No earthly mean to save him, but that either
> You must lay down the treasures of your body
> To this suppos'd, or else to let him suffer:
> What would you do? [II, iv, 88–98]

The verbosity and the staccato rhythm of the verse, attributable to the irregularity of the caesurae, draw attention to Angelo's deviousness as well as to his moral cowardice: he does not yet dare to identify himself as Isabella's would-be seducer, but speaks vaguely of 'this suppos'd', 'such a person' who has

---

[23] Cf. Satan in Milton's *Paradise Lost*, IX, 532–732.

influence or status sufficient to save Claudio from execution. His language also seeks to give greater respectability to the sordid transaction that he is proposing, his reference to 'the treasures of [Isabella's] body' presenting her desired sexual acquiescence as a means of ransom as legitimate as a payment of family 'treasure' to secure the liberty of a convicted criminal.

Although the outraged Isabella rejects Angelo's indecent proposal, her response encourages him to pursue his shameful objective even more ardently. Her language (lines 99–104) is suffused with potentially erotic images: 'wear as rubies'; 'strip myself'; 'a bed / That longing have been sick for'; 'yield / My body up'. An audience might recognise that such speech would suggest to Angelo a sexual awareness in Isabella comparable to his own recent erotic awakening.[24]

As the verbal combat intensifies, Angelo searches for a weakness in Isabella's defences while Isabella parries his attacks. First, he proposes that her inflexible morality is just as harsh as the capital sentence that he is imposing under the statutes of Vienna (lines 109–10). When she skilfully refutes his suggestion by distinguishing between 'lawful mercy' and 'foul redemption' (lines 112–13), he seeks to regain the upper hand in the struggle by reminding Isabella that she has belittled the significance of her brother's crime in pleading for his pardon (lines 114–16). Having gained an advantage over the chastened Isabella, Angelo seizes the opportunity for further insidious attacks. When he suggests that all human beings are weak, an audience may suspect that he is seeking for the advantage that an admission of frailty from Isabella would give him; however, her response (that the corollary of Angelo's words is that her brother's sin has been and will be committed by many other men) frustrates such an intention. He therefore focuses more specifically on female susceptibility:

Nay, women are frail too. [II, iv, 123]

---

[24] Cf. Isabella's inadvertent 'temptation' of Angelo at II, ii, 137–47.

In response, Isabella's vigorous condemnation of women's weakness, particularly their vulnerability to sexual temptation, may appear to an audience as a reflex conditioned by her familiarity with the misogynistic tradition of her faith; but it also provides Angelo with the opportunity that he has sought, through persistent verbal probing, to launch his final assault.

Angelo's language becomes at once impulsive, impassioned, and imperative:

> . . . let me be bold.
> I do arrest your words. Be that you are,
> That is, a woman; if you be more, you're none.
> If you be one—as you are well-express'd
> By all external warrants—show it now,
> By putting on the destin'd livery. [II, iv, 132–7]

The jerky, disjointed syntax and strong, irregular caesurae clearly show his excitement as he commands Isabella to comply with his will. She has condemned the frailty of all women and, in so doing, implicitly admitted to her own susceptibility, which Angelo desires to exploit. Her 'destin'd livery' is no longer her nun's garb; rather, as a woman, she is ordained to accept a man's 'livery' by submitting herself to his pleasure.[25] Angelo's implication could be clarified with reference to John Donne's elegy, 'To His Mistress Going to Bed', where the woman undressing is presented with the ultimate (and ambiguous) question, 'What need'st thou have more covering than a man?' (Elegy XX, 47–8). Stripped of all other garments, the female should be covered by the male. Such is Angelo's meaning, however distasteful.

---

[25] The image of dressing (or perhaps, undressing) is an extension of Angelo's meditation in his second soliloquy on how 'habit' (that is, 'clothing') creates 'false seeming' (II, iv, 14-15). The nun's habit might disguise the carnal woman.

Isabella's earnest plea for Angelo to revert to his 'former language', abandoning his aggressively sexual proposition, draws from him an open admission:

Plainly conceive, I love you. [II, iv, 140]

Such words might have seemed touchingly simple or endearingly frank in another context, but not here: it is lust, not love, that would seek to strike such a sordid bargain as Angelo is pursuing. His words are striving to present raw, unrestrained sexual desire as something more noble. When Isabella deplores the hypocrisy of Angelo's position—that he is seeking the same sexual gratification for which he has condemned Claudio to death (lines 141–2)—Angelo promises to pardon her brother in return for what he calls Isabella's 'love', by which he clearly means her sexual favours (line 143). Ironically, he swears by his 'honour' and protests that his 'words express [his] purpose' (lines 146–7) when the preceding exchanges have confirmed that his honour is tainted and that his words are slippery.

When the outraged Isabella condemns Angelo as a hypocrite and threatens to expose him publicly unless he should give her the pardon for Claudio that she demands (II, iv, 148–53), the simplicity of Angelo's refutation is devastating:

Who will believe thee, Isabel?
My unsoil'd name, th'austereness of my life,
My vouch against you, and my place i'th'state
Will so your accusation overweigh,
That you shall stifle in your own report,
And smell of calumny. [II, iv, 153–8]

Her threat has transformed Angelo from pleading lover into ruthless tyrant. He has returned to the language of authority that he wielded so successfully in the earlier scenes of the play, before he succumbed to his desire for Isabella. Now, however, he is prepared to deny a legitimate accusation and even to allow his righteous accuser to suffer for telling the truth. Angelo's smugness is repulsive, both in his cold initial rhetorical

202

question (line 153) and in his hubristic self-portrait in which he boasts of his spotless reputation, his ascetic previous life, and the supreme authority trustingly bestowed on him by the Duke (lines 154–55). He appears cruelly to relish the prospect of the destruction of Isabella's reputation (lines 157–8),[26] further alienating him from the sympathy of the audience.

But worse is to follow as Angelo, abandoning all moral scruples, degenerates from seducer to rapist:

> I have begun,
> And now I give my sensual race the rein:
> Fit thy consent to my sharp appetite;
> Lay by all nicety and prolixious blushes
> That banish what they sue for. [II, iv, 158–62]

The Duke had characterised the 'strict statutes and most biting laws' of Vienna as 'The needful bits and curbs to headstrong jades' (I, iii, 19–20), using an equine image to refer to the necessary control of animalistic passions. Criminal desires were thus presented by the Duke as unruly horses requiring firm government.[27] Now Angelo, the very man chosen by the Duke to administer those laws formulated to control unruly passions in the state, wilfully abandons the self-control that should govern his own illicit desires. Instead, he offers complete freedom to his lustful urges, 'give my sensual race the rein' extending the earlier equine metaphors by presenting his desires as wild horses deliberately freed from restraint. Having abandoned all conscience and morality, Angelo brutally addresses Isabella with a series of imperatives, demanding her acquiescence. 'Fit thy consent to my sharp appetite' is more than a mere command by Angelo for Isabella to obey his

---

[26] Cf. his destruction of Mariana's reputation to justify breaking his oath of marriage (III, i, 226–7).

[27] Further evidence of Shakespeare's strain of imagery occurs when Claudio refers to 'the body public' as 'A horse whereon the governor doth ride' (I, ii, 148–9), the metaphor presenting Angelo as responsible for controlling bestial urges in Vienna.

wishes. Freudian critics will no doubt identify a phallic symbol in the phrase 'sharp appetite' and consider the whole line—governed by the command 'fit'— to be a metaphor describing the sexual act between man and woman. Shakespeare's choice of the word 'sharp' carries further connotations, suggesting not merely the powerful intensity of Angelo's desire but also that his appetite is a dangerous weapon simultaneously threatening Isabella while deeply wounding himself. His demand that she should 'Lay by' the trappings of her modesty represents her 'nicety and prolixious blushes' as garments to be cast aside as a prelude to their sexual encounter. Again, Shakespeare's lines encourage comparison with the conclusion of Donne's elegy, 'To His Mistress Going to Bed':

> Cast all, yea this white linen, hence:
> There is no penance, much less innocence!
> [Elegy XX, 45–6]

Like Donne, Angelo refuses to consider modesty as a sign of 'innocence', regarding it rather as a provocation to inflame desire. Angelo's commands admit of no shame or delay, either on his part or hers: he has deliberately rejected all such virtuous constraints, and now demands the same from Isabella. Any modest 'blushes' from her—'prolixious' because they would seek delay—would merely serve further to whet his 'sharp appetite'.

Just when an audience may think that Angelo can sink no lower ethically, he further compounds his offences against Isabella, Claudio, the law, and all morality:

> Redeem thy brother
> By yielding up thy body to my will;
> Or else he must not only die the death,
> But thy unkindness shall his death draw out
> To ling'ring sufferance. [II, iv, 162–6]

Significantly, this shocking threat to torture Claudio to death if Isabella should refuse to comply with Angelo's sexual demands is not found in any of the possible sources for the plot of *Measure for Measure*. Shakespeare's corrupt judge plumbs depths of depravity not fathomed in other versions of the tale. Angelo's attempt to make Isabella's 'unkindness' responsible for her brother's agony and death is insidious. The word is carefully chosen for its ambiguity. It could mean 'unkindness' in the erotic sense, that Isabella is the unpitying lady of the courtly tradition, rejecting the suit of the woeful lover (in this case, Angelo); but there is the further meaning that her 'unkindness' is her 'unnatural' course of abandoning her own brother to his fate.[28] In addition, Angelo's manipulative malice is insinuated in the phrase 'draw out / To ling'ring sufferance': it hints either at the torment of being disembowelled while still alive, as practised in the contemporary punishment of hanging, drawing and quartering; or suggests the horrors of the rack, which Escalus later confirms is a torture device that will 'touse you / Joint by joint' (V, i, 309–10). The threat to Claudio is horrifying, and therefore the pressure exerted on Isabella is brutally increased.

Although this speech may lead to a physical confrontation between Angelo and Isabella in certain productions, Angelo must show sufficient restraint to delay the consummation of his desires:

> Answer me tomorrow,
> Or, by the affection that now guides me most,
> I'll prove a tyrant to him. As for you,
> Say what you can: my false o'erweighs your true.
> [II, iv, 166–9]

Boasting of his descent into lust and tyranny, Angelo here revels in the authority to abuse. The sneer in his final line indicates the scorn that he now feels both for Isabella's virtue

---

[28] Until the end of the Middle Ages, the principal meaning of 'kind' was 'natural'. Shakespeare plays on the contrasting mediaeval and renaissance meanings of 'kind' elsewhere, e.g. in *King Lear*, Act I, *passim*.

and for the laws that have been entrusted to him to enforce: under his direction, hypocrisy more than counterbalances honesty in the scales of justice.

How should the actors portraying Angelo and Isabella conduct themselves in the course of Angelo's long speech (II, iv, 153–69)? The preceding exchanges are likely to have been predominantly static, relying on language for dramatic effect. Here, though, is a clear opportunity for significant physical activity. For example, in David Thacker's 1994 production for the BBC, Corin Redgrave's predatory Angelo gave his 'sensual race the rein' by pursuing Juliet Aubrey's terrified Isabella around the imposing desk of his presence-chamber. A blazing fire, suggestive both of unbridled passion and of incipient damnation, was the backdrop as he seized her violently, threw her down on a couch and spat his lines about desire, death, and torture into her agonised face. With his final words in the scene, he hurled Isabella out of the door into the antechamber, where he left her sprawling on the floor to deliver her soliloquy. This Angelo abused not only his judicial power but also his masculine, physical dominance.

Angelo *in Absentia*

Angelo will not be seen again on stage for more than one and a half acts (not until Act IV, scene iv, which includes his third and final great soliloquy); but Shakespeare ensures that his character, words, and actions are constantly kept in view by the audience during this long absence. Angelo was presented as the strict, virtuous ascetic in Act I and the earlier part of Act II, and as the brutal, lecherous tyrant towards the end of Act II. Even in his earlier manifestation as the bastion of the law, he had not—because of his unsympathetic inflexibility—excited universal approval. In his fallen state, he will suffer still greater condemnation, even from those who do not recognise the full extent of his corruption.

Isabella, victim of his tyranny and object of his lust, associates Angelo with devils, hell and damnation. He shows 'a devilish mercy' (III, i, 64); he 'is yet a devil', whose 'filth . . . as deep as hell' is disguised under 'the cunning livery of hell' (III, i, 91–4). On learning of the execution of her brother, she styles him 'most damned Angelo!' (IV, iii, 122), while on learning of Angelo's cruel desertion and slandering of Mariana, her exasperation with earthly justice—of which Angelo is the embodiment—breaks forth: 'What corruption in this life, that it will let this man live!' (III, i, 232–3). In short, Isabella is consistent and morally clear-sighted in her judgement of Angelo after her encounter with him at the end of the Second Act.

By contrast, Angelo's hypocrisy serves to confuse Claudio morally. Because Angelo has promised to reprieve Claudio's capital sentence if allowed to commit the same crime for which Claudio was condemned to death, Claudio attempts to convince himself that his offence is being condoned by the Deputy (III, i, 107–14). Claudio wildly grasps at the belief that a figure as judicious as Angelo would not contemplate involvement in a damnable act, and that therefore Claudio's comparable offence must be venial rather than mortal. As in the image of the carrion lying by the violet in the sun (II, i, 165–8), Angelo's corruption is seen to be polluting the moral judgement of those around him.

But it is not merely Angelo the fallen angel who is condemned in Acts III and IV. Angelo's severity is condemned by the Provost—'It is a bitter deputy' (IV, ii, 76). Less obvious is the unintentional irony at Angelo's expense of Elbow's words on arresting Pompey:

. . . . we have found upon him, sir, a strange pick-lock, which we have sent to the deputy. . . . The deputy cannot abide a whoremaster. If he be a whoremonger and comes before him, he were as good go a mile on his errand. [III, ii, 15–36]

It has been ingeniously suggested by several editors that the pick-lock is to gain access to female chastity belts (hence the immediate assumption at III, ii, 18 by the Duke, in disguise as Friar Lodowick, that Pompey is 'a bawd, a wicked bawd').[29] The reference subtly reminds the audience of Angelo's attempts, only two scenes before, to pick the lock of Isabella's chastity, while more obviously stressing Angelo's hypocrisy in condemning 'whoremasters' and 'whoremongers' while seeking surreptitiously to participate in the flesh-trade himself.

Not surprisingly, Angelo's (former) puritanical morality is mocked by the hedonistic Lucio as it is threatening Lucio with retribution for his lax sexual habits, as well as condemning his friend, Claudio, to death. Angelo's stringent administration of the laws on sexual morality seems particularly distasteful and unnatural to the sensualist, Lucio: it is 'a ruthless thing . . . for the rebellion of a codpiece to take away the life of a man!' (III, ii, 110–12). In a series of 'fantastical' remarks, Lucio presents Angelo as a freak of nature:

> They say this Angelo was not made by man and woman, after this downright way of creation. . . . Some report, a sea-maid spawned him. Some, that he was begot between two stockfishes. But it is certain that when he makes water, his urine is congealed ice. . . . And he is a motion ungenerative. . . . [III, ii, 99–108]

Lucio's repeated suggestions that there is something fishy and cold about Angelo's lack of empathy leads to his conclusion that the deputy is 'a motion ungenerative', a mere puppet, incapable of sexual reproduction. Similarly, Lucio will later refer to Angelo as an 'ungenitured agent', a eunuch upon whom power has been bestowed—sufficient power to destroy the state by enforcing sexual abstinence (III, ii, 167–9).

The most important source of remarks about Angelo in Acts III and IV is, nevertheless, the Duke. Vincentio presents an

---

[29] See Lever, pp. 82–83n. As a modern audience is scarcely likely to recognize this implication, Pompey might wear around his neck a punitive placard announcing him to be a 'bawd'.

idealised picture of Angelo to the Provost, feigning ignorance of Angelo's recent moral degeneration:

> . . . his life is parallel'd
> Even with the stroke and line of his great justice.
> He doth with holy abstinence subdue
> That in himself which he spurs on his power
> To qualify in others: were he meal'd with that
> Which he corrects, then were he tyrannous;
> But this being so, he's just. [IV, ii, 76–83]

Despite their literal meaning, these lines should convey to an audience the extent to which Angelo has failed in his duties as deputy. His 'life' and his 'great justice' are no longer congruent. He has not succeeded to 'subdue' the illicit desires that he seeks to 'qualify in others'. Accordingly, he is 'meal'd with that / Which he corrects' and is therefore 'tyrannous' rather than 'just'. Clearly, the ducal definition of a tyrant is one who indulges in vices that he punishes in others.[30] Such a man is Angelo, who has abandoned the 'holy abstinence' worthy of his angelic name. Vincentio's lines, literally a defence of Angelo to one of his officers, are ironically a condemnation of the Deputy to the audience.

At the end of the same scene, in gnomic couplets, the Duke considers those qualities to which Angelo should have aspired and the extent to which Angelo has fallen short of those ideals (III, ii, 254–65).[31] Angelo deserves not only 'shame' for his 'cruel striking' at the life of a condemned man whose offence he shares, but also '[t]wice treble shame' for fostering in himself those very vices that he was appointed to prosecute in

---

[30] In this respect, Shakespeare's Duke would be echoed by England's King. In a speech to Parliament in March, 1610, James I declared that 'a King governing in a setled Kingdome, leaves to be a King, and degenerates into a Tyrant, assoone as he leaves off to rule according to his Lawes' (quoted by Braunmuller and Watson, p.182n.).

[31] The passage is discussed in detail in Chapter 2, 'The Duke's Monologues', pp. 89–90.

the state. This at times highly-compressed lecture reflects on both the Duke and Angelo, presenting the former as a wise, righteous arbiter and the latter as a despicable hypocrite.

There is, however, further evidence known to the Duke against 'this wretch' (IV, iii, 133), Angelo:

[Mariana] should this Angelo have married: was affianced to her oath, and the nuptial appointed. Between which time of the contract and limit of the solemnity, her brother Frederick was racked at sea, having in that perished vessel the dowry of his sister. . . . There she lost a noble and renowned brother, in his love to her ever most kind and natural; with him, the portion and sinew of her fortune, her marriage-dowry; with both, her combinate husband, this well-seeming Angelo. . . . Left her in her tears, and dried not one of them with his comfort: swallowed his vows whole, pretending in her discoveries of dishonour: in few, bestowed her on her own lamentation, which she yet wears for his sake; and he, a marble to her tears, is washed with them, but relents not. . . . His unjust unkindness, that in all reason should have quenched her love, hath, like an impediment in the current, made it more violent and unruly. [III, i, 213–43]

The parallels and contrasts between the circumstances of the judge, Angelo, and the condemned man, Claudio, are striking.[32] Both were 'affianced' by 'oath' to a woman whose 'dowry' was lacking. Claudio remained faithful to his sworn love, although he broke the law (according to Angelo, at least) by consummating the relationship before the marriage had been authorised. Angelo deserted his love cruelly, exacerbating his offence by fraudulently blackening her reputation to justify his abandonment of her. Claudio has been presented as well-intentioned but unfortunate. Angelo, by contrast, appears faithless, avaricious, mendacious, and cowardly. Certainly, the

---

[32] For details of Claudio's similar circumstances, see I, ii, 134–44. These two contexts are compared in Chapter 5, 'Doomed Betrothal', pp. 292–295.

Duke's words here are strongly judgemental, encouraging the audience to despise his 'well-seeming' deputy: Angelo, with 'unjust unkindness', has denied 'comfort' to a woman of a 'noble and renowned' family whose reputation he has tarnished by 'pretending . . . dishonour' in her.

Although, in Shakespeare's time, loss of a dowry might have been considered appropriate grounds for a man's termination of his pledge of marriage, a modern audience is likely to be less sympathetic to Angelo, seeing him as venal and treacherous. His action in abandoning Mariana suggests that he looked on his alliance with her as a transaction that was invalidated when his opportunity for profit was lost, circumstances uncomfortably close to the kind of sexual bargaining that is conducted in Vienna's 'houses of resort', such as that run by Mistress Overdone. In addition, Angelo's blackening of Mariana's reputation smacks of guilt on his part: it seems a devious attempt to forestall the suspicion that he is forsworn and that his motives were unworthy when he terminated their relationship. His malicious slander of his betrothed is further evidence of Angelo's preoccupation with his public image, to which he referred so guardedly in his second soliloquy. Fittingly, then, he will ultimately be punished by the permanent loss of this reputation that he values so highly, and must look to the virtue of the woman whom he slighted to be the guardian of his future honour.

Perhaps it would be ill-advised fully to reappraise Act I of the play in the light of the Duke's words about Mariana and Angelo. If the extent of Angelo's deceitfulness, avarice, and corruptibility was known to the Duke from the outset, then it would have been a profoundly irresponsible act to promote such a man to supreme authority in Vienna: suffering and injustice should have been recognised as the likely consequence. But such a judgement overlooks the influence of folk-tale on this aspect of the plot. The story of Mariana's betrayal, slander, and abandonment by Angelo is introduced here by the Duke as the necessary preliminary to unravelling all the complex moral and political problems that have become entangled in the play so far. Until Angelo has been corrupted by his lust for Isabella, no direct reference has been made to his shameful treatment of Mariana—indeed, no direct reference has been made to Mariana at all in the first half of the play. During a performance, therefore, an audience might assimilate this information about Mariana as further evidence of Angelo's malfeasance in his 'fallen' state. The alternative is to recognise that the Duke is presented as knowing of Angelo's corruption at the beginning of the play, and that Angelo was therefore an entirely inappropriate candidate for high office.[33]

The Duke's words about Mariana's betrayal are necessary to prepare the audience for the plan that Vincentio will reveal to dupe Angelo: the 'bed-trick', exchanging Mariana for Isabella (III, i, 243–57). When Angelo's missive arrives at the jail on the night on which the 'bed-trick' has taken place, the Duke predicts the content of the note in neat couplets full of high sentence (IV, ii, 106–11). He assumes that Angelo is a paradigm for corrupt authority: pardon will be granted to Claudio because the judge has now committed the very sin that he had previously condemned in the accused. The Duke's expectation, however, proves erroneous. Angelo's moral degeneration is greater than even the Duke has predicted, as the Deputy's letter to the Provost confirms:

---

[33] Although the Duke might plausibly have learned of Angelo's mistreatment of his betrothed *after* Vincentio transformed himself into a friar—for example, during the confessional between Friar Lodowick and Mariana to which the Duke refers at V, i, 524—the time-scheme of the play does not fit comfortably with such an interpretation (see Appendix 1). Additionally, such speculation risks treating characters in a drama as 'real' people with lives beyond those portrayed on stage. Suffice it to say that the Duke's early speech to Friar Thomas (at I, iii, 50–54) scarcely suggests approval of Angelo (labelling him as a 'seemer' and accurately predicting that 'power' will reveal his hypocrisy) but makes no specific charge of criminality against him. See also the interpretation of I, i, 27–9 offered earlier in this chapter, pp. 160–161, and also in Chapter 2, 'The Problems of Act I', p. 101.

Whatsoever you may hear to the contrary, let Claudio be executed by four of the clock, and in the afternoon, Barnadine. For my better satisfaction, let me have Claudio's head sent me by five. Let this be duly performed, with a thought that more depends on it than we must yet deliver. Thus fail not to do your office, as you will answer it at your peril. [IV, ii, 118–24]

These are the only words attributed to Angelo in his lengthy absence from stage during the second half of the play, and they serve further to alienate the sympathies of the audience from him. Having succeeded, as far as he is aware, in taking Isabella's virginity, this known oath-breaker who previously betrayed Mariana now refuses to fulfil his solemn pledge to pardon Claudio (II, iv, 143–6), but rather demands evidence of his speedy execution. Furthermore, Angelo feigns some unspecified danger to the state and threatens dire retribution should the Provost fail to carry out the Deputy's commands. The Duke must reassure the Provost that 'Claudio, whom here you have warrant to execute, is no greater forfeit to the law than Angelo who hath sentenced him' (IV, ii, 156–7). For the audience, who can compare the offences of Claudio and Angelo, the former is vindicated but the latter further degraded. During his absence from stage, any residual sympathy that might have been felt for Angelo would seem to have been dissipated totally: the audience relishes the prospect of Angelo's exposure and downfall as letters and instructions are issued concerning the Duke's return (IV, iii, 92ff).

After the Fall: The Third Soliloquy

Angelo's third soliloquy occurs in a scene in which he has clearly lost his decisiveness and perspicacity. The Duke's letters have succeeded in their objective of confusing the Deputy and arousing his guilt. There is panic in his tone as he addresses the noble Escalus:

And why meet him at the gates and redeliver our authorities there? . . . And why should we proclaim it an hour before his

213

entering, that if any crave redress of injustice, they should exhibit their petitions in the street? [IV, iv, 4–9]

That Angelo's questions here stem from a conscience in turmoil is suggested by Escalus's measured response (IV, iv, 10–12) in which he simply reiterates the answer to Angelo's second question as it appears in the Duke's letter. Angelo, in his guilt-ridden state, has proved incapable of assimilating Vincentio's brief.

Angelo acknowledges as much in the opening lines of his final soliloquy:

> This deed unshapes me quite; makes me unpregnant
> And dull to all proceedings. [IV, iv, 18–19]

The word 'unshapes' is as unexpected as it is apposite. It suggests more than that Angelo simply does not recognise himself in his fallen state (as was indicated in his first soliloquy when he asked, 'What dost thou, or what art thou, Angelo?' [II, ii, 173]): it confirms that Angelo's vice has transformed him into something monstrous in his own eyes. Sensual indulgence has paradoxically left him 'unpregnant', that is, incapable of 'conceiving'—not sexually, but mentally. His preoccupation with his offence has blunted the intellectual edge of a man who spoke so eloquently and confidently of the law at the beginning of Act II: he has become 'dull to all proceedings'. Guilt is disfiguring both his image and his acuity.

The language that he speaks as he contemplates his shameful act is now tainted with physical, potentially sexual, diction—further evidence that his preoccupation with Isabella is overwhelming his previously lucid, dispassionate mind:

> A *deflower'd maid*;
> And by an eminent *body*, that *enforc'd*
> The law against it! But that her *tender* shame
> Will not proclaim against *her maiden loss*,
> How might she *tongue me*! Yet reason dares her no,

For my authority bears so credent *bulk*
That no particular scandal once can *touch*,
But it confounds the *breather*.
                [IV, iv, 19-26; italics added]

The italicised words accumulate to suggest subliminally how his sensual preoccupations are distracting Angelo from his public duties. Guilt and shock, conveyed in the first two sentences by his contemplation of what he has done and what the consequences might be, are emphasised by the exclamation-marks. The consolation that he offers himself in the third sentence is ironic: he believes that his office and reputation are so substantial that he is proof against any allegations: accusations against him would merely incriminate the accuser. The audience, however, should immediately register that his ultimate accuser, who knows the whole truth of his circumstances, will be the Duke, whose 'authority' is of greater 'credent bulk' than Angelo's own. Angelo's deliberations therefore lead the audience more eagerly to anticipate the retribution that fast approaches him.

This part of his soliloquy is, nevertheless, important in that the 'monstrous' Angelo, whom we have heard so roundly condemned by the Duke, Isabella, and Lucio since his last appearance, may be partially redeemed in our eyes by the anguish to which his conscience is subjecting him: his punishment has already begun in the shame, fear, and self-disgust that he is experiencing. Although he has tried to convince himself that he is safe from public reproof (lines 23–26), his remorse reappears when he contemplates Claudio, whom he believes executed on his command, in breach of his sordid contract with Isabella:

                    He should have liv'd;
Save that his riotous youth, with dangerous sense,
Might in the times to come have ta'en revenge
By so receiving a dishonour'd life
With ransom of such shame. Would yet he had lived.
                            [IV, iv, 26–30]

The dramatic irony should not be lost on the audience, fully aware of the Duke's secret intercession: ultimately, Angelo's wish will be fulfilled that Claudio should survive his death-sentence. The contradiction in this section of Angelo's soliloquy—fear of reprisal justifying Claudio's execution, set against remorse deploring Claudio's death—is summarised in a gnomic couplet reminiscent of the Duke's choric function elsewhere in the play:

> Alack, when once our grace we have forgot,
> Nothing goes right; we would, and we would not.
>
> [IV, iv, 31–32]

For a moment, we glimpse the wisdom and incisiveness of the former, prelapsarian Angelo as he recognises that a fall from divine grace produces the chaos of self-contradictory desires from which he is now suffering. Angelo's tragedy is that he can recognise this terrible consequence but has been too weak to avoid it.

Fathoming the Silences

The fate of Angelo—whether he will escape unpunished, or what his ultimate sentence will be when his crimes are revealed—is the overriding issue as the play draws to its conclusion. Throughout Act V (which is one unbroken scene), Angelo will be the primary focus, both of the other characters and of the audience; however, although he never leaves the stage, he speaks surprisingly little. He is apportioned only forty-three of the total of 535 lines during this great trial-scene. These silences make considerable demands on the actor: how should Angelo be portrayed when not speaking?

Angelo's protracted silences are both eloquent and problematical, eloquent because they communicate so suggestively, but problematical when determining precisely *what* is communicated in each context. Shakespeare provides some clues. Twenty-five of Angelo's lines (nearly sixty percent

216

of his total in this final Act) occur in just three speeches: lines 215–23 sound defensive and hesitant, suggesting how Angelo might conduct himself throughout the early part of the scene; lines 232–8 are agitated and irascible, moods that an actor could plausibly maintain until the unhooding of Friar Lodowick; and lines 364–72 are humble and penitent, in keeping with Angelo's few other words between this point and the ending of the play.

At the start of the final scene, the Duke (speaking in propria persona) is careful to encourage his deputy to persevere in that false sense of security that Angelo himself had fabricated in his final soliloquy. The Duke refers to the 'goodness' of Angelo's and Escalus's 'justice', and to 'thanks, / Forerunning more requital' (V, i, 7–8). The word 'requital', however, may be ominous, as it could signify that a severe reckoning, rather than a reward, might follow for Angelo. An audience may also anticipate the Duke's exposure of Angelo's crimes when Vincentio uses highly ambiguous lines apparently in praise of Angelo:

> O, but your desert speaks loud, and I should wrong it
> To lock it in the wards of covert bosom,
> When it deserves with characters of brass
> A forted residence 'gainst the tooth of time
> And razure of oblivion. [V, i, 10–14]

The image 'lock it in the wards' derives from imprisonment (a 'ward' is a cell, as at IV, iii, 62), which introduces the concept of punishment for crime. Additionally, the word 'brass' subliminally draws attention to Angelo's 'brazen' behaviour, both hitherto and in the exchanges immediately following this reference. Finally, the Duke's pledge that Angelo's reputation will transcend time is an equivocation foreshadowing Angelo's ultimate punishment: after public humiliation, his name would be chronicled for perpetuity in association with his offences.

The appearance of Isabella begins Angelo's ultimate test. She identifies him as 'the devil', (V, i, 30), reminding the audience of her infernal imagery in acts III and IV when referring to his offences. Angelo, in cowardly fashion, seeks to discredit Isabella before she has had the opportunity to articulate her accusations against him:

> My lord, her wits I fear me are not firm.
> She hath been a suitor to me for her brother,
> Cut off by course of justice. . . .
> And she will speak most bitterly and strange. [V, i, 35–8]

Using a partial truth in an attempt to validate his testimony, Angelo bears false witness against a woman whom he has abused, entirely in keeping with his earlier treatment of Mariana, whose reputation he attempted to discredit to justify his heartless betrayal of her love (as revealed at III, i, 213–43). Isabella, nevertheless, articulates her accusations against him, all of which Angelo believes to be true, but none of which he is prepared to acknowledge as true before the Duke and the people of Vienna: he is portrayed as 'forsworn', 'a murderer', 'an adulterous thief', '[a]n hypocrite' and 'a virgin-violator' (V, i, 40–3). By denying his guilt when justly accused, Angelo compounds his offences.

Isabella presents a portrait of Angelo as the arch-hypocrite, confirming her earlier words and those of the Duke that the puritanical Deputy is an outrageous 'seemer':

>   'Tis not impossible
> But one, the wicked'st caitiff on the ground,
> May seem as shy, as grave, as just, as absolute,
> As Angelo; even so may Angelo,
> In all his dressings, caracts, titles, forms,
> Be an arch-villain. Believe it, royal Prince,
> If he be less, he's nothing; but he's more,
> Had I more names for badness. [V, i, 55–62]

Shakespeare is subtly echoing Angelo's second and third soliloquies, in which the deputy referred to the importance to him both of his public reputation and of the trappings of office (II, iv, 7–14 and IV, iv, 23–6). Here, Isabella identifies

Angelo's vanity concerning his public image: he wishes to appear to the people as 'shy' (reserved), 'grave', 'just' and 'absolute' (of unqualified virtue), while he takes pride in his 'dressings', 'caracts', 'titles', and 'forms' (the decorations, distinctive marks, ranks, and badges that accompany his pre-eminent position in society). Any viewer or reader who assumes that Angelo is leniently treated at the end of the play should consider the mortifying humiliation that such a man would suffer in being publicly stripped of all these aspects of reputation and office which—as these words imply—he so highly values and with which he so entirely identifies himself.

Angelo is silent from the point at which he attempts to pre-empt Isabella's testimony against him (lines 35–7) until Mariana has completed her account of her sexual encounter with him (line 199); yet the actor playing Angelo must respond frequently to the discussion between the Duke, Isabella, Lucio, Friar Peter, and Mariana. He might brazenly laugh at his accusers, further alienating the sympathy of the audience; but such a reaction would undermine Angelo's 'gravity, / Wherein —let no man hear me—I take pride' (II, iv, 9–10). The text itself implies that Angelo should not appear to ridicule those who testify against him, for the Duke's words, 'Do you not smile at this, Lord Angelo?' (line 165) question why Angelo has not responded with derision. Angelo might remain grim-faced and tense throughout, hinting at the very palpable hits on his character with suppressed grimaces, winces, or other nervous tics.

There are numerous occasions when the actor playing Angelo might subtly react to what is said about him. Isabella condemns 'this pernicious caitiff Deputy' (line 91), deploring his 'concupiscible, intemperate lust' (line 101) and his 'vile conclusion' (line 98) when she 'did yield to him' (line 103), a surrender that has brought her to 'grief and shame' (line 99). Mariana claims, 'I had him in my arms / With all th'effects of love' (lines 197–8), the precise point at which Angelo breaks his long silence. These are among the character-slurs and reminders of guilt to which Angelo might offer some appropriate but surreptitious reaction; but Angelo might also respond when he hears testimony in his support, especially that from the Duke, who wields the ultimate power to punish or exonerate him. The Duke claims that Angelo's 'integrity / Stands without blemish' (lines 110–11) and seems determined not to allow 'a scandalous breath to fall / On him so near us' (lines 125–6). Friar Peter calls Angelo 'this worthy nobleman / So vulgarly and personally accus'd' (lines 161–2). As he hears these testimonies for and against him, discreet physical responses, suggesting how Angelo is fluctuating between anxiety and complacency, might increase the dramatic tension: will he or will he not be obliged to acknowledge his crimes and to atone for his abuses?

One silent reaction definitely required from Angelo is when the Duke invites him to be judge in a trial in which Angelo himself stands accused:

> Give us some seats.—Come, cousin Angelo,
> In this I'll be impartial: be you judge
> Of your own cause. [V, i, 167–9]

This is a development in Duke's test of Angelo: in accepting the judgement-seat, Angelo will sink still deeper into injustice as he will have power to punish those who testify righteously against him. Although Angelo does not offer any immediate verbal response to the Duke's invitation, and although there is no stage-direction to indicate Angelo's reaction, there can be no doubt that he does assume this position of authority (with what alacrity, the actor and director must decide) as he is soon participating in the interrogation of Mariana after his long silence.

Ultimately, Angelo recognises that he must testify in his own defence when Mariana claims that he is now her husband, having consummated their vows 'at [his] garden-house' (line 211):

> My lord, I must confess I know this woman;

And five years since, there was some speech of marriage
Betwixt myself and her; which was broke off,
Partly for that her promised proportions
Came short of composition; but in chief
For that her reputation was disvalu'd
In levity: since which time of five years
I never spake with her, saw her, nor heard from her,
Upon my faith and honour. [V, i, 215–23]

The intrusion of irregular caesurae creates a jerky rhythm
suggesting uncertainty, especially in line 222, where Angelo
swears an oath that is a lie, albeit an inadvertent lie. Although
he may believe much of his testimony to be true, Angelo's
report is tainted for two reasons. First, the audience knows that
Angelo has offended against his own interpretation of Vienna's
statutes against fornication, even though he believed that he
was embracing Isabella when he was actually in Mariana's
arms. Second, the Duke's earlier testimony against Angelo to
Isabella had discredited Angelo's accusation against Mariana's
reputation, accusing Angelo of '*pretending* in her discoveries of
dishonour' (III, i, 226–7; italics added). As Angelo has long
been established as a 'seemer', Angelo's repetition of this self-
justification before the Duke should be recognised by the
audience as a malicious lie. To preserve his own reputation for
'faith and honour', Angelo is prepared to bear false witness
against Mariana's reputation for chastity.

Angelo does not remain long in the subordinate role of
witness in his own defence. After Mariana has repeated her
claim that 'Tuesday night last gone, in's garden house / He
knew me as a wife' (lines 228–9), Angelo turns tyrant.
Recognising the power that the Duke has offered him to try his
own case, Angelo seizes his opportunity:

I did but smile till now:
Now, good my lord, give me the scope of justice.
My patience here is touch'd: I do perceive
These poor informal women are no more
But instruments of some more mightier member

That sets them on. Let me have way, my lord,
To find this practice out. [V, i, 232–8]

The first line might suggest that, during his long silence (lines
39–198), Angelo's face bore the smug grin of a malefactor
secure from accusation; but that would run counter to the
implications of the whole of Act IV scene iv, when Angelo had
seemed close to panic at the prospect of the return of the Duke
and the general invitation to publish petitions seeking for
'redress of injustice' (IV, iv, 8). More plausibly, the line 'I did
but smile till now' is figurative: Angelo is claiming that,
hitherto, he did not feel substantially threatened by the
accusations. Now, his 'patience' is 'touch'd', an admission
suggesting that the panic and confusion that afflicted him when
the Duke's return was announced are now seeking to disguise
themselves in anger. Indeed, in another context, the remainder
of this speech might seem paranoid, as Angelo imagines a
mighty conspiracy against him. He claims that the women are
'informal', that is, mentally deranged (a further attempt to
preserve his own reputation by blackening the reputation of
others), and that their accusations have been orchestrated by
some secret, powerful prime-mover. Of course, the audience is
well aware of the dramatic irony as that prime-mover is
standing before Angelo in the figure of the Duke himself.

Immediately before he withdraws, entrusting the process of
trial and sentencing to Angelo, the Duke clearly suggests
partiality towards Angelo and prejudice against the accusers. In
granting his deputy's request for leave 'to find this practice out'
(line 238), Vincentio bolsters Angelo's complacency. The Duke
condemns Angelo's three accusers as 'these slanderers' (line
258), censuring them individually as the 'foolish friar' and the
'pernicious woman, / Compact with her that's gone' (lines 240–
1, referring to Friar Peter, Mariana, and Isabella respectively).
Furthermore, he publicly confirms Angelo's 'worth and credit, /
That's seal'd in approbation' (lines 243–4). Angelo is being
offered further scope to play the seemer.

Vincentio's withdrawal, however, is an additional ploy by the Duke to encourage Angelo's belief that his position is secure. Such 'security'—that is, complacency, a false sense of security—is represented elsewhere in Shakespeare's works as potentially damnable. In *Macbeth*, the Weird Women's equivocations are explained by Hecate as the means of promoting such self-destructive 'security'.[34] Like Macbeth, Angelo is being tricked by deliberately misleading words into believing that he is invulnerable to retribution and free to commit any atrocity that he chooses.

Angelo has assumed the role of judge and jury in his own trial. His hypocrisy, however, will be counterpoised by the deception practised by the Duke, who appears in the guise of Friar Lodowick to condemn Viennese justice roundly:

> . . . let the devil
> Be sometimes honour'd for his burning throne.
> . . . The Duke's unjust
> Thus to retort your manifest appeal,
> And put your trial in the villain's mouth
> Which here you come to accuse. [V, i, 290–301]

In his last speech before leaving the stage to don his disguise, the Duke had praised Angelo as his 'noble and well-warranted cousin' (line 253). Now, under forty lines later and under the alias of Friar Lodowick, he condemns Angelo as a 'villain', comparing him with 'the devil' seated on 'his burning throne'.[35] Although both Angelo and the Duke are indulging in 'seeming',

---

[34] Hecate's lines (*Macbeth*, III, v, 30–3) suggest how Macbeth's false belief that no retribution will befall him will contribute directly to his damnation.

[35] The Duke's reference to the Devil, echoing the infernal imagery that Isabella had directed against Angelo in Acts III and IV, is an ironic comment on Angelo's name that might otherwise associate him with divine rather than devilish agency. Implicitly, Angelo is to be identified as the *fallen* angel: Lucifer transformed into Satan.

Angelo's objective is to conceal, whereas the Duke's objective is to reveal, Angelo's crimes.

Yet again, Angelo is entirely silent for a considerable period (lines 238–322). Escalus conducts the prosecution of Friar Lodowick, whilst Angelo tacitly presides. The dialogue offers no evidence of any workings of conscience afflicting Angelo during these exchanges. Facial expressions and body-language might plausibly suggest that Angelo gradually strengthens in confidence as his position becomes increasingly secure, with all those who accuse him apparently facing dire punishment.

When Friar Lodowick is threatened by Escalus with a savage racking for his 'slander to th'state' (line 320), Angelo finally intervenes, demanding evidence from Lucio against the friar (lines 322–3). On the basis of Lucio's brief, untrustworthy allegations, Angelo condemns the friar as a 'villain' guilty of 'treasonable abuses' (lines 340–1). Angelo now appears to recognise in Friar Lodowick the 'more mightier member' (line 236) who co-ordinated the evidence presented against him by Isabella, Friar Peter, and Mariana. Angelo shows no qualms about the terrible penalties proposed for these righteous accusers. In seeking to hasten his own vindication, however, Angelo ironically precipitates his own 'unhooding', when he commands Lucio—his fellow bearer of false witness—to lay hands on Friar Lodowick (line 348).

Final Judgement

The Deputy's hubris leads directly to his nemesis: when the friar is unhooded by Lucio to reveal the Duke, Angelo suffers his *peripeteia*, that sudden reversal of fortune frequently encountered in Greek classical tragedy. Angelo is left to suffer in agonised silence, contemplating his doom, while the Duke addresses Lucio, the Provost, and Escalus (lines 354–60). When the Duke ultimately confronts Angelo, his first act is to force his Deputy to abdicate the judgement-seat with the ironically polite, 'Sir, by your leave' (line 361). Much can be made theatrically of Angelo's descent from his position of power, perhaps as slow a process as when the Duke compelled Angelo to accept his commission in the first scene of the play. Authority, at first difficult to assume, ultimately becomes just as difficult to relinquish. Finally, stripped of all rank and privilege, Angelo must endure interrogation by an accuser whose authority, veracity, and apparent omniscience he cannot challenge:

> Hast thou or word, or wit, or impudence,
> That yet can do thee office? If thou hast,
> Rely upon it till my tale be heard,
> And hold no longer out. [V, i, 361–4]

Angelo's collapse (literally, in the case of Corin Redgrave, who played Angelo in the 1994 BBC television-production) is as sudden as it is complete. He capitulates to the Duke:

> O my dread lord,
> I should be guiltier than my guiltiness
> To think I can be undiscernible,
> When I perceive your Grace, like power divine,
> Hath looked upon my passes. [V, i, 364–8]

Having compounded his initial crime with further offences, Angelo at last acknowledges that to persevere in denying his guilt would augment his misdeeds. His comparison between the Duke and 'power divine' might momentarily lead an audience to suspect him of a sycophantic attempt to lessen his likely capital sentence, but the conclusion of his speech refutes any such possibility:

> Then, good prince,
> No longer session hold upon my shame,
> But let my trial be mine own confession.
> Immediate sentence, then, and sequent death
> Is all the grace I beg. [V, i, 368–72]

In a wonderfully ironic piece of theatre, Angelo, who imposed unjust sentence on others when he occupied the judgement-seat, now passes what will prove to be an unjust sentence on himself: he wrongly believes himself to be 'a murderer', 'an adulterous thief', and a 'virgin-violator' (Isabella: V, i, 41–3), three offences any one of which might condemn him to death. His words, nevertheless, suggest an attempt to lessen his suffering: 'immediate sentence' and 'sequent death' will be a 'grace' because his conscience will be assuaged and his public humiliation speedily concluded. His reference to 'grace', however, in echoing the key word in the closing couplet of his final soliloquy (IV, iv, 31–2), may imply that he is seeking to regain that divine grace that he formerly feared lost to him. Angelo's confession is expressed in few words: 'my guiltiness' (line 365) and 'mine own confession' (line 370). This suggests how painful such a man—so proud of his reputation and his high office, and previously so disdainful of the sins of lesser mortals—would find it were his crimes further to be scrutinised before an assembly '[w]here youth, and cost, witless bravery' (the Duke: I, iii, 10) have flocked to celebrate Vincentio's return.

Angelo has, nevertheless, shown in this speech that he is worthy of the Duke's mercy: under the sacrament of penance as understood in Shakespeare's time, contrition, confession, and restitution were the necessary precursors to absolution. Clearly, the tone of Angelo's language indicates that he is contrite (confirmed later when he speaks to Escalus of his 'penitent heart' at V, i, 472–3); he has confessed, however briefly; and he is eager to make restitution, even at the expense of his own life. He therefore does not plead for mercy when the Duke condemns him in the language of inflexible authority that Angelo himself had assumed in his time as Deputy:

'An Angelo for Claudio; death for death. . . .'
We do condemn thee to the very block
Where Claudio stoop'd to death, and with like haste.
[V, i, 407–13]

The restitution exacted from Angelo will, however, prove very different. As the sacrament of marriage assumes pre-

226

eminence on the stage, Angelo is compelled to make amends to the woman whom he abandoned: Mariana. Once Friar Peter has performed the marriage-ceremony between the two offstage, marriage will prove Angelo's salvation. His new wife, Mariana, intercedes for him, and recruits his intended sexual victim, Isabella, to plead for the repeal of the Duke's capital sentence on him. By means of these dramatic interventions, Shakespeare achieves an ironic coup de théâtre: the two women whom Angelo had wronged most profoundly, and whom Angelo so harshly condemned when he was judge in his own case, now pass their merciful judgements on him by pleading to the Duke for his repeal.[36] As elsewhere in this concluding scene, although vengeance may have been expected, it is forgiveness that prevails.[37]

Angelo's last words in the play should be weighed carefully. Judgement has been suspended while the Provost is sent by the Duke on an errand to the prison. Angelo takes the opportunity to reiterate his remorse while expressing his eagerness to make reparation for his crime:

> I am sorry that such sorrow I procure,
> And so deep sticks it in my penitent heart
> That I crave death more willingly than mercy;
> 'Tis my deserving, and I do entreat it. [V, i, 472–5]

His pride is clearly broken, while his perspicuity and deference for justice (loss of which he lamented in his second and third soliloquies) have returned. He recognises execution as his 'deserving', for which he petitions the court. This will end the

---

[36] In Peter Brook's 1951 production, John Gielgud's Angelo uttered an inarticulate sob (of incredulity? of remorse? of gratitude?) during Isabella's intercession on his behalf at lines 442 ff. This intensely dramatic cry is recorded by Richard David in 'Measure for Measure on the Modern Stage', SS 4 (1951), reprinted by Stead, p. 70.
[37] The context is comparable with the concluding scene of The Tempest, when Prospero determines that 'the rarer action is / In virtue than in vengeance' (V, I, 27–8).

suffering caused by remorse which inflicts such 'deep' wounds. In the course of this speech, he completes the prerequisites for absolution demanded by the sacrament of penance: his contrition is shown by his reference to his 'penitent heart', he confesses to having 'procure[d] sorrow' for others by his misdeeds, and finally he has made restitution to Mariana by marring her.

Although the rest is silence (for he speaks no more), Angelo still responds in gesture and mien to words and events as the play concludes. For example, at the moment when Claudio is 'unmuffled', a revelation that should lift a great burden from Angelo's conscience, he registers his relief in his facial expression:

> By this Lord Angelo perceives he's safe;
> Methinks I see a quickening in his eye. [V, i, 492–3]

Angelo is 'safe' because he at last recognises that both the principal crimes of which he previously believed himself guilty—the violation of Isabella, and the murder of her brother—were illusory. The Duke's immediately following words also demand an appropriate reaction:

> Well, Angelo, your evil quits you well.
> Look that you love your wife: her worth, worth yours.
>   [V, i, 494–5]

Like Bertram in the final scene of *All's Well that Ends Well*, Angelo is compelled by supreme authority to accept as his wife the woman whom he had previously so wilfully rejected. Although there is no verbal response and no stage-direction to provide clear evidence, Angelo could scarcely be grudging, for the Duke is offering him the opportunity to atone for the sins that had so disgusted Angelo in himself and that had robbed him of his sense of identity, as revealed in his soliloquies.[38] In

---

[38] Nevertheless, in the RSC's 2003 production, directed by Sean Holmes, Angelo appeared a reluctant participant in his own nuptials,

being thwarted of his wicked designs, he has fared 'well' despite his 'evil', and has now been given the chance to re-establish his 'worth' with a partner of surpassing 'worth'. This, then, is an occasion when silence, 'the perfectest herald of joy',[39] may reasonably be assumed to indicate consent: Angelo might respond with suitable gestures of affection and gratitude to the Duke's injunction to love Mariana. The final speech of the play reinforces such an interpretation, when the Duke invites Angelo to embrace virtue in the form of his newly-wedded wife:

> Joy to you, Mariana; love her, Angelo:
> I have confess'd her, and I know her virtue. [V, i, 523–4]

In addition, the Duke invites Angelo to show forgiveness to the Provost, who used deception to save Claudio from the unjust execution that Angelo had commanded (lines 529–31). These words involve a further test of Angelo's reformation, as he is encouraged to forgive another as he hopes himself for forgiveness.[40] Angelo should acknowledge his debt to the Provost with a suitable gesture to confirm reconciliation. It would be plausible for a regenerate Angelo to show unalloyed gratitude to all those instrumental in securing his amnesty.

How, though, should an audience respond to Angelo's reprieve? Is it appropriate to conclude, with Samuel Taylor

---

avoiding physical contact and even eye-contact with Mariana. This stage-business is recorded by Rachod Nusen in 'English Productions of Measure for Measure on Stage and Screen: The Play's Indeterminacy and the Authority of Performance' (PhD thesis), Lancaster University, 6 May 2016, p. 309, https://eprints.lancs.ac.uk/id/eprint/79345/1/2016rachodphd.pdf.

[39] These are the words of another Claudio, the rash young lover in *Much Ado About Nothing*, II, i, 275.

[40] The words of St. Matthew's Gospel suggest this interpretation: 'For, if ye do forgive men their trespasses, your heavenly Father will also forgive you' (Matthew 6: 14). Cf. The Lord's Prayer: 'And forgive us our trespasses / As we forgive those who trespass against us' (lines 7–8).

Coleridge (*Table Talk*: June 1827), that 'our feelings of justice are grossly wounded in Angelo's escape'?[41] A dispassionate consideration of the play challenges such a claim. Angelo has not escaped. He has lost his self-esteem, all authority in the state, and his reputation. He has been exposed to public humiliation, becoming a paradigm for corrupt government. This is the man who, according to the Duke, was 'precise' and stood 'at a guard with envy', scarcely confessing to his bodily appetites (I, iii, 50–3), a man who presented himself as superior to the rest of humanity. That image is now thoroughly defaced. Angelo himself, in his second soliloquy, was dismayed to recognise the loss of his piety, the collapse of his professional dedication, and the empty vanity of his austere demeanour (II, iv, 4–12). Now that these failures are common knowledge, he must endure shame and notoriety. For such a proud man, 'immediate sentence' and 'sequent death' might well be a 'grace' (V, i, 371–2), as execution would release him from the ordeal of mortification through prolonged humiliation. By contrast, his reprieve would not offer him the 'escape' that Coleridge alleged, but rather the painful and enduring punishment of universal opprobrium.

The Duke, however, has given Angelo the opportunity to recover the divine grace that the Deputy (in his final soliloquy at IV, iv, 31–2) feared he had lost. In saving Claudio from execution, the Duke has prevented Angelo from committing the crime of tyrannical murder. In substituting Mariana for Isabella, the Duke has ensured that Angelo has not committed rape or broken his marriage-oath *per verba de futuri*. In stripping Angelo of authority, the Duke has removed the corruptive influence of absolute power from a man who was overwhelmed

---

[41] Those who have expressed disapproval at Angelo's 'escape' from punishment include Charlotte Lennox in 1753 (Braunmuller and Watson, p. 143), Samuel Johnson in 1765 (*Dr. Johnson on Shakespeare*, ed. W. K. Wimsatt [Harmondsworth: Penguin, 1969], p. 105), Elizabeth Griffiths in 1775 (Braunmuller and Watson, p. 143), and Algernon Charles Swinburne in 1880 (Geckle, pp. 194–5).

by it. In marrying Angelo to Mariana, the Duke has given his former deputy a faithful and virtuous wife, a domestic consolation for his loss of public office. In encouraging Angelo to forgive the Provost for disobeying and deceiving him, the Duke has offered Angelo the chance to earn divine forgiveness, 'For with what judgment ye judge, ye shall be judged, and with what measure ye mete, it shall be measured unto you again' (Matthew 7: 2). In short, the Duke is presented as Angelo's saviour: 'like power divine' (line 367) he has rescued a sinner sinking ever deeper into the mire of crime by offering him redemption through the twin sacraments of penance and marriage.

With divine judgement impending—like Everyman, Mankind, or Youth, protagonists in three of the most prominent morality plays—Angelo is presented with the opportunity to step back from the infernal brink and to pursue a more virtuous path. The evidence strongly suggests that Angelo's final act in the play should be willingly to join the Duke's procession, hand in hand with Mariana, looking gratefully and lovingly on her as the instrument of his salvation. The tableau might imply that Angelo willingly embarks on marriage as a pilgrimage that will cleanse him spiritually. Reunification and reconciliation, as in the final scene of so many of Shakespeare's plays, have led to the restoration of happiness.

What, then, should be our final judgement of Angelo? He is initially presented as a man striving to transcend all human imperfections. Once he is guilty of a major lapse, however, he plummets from grace, losing his sense of identity and, with it, all moral restraint, as he descends further and further into iniquity. There is, however, a paradox here. Although he might have remained a morally superior being had he never been tempted and fallen, his early appearance as a cold, supercilious character made him less dramatically interesting and certainly less likable to an audience. Angelo's faults humanise him, and the agony of conscience revealed in his soliloquies makes him more worthy of sympathetic understanding. After the first scene, Angelo's frigid virtues provoke few warm compliments

231

but a plethora of icy criticisms: from Claudio, the Duke, Lucio, Isabella, Escalus, the anonymous Justice, and the Provost. Such comments ensure that the puritanical Angelo, once established as deputy in the Duke's absence, is too remote and aloof to engage the audience's sympathy. By contrast, both the soul-searcher of the soliloquies and the penitent sinner of the conclusion are recognisably fallible, which encourages an audience to engage empathetically with Angelo. He epitomises the human condition: the aspiration towards virtue counterbalanced by the temptation towards vice. His immoderate behaviour illustrates the truth of Voltaire's maxim that neither abstinence nor excess ever procures human happiness.[42] With his salvation secured just as dire retribution seems imminent, he embodies the hopes of Shakespeare's Christian audience for ultimate redemption from sin. For a modern audience, all too familiar with stories of the corruptive influence of power and sexual desire (especially when the two are combined), he is an object lesson in the terrible personal cost of yielding to temptation.

---

[42] 'Cinquième discours: sur la nature de plaisir' in *Sept discours en vers sur l'homme* (1738).

232

Chapter 4

Isabella

No role in *Measure for Measure*—perhaps no role in the whole of Shakespeare's dramatic works—has provoked more extreme and conflicting critical judgements than Isabella's. What are we to make of her? Persecuted saint? Prudish virago? Shameless hypocrite, as morally compromised as Angelo, her tormentor? Such extreme judgements often reveal more about the era in which they were written—or about those who expressed them—than they do about the Isabella revealed by careful consideration of *Measure for Measure* in its entirety. Although mutually contradictory interpretations that either idealise or demonise Isabella may apparently be validated by close examination of a specific context (or a limited range of contexts) in the play, we should be wary of such approaches. They tend to disregard evidence to the contrary elsewhere in the text by treating Isabella as a 'static' character, rather than as one developing organically under the influence of internal and external forces in traumatising conflict.

Although Lucio's address to Isabella on their first meeting— 'I hold you as a thing enskied and sainted / . . . an immortal spirit' (I, iv, 34–5)—seems at least hyperbolical or even sarcastic in tone, it is surprising how many critics have venerated Isabella in similar terms.[1] This tendency was especially prevalent when polite society was generally disgusted by illicit sexual activity, and women were idealised as pure, pious, and (perhaps) prim. For example, in the first half of the Nineteenth Century, Isabella was variously described as 'a

---

[1] Even the most recent editors, Braunmuller and Watson, suggest that 'Isabella is a model of female virtue under Catholicism . . .' (p. 32).

very angel of light' (August Wilhelm von Schlegel: 1809–11), 'a ministering spirit from the throne of grace' (Nathan Drake: 1817), a character of 'a saintly grace, something of vestal dignity and purity' (Anna Brownell Jameson: 1832), and 'as nearly approaching perfection as is consistent with possible reality' (J. D. Halliwell: 1850); while Edward Dowden, writing in 1875, clearly saw Isabella as the embodiment of Victorian values when he referred to 'this pure zeal, this rectitude of will, this virgin sanctity'.[2] Even in the Twentieth Century, some critics retained this notion of Isabella as one of Shakespeare's 'ideal women' (for example, E. C. Morris in 1940). There were, however, dissenting voices: In 1753, Charlotte Lennox branded Isabella as 'a mere Vixen in her Virtue';[3] William Hazlitt (1817) questioned Isabella's 'rigid chastity'; various commentators in the 1850s 'deemed her piety cold, pitiless, excessive, self-regarding, unnatural, unattractive and/or unfeminine';[4] while Arthur Quiller-Couch (1922) went so far as to call her chastity 'rancid', accusing Isabella of becoming 'a bare procuress' in the second half of the play. The notion of Isabella as a changing character has had its advocates, although initially there may have been a tendency to regard this transformation as an inconsistency on Shakespeare's part rather than as an evolution in Isabella's presentation: thus, J. S. P. Tatlock (1916) agreed with Lucio's initial assessment that she was 'a thing enskied and sainted'—that is, a saintly and ethereal being—before her descent into 'a dubious intrigue' in the latter half of the play.

Is Isabella, then—like the Duke—a dramatic device, inconsistently portrayed? The Isabella who speaks her concluding lines of forgiveness and reconciliation in Act V may appear a much more humane and amiable character than the prudish, ascetic novice encountered during the first two Acts,

---

[2] Many of the critical attitudes to Isabella cited in this paragraph derive from Geckle, *passim*, especially pp. xviii–xxi and 169.
[3] Braunmuller and Watson, p. 73, quoting from Lennox's *Shakespear Illustrated*, p. 32.
[4] Braunmuller and Watson, p. 73, citing Geckle, pp. 128–33.

and entirely alien from the ferocious sister who condemns Claudio to an agonising death early in Act III. Yet all these conflicting characteristics might coexist convincingly in a single protagonist if they were recognised as the products of specific circumstances at specific times affecting a developing character. Perhaps Isabella is not a casualty of inconsistent characterisation on the part of Shakespeare, but rather an evolving portrayal of a woman responding to, and learning from, her changing circumstances.

Religion, Chastity, and Authority

The Isabella whom we encounter at the beginning of the play is a novice seeking admission to 'the votarists of Saint Clare' (I, iv, 5), the most stringent of the Christian female religious orders.[5] Yet even their rule is insufficient to satisfy Isabella, who desires sterner regulations, 'a more strict restraint' (I, iv, 4) upon her. From the outset, she is presented by Shakespeare as a woman yearning for a system that ensures order and obedience by exerting complete authority over the individual.

Even before Isabella's earliest appearance in the play, Shakespeare had been careful to supply clues as to why a virtuous young Viennese woman might seek to be encompassed by such severe regulations. In the second scene of *Measure for Measure*, the conversation of Lucio and his two associates, saturated in references to violence, crime, irreligion, and sexually transmitted diseases, immediately preceded a dialogue between a brothel-keeper and her pimp about the dire consequences of sexual indulgence. This exchange merged into a tableau of the public humiliation of a betrothed couple, whose sexual licence brought disaster upon them. In the very next scene, the Duke characterised Vienna as a society in which

---

[5] Their thirteenth-century founder, St. Clare, had resisted the more lenient Ugolino Rule, promoting the original and more restrictive protocols that were retained by the 'Poor Clares'.

. . . Liberty plucks Justice by the nose,
The baby beats the nurse, and quite athwart
Goes all decorum. [I, iii, 29–31]

Clearly, criminal (especially sexual) misconduct is rife in this city. A virtuous young woman, conscious of her vulnerability in such depraved times, might well seek refuge in a convent as a place of safety. The stricter the restraint, the greater the security.

Isabella's early request for a closely-regulated life in an ascetic community is a vital clue as to why she might be expected to react in the ways that she does later in the play. For example, her opening words to Angelo express her abhorrence of fornication. Later, in a harrowing confrontation in the prison, she cruelly condemns her brother for begging her to save his life by yielding her virginity to the Deputy. Isabella, threatened by the licentiousness that is so rife in Vienna, is presented as fearful of sexual indulgence: she is seeking to sequester herself from the deed, its participants, and its consequences.

Catholicism is a patriarchal religion (despite its reverence for the Virgin Mary). The Vienna of *Measure for Measure* is a patriarchal society. Outside the nunnery (or the brothel), power resides entirely in the hands of men, while women are subordinate. For this reason, despite her 'prosperous art / When she will play with reason and discourse' (as attested by Claudio at I, ii, 174–75), Isabella characteristically defers to male authority. If the directive threatens her chastity, she will resist, as her virginity is pledged to that transcendent male authority-figure, Christ; otherwise, if an assertive man assumes responsibility for the decision, she will quell her moral objections or even compromise her integrity. Especially in the latter half of the play, she sets aside her own principles and allows herself to be persuaded by male authority to a course of action that an audience might otherwise expect her to find morally abhorrent.

From her first appearance in the play, Isabella's respect for authority is manifest. Her desire for stringent regulation, and her tacit welcome of the power and influence of the Prioress over the lives of the nuns, are conveyed by her exchanges with Sister Francisca. More subtly revealed in that same scene is her tendency to accept the authority of males. Even though he is an embodiment of those same corruptive influences in society from which she is retreating, Isabella responds obediently to the many imperatives of Lucio:

Do not believe it. [I, iv, 38]

Assay the power you have. [I, iv, 76]

Go to Lord Angelo,
And let him learn to know, when maidens sue,
Men give like gods. . . . [I, iv, 79–81]

But speedily. [I, iv, 84]

Ultimately, she obeys each of Lucio's commands.

When first appearing before Angelo in Act II, scene ii, she is propelled in contrary directions by the Deputy and by her companion, Lucio. When Angelo rejects her initial plea to save the life of Claudio [II, ii, 37–41], she immediately capitulates to male authority and seeks to withdraw:

O just but severe law!
I had a brother, then: heaven keep your honour.
[II, ii, 41–2]

She is, however, forcibly redirected by the multiple imperatives of Lucio:

Give't not o'er so.—To him again, entreat him,
Kneel down before him, hang upon his gown. . . .
To him, I say. [II, ii, 43–7]

With the support of such frequent brief encouragements from Lucio, a male (however dissolute) taking command of the situation, she confidently challenges that embodiment of patriarchal power, Angelo.

When Lucio is absent on her return to Angelo's presence-chamber in Act II scene iv, however, she immediately accepts the Deputy's sentence on her brother without the slightest demurral, even though Angelo's words the previous day had left her in hope of a reprieve:

> *Ang.* Your brother cannot live.
> *Isab.* Even so. Heaven keep your honour. [II, iv, 33–4]

There is no obvious dismay expressed at the confirmation of her brother's fate, no exclamation of disappointed expectation, no recriminations against the judge, but only passive acquiescence. Her resilience and resistance against Angelo will reappear only when her chastity is threatened later in the scene.

Whence comes this tendency to capitulate to male authority? As a Roman Catholic in seventeenth-century Europe, Isabella would recognize the subordination of women to men as exemplified in the all-male priesthood and in the Genesis-story, which attributes the origin of sin to a woman succumbing to temptation. As a nun, Isabella would accept the authority of the male clergy over women in holy orders, as we shall see in her encounters with Friar Lodowick (the Duke's alias).[6] Isabella's misgivings about female frailty are made manifest by her extraordinary diatribe against women in response to the briefest of prompts by Angelo (II, iv, 123–9). This condemnation of all women, uttered by a woman, suggests how the prevalence of religious misogyny might corrupt a devotee's perceptions.

---

[6] Isabella is a postulant to the Poor Clares, founded as the sister order to the Franciscans. As the Duke poses specifically as a Franciscan friar (at III, ii, 39, Elbow identifies Lodowick as a Cordelier—a Franciscan—by the cord around Lodowick's waist), a Clarisse would be obliged to defer to his spiritual authority.

Isabella admits of no redeeming features in women: they are all weak, fallen creatures, particularly susceptible to sexual temptation and exploitation. This notion offers to an audience a plausible explanation of Isabella's reasons both for joining the Poor Clares and for accepting the authority of men: she is presented as fearful that her inherent weakness as a woman might cause her downfall. Entry into a convent might thus enable her to fulfil the wish expressed in the Lord's Prayer: '. . . lead us not into temptation, but deliver us from evil' (Matthew 6: 13). However, her wish to avoid such temptation and to distance herself from a decadent society is no proof of her vocation as a nun. What textual evidence there is might imply that her motive for joining the Poor Clares is her desire to find a refuge where her chastity will be protected by rigorous safeguards, rather than any desire to devote her life to the contemplation and worship of God.

How might audiences have responded to Isabella's preoccupation with her chastity? It would be unwise to assume that Shakespeare and his contemporaries would have been entirely sympathetic to Isabella's position, despite Catholic veneration of Mary's virginity and Biblical condemnations of fornication.[7] In the Sixteenth Century, William Tyndale, Protestant martyr and translator of the Bible into English, offered evidence that chastity could be a sin rather than a virtue, depending on motive. He condemned the self-destructive chastity of Lucrece, the noble wife of Roman legend,[8] asserting that 'She sought her owne glory in her chastite and not gods . . .which pryde god more abhorreth then the whoredome of anye whor.'[9] As Lucrece and Isabella are both victims of a tyrant's

---

[7] Such prohibitions are particularly prominent in the Pauline Epistles: for example, 'Flee fornication' (1 Corinthians 6: 18); '. . . abstain from fornication' (1 Thessalonians 4: 3); 'Flee also from the lusts of youth' (2 Timothy 2: 22).

[8] Shakespeare had addressed the issue of Lucrece's chastity in his long poem, *The Rape of Lucrece*, published in 1594, ten years before the first recorded performance of *Measure for Measure*.

[9] *The Obedyence of a Chrysten Man* (1561 edition), fol. 39r., quoted by Lever, pp. lxxx–lxxxi.

rapacious intent, Tyndale's words invite our scrutiny of Isabella's motivation. If proud chastity, destructive of life, is regarded as worse than a prostitute's promiscuity, the moral status of Isabella might be deemed lower than that of the whores of Mistress Overdone's 'house of resort'.[10]

There are further reasons to suspect that many in Shakespeare's audience might have been no more sympathetic to Isabella's desperate preoccupation with her virginity than a modern audience is likely to be. In 1604, the date of the first recorded performance of *Measure for Measure*, orders of chaste nuns had long been absent from England. Only those well over sixty-five years of age in Shakespeare's audience might have remembered a foundation of Poor Clares in London, since Henry VIII had closed the Abbey of the Order of St. Clare in Aldgate in 1539, dismissing all the Minoresses. With the accession of Edward VI on his father's death (1547), expectation of celibacy in the clergy sharply declined, and with it, veneration of religious chastity. After the resurgence of Catholicism under Queen Mary (1553–58) was superseded by the establishment of the Church of England (from 1559) under Elizabeth I, any overt devotion to the Virgin Mary was discouraged and her place in the rituals of the Church deliberately diminished. In addition, Queen Elizabeth's refusal to compromise on the matter of her own virginity, despite the frequent petitions of Parliament for her to marry and bear heirs, led to dangerous political instability during her lifetime and, with her death in 1603, the end of the Tudor dynasty founded by her grandfather.

In 1602–4, three years that encompassed the death of England's 'Virgin Queen' (and the accession of a new king, James I, who had already begotten male heirs to secure the succession), female chastity was a major concern of

---

[10] Shakespeare himself had written of 'self-loving nuns' in his 1593 poem, *Venus and Adonis* (line 752); although, in such a context, praise of what the previous line calls 'fruitless chastity' was scarcely to be expected.

240

Shakespeare's so-called 'problem plays', *Troilus and Cressida, All's Well that Ends Well*,[11] and *Measure for Measure*, with the sexual promiscuity of Cressida set against the chaste virtue of Helena, Diana, and Isabella. Significantly, Helena and Parolles conduct an extended discussion of female chastity in *All's Well* (I, i, 104–53). Helena, using the image of a male siege of female virginity, asks for advice from the soldier, Parolles, on how a woman may 'barricado' herself and show 'some warlike resistance' to men. The exchange between Helena and Parolles foreshadows Act II scene iv of *Measure for Measure*, when Angelo begins his assault on Isabella's virtue. Parolles initially dismisses female virginity as 'too cold a companion' and 'a desperate offendress against nature', subsequently condemning it as 'peevish, proud, idle, made of self-love, which is the most inhibited sin in the canon'. Although Parolles is confirmed as a braggart, a liar, and a coward in the course of the play, his opinion here—a strong condemnation of virginity—is not necessarily discredited by his subsequent disgrace. Shakespeare puts some of his most plausible arguments into the mouths of rogues and fools, for example Falstaff on the illusion of honour in *Henry IV* Part 1 (V, i, 127–40), Polonius on precepts for youth in *Hamlet* (I, iii, 58–80), Edmund on the 'excellent foppery' of astrology in *King Lear* (I, ii, 113–27), or Iago on the vicissitudes of reputation in *Othello* (II, iii, 258–263 and III, iii, 159–65). Shakespeare avoids dogmatism and creates dramatic tension by playing off the dubious status of the speaker against the apparent validity of what is spoken. Moreover, at the time of her exchanges with Parolles in *All's Well*, the virtuous Helena is already secretly in love with Bertram and therefore anticipating the loss of her own virginity in marriage. Shakespeare's presentation of compelling arguments against the jealous defence of female virginity in the

---

[11] The date of *All's Well that Ends Well* is much disputed, but 1603–04 seems the most likely hypothesis: Internet Shakespeare Editions, Textual Introduction, 'Dating *All's Well*', 11 January 2019, http://internetshakespeare.uvic.ca/doc/AWW_TextIntro/complete/, reaches this conclusion after weighing a wide range of scholarly evidence.

Parolles/Helena exchanges should temper any praise for Isabella's preoccupation with her chastity in *Measure for Measure*.[12]

Even John Milton, a committed Puritan who condemned illicit sexual indulgence in a work celebrating virginity, recognised the limitations of chastity. Thirty years after the first recorded performance of *Measure for Measure*, he presented his Masque (*Comus*) at Ludlow Castle, in which two brothers converse about their innocent sister, lost in the woods:

> . . . she has a hidden strength. . . .
> 'Tis chastity, my brother, chastity:
> She that has that, is clad in complete steel. . . .
> . . . through the sacred rays of chastity,
> No savage fierce, bandit or mountaineer
> Will dare to soil her virgin purity. . . .
> She may pass on with unblenched majesty,
> *Be it not done in pride, or in presumption.*
>
> [lines 414–30; italics added]

The concession made in that final line is vitally important. Although chastity, the sister's best defence from harm, is a pious virtue, it could be discredited by unworthy motivation. The question in *Measure for Measure*, then, is whether 'pride' and 'presumption'—those very qualities that undermine the power of chastity, according to Milton—are identifiable in Isabella's defence of her virginity. In short, Isabella's chastity might be morally admirable; but, equally, it might be morally deplorable. Closer scrutiny of her role is needed if we are to arbitrate.

---

[12] Additionally, Braunmuller and Watson (pp. 122–3) detect a tendency in Shakespeare's plays for women to renounce the chaste spiritual life for marriage. They cite the Abbess in the *Comedy of Errors* and Thaisa in *Pericles*, while offering further reference to *A Midsummer Night's Dream* and *Two Noble Kinsmen*.

A More Strict Restraint

Before her first appearance on stage, Isabella is introduced to the audience through the words of her brother, Claudio:

> This day my sister should the cloister enter,
> And there receive her approbation.
> Acquaint her with the danger of my state:
> Implore her, in my voice, that she make friends
> To the strict deputy: bid herself assay him.
> I have great hope in that. For in her youth
> There is a prone and speechless dialect
> Such as move men; beside, she hath prosperous art
> When she will play with reason and discourse,
> And well can she persuade. [I, ii, 167–76]

As she is a postulant gifted with persuasive speech, comportment, and appearance, Claudio has 'great hope' (line 172) that she might save his life were she to 'assay' (line 171) the Deputy. He identifies her 'speechless dialect' (line 173) and her 'prosperous art' (line 176) in deploying 'reason and discourse'. Clearly, Claudio admires Isabella's intellectual and rhetorical talents but, in describing them, he unconsciously prefigures the desire that she will provoke when she will 'make friends' (line 170) with Angelo, 'assay him' (line 172), be submissively 'prone' (line 173), 'move' him (line 174), and 'play'—intellectually—with him (line 175).[13] Ironically, his praise of his sister, 'well can she persuade' (line 176), foreshadows the major crisis in the play when Angelo is persuaded by Isabella's behaviour and words to propose the exchange of her virginity for her brother's life. Claudio

---

[13] The case for considering Claudio's words as proleptic irony (rather than as a conscious decision on his part to employ his sister as sexual bait) is presented at greater length in Chapter 5, 'Introducing Claudio', p. 307n. Braunmuller and Watson, however, suggest that 'Everyone seems to have a sense of her sexual power, except maybe Isabella herself— and perhaps she does, too. That would be one way to explain her determination to lock herself into a convent . . .' (p. 78).

inadvertently hints at how Isabella's virtues and talents are potentially a sexual provocation to a susceptible male.

Much, then, has been made of Isabella's persuasive ability before her first appearance in the play, but nothing yet has yet been said of her rigorous asceticism. Her first words, an enquiry about the privileges available to the Poor Clares, are therefore teasingly misleading:

And have you nuns no farther privileges? [I, iv, 1]

Like Sister Francisca, to whom Isabella is speaking, an audience might suppose Isabella's query to be an implicit request for greater liberty for herself in the convent. Such an expectation, however, is immediately refuted by Isabella's continuation:

. . . I speak not as desiring more [privileges],
But rather wishing a more strict restraint
Upon the sisterhood, the votarists of Saint Clare.[14]
[I, iv, 3–5]

Even the most stringent rule of all the female religious orders is insufficient to satisfy her asceticism, which will find obvious parallels in Angelo's puritanical austerity. Isabella makes no mention of God; nor does she enquire about devotional practices. It may be dangerous to argue from such negative evidence, but the absence here of references to the divine may raise the question of whether Isabella's religious vocation is

---

[14] Shakespeare's Isabella bears comparison with Sainte Isabelle (1225–70), who similarly devoted her life and chastity to God. Sainte Isabelle, younger sister of Saint Louis, King of France, refused to fulfil her marriage contract with a German aristocrat, and resisted pressure from the Pope to marry the son of the Emperor. She founded a Franciscan order of nuns in France but, rather than 'wishing a more strict restraint' like Shakespeare's Isabella, she greatly liberalized the rule of the Clarisses, leading to scandals. [Braunmuller and Watson, p. 68, supplemented by Wikipedia, accessed 12 June 2020, https://en.wikipedia.org/wiki/Isabelle_of_France_(saint)]

well-founded or merely a pretext in her quest to find refuge from a salacious society.[15]

Sister Francesca can reassure Isabella that the Poor Clares are protected from sexual temptation and exploitation:

> When you have vow'd, you must not speak with men
> But in the presence of the prioress;
> Then, if you speak, you must not show your face;
> Or if you show your face, you must not speak.
>
> [I, iv, 10–13]

The promise of an authority-figure (the Prioress) to chaperone her, and Francisca's delineation of the strict rules which will defend the nuns' modesty from potentially predatory males, enable Isabella tacitly to welcome the protection of the religious order. Isabella's silence, in this context relating to a solemn vow, suggests acquiescence: in legalese, *qui tacet consentit*; the person who remains silent consents.

Immediately, Isabella is confronted by a prime representative of the depraved society from which she is striving to protect herself: louche Lucio. His first words to her are a dirty insinuation, and perhaps even a coarse parody of the Annunciation: 'Hail virgin, if you be' (I, iv, 16). Lucio's popular opinion equates a nunnery with the sexual licence of a brothel, as do Hamlet's words in his 'Get thee to a nunnery!' tirade against Ophelia (*Hamlet*: III, i, 121–40). The news that Lucio brings, however, thwarts all of Isabella's attempts to distance herself from the repercussions of sexual activity in licentious Viennese society: her brother, Claudio, 'hath got his

---

[15] Isabella's first appearance in the nunnery immediately follows the Duke's ominous couplet, 'Hence shall we see . . . / . . . what our seemers be' (I, iii, 53–4). Might this line subliminally propose to an audience that the next person to appear or speak should be suspected of 'seeming', that is, of being a hypocrite? If so, then Isabella's integrity will be in question from this moment onwards.

friend with child' (I, iv, 29). The lapse of a close member of her family will make it impossible for Isabella to achieve her objective of finding, among the Poor Clares, immediate refuge from carnal incursions.

Isabella's first reaction, not surprisingly, is defensive incredulity: 'Sir, make me not your story' (I, iv, 30). Apparently, she is seeking to persuade herself that sexual matters—specifically scandal involving her own family—could not so soon have invaded her place of safety. In keeping with her ostensible vocation, she proposes the sacrament of marriage as her remedy for the problem (prefiguring the Duke's ultimate solution for the vices of Vienna in the final scene of the play), only to learn from Lucio that Claudio is already condemned to death by Angelo, 'To make him an example' (I, iv, 68). Her only course, according to Lucio, is to plead for her brother's life to the Deputy. Like Angelo in the very first scene of the play, Isabella twice declines her commission (I, iv, 75–6 and 77) before relenting at the third request (I, iv, 84). Shakespeare is encouraging his audience to recognise the close affinities not only between the unwelcomed commissions thrust upon Angelo and Isabella, but also between their stringent codes of morality. Like Angelo, Isabella is to be put to a severe test by the responsibility imposed upon her.

You Are Too Cold

Once she is before the Deputy, after two lines of formal address, Isabella begins her petition. Her words clearly reveal her priorities. There is no mention of her brother or of his death-sentence, her ostensible reason for appearing before Angelo. Rather, she focuses on her preoccupation with sexual vice, her words confirming the horror with which she regards illicit sexual activity—and perhaps, by extension, any sexual activity:

> There is a vice that most I do abhor,
> And most desire should meet the blow of justice;
> For which I would not plead, but that I must;

For which I must not plead, but that I am
At war 'twixt will and will not.[16] . [II, ii, 29–33]

Astonishingly, although she has been summoned to plead for
Claudio's life, her words to the Deputy, Angelo, fully endorse
the death sentence imposed on her brother. She and Angelo are
entirely in agreement about the need to extirpate illicit sexual
activity by means of harsh punishment. Momentarily, her
brother is forgotten, because of her preoccupation with that
aspect of Viennese society that most threatens her. These five
lines condemn the fault in the most forceful, passionate, and
anguished terms, emphasised by the rhetorical pattern of
superlatives, imperatives, and expressions of contradictory
desire: '. . . most . . . most . . . must . . . must . . . will . . . will
not . . .'

The verb 'abhor' is given particular emphasis here: the
consecutive weak stresses of the pyrrhic foot that precedes it—
'I do'—throws extra weight on to this word as the final foot of
the opening line. 'Abhor' will be echoed by her later in the
play, always with reference to human sexual activity.
Etymologically, its meaning of 'shudder away from' suggests
the fear, as well as the loathing, with which Isabella may
contemplate any sexual conduct. In her only soliloquy in the
play, she will speak of 'such *abhorr'd* pollution' (II, iv, 182)
when contemplating Angelo's proposition, which she will
subsequently convey to Claudio as a deed that 'I *abhor* to
name' (III, i, 101). In these two later instances and here, in her
opening address to Angelo, the word is part of a periphrastic
formula necessary to avoid specific reference to human sexual

---

[16] Braunmuller and Watson (p. 76; citing Anna Kamaralli, 'Writing
about motive: Isabella, the Duke and moral authority', *SS* 58 [2005],
48-59) note that the critic, Ann Barton, believed that 'Isabella's purity
conceals an hysterical fear of sex.' This opinion influenced the RSC's
epoch-making production in 1970 (directed by Ann's husband, John
Barton), when Estelle Kohler's Isabella caused a critical sensation by
rejecting the Duke's two proposals of marriage in Act V.

intercourse. On each occasion, 'abhor' conveys the strength of her disgust in phrasing that avoids specifying precisely what it is that disgusts her. Both her female delicacy and her assumed religious vocation might encourage such prevarication.

Isabella requires a prompt from Angelo before she can fully explain the purpose of her petition:

> I have a brother is condemn'd to die;
> I do beseech you, let it be his fault,
> And not my brother. [II, ii, 33–5]

After the passion of her initial outburst against abhorred vice, these three lines, pleading for the condemnation of the offence rather than of the brother who committed the offence, seem surprisingly brief, lacking in rhetorical force, and unconvincing. Lucio's assessment of these opening words from Isabella to Angelo is highly significant and emphasised by repetition: in seeking a pardon for Claudio,

> You are too cold. [II, ii, 45 *and* II, ii, 56]

Lucio's phraseology and reiteration invite a further comparison between Isabella and Angelo. According to Lucio, Angelo is also too cold: his 'blood / Is very snow-broth' (I, iv, 57–8) and 'when he makes water, his urine is congealed ice' (III, ii, 106–7). In this play, as elsewhere in Shakespeare's works, images of heat are associated with fervour and sexual desire, but images of cold are associated not merely with chastity but also with sterility, austerity, frigidity, and the denial of human compassion. Isabella's 'cold' moral nature inhibits her plea for her brother's life.

Well Can She Persuade

Following Lucio's checks, Isabella gradually 'warms' to her task of pleading, but her words are not so much proof of her devotion to her brother as evidence of the extent to which she relishes the challenge of intellectual argument. Take, for example, her poetical discourse on mercy:

> No ceremony that to great ones longs,
> Not the king's crown, nor the deputed sword,
> The marshal's truncheon, nor the judge's robe,
> Become them with one half so good a grace
> As mercy does. [II, ii, 59–63]

No mention of her brother here; no reference to his worthy family, his previously-unblemished character, his honest intentions in consummating his relationship with Julietta. Even Escalus, no relation to Claudio, had presented a more specific, sympathetic, and personal defence of Isabella's brother in pleading for his life to Angelo (at II, i, 6ff.). Instead, Isabella is focusing on a virtue—mercy—to avoid consideration of the 'vice that most I do abhor'. When she (naturally, as a novice nun) then contemplates divine justice and mercy, she seeks to make Angelo aware of his human subjection to vice, but again any reference to her brother or to his sin is conspicuously absent:

> Why, all the souls that were, were forfeit once,
> And He that might the vantage best have took
> Found out the remedy. How would you be
> If He, which is the top of judgement, should
> But judge you as you are? O, think on that,
> And mercy then will breathe within your lips
> Like man new made. [II, ii, 74–80]

Isabella does make brief passing references to her brother and his plight in these exchanges with Angelo in Act II, scene ii, but is it significant that they are not sustained, detailed, or subjective, as we might have expected from a devoted sister. Rather, she increasingly focuses on Angelo, directing her vehemence against his assumed tyranny, hubris, and self-ignorance in a sustained rhetorical assault:

> So you must be the first that gives this sentence,

And he, that suffers. O, it is excellent
To have a giant's strength, but it is tyrannous
To use it like a giant. . . .
                    Could great men thunder
As Jove himself does, Jove would ne'er be quiet,
For every pelting petty officer
Would use his heaven for thunder; nothing but thunder.
Merciful Heaven,
Thou rather with thy sharp and sulphurous bolt
Splits the unwedgeable and gnarled oak,
Than the soft myrtle. But man, proud man,
Dress'd in a little brief authority,
Most ignorant of what he's most assured—
His glassy essence—like an angry ape
Plays such fantastic tricks before high heaven
As makes the angels weep; who, with our spleens,
Would all themselves laugh mortal.
. . . [A]uthority, though it err like others,
Hath yet a kind of medicine in itself
That skins the vice o'th'top. Go to your bosom,
Knock there, and ask your heart what it doth know
That's like my brother's fault. If it confess
A natural guiltiness, such as is his,
Let it not sound a thought upon your tongue
Against my brother's life. [II, ii, 107–24 and 135–42]

Ultimately (in the last four lines of this lengthy quotation) we have returned to Claudio and his plight, but by what a circuitous route! And the damage has been done. By stressing how natural sexual desire is, and by compelling Angelo to search within himself for such latent erotic feelings, Isabella has inadvertently awakened his lust and made herself its object. Her strategy of questioning the moral probity of the judge, rather than of defending her brother from the charge against him, will have dire consequences, both for herself and for Claudio.

Ignorant of the full effect that her words have had on the Deputy, but aware that 'He will relent' (Lucio: II, ii, 126),

Isabella seeks to secure a reprieve for her brother with her exclamation, 'Hark, how I'll bribe you" (II, ii, 146). Her words are innocent, as her intention is merely to secure his compliance with a pledge of prayers from herself and her sisterhood (lines 148–56). An audience, however, should be aware from Angelo's aside at lines 142–3 of his growing sexual arousal, and should recognise that such words from Isabella might inflame his desire by suggesting the very transaction—her sexual favours in return for her brother's life—that he will propose on his next meeting with her.[17] Again, Isabella seems inadvertently to prompt Angelo's lust for her, just as, equally inadvertently, Claudio's words had suggested she might do, in the first references to her in the play (I, ii, 165–76).

Isabella at Bay

Summoned to return to Angelo the next day, to plead further for her brother's life, Isabella quickly finds herself presented with what might appear a hypothetical choice:

> Which had you rather, that the most just law
> Now took your brother's life; or, to redeem him,
> Give up your body to such sweet uncleanness
> As she that he hath stain'd? [II, iv, 52–5]

Although Angelo tempers the pejorative words 'uncleanness' and 'stained' with the temptation of 'sweet', her responses make it apparent that the prospect of sexual activity, even to secure her brother's life, holds no attraction for the chaste Isabella. Angelo therefore shifts his ground. Perhaps fornication might, in these circumstances, be a virtue, a path to salvation rather than to damnation for the participant:

---

[17] This dramatic situation—of a woman who, in return for a favour involving life and death, promises a 'reward' to a man who then demands her virginity as his recompense—was adapted by Shakespeare's colleague and collaborator, Thomas Middleton, for his 1622 play, *The Changeling* (ed. Michael Neill [London: A & C Black, 2006]), II, ii, 117–32, and III, iii, 17–170.

Might there not be a charity in sin
To save this brother's life? [II, iv, 63–4]

It is worth pausing here to consider the implication of Angelo's words in our judgement of Isabella. The importance of this proposal by Angelo is emphasised by the fact that Claudio will offer exactly the same argument (at III, i, 133–5) during his exchanges in the prison with Isabella. In suggesting that a sin might be transformed into a virtuous act if it achieves a worthy end, Angelo's question encourages an audience to consider the corollary: that there might be circumstances when the inflexible pursuit of a virtue would paradoxically become a vice because of the suffering caused. Is Isabella's jealous guardianship of her virginity selfish, showing her preoccupation with her own salvation, regardless of the fate of others? If so, then it is a moral failing rather than a moral accomplishment.

Although an audience may suspect that Isabella understands Angelo's insinuation here, her words suggest that she misunderstands and has concluded that Angelo is proposing a sin on his part in pardoning the malefactor, rather than a sin on her part in submitting to 'sweet uncleanness' to save her brother. Again, her reluctance to contemplate the 'vice that most I do abhor' is implicit. Shakespeare presents Angelo as having the same doubts about Isabella's understanding as the audience may harbour: 'either you are ignorant, / Or seem so, crafty' (II, iv, 74–5). Recognising the need to speak more plainly, he develops his question about the 'hypothetical' exchange of sexual favours in return for amnesty for Claudio:

> . . . either
> You must lay down the treasures of your body
> To this suppos'd [person], or else . . . let [your brother]
> suffer. . . . [II, iv, 95–7]

Isabella's response, which seizes on Angelo's image of a woman's chastity as her treasure, has rightly been much discussed:

... were *I* under the terms of death,
Th'impression of keen whips *I*'d wear as rubies,
And strip *myself* to death as to a bed
That longing have been sick for, ere *I*'d yield
My body up to shame. [II, iv, 100–4; italics added]

Every one of her lines contains a first-person pronoun, but
Claudio receives no mention, which suggests that Isabella's
obsession with her own abhorrence of the sexual act has
eclipsed her concern for her brother's plight. Yet, in the
confused diction and imagery of the passage, suffering ('terms
of death', 'impression of keen whips', 'to death', 'sick', and
'shame') is implicitly envisaged as an enticing erotic act ('wear
as rubies', 'strip myself', 'as to a bed', 'longing', and 'yield my
body'). In offering herself as a bride of Christ (that is, as a nun),
Isabella apparently sees martyrdom as a consummation
devoutly to be wish'd. She is conflating the extremities of
agony and ecstasy, in keeping with the contemporary
Shakespearian usage of 'death' in the sense of 'orgasm'.
Shakespeare's portrayal of the character of Isabella might even
have been influenced by the writings of St. Teresa of Avila
(1515–82), where divine revelation is presented as an erotic
experience and intense suffering equated with utmost rapture.
Thus, Isabella's language may imply that, in her eagerness to
imitate those female saints who died to preserve their chastity,
she equates martyrdom with a kind of perverse sexual
gratification.

Isabella is stung into defiance by Angelo's indecent
suggestions, particularly when he accuses her of committing a
sin by refusing to compromise her virtue (the corollary of his
question at lines 62–3):

Were you not then as cruel as the sentence
That you have slander'd so? [II, iv, 109–10]

In response, Isabella proves to have as rich a supply as Angelo
of maxims and proverbial wisdom to defend, against the

arguments of an opponent, her conception of justifiable and unjustifiable conduct:

> Better it were a brother died at once,
> Than that a sister, by redeeming him,
> Should die for ever. [II, iv, 106–8]

> Ignominy in ransom and free pardon
> Are of two houses: lawful mercy
> Is nothing kin to foul redemption. [II, iv, 111–13]

> . . . it oft falls out
> To have what we would have, we speak not what we
> mean. [II, iv, 117–18]

Characteristically, Isabella relies on authority when challenged; but here, sententious commonplaces must supply the absence of a male authority-figure to support her.

Despite her formidable command of reasoning and verbal argument, Angelo continues to probe at Isabella's intellectual defences, seeking a place of weakness. He finds it in her dismay at female sexual vulnerability. In encouraging her to admit women's susceptibility, Angelo prompts (with only five words) an extraordinary response from Isabella:

> *Ang.*   Nay, women are frail too.
> *Isab.*   Ay, as the glasses where they view themselves,
> Which are as easy broke as they make forms.
> Women?—Help, Heaven! Men their creation mar
> In profiting by them. Nay, call us ten times frail;
> For we are soft as our complexions are,
> And credulous to false prints. [II, iv, 123–9]

An audience may again observe how Isabella's language has been infected by Angelo's sexual insinuations. Although the image of 'glasses' (lines 124–5) might seem to suggest vanity (female posturing before a mirror) rather than lechery, glass was traditionally associated with female virginity, in which context the words 'broke as they make forms' carry with them connotations of deflowering and conception. In addition, in condemning males (lines 126–7), Isabella deplores how men exploit female sexual susceptibility. Finally, her metaphor of women being 'credulous to false prints' is redolent of Angelo's earlier image (lines 44–6) about illegitimate offspring being stamped as false coin. Isabella's speech, rather than being a general condemnation of female moral weakness, is a more specific diatribe against women's susceptibility to sexual corruption.

Isabella's exclamation against women has left her vulnerable to Angelo. He is quick to seize the advantage offered by this admission, on Isabella's part, of feminine weakness:

> Be that you are,
> That is, a woman; if you be more, you're none.
> . . . [S]how it now
> By putting on the destin'd livery. [II, iv, 133–7]

Perhaps there is a play on words here, 'none' in line 134 reminding the audience that Isabella is a 'nun' rather than a woman, and that her 'destin'd livery' should therefore be the religious veil rather than feminine frailty. In performance, the effect of these lines may be accentuated by Isabella's appearance in her nun's habit before Angelo—a perpetual visual reminder that her chaste vocation should protect her from what she believes to be the 'destin'd livery' of her sinful womanhood.

When Angelo has plainly revealed his indecent proposal (lines 129–43), Isabella is fired into open rebellion against his authority. The respectful vocatives that she had persistently attached to her petitions to the Deputy earlier in the scene ('Your honour,' 'Sir', 'My lord', 'Gentle my Lord') are now abandoned as she addresses him directly by name rather than by title, no longer respecting his position as judge, but rather reversing their positions and standing in judgement on him:

Ha? Little honour, to be much believ'd,
And most pernicious purpose! Seeming, seeming!
I will proclaim thee, Angelo, look for't.
Sign me a present pardon for my brother,
Or with an outstretch'd throat I'll tell the world aloud
What man thou art. [II, iv, 148–53]

Her righteous indignation is apparent in her condemnation of
her tormentor: 'Little honour'; 'most pernicious purpose';
'Seeming, seeming!' She no longer employs the respectful
second person pronoun, 'you', in addressing the magistrate who
holds sway over the life of her brother, but rather chooses the
familiar and potentially insulting 'thou' (line 153) and 'thee'
(line 150). At this moment, Isabella appears in the ascendant,
threatening ('I will proclaim thee'), commanding ('Sign me a
present pardon'), and redefining the terms of the bargain
between her and her brother's judge ('Or . . . I'll tell the
world').

Angelo's response is blunt and overwhelming, threatening
Isabella's pious reputation as a nun with the 'smell of calumny'
(line 158) and blaming the fate of her brother on her
'unkindness' (line 165). In both cases, her status as a 'sister'
(nun and sibling) is put in question. We should take this
opportunity to pause on the word 'unkindness'. Angelo now is
threatening not only to execute Claudio if Isabella denies the
Deputy sexual gratification, but also to subject Claudio to
'ling'ring sufferance' (line 166), that is, to torture him to death,
unless she acquiesces. The accusation, 'unkindness', refers
equally to Isabella's treatment of her brother and to her
treatment of Angelo, in denying the former life and the latter
'love'. As the word *kynde* in mediaeval and renaissance English
was synonymous with the Latin *natura*, Shakespeare's audience
might recognise that Isabella was also being accused of
unnatural behaviour, both in denying her feminine favours to a
man and in refusing to save her brother from physical torment
and execution. The word emphasises to the audience Angelo's
cruelty and Isabella's quandary. As we shall see, however,

Isabella refuses to acknowledge the existence of any such quandary.

Isabella's Soliloquy

Angelo gives Isabella one night to consider whether she should save her brother by agreeing to gratify the Deputy's demands. Shakespeare gives Isabella one soliloquy (II, iv, 170–86)—her only soliloquy in the entire play—in which an audience might expect her to be overwhelmed by an agony of indecision. She is nothing of the sort. For Isabella, there is apparently no dilemma.

Isabella seemingly contemplates her predicament with remarkable detachment. Although her soliloquy begins with two questions that convey the injustice of her situation, those questions are not only rhetorical but also curiously brief and subdued:

> To whom should I complain? Did I tell this,
> Who would believe me? [II, iv, 170–71]

The irregular rhythms, the erratic caesurae, and the brevity of expression might lead an audience to conclude that Isabella has been stunned by events, but what follows immediately suggests rather that she is exerting a steely control over her emotions. Her questions lead directly to a substantial, sententious exclamation condemning the hypocrisy of those who distort the law for their own dissolute purposes:

> O perilous mouths,
> That bear in them one and the self-same tongue
> Either of condemnation or approof,
> Bidding the law make curtsey to their will,
> Hooking both right and wrong to th'appetite,
> To follow as it draws! [II, iv, 171–6]

There may be righteous indignation here, but personal anguish is strictly suppressed in this generalised condemnation of corrupt magistrates. An audience would have expected Isabella to direct her tirade against Angelo, her antagonist, but that would have obliged her to contemplate more specifically—and therefore more painfully—her circumstances and those of her brother. Her language here seems too dignified, too restrained, too cerebral to explore the emotional depths of her predicament.

With her next words, 'I'll to my brother' (line 176), Isabella once again contemplates a retreat to a place of (imagined) safety. There is, nevertheless, a wishful complacency in her expectation of Claudio's reaction to her news:

> Though he hath fall'n by prompture of the blood,
> Yet hath he in him such a mind of honour,
> That had he twenty heads to tender down
> On twenty bloody blocks, he'd yield them up
> Before his sister should her body stoop
> To such abhorr'd pollution. [II, iv, 177–82]

Isabella is seeking to convince herself that her brother would consider his imminent suffering to be paltry in comparison with her sexual ordeal necessary to redeem him. In so doing, she seizes on the word 'honour' as her vindication. In its immediate context (lines 178–80), this word denotes Claudio's noble nature but, as the sentence develops, 'honour' extends its associations to encompass familial obligations, sexual conduct, and female virginity. In accepting death, Claudio will preserve the family 'honour' by safeguarding Isabella's 'honour', her chastity; however, the word also implies that, in Isabella's eyes, he faces the capital sentence because he has jeopardised his own 'honour' in begetting an illegitimate child with Julietta.

Isabella begins and ends her sentence with a characteristic condemnation of sexual activity. Claudio is 'fall'n'—the word is laden with Christian connotations of damnation—because of his inability to restrain the 'prompture of the blood'. That same male sexual desire to which Claudio succumbed has corrupted Angelo and now threatens Isabella with 'abhorr'd pollution', words that remind the audience of the extent of her previous revulsion at, and fear of, carnal indulgence. Isabella is reassuring herself that Claudio will readily accept the terrible prospect of his own agonising death when weighing it against the deed that she would have to perform to save him; but how convincing is that reassurance?

The conclusion of her soliloquy presents us with further challenges to our responses to Isabella. First, we encounter the glib jingle of the couplet,

> Then, Isabel live chaste, and brother, die:
> More than our brother is our chastity. [II, iv, 183–4]

By commencing with 'Then', a term that suggests a conclusion reached after scholarly consideration, Isabella attempts to establish a tone of dispassionate rationality. Having persuaded herself that Claudio possesses 'such a mind of honour' that he will not demand the sacrifice of her chastity to save his life, Isabella is seeking to repress her fears with a consoling, pseudo-logical formula. The reference to herself in the third person and her recourse to nosism—that is, to the royal 'we' (or 'majestic plural')—may denote her attempt to bolster her self-respect; but her words seem hubristic. Isabella's preoccupation with her virginity unbalances the equation in the second line: her chastity is, she maintains, worth *more* than her brother's life. She clings to the belief that her brother would undergo execution twenty times over (lines 179–80) before he would expose her to the horrors of Angelo's lascivious embraces. The very title of the play, *Measure for Measure*, invites the audience to question the validity of Isabella's formula that chastity, when weighed in the balance, is over twenty times more important than human life.

But her implausible hyperbole hints at her underlying uncertainty. The staccato rhythms and erratic caesurae of the first line of this couplet undercut the assertive tone of the diction to suggest a stumbling attempt at rationality. The second line may seem more assured, but the seven weak stresses ('than our', '. . . -ther is our', '. . . -tity') in a line of ten syllables, coming after the emphatic inversion of the first foot (a trochee rather than an iamb), suggest stumbling simulation rather than confident resolve.

Her final couplet (the one that concludes the Act) is just as problematical for an audience that might otherwise wish entirely to sympathise with the persecuted Isabella:

> I'll tell him yet of Angelo's request,
> And fit his mind to death, for his soul's rest.
>
> [II, iv, 185–6]

Her complacent plan is doomed to failure. At the start of the very next scene, the audience will witness how successfully the Duke prepares Claudio for his execution, fully reconciling him to his fate (III, i, 5–43). When Isabella ultimately fulfils her stated intention to tell Claudio of 'Angelo's request', far from 'fit[ting] his mind for death', the possibility of amnesty will destroy his resolve to suffer execution nobly, leading to an agonising confrontation between sister and brother.

Isabella's apparent confidence in the rectitude of her decision to preserve her chastity at the expense of her brother's life contrasts sharply with the tearful uncertainties of the operatic heroine, Tosca, when facing almost identical circumstances. In Puccini's 1900 opera, Scarpia has demanded that Tosca should yield to him sexually to save from execution her lover, whose agonies under torture she has already been forced to overhear. The dispassionate statements in which Isabella seeks to suppress emotion with logic are thrown into stark relief by Tosca's despairing questions, in her aria *Vissi d'arte*, to a seemingly remorseless God who has delivered her and her lover into the hands of a cruel tormentor.

But opera wears its heart upon its sleeve, whereas Shakespeare's art is more emotionally subtle. Could the depth and complexity of Isabella's feelings be suggested, paradoxically, by her seemingly composed rationality? Her apparent confidence in her brother's willingness to throw down

260

his life to protect her honour would then be not so much a prediction as a desperate hope. Does Isabella's one soliloquy in the play, in its very *certainty*, confirm how *uncertain* she is of her brother's acquiescence in her desperate attempt to preserve her virginity? Such an interpretation of her soliloquy is strongly supported when the immense power of her concealed emotions is revealed in her confrontation with Claudio in the very next scene (III, i, 135–50), and subsequently in her agony when she is (falsely) informed of her brother's execution (IV, iii, 116–22). Shakespeare's achievement in Isabella's one soliloquy is to imply that she is repressing painfully intense feelings beneath a dispassionate facade.

O, I do Fear Thee, Claudio

Isabella's resolve changes radically between her soliloquy and her re-entry only 50 lines later. Once she is facing her brother in his prison-cell, her assumed moral certainty—that Claudio will die willingly rather than demand the sacrifice of her chastity—fails her. She resorts to the kind of equivocation that the audience witnessed in Angelo when he propositioned Isabella sexually. In both cases, such equivocation clearly suggests doubt that the person addressed will comply with the wishes of the speaker. To her brother, Isabella speaks of 'such a remedy as, to save a head, / To cleave a heart in twain' (III, i, 61–2), of 'a devilish mercy in the judge / . . . that will free your life, / But fetter you till death' (lines 63–5), of 'perpetual durance, a restraint, / Though all the world's vastidity you had, / To a determin'd scope' (lines 67–9). Despite Claudio's earnest attempt to understand the bargain that Angelo has offered— 'But in what nature?' (line 69)—Isabella remains evasive:

> In such a one as, you consenting to't,
> Would bark your honour from that trunk you bear
> And leave you naked. [III, i, 70–2]

After the seemingly assured statements of the soliloquy, these prevarications are a sorry decline. Although the exasperated Claudio now demands, 'Let me know the point' (line 72),

Isabella procrastinates for a further twenty lines or more, emphasising Claudio's need to be worthy of his late noble father and to preserve his 'perpetual honour' (line 76). Her contention is that Claudio's honour is synonymous with hers: he must accept death honourably to preserve her female honour, her chastity.

The words that explain this change in Isabella from confident statements in her soliloquy to prevarications in speaking to her brother are, 'O, I do fear thee, Claudio' (III, i, 73). In soliloquy, after Angelo's departure, Isabella had sought to convince herself that her brother would reject Angelo's lecherous proposal just as firmly as she does. On having to face Claudio in person, however, her complacency is shown to crumble as she hesitates to tell him of Angelo's proposition for fear that Claudio should plead that she should indeed undergo 'such abhorr'd pollution' (II, iv, 182) to save a brother's life. We see how consistently Shakespeare has constructed the character of Isabella. Her need for moral absolutes, indicated by her first words in the play, and her fear of the 'vice that most I do abhor' (II, ii, 29), emphasised in her first words to Angelo, have pre-determined her response to the Deputy's immoral bargain; but now she is seeking the compliance of the man who must pay the price for her moral inflexibility: his own life. She is fearful that her brother, threatened with a terrible death, might not endorse her refusal to compromise her virtue.

There follows one of the most painful exchanges in Shakespeare, as agonising for the audience as the 'Brothel Scene' in *Othello* (IV, ii, 1–110), where the innocent Desdemona is tormented by the jealous accusations of her misguided husband. Isabella finally reveals to Claudio the proposed exchange of the sister's virginity in return for the brother's life (III, i, 95–7) and awaits his response. To her dismay, Isabella will see Claudio weaken after his initial indignant rejection of Angelo's bargain ('Thou shalt not do't': line 102). Her reassurance to him—

O were it but my life,

I'd throw it down for your deliverance
As frankly as a pin [103–5]—

merely serves to remind Claudio that it is not Isabella's 'life'
that is in question, but his. Because she refuses to secure his
'deliverance' by sacrificing her chastity, his 'life' must be
'throw[n] down . . . / As frankly as a pin' to ensure Isabella's
'deliverance' from Angelo's proposed bargain. After a
nightmarish meditation on death (lines 117–31), Claudio pleads
for his life in words that echo Angelo's argument (at II, iv, 63–
4) that a sin committed by Isabella for a benevolent purpose
would be transformed into a virtue (III, i, 133–5). In response,
Isabella attempts no logical refutation of Claudio's argument;
rather, she condemns him in a horrified outburst of
exclamations and rhetorical questions, one of the cruellest
speeches in Shakespeare:

O, you beast!
O faithless coward! O dishonest wretch!
Wilt thou be made a man out of my vice?
Is't not a kind of incest, to take life
From thine own sister's shame? What should I think?
Heaven shield my mother play'd my father fair:
For such a warped slip of wilderness
Ne'er issued from his blood. Take my defiance,
Die, perish! Might but my bending down
Reprieve thee from thy fate, it should proceed.
I'll pray a thousand prayers for thy death;
No word to save thee. [III, i, 135–46]

E. M. W. Tillyard proposes that Isabella's scorn for Claudio
is fully justified and 'perfect', choosing this speech as the
quintessential representation of her character: 'That is the true
Isabella.'[18] His words might seem to invite admiration for her
'scorn of Claudio's weakness'; but what is perfect or admirable
about this bitter, pitiless condemnation? She vilifies Claudio

---

[18] *Shakespeare's Problem Plays* (London: Chatto & Windus, 1950;
repr. Harmondsworth: Penguin, 1970) p. 127.

263

unrestrainedly, denying him any hope of reprieve from his capital sentence. An audience at this point might recall Angelo's question to Isabella during their last confrontation:

Were you not then as cruel as the sentence
That you have slander'd so? [II, iv, 109–10]

Her condemnation of Claudio would seem to validate Angelo's insinuation: Isabella is as remorseless and inflexible a judge as Angelo himself.

What, though, is Shakespeare conveying in Isabella's speech condemning Claudio: her moral indignation at a brother's unworthy request; or her mortal terror at being requested to 'do what I abhor to name' (III, i, 101) to redeem him? The virulence of the emotional reaction suggests the latter rather than the former. Were Shakespeare portraying an Isabella merely deeply disappointed in her brother, her reaction should have been tempered with at least some sympathy for his predicament. Her horror appears to be less with what he is trying to do—to save his life by ignoble means—and more with what he is asking of her—to yield her chastity to Angelo. From the beginning of the play, we have witnessed Isabella retreating from the dreaded contamination of sexual activity; but repeatedly, first through Lucio, then through Angelo, and now through Claudio, she has been dragged from her place of safety, by men whom she regards as dishonourable, to contemplate carnality's stark reality. It terrifies her. Her frenzied response suggests the depth of her panic rather than the strength of her Christian virtue.

At the heart of her speech lies a reference to her respect for her father (lines 140–2). This is not the first time in this scene that she has spoken with such admiration for this epitome of the male authority figure (see lines 85–86). Isabella will implicitly identify the Duke as such a paternal figure when he re-enters the scene after her confrontation with Claudio: she will address the disguised friar as 'father' as early as line 174. In this previous context, when addressing Claudio, she refuses to acknowledge that such a noble figure as her father could have produced such a dishonourable offspring as her brother. She therefore beseeches heaven to grant that her mother was sexually disloyal to her father, so that Claudio would share none of his virtuous father's blood.[19] As before (especially at II, iv, 124–9), Isabella associates frailty, especially in the sense of sexual corruption, with women, her prejudice extending even to her own mother, whom she would rather believe to be an adulteress than accept Claudio as her father's legitimate son. Women are corruptible figures to be suspected and condemned; men are authoritative figures to be respected and obeyed— provided that they defend rather than threaten Isabella's chastity.

Isabella's last words to her brother in this scene, because they come from a sister (nun and sibling), are as brutal a condemnation as Angelo's sentence on him:

> O fie, fie, fie!
> Thy sin's not accidental, but a trade;
> Mercy to thee would prove itself a bawd;
> 'Tis best that thou diest quickly. [III, i, 147–50]

The disproportion of her response should be obvious to the audience: Claudio's 'true contract' with Julietta and his attempt to save his life are wildly equated by his sister with what the audience knows of the disreputable 'trade' of the 'bawd', Mistress Overdone, and of her pimp, Pompey. These are Isabella's last words to her brother in the play, and they leave a bitter taste.

---

[19] Freudian—or rather, Jungian—critics might use this evidence to suggest an Electra complex on Isabella's part. It then follows that Isabella's accusation that Claudio is committing 'a kind of incest' (V, i,138) in taking life from his sister's shame would sit uncomfortably beside her relationship with her father—and even beside her relationship with the Duke, whom she calls 'father' and who calls her 'sister' later in this same scene, when they conspire to satisfy Angelo's lust.

Lever proposes[20] that there should be a mimed reconciliation between brother and sister soon after Isabella's tirade (between lines 170 and 178). What makes the suggestion implausible is the absence of any stage-direction to imply, or any dialogue to confirm, any harmonious reunification between brother and sister. Why should Shakespeare have left such a dramatic opportunity for dialogue to mere dumb-show? Even if Claudio's line, 'Let me ask my sister pardon' (III, i, 170), is addressed to Isabella rather than to the Duke (which seems implausible), there is insufficient substance in the speech to confirm reconciliation between brother and sister, no stage-direction to authorize it, and no scripted response from Isabella to suggest it. Nevertheless, in Dominic Dromgoole's 2015 production of *Measure for Measure* at The Globe Theatre, London, Isabella and Claudio did briefly join hands at this point, looking forgivingly into each other's eyes; but the tableau was too brief to be dramatically convincing, and was upstaged by the dialogue between the Duke *qua* friar and the Provost.[21] Isabella's condemnation of her brother when he pleads for her to save his life is so sustained and so venomous that only a correspondingly substantial dialogue between the siblings could convince an audience of their full reconciliation. But there is none here. And there will be none later.

The aftermath of the confrontation between brother and sister was addressed more convincingly in the 2019 RSC production directed by Gregory Doran. The Duke physically restrained Claudio from approaching Isabella on the line 'Let me ask my sister pardon' (III, i, 170), deliberately delaying any potential reconciliation until later. The ultimate reunion of Claudio and Isabella at V, i, 487 was all the more poignant: their joy could not fully expunge the bitterness of their parting in the prison.

---

[20] Three times: pp. xxvi, lxxxii, and 77.
[21] Braunmuller and Watson imply that any dumb-show of reconciliation in this context would, in all likelihood, be unconvincing: 'the dramaturgy remains awkwardly blunt' (p. 266n.).

The Evolution of Isabella

The Isabella with whom the Duke (disguised as Friar Lodowick) requests an interview on her departure from her brother is officious and grudging as she attempts to regain her composure (further evidence that a reconciliation with her brother is unlikely to have occurred):

> I have no superfluous leisure; my stay must be stolen out of other affairs: but I will attend you a while. [III, i, 156–8]

The cold stiffness of this response may suggest to an audience that her faith in male integrity has been profoundly shaken by her brother's capitulation, following so closely after Angelo's attempt at sexual extortion. Undeterred, the disguised Duke proposes to Isabella a typical folk-tale formula whereby a series of seemingly insoluble conundrums may be resolved:

> I do make myself believe that you may most uprighteously do a poor wronged lady a merited benefit; redeem your brother from the angry law; do no stain to your own gracious person; and much please the absent Duke, if peradventure he shall ever return to have hearing of this business. [III, i, 198–204]

Here, a male authority-figure—apparently a man in holy orders who should be well experienced in determining moral courses—proposes to Isabella how she may act 'uprighteously' and 'do no stain to [her] own gracious person' in resolving her difficulties. Reassured that her integrity is no longer under threat and that she may escape from the demands of Angelo and Claudio, Isabella's mood seems to change abruptly at these words. She appears eager to participate—in stark contrast to her initial frosty response to the Friar:

> Let me hear you speak farther. I have spirit to do anything that appears not foul in the truth of my spirit. [III, i, 205–7]

If considered objectively, the Duke's proposal is astonishing: he encourages Isabella to lie to Angelo that she will acquiesce to his sexual demands, and then to 'advise' Angelo's betrothed, the rejected Mariana, to take Isabella's place in the act of sexual consummation. How could such a course of action be reconciled with Isabella's previous moral inflexibility? Isabella's response is still more astonishing:

> The image of it gives me content already, and I trust it will grow to a most prosperous perfection. [III, i, 260–1]

What has happened to Isabella's moral scruples, her wish for a 'more strict restraint', her condemnation of sexual activity as 'such abhorr'd pollution'? On the appearance of a male authority figure in the guise of a member of a religious order, she promptly capitulates to his proposed course of action. How could consummation between Angelo and his betrothed be in any way more justified morally than the 'true contract' by which Claudio 'got possession of Julietta's bed' and which Isabella has so roundly condemned since first she heard that 'He has got his friend with child'? Julietta was 'fast [Claudio's] wife' and their 'sin' was 'most mutually committed', whereas Angelo has rejected Mariana and has no wish to embrace her. The former relationship may have been conducted with modest 'stealth', but the latter will be consummated by means of deceitful ploys. In this very scene, just over 100 lines before, Isabella had condemned Claudio with the words, 'Thy sin's not accidental, but a trade' (III, i, 148). Now, she is entering that same flesh-trade in procuring Mariana for the reluctant Angelo. Worse, she is agreeing to use lies and deception to bring them together.

What are we to make of these apparently perplexing inconsistencies in Isabella's characterisation? Some audiences might overlook the contradictions by accepting her behaviour as a comic convention, one of the many implausibilities necessary to resolve such a folk-tale as that dramatized in the second half of *Measure for Measure*. Were an audience to consider more closely, however, the apparent inconsistencies might resolve themselves. In a traumatic confrontation, Isabella has condemned her brother in order to save her chastity. Now, she is offered a course of action that might preserve both her virginity and her brother's life. Her eagerness to achieve these seemingly irreconcilable objectives might plausibly blind her to all moral objections to the strategy proposed by the friar. Moreover, as a male authority-figure in holy orders, the friar has taken responsibility for the deception, and Isabella has been invited to become the instrument whereby a happy outcome should be achieved. Most importantly, Isabella will no longer be under pressure to commit the deed 'that I abhor to name'.

Isabella's acquiescence might even suggest that she has come to recognise the need for compromise. The inflexibility of her moral code has generated appalling conflict with her brother. Reconciliation might still be possible were she prepared to condone lesser evils to effect Claudio's redemption from a terrible injustice. In her private interview with Angelo, Isabella had recognised that, although in heaven all sins are condemned, on earth some sins are deemed less culpable: ''Tis set down so in heaven, but not in earth' (II, iv, 50). Now is her opportunity to apply her distinction to her brother's disproportionate sentence. A desire to make amends for her terrible curse on Claudio at their moment of crisis might plausibly lessen her objections to the dubious morality of the conduct to which she is agreeing.

By the time of her meeting with the Duke and Mariana, Isabella has eagerly—and seemingly without moral qualms—engaged in the deception of Angelo:

> There [in his 'garden circummur'd with brick'] have I
> made my promise
> Upon the heavy middle of the night
> To call upon him. . . .
> . . . I have possess'd him my most stay
> Can be but brief: for I have made him know
> I have a servant comes with me along,
> That stays upon me; whose persuasion is

I come about my brother. [IV, i, 34–48]

Not only has Isabella carried out the instructions of the disguised Duke in lying to Angelo about her willingness to yield to him her virginity, but she has even elaborated on the deception, on her own initiative, by creating the device of the accompanying servant. She thereby earns approval for her ruse from her male authority-figure: ''Tis well borne up' (IV, i, 48). Isabella may seem to be acquiring a taste for intrigue and duplicity comparable to the Duke's.

In a further extraordinary dramatic twist, the Duke/friar now entrusts Isabella with the task of informing Mariana of the plan to deceive Angelo and of persuading her to take Isabella's place in the bed-trick. Isabella readily agrees to bring procreants together in the act that previously she loathed to name. The exchanges between Isabella and Mariana take place almost entirely off-stage (the Duke offering an implausibly short and apparently irrelevant moral monologue during this interlude), but Shakespeare gives us a clue as to Isabella's changing priorities in the one line that we *do* hear her deliver to Mariana:

Little have you to say
When you depart from him, but, soft and low,
'Remember now my brother'. [IV, i, 68–70]

Her earlier preoccupation with 'a vice that most I do abhor', which could have been regarded as a selfish quest for her own salvation, has been replaced here by a more charitable concern for her brother's welfare. Of course, a less favourable interpretation on the audience's part would be that Isabella is prepared to sacrifice another woman's virginity to preserve her own. As if to forestall such a negative view of Isabella (and Mariana), Shakespeare immediately seeks to justify the deception practised by the two women when the disguised Duke assures Mariana that Angelo is her 'husband on a pre-contract' and that consummating her relationship with him is 'no sin' but rather 'justice' (IV, i, 72–5). Regardless of whether the audience considers these words to have been spoken by the

Duke in propria persona, or by his alter ego, Friar Lodowick (in his assumed capacity as a man of religious authority), the speech will be seen potentially to legitimise the union of Angelo and Mariana and to free the two women from any blame for the duplicity that they are intending.

Having practised deception herself at the instigation of the Duke, Isabella soon becomes the victim of deception *by* the Duke, who seeks to justify his lies on a dubious pretext:

> . . . I will keep her ignorant of her good,
> To make her heavenly comforts of despair
> When it is least expected [IV, iii, 108–10]

Isabella has come to 'so holy a man' (IV, iii, 112), as she innocently believes Friar Lodowick to be, to learn whether Claudio's pardon has yet arrived. The man whom she trusts lies to her bluntly, showing no attempt to lessen the terrible impact of his dishonesty:

> [Claudio's] head is off and sent to Angelo. [IV, iii, 115]

Unsurprisingly in the circumstances, her emotions again take control of Isabella; but, this time, fury and misery rather than terror govern her:

> O, I will to him and pluck out his eyes! [IV, iii, 119]

> Unhappy Claudio! wretched Isabel!
> Injurious world! most damned Angelo! [IV, iii, 121–2]

Might Isabella's expressions of dismay also be tinged with guilt? Her exclamation, 'Wretched Isabel!' encourages an audience to consider the likely response to news of Claudio's death by a woman whose last words to her brother were a cruel curse, condemning him to torture and execution.[22] Like Angelo,

---

[22] At this point, in the RSC's 2019 production, directed by Gregory Doran, Isabella (Lucy Phelps) tore off her wimple and flung herself

Isabella must suffer remorse for her unjust sentence before she can ultimately be redeemed. Whether such an intention—to elicit contrition from Isabella—could be attributed to the Duke is questionable. An audience may, nevertheless, be inclined to regard Isabella more sympathetically because her responses to adversity here show touching human frailty rather than saintly patience. She may warrant further sympathy because her trust is being abused by Friar Lodowick (the Duke in disguise) who, while lying to her, falsely claims 'a faithful verity' (IV, iii, 126) in his every word. Isabella is again a victim of male machinations, but this time her reactions to her predicament should endear her to an audience.

Ultimately, the Duke/friar consoles Isabella with an elaborate series of imperatives, instructions, and pledges, attempting to restore her to patience. He promises her that

. . . you shall have your bosom on this wretch,
Grace of the Duke, revenges to your heart,
And general honour. [IV, iii, 134–6]

This prophecy from Friar Lodowick, in the folk-tradition of addressing multiple tasks that are seemingly impossible to reconcile, predicts that Isabella will achieve the full measure of vengeance on Angelo that she desires, that she will receive the Duke's favour when he returns on the morrow, and that (most importantly) she will preserve her virtuous reputation. In response, Isabella sobs her acquiescence to the instructions of the male authority-figure:

I am directed by you. [IV, iii, 136]

---

down, beating the stage with her fists in despair. Symbolically, Isabella's emotions were breaking free from the religious constraints imposed on them. This stage-business might further have signified Isabella's renunciation of the sisterhood's doctrine of forgiveness, or betokened, because she had abandoned her brother to his fate, that she now deemed herself unfit for a religious vocation.

She thereby agrees to become a menial to the Duke/friar, delivering his letter, bearing his message by word of mouth, and obeying all his commands concerning her words and deeds. Her spirit, though, seems broken by grief for her brother's death, as the Duke/friar notes in observing the 'fretting waters' in her eyes (line 146).

Although, on the entry of Lucio, Isabella mysteriously disappears from this scene (there is no stage-direction to indicate her departure), the last reference to her confirms her new-found humanity:

O pretty Isabella, I am pale at mine heart to see thine eyes so red: thou must be patient. [IV, iii, 150–1][23]

The ice-maiden of Acts I–III has melted, and here she shows her distress so openly and frankly that it draws unalloyed sympathy even from the usually cynical, brash Lucio. An audience should be similarly moved by her plight, as her tears are testimony to her rehabilitation after her cruelty in the prison-scene with her brother.

Speaking Indirectly

At the conclusion of the play, Isabella, under instruction from her friar, participates in the pageant of equivocations and deceptions that the Duke has devised to entrap Angelo. Shakespeare is careful, however, to show that Isabella has misgivings about assuming such a morally questionable role in this denouement:

To speak so indirectly I am loth;
I would say the truth, but to accuse him so
That is your part; yet I am advis'd to do it,
He says, to veil full purpose. [IV, vi, 1–4]

---

[23] This sentence was the cue for Isabella's departure from the stage in the RSC's 2019 production.

Characteristically, Isabella is torn between concern for her integrity and obedience to the male authority-figure. Encouraged by Mariana and Friar Peter, however, she accepts the task of speaking according to the precise instructions that she has received: rather than uttering nothing but 'the truth', she adopts the moral compromise that she must 'veil full purpose' by speaking 'indirectly'; that is, she will equivocate.

Accordingly, on the Duke's re-entry into Vienna to greet Angelo, Escalus, and his people, she is prompted by Friar Peter to step forward to make her accusation against Angelo. From the outset, her script relies on prevarications and evasions—speaking indirectly:

> Vail your regard
> Upon a wrong'd—I would fain have said, a maid.
> [V, i, 21–2]

Subtly, Isabella (or her script, provided by the disguised Duke) does not actually confess that she has lost her virginity, as claiming to be a 'maid' (which we must consider she is) would invalidate the accusation that follows; but clearly her words imply that she has indeed lost her virginity. The profusion of short exclamations in Isabella's opening speech in this final scene suggests that her words must be desperately impassioned, confirmed when Angelo observes,

> And she will speak most bitterly and strange. [V, i, 38]

Taking her cue from Angelo's final word, 'strange', Isabella utters a list of accusations against Angelo, each of which she delivers with all the force that rhetoric can lend:

> That Angelo's forsworn, is it not strange?
> That Angelo's a murderer, is't not strange?
> That Angelo is an adulterous thief,
> An hypocrite, a virgin-violator,
> Is it not strange, and strange? [V, i, 40–4]

What is an audience to make of these charges against Angelo? Does Isabella believe all her accusations to be true? Some clearly are true, but some are problematical. If one or more of her accusations is untrue, is she bearing false witness, in direct defiance of the ninth Commandment?

Her accusations that Angelo is 'forsworn' and a 'hypocrite' present no problem: Angelo is clearly guilty, as any audience well knows. 'Murderer' should elicit no major objection from the audience, as Isabella believes that Angelo has executed Claudio, despite his oath to free her brother in return for sexual gratification. Furthermore, Angelo has forfeited his right to sit in judgement on her brother by offending against the very statute under which he condemned Claudio.

How, though, could Angelo be 'an adulterous thief'? With whom has he broken the seventh (perhaps, also, the eighth) Commandment? We might respond that, in his desire for Isabella, he was betraying his (lapsed) vows to Mariana to whom the Duke had declared, 'He is your husband on a pre-contract' (IV, i, 72). Thus, Angelo might be considered a married man, intent on the theft of the virginity of a woman (Isabella) who is not his wife. A sin intended could be considered as culpable as a sin committed, and was often declared to be so in mediaeval and renaissance sermons, echoing Christ's words in the Sermon on the Mount (Matthew 5: 28). Would, though, such a justification for the accusation occur to an audience, or convince an audience if it were considered? Besides, Isabella herself will argue, later in the scene (V, i, 448–52), that intent is *not* equivalent to actual sin.

Then there is the accusation that Angelo is 'a virgin violator'. 'Violator' insinuates that Angelo is a rapist. Mariana gave herself to Angelo willingly, and so it is difficult to conceive of her as the ravished 'virgin' of the accusation. Isabella well knows that, although she herself might have been the unwilling virgin whom Angelo wished to violate, 'His act did not o'ertake his bad intent' (as she will later plead in extenuation of his offences at V, i, 449).

275

To resolve the problem, we should look more carefully at the wording that Shakespeare/the Duke/Friar Lodowick has given to Isabella. She does not state that Angelo is forsworn, a murderer, an adulterous thief, a hypocrite and a virgin-violator. Instead, she asks a series of rhetorical questions, each based on the repeated, interrogative main clause: "Is it not strange?" Angelo is renowned throughout Vienna for purity, rigour, and self-denial. Such accusations against him would therefore undeniably be 'strange' to consider. Isabella is, then, equivocating by seeming to accuse Angelo of all these offences while cleverly using his reputation, the very thing that Angelo believed would protect him from slander (see II, iv, 153–58), to avoid any charge of bearing false witness on her part. Thus, although Isabella draws to public attention five accusations against Angelo, some of which she might know to be misleading or untrue, she never actually asserts that they are all true. When she does claim truth to be on her side in another rhetorically elaborate speech, her use of pronouns ('it'; 'this'; 'it') seems deliberately vague and confusing:

> It is not truer he is Angelo,
> Than this is all as true as it is strange;
> Nay, it is ten times true, for truth is truth
> To th'end of reck'ning. [V, i, 46–9]

If the admittedly Byzantine argument offered above fails to convince, then we must conclude that Isabella is not equivocating but lying, bearing false witness. Her only defence in that case would be that she was acting under instruction from the disguised Duke, acknowledging his spiritual authority over her; but how could we square that course of action with her scrupulous moral integrity in the first two Acts of the play? Perhaps we could do so by asserting that Isabella might plausibly have come to recognise the validity of the argument that was used against her by both Angelo (II, iv, 63–4) and Claudio (III, i, 133–5): a sin committed with righteous intentions is transformed into a virtue.

Ultimately, though, the dramatic justification for Isabella's words here is not to present the audience with a quandary concerning Isabella's moral status. The point is that Angelo, in the audience's opinion, would believe every part of every accusation to be true. In his ignorance of the exchange of Mariana for Isabella in his bed, and of the Duke's scheme to preserve Claudio's life, he would be certain that his every offence has been made public by Isabella.

Isabella's next speech is less problematical to justify. She offers a synopsis of the process whereby she pleaded for her brother's reprieve, provoking from Angelo the bargain for her to secure Claudio's release in exchange for her virginity. The lines requiring more careful consideration are,

> . . . and after much debatement,
> My sisterly remorse confutes mine honour,
> And I did yield to him. [V, i, 102–4]

The accusation that this is a lie by Isabella is relatively easy to refute. Although the apparent meaning is that Isabella gave her virginity ('honour') to Angelo, she has actually said no more than that she agreed to his dishonourable demand (having arranged for Mariana to take her place). Again, by equivocating (speaking indirectly), Isabella might avoid the charge that she is bearing false witness.

An Assay of Her Virtue

Although the principal dramatic focus of this final scene is the trial of Angelo, it also comprises the trial of Isabella, by way of a series of tests devised by the Duke. First, her obedience is tested, as she makes her accusations against Angelo, striving subtly to avoid perjury by speaking 'indirectly', according to the instruction that she has received from the spiritual authority-figure whom she knows as Friar Lodowick. When the Duke, in propria persona, intervenes to pass judgement on her evidence, he feigns disbelief and accuses her of being suborned to slander his Deputy (V, i, 108ff.). As

277

Isabella's response suggests—'O you blessed ministers above, / Keep me in patience' (V, i, 118–19)—this is now a test of her patience. She passes the test, maintaining her dignity even when committed to prison by the Duke, and led offstage. An audience is likely to feel a growing respect for her, as her stoical silence here contrasts sharply with her violently emotional condemnation of Claudio that might earlier have alienated audience sympathy.

The testing of Isabella continues when, at Escalus's command, she is summoned to reappear before the tribunal, arriving immediately before Friar Lodowick is unhooded to reveal Duke Vincentio. Once his disguise is abandoned, the Duke, in summoning Isabella to come forward, reassures her of his continuing support for her (V, i, 379–83). Her response is not to seek advantage from her new-found prestige and potential influence as 'an inward of' the Duke (to misappropriate Lucio's earlier boast at III, ii, 127), but instead to emphasise her sense of unworthiness to have claimed his assistance:

> O, give me pardon,
> That I, your vassal, have employ'd and pain'd
> Your unknown sovereignty. [V, i, 83–5]

Thus, she passes the test of humility. When the Duke, continuing in his manipulative deception of Isabella, informs her that he was unable to use his power to save her brother because of 'the swift celerity of [Claudio's] death' (V, i, 392), Isabella does not remonstrate with the Duke or lament her loss. The Duke instructs her, 'Make it your comfort, / So happy is your brother,' and she replies with simple, modest obedience, 'I do, my lord' (V, i, 96–7). Her meekness and patience are manifest throughout these exchanges.

The final and greatest test of Isabella—a test of compassion and forgiveness—comes with the Duke's condemnation of Angelo. Isabella's fury and distress on being told that her brother had been executed despite Angelo's pledge to free him

278

had been calmed by the disguised Duke with a promise of 'revenges to your heart' (IV, iii, 135). Now, Isabella has the opportunity to enjoy such revenge merely by remaining silent, thereby allowing the Duke's sentence of death to be carried out on Angelo. Nevertheless, Isabella, however cruelly she has been treated by Angelo, is a novice nun, subject to the Christian doctrines of forbearance and forgiveness. Perhaps more significantly, it is Mariana who is pleading with Isabella to intervene on behalf of her newly-wedded husband—the same Mariana who saved Isabella from 'abhorr'd pollution' by taking her place in Angelo's bed:

> . . . sweet Isabel, take my part;
> Lend me your knees, and all my life to come
> I'll lend you all my life to do you service. [V, i, 428–30]

Mariana's generosity to Isabella in saving her from shame demands recompense, but Mariana's words confirm that there is no immediate response, verbal or physical, from Isabella. Mariana is obliged to ask for a simple gesture from Isabella, rather than any words in favour of Angelo:

> Sweet Isabel, do yet but kneel by me;
> Hold up your hands, say nothing: I'll speak all.
> [V, i, 434–6]

There is evidently still no reaction from Isabella, as a despairing Mariana exclaims several lines later:

> O Isabel! Will you not lend a knee? [V, i, 440]

This is the greatest test of Isabella's virtue, demanding of her a selfless rather than self-interested response.

Isabella's humanity is confirmed by her hesitation, suggesting the quandary that she faces. The contrast with her one soliloquy in the play is emphatic: there, she acknowledged no dilemma over Angelo's shocking proposition, as 'more than our brother is our chastity' (II, iv, 184); whereas here, her debt to Mariana conflicts with her obligation to Claudio. As the Duke has already suggested (V, i, 431–4), were she to plead in favour of Angelo, she would betray the memory of her brother, whom she believes executed at Angelo's command; but were she to refuse the request to plead for Angelo, she would betray the friendship and the gratitude that she owes to Mariana.

Unlike the moment when Angelo demanded her virginity in exchange for her brother's life, Isabella now encounters a moral dilemma that causes her to pause and to consider. The director and the actress playing Isabella might agree on a particularly long pause at this point to give the audience time to ponder Isabella's predicament. So it was that, in the 1950 production at Stratford, Barbara Jefford was instructed by director Peter Brook to stretch the silence for as long as she thought the audience could tolerate the break in the action. More recently, in the 2015 production at the Globe Theatre, Isabella (Mariah Gale) turned her back on the pleading of Mariana (Rosie Hilal) and walked slowly away, apparently acquiescing in silence to Angelo's execution; but, by a circuitous route, she arrived upstage of Mariana, where she turned back, as if having reconsidered her decision, before kneeling to join her companion in petitioning the Duke.

It may be significant that Isabella intervenes only after the Duke's line,

He dies for Claudio's death. [V, i, 441]

The name of Claudio serves to remind the audience of the last meeting between Isabella and her brother, when Isabella's terror of the vice that 'I abhor to name' led her to such a cruel condemnation of Claudio, very far from the Christian charity that one of her vocation should profess. In that context, she had sworn that she would not even bow down to request his repeal (III, i, 143–44). Here is her opportunity to redeem herself, by showing to Mariana, in her hour of need, the compassion that she refused to her brother in his. She relents by kneeling to the Duke:

> Most bounteous sir:
> Look, if it please you, on this man condemn'd
> As if my brother liv'd. I partly think
> A due sincerity govern'd his deeds
> Till he did look on me. Since it is so,
> Let him not die. My brother had but justice,
> In that he did the thing for which he died:
> For Angelo,
> His act did not o'ertake his bad intent,
> And must be buried but as an intent
> That perish'd by the way. Thoughts are no subjects;
> Intents, but merely thoughts. [V, i, 441–52]

These, perhaps surprisingly, are Isabella's last lines in the play. New compassion and forgiveness are certainly apparent in her final speech, but Shakespeare's masterstroke is that the speech is still characteristic of the former Isabella. The restriction of her moral vision, previously shown in her jealous guardianship of her virginity, is again apparent. She claims here that Claudio 'did the thing for which he died' whereas Angelo's 'act did not o'ertake his bad intent' (lines 447 and 449). Certainly, Angelo did not take *Isabella's* virginity, which is clearly what he desired and what Isabella appears to be considering in her line here; but he did take Mariana's virginity instead, in circumstances comparable to those in which Claudio took Julietta's, and for which Claudio was condemned to death, both by the statutes against fornication and by his sister, Isabella, in the prison-scene. Isabella's distinction is, therefore, a false one: Angelo is deserving of precisely the same penalty as Claudio. The audience, however, will be aware that Claudio, although suffering the anguish of facing the death-penalty, has been saved; and so Angelo's reprieve can be dramatically justified after he has suffered, as his penance, the same public exposure and threat of capital punishment.

Regardless of whether an audience identifies the false distinction that her speech contains, Isabella is seen to have passed her test by showing extraordinary forbearance and mollifying the hard-heartedness apparent in her treatment of her brother in the prison-scene. Her reward for passing the test is that her brother, whom she believed dead, is now restored to her by the Duke.

The director and the actors playing Claudio and Isabella must agree the precise mood of this reunification and reconciliation sequence, of a general type so frequently encountered as a joyous interlude in the final scene of Shakespeare's plays. Here, however, there is no textual guidance as to the tone of the reunion: neither Isabella nor Claudio is given a word of speech, and there is no stage-direction. An orthodox interpretation might be that the siblings show unalloyed joy, fitting for the ending of a Shakespearian 'happy comedy'; but, if that joy is to be psychologically convincing, should it not be tempered with a degree of shame and discomfort? When last these two met and spoke together in the play, Claudio pleaded to a horrified Isabella that she should sacrifice her virginity to save his life; and Isabella condemned a terrified Claudio to death with savage intensity. If we look for psychological truth here, Isabella should be profoundly disturbed by the unhooding of Claudio, torn between extremes of emotion: relief, delight, and mortification. Thus, the reunification between Lucy Phelps's Isabella and James Cooney's Claudio in the 2019 RSC production was painfully rather than joyously moving.

Proposal or Proposition?

At the unhooding of Claudio, the Duke petitions Isabella immediately:

> If he be like your brother, for his sake
> Is he pardon'd; and for your lovely sake
> Give me your hand and say you will be mine.
> He is my brother too. [V, i, 488–90]

Just as Isabella would be at her most emotionally vulnerable, the Duke proposes marriage to her. Or should we say, more coarsely, 'propositions her', for the Duke is attempting to exploit her circumstances just as surely as Angelo did. Like Angelo, he is taking advantage of her love for her brother to blackmail her emotionally. Worse than Angelo, the Duke has systematically lied to Isabella, manipulating her circumstances to ensure his unfair advantage.

How is Isabella to react? Again, the silence is pregnant with possibilities. Perhaps Isabella is surprised by joy; but the implication of the Duke's very next words—'but fitter time for that' (V, i, 491)—is surely that Isabella does not respond acquiescingly. This is characteristic of her, as we have already witnessed her reluctance to commit herself to a course of action which is unexpectedly sprung upon her. For example, three separate petitions were necessary to secure her agreement when Lucio attempted to persuade her to plead for her brother (in I, iv), and when Mariana begged with her to intercede for Angelo (earlier in V, i). But what if the actor playing Isabella were to show distress or indignation at the Duke's proposal—as she did when similarly propositioned by Angelo in Act II, scene iv? Such a response would radically change the mood of the performance, producing a much more sombre atmosphere at the play's conclusion. What is certain is that the Duke reacts to the response that he sees from Isabella by changing the focus of his speech, first to Angelo and then to Lucio.

Isabella has proved herself worthy of the Duke by passing the final test of forgiveness and compassion; the devious Duke now needs to prove himself worthy of her virtues. He does so by finding 'an apt remission in myself' (V, i, 496), whereby first he pardons Angelo, and then, after much elaboration, mitigates the sentence on Lucio. This latter act is the more significant, as Lucio's was a personal offence against the Duke, slandering his name and then seeking to attribute that slander to Friar Lodowick, the Duke's alias. The Duke is showing the same qualities of compassion and forgiveness to Angelo and Lucio that Isabella showed in interceding on Mariana's behalf for Angelo; and so the Duke may have proved himself worthy of Isabella's acceptance of his offer. From this stronger moral position, Vincentio makes a second bid for her consent to his proposal of marriage:

> Dear Isabel,
> I have a motion much imports your good;
> Whereto if you'll a willing ear incline,
> What's mine is yours, and what is yours is mine.
>
> [V, i, 531–4]

Unlike the Duke's first proposal, the emphasis here is on the benefits that Isabella will accrue—'much imports your good'— and on the reciprocation, the 'measure for measure', involved in the marriage-exchange. Isabella is offered status and wealth as the Duke's Duchess, but in return, 'what is yours is mine'. Of course, the Duke will acquire Claudio as a brother (as he indicated at line 491), but this is not the obvious meaning that will occur to the audience. The Duke is acquiring Isabella's virtues in the exchange, and prominent among her virtues is the virginity with which she has been so preoccupied since the beginning of the play. The Duke is proposing the exchange of his material treasures for what Angelo called 'the treasures of [Isabella's] body' (II, iv, 96). Will the chaste Isabella yield to the Duke the honour that she so jealously—even hysterically— defended when propositioned by Angelo and when petitioned by Claudio? Again, there is no word from Isabella and no stage direction to provide a clue.

Isabella is obliged to make three major decisions in the play: otherwise, decisions tend to be made for her or thrust upon her, by circumstances or by devious men. Angelo compels her to make her first decision—between her brother's life and her chastity. Her decision in favour of her chastity causes bitter division between her and her brother, the open silence when they are reunited at the end of the play leaving the mood of their reconciliation unresolved textually. Then, Mariana asks for her intercession to plead for the life of Angelo, the man who has tormented Isabella most. A decision must be made between revenge and the obligations of friendship. Like Prospero, Isabella discovers that 'the rarer action is / In virtue than in vengeance' (*The Tempest*: V, i, 27–8), and pleads Mariana's cause. Finally, she must decide between the Duke's offer of marriage and her commitment to 'the life remov'd' (Vincentio: I, iii, 8). The open silence at the very end of the play offers no definitive evidence of her response.

It is for the director and the actor working together to determine—not simply at this point of the play, but by the way in which they have presented Isabella's development throughout the performance—whether Isabella can or cannot accept the Duke's offer of marriage. A 'traditional' interpretation, in keeping with the convention of multiple marriages at the end of Shakespeare's 'happy comedies', would be that Isabella accepts the Duke's offer with a suitably gracious gesture and then processes from the stage, hand-in-hand with the Duke, followed by the other characters. Such an interpretation of Isabella's final actions in the play might be justified by reference to the legal convention that silence represents consent. And, of course, in the tradition of folk-tale, the noble male frequently rewards the woman of humbler origin by taking her as his bride after testing and proving her virtue. Far be it, in these circumstances, for Isabella to demur. Such, then, was the conclusion to the BBC's 1979 television-production directed by Desmond Davis, as Kate Nelligan's Isabella accepted Kenneth Colley's ducal hand to popular acclaim, followed by a final triumphal procession.

How different was the ending of BBC television-production directed by David Thacker fifteen years later! The Duke's second proposal to Isabella was not a public declaration but a private whisper, uttered when all other characters had departed from the council-chamber in which the final scene of this production was set. Juliet Aubrey's Isabella appeared horrified by the Duke's attempt to take advantage of her predicament, maintaining a distance of several feet from Tom Wilkinson's Duke and fixing on him a stare down which the Duke would not dare to advance. The Duke's leniency in the final scene, pardoning all malefactors, had not impressed this Isabella, perhaps because his leniency signified the reinstatement of the

285

lax government from which Isabella had attempted to escape when entering a religious order at the beginning of the play. The final tableau, a stand-off between nun and duke, was maintained as the credits for the production ran up the screen, leaving viewers with a disquieting limbo. Here, Isabella's silence certainly did not indicate consent. The vice that 'I abhor to name' continued to dominate her responses, and her stare was a condemnation of yet another corrupt and sexually predatory male: the Duke.[24]

This concluding impasse, however, was achieved in the BBC's 1994 production by the omission of the final couplet of the text:

> So bring us to our palace, where we'll show
> What's yet behind that's meet you all should know.
>   [V, i, 535–6]

Here, the Duke's first word, 'So', might be understood to mean 'with these things agreed'. This would suggest a positive response from Isabella as he commands what appears to be a procession to celebrate the success of all his designs, including his marriage-proposal.

By contrast, if a pause were added after the word 'So', it might become the Duke's stoical acknowledgement of his rejection by Isabella, as he turns his focus from amatory affairs to the business of 'unfold[ing]' to the court of Vienna the 'properties' of his recent 'government', as anticipated by his first line in the play. In this interpretation, Isabella might remain behind on stage, implicitly as a preliminary to returning to her convent. Despite having learned from circumstances— and from the Duke—the need to compromise, she has reverted

---

[24] A similar stand-off concluded the RSC's 2019 production: as the stage emptied of all other characters, Lucy Phelps's Isabella was left in paralysed confusion. Three yards from her, as the lights faded, Antony Byrne's Duke looked on, awaiting a response that never came.

to her previously inflexible principle of safeguarding her chastity. She will be the bride of Christ, not of the Duke.

An intriguing compromise was presented in the 2015 production that Dominic Dromgoole directed for the Globe Theatre, London. After the Duke's second proposal, Mariah Gale's Isabella slowly rose to her feet, but averted her gaze. The Duke's 'So' was delivered as a disappointed recognition of the failure of his proposal, as he turned away to speak the remaining lines. With the final couplet concluded, a slow, mournful air commenced on a solo violin, seemingly casting a sad spell over the silent characters on stage. Eventually, however, Isabella drifted towards the Duke, where she smiled and took his hand, as if accepting his proposal; but then she bent her arm and his into an arch for the choreographed finale. Was this harmonious meeting the conclusion of the play, with Isabella accepting the Duke's offer of marriage, or rather a coda in which the actors had relinquished their stage-characters to participate in the general dance with which all Globe productions end? Cleverly (and tantalisingly), the decision was left to the individual members of the audience.

Such an ambiguous ending was not unprecedented. Paul Taylor records that, in the 1994 RSC production directed by Steven Pimlott, Isabella was violently torn between conflicting emotions:

. . . at the end, Stella Gonet's Isabella fetches the Duke (Michael Feast) a stinging slap across the chops when he makes his tactless, last-minute pitch to become an item with her.

No sooner has she hit him than she's passionately kissing him better, though, and then she has second thoughts about that response, too, abruptly recoiling with little sobs, still clearly in shock from the emotional turmoil his scheming has caused.

Pimlott brings out the grim farce of the drama's wilfully cobbled-together happy ending by allowing the lights to fade very slowly on a state of ludicrous wavering. It's like looking at a couple paralysed with hapless indecision before a revolving door. [25]

As Juliet Stevenson shrewdly observed, having played Isabella in the RSC's 1983 production, 'There isn't a fixed end to the play. The *script* ends. The words run out. But the ending— that's something that has to be negotiated every performance.'[26]

Reconciling the Contradictions

Is it possible, then, to conclude that Shakespeare presents us with an entirely coherent and credible (rather than an idealised or fanciful) protagonist in his portrayal of Isabella? First, we should acknowledge that to argue that Isabella is a flawed character is not to allege that there are flaws in Shakespeare's characterisation of her. This is an important distinction in a study which has argued that the characterisation of the Duke *is* flawed. *His* inconsistent behaviour is implausible; *hers* is both plausible and defensible. One who is reputed 'a very virtuous maid' (II, ii, 20) or even 'a thing enskied and sainted' (I, iv, 34) may suffer from defects of personality that would not be readily apparent to those testifying to her worth. Isabella's inconsistencies, weaknesses, and foibles are credible facets of a young postulant threatened by a dissolute society.

During her first mention in the play, her brother's reference to 'her youth' (I, ii, 172) might suggest that she is no more than

---

[25] Paul Taylor, 'Better than a slap in the face: *Measure for Measure—* RSC, Stratford', *The Independent*: 22 October 1994, https://www.independent.co.uk/arts-entertainment/theatre-better-than-a-slap-in-the-face-measure-for-measure-rsc-stratford-1444345.html.
[26] Quoted by Kate Chedzgoy, 'Measure for Measure: what's the problem?' The British Library, 15 March 2016, https://www.bl.uk/shakespeare/articles/measure-for-measure-as-a-problem-play.

adolescent, her character and opinions not yet fully formed. The eagerness with which she seeks 'a more strict restraint' (I, iv, 4) among the Poor Clares might, then, be attributable to youthful zeal rather than to any pusillanimity in seeking refuge from the 'vice that most I do abhor' (II, ii, 29). Her idealisation of chastity might be that of an innocent not far beyond childhood, one who—like Angelo (although we may assume, from his history of public service implied in the first scene, that he is older)—has never experienced 'The wanton stings and motions of the sense' (I, iv, 59). In this reading, the play charts her development from innocence to experience, a voyage in which her attitudes and values are severely tested before she reaches her eventual destination of mature understanding and proven piety. If so, then she should be judged by what she ultimately becomes, rather than by how she conducted herself on her long journey. Such, according to Christ's Parable of the Vineyard (Matthew 20: 1–16), is how God judges. If an audience is to comply with the implications of the title of this play, with its reference to the doctrine of the Sermon on the Mount (Matthew, Chapters 5–7), then Isabella should be absolved from blame on the basis of the compassion and forgiveness that she shows in her final speech in the play, pleading for Angelo's life.

If Isabella is portrayed as very young, the implications for other aspects of the play are considerable. Isabella's respect for male authority-figures becomes the awe felt by a female child in the presence of an adult male. This might reinforce the suspicion that her praise for her father in her exchanges with Claudio (III, i, 85–6 and 140–2) hints at a youthful daughter's Electra Complex. Angelo's indecent proposal becomes even more loathsome to a modern audience, his attempted seduction smacking of paedophilia, although Shakespeare's audience might more readily accept that a pubescent girl could be the object of such desire.[27] The offer by the 'old Duke' of marriage

---

[27] In renaissance Europe, girls as young as twelve were legally permitted to marry. See, for example, the exchange between Capulet and County Paris (*Romeo and Juliet*: I, ii, 8–13), with its acknowledgement of (but warning against) such youthful marriages.

at the end of the play becomes an obvious mismatch—inappropriate and distasteful—if Isabella is little more than a child and he 'grave and wrinkled' (I, iii, 5).[28] As was illustrated by Chaucer's 'Merchant's Tale', old Januarie and young May cannot happily coexist in marriage.[29]

At the beginning of this chapter, it was suggested that extreme judgements on Isabella's moral status—saint? virago? hypocrite?—are suspect as they tend to be based on the examination of brief contexts, ignoring contradictory detail encountered elsewhere in *Measure for Measure*. A conclusion that reconciles some of these polar opinions is that she is neither entirely admirable nor entirely deplorable, but ultimately (and, rather more endearingly) human. Circumstances oblige her to recognise that, to achieve virtuous ends, it is sometimes necessary to compromise morally. In creating Isabella as an organic, developing character, Shakespeare encourages his audience to sympathise with her gradual maturation from moral inflexibility and (arguably) terrified abhorrence of sexual activity to a more compassionate understanding of the human predicament.

---

[28] For the presentation of this disquieting age-discrepancy between Isabella and the Duke in modern productions of the play, see Chapter 8, 'Performances in More Recent Years', especially pp. 539–542.

[29] Chaucer's tale (strongly influenced by, among others, Jean de Meun, Giovanni Boccaccio, and Eustache Deschamps) drew on a European narrative tradition of representing mismatches between young women and old men. The inability of the latter to satisfy the former was the subject of much literary ridicule.

Chapter 5

The Lovers

Although Isabella is the most obvious of Angelo's victims, his ruthlessness causes excessive suffering to others in the play, most notably, to the lovers. First, we encounter a young couple whose only offence is to consummate their relationship before their marriage has been ratified by the Church or the state. Claudio and Julietta[1] are prosecuted to the full extent of the law—and beyond—by Angelo. He appears determined to intimidate others and to enhance his own reputation for severity by humiliating the couple through public exposure, before subjecting them to more extreme punishment. The case of Mariana reflects even more adversely on Angelo. He is presented as having made vows to her very similar to those exchanged between Claudio and Julietta, subsequently breaking those vows out of materialistic considerations while seeking to justify his actions by blackening her reputation. Since then, she has lived in mourning for her lost love, exiled from society. Although an audience may feel ambivalent towards another of Angelo's victims—Isabella—because of *her* moral inflexibility, that same audience is likely to feel more strongly sympathetic towards Claudio, Julietta, and Mariana because, through love, they fall victim to that epitome of moral inflexibility, Angelo.

---

[1] Although her name appears as 'Juliet' in the dramatis personae, Claudio uses the extended version of her name, 'Julietta', when first he mentions her (I, ii, 135). Given the more famous Juliet in another play about young lovers, I have sought to avoid any confusion by consistently adopting 'Julietta' as the name for Claudio's betrothed.

Doomed Betrothal

Angelo dooms two betrothals: his own to Mariana and Claudio's to Julietta. Shakespeare is careful to establish striking similarities between these two handfastings, to convey to the audience the extent both of Angelo's hypocrisy and of the suffering that he causes. Two significant passages invite close comparison.

In the first, Claudio explains to Lucio the circumstances of his betrothal and subsequent prosecution:

> Thus stands it with me: upon a true contract
> I got possession of Julietta's bed.
> You know the lady; she is fast my wife,
> Save that we do the denunciation lack
> Of outward order. This we came not to
> Only for propagation of a dower
> Remaining in the coffer of her friends,
> From whom we thought it meet to hide our love
> Till time had made them for us. But it chances
> The stealth of our most mutual entertainment
> With character too gross is writ on Juliet.
>
>   . . . this new governor
> Awakes me all the enrolled penalties
> Which have, like unscour'd armour, hung by th'wall
> So long, that nineteen zodiacs have gone round,
> And none of them been worn; and for a name
> Now puts the drowsy and neglected act
> Freshly on me: 'tis surely for a name.
>
>   [I, ii, 134–44 and 154–60]

In the second passage, the Duke informs Isabella of Mariana's misfortunes:

> She should this Angelo have married: was affianced to her oath, and the nuptial appointed. Between which time of the contract and limit of the solemnity, her brother Frederick

was wracked at sea, having in that perished vessel the dowry of his sister. But mark how heavily this befell to the poor gentlewoman. There she lost a noble and renowned brother, in his love towards her ever most kind and natural; with him, the portion and sinew of her fortune, her marriage dowry; with both, her combinate husband, this well-seeming Angelo . . . [who] Left her in her tears, and dried not one of them with his comfort: swallowed his vows whole, pretending in her discoveries of dishonour: in few, bestowed her on her own lamentation, which she yet wears for his sake; and he, a marble to her tears, is washed with them, but relents not.

[III, i, 213–30]

Four key elements are shared between the two passages: the binding force of the mutual exchange of marriage-vows; the vital role of the woman's dowry in determining the destiny of the marriage; the importance of family support for the lovers; and the significance of personal reputation in determining the fate of the relationship. Furthermore, in both passages, Angelo's behaviour is deplored, while the other three lovers are represented at least sympathetically or even as entirely blameless.

Claudio defines his relationship with Julietta as based on a 'true contract' (I, ii, 134), that is, sincere oaths, mutually exchanged. They have consummated the relationship because Julietta is 'fast [Claudio's] wife' (line 136), where fast signifies 'firmly bound' (rather than suggesting merely that they are 'well-nigh' married). That each welcomed the opportunity for discreet intimacy is suggested by Claudio's reference to 'The stealth of our most mutual entertainment' (line 143), where 'stealth' need not imply guilty activity but rather suggests the restraint and privacy with which lovers must conduct their affair. In short, Claudio believed himself happily married.

Claudio's vindication of his relationship with Julietta must be qualified, however: they have not made 'the denunciation . . . / Of outward order' (lines 137–8), that is, there has been no reading of banns or public ceremony to confirm the marriage. It is because of this seemingly venial error that the lovers have been prosecuted and convicted. Claudio explains that he and Julietta had kept their marriage from public knowledge 'Only for propagation of a dower' (line 139), that is, to secure the full extent of Julietta's dowry. Her family—here (as frequently in Shakespeare's works) referred to as 'friends' (line 140)—might have withheld the dowry had they disapproved of the union. The lovers needed time to win the family's support for their nuptials ('Till time had made them for us': line 142) and thereby to secure the full dowry; however, Julietta's obvious pregnancy, 'writ . . . [w]ith character too gross' (line 144), brought retribution from the state before their objective could be achieved. The word 'propagation' (line 139), used of the dowry, therefore takes on an ironic force: while waiting for the dowry to 'breed', Claudio has unintentionally 'propagated' a child with Julietta. As always seems to be the case in *Measure for Measure*, sexual activity and financial considerations—like lovers' vows—go hand in hand.

Having explained and justified his relationship with Julietta, Claudio considers Angelo's treatment of their case. Claudio recognises the injustice that he is being punished under a statute that has been neglected 'So long, that nineteen zodiacs [i.e. years] have gone round' (line 157) since it was last enforced. He believes that the objective of Angelo's severity is to establish 'a name' (lines 158 and 160), that is, a reputation as a strong, decisive ruler. Claudio's words, without seeming maudlin, clearly portray him and his betrothed as victims of a pedantic, inhumane administration, rather than as debauched criminals meriting severe chastisement.

When we re-focus on the Duke's words to Isabella, the similarities between the Claudio-Julietta relationship and the Angelo-Mariana relationship appear far too frequent and significant to be merely coincidental. Again, there is a 'true contract': Mariana was 'affianced' to Angelo by 'oath' and 'the nuptial appointed', that is, the marriage had been arranged (lines 213–14). As in the relationship between Claudio and Julietta, the dowry proved problematical: when Mariana's marriage-portion was lost with her brother's shipwreck, Angelo rejected her (lines 215–23). Unlike Claudio, Angelo treacherously 'swallowed his vows whole' when adversity struck (line 226). Furthermore, to protect his reputation for integrity while extricating himself from his vows, he made false allegations against Mariana's chastity, 'pretending in her discoveries of dishonour' (lines 226–7). He heartlessly abandoned her to her grief ('bestowed her on her own lamentation': line 228), mourning which was not merely for her dead brother, but also for her faithless lover, Angelo (lines 228–30). When the Duke's account of Mariana's fate is compared with Claudio's account to Lucio of his prosecution by Angelo, the integrity of Claudio and Julietta is enhanced, the suffering of the innocent Mariana becomes more poignant, and the treachery and hypocrisy of Angelo appear more sharply defined and deplorable.

Handfasting in the Age of Shakespeare

Shakespeare portrays the relationship between Claudio and Julietta as based on *sponsalia per verba de praesenti*. According to this arrangement, man and woman became husband and wife by means of an exchange of vows ('spousal', 'troth-plighting' or 'handfasting'), using a formula such as, 'I take thee to my wedded husband/wife,' employing the present tense. The only difference in the case of Angelo and Mariana, according to the Duke's account, might be that their vows were made in the future tense, *sponsalia per verba de futuro*, using such a formula as, 'I *shall* take thee to my wedded husband/wife.' According to Mistress Overdone, Lucio made such a commitment to Mistress Kate Keep-down when securing her sexual favours (III, ii, 193–4). We can recognise a further (attempted) handfasting, specifically in the form of *sponsalia per verba de futuro* with the people of Vienna as witnesses, when the Duke proposes to Isabella at the end of the play by saying, 'Give me your hand, and say you will be mine' (V, i, 490).

John Webster's tragedy, *The Duchess of Malfi* (1612–13), incorporates an exchange that perfectly represents the popular belief that endured in England on the issue of such troth-plighting:

I have heard lawyers say a contract in a chamber
Per verba de praesenti, is absolute marriage. . . .[2]

With her serving-woman, Cariola, as witness, the Duchess binds herself in wedlock to her steward, Antonio. Twice, in rhetorical questions, the Duchess insists that spousal *per verba de praesenti* is as valid as marriage in church: 'What can the church force more?' (line 476) and 'How can the church build faster?' (that is, 'more firmly': line 479). Significantly, she insists on the permanence of their marital bond by the same word that Claudio used to confirm Julietta as his wife: 'fast' (*Measure for Measure*: I, ii, 136). The Duchess uses the present tense when affirming, 'We now are man and wife' (I, ii, 480), while belittling the power of the Church, that can 'but echo' the vows that they have exchanged (I, ii, 481). Her tyrannical brothers, however, will refuse to recognise the legitimacy of her secret marriage *per verba de praesenti*, very much in keeping with the tyrannical Angelo in *Measure for Measure*, who refuses to recognise the legitimacy of the closely comparable marriage between Claudio and Julietta.

There are numerous important similarities between the handfasting of Claudio and Julietta and the spousal of John Donne (the poet) and Ann More in 1601. Donne's marriage was based on handfasting in a closed room with only two witnesses. Like Claudio and Julietta, the couple feared that the family might disapprove of their marriage, and so initially kept it secret. Like Claudio, Donne was thrown into prison when the relationship was revealed, although Ann's father, Sir George More, who pursued the prosecution, was ultimately obliged, after a court case, to recognise the legitimacy of the marriage.

---

[2] Brian Gibbons, ed., *The Duchess of Malfi*, 4th ed. (London: Methuen, 1993), I, i, 468–9.

John and Ann Donne lived in penury until Sir George eventually relented by yielding Ann's dowry to the couple. The extraordinary coincidence of details in these two histories, one factual and one fictional, makes it possible that John Donne's marriage to Ann More might have been the topical prototype for the presentation of the Claudio-Julietta relationship in *Measure for Measure*.

Both types of vow (*de praesenti* and *de futuro*) had long been considered binding, although there was some dispute as to whether witnesses were required to validate such oaths. Before the tradition of troth-plighting was challenged, those who took their vows in the present tense might blamelessly consummate the marriage, while those who took the vows in the future tense were man and wife whose vows might later be sealed by the physical consummation of their union. Thus, when the Duke, disguised as Friar Lodowick, reassures Mariana that she may irreproachably take Isabella's place in Angelo's bed, he emphasises the binding nature of *sponsalia per verba de futuro*:

> Nor, gentle daughter, fear you not at all.
> He is your husband on a pre-contract:
> To bring you thus together 'tis no sin,
> Sith that the justice of your title to him
> Doth flourish the deceit. [IV, i, 71–5]

According to the Duke's words, in accepting Angelo's embraces, Mariana is legitimately consummating the marital relationship that was anticipated with the oaths that the two exchanged when 'the nuptial' was 'appointed' (III, i, 214).

Shakespeare had good cause to present the plight of such lovers sympathetically, having learned at an early age how a young man's sexual activities were subject to regulation by higher authority. When he married at eighteen, Shakespeare was under the age of consent (twenty-one in England) and his wife, Anne, was three months into her pregnancy with their first child, Susanna. A £40 bond, issued by the Bishop of Worcester, was required for a special dispensation that enabled them to marry with only one reading of the banns—usually deemed insufficient 'denunciation . . . of outward order' (I, ii, 137–8). Under any statute against fornication comparable with that enforced by Angelo in *Measure for Measure*, Shakespeare's life would have been 'a forfeit of the law' (II, ii, 71) before he was out of his teens.

The issue of handfasting continually engaged Shakespeare's attention. In 1604, the year in which *Measure for Measure* was first performed before the new King, Shakespeare was witness to such a betrothal. The dowry was still under dispute some eight years later, when Shakespeare was summoned to testify on the matter. A year or two before the case of the dowry came to court, Shakespeare incorporated a handfasting scene between young lovers into what was probably the last play for which he was solely responsible as author: *The Tempest* (III, i, 81–90). Miranda, in 'plain and holy innocence', offers herself in marriage to Ferdinand as 'your wife, if you will marry me' (lines 82–3), modestly questioning whether Ferdinand agrees to be '[m]y husband' (line 87). Ferdinand accepts 'with a heart as willing / As bondage e'er of freedom' (lines 88–9). The handfasting confirms this exchange of vows: Ferdinand seals the oral contract of marriage with, 'Here's my hand,' to which Miranda responds with, 'And mine, with my heart in't' (lines 89–90). Although the lovers believe themselves alone, their troth-plighting has been witnessed by Miranda's father, Prospero, who later confirms their marriage by addressing Ferdinand with the words 'she is thine own' (*The Tempest*: IV, i, 32). He further provides the masque of the three goddesses, 'A contract of true love to celebrate' (line 84), the word 'contract' being identical to that employed by Claudio to describe his handfasting with Julietta (*Measure for Measure*: I, ii, 134).

In addition, Prospero's caution to Ferdinand is highly relevant to Claudio's situation in *Measure for Measure*:

>If thou dost break her virgin-knot before
>All sanctimonious ceremonies may

With full and holy rite be minist'red,
No sweet aspersion shall the heavens let fall
To make this contract grow. . . .

[*The Tempest*, IV, i, 15–19]

Ferdinand is warned of the penalties that will follow if, like
Claudio and Julietta, the lovers delight in '[t]he stealth of . . .
most mutual entertainment' without 'the denunciation . . . / Of
outward order' (*Measure for Measure*: I, ii, 137–43). Prospero
resembles Angelo in that, as the character in authority, he seeks
to prevent sexual union between a couple joined by handfasting
until '[a]ll sanctimonious ceremonies' with 'full and holy rite'
have been concluded.

Like Prospero's, Angelo's measures involving young lovers
are entirely congruent with the edicts of the Council of Trent
(1563) and the statutes of the Canons of the Church of England
(1604): marriage must be ratified by the church before it can be
considered valid. Specifically, marriage needs banns and
witnesses ('the denunciation . . . / Of outward order') to
confirm its legitimacy. Angelo therefore refuses to recognise
Claudio's and Julietta's 'true contract' (I, ii, 134), condemning
them for consummating their relationship and producing a child
which he deems illegitimate. The danger of Angelo's position is
that it does not distinguish between the relationship between
Claudio and Julietta, one of exchanged oaths, mutual love, and
fidelity, and such a relationship as that between Lucio and
Mistress Kate Keep-down, a squalid sexual transaction
(according to Lucio, at least). Angelo's moral inflexibility here
appears unreasonable. Additionally, even if he does not
recognise the full validity of *sponsalia per verba de futuro*, his
breach of his vow to Mariana and his untruthful blackening of
her reputation to justify his abandonment of her are two
indisputably disreputable actions.

By contrast, the Duke has a belt-and-braces approach to the
issue of marriage. Although he reassures Mariana that she may
consummate her relationship with Angelo as 'He is your
husband on a pre-contract' (IV, i, 72), he commands Friar Peter

in the final scene to marry her to Angelo, subsequently explaining to Mariana why this was necessary:

> Consenting to the safeguard of your honour,
> I thought your marriage fit: else imputation,
> For that he knew you, might reproach your life,
> And choke your good to come. [V, i, 417–20]

Clearly, then, in Vincentio's Vienna, Angelo is not the only person who might look disdainfully on a woman who consummated her vows *per verba de futuro* without the authorisation of Church or state. Mariana's marriage to Angelo must therefore be conducted before a priest to protect her virtuous reputation. Similarly, the Duke's last words to Claudio are, 'She . . . that you wrong'd, look you restore' (V, i, 522). As the 'She' is Julietta,[3] it follows that the 'wrong' is Claudio's sexual union with his betrothed before their marriage had been ratified by Church or state. Yet, in authorising Mariana to consummate her relationship with Angelo, the Duke had endorsed such sexual activity after troth-plighting, claiming that ''tis no sin' (IV, i, 73). Moreover, Claudio has been prosecuted under Vienna's statutes against fornication, strict laws which the Duke had not enforced for many years. An audience could conclude that the Duke might have demurred in enforcing such statutes because he recognised their unfairness but, by implicitly condoning such sexual activity, he might plausibly have prompted Lucio to remark, 'He had some feeling of the sport' (III, ii, 115–16). The Duke has defended the strict statutes publicly (e.g. at III, ii, 96), but has laboured secretly to save Claudio (and, thereby, Julietta) from their consequences. In the final exchanges of the play, the Duke even remits Lucio's other punishments, merely requiring him to marry the woman who bore his child and to whom (according to Mistress Overdone, at least: III, ii, 193–6) he had sworn a false marriage-vow *per verba de futuro*. The Duke is, then, the

---

[3] The line cannot refer to Isabella: in what way could Claudio 'restore' Isabella? By contrast, he can 'restore' Julietta's virtuous reputation by legitimising their marriage with banns, ceremony, and witnesses.

embodiment of the ambivalence of opinion concerning *sponsalia per verba de praesenti* and *sponsalia per verba de futuro* early in the Seventeenth Century. The validity of handfasting is neither fully confirmed nor fully denied. The lovers in *Measure for Measure* are the casualties of this enduring ambiguity.

Introducing Claudio

In *Measure for Measure*, Claudio is not merely a victim of that stock-in-trade of the opening scenes of Shakespearian comedy, 'the imposition of irrational law';[4] he is also, like the Duke, a fount of philosophical reflection. His ruminations when under arrest explore many of the themes central to the play. He offers the audience important guidance as to how they should respond to other major characters, particularly his sister, Isabella, and her persecutor, Angelo. In addition, on the eve of his execution, he utters one of the most moving and disturbing speeches in the Shakespearean canon as he contemplates his fate after death. Although this latter context has caused some in the critical tradition to judge Claudio harshly as the 'faithless coward' that his beleaguered sister accuses him of being (III, i, 136), his understandable trepidation as he confronts death should not detract from his noble and dignified character reflected elsewhere in the text. Overall, Claudio might even be considered the most exemplary secular male character in the play, his only possible rival to the title being the Provost.

There can be little doubt that, even before Claudio first appears, the audience has been invited to feel respect and sympathy for this victim of Angelo's moral crusade against illicit sexual activity. According to Mistress Overdone, he is '*Signior* Claudio' (I, ii, 59; italics added), given the title of a

---

[4] The phrase derives from the lectures on the patterns of Shakespearian comedy given by Dr. John Wilders at the University of Oxford, 1970–1.

gentleman.[5] He is highly regarded by her as 'worth five thousand' (I, ii, 57) of those more dissolute 'gentlemen' who frequent her 'house of resort'. Nevertheless, he has been 'arrested and carried to prison' (I, ii, 56–7) where 'his head [is] to be chopped off' (I, ii, 63) for 'getting Madam Julietta with child' (I, ii, 67–8). The bluntness of the language and the savagery of the sentence are a shock, particularly to a modern audience: the punishment seems grossly disproportionate, especially when the lines may be delivered in the setting of a brothel, where much more dubious sexual transactions are seemingly flourishing.[6]

From the moment of his entry, Claudio's dignity is suggested by the fact that he speaks consistently in verse:[7] he and his lover, Julietta, are the only characters to do so throughout the play, which might serve to confirm their noble lineage and characters. In addition, much of the verse that he speaks is based on antithesis, 'weighing' disparate things in the manner of the scales of justice which, as the title of the play suggests, is the central symbol of *Measure for Measure*.

From his first entry, Claudio is likely to elicit both compassion and a degree of admiration from an audience.[8]

---

[5] He is also referred to as 'signior' by Pompey (I, ii, 106) and the Provost (III, i, 49), confirmation of Claudio's elevated social status.

[6] The text of the First Folio gives no setting for this scene. Lever suggests 'A public place' (p. 9), but both BBC productions (1979 and 1994) plausibly set Mistress Overdone's dialogue in her brothel, thereby creating a stark contrast with the courtly setting of the previous scene.

[7] The only lines from Claudio that are presented by Lever in prose might be scanned as rough-hewn iambic pentameters, thus: 'Let me ask / My sister pardon; I am so out of love / With life that I will sue to be rid of it' (III, i, 170–1). The slight metrical irregularity here might suggest Claudio's anguish at his painful interview with his sister.

[8] Braunmuller and Watson find Claudio in this scene 'rather priggish, naïve and moralizing' (p. 175, n.), but any priggish moralizing could be attributed to the efforts of a young man in mortal danger to understand his circumstances and to seek consolation in philosophy.

Despite his distress on being paraded through the streets as a sexual offender, he addresses the Provost with restraint when questioning why he has not been dispatched to prison immediately (I, ii, 108–9). He and Julietta might be dressed penitentially, for example in a white sheet prescribed by the Church in Shakespeare's day for such offenders.[9] On learning that public humiliation is part of the punishment imposed by Angelo, Claudio becomes philosophical:

> Thus can the demi-god, Authority,
> Make us pay down for our offence by weight.
> The words of heaven; on whom it will, it will;
> On whom it will not, so; yet still 'tis just. [I, ii, 112–16]

Claudio is here expressing some of the central concepts of the play: that justice is divinely ordained to ensure that punishment is proportionate to crime; and that justice retains its legitimacy although it may punish only certain offenders while other such criminals go free. The tone of Claudio's speech is, nevertheless, open to question. If taken literally, the speech is a stoical acknowledgement of the validity of his sentence; but it could be revealing, through thinly-veiled irony, the injustice of his condemnation when others who are guilty of similar or greater offences escape the law.

Claudio's capacity for perspicacity and philosophical reflection—remarkable (some might argue, implausible) in a man under sentence of death—remains apparent after he encounters his friend, Lucio. Claudio, like the Duke elsewhere in the play, performs a choric function, extrapolating from experience to formulate dispassionate maxims of universal human significance. When questioned about his 'restraint', Claudio explains that it derives

> From too much liberty, my Lucio. Liberty,

---

[9] In the 1978 RSC production directed by Barry Kyle, Claudio's arms were bound and he was obliged to wear, on his head, a paper mitre depicting the flames of hell.

As surfeit, is the father of much fast;
So every scope by the immoderate use
Turns to restraint. Our natures do pursue,
Like rats that ravin down their proper bane,
A thirsty evil; and when we drink, we die. [I, ii, 117–22]

Fittingly in a play entitled *Measure for Measure*, this speech is based entirely on antithesis and comparison. It develops Claudio's previous image concerning the scales of justice whereby authority can 'Make us pay down for our offence by weight' (line 113). 'Liberty' is counterbalanced by 'restraint': Claudio explains that over-indulgence, whether it be excessive consumption of food and drink ('surfeit') or other loose behaviour such as sexual misconduct ('liberty'), will result in 'fast', that is, obligatory abstinence, with perhaps a hint at being held 'fast' in prison. Accordingly, he can argue that *every* scope' when used immoderately (that is, any indulgence or freedom when not subject to 'measure') will lead to the imposition of dire penalties. Claudio's concluding simile has close affinities with those other strains of animal imagery in the play which suggest that, without 'restraint' (imposed either by the law or by the exercise of reason), humanity will revert to bestial behaviour. Just as rats eagerly devour poison, so human beings crave those things that will kill them. Unrestrained freedom in humans promotes self-destructive indulgence, 'a thirsty evil' that recalls the earlier reference to 'surfeit', with its connotations of the damage deriving from excessive drinking— for example, the thirst and discomfort caused by a hangover. The expression 'when we drink, we die' concedes that, just as arsenic induces thirst in rats as it kills them, so too much liberty makes humans thirst for that which will destroy them. The image, nevertheless, may be less philosophically self-critical, and more a complaint against injustice: as Claudio will protest that 'nineteen zodiacs have gone round' since the law against fornication was last enforced (I, ii, 157), the ratsbane-image may suggest that, in seeming for so long to condone sexual intercourse outside authorised wedlock, the state has deliberately lured lovers with poison, tempting them towards their destruction.[10]

Having employed generally measured language to protest the legitimacy of his relationship with Julietta (I, ii, 134–44), Claudio lapses into more disjointed speech when considering the injustice of the sentence of death imposed on him. His emotion is obvious in a sentence of considerable length (fifteen lines) that breaks down syntactically into a complex, periodic structure after its very first line:

> And the new deputy now for the Duke—
> Whether it be the fault and glimpse of newness,
> O[r] whether that the body public be
> A horse whereon the governor doth ride,
> Who, newly in the seat, that it may know
> He can command, lets it straight feel the spur;
> Whether the tyranny be in his place,
> Or in his eminence that fills it up,
> I stagger in—but this new governor
> Awakes me all the enrolled penalties
> Which have, like unscour'd armour, hung by th'wall
> So long, that nineteen zodiacs have gone round,
> And none of them been worn; and for a name
> Now puts the drowsy and neglected act
> Freshly on me: 'tis surely for a name. [I, ii, 146–60]

The actor playing Claudio might scarcely pause to draw breath as the indirect questions accumulate between subject (line 146) and predicate (line 155), some of these subordinate clauses themselves fragmented by intervening clauses and phrases (see lines 150–1). Claudio's confusion in the first half of this speech is reflected by the tormented syntax, as he conjectures desperately on Angelo's motivation for persecuting him, characterising Angelo as a tyrant, either by nature, or because

---

[10] For a fuller discussion of this idea, see C. K. Stead, ed., *Shakespeare*: Measure for Measure: *A Casebook* (London: Macmillan, 1971), pp. 33–34.

of the corruptive influence of the power bestowed upon him as Deputy (lines 152–3). Claudio's words rush towards his exasperated conclusion, that his life is to be forfeit simply to enhance the reputation of the new deputy. His imagery involves a sharp antithesis: Angelo, newly in authority, is like a horseman intent on immediately establishing his control of a potentially unruly mount by imposing discipline on it; while the law under which Claudio has been punished was old and neglected, 'unscour'd armour' rusting in disuse for nineteen years. The two images fuse to create the picture of Angelo as part of an equestrian statue, mounted on the steed of state and clad in the renovated armour of the 'old law' which, like the Old Law of the Bible, seems outmoded, cold, and hard.

Claudio's dignity and distress are established partly by the form, tone, and content of the verse that he speaks, and partly by contrast with Lucio's flippant interjections in prose. Claudio must, nevertheless, rely on the irreverent Lucio to recruit the assistance of his sister, Isabella:

> I prithee, Lucio, do me this kind service. . . .
> Acquaint her with the danger of my state:
> Implore her, in my voice, that she make friends
> To the strict deputy: bid herself assay him. [I, ii, 166–71]

Claudio's language is more measured than in his previous speech about his sentence under Angelo, but the urgency of his circumstances is still apparent in the profusion of imperatives that he directs towards his friend: 'do', 'acquaint', 'implore', and 'bid'. Claudio's references to his sister's persuasive abilities conveys both his respect for her and the desperate hope to which he clings that she might save his life by pleading his cause:

> . . . in her youth
> There is a prone and speechless dialect
> Such as move men; beside, she hath prosperous art
> When she will play with reason and discourse,

And well can she persuade.[11] [I, ii, 172–5]

The speech performs the function of introducing Isabella and her reputation to the audience two scenes before she first appears on stage, reminding us that Claudio's plight is a dramatic device, as indispensable a part of the induction to the play as the Duke's decision to quit the Viennese court and to don his disguise as a friar.

---

[11] William Empson's suggestion, developed by Jonathan Bate, that the word 'prone' in this speech could have sexual connotations, is discussed at some length by Frank Kermode, *Shakespeare's Language* (London: Penguin, 2001), pp. 150–156. In conjunction with 'youth', 'move', and 'play', 'prone' might suggest that Claudio's words are anticipating the erotic effect of Isabella's presence on Angelo in Act II. If so, then surely an audience would consider this context as proleptic irony in which Claudio appears unaware of the possibly scurrilous dimension to his speech. The alternative is to imagine that Claudio would intentionally send his sister, a postulant, as potentially flirtatious sexual bait to the Deputy, an interpretation that would transform Claudio into a pimp and Isabella into a tart on their first introduction to the audience. Such a perverse interpretation of their characters is not borne out by any subsequent context in the play. Claudio's assumed meaning for 'prone' might be 'willing to hear', a gloss supported by language-scholar Hilda Hulme with reference to a Latin thesaurus written by Bishop Thomas Cooper (c.1517–94). This is just one of several plausible 'innocent' alternatives offered by Kermode. Claudio would thus present his young sister as an attentive and silent listener, as well as a talented debater and rhetorician, one who in both roles might sway the Deputy in Claudio's favour. The word 'prone' might appear to have two diametrically-opposed meanings—one erotic and one innocent—to the ingenious observer (perhaps even to Lucio, the recipient of this speech, who is always quick to recognise and to utter innuendo); but Claudio, the speaker, should be presented as unaware of any such 'laddish' ambiguity. For an audience to believe otherwise would seriously undermine his tragic stature in subsequent scenes.

Claudio *in Absentia*

Although absent from the stage, Claudio is the focus of much of the Second Act. His capital sentence is the ostensible subject of the great debate that takes place between Isabella and Angelo in Act II, scenes ii and iv—although Angelo's illicit desire for Isabella gradually usurps that discussion. When Angelo eventually makes his carnal intentions clear to her, she demands 'a present pardon for my brother' (II, iv, 151), otherwise threatening to expose Angelo. In dismissing her threat, he responds with a threat of his own: to torture Claudio to death if she refuses to accede to the sexual bargain (II, iv, 162–6). Although Claudio's fate is being decided, he himself plays no direct part in these proceedings.

During his absence from the stage (between Act I, scene ii and Act III, scene i), Claudio is the object of frequent reference by other characters, enabling the audience to establish an informed judgement of his crime and the penalty imposed on him. Shakespeare balances the arguments for and against harsh punishment on Claudio by allocating dramatic voices to either side of the case. For Lucio, Claudio deserves praise rather than blame for consummating his relationship with Julietta:

> . . . if myself might be his judge,
> He should receive his punishment in thanks:
> He has got his friend with child. [I, iv, 27–9]

In one remarkable speech, the usually cynical, frivolous Lucio produces a memorable celebration of human erotic love with reference to Claudio and Julietta:

> Your brother and his lover have embrac'd;
> As those that feed grow full, as blossoming time
> That from the seedness the bare fallow brings
> To teeming foison, even so her plenteous womb
> Expresseth his full tilth and husbandry. [I, iv, 40–4]

Lucio's panegyric emphasises how natural is the development of the relationship between the two lovers. Their intimacy is expressed by the affectionate delicacy of the participle 'embrac'd'. Its consequence (of Julietta becoming pregnant) is conveyed through imagery relating to how nourishment produces growth and to how the natural cycle of the seasons brings abundance to harvest. The concluding metaphor envisages Claudio as the assiduous husbandman, labouring to produce his crop of offspring from Julietta's fruitful body. When sexual intercourse is described in this way, nothing could seem more wholesome, laudable, or inoffensive than such pursuits between lovers.

By contrast, Isabella's horror at Claudio's offence is apparent throughout the opening words of her petition to Angelo:

> There is a vice that most I do abhor,
> And most desire should meet the blow of justice;
> For which I would not plead, but that I must;
> For which I must not plead, but that I am
> At war 'twixt will and will not. [II, ii, 29–33]

This speech is remarkable for what it does *not* say. Isabella avoids identifying Claudio as the offender. Nor does she specify his offence. Instead, the whole emphasis of the speech—deploying the personal pronoun ('I') five times in as many lines—is on the anguish that *she herself* is suffering because of her moral dilemma, rather than on the imperative to absolve her brother. In that respect, it is a selfish speech, which calls into question the piety of the speaker's seemingly virtuous sentiments. By entirely failing to plead in Claudio's defence while expressing her abhorrence of the deed that her brother has committed—that same deed that Lucio celebrated so lyrically— she succeeds in this speech in doing no more than to condemn her own brother and to confirm the justice of his capital sentence.

With the exception of Angelo, the officers of the law are sympathetic to Claudio's cause. The harshness of Angelo's sentence on Claudio is summarised in the only context in the play when Escalus's anonymous fellow magistrate speaks: 'Lord Angelo is severe' (II, i, 279). The Provost considers that the offence is like a figment of the imagination: 'He hath but as offended in a dream' (II, ii, 4). Furthermore, he is indignant that Claudio is to be executed when such sexual activity has been universal from time immemorial:

> All sects, all ages smack of this vice, and he
> To die for't! [II, ii, 5–6]

The Provost endorses Lucio's opinion when he comments to the disguised Duke that Claudio is 'More fit to do another such offence, / Than die for this' (II, iii, 14-15). Like Lucio, the Provost regards Claudio as a worthy future parent rather than as a criminal deserving execution. Familial considerations recur in Escalus's opinion that Claudio's honourable parentage is an important consideration:

> Alas, this gentleman,
> Whom I would save, had a most noble father. [II, i, 6–7]

These words foreshadow the contrast between Claudio's 'noble' conduct in his personal relationship with Julietta and the ignoble behaviour of 'the drabs and the knaves' to whom Pompey will refer later in the scene (II, i, 231–32), frequenters of 'hot-house[s]' (II, i, 65) such as Mistress Overdone's brothel. Escalus's frustration at the injustice of Claudio's sentence is readily apparent in the gnomic couplet with which he concludes his interview with Angelo:

> Some run [through brakes of Vice] and answer none,
> And some condemned for a fault alone. [II, i, 39–40]

The antithesis in these two lines is clarified by Rowe's emendation (enclosed above in square brackets) of the Folio reading: those who sport themselves 'in thickets of depravity'

310

(places so dark and impenetrable to the law that offenders cannot readily be identified there) may never face prosecution for their crimes; whereas unfortunates like Claudio (who, implicitly, do not frequent such 'brakes of Vice') suffer the extreme penalty for a single, trivial lapse.[12] Escalus, whose knowledge of the 'nature of our people' and the 'terms / For common justice' was highly praised by the Duke (I, i, 9–13), would seem to judge Claudio's action not as an offence, but rather as a misdemeanour at worst.

Unlike the anonymous Justice, the Provost, and Escalus, Angelo refuses to consider any mitigating circumstances such as family ties:

> It is the law, not I, condemn your brother;
> Were he my kinsman, brother, or my son,
> It should be thus with him. . . .
> [I] do him right that, answering one foul wrong,
> Lives not to act another. [II, ii, 80–2 and 104–5]

There need be no implication in those latter two lines that Angelo believes Claudio to be sexually promiscuous: for Angelo, each further child begotten from the 'true contract' between Claudio and Julietta would be another 'foul wrong' as neither Church nor state has endorsed their relationship. Angelo goes further in his second meeting with Isabella, equating the begetting of an illegitimate child with two indisputably capital offences:

> Fie, these filthy vices! It were as good
> To pardon him that hath from nature stolen

---

[12] That 'fault' represents 'a trivial lapse' is implied by the context: Angelo has suggested a distinction between a fault and a more serious 'offence' only twelve lines earlier. In addition, the pyrrhic foot ('-ed for') throws extra emphasis on to the next heavy stress, the short-vowelled monosyllable 'fault' which, accompanied by the word 'alone', implies that such an isolated 'fault' does not fully constitute an offence.

A man already made, as to remit
Their saucy sweetness that do coin heaven's image
In stamps that are forbid. 'Tis all as easy
Falsely to take away a life true made,
As to put mettle in restrained means
To make a false one. [II, iv, 42–9]

Claudio is thus condemned by 'the voice of the recorded law' (II, iv, 61) as guilty of a crime that warrants the same death-penalty as murder or forgery.

By these means, Shakespeare implicitly invites the audience to arbitrate between a range of judgements on Claudio's relationship with Julietta. For Lucio, it is an entirely praiseworthy union. For the officers of the law other than Angelo (that is, for the Provost, Escalus, and the Justice), it is a venial lapse. For Isabella, it is an abhorrent vice, nonetheless one committed by a beloved brother. For Angelo, it is a capital offence that cannot be mitigated by any extraneous consideration. It is, however, Angelo himself who will offer to remit Claudio's sentence in return for Isabella's sexual acquiescence. For the audience, the sordid transaction that Angelo suggests both invalidates his capital sentence on Claudio (by calling his judgement into question) and elevates Claudio's relationship with Julietta (by comparison with Angelo's indecent proposal). Angelo's threat to torture Claudio to death should Isabella refuse to accept the terms of his improper bargain (II, iv, 162–66) finally and entirely discredits any judgement that Angelo might have passed on Claudio. His verdict, tainted by association with a depraved tyrant, is unworthy of support.

Set against Angelo's malicious exploitation of Claudio's misery, we encounter the simplicity and sincerity of Julietta's account of her relationship with her betrothed. She loves Claudio 'as I love the woman that wrong'd him' (II, iii, 25), that is, as herself. Their lovemaking was 'mutually committed' (II, iii, 27), in contrast to the compulsion of Isabella that Angelo wishes to enforce. Finally, her distress on learning of the imminence of Claudio's sentence of death is harrowing:

> Must die to-morrow! O injurious love,
> That respites me a life, whose very comfort
> Is still a dying horror! [II, iii, 40–2]

Julietta's impassioned words create deep pathos and a profound sense of injustice. Her life has been spared because of her pregnancy, but the child that she will bear will be a constantly distressing reminder of its dead father, Claudio, executed for consensual sexual activity that sealed a mutual exchange of vows.

Claudio in Prison

An audience is therefore likely to be particularly sympathetically disposed towards Claudio when he re-appears in the prison at the start of the Third Act. His first words there invite the audience's compassion as he refers to hope as his solace in misery, presenting himself as reconciled to either life or death:

> The miserable have no other medicine
> But only hope:
> I have hope to live, and am prepar'd to die. (III, i, 2–4)

His stoical dignity is particularly well conveyed by that final line, with its careful syntactical balance of the antitheses 'live' and 'die' implying that he has weighed the outcomes dispassionately and is calmly reconciled to either possibility. Once he has heard the disguised Duke's long speech, that fusion of philosophical consolation and contempt for the world, Claudio calmly expresses his acceptance of the inevitability of present death:

> To sue to live, I find I seek to die,
> And seeking death, find life. Let it come on. [III, i, 42–3]

The antitheses ('live'/'die' and 'death'/'life') and the compressed expression may initially puzzle an audience, but the sense seems to be strongly Christian,[13] even though the Duke's speech contained not a single overtly Christian reference. Claudio had initially recruited his sister 'to sue to live' for him: she was to plead with Angelo to save Claudio's life. Now, Claudio has set aside such worldly concerns and is petitioning, not the Deputy for temporal life, but God for eternal life. He trusts that, in preparing himself spiritually for death, he can achieve eternal salvation. He has transformed the disguised Duke's injunction, 'Be absolute for death' (III, i, 5), into heroic steadfastness: 'Let it come on.' In this frame of mind, a condemned man such as Claudio might die in a state of grace.

Tragically, his sister's intervention will be shown to destroy his resolve. Claudio's transformation from stoic resignation to death into desperate pleading for life must strike an audience as painfully ironic. Isabella's last words in Act II had announced her intention to inform Claudio of Angelo's 'request' in order to 'fit [Claudio's] mind to death, for his soul's rest' (II, iv, 185–6). Before her arrival at the prison, however, the Duke has already persuaded Claudio to be 'absolute for death' (III, i, 5), as death would release him from the afflictions of life—accentuated in prison—and as there seemed no prospect of a repeal from Angelo. When Isabella informs Claudio of Angelo's proposal—Isabella's virginity in return for her brother's life—the foundations on which Claudio's resolve was built are undermined by vain hopes of acquittal, and the whole edifice topples.

That Claudio should lose his resolve is entirely credible in this most painful of scenes. Isabella prevaricates for over forty lines (III, i, 54–96), tantalising Claudio by hinting at the possibility of ignoble reprieve but refusing (despite Claudio's frequent interjections) to specify how he might save his life.

---

[13] Lever suggests an echo of Matthew 16. 25: 'For whosoever will save his life, shall lose it: and, whosoever shall lose his life for my sake, shall find it.'

Goaded by Isabella's 'fear' that he might jeopardise his 'perpetual honour' to escape death (III, i, 73–6), and by her conceit that 'apprehension' of death is all that distinguishes between the death-pangs of a beetle and those of a giant (III, i, 77–80), Claudio responds heatedly:

> Why give you me this shame?
> Think you I can a resolution fetch
> From flowery tenderness? If I must die,
> I will encounter darkness as a bride
> And hug it in mine arms. [III, i, 80–84]

He appears insulted that his sister doubts his courage, and contemptuous of her belief that she can strengthen his 'resolution' by words of 'flowery tenderness'. Again, his language is based on antithesis: here the sharp contrast between manly strength and delicate affection refutes any suggestion that the latter could fortify the former. This leads logically (but, nevertheless, rather surprisingly) to the erotic image with which he concludes the retort. As courage was equated with male sexual potency, and as 'death' was the standard euphemism for orgasm in the age of Shakespeare, Claudio imagines the throes of death as a passionate embrace that he will welcome.[14] Of course, there is a sadly ironic appropriateness in his words, as his sentence of death has resulted directly from his 'encounter' with Julietta 'as a bride' whom he embraced 'in mine arms'.

Still Claudio is denied the knowledge of how he might save his life, the delay plausibly weakening his resolve to 'be absolute for death'. Although Isabella rejoices to learn of Claudio's resolve, she further prevaricates for a dozen lines (III, i, 85–96) before finally revealing the terms of the bargain with Angelo:

> If I would yield him my virginity

---

[14] There may be a deliberate echo here of Isabella's speech to Angelo in which she conflates notions of painful death and of erotic fulfilment (II, iv, 100–04). Like sister, like brother.

315

Thou mightst be freed[.] [III, i, 97–8]

Such prolonged evasiveness can signify only one thing: that, despite her complacent certitude before her encounter with her brother that he would suffer death twenty times over rather than subject her to 'such abhorr'd pollution' (II, iv, 177–82), she now believes that he will falter and fail her: 'O, I do fear thee, Claudio, and I quake' (III, i, 73). Although she encourages him to be 'ready . . . for your death tomorrow' (III, i, 106), her doubts in his noble resolution are instrumental in eroding his courage: it is most difficult to maintain resolve when expected by a beloved devotee to falter.

After Claudio's initial reactions to Isabella's revelation of Angelo's intentions—the disbelief of 'O heavens, it cannot be!' (III, i, 98), followed by the revulsion of 'Thou shalt not do't' (III, i, 102)—irresolution, confusion, and fear appear gradually to tighten their grip on him:

> Has he affections in him,
> That thus can make him bite the law by th'nose
> When he would force it?—Sure, it is no sin;
> Or of the deadly seven it is the least. . . .
> If it were damnable, he being so wise,
> Why would he for the momentary trick
> Be perdurably fin'd?—O Isabel!
> . . . Death is a fearful thing.
> [III, i, 107–15]

During this speech, Isabella's contributions are reduced to two brief interjections, as she is no longer governing Claudio's thoughts. His speech (four sentences in the pattern question / statement / question / statement) shows him sifting the evidence and reaching his own conclusions, no longer listening to his sister's objections. Because Angelo desires to commit the same offence for which he prosecutes others, Claudio leaps to the conclusion that either he (Claudio) has been guilty of no offence at all, or that lechery is subordinate to other sins. Claudio's second question seems rhetorical in the context of the conclusion that he has just drawn: as Angelo is such a learned judge, he would not risk damnation for the fleeting trifle of sexual gratification. Believing himself exonerated from any serious offence involving Julietta, and reminded by his sister that he is still to suffer execution (III, i, 105), Claudio now turns the tables on Isabella: if any sexual activity that a sister might undertake to save him is not damnable, then it is a preferable alternative to what he faces.

The Sense of Death is Most in Apprehension

Claudio contemplates with horror his imminent encounter with death in an implicit response to the Duke's earlier monologue expressing contempt for life. Yet again, Claudio's speech is based on balance and antithesis, as he weighs the hellish torments of death against the 'paradise' of any kind of life, however arduous or painful:

> Ay, but to die, and go we know not where;
> To lie in cold obstruction and to rot;
> This sensible warm motion to become
> A kneaded clod; and the delighted spirit
> To bath in fiery floods, or to reside
> In thrilling region of thick-ribbed ice;
> To be imprison'd in the viewless winds
> And blown with restless violence round about
> The pendent world: or to be worse than worst
> Of those that lawless and incertain thought
> Imagine howling,—'tis too horrible.
> The weariest and most loathed worldly life
> That age, ache, penury and imprisonment
> Can lay on nature, is a paradise
> To what we fear of death. [III, i, 117–31]

The word 'Ay' with which Claudio commences does not indicate agreement with Isabella; rather, it represents an attempt to wrest the initiative in their exchanges from her, to silence her with apparent acquiescence so that he can freely articulate his fear of death. His apprehension seems initially to derive from the fact that what happens after death is unknown (line 117), and yet the remaining images that he deploys are horrifyingly specific.

The tortured first sentence does not find the resolution of a main clause until its final five syllables: ''tis too horrible' (line 127); before that, it was an accumulation of subordinate phrases for ten lines of nightmarish detail. The verbs, all infinitives and therefore unspecific in either subject (usually) or tense, are suggestive of the universality and infinity of the experiences that they describe. The images are jumbled, as the frantic Claudio conflates the respective fates of soul and body after death into a terrifying inventory of the tortures that might befall those who are to be 'perduraby fin'd' (that is, eternally punished: line 114). The dead body will be deprived of all warmth and motion (line 118), decaying noisomely as the 'carrion' does in Angelo's first soliloquy (II, ii, 165–8).[15] The corpse will be transformed into a 'kneaded clod' (line 120), suffering the degradation of being trampled underfoot as it becomes indistinguishable from the earth from which it came. By contrast, the living body had previously been a 'sensible warm motion' (line 119) with freedom to move at will and to enjoy sensations such as the warmth of life and love. Warmth is a comfortably moderate state, contrasting sharply with the extremes of the 'fiery floods' and the 'region of thick-ribbed ice' which, Claudio fears, the soul will suffer after death.

The phrase 'delighted spirit' (line 120) is problematical: perhaps, as Hanmer suggested in his 1744 edition of Shakespeare, 'delighted' is a misreading for 'dilated', for the immortal spirit will expand into new zones of terrifying experience while the dead body moulders. If 'delighted' is the correct reading, then perhaps the word indicates the heights of ecstasy that the spirit once attained in life, before its sensitivity

---

[15] The notion that the body will degenerate into a mere 'obstruction' (line 118) is reminiscent of Hamlet's meditation on death in the Gravedigger Scene: 'Imperious Caesar, dead and turn'd to clay, / Might stop a hole to keep the wind away' (*Hamlet*: V, i, 207–8).

was subjected, in the afterlife, to the agonies of being engulfed in a raging inferno, or trapped and shuddering within the ribs of some monstrous ice-beast, like Jonah in his whale.[16]

Angelo had threatened Claudio with 'ling'ring sufferance' should Isabella not agree to Angelo's demands (II, iv, 164–6). Although not informed of that threat by his sister, Claudio is now envisaging far worse 'ling'ring sufferance': not merely temporal, but *endless* torment. His imagination strays back to the corporeal in his vision of the clay, to which the body has returned, further degenerating into dust, to be 'blown . . . about' in the 'viewless winds', suffering 'restless violence'—that is,

---

[16] Jonah's descent into the belly of the whale before re-emerging after a period of suffering was regarded throughout the Middle Ages as symbolic of the passage of the soul through Purgatory, where sinners would atone through suffering for their misdeeds on Earth. Claudio's language reflects medieval conceptions of purgatory in his reference to 'bath[ing]' in 'fiery floods' (line 121), as if to wash off mortal sin. The only difference between Purgatory and Hell (according to the medieval conception) was that suffering in the former would ultimately be terminated, however prolonged; whereas suffering in the latter was eternal, offering neither respite nor hope. The notion of the dead in the afterlife being tormented by cold (as well as heat) can be encountered in the classical tradition (for example, in Virgil: *Aeneid*, VI). Medieval iconography sometimes depicted hell as comprising zones of fire (red pigment predominating) and of ice (blue pigment predominating), each zone overflowing with tormented souls. In literature, this duality can be traced from Dante through Shakespeare to its most accessible synopsis in Milton:

Thither by harpy-footed Furies haled,
At certain revolutions all the damned
Are brought: and feel by turns the bitter change
Of fierce extremes, extremes by change more fierce,
From beds of raging fire to starve in ice
Their soft ethereal warmth, and there to pine
Immovable, infixed, and frozen round,
Periods of time, thence hurried back to fire.
[*Paradise Lost*: II, 596–603]

eternal battering (lines 123–4).[17] The winds are 'viewless' because they are invisible, as are the specks of human dust (or, possibly, the human souls) that the winds bear along. Human destiny, in this terrible vision, is to become absolutely helpless, eternally tormented, and entirely abandoned, while denied the refuge of oblivion. The four elements of fire, water, earth, and air jointly conspire to accentuate the suffering, as the spirit is tortured by moving between flames and ice, while the body is reduced to soil and then vanishes into the wind as dust.

Claudio recognises that the imagination is limited to human experience in this 'pendent world' (line 125), suspended between Heaven and Hell but ignorant of both. The experience of the afterlife could therefore be even 'worse' than the 'worst' that the human mind could conceive: even when the mind is 'lawless' (that is, not subject to regulation by such influences as reason or Christian doctrine) and 'incertain' (that is, given to wild surmise), it might not be capable of envisaging the full horrors of punishments in the afterlife (lines 125–7). The 'howling' would be 'too horrible' for the living to conceive (line 127).

Having contemplated the potential agonies of the afterlife, Claudio must now reject the doctrine offered to him in the Duke's speech, 'Be absolute for death' (III, I, 5–41), that catalogued the miseries of earthly life and presented death as a release from suffering. To Claudio, faced with execution but snatching at the chance of reprieve, even the most excruciating life is a 'paradise' when set against the terrible possibilities of what will be experienced after death. Negative superlatives abound—'worst', 'too horrible', 'weariest', 'most loathed'—as he weighs the pains of life against the potentially far greater pains to be encountered in the afterlife. In an agonisingly ponderous line, he contemplates the very worst that 'worldly

---

[17] Alternatively, this image may represent a further experience of the soul. As with the references to extreme heat and cold, the notion here would be that the soul undergoes agonising physical pain, not merely spiritual anguish, as its punishment in the afterlife.

life' can impose on 'nature' (that is, on humanity): 'age, ache, penury and imprisonment' (line 129). The long vowels (those initial *a*-sounds) and the strong caesurae (indicated by the commas) combine with three consecutive heavy stresses on the first three syllables ('age, ache, pen . . .') to stretch the line agonisingly, expressing the distress caused by accumulating afflictions. The nouns increase in syllabic length until the final noun, with its four syllables, seems to suggest a line stretching out to the crack of doom. Yet, to the tormented Claudio, this anguished life is greatly preferable to the inconceivable horrors to be faced after death.[18]

As his sister's reaction to his words is ambiguous—Claudio might plausibly appear to interpret her sobbed 'Alas, alas!' (III, i, 131) as sympathy rather than condemnation—Claudio ventures to plead with her:

Sweet sister, let me live.
What sin you do to save a brother's life,
Nature dispenses with the deed so far
That it becomes a virtue. [III, i, 132–5]

---

[18] This speech and the reaction that it provokes from Isabella are the most emotionally intense moments in the play. Claudio's language, reflective of his own mental agony, is also deeply distressing to an audience. This is not the customary territory of comedy: Claudio's words are very close in substance to those encountered in two of Shakespeare's great tragedies written in the period between 1600 and 1606, the same period that produced *Measure for Measure*. Claudio's reference to death as an unknowable destination recalls Hamlet's image that the afterlife is 'The undiscover'd country, from whose bourn / No traveller returns' (*Hamlet*, III, i, 79–80). Certainly, Claudio's meditation on the decay of the body echoes Hamlet's preoccupation with physical corruption in his remarks to Horatio in the Gravedigger Scene (*Hamlet*, V, i, 196–210). Furthermore, Claudio's speculation on what might be 'worse' than the 'worst' that is imaginable anticipates Edgar's soliloquy on despair in *King Lear* (IV, i, 1–29), first performed two years after *Measure for Measure*.

The first line is moving in its simplicity. The subsequent three lines, however, are a painful reminder of the words of Angelo (II, iv, 63–4), expressing the same meaning to the same purpose: if Isabella were to sacrifice her virginity to save Claudio's life, her seemingly immoral deed would be redeemed by its virtuous intention. It is therefore entirely credible that Isabella, in response, should unleash such a hysterical and pitiless tirade against her brother. She had no power to condemn her would-be seducer, Angelo; but she can condemn her brother for deploying Angelo's arguments to promote Angelo's cause.

Claudio, his protests floundering (III, i, 146 and 150) as he is overwhelmed by his sister's invective, is rescued from despair by the intervention of the Duke. The tissue of lies that the Duke utters (III, i, 160–66) has a seemingly benevolent purpose: once again to reconcile Claudio to death by convincing him that there is no hope of reprieve. The audience has (as yet) no knowledge of the Duke's intention to save Claudio's life, and ultimately to claim Isabella's hand, seemingly as his reward for redeeming her brother. The Duke's instructions to Claudio may, therefore, appear a sincere attempt to offer Claudio his opportunity for peace of mind rather than an example of self-interested manipulation by the Duke:

> Do not satisfy your resolution with hopes that are fallible; tomorrow you must die; go to your knees, and make ready.
> [III, i, 167–9]

Claudio appears entirely taken in by the deception, regretting his petition to his sister and, like Angelo at the end of the play, craving death as a release from the shame that he has brought upon himself by his words:

> Let me ask my sister pardon; I am so out of love with life that I will sue to be rid of it. [III, i, 170–1]

In response both to Claudio's opening clause here (concerning his yearning for his sister's forgiveness) and to J.

W. Lever's editorial suggestion, a director might venture a mimed reconciliation between sister and brother during the disguised Duke's discourse with the Provost; but the brevity of the six-line exchange between Duke and Provost (III, i, 173–8) and the absence of any dialogue between brother and sister would render such a short, silent reconciliation dramatically unconvincing.[19] Better to leave the bitterness between Claudio and Isabella unresolved until the siblings are reunited in the final scene, when forgiveness is paramount and universal.

A Man Condemned

Although Claudio has under three full lines remaining in the play, his fate remains central to the action throughout Acts III–V. Both the 'bed-trick' and the 'head-trick', the dramatic events that dominate Acts III and IV, are devised to save Claudio from death. The latter device must be improvised when the former ploy fails in this objective. Mariana, incognito, takes Isabella's place in Angelo's bed, in return for which Angelo has pledged to issue Claudio's pardon. When the corrupt Deputy breaks his word, insisting on seeing Claudio's severed head as proof of his execution, an alternative victim must be found. Barnadine proves too recalcitrant (and physically too dissimilar to Claudio) to be a suitable substitute; but the death of Ragozine, a pirate of Claudio's age and appearance, provides the necessary prop. Angelo is deceived, and Claudio's life is saved.

Claudio's final speech in the play is brief but worthy of comment. The Provost, holding the warrant for his execution, informs Claudio that he 'must be made immortal' by eight o'clock the following morning (IV, ii, 62–3). As it is 'dead midnight' when the Provost speaks, Claudio could count the remaining hours of his life on the fingers of two hands. Were he frantically fearful, it would be entirely understandable. But he

---

[19] Such a reconciliation was presented at this point in the text in the 2015 production at the Globe Theatre, but it was the briefest of interludes and seemed perfunctory as it was upstaged by the dialogue involving the Duke and the Provost.

appears ethereally serene. He speaks no word of himself or of his own plight. Instead, he characterises Barnadine, his fellow prisoner who is to share his fate: Barnadine is

> As fast lock'd up in sleep as guiltless labour
> When it lies starkly in the traveller's bones.
> He will not wake. [IV, ii, 64–6]

The image of 'guiltless labour' at rest finds its origin in the Bible: Ecclesiastes 6: 12 records the sweet sleep of the labouring man (Claudio's word 'traveller' might be pronounced 'travail-er' to make the biblical echo more apparent). The words that he applies to the resting Barnadine reflect the spiritual tranquillity of Claudio himself. In fact, Barnadine is in a drunken stupor (see IV, ii, 140–51 and IV, iii, 21–62), but Claudio, in his state of grace, sees it as innocent slumber. Claudio's words are dignified and lyrical, clearly suggesting that he is reconciled to death. The Provost's injunction, 'Well, go; prepare yourself' (IV, ii, 67), is a further indication that Claudio would be 'absolute for death' were his execution as imminent as he believes.

When the Duke seeks to recruit Isabella to his plan to thwart Angelo, the assumption is always that she still desires to save Claudio, despite her earlier rancorous words condemning him: 'How will you do . . . to save your brother?' (III, i, 186–7); 'redeem your brother from the angry law' (III, i, 200–1); and 'by this is your brother saved' (III, i, 253–4). The Duke's assumption is proved correct when Isabella instructs Mariana how to conduct herself after the consummation of her relationship with Angelo:

> Little have you to say
> When you depart from him, but, soft and low,
> 'Remember now my brother'. [IV, i, 68–70]

Isabella's anguished reaction when she is told by the disguised Duke that her brother is dead confirms that her sisterly love for

Claudio has survived their bitter encounter in the prison, and that her consequent detestation of Angelo has intensified:

> O, I will to him and pluck out his eyes! . . .
> Unhappy Claudio! wretched Isabel!
> Injurious world! most damned Angelo! [IV, iii, 119–22]

Although she cruelly condemned her brother to his fate during their confrontation in the prison, Isabella has laboured to save Claudio's life and now will strive until the final scene to bring his (and her) persecutor to justice.

Lucio also remains a strong defender of Claudio's interests. He condemns Claudio's judge: 'Why, what a ruthless thing is this in [Angelo], for the rebellion of a codpiece to take away the life of a man!' (III, ii, 110–12); he enquires anxiously about his friend's fate: 'Canst thou tell if Claudio die tomorrow, or no?' (III, ii, 163–4); and he ridicules the triviality of Claudio's offence: 'Marry, this Claudio is condemned for untrussing' (III, ii, 173). On meeting the weeping Isabella, who has been convinced by the disguised Duke that Claudio is dead, Lucio exclaims earnestly, 'By my troth, Isabel, I loved thy brother' (IV, iii, 155). Claudio is clearly seen to inspire deep affection and loyalty in his otherwise dissolute friend.

Claudio is also the subject of the sympathy and benevolence of Angelo's deputies in administering the law. The Provost confirms that Claudio 'has my pity' (IV, ii, 59) and seeks to discover 'What comfort is for Claudio?' (IV, ii, 75) before condemning Angelo as 'a bitter deputy' (IV, ii, 76). He addresses Claudio compassionately, having shown him the warrant for his execution: 'Heaven give your spirits comfort!' (IV, ii, 68). Escalus intercedes earnestly on Claudio's behalf as he is convinced that Angelo's judgement is too severe: 'I have laboured for the poor gentleman to the extremest shore of my modesty' (III, ii, 244–6); yet 'Claudio must die tomorrow. . . . If my brother wrought by my pity, it should not be so with him' (III, ii, 202–5). Although unsuccessful in pleading to save Claudio's life, the conscientious Escalus makes careful provision to save Claudio's soul, instructing the Provost, 'Let him be furnished with divines, and have all charitable preparation' (III, ii, 202–3). Escalus therefore appears delighted to learn from Friar Lodowick (the Duke in disguise) that Claudio now 'humbles himself to the determination of justice' (III, ii, 237–8) and that 'now is he resolved to die' (III, ii, 241–2), having benefited from the spiritual advice that he has been offered. Friar Lodowick receives Escalus's thanks for saving Claudio from despair and reconciling him to execution: 'You have paid the heavens your function, and the prisoner the very debt of your calling' (III, ii, 243–4). In short, there is widespread sympathy for the prisoner, and widespread disquiet at the severity of his judge.

Angelo, although tormented by conscience, remains intransigent in his condemnation of Claudio. In this respect, Angelo defies even the expectation of the Duke, who predicts that his Deputy, believing that Isabella has yielded her virginity to him, will pardon her brother. Instead, the audience is shocked by the treachery and tyranny of Angelo's note to the Provost:

> . . . *let Claudio be executed by four of the clock. . . . For my better satisfaction, let me have Claudio's head sent me by five. . . . Thus fail not to do your office, as you will answer it at your peril.* [IV, ii, 118–24]

Angelo's conscience, however, exacts severe retribution, tormenting him over the injustice of Claudio's execution and forcing him to recognise his own cowardice:

> [Claudio] should have liv'd;
> Save that his riotous youth, with dangerous sense,
> Might in the times to come have ta'en revenge
> By so receiving a dishonour'd life
> With ransom of such shame. Would yet he had lived.
> Alack, when once our grace we have forgot,
> Nothing goes right; we would, and we would not.
> [IV, iv, 26–32]

The once resolute and unambivalent Angelo is afflicted by confusion and anxiety after Claudio's supposed execution, as he fears loss of divine favour ('grace': line 31). The 'dangerous . . . revenge' that Angelo would face from Claudio is the justification for denying Claudio the promised pardon, but Angelo's troubled conscience nevertheless wishes Claudio alive again. He recognises the torment that Claudio would have undergone in living 'a dishonour'd life' of 'such shame', ironic as Angelo himself is here privately acknowledging his own dishonour and shame in abusing the law for his own gratification. Furthermore, to Angelo's utter mortification, he himself will suffer public disgrace at the end of the play, when his secret abuses are revealed. Here, and elsewhere, Shakespeare is careful to establish how closely the respective fates of Claudio and Angelo are linked.

Both Claudio and Angelo will be rescued by the grace of the Duke from the capital penalty for their misdeeds. When Escalus calls Angelo 'indeed Justice' (III, ii, 248)—that is, Justice personified—the disguised Duke replies ominously that 'If his own life answer the straightness of his proceeding, it shall become him well: wherein if he chance to fail, he hath sentenced himself' (III, 249–51). This line foreshadows the climax of the play, when the Duke, speaking in propria persona, will proclaim, 'An Angelo for Claudio; death for death' (V, i, 407). As Angelo himself declared, having sentenced Claudio to death, 'When I that censure him do so offend, / Let mine own judgement pattern out my death, / And nothing come in partial (II, i, 29–31). In condemning Claudio, Angelo has condemned himself.

Ultimately, justice allows that Angelo's life may be spared *because* Claudio escapes the penalty imposed upon him by the Deputy. It is a particularly powerful irony that, despite Angelo's best efforts to secure his victim's execution, Claudio's survival preserves Angelo's life.

327

Claudio Unmuffled

Claudio does not speak in the final scene, but his appearance on stage precipitates one of Shakespeare's most effective and frequently-deployed dramatic devices: pageants of recognition, reunification, and reconciliation deeply affect audiences emotionally at the end of so many of Shakespeare's plays, particularly the comedies.[20] The audience of *Measure for Measure*, having the advantage over the characters on stage who would believe Claudio to be dead, can anticipate with relish the likely effects on others of the unhooding of Claudio. The resultant tableau (when Claudio's face is finally revealed at V, i, 487) should present a wide range of contrasting emotions.

Isabella, although not the only character to be affected by the unhooding of Claudio, is most likely to be the major focus of the audience's attention. Claudio's desperate plea to her to save him by sacrificing her virginity, which provoked her bitter condemnation of her brother—arguably the most powerful exchange in the play—could not be forgotten or disregarded by any audience. As no words have passed between brother and sister since then, this should not be a meeting of unalloyed joy. Both Claudio and Isabella have had occasion to be chastened by events and have had time to experience the remorse caused by rash words. Their reunion should be an exquisite fusion of pain and delight, regret and love.

The fate of other characters is linked to Claudio's. Lucio could show his relief and joy that the friend has survived, but such positive emotions might be tempered by apprehension at his own fast-approaching doom. Lucio is, after all, awaiting the Duke's sentence for slander against the head of state as well as for begetting an illegitimate child. Lucio's unselfish happiness at Claudio's redemption should, however, remind the audience

---

[20] For example, *The Two Gentlemen of Verona*, *The Comedy of Errors*, *The Merchant of Venice*, *Much Ado About Nothing*, *Twelfth Night*, *As You Like It*, *The Winter's Tale*, *Cymbeline*, *King Lear*, and *The Tempest*.

of his loyal efforts to secure his friend's reprieve, proving him worthy of mercy when the Duke repeals his sentence (V, i, 517–18).

Neither should Angelo's response to Claudio's unhooding be overlooked by the audience. Although Angelo has already been informed that he did not take the virginity of the unwilling Isabella, but rather that of the willing Mariana, he would still have every reason to believe that he has executed a man for the very same offence that he himself has committed: the consummation of a relationship based on no more than a mutual exchange of vows. He can now recognise that his worst offence is merely 'seeming'—hypocrisy and bearing false witness—as he is neither a rapist nor a murderer. Profound relief as well as astonishment should figure in his expression. Because of Claudio's survival, Angelo has been saved from himself, avoiding the greatest of the crimes that his lust so ardently pursued but that his conscience so passionately loathed.

The last word on Claudio belongs to the Duke:

> She, Claudio, that you wrong'd, look you restore.
>
> [V, i, 522]

Since his unhooding some thirty-five lines earlier, no speech has been directed to Claudio. Now, he is given an injunction that replaces the death-sentence under which he has languished with instruction on how to make amends. No further retribution need be demanded by the state, nor any further restitution by the Church. Claudio had recognised from the outset that his union with Julietta lacked 'the denunciation . . . / Of outward order' (I, ii, 137–38), which is all that he needs to 'restore' the 'wrong' that he did to Julietta. In simpler terms, he needs to undergo the formal ceremony of marriage to legitimise his union with his partner. The stage-business at this point often involves the reintroduction of Julietta, new-born babe in arms, to the delighted Claudio. This might contrast ironically—even amusingly—with the simultaneous reintroduction of Mistress Kate Keep-down and her illegitimate child to the reluctant

Lucio.[21] If his sister were to accept the Duke's offer of marriage—'He is my brother too' (V, i, 491)—then Claudio would become a member of the ruling family of Vienna who could, arm-in-arm with Julietta, respond to Vincentio's invitation, 'So bring us to our palace' (V, i, 535), by accompanying the Duke in a joyful procession from the stage.

In the critical tradition, it might be surprising to encounter harsh judgements on the unfortunate Claudio, were not every character, incident, and theme in *Measure for Measure* subject to controversy. Samuel Taylor Coleridge (in 1827) dismissed Claudio as 'detestable', while Edward Dowden (in 1875) referred to him as 'this disgrace of manhood'.[22] One can only assume that their conceptions of appropriate masculine conduct—valour, stoicism, and duty towards women—had been offended by Claudio's plea to Isabella in the prison. Disgust at this behaviour was not, however, unanimous among Victorian critics: in a rather cloying simile, Walter Pater (writing in 1889) characterised Claudio as 'a flowerlike young man' dressed in 'all the bravery of youth'.[23] Adverse judgements of Claudio nevertheless persisted into the Twentieth Century, conceptions of male virtue continuing to colour critical judgement: in 1951, William Empson suggested that Claudio 'is drawn as a weak character' because he fails to say 'the *manly* thing'.[24] In the present century, however, when gender stereotypes are more likely to be regarded with suspicion, Claudio should appear, to a sympathetic audience, less deserving of moral disapproval and more human in his fears.

---

[21] Such was the stage-business successfully employed in David Thacker's 1994 production for the BBC.

[22] Geckle, pp. 80 and 170.

[23] *Appreciations: With an Essay on Style* (London and New York: Macmillan, 1901), p. 180.

[24] 'Sense in *Measure for Measure*' in *Shakespeare*: Measure for Measure: *A Casebook* ed. C. K. Stead (London: Macmillan, 1971), p. 209.

Claudio's is a surprisingly small part as far as the number of lines that he speaks is concerned, but he is hugely influential in relation to the plot and themes of *Measure for Measure*.[25] In a play so intimately concerned with the business of good government, Claudio's fortunes illustrate the injustice of prosecuting someone who has acted in good faith and in apparent ignorance of the law. In a play in which oppression, deception, and hypocrisy abound, Claudio is always the victim and never the perpetrator. In a scurrilous world, he conducts himself with dignity (arguably, even in his exchanges in the prison with Isabella), proving himself worthy of his 'most noble father' (II, i, 7). He remains loyal in love to his partner, Julietta, when the other two male lovers in the play, Angelo and Lucio, are unfaithful to theirs. He openly expresses contrition for distressing his sister (III, i, 170–1) when others (for example, Angelo) suppress their remorse or (like the Duke and Isabella) indicate no regret at all for their mistreatment of others. An audience, never in doubt that this is a young man worthy of redemption, should feel uplifted by his ultimate vindication.

Mariana's History

Like every other significant character in the play, Mariana has prompted startlingly extreme opinions, the adverse ones mainly from those who disapprove of the 'bed-trick'. Her virtue, however, never appears coldly self-interested (as Isabella's may sometimes seem to be): she is love's martyr who, in response to what she believes to be religious advice, finds the path to fulfilment while avoiding the snares of materialism. It is important to recognise that she is represented as having fallen victim to Angelo's abuse of women long

---

[25] L. C. Knights claimed that Claudio is 'scarcely a "character" at all', despite the fact that 'he is the central figure of the plot': 'The Ambiguity of *Measure for Measure*', *Scrutiny* X (1942), in Stead, pp. 141 and 144. The fact that Claudio speaks under three lines in the second half of the play (after III, i, 171) should not, however, divert attention from how deftly—and fully—his character has been established in the 'tragic' first half.

before his assault on Isabella; hence, she must wait much longer than Isabella for justice. She is the female equivalent of Claudio: a lover redeemed from blame by sincerity, humility, and dignity.

Like several other prominent characters in the play, Mariana is first depicted a considerable time before her initial appearance on stage. Although she is not mentioned directly in the first two acts of the play, the Duke's opening words to Angelo in the first scene might, with the benefit of hindsight, be regarded by an audience as an equivocation disguising reference to Mariana:

> There is a kind of character in thy life
> That to th'observer doth thy history
> Fully unfold. [I, i, 27–9]

To a seventeenth-century audience, the familiar meaning of 'character' was 'script' or 'lettering'. Shakespeare's audience would have understood that Angelo's past ('history') was recorded in a figurative written account ('kind of character'), the obvious sense being that the chronicle of Angelo's life is apparent from his current status and achievements. On the surface, this would appear to be a compliment but, in the third Act, the audience will learn from the very same speaker, the Duke, of Angelo's abuse of Mariana. The record of Angelo's life is not, therefore, free from blame. The hidden implications might be more apparent to a modern audience. Our contemporary sense of 'character' as 'a person (in a play)' makes the sinister sense of the Duke's words even more apparent: a 'character' (Mariana) from Angelo's earlier 'life' has entirely revealed ('fully unfold[ed]') his past ('thy history') to the Duke ('th'observer'). In either reading, the Duke is hinting at his knowledge of Angelo's perfidy towards Mariana while seeming to compliment him for an unblemished reputation.

The first overt references to Mariana in the play emphasise her status as a victim of misfortune and injustice. Although the

Duke's speeches to Isabella concerning Mariana's calamities (III, i, 208–43) were considered at the opening of this chapter, certain issues from that important context in the play merit further comment. Mariana has suffered disaster after disaster, some the product of ill-fortune, but most the result of Angelo's perfidy. Ill-fortune accounted for the death of her brother at sea, and the concomitant loss of her marriage-portion. Angelo, however, inflicted the heaviest blows, first in breaking his oath to marry her, second in blackening her reputation, and third in compelling her thereby to withdraw in shame from society. Like Claudio, she is a respected citizen who has been publicly humiliated by Angelo. It will therefore be poetic justice when Angelo's own punishment will be to suffer similar public mortification and loss of respect.

Even before she has been named, the Duke refers to Mariana as a 'poor wronged lady' (III, i, 199–200), immediately establishing (in only three words) her nobility, her misfortune, and the injustice of her predicament. Like Claudio, Mariana is from a well-respected family: her brother is described as 'the great soldier' (line 210), 'noble and renowned' (lines 219–20). She herself had a virtuous reputation: according to Isabella, 'good words went with her name' (lines 211–12). This is the reputation that Angelo has stolen from her by 'pretending in her discoveries of dishonour' (lines 226–7). To safeguard himself from accusations of callous materialism and breach of promise, he has sought to justify his rejection of her by insinuating that he found Mariana to have been unchaste. The social penalty for a woman so reputed in Shakespeare's society would have been heavy: even a moderate preacher like William Perkins warned that no Christian man should take to wife 'a defamed woman . . . though she be repentant'.[26] The slander is made still more shocking dramatically because this information about Mariana is being imparted to Isabella, who is all too painfully aware of

---

[26] *Christian oeconomie* (London: 1609), Chapter 5: 'Of the Choice of Persons Fit for Marriage', p. 66, accessed through Early English books, 21 January 2020, https://quod.lib.umich.edu/e/eebo/A09377.0001.001?

the terrible consequences to a woman of sexual 'dishonour', and who has been threatened with defamation by the same Angelo who disgraced his betrothed. Mariana the pariah has retreated to 'the moated grange' at 'Saint Luke's' (III, i, 265), like Isabella seeking refuge from a dishonest society within the walls of what sounds to be a religious community, the customary last resort of 'fallen women' of noble birth.

Angelo's fickleness is carefully contrasted with Mariana's constancy: he has abandoned her, but she has not abandoned him. He has 'bestowed her on her own lamentation, which she yet wears for his sake' (III, i, 228–9), that is, encouraged her to wear not a bridal gown but a garb of mourning, with which she still commemorates her loss of him. Rather than alienating her affections, Mariana's rejection by Angelo has served to intensify her love for him: 'His unjust unkindness, that in all reason should have quenched her love, hath, like an impediment in the current, made it more violent and unruly' (lines 240-3). A celebrated context in the Sonnets suggests that Mariana's unstinting fidelity, far from warranting any scepticism or derision on the part of the audience or critic, is presented by Shakespeare as an ideal:

> Love is not love
> Which alters when it alteration finds,
> Or bends with the remover to remove.
> [Sonnet 116: lines 2–4]

By this definition, Mariana represents perfection in relationships between the sexes: she does not quell her love for Angelo nor allow it to diminish, even when he has withdrawn his love from her.

Evidence suggests that Shakespeare was working on *Othello* at the same time as *Measure for Measure* (1603–4): the earliest recorded performance of the former occurred at the Banqueting House at Whitehall in the month before James I attended the first verified performance of the latter.[27] Mariana shares with Desdemona, Othello's wife, many of the qualities of the tragic heroine. Both women are gracious, compassionate, and eager to believe the best in others. Neither proves in the least vengeful, even when undergoing extreme suffering: each, devoted to a cruel male partner, seeks to save his life, even when he has done his worst to destroy their relationship and to harm the woman who so loves him. In Desdemona's case, her last words are an attempt to protect Othello from the consequences of her murder, while Mariana's final speeches labour to redeem Angelo—who abandoned her and wilfully ruined her reputation—from the sentence of death that the Duke has imposed on him. Shakespeare presents these women as ideals of fidelity in love.

Mariana *at the Moated Grange*

Like Desdemona with her 'song of "willow"' (*Othello*: IV, iii, 25–55), Mariana is memorably associated with the sad music of lost love. She first appears to the accompaniment of a simple song that succinctly conveys her ambivalence concerning her relationship with Angelo:

> *Take, o take those lips away*
> *   that so sweetly were forsworn,*
> *And those eyes, the break of day*
> *   lights that do mislead the morn:*
> *But my kisses bring again,*
> *   bring again;*
> *Seals of love, but seal'd in vain,*
> *   seal'd in vain.*
> [IV, i, 1–6]

The song beseeches that the lips and eyes of the beloved should no longer attend her, because they are 'forsworn' and 'mislead';

---

[27] Gamini Salgado, *Eyewitnesses of Shakespeare: First Hand Accounts of Performances 1590–1890* (New York: Harper and Row, 1975), pp. 23–24.

yet the lips break their oaths 'sweetly', while the eyes deceive the dawn by burning so brightly that they become 'break of day / Lights'. Clearly, the faithless lover is still the object of desire. The song asks for the kisses given to the beloved to be returned—but how could they be returned other than by the faithless lover bestowing more kisses on her whom he has abandoned? The kisses are a reminder of the exchange of vows between Angelo and Mariana as they are 'seals of love', but like those vows, they were 'seal'd in vain', in that the vows were broken by him. Through the medium of a simple lyric, Shakespeare poignantly reminds the audience of Mariana's plight and of her continued love for the man who wronged her.

Mariana speaks seldom in her first scene, but her words characterise her as modest, dutiful, and sincere, while serving to create a back-story for her relationship with the disguised Duke. Her longest speech in the scene is her first, where she identifies Friar Lodowick as a 'man of comfort' who has 'often' assuaged her 'brawling discontent' with his 'advice' (IV, i, 8–9). Her words suggest a long association between the friar and the grieving woman, in which she has confided in him and benefited from his consolation. They anticipate the Duke's speech to Angelo at the very end of the play, where Vincentio testifies to Mariana's worth by claiming that 'I have confess'd her, and I know her virtue' (V, i, 524). In the first words that she addresses to the disguised Duke, Mariana expresses her apologies for indulging her grief:

> I cry you mercy, sir, and well could wish
> You had not found me here so musical.
> Let me excuse me, and believe me so;
> My mirth it much displeas'd, but pleas'd my woe.
> [IV, i, 10–13]

The delicacy of her sentiments is apparent here: she is ashamed that her musical pursuits might be thought trivial or hedonistic, seeking to justify them not as a source of frivolous delight, but rather as a means of assuaging her anguish.

None of Mariana's further verbal contributions to the scene is longer than a line, but this does not mean that their sense is unimportant. Her admission that 'I have sat here all day' (IV, i, 19–20) is characteristic of her passive suffering: it is as if her life has been indefinitely suspended, her dwelling a kind of limbo until she is rescued by her friar's plan. Her dutiful words, 'I am always bound to you' (IV, i, 25), not only express her gratitude to the Duke/friar but also imply her reliance on him for succour. Before Friar Lodowick introduces her, via Isabella, to his proposed 'bed-trick', he seeks assurance of her recognition 'that I respect you', to which she responds with wholehearted confirmation (IV, i, 53–4) before conducting Isabella to their private conference (IV, i, 59). Her modesty is such that it is Isabella, rather than Mariana herself, who confirms Mariana's willingness to take Isabella's place in Angelo's bed: 'She'll take the enterprise upon her, father' (IV, i, 66). Mariana's silence on the subject is eloquent: with delicate restraint, she allows her new companion to be her spokesperson, lest she should appear unseemly by acknowledging in words her willingness to employ deception to fulfil her desires. She also requires confirmation that the course of action to which she is being persuaded has the sanction of a holy man: she will comply, 'If you [Friar Lodowick] advise it' (IV, i, 67). Her only other words are to reassure the anxious Isabella that, before leaving Angelo, she will remind him of his pledge to pardon Claudio: 'Fear me not' (IV, i, 70). Throughout these exchanges, the audience should sense the implication that Mariana might well believe herself the passive instrument of a divine providence working through the friar (Vincentio) and the novice nun (Isabella).

In response to her acquiescence, the Duke/friar rewards Mariana with the strongest reassurance that her chosen course of action is divinely sanctioned (IV, i, 71–5). Mariana is addressed as a 'gentle daughter', that is, a noble child of the Church, who should be 'not at all' apprehensive because Angelo is already her 'husband' because of their 'pre-contract' *per verba de futuri* (lines 71–2). Their sexual union will be 'no sin' as her prior 'title' to Angelo transforms the 'deceit' involved into a legitimate adornment or 'flourish' on their contract of love (lines 73–5). Like Isabella, Mariana is a woman who accepts Friar Lodowick's male spiritual authority without question. With no imputation of wantonness or deviousness, but rather with associations of piety, courage, and legitimacy, she embarks on her nocturnal enterprise.

Her role with Isabella is reversed when next the audience encounters Mariana: Isabella had persuaded Mariana to undertake the 'bed-trick'; Mariana must now persuade Isabella to 'speak . . . indirectly' in accusing Angelo (IV, vi, 1). Mariana's is a message of simple trust in the wisdom and benevolence of the friar's advice: 'Be rul'd by him' (IV, vi, 4). In the absence of the disguised Duke, however, she longs for the reassurance of a pious male authority-figure to support them when they confront the full power of the state: 'I would Friar Peter—' (IV, vi, 8). Her wish is granted with Friar Peter's immediate appearance: he will conduct her before the judgement-seat in the final scene. As before, Mariana's modesty and piety are evident in her words and deeds.

The Test of Fortitude

When Shakespeare re-introduces Mariana for the final time, she is the dramatic means by which he creates delicious ironies, mysteries, and riddles. She is presented as a witness for the defence of Lord Angelo against the multiple accusations that Isabella has made. Mariana is not named by Friar Peter when she approaches Angelo, and the veil that she wears initially would prevent the Deputy from recognising her. When the Duke, speaking in propria persona, asks Mariana to reveal her face, she demurs, despite his authority:

> Pardon, my lord; I will not show my face
> Until my husband bid me.[28] [V, i, 171–2]

---

[28] Cf. *Much Ado About Nothing*: V, iv, 55–57, where Claudio is not allowed to see Hero's face until he has pledged to accept her as his bride.

To most of the characters on stage (especially Angelo), the identity of the veiled woman should be a mystery, but the audience should be able readily to identify Mariana, not only from her voice but also from her costume, witnessed earlier in her exchanges with Isabella and Friar Peter (IV, vi). She answers calmly, concisely, and frankly to each of the Duke's questions about her status as a woman (V, i, 172–7). She stoically endures derision when the Duke's pretended bafflement—'Why, you are nothing then: neither maid, widow, nor wife!' (V, i, 178–9)—leads directly to Lucio's insinuation that she may be a 'punk', or whore (V, i, 180). Maintaining her restraint and dignity, she presents her circumstances to the court:

> My lord, I do confess I ne'er was married;
> And I confess besides, I am no maid.
> I have known my husband; yet my husband
> Knows not that ever he knew me. [V, i, 185–8]

In keeping with her immediately preceding exchanges with the Duke, Mariana expresses herself in paradoxical riddles. Such riddles are the province of folk-tales, where seemingly impossible circumstances are ultimately explained and resolved. As the 'damsel in distress' of Shakespeare's folk-tale, then, her language here is entirely appropriate—but Shakespeare again allows himself the bold comic intrusion of an irreverent remark from Lucio, who suggests that Mariana's husband must have been 'drunk' at the time of their encounter (V, i, 189). With calm dignity, Mariana ignores the jibe, developing her case with a further kind of riddle:

> She [Isabella] that accuses him [Angelo] of fornication
> In self-same manner doth accuse my husband,
> And charges him, my lord, with such a time
> When I'll depose I had him in mine arms
> With all th'effect of love. [V, i, 194–8]

339

The language is now legalistic and precise: 'accuses', 'fornication', 'self-same manner', 'doth accuse my husband', 'charges him', 'such a time', and 'I'll depose'. The iambic pentameters are regular, while frequent enjambement with no heavy end-stopping or caesurae ensures the fluency of the verse. The suggestion is that Mariana is serenely confident in her delivery of this seeming exoneration of Angelo: she is providing her 'husband' with an apparent alibi to refute Isabella's accusations against him.

As they can readily resolve the conundrum, audiences enjoy Mariana's mysterious words while observing Angelo's apparent bafflement: he can make sense of Mariana's speech only if she is speaking of two distinct men: of him, and of a different man to whom she is married (V, i, 199). In response to Angelo's confusion and to the Duke's prompting to identify her husband, Mariana explains,

> Why just, my lord, and that is Angelo,
> Who thinks he knows that he ne'er knew my body,
> But knows, he thinks, that he knows Isabel's.
>
> [V, i, 201–3]

The words are simple, but they are woven into a complex and witty pattern of pun and paradox, which may make their sense less than immediately comprehensible. Having, in her first line, fused two seemingly distinct men into one man—the husband to whom she refers, and Angelo in support of whom she is ostensibly testifying—Mariana embarks on a clever interplay between the words 'thinks' and 'knows'. Both words express a belief in something, although 'knows' suggests greater certitude than 'thinks'. 'Knows', however, has the additional biblical sense of 'carnal knowledge', sexual union which is the foundation of the accusation against Angelo. To paraphrase lines 202–3: Angelo believes that he can be certain that he never 'knew' Mariana in the biblical sense; but he is certain—or so he believes—that he has had 'carnal knowledge' of Isabella. The audience is reminded that what Angelo believes to be untrue is true, and that what he believes to be true is untrue.

Shakespeare has carefully prepared for this moment, the first of three dramatic tableaux (the others involving Friar Lodowick and Claudio) where concealment is cast aside to provoke astonished recognition among the previously unsuspecting characters deployed on stage. In response to Angelo's perplexed demand to see her face, Mariana obediently unveils:

> My husband bids me; now I will unmask.
> This is that face, thou cruel Angelo,
> Which once thou swor'st was worth the looking on:
> This is the hand which, with a vow'd contract,
> Was fast belock'd in thine: this is the body
> That took away the match from Isabel
> And did supply thee at thy garden-house,
> In her imagin'd person. (V, i, 205–12)

The language is strongly rhetorical: Mariana deploys anaphora in the repeated introductory phrasing ('This is . . .'), on each occasion linked with a different part of her physical self which sealed her compact with Angelo. With characteristic modesty, she describes her face as one that 'once thou swor'st was worth the looking on': she makes no boast about her beauty, but rather presents her face as the subject of a broken oath on Angelo's part. This introduces the central reference to Angelo's betrayal of his vows to Mariana, where the language that she uses— 'contract' and 'fast'—significantly echoes Claudio's reference to his 'true contract' with Julietta who is 'fast my wife' (I, ii, 134–6). Angelo has prosecuted Claudio and Julietta for keeping the same vows that he has broken to Mariana. Finally, Mariana can reveal, with considerably delicacy of phrasing, avoiding any gross references, how the 'bed-trick' was performed on Angelo. The preceding references to Angelo's perjury are implicitly a vindication of Mariana's successful ploy to consummate their relationship: their sexual union confirmed Angelo as Mariana's husband, as he had vowed to become when first they exchanged oaths and as she has consistently claimed him to be in her testimony to the court.

Mariana has transformed herself from a witness in defence of Angelo (replying to Isabella's accusations) into the plaintiff seeking redress from Angelo. In response, Angelo offers a testimony in his own defence and swears an oath in support (V, i, 215–23). Both, however, are suspect, either because of wilful misrepresentation or because of ignorance. Angelo admits that he abandoned Mariana, but maintains his shameless slander that he did so primarily because 'her reputation was disvalu'd / In levity' (V, i, 220–1; cf. III, i, 226–7). In addition, apparently still not understanding the 'bed-trick', Angelo swears that he has not spoken with, seen, or heard from Mariana in the 'five years' since he broke contact with her (lines 222–4). Angelo's words further increase an audience's sympathy for Mariana: she has been condemned to fully five years of ostracism, tantamount to solitary confinement, because Angelo undermined her honour with an unfounded allegation that he now repeats before the assembled people of Vienna.

In response, Mariana concludes her case with an impassioned oath to the Duke, seeking not to condemn Angelo but rather to confirm that she is his lawful wife:

> Noble prince,
> As there comes light from heaven, and words from breath,
> As there is sense in truth, and truth in virtue,
> I am affianc'd this man's wife, as strongly
> As words could make up vows. And, my good lord,
> But Tuesday night last gone, in's garden house,
> He knew me as a wife. As this is true
> Let me in safety raise me from my knees,
> Or else for ever be confixed here,
> A marble monument. [V, i, 223–32]

Again, understanding of *sponsalia per verba de futuri* is necessary fully to appreciate the force of Mariana's words. She refers to the 'vows' that she exchanged with Angelo as having 'affianc'd' them 'strongly'. Therefore, when Angelo 'knew' her (in the biblical sense of carnal knowledge), he was consummating their union according to his 'vows', and she became his 'wife'. Mariana has kept her oath to Angelo, despite his devious attempt to reject her. She now swears a further elaborate vow, phrased in characteristically modest language, to confirm the truth of her consistent testimony that Angelo is her husband. Until the Duke accepts the truth of her account by acknowledging her marital status, she undertakes to kneel in silent supplication, characteristic of her humility and piety.

Mariana does not participate again until summoned by the Duke to marry Angelo, 140 lines later: she remains silently and patiently kneeling, even when falsely accused on all sides and threatened with dire consequences. Angelo blackens Mariana's reputation by calling her 'informal' (line 235)—that is, mentally deranged.[29] Furthermore, he insinuates that she is guilty of treason by claiming that she is instrumental in a conspiracy against him (V, i, 235–8). The Duke dismisses Mariana as a 'pernicious woman' (line 240), one of 'these slanderers' (line 258) to be prosecuted by Angelo, who has now been granted the power to preside over a trial in which he himself was previously the accused. Even Friar Peter seems to concur with the conspiracy theory when he refers to Friar Lodowick as the man who has 'set the women on to this complaint' (line 250), where 'set . . . on' suggests seditious intent, with Isabella and Mariana complicit.

After this prolonged test of Mariana's fortitude, however, the Duke will cast off his disguise as Friar Lodowick, oblige his deputy to confess his guilt, and call Mariana forward to be married to Angelo by Friar Peter (V, i, 372–77). Now, the depth and sincerity of Mariana's love for Angelo are about to be tested.

---

[29] Although, elsewhere, Shakespeare uses the word 'formal' to mean 'sane' (*The Comedy of Errors*: V, i, 105), this context is the only recorded usage in OED of 'informal' in the sense of 'mentally deranged'. The alternative, however, seems unconvincing: that Angelo is alleging that the women's complaints against him are 'unofficial', that is, not conducted through the proper channels.

The Test of Fidelity

It is characteristic of Mariana's modest acquiescence that she is silent both immediately before and immediately after her marriage (which occurs offstage). When the Duke sentences Angelo to death (V, i, 401–14), however, she immediately and boldly challenges the judgement:

> O my most gracious lord,
> I hope you will not mock me with a husband.
>
> [V, i, 414–15]

Although the vocative is respectful and the response expresses a wish, it thinly disguises an accusation of irrationality against the Duke: having granted Mariana the husband whom she desires, he is now proposing, immediately and perversely, to dispossess her of that same husband. Vincentio confirms that her marriage will have been legitimized, even in previously sceptical eyes, by the ceremony conducted by Friar Peter (V, i, 417–20). Her reputation for chastity is therefore secure. Now comes the temptation: all Angelo's wealth, confiscated by the state, is offered to Mariana, 'To buy you a better husband' (V, i, 423).

Once again, a woman's integrity is being tested by an all-powerful male figure as she labours to save a man whom she loves from the death-sentence. If the dowry that Mariana lost with her brother's shipwreck were to be so handsomely restored by the Duke, she could have her choice of eligible men. Therefore, were Mariana's devotion to Angelo less than absolute, or if materialism could sway her choice, she might succumb to temptation by abandoning her newly-married husband to his fate. Instead, she remains resolute, expressing herself with an earnest simplicity:

> O my dear lord,
> I crave no other, nor no better man. [V, i, 423–4]

In passing the test that the Duke has set for her, she rejects materialism. Furthermore, she exemplifies faithful love, defined in Shakespeare's Sonnet 116 as an 'ever-fixed mark' that will not alter 'when it alteration finds' (lines 3–5).

When the Duke refuses to remit his sentence, despite Mariana's continued, respectful pleading (V, i, 426 and 428), she seeks to recruit help in her desperate attempt to save her husband's life:

> . . . sweet Isabel, take my part;
> Lend me your knees, and all my life to come
> I'll lend you all my life to do you service. [V, i, 428–30]

Isabella, deeply indebted to Mariana for preserving her chastity, might now petition the Duke to repeal the sentence on her friend's husband; but Isabella has good reason to avenge herself on Angelo, and could do so simply by remaining silent. Mariana nevertheless persists in her determination to recruit Isabella to her cause:

> Isabel!
> Sweet Isabel, do yet but kneel by me;
> Hold up your hands, say nothing: I'll speak all.
> They say best men are moulded out of faults,
> And, for the most, become much more the better
> For being a little bad. So may my husband.
> O Isabel! Will you not lend a knee? [V, i, 434–40]

The whole of this speech is addressed to Isabella (it is bracketed by two vocatives directed to her); but at its heart is a problematical three-line defence of Angelo. Could Isabella accept that her would-be rapist and the (supposed) murderer of her brother, Claudio, is merely 'a little bad'? If we consider more carefully, however, we recognise that Mariana's special pleading for her new husband is characteristic of her delicacy. Unlike the Duke when he philosophises, Mariana does not confidently assert the truth of her moral maxim; rather, she invokes popular opinion as her authority—'They say' (line

437)—and uses a modal verb to express her *wish*, rather than her certainty, that her husband 'may' improve (line 439). According to her report, 'best men' are not made of faults; rather, their faults shape them into something better: they are 'moulded' by their misdeeds (line 437). Her implication would seem to be that, if most men are ultimately improved morally by 'being a little bad' (line 439), so her husband might be transformed into a paragon of virtue after his more serious moral lapses. Mariana's words are not a vindication of Angelo, but rather an expression of her faith and love: she needs to believe that his evil actions can transform him into a worthier husband.

That final question, 'Will you not lend a knee?' is a cry of dismay at Isabella's inaction. Three times, Mariana has begged Isabella to kneel (lines 429, 435, and 440). Never once, though, has she taxed her friend with ingratitude by reminding Isabella of the service that she, Mariana, has done in attempting to save Claudio's life while simultaneously preserving Isabella's virginity. Such delicacy of feeling, especially when Mariana is so sorely beset, should appear admirable to an audience. All eyes will be on Isabella as she ponders her quandary, but Isabella's eyes should be on Mariana, a woman who, like her, has been estranged from a man whom she loves dearly by a bitter dispute in which her virtue was at stake; but also a woman who, unlike her, has forgiven the man and is willing to plead for his life. Mariana embodies the humility, compassion, and forgiveness that Isabella has yet to discover in herself.

Isabella slowly absorbs the lesson and, on hearing the Duke speak her brother's name—'He dies for Claudio's death' (V, i, 440)—she kneels beside the woman to whom she owes such a debt of gratitude, supporting her plea for Angelo's life with a substantial and persuasive speech of her own. Mariana's last three words in the play (V, i, 452) serve as a coda to Isabella's speech, endorsing the argument of her friend and supporter. This tableau of two women kneeling disconsolately before a judge was anticipated structurally by the words of Lucio in Isabella's very first scene:

> . . . when maidens sue,
> Men give like gods; but when they weep and kneel,
> All their petitions are as freely theirs
> As they themselves would owe them. [I, iv, 80–3]

Mariana achieves the objective of her petition—but not immediately: Angelo is not reprieved for another 40 lines. She must endure hearing her husband plead for death to release him from shame (V, i, 472–5) and then witness his misery transformed into 'a quickening in his eye' (line 493) by the revelation that Claudio, his intended victim, has escaped execution. When the Duke does eventually pardon Angelo, it is with the proviso that he should recognise his debt to Mariana:

> Well, Angelo, your evil quits you well.
> Look that you love your wife: her worth, worth yours.
>   [V, i, 494–5]

That he should love Mariana is axiomatic: her love has saved him from committing an offence against Isabella that should have cost him his life, even if he had then pardoned Claudio. Angelo must also transform his 'evil' into sufficient 'worth' to counterbalance Mariana's 'worth'; that is, in the equation of 'measure for measure', he should aspire to the virtuous ideals that his wife embodies. The Duke's words echo the sense of Mariana's speech in defence of her husband (V, i, 437–9), in which she hoped that Angelo, a man 'moulded out of faults', would become 'much more the better'.

The fortunes of Mariana in the play illustrate the common dramatic convention in comedies, that virtue is ultimately rewarded. In the final speech of the play, in which the Duke pardons and rewards those who accompany him in procession to his palace, he turns to the newly-married couple:

> Joy to you, Mariana; love her, Angelo:
> I have confess'd her, and I know her virtue. [V, i, 523–4]

The last words to Mariana are a blessing bestowing 'joy'; the last words to her husband are a command to 'love her'; and the last words concerning Mariana publicly reaffirm her 'virtue', corroborated by a solemn sacrament of the Church. Implicitly, her reputation, her husband, her prosperity, and her future happiness are now secured, the result of her constancy in love. In this respect, Mariana is cast in the same mould as the heroines of Shakespeare's 'happy comedies'. She bears a particularly strong resemblance to Hero in *Much Ado About Nothing*, rescued into joyous matrimony after public denigration and rejection by the man whom she loves.

Mariana has offered one of the most important moral judgements in the play. Her plea to redeem her husband should be more influential in convincing the audience that Angelo is capable of redemption than anything said by the two principal male protagonists, the Duke and Angelo himself:

> They say best men are moulded out of faults,
> And, for the most, become much more the better
> For being a little bad. So may my husband. [V, i, 437–9]

Mariana's optimistic forgiveness of her beloved epitomises the central concept in *Measure for Measure*: that judgement should be merciful and compassionate. Mariana embodies this fundamental doctrine of the play: she, who has suffered the longest from the perfidy of Angelo, is the quickest to forgive him. An audience learns, with Isabella, to absolve Angelo for Mariana's sake, in recognition of 'her worth' (V, i, 495).

Julietta

Although Julietta appears in only three scenes in the play, and speaks in only one, she is another example of a minor role with a major dramatic impact. Like Claudio, Julietta is presented sympathetically and distinguished from the lower orders by reference to her social status. Mistress Overdone refers to her with respect as '*Madam* Juliet' (I, ii, 107; italics added), while to the Provost she is 'a *gentle*woman' (II, iii, 10;

348

italics added), both appellations suggesting that she is regarded as a lady rather than as a commoner. Claudio refers to her as such—'the lady' (I, ii, 136)—and one who has 'a dower / Remaining in the coffer of her friends', words that suggest that she is of a wealthy family. Like Claudio, she is implicitly attributed with delicacy of birth, breeding, and manners; but, because of 'falling in the flaws of her own youth' (that is, succumbing to the blustery impulses to which the young are susceptible), she has 'blister'd her report' (II, iii, 11–12). Her reputation, like Mariana's, has been jeopardised by her relationship with the man whom she loves: her good name ('report') now bears a mark of shame, 'blister'd' like the brand on the brow of a whore.[30]

Her distress, then, should be made obvious to the audience when she is paraded through the streets by the Provost, on the orders of Angelo (I, ii, 108ff.). Her humiliation should be accentuated by the fact that 'The stealth of our most mutual entertainment / With character too gross is writ on Juliet' (I, ii, 143–4)—that is, she is heavily pregnant. This evidence of her sexual intimacy with the man with whom she has exchanged vows of love is being displayed as an object of public derision, and she exposed to vilification. The severity of her treatment should excite pity and sympathy from the audience.

Like Claudio, Julietta evokes compassion from other characters, but not from Angelo. Although the Provost assiduously enquires about provision for Julietta now that she has gone into labour (II, ii, 15–16), Angelo proves unmoved by her predicament. When he commands, vaguely, that she should 'with speed' be '[d]ispose[d]' to 'some more fitter place' (II, ii, 16–17), he appears impatient with and dismissive of the disruption caused by her condition. When subsequently he amplifies his command, he depersonalises Julietta, identifying

---

[30] Cf. Hamlet's condemnation of his mother's second marriage: 'Such an act / That blurs the grace and blush of modesty; / Calls virtue hypocrite; takes off the rose / From the fair forehead of an innocent love / And sets a blister there' (Hamlet: III, iv, 40–4).

her by her crime and denying her any comforts: she is 'the
fornicatress' to be allowed no more than 'needful . . . means'
(II, ii, 23–4). Angelo's evident lack of sympathy is likely to
provoke an equal and opposite surge of sympathy in an
audience—and further to alienate Angelo from favour.

In the one scene in which she speaks in *Measure for
Measure* (Act II, scene iii), Julietta's surroundings should be
spartan and she herself 'groaning' because 'very near her hour'
(II, ii, 15–16). So it was that, when David Thacker directed the
play for the BBC in 1994, Sally George's Juliet was in her shift,
soaked in sweat, frequently wracked by agonising spasms, and
sprawling on a disordered metal bed of a type common in
underfunded institutions. Her replies to Friar Lodowick (that is,
to the Duke in disguise, as he 'confesses' her) are brief and
punctuated by heavy caesurae, suggesting breathlessness caused
by the pangs of her labour. Her penitence, piety, and sincerity
are thereby accentuated. She expresses contrition for
conceiving her unborn child ('the sin you carry'), and bears it
without complaint ('patiently') (lines 19–20). When Friar
Lodowick enquires about her feelings for 'the man that wrong'd
you', she proudly asserts her love for Claudio to be as strong as
her feelings for 'the woman that wrong'd him', that is, for
herself (lines 24–5). She will not allow Claudio solely to
shoulder the blame for what Friar Lodowick calls a 'most
offenceful act' (line 26): it was, she promptly confirms,
'mutually committed' (line 27). She goes further: when the friar
proposes that her sin is therefore greater than Claudio's (in the
theological tradition of blaming Eve, the temptress, for Adam's
Fall), she does not demur, but rather is prepared to 'confess it,
and repent it' (lines 28–9), accepting the heavier burden of
blame to lessen Claudio's responsibility. When the friar further
suggests that her penitence may be shallow—sorrow for her
own suffering rather than sorrow for offending God—she
interrupts him with a refutation that is both spirited and
unequivocal:

> I do repent me as it is an evil,
> And take the shame with joy. [II, iii, 35–6]

In such trying circumstances (in prison and in labour), Julietta's piety and fidelity to her beloved are both admirable and moving.

The response of the disguised Duke seems scant reward for Julietta's patient dignity. His words—'There rest. / Your partner, as I hear, must die tomorrow' (II, iii, 36–7)—are so terse as to be brutal. With that Parthian shot, he leaves Julietta suffering from the shock of his revelation of Claudio's imminent execution:

> Must die to-morrow! O injurious love,
> That respites me a life, whose very comfort
> Is still a dying horror! [II, iii, 40–2]

These three lines comprise her longest speech in the play, and they constitute the only time that she complains, despite her many misfortunes. If the Duke's words are regarded as a test of Julietta's patience, then she may have failed it, but how understandably, and with what pathos! Her repetition of the vital phrasing, 'Must die to-morrow,' suggests either that she did not know of the death-sentence pronounced on Claudio, or that she did not realise how imminent his execution was. Her lament is that love could be so harmful as to spare her 'a life'—either her own life, spared because she is pregnant, or that of her child—when depriving her of that other precious life, Claudio's. The 'comfort' that she derives from 'a life'—either hers or her child's—will always ('still') be transformed into 'a dying horror' as she will be unable to forget Claudio, their child being a constant reminder. Her suffering here may seem cruel but, with the benefit of hindsight, it may be regarded as the penance that earns her, in the final scene, reunification with Claudio, ultimate pardon, and future happiness.

Julietta is silent, unmentioned, and absent from the stage until sixty lines before the end of the play, when she is re-introduced (at V, i, 475) as part of the pageant in which Claudio will be discovered to have escaped death. As she comes onstage

351

with the disguised Claudio, an audience must assume her prior knowledge of Claudio's survival. It would, therefore, be unnecessary for Julietta to react with delighted astonishment to Claudio's 'unmuffling'. This is important in the staging, as Claudio's survival must be a startling revelation to at least three other characters—Lucio, Angelo, and (particularly) Isabella—whose responses will be the focus of audience-attention. The amazement of a fourth character might make the dramatic effect too diffuse.

Julietta herself is never addressed directly in this final sequence but, when the Duke speaks to Claudio, it is Julietta who is the subject of the princely command:

> She, Claudio, that you wrong'd, look you restore.
> [V, i, 522]

Now that he has cast off the disguise under which he acted as her confessor, the Duke implicitly exonerates Julietta by placing responsibility for her condition on Claudio who 'wrong'd' her and by making it Claudio's responsibility to 'restore' her. This might be achieved by a formal ceremony of marriage involving 'the denunciation . . . of outward order' (I, ii, 137–8) that they previously neglected when swearing their mutual vows. The stage-business here is often for Julietta to present Claudio with their child and for the lovers to embrace, before processing with the Duke off-stage, to attend him at his palace. After all, if Isabella accepts the Duke's proposal of marriage, Julietta will now be sister-in-law to the Duke and therefore promoted to the rank of the nobility. As is the case with Mariana, after a period of anguish, her fidelity and piety have earned her a husband and a prosperous future. All three of the lovers persecuted by Angelo—Claudio, Mariana, and Julietta—are vindicated and rewarded at the end of the play.

Lovers in Shakespearean Comedy

Like so many of Shakespeare's 'happy comedies', particularly those of the middle period (c.1596–1604), *Measure*

352

for Measure ends in multiple marriages. These plays illustrate the adage that 'The course of true love never did run smooth' (*A Midsummer Night's Dream*, I, i, 134). The lovers must endure prolonged separation, undergoing hardships and sometimes harsh tests of their fidelity, before attaining their ultimate union. Implicitly, because their love has survived such trials and tribulations, their marriage will be the stronger and their future will be free from strife: they have learned forbearance and patience from their suffering, and appreciation of how painful it is to be separated from the beloved.

Dramatically to counterpoint the relationships of the true lovers, Shakespeare sometimes includes the nuptials of a more frivolous couple on the concluding marriage merry-go-round; for example, Maria and Sir Toby in *Twelfth Night*, Touchstone and Audrey in *As You Like It*, and Mistress Kate Keep-down and Lucio in *Measure for Measure*. These less serious unions heighten, by dramatic contrast, the solemnity of the marriages of the true lovers—in *Measure for Measure*, those between Angelo and Mariana, and Claudio and Julietta.

Sometimes, a woman who has remained true to her beloved since the first Act, despite rejection or neglect, is rewarded at the end of the play by his acknowledgement and acceptance of her; for example, Helena in *A Midsummer Night's Dream*, Viola in *Twelfth Night*, and a second Helena in *All's Well that Ends Well*. Although she is not mentioned until Act III of *Measure for Measure*, Mariana is comparable to these earlier heroines of Shakespearian comedy. The 'middle-period' comedies establish a pattern whereby women are constant and men are capricious. The woman's patient fidelity ultimately earns the love of the fickle man.[31]

---

[31] It is tempting to speculate whether the history of the Tudor dynasty affected Shakespeare in this respect. Most of Shakespeare's plays were written in the reign of Elizabeth I, whose jealous father, Henry VIII, had executed her mother on suspicion of infidelity, despite the latter's protests of innocence and of continued devotion to her husband. Among Shakespeare's male protagonists, sexual jealousy

Which brings us back to that ultimate enigma: does Isabella accept the Duke's offer of marriage at the end of the play? Were *Measure for Measure* a 'happy comedy', there would be little dispute: the play would end with a general marriage-fest. With the unions of Angelo and Mariana, Claudio and Julietta, and Lucio and Kate secured, Isabella's acceptance of the Duke's second offer of marriage would complete the established pattern. Love would have triumphed. But, unlike the Shakespearian comedies with which it has been compared in this chapter, *Measure for Measure* is not principally concerned with love in its main plot, but rather with issues of government and the law. Of course, a bond between the Duke and Isabella would sweeten the ending of a sometimes bitter play, but the union might seem less appropriate and convincing than those between Angelo and Mariana, and Claudio and Julietta. Does 'the old, fantastical Duke of dark corners' (IV, iii, 156) deserve the 'youth' (I, ii, 172) of Isabella? For that matter, does the erstwhile neurotic, self-absorbed Isabella deserve marriage to a duke? Until the concluding lines the play, has the Duke ever expressed amatory interest in Isabella? Furthermore, has Isabella ever expressed amatory interest in *any* man, let alone a duke who (according, at least, to that unreliable source, Lucio) is 'now past it' (III, ii, 176)? The comic imperative may, nevertheless, override these uncertainties. Directors and actors, audiences and readers must arbitrate.

---

proves unfounded: in *Othello*, the Moor murders Desdemona before discovering her innocence and weeping over her corpse; Leontes condemns Hermione in *The Winter's Tale,* only to repent after her apparent death and to suffer sixteen years of agonising regret before their reunion; while, in *Cymbeline*, Posthumus Leonatus plots to kill the innocent Imogen who, by quirks of fate, survives, ultimately to be reunited with her penitent love. In each of these cases, the husband suspects the wife of infidelity, but the wife proves innocent and remains devoted to the husband, despite his jealous cruelty. There may be grounds for suspicion that Shakespeare, in these plays, was undertaking historical revisionism out of respect for his first royal patron, Queen Elizabeth I.

Chapter 6

The Underworld

Much of *Measure for Measure* is set in or immediately outside a brothel or a prison, respectively the playground and the purgatory for those who frequent the underworld of the play. The close relationship between these two establishments is confirmed in Pompey's speech (IV, iii, 1–20) recording that many of those who patronized Mistress Overdone's tavern and hot-house have accompanied her pimp to gaol, implicitly as a consequence of the strict enforcement of the statutes by the recently-appointed Angelo:

> I am as well acquainted here as I was in our house of profession: one would think it were Mistress Overdone's own house, for here be many of her old customers.
>
> [IV, iii, 1–4]

Pompey names ten such clients, indicating their offences, before referring more generally to 'forty more' former whoremasters ('all great doers in our trade') who have since been incarcerated and forced to beg through the bars ('"for the Lord's sake"') to survive (lines 18–20). The fuller significance of the names and the crimes of these wrongdoers will be considered later. Suffice it for the present to confirm that the inmates of Vienna's brothels and prison—through their English-sounding names and their association with offences so prevalent in London—would undoubtedly have been types readily recognizable to those attending any early performance of Shakespeare's play.[1]

---

[1] Although the first (and only) recorded performance of *Measure for Measure* during the Jacobean era was that of 26 December 1604 at

Shakespeare's Southwark

Measure for Measure did not require Shakespeare's audience to make any great imaginative leap into a Viennese underworld profoundly different from that encountered in London. Shakespeare's Globe Theatre, together with the Rose Theatre and the Swan Theatre, was situated in an area where brothels proliferated.[2] Some of these brothels (like Mistress Overdone's) doubled as taverns, bath-houses, or ordinaries (eating-places), attempting to avoid regulation or prosecution by creating the illusion of respectable business. This was Southwark, on the south bank of the Thames, immediately to the west of London Bridge. The area had grown up beyond the jurisdiction of the City of London and its powerful, morally conservative guilds. As the 'Liberty of Winchester', Southwark was administered under the authority of successive Bishops of Winchester—hence the popular soubriquet 'Winchester geese' for the local prostitutes.[3] By the Sixteenth Century,

---

court, there is a consensus among modern scholars that there had most probably been earlier performances of the play at the Globe (following its reopening on 10 April 1604, after the major outbreak of the plague in 1603). See, for example, Braunmuller and Watson: 'This [the December 1604 performance before James I] is unlikely to have been the play's first performance, as court performances were normally of plays that had already been tested in the commercial playhouses.' (p. 373). Dr Martin Wiggins offers a more detailed argument in support of this claim in his programme-notes to the RSC's 2019 production of *Measure for Measure*.

[2] Michelle A. Laughran: 'The Bankside Stews: Prostitution in London 1161–1546', accessed 20 July 2020, http://www.academia.edu/234490/_The_Bankside_stews_prostitution _in_London_1161–1546. The three theatres mentioned were all open at the time that Shakespeare was writing *Measure for Measure*. They would be joined by the Hope Theatre in 1614 although, by that time, the Rose had closed and the Globe had just been reconstructed after it was burnt down in 1613.

[3] Paul Slade, *Cross Bones*, 2013, Chapter 5, 'Birth of the Liberty', accessed 20 July 2020, http://www.planetslade.com/cross-bones-05.html.

Southwark—or Bankside—had become popularly known as 'Stews' Bank', the name 'stew' deriving from bath-houses that (like Mistress Overdone's hot-house) doubled as brothels.[4]

Attempts to regulate these establishments led to limited or temporary success at best. Escalus's powerlessness to prosecute Froth and Pompey in Act II scene i of *Measure for Measure* is symptomatic of the similar difficulty of policing illicit sexual activity in England. The extent to which the brothels of Bankside had proliferated and become a social problem during the Twelfth Century is suggested by Henry II's *Ordinances Touching the Government of the Stewholders in Southwark Under the Direction of the Bishop of Winchester* of 1161: despite over fifty years of episcopal supervision, the abuses occurring in Southwark's stews had become notorious enough to prompt royal intervention.[5] Reference to a selection of further legislation should establish a pattern of concern over promiscuous sexual activity in London in general, and in Southwark in particular. In 1277, prostitutes were banned from living in the City of London, in an effort to limit their trade to Southwark; while thirty-three years later, Edward II (like Angelo) attempted to close all of London's brothels.[6] In 1483, Edward V reintroduced legislation to ban prostitutes from the City of London, a sure sign that any earlier attempts to limit them to the suburbs had been unsuccessful.[7] Henry VIII, fearful of the spread of syphilis, passed a law in 1511 that all whores should be branded.[8] Subsequently, in an attempt to check the spread of the plague, he ordered the closure of Southwark's brothels in 1546;[9] but they continued to operate surreptitiously

---

[4] Gamini Salgado, *The Elizabethan Underworld* (London: Dent, 1977; repr. Stroud: Alan Sutton, 1992), pp. 40–41.

[5] The text of these ordinances is offered by Slade, Chapter 5.

[6] 'Prostitution in the United Kingdom', Wikipedia, accessed 18 July 2020, https://en.wikipedia.org/wiki/Prostitution_in_the_United_Kingdom.

[7] Laughran, pp. 70–71.

[8] Salgado, p. 41.

[9] Laughran, pp. 74–75.

until legitimate regulation of brothels was reinstated under Henry's son, Edward VI.[10] In Elizabethan and Jacobean times, they flourished, despite persistent opposition from Puritans and frequent closure during outbreaks of disease. For example, during the plague of 1603, at a time when *Measure for Measure* was probably being prepared for the stage, James 1 ordered the demolition of suburban brothels in an attempt to contain the disease.[11] As Pompey wryly observes to Mistress overdone, however, 'though you change your place, you need not change your trade' (I, ii, 99–100): when one brothel was 'plucked down', another would promptly spring up nearby.

The services of prostitutes, therefore, could be procured not only in theatres such as the Globe, Rose, and Swan, where they might ply their trade while mingling with the audiences, but also in the immediately-surrounding establishments of Southwark, the supervision of which had been, for five hundred years, the responsibility of prominent English clergymen. Successive Bishops of Winchester must have 'had some feeling of the sport' (Lucio: III, ii, 115–16), as they profited greatly from it. In their defence—and as if to endorse Pompey's pragmatic justification of his 'trade' as a pimp (II, i, 216–40)—they might have cited the opinions of two of the most influential figures in the history of Christian theology: St. Augustine of Hippo (354–430) and St. Thomas Aquinas (1225–74). The two scholars agree that prostitution is a practical necessity, Aquinas describing it as a receptacle for human foulness, like a cesspool.[12] In applying Aquinas's image to sixteenth-century London, Gamini Salgado observes how some of those most prominent in the theatres also made money from prostitution (just as Pompey and Mistress Overdone make their living in *Measure for Measure*):

> . . . Southwark was the cesspool which drained the city, offering rich pickings to the substantial burghers to whom

---

[10] Laughran, p. 76.
[11] Lever, pp. xxxii–xxxiii.
[12] Salgado, pp. 37–39.

the Bishop of Winchester farmed it out. . . . [B]oth Philip Henslowe, the best-known impresario of the Elizabethan theatre, and his son-in-law Edward Alleyn, the most celebrated actor of the day, found brothel-owning as profitable as the theatre.[13]

When sanctioned by the Church, brothels could indeed prove a lucrative investment: by 1619, Alleyn's fortune was sufficiently large for him to found Dulwich College as 'God's Gift', for the education of twelve poor scholars.[14] When Pompey talks of the 'wise burgher' who intervened in support of the brothels in the city of Vienna (I, ii, 91–2), Shakespeare's audience would have been reminded of the similar vested interests in the flesh-trade of those powerful personages with property in Southwark.

Like brothels, prisons proliferated on Bankside. John Taylor's verse-pamphlet of 1623, ironically entitled *The Praise and Virtue of a Jail and Jailers,* records no fewer than five prisons in Southwark, more than a quarter of the total of eighteen for the whole of London:

> Five jails or prisons are in Southwark place[d],
> The Counter (once St Margaret's Church defaced),
> The Marshalsea, the King's Bench and White Lion. . . .
> Then there's the Clink, where handsome lodgings be.[15]

---

[13] Salgado, p. 39. Like Claudio and Julietta, Henslowe's stepdaughter, who was also Alleyn's wife, suffered the humiliation of public punishment for a sexual offence in 1593. She was hauled through the streets behind a cart, probably either for prostitution or for failing to close a brothel, as demanded by the authorities, during the outbreak of the plague that year (Salgado, p. 49).

[14] 'Dulwich College', Wikipedia, accessed 20 July 2020, https://en.wikipedia.org/wiki/Dulwich_College. One wonders if 'God's Gift' might have been an ironic acknowledgement of the role of the Bishop of Winchester's licentious policies in augmenting Alleyn's fortune.

[15] Quoted by Salgado, pp. 185–186.

As the Marshalsea was particularly associated with religious and maritime offences,[16] it would have been an appropriate venue in which to encounter a Claudio, imprisoned for the kind of illicit sexual activity condemned by the Church, alongside a Ragozine, 'a most notorious pirate' (IV, iii, 70). Moreover, the Marshalsea was only a few hundred metres from Shakespeare's Globe Theatre.

Closer still was the Clink, the most infamous of Southwark's prisons. It was particularly associated with offences committed locally, and with religious crimes.[17] Like the brothels, the Clink was the administrative responsibility of the Bishop of Winchester. In *Measure for Measure*, the Vienna of Duke Vincentio harbours numerous places of 'fornication, adultery, and all uncleanliness' (Elbow: II, i, 80), despite the deterrence of a grim place of correction nearby. Similarly, the Bishop of Winchester's Liberty of Southwark was home to a profusion of brothels, despite the threatening proximity of the Clink Prison. There is little distinction between the underworld of *Measure for Measure* and the underworld of Shakespeare's Southwark: in the scenes set in or around the brothel and prison in *Measure for Measure*, Shakespeare is portraying characters and an environment entirely familiar to him and to his audiences.[18]

The administration of many London prisons was 'farmed out' to the highest bidders. Profits could be made by overcharging the prisoners for food, extorting payment for privileges, and offering overnight accommodation to ne'er-do-wells. Prison governors acquired a deserved notoriety for harsh rapaciousness; hence Duke Vincentio's maxim,

---

[16] Salgado, p. 184.

[17] Salgado, p. 181.

[18] In this respect, Shakespeare's play anticipates the comedies that Ben Jonson set overtly in London: the seamy side of Jacobean urban life would be represented directly and unambiguously in works such as *Eastward Ho!* (1605), *The Alchemist* (1610), and *Bartholomew Fair* (1614).

> . . . seldom when
> The steeled gaoler is the friend of men. [IV, ii, 84–8]

There was sometimes little distinction between the prison and the brothel in London. One of the prisons in the City, the Wood Street Counter, charged fourpence a night to house known thieves and whores.[19] As a detention-centre particularly associated with the correction of prostitutes, Bridewell had been promoted by Edward VI as a place of enlightened reform, but its administration passed into the hands of a business consortium in 1602, only two years before the first recorded performance of *Measure for Measure*. The four businessmen involved transformed Bridewell into an extravagant hostelry-cum-brothel, while poor inmates were neglected or expelled. Although the consortium's licence was eventually revoked, the businessmen appear to have escaped without further retribution.[20] It is scarcely surprising, therefore, that Shakespeare should represent Pompey as encountering so many of Mistress Overdone's former customers in Vienna's prison: by the time that *Measure for Measure* first appeared on stage, the distinction between London's brothels and prisons had become blurred.

Although, morally, both the brothel and the prison in *Measure for Measure* may 'stink in some sort' (Pompey: III, ii, 27), Shakespeare gives them a surprising vitality. The underworld may, at first glance, seem more appealing because it is set against the tarnished authority of flawed characters such as the Duke and Angelo. The statutes have been mismanaged by the hapless Duke, as he himself admits (I, iii, 19–39), while the law is further discredited by the repugnant behaviour of Angelo towards Claudio, Julietta, Mariana, and (especially) Isabella. In the inaptitude of its minor officials, Elbow the constable and Abhorson the executioner, the reputation of the

---

[19] Salgado, p. 174.
[20] Salgado, pp. 195–196.

state is further compromised.[21] Additionally, the practitioners of abstinence—Isabella and Angelo—can appear bigoted, smug, and ruthless.

By contrast, the agents of anarchy and indulgence include in their ranks two seemingly engaging, free-spirited characters: Pompey and Lucio display endearing vitality, ingenuity, and resilience. Pompey is resourceful, cheerful in adversity, and even (on occasion) profound in his philosophy; while Lucio is the most prominent, the most complex, and the most fascinating of those who flout the rule of law. We should, nevertheless, beware of concluding prematurely that anarchy and indulgence in *Measure for Measure* are ultimately more attractive than their opposites: authority and abstinence. It would be wise to look more closely at Shakespeare's presentation of Vienna's various underworld characters before reaching any final decision.

Introducing Lucio

Lucio is a multi-faceted character. His name, with its connotations of 'light', might hint at the 'light' or dissolute behaviour that is so significant a part of his personality. In the dramatis personae appended to the text of *Measure for Measure* in the First Folio, he is categorized as 'a fantastique', a preparation for the outrageous things that he will say and the unpredictable ways in which he will behave as the play develops. Additionally, the word 'fantastique' had, during Elizabeth's reign, developed connotations of foppishness.[22]

---

[21] Granted, in the Provost and Escalus, the law finds two worthy practitioners—but even Escalus may seem rash and brutal in his exercise of power when he summarily condemns Friar Lodowick to the rack for his criticism of the state, grimly threatening, 'We'll touse you / Joint by joint' (V, i, 309–10).

[22] *OED* n. 2 indicates that, from 1598 onward, 'fantastique' could denote a fop, a connotation reflected in many modern productions. For example, both Brendan O'Hea's effete Lucio at the Globe in 2015 and Joseph Arkley's rather more robust Lucio for the RSC in 2019 dressed and strutted like dandies throughout their performances.

From the outset, then, Lucio should appear decadent, quirky, and pretentiously overdressed; but he also proves consistently amusing and a frequent source of important truths. He provokes conflicting responses in an audience: although many of his words and deeds may seem difficult to condone, he is often redeemed by the fertility of his imagination, the incisiveness of his judgement, and the strength of his loyalty (to Claudio and Isabella, at least, if not to his associates in the underworld).

Lucio indulges in coarse banter with two 'gentlemen' on his first appearance (Act I scene ii). That all three men are soldiers is strongly suggested when one of Lucio's companions remarks, 'There's not a soldier of us all that, in the thanksgiving before meat, do relish the petition well that prays for peace' (I, ii, 14–16). In saying 'of *us* all' rather than 'of *them* all', the speaker would seem to include himself and his two colleagues in the ranks of the military. Their language, studded with mutual insults, is coarsely amusing, ranging across topics suitable for discussion by soldiers in Shakespeare's time: war and peace, piracy and theft, irreligious behaviour, drink, and (especially) sexually transmitted infections (I, ii, 1–55). These exchanges introduce the audience to Lucio's preoccupations, to his dissolute life, and to his profane tongue.

Subsequently, Lucio will inform Isabella that he was one of many 'gentlemen' deceived by the Duke's departure from Vienna into 'hope of action' (I, iv, 50–2); that is, Lucio expected to be employed in military service. The evidence strongly suggests that Lucio and his two companions (whose only appearance in the play is in the second scene) make their living by following the wars, just as the braggart Parolles does in Shakespeare's nearly contemporary and closely comparable play, *All's Well that Ends Well*.

It is significant that Lucio is associated with the military because his literary origins may lie in the *miles gloriosus*, the braggart soldier who was a stock character of Roman drama.[23] Lucio shares important affinities with the loud-mouthed mercenaries, based on the Roman archetype, who are encountered elsewhere in Elizabethan and Jacobean drama: for example, Ancient Pistol in *Henry IV Part 2*, *Henry V*, and *The Merry Wives of Windsor*, Parolles in *All's Well that Ends Well*, and Captain Bobadil in Ben Jonson's *Every Man in His Humour*. Like the classical *miles gloriosus*, these characters created by Shakespeare and Jonson are shameless boasters who, to the audience's delight, are sure to be exposed and humiliated. Although the other soldiers in the tradition tend to boast of their military prowess and physical accomplishments, Lucio brags of his intimate association with the Duke, as if he were captain of Vincentio's equivalent of the Praetorian Guard and therefore privy to his ruler's personal secrets.

At first, Lucio's boasts concerning the Duke may appear to an audience as the spontaneous product of his 'fantastical' imagination, rather than as premeditated malice. In conversation with Friar Lodowick (the Duke in disguise), Lucio has been critical of Angelo's cold, inhumane administration of the law (III, ii, 91–112). Seeking to contrast the previous liberal regime under the Duke, Lucio is characteristically hyperbolical, claiming that the Duke was as sexually promiscuous then as Angelo is ascetically abstemious now. The diametrical contrast seems necessary to imply that government in Vienna has gone from one extreme to the other, from condoning to condemning sexual activity—and Claudio, Lucio's friend, is the victim of this inconsistency. When challenged to give authority for his

---

[23] During the English renaissance, the influence of Plautus's play, *Miles Gloriosus*, was particularly extensive. It is even possible that Lucio's name recalls Lurcio, the drunken slave in *Miles Gloriosus*. Alternatively, Lucio may owe his origins to the satirical tradition: 'Perhaps Lucio is an escapee from another genre: the verse-satires blocked by the Bishops' Ban of 1599 that morphed into the satiric characters of late-Elizabethan plays' (Braunmuller and Watson, p. 94).

accusation of debauchery against Vincentio, Lucio rashly represents himself as a courtier with close personal knowledge of the Duke:

Sir, I was an inward of his. A shy fellow was the Duke; and I believe I know the cause of his withdrawing.

[III, ii, 127–9]

When Lucio subsequently refuses to be drawn on the reason for the Duke's departure from court, he may seem to be feigning the tact of a courtier in whom a state secret has been confided; but simultaneously Lucio is making a coarse insinuation, in support of his slander of the Duke. Coming so soon after Lucio's accusations that the Duke was a drunken lecher of indiscriminate amatory tastes, the implication is that Vincentio has withdrawn for sexual reasons, either further to gratify his appetite or, more likely, to seek treatment for the inevitable diseases that he would have acquired. Sexual infections were, after all, a favourite topic of the banter between Lucio and his two companions at the start of Act I scene ii.

Seemingly carried away by his own rhetoric, Lucio compounds his offence by attributing to the Duke further outrageous behaviour, repeatedly seeking to validate his accusations by maintaining that he was a close associate of Vincentio (e.g. at III, ii, 145 and 148). His braggart's confidence even leads him to identify himself to his interlocutor whom, amusingly, he does not recognise as the very Duke with whom he is boasting such intimate acquaintance:

Sir, my name is Lucio, well known to the Duke. [III, ii, 155]

Of course, the audience is fully aware of the delicious irony that Lucio is now indeed 'well known to the Duke' who, in his disguise as Friar Lodowick, has heard himself roundly slandered and will have the opportunity to exact retribution from Lucio in due course.

Lucio's bragging leads directly to his downfall. On their second meeting, he repeats his slanders against the Duke to Friar Lodowick, again boasting of his close personal relationship with Vincentio (IV, iii, 160–1 and 163–4). In support of this latter claim, Lucio specifies the one time (before these exchanges) when an audience might confidently believe that he was indeed in the presence of the Duke:

> I was once before him for getting a wench with child. . . . marry, did I: but I was fain to forswear it; they would else have married me to the rotten medlar. [IV, iii, 167–72]

The audience, recognising Lucio's boast as an admission not only of perjury but also of an offence against the very statutes under which Claudio stands condemned, will eagerly anticipate the retribution that must follow when the Duke doffs his disguise to deal justice.

Lucio the Lecher

A hint of Lucio's ultimate downfall is given as early as the first scene in which he appears. On seeing Mistress Overdone's approach, he admits, whether jocularly or in earnest, 'I have purchased as many diseases under her roof as come to—' (I, ii, 42–3). This willingness to speak openly and flippantly about his association with brothels and prostitutes is further illustrated when Lucio boasts to Friar Lodowick of begetting his illegitimate child. In the closing moments of the play, Lucio will be obliged by the Duke to marry the alleged 'whore' whom he has wronged (V, i, 505–21), to make amends for his dissolute behaviour.

Lucio speaks of sexual activity in a variety of ways: crudely, jocularly, and even lyrically. When exasperated by the sentence imposed on his friend, he flippantly characterises Claudio's crime as a pastime, 'a game of tick-tack' (I, ii, 180–1) or as a domestic activity, 'filling a bottle with a tun-dish' (III, ii, 166). Both analogies imply comic but obscene reference to the male and female sexual organs, tick-tack being a game scored by

366

thrusting pegs into holes, and a tun-dish being a funnel pushed into a bottle for the transfer of fluids.

By contrast, Lucio offers the most poetical description of human sexual relations in the entire play:

> Your brother and his lover have embrac'd;
> . . . as blossoming time
> That from the seedness the bare fallow brings
> To teeming foison, even so her plenteous womb
> Expresseth his full tilth and husbandry. [I, iv, 39–44]

The extended idyllic image presents the relationship of Claudio and Julietta as entirely natural and implicitly free from blame, the product of their union being cause for rejoicing rather than for censure. Their child will be the 'foison' of her 'plenteous womb', an abundance of riches resulting from the 'full tilth and husbandry'—that is, the assiduity and honest labour—of the male. Although the actor playing Lucio could deliver this short speech in a cynical tone, to 'blaspheme the good, in mocking'—to use Isabella's immediately preceding accusation against Lucio (I, iv, 38)—there is nothing in the speech itself to suggest that it should be spoken in any way other than sincerely, offering a lyrical celebration of erotic love.

Generally, however, Lucio is forthright when discussing sexual matters, perhaps in keeping with his military image. He first informs the demure Isabella of her brother's plight with the stark, monosyllabic statement, 'He hath got his friend with child' (I, iv, 29). In his defence, it should be said that such directness is preferable to tactful prevarication when the situation is so urgent, Claudio's imminent execution demanding immediate action. Furthermore, such a simple sentence without the slightest embellishment implies that Claudio's sexual activity is commonplace rather than morally offensive. Similarly, in Lucio's first exchanges with the disguised Duke, his exasperated explanation of his friend's prosecution is that 'this Claudio is condemned for untrussing' (III, ii, 173). 'Untrussing'—the untying of the tabs between doublet and hose (or codpiece), inevitable for urination—is implicitly a necessary daily activity prohibited by an irrational law.

With earthy pragmatism, Lucio twice proposes that legislation against lust is unreasonable because the necessary partaking of food and drink is the inevitable precursor to carnal indulgence. For him, the sexual appetite is as natural as hunger or thirst, and therefore as necessary to satisfy:

> . . . but it is impossible to extirp [lechery] quite, friar, till eating and drinking be put down. [III, ii, 98–9]

He revisits this opinion in a later scene, in lines that include clearer reference to the capital sentence now imposed on fornicators:

> I dare not for my head fill my belly: one fruitful meal would set me to't. [IV, iii, 152–4]

His words convey concisely how oppressive legislation denies him even the simple pleasure of eating well, as sating one appetite would stimulate another—erotic desire—that would have fatal consequences. Shakespeare presents such sexual references as a natural, spontaneous part of Lucio's speech.

An audience may, nevertheless, be startled by how many of Lucio's imperatives and exclamations to Isabella, during her first encounter with Angelo, sound uncomfortably like sexual innuendos. They resemble the encouragements of a pimp to an inexperienced prostitute entertaining a client: 'Give it not o'er so.—To him again. . . . You are too cold. . . . To him, I say. . . . You are too cold. . . . Ay, touch him: there's the vein. . . . O, to him, to him, wench! . . . He's coming: I perceive't. . . . more o' that. . . . Art avised o'that? More on't' (II, ii, 43–133). Shakespeare may be ensuring consistency with Lucio's portrayal elsewhere; after all, Lucio is particularly aware of such potential sexual innuendos during the comparable legal proceedings with which the play concludes (e.g. at V, i, 180–1, 272, 274–6, and 278). Lucio, whose language is as infected as his body by the brothel, is no great respecter of place, person, or circumstance.

In his ribald, anarchistic way, however, he proves something of a practical philosopher when discussing erotic matters. In his first encounter in the play with the Duke/friar, Lucio explores the relationship between the law and human sexual conduct, beginning with his adverse judgement of Angelo's administration of the statutes:

A little more lenity to lechery would do no harm in him.

[III, ii, 94–5]

The phrase 'lenity to lechery' is well-wrought: the two nouns, by mirroring each other alliteratively and metrically (both are dactyls), reinforce his argument that judicial clemency and sexual indulgence should be entirely compatible. His justification for this premise is that

. . . the vice is of a great kindred; it is well allied. . . .

[III, ii, 97–8]

The ambiguity is cleverly managed: 'great kindred' and 'well allied' could suggest either that the vice has 'many relations' or, more specifically, that it has '*noble* relations'. Lucio, by presenting lechery's 'family' through personification, is arguing that sexual licence is very widely prevalent while simultaneously (and mischievously) suggesting that it is particularly favoured by the wealthy and powerful. In this way, Lucio achieves three objectives: he offers lechery a 'respectable' pedigree; he implies that it would be hypocritical of legislators to prosecute lechery when they so often indulge in it themselves; and he prepares the ground for his slander of the Duke, whom he will soon accuse of having 'some feeling of the sport' (III, ii, 115–16).

Because Lucio presents sexual activity as natural and spontaneous, he is strongly opposed to strict legislation against this aspect of human conduct:

369

Why, what a ruthless thing is this in him, for the rebellion of a codpiece to take away the life of a man! [III, ii, 110–12]

This indignant exclamation against Angelo's capital sentence on Claudio uses bathos to suggest the pettiness of the law. Rebellion against the state would indeed be a capital offence, but lechery is 'the rebellion of a codpiece', that is, the uprising of an unruly organ under a man's clothing. Lucio's ridiculous personification of the stirrings of male sexual desire invites the hearer to laugh the charge out of court. Such anarchic ripostes, challenging orthodox moral and legal opinions, are likely to endear him to a modern audience.

Lucio's Loyalty

Audiences who enjoy the character of Lucio because he is so amusingly outrageous may also admire him because his loyalty never wavers to his noble friend, Claudio. On Lucio's first appearance in the play, Mistress Overdone reports to him that 'There's one yonder arrested and carried to prison, was worth five thousand of you all' (I, ii, 56–7), identifying the victim whom she has so praised as 'Claudio; Signor Claudio' (I, ii, 59). Mistress Overdone's hyperbolical appraisal of Claudio's 'worth' and the respectful title of 'Signor' identify Claudio as deserving of the support of loyal friends. Lucio responds with alacrity—'Away! Let's go learn the truth of this' (I, ii, 74)—and thirty lines later he has sought out and found Claudio. The difference in social—and perhaps moral—status between these two friends may immediately be suggested by the fact that Claudio consistently speaks to Lucio in dignified verse, whereas Lucio predominantly replies in offhand prose. The normally garrulous Lucio nevertheless shows his respect and sympathy by listening in relative silence to Claudio's lengthy account of the progress of his relationship with Julietta, his prosecution by Angelo, his fruitless petition to the absent Duke, and his final hope: to persuade Lucio to recruit his sister, Isabella the novice nun, to plead for his life to the Deputy (I, ii, 134–76). Without demur, Lucio undertakes to complete the task 'within two hours' (I, ii, 183), thereby encouraging his friend with expectation of a speedy reprieve. Lucio performs the duties of friendship with alacrity.

In the presence of Isabella two scenes later, Lucio battles against two obstacles that threaten to thwart his attempt to redeem Claudio: first, Isabella's scepticism concerning Lucio's character and truthfulness; and second, Isabella's fear that she lacks the ability to secure her brother's repeal. Lucio proves equal to both tasks. He defends his friend's reputation by asserting that Claudio has been sentenced

> For that which, if myself might be his judge,
> He should receive his punishment in thanks:
> He hath got his friend with child. [I, iv, 27–9]

Lucio prepares his potentially shocking revelation skilfully, by suggesting that Claudio deserves praise rather than prosecution for the successful consummation of his relationship with Julietta. When Isabella refuses to believe Lucio's 'story' (line 30), Lucio earns her credence with an elaborate and apparently earnest speech (lines 39–44, already discussed) celebrating the love between Claudio and Julietta. On learning subsequently that her brother requires her to plead before Angelo for his life, Isabella twice expresses doubts in her ability to succeed (I, iv, 75–6 and 77), prompting Lucio to assume command with authoritative statements based on a seemingly profound understanding of human behaviour:

> Our doubts are traitors,
> And make us lose the good we oft might win
> By fearing to attempt. Go to Lord Angelo,
> And let him learn to know, when maidens sue,
> Men give like gods; but when they weep and kneel,
> All their petitions are as freely theirs
> As they themselves would owe them. [I, iv, 77–83]

Lucio's initial metaphor is entirely appropriate both to his anarchic character and to the request that he is making of

Isabella: petitioning Angelo is a kind of rebellion against the authority of the law, an 'attempt' that Isabella might 'win' if she could overcome her 'doubts' which, like 'traitors', threaten to betray her cause. Lucio supports his sententious opening words with a strongly rhetorical appeal, beginning with imperatives ('go' and 'let') supported by pledges of inevitable success if his directives are followed. In the service of his friend, Lucio has transformed himself from an irreverent cynic into an earnest, resourceful, and effective pleader.

Throughout these exchanges with Isabella in Act I scene iv, Lucio speaks in verse rather than prose. This change corresponds with the transformation of his language from bawdy banter (in Act I, scene ii) to reasoned discourse. Because of his earnestness, the advice that he gives Isabella here about how a woman should petition a man will guide her future conduct: not only when she appears before Angelo in Act II, but also when she intercedes before the Duke on behalf of Angelo in the final scene of the play. Implicitly, Lucio's speech might also influence her cruel words to her brother in Act III, when she will refuse even a gesture as effortless as 'bending down' (III, i, 143) to redeem him from sentence of death. Lucio claims that a woman who kneels to a man in authority will readily secure her petition. It is sharply ironic, then, that the advice that Lucio gives as a faithful advocate of Claudio's cause might be influential when Isabella confirms her total abandonment of support for her brother.

Lucio repeatedly shows his determination to redeem Claudio from his death-sentence when he boldly accompanies Isabella into the presence of Angelo. Initially, her irresolution is such that she is soon deferring to the dogmatic Deputy and preparing to withdraw from the presence-chamber (at II, ii, 41–2). It takes a decisive intervention from Lucio to save the day:

> Give't not o'er so.—To him again, entreat him,
> Kneel down before him, hang upon his gown;
> You are too cold. If you should need a pin,
> You could not with more tame a tongue desire it.

To him, I say. [II, ii, 43–7][24]

The jerky rhythm of the passage, created by the metrical irregularities and the profusion of caesurae, vividly conveys the strength of Lucio's anxiety when he fears that his friend's fate will be sealed for lack of sustained pleading on Isabella's part. Lucio uses five imperatives in the first two lines to demand further petition, immediately followed by a blunt indictment of the demure Isabella. The coldness that he criticises in her suggests by contrast his ardent desire to secure his friend's safety. After the domestic image condemning Isabella's 'tame tongue', his further imperative ('To him, I say') suggests stage-business: Lucio, having seized the retreating Isabella, might physically turn her about, and propel her back towards the Deputy. Nine lines later, he is again compelled to comment that her pleading is 'too cold' (II, ii, 56). Lucio faithfully perseveres in Claudio's cause when even Claudio's own sister is ready to capitulate.

These interventions persuade Isabella to argue her cause more forcibly, at which Lucio's adverse comments become pithy encouragements (at II, ii, 70, 90, and 111). Soon, Lucio's anxiety is transformed into excited anticipation as he appears to believe that Isabella is winning the argument with Angelo and that Claudio's life may be secured:

O, to him, to him, wench! He will relent;
He's coming: I perceive't. [II, ii, 125–6]

Thou'rt i'th'right, girl; more o'that. [II, ii, 130]

---

[24] It was during this speech, in the 2004 National Theatre production directed by Simon McBurney, that Toby Jones's Lucio transformed Isabella into sexual bait by unbuttoning her blouse before spinning her back towards Angelo. Although this stage-business runs counter to Lucio's firm belief, consistently expressed elsewhere in the play, that Angelo is impervious to sexual desire, it is fully congruent with Lucio's sexually-charged language throughout this scene. As illustrated previously in this chapter (pp. 368–369), Lucio is assuming the role of Angelo's procurer.

Art avis'd o' that? More on't. [II, ii, 133]

In each of these interventions, which might be delivered as asides but would be more effective dramatically as messages whispered to Isabella as encouragements, Lucio's fervent optimism, his anticipation of success on his mission from Claudio, is suggested by his jerky, colloquial language, studded with frequent informal abbreviations. Finally, it is Lucio who intervenes to prompt Isabella to withdraw when he recognises that Angelo needs time to reconsider his position:

Go to: 'tis well; away. [II, ii, 157]

Although the volume of his contribution to the dialogue may seem insignificant when set against Isabella's lengthy solicitations to Angelo, Lucio has been the controlling influence in the appeal, judging when Isabella was 'too cold', when her arguments were succeeding, and when it was appropriate to end the debate. Lucio's interventions suggest skill and experience in negotiation. He has assiduously carried out his duty to his beleaguered friend in ensuring that the very best case has been made for Claudio's repeal. In addition, he has performed an important dramatic function by acting as chorus, commenting on the action and encouraging appropriate responses in the audience.

Lucio's preoccupation with Claudio's fate is again evident in his first meeting with Friar Lodowick (the Duke in disguise). After making facetious and slanderous remarks about Angelo and the Duke, Lucio's anxiety for his friend breaks through:

But no more of this.—Canst thou tell if Claudio die tomorrow, or no? [III, ii, 163–4]

When the Duke/friar feigns ignorance of the case, Lucio's exasperation at the injustice of his friend's continued imprisonment bursts forth in a speech in which he repeatedly belittles Claudio's offence, rails against Angelo's phlegmatic ruthlessness, and longs for the restoration of the old Duke's indulgent regime (III, ii, 166–73).[25] Lucio's ardour for the cause that he undertook in Act I scene ii has clearly not abated: Claudio's safety remains his major concern, and is in part the justification for his adverse verdicts on Angelo and the Duke.

On his second meeting with the Duke/friar, Lucio apparently deduces the ill tidings of Claudio's execution from Isabella's tearful appearance. It leaves him 'pale at mine heart' (IV, iii, 150) and leads to his impassioned exclamation,

> By my troth, Isabel, I loved thy brother; if the old fantastical duke of dark corners had been at home, he had lived.
> [IV, iii, 155–7]

Lucio's exasperation at the continued absence of the Duke, the one person (however pejoratively described) who might have saved his friend from death, must impress the audience with its earnestness. Like Isabella, Lucio displays intense grief at the presumed loss of Claudio.

If his friend were indeed dead, then Lucio would recognise the failure of his mission, despite his best efforts. This should have a bearing on the stage business towards the end of the final scene when the 'unmuffling' of Claudio reveals that he has been saved from execution. The reconciliation between brother and sister is the sole focus in most productions, but what of the reunion of the old friends, Lucio and Claudio? At a time when Lucio is at bay, apparently about to be condemned to severe punishment by the Duke whom he has so outrageously slandered, the audience—and, indeed, certain characters on

---

[25] At the conclusion of this tirade against puritanical injustice, Rob Edwards's Lucio, in David Thacker's 1994 television-production for the BBC, leaned back against a wall and uttered the line 'Farewell, good friar, I prithee pray for me' (III, ii, 174) as a world-weary sigh, with his eyes closing in despair. This was the most revealing moment in a thoroughly convincing performance, Lucio seemingly sickened by injustice, hypocrisy, and lies—his own included.

stage—might be reminded of Lucio's most redeeming characteristic: his loyalty to his friend. Some mutual gestures of affection could be offered to show both Claudio's gratitude to Lucio and Lucio's delight that Claudio has survived. The Duke's relatively lenient final sentence on Lucio, to marry the woman whom he has impregnated, would thereby appear to be in response (in part, at least) to Lucio's merit in persevering in Claudio's cause—a cause that the Duke has shared.

Lucio's loyal support of his worthy friend, Claudio, contrasts sharply with his betrayal of his underworld associates. When Pompey is arrested, he, like Claudio, appeals to Lucio for assistance:

> I spy comfort, I cry bail! Here's a gentleman, and a friend of mine. [III, ii, 40–1]

An audience will accept that Lucio must be well acquainted with Pompey the pimp, as both frequent Mistress Overdone's brothel. Far from lending a sympathetic ear to Pompey's plight, however, Lucio mocks both him and his mistress at length (III, ii, 42–61). In a disquieting turn of phrase, on confirmation that Pompey is committed to prison, Lucio sneers,

> Why, 'tis not amiss, Pompey. Farewell: go, say I sent thee thither. [III, ii, 61–2]

Lucio's lack of sympathy here for the man who claims him as a friend—indeed, his mocking endorsement of Pompey's sentence in the words "'tis not amiss' (line 61)—is diametrically opposed to his concern for Claudio's plight in Act I scene ii. His boast, 'I sent thee thither' (lines 61–2), is more problematical. Of course, this could be Lucio the braggart declaring that he would happily acquire notoriety for doing something for which he had actually no responsibility (other than by refusing to bail his associate); but a more sinister interpretation would be that Pompey has been committed to prison on Lucio's testimony, raising the issue of whether Shakespeare is presenting Lucio as an informer to those same

376

authorities that he otherwise so reviles. Certainly, Lucio testifies against Pompey just a few lines later, when he exclaims,

> If imprisonment be the due of a bawd, why, 'tis his right. Bawd is he doubtless, and of antiquity, too: bawd born.
> [III, ii, 64–6]

Although this testimony is not given in a court of law, it might still strike an audience as admissible evidence for the prosecution of the tapster who had thought Lucio his friend.[26]

Lucio, having taken his sexual pleasure at Mistress Overdone's brothel for so long (according, at least, to his words at I, ii, 42–3), appears eager to purge himself of his former associates, allowing Pompey (and elsewhere, Mistress Overdone) to bear the blame and to pay the penalty. Certainly, Pompey appears disappointed to be abandoned by one whom he had thought his friend and whom he now attempts to flatter into compliance with a bogus title, as if Lucio were the magistrate judging his case: 'I hope, sir, your good worship will be my bail?' (III, ii, 70). Lucio's response to Pompey's plea is callously vindictive in proposing a more severe sentence:

> No, indeed will I not. . . . I will pray, Pompey, to increase your bondage. . . . [III, ii, 71–2]

An audience may find it distasteful that Lucio, showing neither friendship not gratitude to Pompey for his previous offices, gleefully invites even heavier restraints to be imposed on his former associate.[27]

---

[26] The issue of the sources of evidence admissible in 'bawdy courts' is considered in Chapter 7, pp. 428–429.

[27] Cf. Isabella's hope for 'a more strict restraint' among 'the votarists of Saint Clare' (I, iv, 4–5), and Claudio's philosophical observation that 'every scope by the immoderate use / Turns to restraint' (I, ii, 119–20).

It is conceivable that a character such as Lucio might condemn a colleague in this callous manner because he is therefore less likely to face retribution for his own misdeeds. Lucio knows that his friend, Claudio, has been condemned to death for fathering an illegitimate child. Lucio, like Claudio, also admits to having fathered a child of dubious birth, but Lucio has abandoned his sexual partner, claiming the woman to be a whore. He boasts as much to the disguised Duke (IV, iii, 167–72). Lucio might deliberately forestall any testimonies against him under the statutes against fornication by ensuring that potential accusers are imprisoned first under those same statutes. Such a hypothesis gives greater credence to Mistress Overdone's impassioned complaint when she is arrested by Escalus for being 'a bawd of eleven years' continuance' (III, ii, 190):

> My lord, this is one Lucio's information against me, Mistress Kate Keep-down was with child by him in the Duke's time, he promised her marriage. His child is a year and a quarter old come Philip and Jacob. I have kept it myself; and see how he goes about to abuse me.
> [III, ii, 192–7]

It would seem from this speech that Lucio is presented by Shakespeare as analogous to Angelo: guilty both of breach of promise to his betrothed and of blackening another's reputation to avoid the consequences of his misdeeds. Of course, Mistress Overdone might be regarded as attempting to alleviate her sentence by making false allegations against a fellow offender; but her reference to the existence of Lucio's illegitimate child, the plausibility of which is confirmed by Lucio's boast to the Duke, suggests that Shakespeare is presenting Lucio as indebted to Mistress Overdone for caring for his offspring and for keeping his guilty secret about its origins. Informing against Mistress Overdone would clear his financial debt for child-maintenance and silence a possible witness against him. Were Lucio recognised to be acting as an informer, a 'base . . .

intelligencer'[28] to the state, an audience might consider his conduct even more reprehensible than that of the underworld associates whom he has condemned.

Here, then, is the paradox at the heart of Shakespeare's characterisation of Lucio. He is both admirably loyal and deplorably disloyal in his relationships. He is loyal to those associates whom he might regard as his moral as well as his social superiors: 'Signior' Claudio and the 'very virtuous maid', Claudio's sister Isabella. By contrast, he betrays the trust of those acquaintances in whom he might see his own degenerate life reflected, or who might bear witness against him to the authorities: Pompey the Pimp, Mistress Overdone the madam, and Mistress Kate Keep-down the (alleged) punk. In short, Lucio's fickleness seems based on his conception of who is deserving—and who is undeserving—of faithful friendship.

Lucio the Social Commentator

One of Lucio's most important dramatic functions in the play is to comment on other prominent characters and on aspects of Viennese society. In this respect, his role as a kind of Grecian chorus is analogous to the Duke's in several of Vincentio's 'soliloquies'. Lucio's judgement on the Duke's new Deputy is particularly important in guiding an audience's initial responses to Angelo,

> . . . a man whose blood
> Is very snow-broth; one who never feels
> The wanton stings and motions of the sense;
> But doth rebate and blunt his natural edge
> With profits of the mind, study and fast.
> He, to give fear to use and liberty,
> Which have for long run by the hideous law
> As mice by lions, hath pick'd out an act

---

[28] The phrase is used of himself, with disgust, by Bosola in John Webster's *The Duchess of Malfi* (ed. Brian Gibbons, 4th ed. [London: Methuen, 2001]), III, ii, 322–3.

Under whose heavy sense your brother's life
Falls into forfeit: he arrests him on it,
And follows close the rigour of the statute
To make him an example. [I, iv, 57–68]

Although it may be partial in some respects, Lucio's account is not malicious slander: he accurately characterises Angelo's ascetic nature (to which, the tone suggests, he pays grudging respect); he identifies Angelo's desire to use the existing statutes to threaten those who live sexually indulgent lives; and he confirms that Claudio's harsh sentence is intended as a deterrent. Lucio thus proves a shrewd adjudicator of character and motive, a capability that we should bear in mind when he passes judgement on the Duke.

When in the company of Friar Lodowick (the Duke in disguise), Lucio's instincts again prove sound. He lives up to his description as a 'fantastique' by indulging in outrageous fantasies about Angelo:

They say this Angelo was not made by man and woman, after this downright way of creation. . . . Some report, a sea-maid spawned him. Some, that he was begot between two stockfishes. But it is certain that when he makes water, his urine is congealed ice; that I know to be true. And he is a motion ungenerative; that's infallible. [III, ii, 99–108]

Although blatantly fictitious in their specifics, these speculations find their common ground in an undeniable truth: that there is something 'fishy' about a man who appears so cold that he shows no human emotion, presenting himself as impervious to desire.[29]

---

[29] There is irony, however, in Lucio's claim that Angelo is a 'motion ungenerative', a mere puppet, incapable of reproduction. Lucio is ignorant of what the audience has witnessed: Angelo's transformation into a sexual being as a result of his encounter with Isabella.

Lucio's judgements of the Duke are predominantly of a different order: they appear to be fantasies with little foundation in truth, although they derive from Vincentio's self-confessed leniency as a ruler. In seeking to increase his own prestige, Lucio presents himself as an intimate associate of the Duke, a source of salacious secrets about Vincentio's predilections:

> Ere he would have hanged a man for the getting a hundred bastards, he would have paid for the nursing a thousand. He had some feeling of the sport; he knew the service. . . . Yes, your beggar of fifty; and his use was to put a ducat in her clack-dish. . . . [III, ii, 113–23]

Lucio appears to be carried away by his own rhetoric. In seeking to compare the liberal regime of the Duke with the repressive regime of the fiercely ascetic Angelo, he creates an image of a debauched Vincentio to strengthen the contrast between past and present government in Vienna. Lucio seems deliberately to distort what might simply be charitable acts by the Duke (supporting orphans; giving alms to the poor) by claiming that Vincentio was actually funding his vices by paying for the upkeep of his illegitimate children and by purchasing sexual favours, however unalluring the woman. Lucio deliberately creates an outrageous innuendo in the phrase 'put a ducat in her clack-dish' where the ducat, the Duke's token conveying his image, and the clack-dish, the beggar-woman's open bowl, conjoin to imply an obscene image of the union of their sexual organs.

Unabashed by the objections of the disguised Duke, Lucio repeats, before his departure, his damaging allegations about Vincentio's sexual exploitation of impoverished women:

> The Duke, I say to thee again, would eat mutton on Fridays. He's now past it; yet, I say to thee, he would mouth with a beggar though she smelt brown bread and garlic. . . .
> [III, ii, 174–8]

Again, Lucio employs innuendo: eating meat on Friday might certainly be forbidden in Catholic Vienna; but Lucio's accusation involves the specific word 'mutton', and 'mutton' was a euphemism for a prostitute. Lucio is again insinuating that the Duke indulged in illicit sexual activities. Similarly, in his later encounter with the Duke/friar, Lucio will call Vincentio 'a better woodman than thou tak'st him for' (IV, iii, 161), where a woodman is, by editorial consensus, specifically a hunter of women, a wood being a suitably private place for sexual pursuits. An added insult is contained in Lucio's offhand remark, 'He's now past it,' the likely implication being not that the Duke has reformed his behaviour for moral reasons but rather that he has been incapacitated by age, diseases, and sexual excess. In his first encounter with the Duke/friar, Lucio makes two further unsubstantiated allegations against Vincentio, that he 'would be drunk' and that he is a 'very superficial, ignorant, unweighing fellow' (III, ii, 124–36). It might be concluded that Lucio is creating an impression of the Duke in his (Lucio's) own image: a frequenter of brothels, an exploiter of vulnerable women, and a drunken buffoon.

Set against this, though, are the important truths about the Duke that Lucio stumbles upon in his banter. His judgement of the Duke's disappearance from Vienna requires careful consideration:

> It was a mad, fantastical trick of him to steal from the state and usurp the beggary he was never born to. [III, ii, 89–90]

Earlier in the play (I, iii, 31–4), Friar Thomas had expressed misgivings about Vincentio's course of action in withdrawing from government but had been overruled by the Duke. Lucio now characterises Vincentio's actions at the start of the play as 'a mad, fantastical trick', a more extreme statement of Friar Thomas's position, and indicative of Lucio's tendency to create a portrait of the Duke in his own 'fantastical' image. But there is more here: Lucio accuses the Duke of usurping beggary. Friars were a mendicant order, that is, they were pledged to live by begging. Of course, Lucio does not recognise that the figure whom he is addressing is the Duke disguised as a Friar,[30] but Shakespeare ensures that his words cut to the heart of the matter. The Duke, in becoming a friar, has not merely disregarded the great chain of being that bestowed on him the highest social and political status, but has also 'usurped' the function of a friar without ever being admitted into holy orders.[31] Lucio's criticism of the Duke has firmer foundations than Lucio himself could suspect, and creates a powerful

---

[30] Nevertheless, the use of the word 'beggary' in this context led Nevill Coghill ('Comic Form in Measure for Measure', *SS* 8 [1955], p. 24) to postulate that Lucio has seen through the Duke's disguise: Lucio might enjoy baiting the Duke with insults, knowing that Vincentio could not respond without revealing his identity. Tempting as this interpretation might initially seem, it would negate the delight that the audience will take in hearing Lucio (when boasting that he has fathered an illegitimate child) inadvertently incriminate himself before the figure most able to exact retribution from him. Furthermore, it would entirely destroy one of the most powerfully dramatic moments in the play: when Lucio unhoods Friar Lodowick to reveal Duke Vincentio, he is, of necessity, ignorant that he is immediately unleashing the full force of the law against himself. Otherwise, he should seek to escape rather than choose to unveil his nemesis. It follows that Lucio's use of the word 'beggary' must here denote no more than 'poverty': in absenting himself from Vienna, Duke Vincentio has abandoned all his trappings of wealth and privilege. The audience will be amused by the irony of Lucio's inadvertent joke, but Lucio himself must appear ignorant of the full truth.

[31] As noted elsewhere in this study (e.g. Chapter 7, 'The Mendacious Mendicant and the Prudish Postulant', especially pp. 446–447), Vincentio has 'usurped', that is, seized without authority, four of the seven Christian sacraments: the sacraments of holy orders, penance, marriage, and extreme unction. In addition, in radically changing his social function, the Duke is defying the concept of the three estates. According to mediaeval and renaissance political theory, there was no promotion, demotion, or interchange between three estates of nobility, clergy, and commons: they were ordained by God and were inviolate. Just as Chaucer's Monk in *The Canterbury Tales* was culpable in attempting to elevate himself to the status of the aristocracy, so Vincentio is defying established social order by debasing himself from the aristocracy to the level of a mendicant friar.

dramatic irony that should be recognised by an attentive audience.

Of similar significance is Lucio's indignant remark on his second encounter with the Duke/friar:

. . . if the old fantastical duke of dark corners had been at home, [Claudio] had lived. [IV, iii, 156–7]

Lucio is entirely unaware of the activities of the Duke in Acts II–IV, but the audience should readily recognise the justice of Lucio's description. The Duke has indeed lurked in 'dark corners', metaphorically by assuming a disguise, intermittently when frequenting the dark prison, and particularly when eaves-dropping on the discourse between Isabella and Claudio. His behaviour, like Lucio's, has frequently seemed 'fantastical' to the audience: concealing his true identity under the garb of a friar; devising ingenious and convoluted tricks to save Isabella's chastity and Claudio's life; and deceiving both Isabella about her brother's death and Claudio about his intended reprieve. As was the case with his early description of Angelo, it appears here that Lucio has the happy knack of nailing his target at a stroke. His social commentary can be trenchant.

Last Judgement on Lucio

In the final scene of the play, Lucio's progress significantly resembles Angelo's: both bear false witness in attempting to exonerate themselves and, just as they believe that they have triumphantly escaped all retribution, they suffer an abrupt reversal of fortune (*peripeteia*) that leads directly to judgement by the Duke. Lucio's fate is thus a skilfully-wrought comic counterpoint to the more serious main issue of the last act of the play: the fall of Angelo.

When Lucio is interrupting legal proceedings in support of Isabella (as he did in Act II scene ii), he is silenced several times by a harsh snub from the otherwise equable Duke, who gives him sinister warnings:

> . . . when you have a business for yourself,
> Pray heaven you then be perfect. . . .
> The warrant's for yourself: take heed to't. [V, i, 84–6]

The Duke's words alert the audience to the likely severity of his forthcoming judgement on his slanderer. Meanwhile, the hubristic Lucio, eager to boast of his participation in the events being examined in court, proceeds in seemingly blissful ignorance of his fast-approaching nemesis.

As Shakespeare had earlier suggested that Lucio had informed to the state against both Pompey and Mistress Overdone, condemning them in hope of avoiding the consequences of his own misdeeds, Lucio's next actions should come as no surprise to an alert audience. When Friar Lodowick is summoned to testify, Lucio prepares his defence in advance, seeking to prejudice the court by attributing to the friar his (Lucio's) own slanders of the Duke:

> My lord, I know him. 'Tis a meddling friar;
> I do not like the man; had he been lay, my lord,
> For certain words he spake against your Grace
> In your retirement, I had swing'd him soundly. . . .
>   . . . a saucy friar,
> A very scurvy fellow. [V, i, 130–39]

As no-one else was present during their exchanges (in Act III, scene ii and Act IV, scene ii), it will be Lucio's word against the friar's—and Lucio appears determined to manipulate opinion before the arrival of his adversary, reckless of the fact that he is compounding his offence by bearing false witness.

Once the court has established the link between Friar Lodowick and the two apparently discredited women who have accused Lord Angelo (Isabella and Mariana), Escalus invites Lucio to testify as a witness for the prosecution of the Friar:

Esc. Signior Lucio, did not you say you knew that Friar Lodowick to be a dishonest person?

Lucio. Cucullus non facit monachum: honest in nothing but in his clothes, and one that hath spoke most villainous speeches of the Duke. [V, i, 259–63]

Shakespeare here handles the response particularly skilfully. The concluding clause is clearly Lucio's attempt to transfer to Friar Lodowick the responsibility for his own slanders of the Duke, but the earlier part of his speech is shot through with dramatic irony. Lucio turns to a popular proverb, that 'the cowl does not make the monk', that is, that a man in monastic garb is not necessarily a worthy member of the order. Lucio's obvious meaning is that a monk may not epitomise Christian virtue, but the audience should realize that Lucio is inadvertently referring to a friar who is not a friar at all, but rather a duke in disguise— or rather (if the audience recognizes the bold metatheatrical stroke) an actor playing a duke playing a friar. In addition, the reference to the *cucullus* ('cowl') that conceals the true man ironically foreshadows that moment when Lucio will unhood Friar Lodowick to reveal the Duke. As for the allegation that Friar Lodowick is honest in nothing but his clothes, an alert audience may recall that the Duke has been dishonest to both Claudio and Isabella, disguising his lies behind religious vestments and swearing falsely by his holy order. As on other occasions, Lucio's words contain greater truths than he could recognise.

Lucio's nemesis is at hand, as the audience anticipates but he cannot. On the re-entry of the Duke, who has now reassumed his disguise as Friar Lodowick, Lucio twice identifies the friar as the 'rascal' of whom he spoke (lines 281 and 302), and is delighted when Friar Lodowick's outspoken testimonies seem to confirm Lucio's prejudicial account of him. Having heard his adversary summarily condemned to prison and the rack (lines 309–10 and 321), Lucio sees his chance to attribute all his own slanders of the Duke to the hapless Friar Lodowick, further discrediting the only witness against him and simultaneously exonerating himself:

And was the Duke a fleshmonger, a fool, and a coward, as you then reported him to be? [V, i, 331–3]

So convincing is Lucio's testimony for the prosecution of Friar Lodowick that he is even enlisted by Angelo as an agent of the court to assist the Provost in arresting the struggling friar (line 348). Then, at the very moment of his seeming triumph, Lucio encounters two of the experiences suffered by the protagonist at the conclusion of a classical tragedy: *anagnorisis*, a moment of profound revelation, and *peripeteia*, a sudden reversal of fortune. Lucio, the newly-appointed court-official who tears aside the Friar's protective cowl, is instantaneously transformed into Lucio, the guilty wretch suffering arrest at the Duke's command:

Thou art the first knave that e'er mad'st a duke. . . .
Sneak not away, sir, for the friar and you
Must have a word anon.—Lay hold on him. [V, i, 354–7]

With these words, Lucio is left for over 130 lines (V, i, 360–496) to suffer public exposure in silence. As the actor portraying Lucio has no lines during this lengthy interim, he faces the challenge of conveying his constant anxiety at the forthcoming judgement, perhaps, at appropriate junctures, by grimacing and by resisting the hands that are laid on him by court-officials.

A momentary respite from Lucio's ordeal should come during the long pause in the dialogue at line 487, when Claudio is unhooded. The eyes of the audience will most obviously be on Isabella and on Angelo, both of whom cruelly condemned Claudio to death; but they should also glance at Lucio, whose support for Claudio never wavered. All three will be judged on their spontaneous responses to the discovery that Claudio, whom they had thought dead at Angelo's command, has been saved. Lucio, who laboured so hard to effect Claudio's reprieve, should register both relief and delight. A close embrace between the two friends might impress the audience and appear to sway the Duke to leniency in his ultimate sentence.

When judgement finally comes for Lucio, his fears that his punishment 'may prove worse than hanging' (line 359) at first seem well-founded. Although he requests relative clemency from the Duke, that 'I might be whipped' (line 504), the Duke is severe:

Whipp'd first, sir, and hang'd after. [V, i, 505]

For Lucio, misery is piled upon misery, as the Duke insists that Lucio should make amends by marrying the woman whom he wronged (lines 506–10), after which the Duke's original sentence will still be carried out:

. . . The nuptial finish'd,
Let him be whipp'd and hang'd. [V, i, 510–11]

The severity of the sentence is likely to shock the audience for two reasons. First, it reflects adversely on the Duke, as he has been remarkably merciful in his judgement of cases in which others were wronged, but now seems excessively severe in the one case where he personally is the plaintiff. Second, the harsh sentence is being imposed on a character for whom the audience has developed a measure of affection and even admiration, one who has been frequently (albeit coarsely) amusing and consistently loyal to his friend, Claudio, with whom he has recently been reunited.

Lucio, to the audience's delight, retains his wit and his effrontery, even when under such severe judgement:

Your Highness said even now, I made you a duke; good my
lord, do not recompense me in making me a cuckold.[32]

[V, i, 513–15]

The Duke relents so readily that his earlier sentence may seem
to have been intended merely to incite fear and penitence in
Lucio: as the Duke agrees to '[r]emit thy other forfeits' (line
518), Lucio will no longer suffer whipping and hanging.[33]
Vincentio insists, nevertheless, that 'thou shalt marry her' (line
516), forcing Lucio to make restitution to Mistress Kate Keep-
down, who bore his child. Lucio thus becomes the comic
counterpart to Angelo, compelled by the returning Duke to
marry the woman to whom he once swore vows *per verba de
futuro*, but whose name he has subsequently blackened to
justify her abandonment.

For Lucio, however, marriage to Mistress Kate Keep-down
is the most severe of all the punishments— at least, according
to his last words in the play:

Marrying a punk, my lord, is pressing to death,
Whipping, and hanging. [V, i, 520–1]

Although this response to the Duke's sentence may appear
characteristically hyperbolical on Lucio's part, it should be
remembered that Lucio is not simply being disparaged, that is,
forced into marriage with a woman whom he considers
unworthy; he is also facing utter humiliation. For the others at
the end of the play—for Claudio and Julietta, for Mariana and
Angelo, for Isabella and the Duke—marriage may come as a

---

[32] In the 2019 production for the RSC, Joseph Arkley's Lucio, dressed
as a dandy, commenced his appeal for leniency by kneeling on a
handkerchief that he produced from his top pocket, unfolded, and
carefully spread on the stage. This attempt to preserve his dapper
appearance, even when his life was in the balance, prompted both
laughter and applause from the audience.
[33] This important concession from the Duke seems to have been
overlooked by Kamps and Raber, pp. 145–148.

blessing; for Lucio, it is a curse, as he will become that most ridiculed of men in the Elizabethan and Jacobean drama: the cuckold, wedded to a promiscuous woman.[34] To an audience, however, the justice of the sentence may well be pleasing, as Lucio the whoremaster has received measure for measure in his entirely appropriate comeuppance.

Lucio may be accommodated into the otherwise celebratory final procession from the stage when he is escorted to prison, there to face his sentence of marriage. It is unlikely that sympathy for his plight will adversely affect the mood of the end of the play, unlike *Twelfth Night*, where so often an audience's dismay at the cruel treatment of Malvolio (and, to a lesser extent, of Sir Andrew Aguecheek) darkens the mood of the final scene. Although the audience will have enjoyed Lucio's anarchical behaviour, that same audience should recognise that the potential disruption to the state caused by his unregulated words and deeds would need to be checked as the precursor to the restoration of the Duke's authority and (implicitly) of improved government in Vienna. Had the Duke not so firmly restrained the influence of Lucio's 'fantastical' behaviour, an audience might have concluded that anarchy would continue to flout the law after Vincentio's restoration to power, and that 'all decorum' in Vienna would continue to go 'quite athwart' (I, iii, 30–1).

Pompey the Wily Servant

Pompey is more resilient than Lucio when thwarted by misfortune. He is also consistently likeable as, unlike Lucio, he is never seen on stage to perform a malicious or a hurtful act. His appellation in the First Folio, *Clowne*, suggests that he is a major source of laughter and amusement. Although the crudest of this amusement stems from his rather tedious punning on the

---

[34] For example, the language of Benedick in *Much Ado About Nothing* (1598–99) abounds in references to cuckolds and their humiliating horns as his justification for his refusal to commit to a relationship with any woman, e.g. I, i, 88–91, 170–5, and 206–32.

word 'done', which he employs repeatedly as a sexual innuendo, he also proves to be capable of more sophisticated wit and humour. At times, his wisdom and resourcefulness have considerable dramatic significance, for example when his accomplished performance before Angelo and Escalus illustrates how difficult it is for the authorities to take effective action against those involved in the sex-trade.

Pompey's respectable title is 'Thomas tapster' (I, ii, 104). At the beginning of the play, he works in what purports to be a tavern; but the tavern doubles as a brothel in which he functions as a pimp, a charge on which Elbow, the constable, twice arrests him, the second time successfully. Although imprisoned and apparently excluded from the general amnesty at the end of the play, Pompey seems satisfied to be accommodated as a hangman's apprentice, thus avoiding the whipping to which he was sentenced.

Pompey begins the play as Mistress Overdone's servant. Just as Lucio may owe his boastful character to a classical archetype—the *miles gloriosus* of Roman comedy—so Pompey bears a strong resemblance to the resourceful servants encountered in the comedies of Plautus, deriving ultimately from the Greek of Menander. Pompey, like his classical archetypes, performs the dual dramatic function of providing for the audience both exposition and amusement: while initially conveying vital information to his mistress, he is simultaneously enlightening the audience about important issues while entertaining them with his wit and verbal dexterity. He reports two items to Mistress Overdone: a recent arrest for a sexual offence (I, ii, 78–85);[35] and the proclamation that all

---

[35] Editors usually assume this to be a reference to Claudio's arrest, a subject about which Mistress overdone has already spoken to Lucio and the two Gentlemen. This textual anomaly, possibly the result of an interpolation, or an error in composition or transmission, might be justified dramatically if Mistress Overdone is seen deliberately to feign ignorance in order to encourage her tapster's loquacity. When Dominic Dromgoole directed the play for Shakespeare's Globe in 2015, however, Pompey's line was prompted by the flight across the

brothels in the suburbs are to be demolished (I, ii, 85–95). Subsequently, he will perform a simple but valuable function for the audience by identifying other characters when they first appear on stage: 'Here comes Signior Claudio, led by the Provost to prison: and there's Madam Juliet' (I, ii, 106–7). When he calms Mistress Overdone's distress at the imminent destruction of her business-premises, he encourages her to 'change your place' rather than 'change your trade' (I, ii, 99–100). The textual evidence suggests that, on his advice, she abandons her 'tavern' in the suburbs, quickly to establish a 'hot-house', or bath-house, in the city (see Elbow's words at II, i, 62–6), both being fronts for her true occupation as madam of a brothel. As is often the case in classical comedies, the wily servant proves most resourceful in a crisis; thus, Pompey proves indispensable to Mistress Overdone in her hour of need.

Throughout these exchanges, Pompey displays a quick intelligence and a facility with words, although his language (and gestures) can be extremely coarse. On reporting the arrest (presumably, of Claudio) and being asked, 'What has he done?' (I, ii, 80), his prompt repost is, 'A woman', where he characteristically plays on 'done' in the crude, sexual sense. He then describes the offence as, 'Groping for trouts, in a peculiar river' (line 83). The image involves reference to illicit fishing on private property, but the initial words should surely be accompanied by an obscene gesture imitating trout-tickling, where the hand is lowered, palm upward, and the fingers agitated to tempt the fish. The word 'groping' is thus made sexually explicit, while other sexual connotations to Pompey's piscatorial image (tactile and olfactory) are probably best left to the individual imagination. Pompey quibbles with Mistress Overdone's question, 'Is there a maid with child by him?' (line 84) by pedantically insisting that a maid, or virgin, cannot be 'with child'. He corrects her with, 'No: but there's a woman with maid by him' (line 85), where 'maid' might even extend his earlier 'trout' image, as the word sometimes referred to the

stage of one of Lucio's debauched gentleman-friends, hotly pursued by one of Angelo's constables.

young of certain fish. When explaining that only the suburban brothels will be destroyed, Pompey jokes that those in the city 'shall stand for seed' (line 91), suggesting with a phallic metaphor the ability of the sex-establishments to rise again soon after they have been put down. Such sexual innuendos and bawdy references are rife in Pompey's language, and fully appropriate to his calling as a pimp.

Even when indulging in bawdy, explicit patter, Pompey is capable of subtlety in his phrasing. When explaining about the city brothels, he notes that they were saved when 'a wise burgher put in for them' (I, ii, 92). The phrase 'put in for them' is deliberately ambiguous: did the wise burgher simply petition in support of retaining the city brothels, or did he recognise a business-opportunity, making a bid for them at a time when their value was diminished because they were threatened with destruction by the proclamation? Whichever interpretation is preferred, 'wise' is clearly a sardonic comment on the power of wealth and influence to triumph over the law and morality, a repeated theme in *Measure for Measure*. In addition, Pompey wittily consoles Mistress Overdone by presenting her as if she were a learned legal or social consultant whose skills will always be in demand:

> Come: fear not you: good counsellors lack no clients: though you change your place, you need not change your trade: I'll be your tapster still; courage, there will be pity taken on you; you that have worn your eyes almost out in the service, you will be considered. [I, ii, 98–103]

Pompey predicts that, even though Angelo is now seeking to regulate their sexual habits, the people of Vienna will still seek out Mistress Overdone for a consultation because of her reputation for providing the services that they require. In a syntactically well-balanced sentence, Pompey explains that a 'change [of] place' rather than a 'change [of] trade' is all that is required for her to escape the consequences of the proclamation, while retaining her customers. Although blindness was associated with prostitution because Cupid (the 'blind bow-boy', as Mercutio calls him in *Romeo and Juliet*)[36] might appear on a brothel-sign, Pompey's claim that Mistress Overdone has 'worn [her] eyes . . . out in the service' is deliberately ambiguous: it also wittily (but improbably) implies that she has studied her profession assiduously and at length in books, becoming an expert at the expense of ruining her sight. Furthermore, the phrasing suggests that she is providing a valued public utility (a 'service') to Vienna. In short, on his first appearance in the play, the obviously foul-mouthed Pompey has proved particularly knowledgeable, amusing, and inventive in his deployment of language.

Pompey the Pleader

Pompey summons the verbal skills that he has practised earlier when he is obliged to plead his case before Angelo and Escalus in Act II scene i. In defending himself and one of Mistress Overdone's clients, Master Froth, he outmanoeuvres his accuser, Constable Elbow, eventually ensuring that he and Froth face nothing more severe than a warning. The seriousness of the charge is undeniable, but Pompey—by a combination of prolixity, irrelevance, and equivocation in presenting his case— avoids conviction under those same statutes by which Claudio stands condemned to death. He imitates the methods of professional pleaders-at-law, parodying legal language. In a modern production, he might even strut the stage with thumbs hooked under imaginary lapels, in imitation of the clichéd stage-barrister.

Pompey's immediate advantage is that he is much more skilful with words than his accuser, Constable Elbow. Both cause confusion, but Pompey does so deliberately and to his advantage, whereas Elbow does so inadvertently and to his detriment. Elbow frequently chooses the wrong word, sometimes the opposite of his intended meaning, whereas Pompey craftily deploys ambiguous words where possible sexual connotations are hidden under an innocent surface, a

---

[36] *Romeo and Juliet*: II, iv, 16; cf. *Much Ado About Nothing*, I, i, 219.

cunning way of avoiding perjury. From what can be gathered from the Constable's garbled account, the accusation is that Elbow's wife was sexually accosted by Pompey—referred to as 'Mistress Overdone's means' (line 82)—who was procuring for Froth. Pompey allows Elbow to state his rambling, confused case for the prosecution before uttering a simple denial: 'Sir, if it please your honour, this is not so.' (line 84). When invited to present his case for the defence, however, he becomes much more loquacious (and prolix), seeming to portray Mistress Overdone's house as a place of respectable resort, but littering his domestic references with hidden sexual connotations. For example, among the innuendos detected by editors are 'stewed prunes' (line 89), 'but two' (line 90), 'stood' and 'dish' (both line 91), 'china' (line 93), 'pin' (line 96), 'point' (line 97) and 'cracking the stones' (line 107). Although these vulgar puns (unless accompanied by appropriately obscene gestures) will almost certainly be lost on a modern audience, other instances of Pompey's bawdy banter will be more readily appreciable: Escalus's language is seized upon as an opportunity for ribald humour when the words 'come' and 'done' (line 117) are transformed into innuendos in Pompey's response. Thereafter, Pompey launches into filibustering exchanges with Master Froth about the latter's personal circumstances, concluding with superfluous details of his visit to Mistress Overdone's house. The innuendo-strewn prattle and profusion of irrelevant specifics prove too much for the impatient Angelo, who withdraws, deputing the judgement on the case to the more indulgent Escalus. Pompey has thus achieved his first success as advocate: the very judge responsible for enforcing the statutes against fornication has (in this instance, at least) abandoned the case.

Pompey continues to employ diversionary tactics before Escalus, his instinct being that the best defence is to avoid addressing the charge directly. When Escalus demands to know 'What was done to Elbow's wife, once more?' (line 138–39) Pompey characteristically takes advantage of the bawdy sense of the word 'done' (as he did in his first innuendo in the play, at I, ii, 81). He claims that there was 'nothing done to her once' (line 140), presenting Mistress Elbow as a wanton, an accusation that he will repeat more explicitly later, while simultaneously incriminating his accuser, Elbow:

> . . . his wife is a more [sus]pected person than any of us all. . . . . Sir, she was [sus]pected with him, before he married with her. [II, i, 162–8]

Pompey thus deflects the charge away from himself and his co-defendant, Froth, and on to the plaintiff, Elbow, and his wife.

In the interim, he has ridiculously presented Froth's face as evidence for the defence. Presumably, Escalus would find it impossible to imagine that Froth's face, that of an innocuous simpleton, could conceal criminal intent:

> I beseech you, sir, look in this gentleman's face. Good Master Froth, look upon his honour; 'tis for a good purpose.—Doth your honour mark his face? . . . Nay, I beseech you, mark it well. . . . Doth your honour see any harm in his face? . . . I'll be supposed upon a book, his face is the worst thing about him.—Good, then: if his face be the worst thing about him, how could master Froth do the constable's wife any harm? I would know that of your honour. [II, i, 145–57]

This is a travesty of the submission of material evidence in a court of law. Froth's face becomes Exhibit A for the defence—and carries the day because Froth looks so gormless. Pompey's parody of the techniques of a professional pleader is as successful as it is hilarious. Because of Elbow's failure to present any corresponding material evidence for the prosecution, Escalus has insufficient grounds to convict Pompey, and must 'let him continue' (lines 183–4) until he incriminates himself incontrovertibly.

Pompey the Philosopher

After Froth has been dismissed with a warning, Escalus, the wise magistrate, seeks first to persuade Pompey to confess his past and second to warn him from offending in future. In both respects, Escalus is unsuccessful, as the witty, resilient Pompey proves a shrewd adversary, capable of deploying convincing arguments in support of his vocation.

Pompey will not admit to being a pimp, even when Escalus promises that a confession 'shall be the better for you' (II, i, 218–19). Pompey prevaricates, conceding merely that he is 'a poor fellow that would live' (line 220): he is presenting himself as an unfortunate man seeking to earn his living by working in his (unspecified) trade.[37] An audience may be reminded of that other amiable Shakespearian rascal, Falstaff, who justifies highway robbery by quipping that it is 'no sin for a man to labour in his vocation' (1 *Henry IV*, I, ii, 101). Escalus's next questions draw from Pompey one of the simplest yet most profound responses in the play: asked if he thinks 'being a bawd' to be 'a lawful trade' (lines 221–3), Pompey replies,

If the law would allow it, sir. [II, i, 224]

Pompey's seemingly innocent answer cuts to the very heart of the matter, raising the issue of whether it should be a function of the law to impose standards of sexual behaviour on society. The statutes prohibiting fornication that the Duke neglected and that Angelo is now so obsessively enforcing are not *natural law*, which should be universal and inviolable, but rather *positive law*, specific to Vienna. Had these laws not been

---

[37] Braunmuller and Watson point out that, although some productions and critics consider the sex industry in *Measure for Measure* 'a hedonistic resistance to a puritanical state', others represent it as 'a grim business run for survival' (p. 72). Pompey's exclamation here— 'Truly, sir, I am a poor fellow that would live' (II, i, 220)—lends support to this latter view.

included in the statute-book, then no offence would have been committed.

Escalus, however, will not accept such an answer, as the sex-trade 'shall not be allowed in Vienna' (lines 225–6), at which Pompey offers a shrewd riposte:

> Does your worship mean to geld and splay all the youth of the city? . . . Truly sir, in my poor opinion, they will to't then. [II, i, 227–30]

For Pompey, like Lucio, sexual desire is a natural appetite that cannot be denied. As it is particularly strong among youths, only neutering both males and females—'geld[ing] and splay[ing]'—would prevent them from offending under the law. Pompey is implicitly condemning the savage and unnatural sanctions necessary to enforce Vienna's statutes against fornication. His sardonic solution to the social problem challenges the foundation of the statutes and the attitudes of those in authority:

> If your worship will take order for the drabs and the knaves, you need not fear the bawds. [II, i, 231–2]

The pragmatic argument here is based on the concept of supply and demand: were there no longer a commercial demand for 'bawds', then no-one would be obliged to find employment in facilitating sexual activity. There would be no procurers such as Pompey and Mistress Overdone to pursue if the law were to prosecute only those low-life characters who revel in promiscuous sexual intercourse (a contention that implicitly vindicates faithful lovers like Claudio and Julietta).

When Escalus remains firm, threatening not gelding and splaying but rather 'heading and hanging' (line 234) for all those who offend under the statutes against fornication, Pompey produces his masterstroke:

If you head and hang all that offend that way but for ten years together, you'll be glad to give out a commission for more heads: if this law hold in Vienna ten year, I'll rent the fairest house in it after three pence a bay. If you live to see this come to pass, say Pompey told you so. [II, i, 235–240]

Pompey's argument is difficult to refute. As the laws of Vienna are intent on suppressing all human sexual activity outside marriage by imposing capital punishment on offenders, and as sexual activity is universal and irresistible, Pompey predicts that there will soon be a collapse in both the population and the economy of Vienna. He foresees that this will force the state to relent and to reverse its policies, putting out 'a commission for more heads', presumably by encouraging procreation regardless of wedlock.

Although Escalus remains unmoved by Pompey's prophecy, pledging to have him whipped if he is ever brought before Escalus again, Pompey responds in an aside that the demands of 'flesh and fortune' are 'better' persuaders (lines 250–51)— that is, his future behaviour will be governed by sexual and financial imperatives, rather than by any threat of judicial correction. Pompey cheerfully refuses to be intimidated:

> Whip me? No, no, let carman whip his jade;
> The valiant heart's not whipt out of his trade.
>
> [II, i, 252–3]

Pompey, having persuaded the audience of the validity of his pragmatic opinions, now jauntily leaves the stage with a jingling couplet suggesting his delight at his success. Anarchy has triumphed over the law—temporarily, at least.

Pompey Arrested

Pompey re-appears in Act III scene ii when, led to prison by a now triumphant Elbow, he encounters first the Duke (disguised as Friar Lodowick) and then Lucio. There is a parallel with Act I scene ii, where Claudio encountered Lucio as he was being paraded on the streets of Vienna by the Provost before being escorted to prison, condemned under the same statutes. In that scene, Lucio had proved a faithful friend to Claudio, striving to rescue him from the rigour of the law; but here, in this later scene, Lucio disdainfully abandons his former confederate to his fate.

On this re-entry, Pompey seems as resiliently philosophical and quick-witted as in his earlier confrontation with Escalus. In his speech about the 'two usuries' (III, ii, 6–10)—which may be addressed to the Duke/friar, or to Elbow, or may even be a choric statement for the benefit of the audience—he observes how unjust it is that the joyless pursuit of breeding financial interest is permitted to prosper under the law while the 'merriest' comparable activity, sexual intercourse, is suppressed. When the Duke/friar upbraids him at length (lines 18–26) for 'living . . . a life / So stinkingly depending', Pompey seizes on the word 'stinking' as if to begin a characteristically vigorous defence of his calling as a pimp: 'But yet, sir, I would prove—' (lines 27–8). This time, however, he is quickly silenced by the Duke/friar's peremptory response (lines 27–32). He will not be allowed a second opportunity to play the barrister, flouting the law when under arrest as he did before Escalus.

Pompey's spirits appear to rise on the appearance of Lucio:

I spy comfort, I cry bail! Here's a gentleman, and a friend of mine. [III, ii, 40–1]

His expectation is obviously that he will again evade the clutches of the law, this time as a result of Lucio's intercession. Lucio, however, mocks and scorns him, giving him scarcely an opportunity to respond. Pompey's more tentative and insinuating enquiry, 'I hope, sir, your good worship will be my bail?' (line 70) elicits from Lucio nothing but further sneers, confirming Pompey's worst fears:

You will not bail me then, sir? [III, ii, 78]

Although Lucio dismisses Pompey to prison in peremptory fashion, Shakespeare gives Pompey no words of complaint about this betrayal.[38] As ever, the good-natured Pompey seems to accept the slings and arrows of outrageous fortune with equanimity, as if the prospect of a sojourn in prison might not seem substantially worse than unremitting service in Mistress Overdone's brothel.

The Executioner's Apprentice

Having pointed out the injustice of the law in permitting usury but persecuting sexual activity, Pompey's quick perceptions recognise an even greater inconsistency in the law after he is committed to prison. When the Provost invites Pompey to become Abhorson's apprentice executioner, Pompey quips,

Sir, I have been an unlawful bawd time out of mind, but yet I will be content to be a lawful hangman. [IV, ii, 14–16]

The lines are reminiscent of his response to Escalus's enquiry whether being a bawd is a lawful trade: 'If the law would allow it' (II, i, 224). From Pompey's perspective, the law is arbitrary and unjust, punishing those who seek sexual pleasure or facilitate sexual activity, but commissioning and rewarding those prepared to torture and kill by hanging, disembowelling, or cutting off heads.

There follows a ridiculous exchange between Abhorson and Pompey where each, with tenuous logic, seeks to argue that his occupation is a 'mystery'—that is, a skilled profession. Pompey

---

[38] Pompey's arrest here might have been occasioned by Lucio's testimony against him, as suggested earlier (pp. 376–377). In an ironic quid pro quo, Pompey has already suggested that the law should be directed, not against bawds, but against 'the drabs and the knaves' (II, i, 231–2), among whom Lucio and his paramour, Mistress Kate Keepdown, might be prominent.

bases his witty claim on the fact that pimps associate with prostitutes who use cosmetics or face-paint, and painting is recognised as a professional skill worthy of a guild or mystery:

Painting, sir, I have heard say, is a mystery; and your whores, sir, being members of my occupation, using painting, do prove my occupation a mystery. But what mystery there should be in hanging, if I should be hanged, I cannot imagine. [IV, ii, 34–8]

This is an amusing riposte to Abhorson's sneer that employing a bawd as an executioner would discredit Abhorson's profession (lines 25–6). Pompey challenges Abhorson with this specious logic, and Abhorson, as if failing to recognise how ridiculous Pompey's argument is, attempts to respond in kind. Either because of a defective text or because of a defective intellect, Abhorson's response falls flat. Either way, Pompey has won yet another battle of wits with a representative of the law, and the audience will enjoy this further triumph.

As in his dealings with Elbow, Pompey runs verbal rings around a minor law-officer. Abhorson expressed his disdain for his new apprentice when he addressed Pompey as 'bawd' and 'thee' (the familiar and sometimes condescending second-person singular pronoun) on summoning him to instruction (IV, ii, 52–3). In response, Pompey uses the subtlety of irony:

I do desire to learn, sir; and I hope, if you have occasion to use me for your own turn, you shall find me yare. For truly, sir, for your kindness I owe you a good turn. [IV, ii. 54–7]

Pompey is sarcastically deferential in addressing Abhorson as 'sir' and 'you' (the respectful second-person singular pronoun). He also refers to Abhorson's 'kindness' to him, a deliberately ambiguous word as it could mean 'compassion' or (in the medieval sense of 'kynde') 'characteristic behaviour' which, in a hangman's case, would most probably be rough and cruel. Although affecting humility in expressing his 'desire to learn' the hangman's trade, Pompey veils in ambiguous phrasing his

402

true aspiration: the 'good turn' that Pompey pledges might not be a favour but rather a grim pun, threatening a turn of the ladder or the rope to hang the hangman himself.

Pompey's final appearance in the play confirms how adaptable he is to conditions and environments. In a substantial speech (IV, iii, 1–20), most probably delivered directly to the audience in choric fashion, he characterises the prison as a counterpart to Mistress Overdone's brothel. He knows the names and circumstances of so many of the prisoners because they were 'all great doers [with the usual sexual pun] in our trade' (lines 18–19). In changing his 'trade', Pompey has not changed his associates. Nor has he lost his sense of humour as he engages in darkly comic banter with the condemned Barnadine:

[We are] Your friends, sir, the hangman. You must be so good, sir, to rise and be put to death. [IV, iii, 27–8]

Pompey's deferential manner is amusingly inappropriate to his stark message of imminent execution. His consolation to the condemned man is ridiculously incongruous:

Pray, Master Barnadine, awake till you are executed, and sleep afterwards. [IV, iii, 31–2]

Pompey seems so much to enjoy his macabre joke that he repeats it as his final line in the play, in response to Barnadine's refusal to comply with his executioners on the grounds of his drunken unpreparedness:

. . . he that drinks all night, and is hanged betimes in the morning, may sleep the sounder all the next day.
[IV, iii, 44–6]

In short, there is no change in Pompey, regardless of circumstances: he is jocular, carefree, and amiable in each of the scenes in which he appears. As the wily and resourceful servant of the Plautine tradition, he will adapt to the environment in which he finds himself, whatever that may be—tavern, hot-house, brothel, or prison—merrily taking on the trade of tapster, clown, pimp, or executioner as necessity demands. He is slow to complain and quick to find a chirpy riposte. His philosophy of life is earthy but pragmatic and compelling. He is not malicious—even the treacherous Lucio escapes without any imprecations—but rather presents a friendly, cheerful demeanour to those whom he encounters. Like Lucio, he endears himself to the audience by bringing the light of laughter into a predominantly dark play.

Mistress Overdone

Pompey's initial employer is simply denoted by the word 'Bawde' in the text of the First Folio. Lucio introduces this woman to the audience under the jocular soubriquet 'Madam Mitigation' (I, ii, 41), presumably because she mitigates desire, reducing its severity by the services provided in her brothel. She is not named in the text until Elbow refers to the involvement of 'Mistress Overdone's means' (II, i, 82) in the corruption of his wife. Mistress Overdone's marital name, deriving from her last husband of nine, is simultaneously a reflection of her sexual state: 'worn . . . out in the service', as Pompey expresses it elsewhere (I, ii, 102). The typical moral response to bawds is articulated by the Duke when he confronts Pompey: he condemns them as 'wicked', 'evil', 'filthy' 'abominable', 'beastly' and 'stinkingly depending' because all their means of sustaining life—food, drink, clothing, and shelter—are furnished from the sexual vices that they promote (III, ii, 18–26). By whichever of these three dubious titles she is identified— 'Madam Mitigation', 'Mistress Overdone', or merely 'bawd'—the corollary is the same: her representation as nothing more than a functionary in the sex-trade depersonalises her.

Not surprisingly, therefore, Mistress Overdone is denigrated by several characters. She is described by Elbow as 'a bad woman; whose house . . . was . . . plucked down in the suburbs' where she now 'professes a hot-house; which I think is a very ill house . . .' (II, i, 63–5). Although Lever (p. 31n.) thinks that the reference to the hot-house is 'a mere gag', it is surely to be taken literally: her tavern/brothel in the suburbs having been demolished, she is presented as now using a bath-house as a front for her continued illicit involvement in the sex-trade. Such a pretext would justify the number of scantily-clad members of both sexes likely to be encountered on the premises. Elbow is confident that her activities there are flouting the statutes against fornication that Angelo is seeking to enforce: 'if it be not a bawd's house . . . it is a naughty house' (II, i, 75–6). The denigration continues when Lucio, in exchanges with Pompey, refers to Mistress Overdone as 'my dear morsel' (III, ii, 52)— an amiable piece of flesh, with perhaps a pun on 'dear' in the sense of 'grievous', reflecting the 'diseases' that he claims to have 'purchased under her roof' (I, ii, 42). When Pompey responds that she is 'in the tub' (III, ii, 55), that is, seeking a cure for venereal disease, Lucio approves her fate: such a condition is an 'unshunned consequence', as the 'fresh whore' always evolves into the 'powdered bawd' (III, ii, 57–8), a clue to the presumed evolution of Mistress Overdone's career in the oldest profession. Finally, on her arrest and imprisonment, the Provost dismisses her summarily as 'a bawd of eleven years' continuance' (III, ii, 190).

Such descriptions present her as unmitigatedly depraved and dissolute. An actor and director might therefore choose to go no further than this evidence in their portrayal of Mistress Overdone: blowsy, loud, and distasteful; amusing to observe from a distance, perhaps, but nevertheless repulsive. In presenting Mistress Overdone as no more than the stereotypical madam, the actor might provide an audience with coarse comic relief. This was how Petra Massey presented Mistress Overdone in Dominic Dromgoole's production at Shakespeare's Globe in 2015.

Shakespeare, however, has provided evidence of potentially a more complex character, for whom an audience might be encouraged to feel at least *some* stirrings of sympathy. Her weakness and susceptibility are apparent at various points in the

405

text. Pompey refers to her as 'a poor widow' who has had nine husbands (II, i, 195–9), a sequence of marital misfortune which, if taken literally, might warrant a measure of compassion amidst the incredulous laughter. Although she never denies her profession as a bawd, her lament (on her first appearance) at the decline of her trade invites sympathetic consideration of her straitened circumstances:

> Thus, what with the war, what with the sweat, what with the gallows, and what with poverty, I am custom-shrunk.
>
> [I, ii, 75–7]

Conflict, disease, execution, and penury, like four apocalyptic horsemen, threaten her livelihood and therefore her survival. To make matters worse, Pompey informs her almost immediately of Angelo's proclamation:

> All houses [of resort] in the suburbs of Vienna must be plucked down. [I, ii, 88–9]

Already suffering from a sharp decline in custom, she must now undergo the loss of her place of business which is also, presumably, her home. Her lament is endearingly human— pathetic in the literal as well as the popular sense, as she conveys to the audience her helplessness and her fear of imminent personal disaster: 'What shall become of me?' (I, ii, 97). Fortunately, she has a resourceful servant who promises her that she need only change her 'place' (that is, her residence), not her 'trade'. Accordingly, she removes her business to the 'hot-house' to which Elbow refers in his indictment of Pompey and Froth. Before long, however, she herself is arrested and appealing plaintively to Escalus:

> Good my lord, be good to me. Your honour is accounted a merciful man. Good my lord. [III, ii, 185–6]

When Escalus appears unmoved, she resorts to accusing her assumed accuser:

'My lord, this in one Lucio's information against me . . . see how he goes about to abuse me' [III, ii, 192–7]

If Mistress Overdone were to shriek and struggle at this point, the scene might deliberately be reduced to slapstick humour, and her fate trivialised. By contrast, an audience's sympathy for a more tearful and subdued Mistress Overdone might increase because of her passive vulnerability.

Mistress Overdone has a further quality worthy of the audience's sympathetic consideration: she can make moral distinctions and ethical choices. Even in her first line in the play, she shows the ability to distinguish between the noble Claudio on the one hand and the dissolute Lucio and his associates on the other:

There's one yonder arrested and carried to prison, was worth five thousand of you all. [I, ii, 56–7]

Her hyperbolical comparison plays an important part in establishing the moral worth of the persecuted Claudio before his first arrival on stage later in the scene. It also suggests that Mistress Overdone is personally afflicted by the news of his arrest and sentence, deploring the shameful fate of such a worthy young man. Furthermore, in her final lines in the play, she gives evidence of selfless moral responsibility:

Mistress Kate Keep-down was with child by [Lucio] in the Duke's time, he promised her marriage. His child is a year and a quarter old come Philip and Jacob. I have kept it myself. . . . [III, ii, 193–6]

Of course, as she is attempting to plead her cause for mercy at this moment, her account might be considered partial; but it cannot be entirely 'fictional', as Lucio elsewhere admits to the conception of his illegitimate child (IV, iii, 167–72). It is plausible that Mistress Overdone might have undertaken the child's upbringing out of maternal compassion (rather than in expectation that the child might grow into a valuable

407

commodity in her 'service'). For example, in the 1994 production, directed for BBC Television by David Thacker, Sue Johnson's Mistress Overdone first appears cradling an infant who is later taken from her arms by the prostitute—presumably Mistress Kate Keep-down—for whose services Lucio is paying. These contexts suggest that she is attributed with at least some potentially worthy principles.

Her initial dramatic function is to convey information to Lucio and his two associates about the fate of Claudio. It is from this information that the action of the rest of the play develops. She also introduces to the audience the earliest evidence of the reforms introduced by Angelo to impose restrictions on sexual excess in Vienna. Her message is stark:

> I saw [Signior Claudio] arrested: saw him carried away: and which is more, within these three days, his head to be chopped off. . . . and it is for getting Madam Julietta with child. [I, ii, 61–7]

The 'chopped' syntax—short clauses with heavy pauses between them—communicates her breathless dismay to the audience at this harsh sentence. By contrast, later in the scene (I, ii, 78–103), she acts as the stooge, supplying 'straight' questions (to which she might be presumed to know the answers) that allow Pompey to crack his gags to provide comic relief for the audience. In her first scene, then, her dramatic contribution to the play is diverse.

Mistress Overdone is an implicit presence at the hearing involving Elbow, Froth, and Pompey in Act II scene i, although she is absent from stage during the scene.[39] Elbow's vilification

---

[39] Although she is not included in the Folio stage-direction at line 40 of this scene (the entry of Elbow, Froth, Pompey, and officers), when Dominic Dromgoole directed the play for Shakespeare's Globe in 2015, Petra Massey's Mistress Overdone, apparently too drunk to testify in the proceedings, was brought on stage in a wheelbarrow to accompany the other accused.

of Mistress Overdone (quoted previously) is suspect as there is reason to assume that Elbow's wife was a willing participant in Froth's (attempted?) seduction of her at Mistress Overdone's 'hot-house':

> There was nothing done to her once. . . . his wife is a more respected [*sic*, for 'suspected'] person than any of us all. . . . Sir, she was respected with him, before he married with her.
>
> [II, i, 140–68]

Of course, Pompey's testimony would be partial, but it goes some way towards decriminalising Mistress Overdone's part in the affair. When she finally appears again before the audience, however, the law is no longer willing to give her the benefit of the doubt:

> Double and treble admonition, and still forfeit in the same kind! This would make mercy swear and play the tyrant. . . . Away with her to prison.—Go to, no more words.
>
> [III, ii, 187–200]

The woman whose lascivious livelihood is embodied in every name attributed to her and every reference made to her in the play is henceforth committed to the oblivion of the prison. We do not see her again.

Barnadine

Through the words of others, several characters in *Measure for Measure* are identified and their essential qualities and circumstances portrayed a considerable time before their first appearance on stage: Angelo, Claudio, Isabella, Mariana and, not least, Barnadine. Barnadine's name may derive from a 'barnard', who lured victims into compromising situations where they could be fleeced; but Shakespeare's Barnadine is a murderer rather than a mere coney-catcher (although the latter activity might plausibly lead to a much more serious offence). In a memorable analogy, William Hazlitt (in 1817) described Barnadine as 'Caliban transported . . . to . . . the prisons of

Vienna.'[40] By contrast, for Harold Bloom in 1998, Barnadine is 'the particular comic genius of this authentically outrageous play.'[41] Although Barnadine is on stage on only two brief occasions (in only one of which he speaks), his role is problematical and highly significant dramatically, both in the challenge that he poses to authority in Act IV and in his stultified silence when the Duke's mercy is extended to him in Act V.

Barnadine is a prisoner scheduled to die on the same day as Claudio (see IV, ii, 6–7). The Provost, whose moral judgement the audience respects, shows no sympathy for him:

> Th'one has my pity; not a jot the other,
> Being a murderer, though he were my brother.
>
> [IV, ii, 59–60]

The Provost believes that such an unregenerate killer does not deserve the same remission of sentence as Claudio, the faithful lover; and yet Barnadine, like Claudio, will benefit from the Duke's general amnesty in the final scene.[42]

Barnadine represents the most significant challenge to authority in the play. He simply refuses to comply with the demands placed upon him by criminal, religious, or moral law, as the audience learns from exchanges between the disguised Duke and the Provost. Barnadine has been a prisoner for nine years, during which time his life has been preserved by repeated appeals by his family or friends. His guilt, however, has recently been established beyond doubt (IV, ii, 128–37).

---

[40] Quoted by Braunmuller and Watson, p. 153, n. 14.

[41] Braunmuller and Watson, p. 91, quoting from *Shakespeare and the Invention of the Human* (New York: Riverhead, 1998) p. 358.

[42] It is curious that Barnadine's pardon has excited relatively little critical demurral, whereas the pardon granted to Angelo—a hypocrite and bearer of false witness, certainly; but neither a murderer nor a rapist, despite his intentions—has provoked outrage among critics (particularly in the Eighteenth and Nineteenth Centuries).

410

Although he does not deny being a murderer, he has shown no sign of penitence:

> A man that apprehends death no more dreadfully but as a drunken sleep; careless, reckless, and fearless of what's past, present, or to come: insensible of mortality, and desperately mortal. [IV, ii, 140–3]

Furthermore, just as he places no value on his life, he has no care for his personal liberty or for his spiritual benefit. He refuses divine counselling:

> He will hear none. He hath evermore had the liberty of the prison: give him leave to escape hence, he would not. Drunk many times a day, if not many days entirely drunk. We have very oft awakened him, as if to carry him to execution, and showed him a seeming warrant for it; it hath not moved him at all. [IV, ii, 145–51]

When an unregenerate prisoner shows no aversion to incarceration or even to execution, how can prison have any corrective or retributive function? How is the law to proceed with a criminal whose conscience is so subdued by crime and whose consciousness so befuddled by alcohol that he is entirely heedless of all aspects of his own welfare? These are the conundrums that Shakespeare dramatizes in the character of Barnadine.

If imprisonment performs neither of its two principal functions—amendment and punishment—what remedy? The Duke's solution is simple: off with Barnadine's head and send it, suitably disguised, to Angelo, to convince the Deputy that it is Claudio's head. Barnadine places no value on either his life or his soul, but in his death might perform a worthwhile function in saving Claudio from execution.

As all the accounts that precede his first emergence from his cell have presented Barnadine as more of a beast than a man, an audience may experience some trepidation as his entrance

411

approaches. Shakespeare takes full dramatic advantage of the situation to create tension. First, Barnadine's disembodied growl from off-stage challenges Abhorson and Pompey when they summon him to appear:

> A pox o' your throats! Who makes that noise there? What are you? . . . Away, you rogue, away: I am sleepy.
>
> [IV, iii, 25–9]

His first words in the play are a curse. His sentences thereafter are short, accusatory, and imperative, his growling like that of 'an o'er-grown lion in a cave'. When Abhorson instructs Pompey to use physical force to extract Barnadine from his cell, fear of the beast is implicit in Pompey's procrastinating response:

> He is coming, sir, he is coming. I hear his straw rustle.[43]
>
> [IV, iii, 34–5]

Rarely in Shakespeare has a character's first entrance been awaited with such a sense of foreboding. It is for the director, designer, and actor to determine whether Barnadine's appearance will confirm or challenge his monstrous reputation. Although an opportunity for comic bathos does offer itself—Barnadine might defy all expectation by proving diminutive or physically (if not vocally) puny—the tendency in production has inevitably been to present him as monstrous, filthy, and repulsive. Thus, in the 2015 Globe Theatre production directed by Dominic Dromgoole, the hulking form of Dean Nolan (previously seen as Constable Elbow) emerged, shaggy and soiled, from under the stage.

All that the Duke requires for his plan to succeed is Barnadine's apathetic submission to his fate—but no such acquiescence is forthcoming. Summoned by his executioners to the block, Barnadine simply refuses to comply:

---

[43] Alternatively, or additionally, Pompey may appear to be repelled by the stench emanating from Barnadine's 'ward'.

You rogue, I have been drinking all night; I am not fitted for't. [IV, iii, 42–3]

Exhorted by a friar (the Duke in disguise) to accept the last rites, he persists in dismissing all attempts to prepare him for death:

I have been drinking hard all night, and I will have more time to prepare me, or they shall beat out my brains with billets. I will not consent to die this day, that's certain.

[IV, iii, 52–5]

Like Escalus in his exchanges with Pompey, the Duke finds himself powerless to proceed against an unregenerate criminal who determinedly frustrates the processes whereby the law seeks to bring him to justice.

Although the much-discussed Barnadine is on stage for fewer than thirty lines in this scene, his intransigence leaves the Duke with a seemingly insurmountable problem:

Unfit to live or die! O gravel heart . . .
A creature unprepar'd, unmeet for death;
And to transport him in the mind he is
Were damnable. [IV, iii, 63–8]

With Barnadine so heedless of the welfare of his soul, the Duke is obliged to undertake its care, at peril of his own soul. To send the prisoner unshriven to the block would not only kill Barnadine in this world but also condemn him to everlasting death in the next. The Duke, unwilling to take such a moral burden on his conscience, spares Barnadine for later judgement.

So it is that, towards the end of the final scene, Barnadine is led on stage to hear his sentence:

Sirrah, thou art said to have a stubborn soul
That apprehends no further than this world,

413

And squar'st thy life according. Thou'rt condemn'd;
But, for those earthly faults, I quit them all,
And pray thee take this mercy to provide
For better times to come. Friar [Peter], advise him.
I leave him to your hand. [V, i, 478–84]

The state thus washes its hands of the intractable criminal,
passing responsibility for instructing him in penitence to the
Church, and responsibility for either punishing or absolving
him to God. Barnadine's 'earthly faults' have been 'quit', but
they have been pardoned by the very Duke who had lamented
in the first act that 'our decrees, / Dead to infliction, to
themselves are dead' (I, iii, 27-28). The Duke was then
acknowledging that, under his previous regime, his failure to
enforce laws caused profound social damage (I, iii, 29–31); yet
this same Duke persists, after the restoration of his power, in
acquitting those whose behaviour is a danger to the state and its
people. Nicholas Hytner's 1987 production for the RSC offered
a fresh perspective on this inconsistency by presenting the
Duke's pardon as a fearful reaction to the threat of Barnadine's
physical presence, which was as intimidating as his
reputation.[44]

Does Barnadine's pardon, then, signal the ultimate triumph
of misrule over authority in Vienna? Although Angelo was
similarly absolved, he was penitent and, as Isabella argued, 'His
act did not o'ertake his bad intent' (V, i, 449). Lucio was
punished by being forced to marry the woman whom he had
wronged, but his 'other forfeits' for his slanders—'[w]hipping,
and hanging'—were remitted (V, i, 518–20). Unlike Barnadine,
neither of these offenders was an impenitent murderer; but
Barnadine enjoys the general amnesty along with all those upon

---

[44] See Rachod Nusen, 'English Productions of Measure for Measure
on Stage and Screen: The Play's Indeterminacy and the Authority of
Performance' (PhD thesis), Lancaster University, 6 May 2016,
https://eprints.lancs.ac.uk/id/eprint/79345/1/2016rachodphd.pdf, p.
293.

whom the Duke exercises his justice on his return to government.

Barnadine remains silent throughout his second and final appearance. This is another of those problematical silences that abound in *Measure for Measure*, particularly in the final scene. How is the actor to portray him: insensible? sullen? surly? or subtly moved towards penitence by the Duke's words of forgiveness? Only the latter interpretation will justify the Duke's general amnesty and leave the audience believing that the Duke's policy of promoting mercy above the strict rule of law has ultimately been vindicated. Thus David Bradley, playing Barnadine in David Thacker's 1994 BBC Television production, responded to the Duke's amnesty with an astonished but chastened look that encouraged the audience to consider the murderer redeemable. By contrast, when Graeme Brookes played Barnadine in the 2019 production for the RSC (directed by Gregory Doran), he left the stage cackling with joy and seemingly unregenerate. Barnadine's pardon by the Duke is unambiguous, but the murderer's reaction to that pardon is an opportunity for widely divergent interpretations.

Master Froth

As his name might suggest, Froth is lacking in substance, like the head on the beer that a tapster such as Pompey might provide for him.[45] He is described in the dramatis personae appended to the text of *Measure for Measure* in the First Folio as 'a foolish gentleman'. Sure enough, the few lines that he speaks indicate that he is ineffectual and frivolous. His pliant, timid nature and his 'fourscore pound(s) a year' of income (II, i, 122 and 192–3) make him an ideal mark for the predators of the Viennese underworld.[46] Accordingly, in the 1979 BBC

---

[45] Braunmuller and Watson (p. 152, n. 11) suggest that his name might even denote 'semen', a coarse reminder of his putative motive for frequenting Mistress Overdone's 'hot-house'.

[46] The reference to Froth's income may involve a topical reference. Braunmuller and Watson (p. 203n.) refer to James I's legislation of

production, Froth was portrayed as a lavishly-dressed fop with a camp manner, entirely reliant on Pompey to defend him from the forces of the law. In the RSC's 2019 production, his lower limbs were exposed, which made him appear like some overgrown infant or some bumpkin caught, literally, with his trousers down. His one (almost mute) appearance in the play is before Escalus in the comic trial-scene (Act II scene i) in which he is accused, with Pompey, of making sexual advances to Constable Elbow's wife at Mistress Overdone's 'hot-house'. He speaks only sixty words in the play, none of them particularly memorable: he is merely compliant and respectful, either intimidated by his encounter with the power of the state, or too impercipient to recognise his predicament.

However, although Froth's cameo role may seem as bland as his character, it provides a good opportunity for an actor with a penchant for slapstick and a range of inane expressions to leave a lasting comic impression on an audience. Froth's face should speak more eloquently than his tongue throughout Pompey's lengthy filibuster before Escalus (II, i, 84–157). Pompey, in defending his client against the charge of sexual assault, appeals to Escalus to accept Froth's face as evidence (II, i, 145–57). In a ridiculous parody of legal proceedings, Froth's innocuous appearance is the entire foundation of the case for the defence. Because of the inept Elbow's inability to articulate a coherent case for the prosecution, the testimony of Froth's face and the absence of incriminating evidence lead to the prosecution being abandoned.

In escaping from the retributive forces of justice, Froth is unique among the representatives of anarchy and disorder

June 1603, under which any man worth forty pounds a year, let alone double that (Froth's 'fourscore pounds a year'), was obliged to pay a fee to the monarch to become a knight—or another fee to avoid that honour! The obvious inappropriateness of Froth as a candidate for the order of knighthood might imply a satirical slur directed at James's money-making scheme, comparable to the one that has been identified in Shakespeare's closely-contemporary play, *Othello*, at III, iv, 43–44.

discussed so far. He departs with an admonition from Escalus to avoid taverns and tapsters like Pompey, who will 'draw' him (line 202). He seems not to recognise Escalus's grim pun which disguises a veiled reference to hanging, drawing and quartering (the fearsome penalty for major criminals) beneath the more obvious sense of 'draw liquor' (the tapster's task in the tavern). Froth's feeble attempt at a riposte suggests the weakness of his mind as well as the meekness of his will: 'I thank your worship. For mine own part, I never come into any room in a tap-house, but I am drawn in' (II, i, 205–7). These, his last words in the play, form his most substantial speech. They indicate his relief at having avoided the clutches of the law, but offer no great testimony to his wit.

Two Gentlemen

Lucio's associates in Act I scene ii, who are described as 'Gentlemen' in the dramatis personae, appear to be soldiers of fortune, eagerly anticipating involvement in conflict with the King of Hungary (I, ii, 1–5). Their association with the military is confirmed early in their dialogue, when the First Gentleman remarks,

> There's not a soldier *of us all* that, in the thanksgiving before meat, do relish the petition well that prays for peace.
> [I, ii, 14–16; italics added]

Soldiers are 'us', and soldiers do not enjoy times of peace (which leave them without an occupation and therefore without money).[47] Although the second gentleman demurs—'I never heard any soldier dislike it [i.e. 'peace']' (I, ii, 14–17)—he, too, is evidently familiar with the world of soldiering, as he can confidently debate the likes and dislikes of military men. This exchange is characteristic of the conversation between the three associates: each will take any opportunity to carp and contradict; their rivalry is jocularly aggressive.

---

[47] The civil disruption that could be caused by such unemployed soldiers is illustrated by Salgado, p. 111.

417

The dramatic function of the two Gentlemen is to provide a contrast to the courtly characters encountered in the first scene, and to establish, at the earliest opportunity, the essential aspects of Lucio's personality. In production, they may be presented as visually contrasting in their stature or dress but, in the text, they are not clearly distinguished from each other in either their language or in their topics of conversation: both might be clad to suggest their military vocation, both are politically well-informed, and both prove capable of defending themselves wittily, if obscenely.

The disparity in language between the opening two scenes is readily apparent. The three speakers in the first scene are dignified and philosophical in their conversation, as befits the most powerful figures whom we encounter in the play: the head of state, his appointed deputy, and his most trusted counsellor. Their exchanges explore the prevailing political situation in Vienna. To confirm the link with this opening scene, the second scene begins with a related topic of conversation as another group of three men—Lucio and the two Gentlemen—considers the likelihood of war. Shakespeare ensures, however, that the conversation quickly degenerates into more squalid topics appropriate to three mercenaries: piracy and theft (lines 7–14), irreligion and immorality (lines 17–29), and sexual diseases and their transmission (lines 30–55). This final topic is the subject of sustained bickering between the three which continues after Mistress Overdone's entry. Just as certainly as the first scene delineated the Duke's concerns over the business of good government, so this second scene demarcates Lucio's spheres of interests: banter, backbiting, and bawdry. The two Gentlemen are indispensable as his sounding-boards.

The language of the two Gentlemen offers an alternative perspective on 'The nature of our people, / Our city's institutions, and the terms / For common justice' (I, i, 10-12) to which Duke Vincentio referred in his discourse with Escalus. Their savvy is apparent when the First Gentleman shows a prior knowledge of Claudio and, implicitly, of his reputation for virtue: 'Claudio to prison? 'Tis not so' (I, ii, 60). He is also conversant with Angelo's measures to suppress vice in Vienna: 'But most of all agreeing with the proclamation' (I, ii, 73). The Second Gentleman is equally familiar with the recent crackdown on sexual offenders as 'it draws something near to the speech we had to such a purpose' (I, ii, 71–2). Here, as elsewhere in the text, no fundamental distinction between these two men is indicated.

The dramatic contrast between the first two scenes of *Measure for Measure* affords an inviting opportunity for the designer. Because Act I, scene i, is set at the court of Vienna, where opulent décor, refined manners, and erudite language prevail, the setting of this second scene should diverge sharply, as the coarse banter of Lucio and the two Gentlemen vividly suggests. The Folio text, however, gives no clue as to where Act I, scene ii, takes place. Although editors have variously suggested 'The Street' (Rowe) or 'A public place' (Lever), recent productions have righty favoured staging the scene in Mistress Overdone's tavern/brothel, to provide the sharpest contrast with the opening perspective on the Viennese court.[48] Thus, the play moves abruptly from the most sophisticated to the most dissolute of locations, encompassing at a stroke the whole gamut of Viennese society. The two Gentlemen might be presented gambling, drinking, and whoring to complement their profane conversation, a sharp contrast to the courtly manners of the opening scene.

Having achieved his dramatic purpose, Shakespeare discards these two decadent Gentlemen from the play in the same scene as they first appear. Although, according to the Folio text, they return with Lucio for his interview with Claudio, they do not speak again, and so they are generally excluded from

---

[48] The two BBC productions of 1979 and 1994 both present the opening of scene ii in the brothel, although the latter dispenses with the two gentlemen, transforming some of their exchanges into a dialogue between Lucio and a prostitute, presumably Mistress Kate Keep-down.

productions after line seventy-four of Act I scene ii. Like Froth, they are not seen to suffer any retribution under the law. Their conversation, however, implies that they might already be paying the price for their dissolute lives with painful and potentially fatal diseases.

Pompey's Clientele

This chapter began with reference to Pompey's speech to the audience about those former clients of Mistress Overdone's brothel whom he encounters in Vienna's prison. Their English names (in contrast with the Italianate style of the more patrician characters in the play) often suggest different types of debtors and brawlers.[49] For example, Pompey's offhand remarks identify the following financial malefactors:

> First, here's young Master Rash; he's in for a commodity of brown paper and old ginger, nine score and seventeen pounds; of which he made five marks ready money: marry, then, ginger was not much in request, for the old women were all dead. Then is there here one Master Caper, at the suit of Master Three-pile the mercer, for some four suits of peach-coloured satin, which now peaches him a beggar. Then we have here young Dizie, and . . . Master Copperspur, and . . . brave Master Shoe-tie, the great traveller. . . .
> [IV, iii, 4–17]

During Shakespeare's lifetime, prosecutions for debt, bankruptcy, and fraud proliferated. In *Measure for Measure*, similar offences appear to have sealed the fate of the five prisoners mentioned above. The impoverished Master Rash has fallen victim to the commodity swindle, a particularly 'English' fraud to which significant reference is made elsewhere in Elizabethan and Jacobean writing.[50] Master Rash's name may

---

[49] Salgado, p. 180, confirms that 'imprisonment for debt or brawling' predominated in London's prisons in the age of Shakespeare.

[50] The fraud involved persuading the dupe to accept a loan which was then supplied, in part or in whole, as a 'commodity' that was grossly

signify more than mere foolhardiness: it could also involve a pun on a type of cloth, suggesting expensive fashion; or a more obvious pun on disease, suggesting sexual excess. The name of Master Caper, who has been ruined by extravagance on costly materials supplied by Master Three-pile the mercer, presumably denotes an enthusiastic dancer (although possibly a sexual athlete). '[B]rave Master Shoe-tie the great traveller' is another aficionado of splendid ('brave') attire that has left him impoverished: he has presumably spent lavishly on fashions such as ornate laces for his footwear. His travels may be literal—a cause of his penury—or figurative, for the popularity of varied, extravagant, and expensive continental fashions in England was the butt of frequent jests among Shakespeare and his contemporaries.[51] Even 'young Dizie', to whom teasingly brief reference is made, may be a bankrupt, as his name could be a corruption of 'dice' or 'dize', suggesting a gambling-habit as well as an unstable ('dizzy') temperament. Finally, 'Master Copperspur' is likely to denote a fraudster or forger, as copper was used as a cheap substitute for gold, to trick gulls. All these prisoners have been guilty of what today might euphemistically be called 'financial misconduct'.

Also strongly represented in Pompey's speech are those involved in the subculture of quarrelling and duelling, 'roaring boys' whose offences had been addressed by the Statute of

---

overvalued and/or difficult to sell (e.g. 'brown paper and old ginger'). The lender might then buy back the 'commodity'—at a greatly reduced price and perhaps through an agent—leaving the dupe struggling to repay the full value originally placed on the loan. For further examples of this device, see Ben Jonson (1572–1637), *The Alchemist*, ed. Gordon Campbell (Oxford: OUP, 1995), II, i, 10–14 and III, ii, 87–99; and Robert Greene (1558–92), *A Defence of Cony-catching*, vol. 11, The works of Robert Greene, ed. A. B. Grosart (London and Aylesbury: Hazell, Watson, and Viney, 1881–86), p. 53.
[51] For example, see *The Merchant of Venice*: I, ii, 66–8, where Portia speaks of her English suitor's eclectic mix of fashions from Italy, France, and Germany. Cf. Joseph Hall's *Virgidemiarum Sixe Bookes* (London, 1597), III, i, 64–9; and Shakespeare's *Much Ado about Nothing*: III, ii, 28–35 and III, iii, 119–26.

Stabbing in 1603. This measure, passed very soon after King James I's accession to the English throne, suggests how serious the issue of street-violence (to this day, a major public concern in London) had become at the time when Shakespeare was preparing *Measure for Measure* for the stage. Those whom Pompey associates with threats, violence, and unlawful killing include

> . . . young Master Deep-vow . . . and Master Starve-Lackey, the rapier and dagger man, and young Drop-heir that killed lusty Pudding, and Master Forthright the tilter . . . and wild Half-can that stabbed pots. . . . [IV, iii, 13–18]

At least three of Pompey's clients would seem to have been committed for serious assault or murder: Master Starve-Lackey is a tyrant in and out of doors: not only a stingy master to his servants ('lackey[s]') at home, but also a 'rapier and dagger man', well-prepared for the duello when he ventures abroad. The name 'young Drop-heir' suggests one who habitually preys on beneficiaries, at least one of whom, the unfortunate 'lusty Pudding', he has murdered.[52] Presumably, 'wild Half-can' is a pint-sized (or easily befuddled) drunkard, crazy enough to attack tapsters (those who carry the 'pots').[53] Master Deep-vow, a swearer of great oaths, sounds like a swaggerer cast in the same mould as Ancient Pistol from Shakespeare's earlier

---

[52] Braunmuller and Watson (p. 308n.) suggest that 'Drop-heir' might suggest 'hair-loss' of the kind caused by syphilis, in which case, 'lusty pudding' would signify a previously active phallus drooping or 'killed' by the disease.

[53] Shakespeare had satirised the vanities of quarrelling in Touchstone's speeches to Jaques and Duke Senior in *As You Like It*: V, iv, 45–97. Shakespeare's close friend and fellow playwright, Ben Jonson (himself guilty of killing a man in a duel in 1598), would later satirise the excesses of quarrelsome behaviour through the character of Kastril, the angry boy, in his play, *The Alchemist* (1610). Lever thinks it possible that Half-can is a tapster who fraudulently alters the volume-marks on ale-pots, but the context, and the violence of the verb 'stabbed', suggests bloody conflict rather than surreptitious swindling.

history plays.[54] There is also the cryptic reference to 'Master Forthright the tilter' to fathom. Like Master Deep-vow, his name (Forthright) suggests that his language—or manner—is aggressive or even profane. Although an obscene thrust of the hips by Pompey might imply that 'tilter' is a euphemism for a male debauchee, a whoremaster,[55] it is more likely from the context that Master Forthright is yet another street-brawler, pugnaciously 'tilting' with his rapier at the breast of opponents.[56]

As we have just seen, Pompey initially names ten of his former clients—'young Master Rash', 'Master Caper', 'young Dizie', 'young master Deep-vow', 'Master Copperspur', 'Master Starve-Lackey', 'young Drop-heir', 'Master Forthright', 'brave Master Shoe-tie', and 'wild Half-Can' (lines 4–18)—as inmates of Vienna's prison. He adds greatly to this total, however, at the end of his speech:

. . . and I think forty more, all great doers in our trade, and are now 'for the Lord's sake'.   [IV, iii, 18–20]

Pompey's characteristic innuendo when he refers to them as 'all great doers in our trade' (where 'doers' signifies fornicators) confirms that at least fifty prisoners who once enthusiastically frequented the brothels of Vienna are now reduced to begging

---

[54] See, for example, *2 Henry IV*: II, iv, 65–193 and *Henry V*: II, i, 26–98; also, *The Merry Wives of Windsor*: I, i, 144–48.

[55] Reference to a lengthy weapon like a lance or pike as a phallic symbol deployed in sexual activity is encountered elsewhere in Shakespeare; cf. Falstaff's words to Doll Tearsheet, the prostitute: 'For to serve bravely is to come halting off; you know, to come off the breach with his pike bent bravely, and to surgery bravely; to venture upon the charg'd chambers bravely—' (*2 Henry IV*: II, iv, 44-7).

[56] Cf. *Romeo and Juliet*: III, i, 155–6: '. . . he tilts / With piercing steel at bold Mercutio's breast. . . .' The ambiguity here in *Measure for Measure*—is Master Forthright a lecher or a brawler?— may suggest that Shakespeare is deliberately blurring the distinction between crimes of 'blood': sex and violence, when ungoverned, are equal threats to social stability.

for sustenance through the bars of the city gaol.[57] Such criminals might have been encountered on passing any of the eighteen prisons in Shakespeare's London.

So many of the prisoners whom Pompey names are young, are associated with crimes of impulsiveness or passion, and are addressed as 'Master'. To Shakespeare's contemporaries, 'Master' was a title that denoted a measure of respect or social rank. Although Pompey's expression may result simply from deference for (or mocking condescension towards) his previous customers, the implication is that many of Pompey's associates formerly enjoyed a degree of prestige in their society.[58] The list suggests how young gentlemen and heirs are subjected to exploitation and driven to crime through their association with establishments such as Mistress Overdone's 'tavern' or 'hothouse'. Having squandered their patrimony, they further regress from brothel to prison.

Retrospective and Reassessment

We are now in a better position to address the question raised earlier in this chapter: whether the world of anarchy and indulgence, as presented in *Measure for Measure*, is more attractive than the world of authority and abstinence that opposes it. If so, then it would be because the offences committed in the name of justice are more odious than those of which the underclasses are guilty. The play may suggests that the Duke was an ineffectual ruler who tacitly encouraged dissolute behaviour before appointing an incipient tyrant to rectify the political situation; but it also confirms that, in any

---

[57] This was a topical issue at the start of the Seventeenth Century. To relieve privations, Elizabeth I's Poor Law Act of 1601 had imposed a weekly levy on Londoners to provide food and drink for the destitute in workhouses and prisons. See Salgado, p. 174, and 'Act for the Relief of the Poor 1601', Wikipedia, accessed 20 July 2020, https://en.wikipedia.org/wiki/Act_for_the_Relief_of_the_Poor_1601.
[58] Salgado, pp. 17–19, discusses the process whereby minor gentlemen so readily became criminals in Shakespearian London.

civilized society, whenever an offence is brought to light, the law must continue to function, even when administered by those who are themselves corrupt (II, i, 19–23). Even an audience that despises the maladministration and hypocrisy of the Duke and Angelo, while relishing the humour and jauntiness of Lucio and Pompey, should recognize that a tainted legal system can still perform an essential and beneficial social function.

Measures against the disorders festering in brothels were topical in Shakespeare's London. Angelo's 'proclamation' that 'All houses in the suburbs of Vienna must be plucked down' (I, ii, 86–8) echoes James I's proclamation of 16 September 1603 that commanded the destruction of houses in the London suburbs to prevent the plague being spread by 'dissolute and idle persons'.[59] Angelo implicitly recognises that moral diseases—as well as the physical ones—proliferate in Vienna's brothels. His strict enforcement of the statutes has purged the streets of such 'dissolute and idle persons', extracting the fifty malefactors mentioned by Pompey (including formerly wealthy and seemingly respectable men) from 'houses of resort', to deposit them behind prison-bars, where they no longer pose a threat to society. Their association with the underworld, although perhaps seductive and exciting initially, has led to criminality which ultimately deprives them of social status, wealth, and freedom.

In *Measure for Measure*, the law (regardless of the moral status of those responsible for its administration) has at least fulfilled its obligation of chastening such corruptive influences. Before the end of the play, Lucio has been condemned to suffer mockery and self-loathing as a cuckold, wedded to a woman whom he considers a whore. Pompey has been compelled to become an executioner's assistant, surviving by imposing, rather than opposing, the full force of the law. Mistress Overdone, exhausted by disease and dissipation, has been committed to the oblivion of indefinite incarceration. Barnadine

---

[59] Lever, pp. xxxii–xxxiii.

has been abandoned to a kind of limbo, with the Church commissioned to save a soul that has degenerated into soporific indifference. Master Froth and two of Lucio's gentlemen-associates may seem to have escaped retribution, but the common fate of so many other dissolute 'gentlemen' suggests that any respite is temporary: Vienna's whoremongers and criminals end the play infected, impoverished, and imprisoned. From the shocking references to sexually-transmitted diseases at the start of the second scene, to the evidence of the sorry fate suffered by such offenders later in the play, the life of irresponsibility and sensual pleasure has progressively shed its allure.

Ultimately, Shakespeare demonstrates that Vienna's underworld—however amusing or animated it may appear on occasion—is distasteful, degrading, and predatory; but he also reveals that Vienna's government—however altruistic or righteous it may purport to be—is administered by inadequate, self-serving, or hypocritical officials. Anarchy, although superficially attractive, emerges as self-destructive; but authority, although politically indispensable, emerges as deeply flawed. Indulgence proves repulsive, but abstinence proves perverse. In the balanced world of *Measure for Measure*, the evils of those who frequent the underworld, and the vices of those who should regulate the underworld, are carefully counterpoised. Between anarchy and authority, between indulgence and abstinence, the play scrupulously maintains the equilibrium.

Chapter 7

Church and State

In the Vienna of *Measure for Measure*, the authority of both the Church and the state are embodied in the figure of the Duke. His power in the state is absolute in the first and last scenes of the play, when he presides in propria persona over his court and his people. Both at the beginning and at the end of the play, however, the Duke concedes that he has neglected Vienna's 'strict statutes and most biting laws' (I, iii, 19–21), as a result of which he has 'seen corruption boil and bubble / Till it o'errun the stew' (V, i, 316–17). By his own admission, there have been deficiencies in his secular rule; but his achievements as a religious figure may seem more considerable in several respects. In the guise of Friar Lodowick, he is the most influential representative of the Church in the play. Not only does he save the life of Claudio, but also he redeems a range of characters from misery and sin. Estimable figures such as Julietta, Isabella, Mariana, Claudio, Escalus, and the Provost hold him in high spiritual regard. Unlike the characters in the play, however, the audience can readily identify the highly dubious means that the disguised Duke *qua* friar employs to achieve his ends.

Although the Duke reverts to his true identity for his final judgement, his choice of the sacrament of marriage to resolve issues at the end of the play implies that the rituals of the Church may prevail where the statutes of the state have failed. The laws of Church and state, nevertheless, seem indistinguishable for much of *Measure for Measure*. The 'strict statutes and most biting laws' (I, iii, 19) over which the Duke of Vienna presides include measures to regulate human sexual activity that, in Shakespeare's England, had for centuries been the preserve of the ecclesiastical courts rather than falling under the jurisdiction of the state. Shakespeare's audience would, nevertheless, have been accustomed to a ruler who held sway over both secular and religious matters, as England's monarch had been head of the Church as well as head of state since Henry VIII's Act of Supremacy in 1534.[1] Such was the authority over and responsibility for secular and religious matters that James I inherited on his accession to the English throne nearly seventy years later. In that same year (1603), Shakespeare had probably begun work on *Measure for Measure*, a play in which the Duke of Vienna flits easily between state affairs and spiritual concerns, assuming authority over both while exploring 'the properties . . . [o]f government' (I, i, 3).

Henry VIII's seizure of power from the Church was prompted by issues relating to marriage and choice of sexual partner,[2] central concerns both of the Duke of Vienna in *Measure for Measure* and of the ecclesiastical courts of Shakespeare's England. The latter became known as the 'bawdy courts' because, although they dealt with other issues of canon law, so many of the cases that came before them concerned sexual impropriety: fornication, adultery, incest, and the begetting of bastards. These courts—between three and four hundred of them nationwide—regulated the piety and morals of the local community, the less prestigious ones relying on the testimonies of neighbours and minor officials such as local

---

[1] There was a brief hiatus between 1554 and 1559, during the reign of Mary I.

[2] Henry had been granted a papal dispensation in 1509 to wed Catherine of Aragon, wife of his dead brother, Arthur. To avoid the imputation of incest, it was initially argued that Arthur had never consummated the marriage. When no male issue resulted from his own union with Catherine, Henry reversed the argument, seeking to divorce Catherine on the grounds that God was displeased with their incestuous nuptial. The Pope, under pressure from Spain, demurred, and so Henry literally took the law into his own hands, asserting his authority as monarch over the English Church and thereby expediting the desired divorce.

constables to convict offenders: hence the role of Elbow and Lucio in the indictment of Pompey and Mistress Overdone.[3] In the Vienna of *Measure for Measure*, Angelo enforces a law that stipulates a capital sentence for a man judged guilty of fathering an illegitimate child. Such an offence was not subject to the death-penalty in the bawdy courts of Shakespeare's England. The courts administered by the state, by contrast, might impose the death-sentence for murder or forgery, the two crimes that Angelo equates with begetting an illegitimate child (II, iv, 42–9).

The penalties for sexual offences could involve public humiliation and corporal punishment. Penitents were forced to confess publicly, sometimes clad in a white sheet and perched on a stool in the aisle of the church. Such a practice is in keeping with Angelo's insistence that Claudio and Julietta should be shown 'to th'world' (I, ii, 108) as offenders against the moral order. Punishment could be exacted even after marriage if it became evident that a child had been conceived before matrimony: a bloody whipping was often the prescribed penalty for such offenders. As for those involved in the sex-trade, prostitutes were taken to Bridewell to be scourged, naked, in public, a sentence comparable with that which Pompey the pimp would have faced in prison had he not agreed to become the executioner's assistant (see IV, ii, 10–13).

Many Puritans, however, were dissatisfied with these punishments, believing stronger measures necessary to eradicate sexual offences. During Elizabeth's reign, William Perkins (1558–1602), although one of the more moderate

---

[3] Shakespeare probably had direct dealings with his local ecclesiastical court in Stratford-upon-Avon over the issue of his relationship with Anne Hathaway (she was three-months pregnant and he was still a minor at the time of their marriage in 1582) but, as no records have survived from the Stratford court that pre-date 1590, we cannot be sure. Certainly, both his daughters are mentioned in the records, one (Susanna) for non-attendance at church, and one (Judith) because, very soon after her wedding, a woman died in childbirth after an illicit sexual relationship with Judith's newly-wedded husband.

voices, cited Biblical authority in support of the death-penalty for adultery.[4] In his *Anatomy of Abuses* (1583), Philip Stubbes ruefully conceded that his contemporary society would not endorse the death-sentence for crimes such as adultery, incest, and prostitution, but he nevertheless recommended branding on some readily-visible part of the face or body to mark out offenders in such cases from the rest of society.[5] The Provost's words about Julietta, that she has 'blister'd her report' (II, iii, 12), possibly refer to this proposed punishment, the blister on Julietta's reputation recollecting the mark of the hot iron on the forehead.[6] On his accession to the English throne in 1603, James I encountered just such clamour among his Puritan subjects for more stringent punishment for sexual offences. This culminated, twenty-five years after his decease, with the introduction of the death-penalty for adultery under the Commonwealth, when the Puritans were in the ascendant. In *Measure for Measure*, the puritanical Angelo goes still further, prescribing capital punishment for the lesser offences of fornication and the begetting of an illegitimate child.

Marriage and the Law

In the Twelfth Century, Peter the Lombard (c.1096–1160), widely influential as academic, theologian, and Bishop of Paris, recognised the legitimacy of two forms of marriage based on the exchange of mutual vows: *de praesenti* for adults and *de futuro* predominantly for minors (as boys could not marry before the age of fourteen and girls before the age of twelve). These 'spousals', 'handfastings', or 'troth-plightings' were legitimate, according to the Lombard, even when witnesses were not present. The situation was re-appraised by the Fourth Lateran Council (1215), which required authorised marriages to be announced publicly in church by priests, to prevent secret

---

[4] 'A Treatise of Conscience' in *Workes* (London, 1635), p. 521.

[5] The relevant extract is quoted by Kamps and Raber, p. 292.

[6] Cf. *Hamlet*: III, iv, 40–4: 'Such an act / That . . . / . . . takes off the rose / From the fair forehead of an innocent love, / And sets a blister there. . . .'

nuptials. Although the response in England, during the reign of Henry III (1216–72), was for common law to reject mere spousals, insisting on banns being read to legitimise marriage, the practice of spousals continued, apparently without effective opposition. By 1563, the Council of Trent had insisted that spousals were null and void until ratified by the church; but, as the edicts of the Council of Trent post-dated the Reformation, they were observed only in Catholic Europe—in the Vienna of Duke Vincentio, perhaps, but not in the London of William Shakespeare.

In 1604, the year of the first recorded performance of *Measure for Measure*, the issue of spousals was particularly topical in England: new legislation was passed challenging the legality of marriages based solely on the exchange of vows between man and woman. 1604 was also the year in which Shakespeare was witness to a 'troth-plighting', the dowry relating to which remained a matter of contention for a further eight years, at the end of which Shakespeare was summoned to offer evidence on the matter. The status of the two betrothals in *Measure for Measure*—between Claudio and Julietta, and between Angelo and Mariana—was therefore a contentious issue to Shakespeare and his audience. Claudio's words about his 'true contract' with a woman who is 'fast my wife' (I, ii, 134–6) suggest that he believes that he is securely married and therefore may legitimately consummate his relationship with Julietta. The Duke's description of the 'oath' between Mariana and Angelo and the arrangements for their marriage indicate a similar binding agreement between man and wife that might be consummated legitimately without the authorisation of the Church (IV, i, 72–5). The only distinction between these two spousals is that Claudio speaks of his marriage in the present tense while, five years before, the 'nuptial' between Angelo and Mariana had been set for an indeterminate future date (see III, i, 214 and V, i, 215–21).

The validity of marriage by mutual vow, as opposed to marriage in a church before a clergyman, was clearly a matter of considerable dispute in Elizabethan and Jacobean England.

Religious writers such as Miles Coverdale (1488–1569), Richard Greenham (1535?–94?) and William Gouge (1575–1653) all condemned the consummation of a contracted marriage before the union had been consecrated by the Church. The 1604 Canons of the Church of England declared marriage valid when conducted in church, and then only after the banns had been read on three different Sundays or holy days (Statute LXII).[7] This new legislation was clearly relevant to *Measure for Measure* and its contemporary audience, as it challenged the prevalent popular opinion that 'a true contract' of handfasting (such as that between the lovers in the play) could be consummated without ecclesiastical ratification.

William Perkins, however, in his *Christian Economy* published in London in 1609, recognised the validity of both types of *sponsalia* (*de praesenti* and *de futuro*), going as far as to say that when sexual union occurs in either case, 'the contract for time to come is, without further controversy, sure and certain'.[8] According to this authority, both the Claudio-Julietta and the Angelo-Mariana relationship were fully confirmed at the moment of consummation. Even as late as 1632, in a work published in London under the title *The Law's Resolution of Women's Rights*, the unidentified 'T.E.' could assert confidently,

> The full contract of matrimony is when it is made by words, *de praesenti* in a lawful consent, and thus two be made man and wife without lying together, yet matrimony is not

---

[7] *1604 Canon Law*, Anglican.net, 5 April 2014, https://www.anglican.net/doctrines/1604-canon-law/. Such provision, directed against marriages which lacked witnesses (or parental assent for the under-21s), ensured that a full register of marriages (together with births and deaths) could be kept in each parish: see Statute LXX.
[8] Kamps and Raber, p. 212. Perkins died in 1602 and so, as his tract was written (in Latin) during Elizabeth's reign, his opinions expressed in this English translation were not his deliberate challenge to the 1604 Canons.

accounted consummate, until there go with the consent of mind and will conjunction of body.[9]

Both these publications challenge the 1604 Canons of the Church of England, not merely by authorising troth-plighting as legitimate marriage, but also by endorsing sexual union as its consummation. *Measure for Measure* reflects these conflicting opinions about the legitimacy of such spousals, merely transferring its investigation of the issue from Protestant London to Catholic Vienna.

Although influential, the clergy whom we encounter in *Measure for Measure* have no political power. There are no cardinals, archbishops, or bishops presiding over the government of Vienna. Rather, the minor clergy whom we encounter in the play must always defer to the state in matters of authority beyond the cloister. Their contribution to the happy outcome of events, however, is considerable. Friar Thomas and Friar Peter are important supporters of the Duke's cause. Sister Francisca and the Prioress offer a place of safety to Isabella. In addition, two of the principal characters in the play, the Duke and Isabella, are identified with religious orders for a substantial part of *Measure for Measure*.

Friar Thomas and Friar Peter

Since the edition of Samuel Johnson, there has been an editorial consensus that Friar Thomas, to whom Vincentio speaks early in the play, and Friar Peter, who appears towards the end of the play, are one and the same character, mistakenly given different names in the First Folio of 1623. Careful consideration of the distinct ways in which the Duke employs and addresses each of the friars, however, suggests that Thomas and Peter should be presented as two different dramatic roles.[10]

---

[9] Kamps and Raber, p. 206.
[10] The Duke's early words to Friar Thomas requesting a friar's habit and instruction in appropriate spiritual conduct in return for 'Moe reasons for this action' (I, iii, 45–9) are cited by Lever, p. xix n., as

At first glance, the role of Friar Thomas may seem insignificant, if only because he speaks no more than thirty-six words in the entire play. The one scene in which he appears (Act I, scene iii) begins in mid-conversation, the Duke responding with an apparently light-hearted dismissal of the friar's suggestion that Vincentio may be withdrawing from the court for amatory reasons. The conversation is respectful on both sides: Vincentio addresses Friar Thomas as 'Holy father' (line 1), 'My holy sir' (line 7) and 'pious sir' (line 16), while the friar tactfully questions the Duke with 'May your Grace speak of it?' (line 6, 'it' being the reason for Vincentio's quasi-abdication). From the outset, Friar Thomas allows the Duke to speak freely, offering only minor prompts: when Vincentio suggests, 'You will demand of me, why I do this' (line 17), Friar Thomas dutifully responds, 'Gladly, my lord' (line18). These exchanges convey the sense that Vincentio is confiding in a trusted and well-respected friend. That impression is confirmed by Vincentio's early remark that 'none better knows than you / How I have ever lov'd the life remov'd' (lines 7–8). The clear implication is that the friar knows the Duke particularly well as the result of long and close acquaintance. Certainly, Vincentio's reverence towards the friar is firmly established by the deferential tone of his address to his spiritual advisor.

Although his first two brief speeches may seem merely to punctuate the much more lengthy and diffuse speeches of the Duke, Friar Thomas's final speech suggests that he has listened attentively. Having learned of the social disorder that has resulted from the Duke's failure to enforce the law to its full extent, Friar Thomas boldly challenges the Duke's plan to

---

anticipating a later meeting in the play between the two men. In that second meeting (IV, v, 1–10), however, the Duke is addressing Friar Peter, not Friar Thomas, according to the Folio text. The friar who attends the Duke in this context is briefed as an agent and employed as a messenger, but is not offered the promised 'moe reasons' for Vincentio's wish to be disguised; nor does the friar offer in return any instruction in appropriate mendicant behaviour.

rectify the situation by absenting himself from the state and by placing Angelo in control:

> It rested in your Grace
> To unloose this tied-up justice when you pleas'd;
> And it in you more dreadful would have seem'd
> Than in Lord Angelo. [I, iii, 31–4]

Friar Thomas's words propose to Vincentio that, in failing to address Vienna's moral crisis personally by re-establishing the laws that had fallen into abeyance, the Duke has been negligent of his duty. Although uttered with tact and restraint, these lines are a surprisingly forthright criticism, presenting Friar Thomas as an earnest, wise, and scrupulous moral arbiter. Even Escalus, so experienced in 'The nature of our people / Our city's institutions, and the terms / For common justice' (I, i, 9–11), had not presumed directly to question the Duke's decision to quit Vienna and to appoint Angelo in his stead. The final impression from the scene is that Friar Thomas is Duke Vincentio's confessor, their mutually respectful addresses, the Duke's reference to the friar's intimate knowledge of him, the friar's moral analysis of the Duke's conduct, and Vincentio's frequently penitential tone all supporting such an interpretation.[11]

Friar Thomas is the only person in whom the Duke confides his plan secretly to observe Angelo's government while disguised as a friar. Thomas is chosen to supply the Duke both with the mendicant robe and with instruction in the proper conduct of a friar. Thomas is also the only person to challenge the authority of the Duke to his (undisguised) face. As such, he is the dramatic device necessary to reveal to the audience both the Duke's plans and the Duke's reasons for undertaking them. Once he has performed these functions, he can be relegated to the wings, never to reappear.

---

[11] In keeping with this reading, the scene was presented as a closed confessional in the 1994 BBC television-production, adapted and directed by David Thacker.

Friar Peter is not mentioned until late in Act IV. The Duke, in disguise as Friar Lodowick, informs Isabella that 'The Duke comes home tomorrow. . . . / One of our co[n]vent, and [i.e. who is] his confessor / Gives me this instance' (IV, iii, 127–9). A few lines later, Vincentio adds:

> This letter then to Friar Peter give;
> 'Tis that he sent me of the Duke's return. [IV, iii, 137–8]

The waters here are muddied by Vincentio's deviousness—or by Shakespeare's deliberate obfuscations. It is obvious to any audience that Friar Lodowick needs no confessor to inform him of the Duke's intentions, as he himself is the Duke. He might, though, plausibly be thought to have informed his confessor of his intentions before asking him to write the letter containing the information, to be given to Friar Peter as evidence of the Duke's imminent arrival. What is undeniable is that Vincentio is making a distinction between the Duke's 'confessor' (plausibly, Friar Thomas, who has been of the Duke's counsel from the outset) and Friar Peter. It seems that it is not until this point in the play that Friar Peter is to be informed of Friar Lodowick's plans:

> Say, by this token I desire [Friar Peter's] company
> At Mariana's house tonight. Her cause and yours
> I'll perfect him withal, and he shall bring you
> Before the Duke; and to the Head of Angelo
> Accuse him home and home. [IV, iii, 139–43]

The speech does not suggest that the Duke/friar has confided in Friar Peter previously; rather, Friar Peter is to meet Mariana and Isabella that evening, to learn of their circumstances from Friar Lodowick, and to present their case in court. No prior knowledge on Friar Peter's part, either of Friar Lodowick's true identity or of his labours to obtain justice for Angelo's victims, is suggested.

The humility and reverence that Vincentio showed towards Friar Thomas, his confessor, are consistently absent from the Duke's manner towards Friar Peter, who appears in each of the last three scenes of the play. In the first, Friar Peter is addressed as a mere menial, his only words being half a line of acquiescence: 'It shall be speeded well' (IV, v, 10). The Duke, apparently in propria persona, has given him a brief and is employing him as a messenger, but never treats him as an intimate confidant or confessor, as he did Friar Thomas:

> These letters at a fit time deliver me.
> ... keep your instruction,
> And hold you ever to our special drift. ...
> Go call at Flavius' house,
> And tell him where I stay. Give the like notice
> To Valencius, Rowland, and to Crassus,
> And bid them bring the trumpets to the gate:
> But send me Flavius first. [IV, v, 1–10]

The respectful vocatives that the Duke consistently addressed to Friar Thomas have entirely disappeared, to be replaced by a profusion of peremptory imperatives—'deliver', 'keep', 'hold', 'Go call', 'tell', 'Give', 'bid', 'send'—without so much as a 'please'. Significantly, the Duke *does* employ thanks and a respectful vocative to Varrius, a courtier whom he greets genially at the very moment that Friar Peter is dismissed, reinforcing the distinction between Vincentio's 'friends' (IV, v, 12) and Friar Peter. The relationship between Duke and friar here seems much more distant and the division of rank much wider than those between Vincentio and Friar Thomas in the earlier scene (I, iii).

An editorial stage-direction (absent from the text of the First Folio) usually indicates that Vincentio has reappeared in his ducal garments when he addresses Friar Peter at the beginning of this scene.[12] Certainly, Vincentio's language is that of a duke

---

[12] For example, 'in his own habit' (Lever; Kamps and Raber) and 'in his own robes' (Coles and Gibson).

addressing a subject. A mere friar, as Lodowick purports to be, would not command a fellow friar to inform eminent courtiers of his whereabouts or to instruct them to supply a fanfare at the city gates (IV, v, 6–10). This raises the issue of whether Friar Peter would now be aware (like Friar Thomas) that the mysterious Friar Lodowick is the Duke in disguise. If Friar Peter is regarded as privy to the Duke's alias, then Peter is the only person on stage in the final scene—other than the Duke himself—who is prepared for the shock of Friar Lodowick's unhooding. There is no evidence that Friar Lodowick has revealed his true identity to anyone outside the cloister, even to the Provost, in whom he has confided so closely. When Lucio plucks off Friar Lodowick's hood to reveal Duke Vincentio, there should be (almost) universal amazement: only one character, Friar Peter, might venture a complacent nod.

Like Angelo in the opening scene, Friar Peter has received a brief concerning how to conduct himself in Vincentio's absence. In the final two scenes of the play, Friar Peter is seen to fulfil the Duke's command to 'keep your instruction, / And hold you ever to our special drift, / Though sometimes you do blench from this to that / As cause doth minister' (IV, v, 3–6). Friar Peter, then, has been given specific directions ('special drift') concerning how to conduct himself before the court, although he has been afforded some leeway to deviate or improvise ('blench from this to that') where appropriate. In dutiful response, he prepares Mariana and Isabella for their encounter with Angelo, instructing them where to position themselves. His lines perform the dramatic function—on the bare stage of Shakespeare's theatre—of creating a vivid image of the splendour of the Duke's return:

> Come, I have found you out a stand most fit,
> Where you may have such vantage on the Duke
> He shall not pass you. Twice have the trumpets sounded.
> The generous and gravest citizens
> Have hent the gates, and very near upon
> The Duke is ent'ring: therefore hence, away.
> [IV, vi, 10–15]

The urgency of those last three words accelerates us into the final scene, where Friar Peter will play his most substantial role.

Like Lucio in the second scene of Act II, Friar Peter prompts Isabella to approach the judgement-seat and to make her appeal, even echoing Lucio's earlier advice to 'kneel before' her judge (V, i, 19–20) to secure success. Unlike Lucio, he then remains silent throughout Isabella's petition (V, i, 21–124). He finally speaks after Lucio has roundly condemned the absent Friar Lodowick to the court. Friar Peter will defend the reputation of his putative fellow friar (V, i, 146–50), but not before he has seemingly condemned the testimony given by Isabella to the court:

> Bless'd be your royal Grace!
> I have stood by, my lord, and I have heard
> Your royal ear abus'd. First hath this woman
> Most wrongfully accus'd your substitute,
> Who is as free from touch or soil with her
> As she from one ungot. [V, i, 139–44]

It may be surprising to the audience that Friar Peter here discredits Isabella's testimony and appears to vindicate the accused Angelo. He is, however, indulging in the same equivocation as Isabella has done immediately before: Angelo may be 'free from touch or soil *with her*' (line 143; italics added), but that exoneration does not extend to all other women with whom Angelo may have had dealings. Friar Peter is preparing the court (and, dramatically, preparing the audience) for the contradictory testimony of the veiled Mariana.[13]

---

[13] Friar Peter's apparent accusation against Isabella of bearing false witness may lead to a reconsideration of an earlier context. When Isabella expressed her reluctance to 'speak so indirectly' before the court, she added, 'yet I am advis'd to do it, / He says, to veil full purpose' (IV, vi, 1–4). Mariana encouraged her to 'Be rul'd by him' (IV, vi, 4), to which Isabella responded, 'Besides, he tells me that, if

Friar Peter successfully stage-manages events until the appearance of Friar Lodowick, but in so doing he appears to perjure himself. Having dutifully defended the reputation of his assumed brother in holy orders (V, i, 146–50), Friar Peter fabricates information to justify his role as Lodowick's delegate, before further discrediting Isabella's testimony:

> Well, [Friar Lodowick] in time may come to clear himself;
> But at this instant he is sick, my lord:
> Of a strange fever. Upon his mere request,
> Being come to knowledge that there was complaint
> Intended 'gainst Lord Angelo, came I hither,
> To speak, as from his mouth, what he doth know
> Is true and false; and what he with his oath
> And all probation will make up full clear
> Whensoever he's convented. First, for this woman,
> To justify this worthy nobleman
> So vulgarly and personally accus'd,
> Her shall you hear disproved to her eyes,

---

peradventure / He speak against me on the adverse side, / I should not think it strange. . . .' (IV, vi, 5–7). An audience was most likely to assume that each singular masculine pronoun ('He', 'him', 'he', 'he') referred to Friar Lodowick—that is, to the Duke in disguise. Friar Lodowick, however, will never speak against Isabella. The Duke may do (e.g. V, i, 108–17, 123–6, and 166), but Isabella does not recognise the Duke as Friar Lodowick until the very end of the final scene. It is therefore possible that the exchanges between the two women in this earlier context are, from the outset of Act IV scene vi, referring to advice offered by Friar Peter: he might be thought to have instructed them how to conduct themselves before the court, while warning Isabella that he might testify against her. This would explain why the very next half-line in this context was Mariana's anxious and incomplete exclamation, 'I would Friar Peter—' (IV, vi, 8). She and Isabella apparently needed the reassurance of Friar Peter's presence to confirm the strategy that he might earlier have persuaded them to pursue. Even if this was the case, however, it would be assumed that Friar Peter's actions had been prompted by Friar Lodowick—that is, by the disguised Duke.

440

Till she herself confess it. [V, i, 152–64]

The audience is fully aware that, as these words are spoken, Friar Lodowick is present in the person of Duke Vincentio. The disguised Duke had lied to Isabella that, when she accuses Angelo, he cannot be present as 'I am combined by a sacred vow' (IV, iii, 144). When Friar Peter now explains that Friar Lodowick is absent because afflicted by 'a strange fever' (line 154), he appears to the audience not so much misinformed as complicit in Friar Lodowick's lies. In justifying himself as Friar Lodowick's proxy, Friar Peter claims to have been briefed fully on the issues of the case and to be ready to speak with Friar Lodowick's voice until his colleague can appear to confirm the testimony (lines 154–60). Having established his authority to speak, Friar Peter dissembles, 'justify[ing]' (vindicating) Angelo as a 'worthy nobleman' (line 161) and apparently representing Isabella as a malicious slanderer (lines 160–4). As he has been briefed beforehand by the Duke/friar, he should know that both representations are false: Angelo is the criminal and Isabella his victim. If Friar Peter is deliberately misleading the court, as it appears, then he might be regarded by the audience as yet another 'seemer' in a Vienna, where 'seeming' is the stock-in-trade of authority figures such as Angelo and the Duke.

This line of argument, however, may be regarded as the result of looking too literally at a character who is essentially little more than a dramatic device, created to supply the place of the Duke's alias, Friar Lodowick, while the Duke himself is appearing in propria persona on stage. The nature of a stage-trial invited Shakespeare to supply a functionary to introduce witnesses in the manner of a barrister. Having already advised Isabella prior to her testimony, Friar Peter summons Mariana, seemingly to bear witness against Isabella on behalf of Lord Angelo (see V, i, 169 and 192). Finally, with his last words in the play, he will instruct the court as to the whereabouts of Friar Lodowick, so that the disguised Duke can be brought before the assembly (V, i, 249–52). That information, however, is imparted under seeming duress, after he has been condemned by the Duke as a 'foolish friar' and apparently arrested, together with Mariana and Isabella (V, i, 239–48).

The Duke never acknowledges the good offices of Friar Peter, nor overtly thanks him, although he does include him, with Mariana and Isabella, among the 'gentle three' whom he bails as his first act after his unhooding by Lucio (V, i, 355). Friar Peter's remaining functions in the play are, nevertheless, significant: to conduct the marriage between Angelo and Mariana—'Do you the office, friar' (V, i, 376)—and to undertake the spiritual instruction of Barnadine—'Friar, advise him' (V, i, 483). On both occasions, the Duke speaks to him in imperatives, adopting that same peremptory tone that he employed in Act IV, scene v, never addressing him with a respectful vocative, never expressing polite thanks, and never offering him praise for his services. Nor does the Duke refer to Friar Peter, directly or indirectly, in the encomium that he bestows in his final speech on those who have assisted him in his triumphant return to government in Vienna. From his first appearance in Act IV scene v, Friar Peter has been treated by the Duke as if he were 'a slight unmeritable man, / Meet to be sent on errands'.[14] The Duke's surprising lack of consideration for an associate who performs so many good offices so obediently is in sharp contrast to the Duke's respect and reverence for Friar Thomas in Act I scene iii.

Shakespeare's text suggests that Friar Thomas should be authoritative and esteemed, a senior friar worthy to be confessor to a duke; whereas Friar Peter should be a junior friar whose energy and efficiency may be assumed, but whose contributions need not be acknowledged. Despite the critical tradition of conflating the two roles, Friar Thomas and Friar Peter are distinct characters, and should be presented as such on stage, as authorised by the First Folio.

---

[14] This is Mark Antony's dismissive opinion of Lepidus in *Julius Caesar*: IV, i, 12–13.

The Votarists of Saint Clare

The primary dramatic purpose of Francisca (who is involved in only fourteen lines of dialogue at the beginning of the fourth scene) is to provide details to the audience of the devotional life that Isabella desires and envisages. Isabella is receiving 'her approbation' (I, ii, 168) from Francisca, who explains to her the rules of the order. Like the Duke in the previous scene, Isabella may 'have ever lov'd the life remov'd' (I, iii, 8), but in her case it is because she wishes 'a more strict restraint' (I, iv, 4) than the stipulations of which she learns. Francisca considers the 'privileges' of the votarists to be 'large enough' to satisfy a novice, not immediately recognising that Isabella would want fewer, not more, freedoms (I, iv, 1–5). Francisca's surprise anticipates that of the audience on learning that a young postulant could wish for a more stringent life than even the notoriously severe Poor Clares would demand of her.

The call of Lucio from off-stage focuses Francisca on the rules protecting an exclusively female society from the incursion of men:

> It is a man's voice! Gentle Isabella,
> Turn you the key, and know his business of him;
> You may, I may not; you are yet unsworn:
> When you have vow'd, you must not speak with men
> But in the presence of the prioress;
> Then, if you speak, you must not show your face;
> Or, if you show your face, you must not speak.
> [I, iv, 7–13]

Francisca here confirms that the cloister is a place where Isabella can find refuge from such depravity as that to which the Duke referred in the previous scene, when he confessed that, due to his lax administration, 'quite athwart / Goes all decorum' in Vienna (I, iii, 30–1). Isabella may hear Lucio's petition because she is 'yet unsworn' (line 9), whereas Francisca must withdraw from male presence, as she does immediately after this speech. Francisca has offered, however, an important clue to Isabella's circumstances: because Isabella is a novice, and can therefore speak to men without impediment, she is not yet protected against the advances of an Angelo—or for that matter, of a Vincentio. She has yet to pledge herself to become a bride of Christ by making her solemn profession.

The Prioress to whom Francisca refers in her speech is the only woman mentioned in the play (with the possible but dubious exception of Mistress Overdone) who wields any kind of authority in the community. If the convent of Saint Clare is the microcosm of the court of Vienna, then the Prioress represents the epitome of good government, a shining example to the Duke. Certainly, the juxtaposition of this scene with the 'confession' of Vincentio in the previous scene invites an audience to contrast the mismanagement of Vienna, to which he admits, with the austere efficiency of the nunnery. The Prioress has not let 'corruption boil and bubble / Till it o'errun the stew' (V, i, 316–17) as the Duke has in neglecting the regulation of morals; she supervises all meetings with men, ensuring that any of the sisterhood attending must remain either veiled or silent (lines 10–13). Although the Prioress never appears on stage, her firm command of discipline in the convent provides a significant contrast with the Duke's indulgent rule in Vienna.

The exchanges between Francisca and Isabella are as important for what they omit as for what they include. Francisca makes no reference to the canonical hours that would determine the shape of a nun's day, no reference to private religious study and devotion, no reference to good works or charitable duties, no reference, even, to God. The discussion is of 'privileges' (line 1) and 'restraint' (line 4), with the emphasis on the latter. In stressing the function of the Prioress in regulating meetings involving men, Francisca is implying that female chastity is particularly closely controlled, and the activities of potentially corruptive males rigorously monitored. As, according to Isabella, sexual indulgence is the 'vice that most I do abhor' (II, ii, 29), Francisca's words would seem to confirm Isabella's motive in seeking to join the sisterhood:

Isabella is seeking refuge from a degenerate society that she loathes and fears. Having performed her dramatic purpose in defining Isabella's overriding preoccupation, Francisca withdraws from the play.[15]

The Mendacious Mendicant and the Prudish Postulant

Before we pass from Church to state, we should revisit two principal characters in the play who are closely associated with Franciscan Orders, although neither has made a solemn profession.[16] The Duke spends most of the play in religious garb: after absenting himself from court in the first scene, he assumes the persona of Friar Lodowick to enable him, incognito, to become 'a looker-on here in Vienna' (V, i, 315). Isabella is a postulant to the Poor Clares when first mentioned to the audience by Claudio—

> This day my sister should the cloister enter,
> And there receive her approbation. [I, ii, 167–68]—

and often appears in her novice's habit throughout stage-productions. Isabella, then, might at first be considered to have a vocation, even if (as suggested in Chapter 4 of this study) her spiritual motives sometimes appear suspect; whereas the Duke is donning religious garb not for devotional purposes but to disguise his person and his intentions while pursuing an essentially political agenda.

By transforming into Friar Lodowick, the Duke intends to 'unfold' the 'properties' of Angelo's 'government' (I, i, 3); at

---

[15] Braunmuller (p. 186, n.) refers to an editorial tradition that Francisca should stay on stage until the end of the scene, to be Isabella's chaperone while she is in Lucio's presence.

[16] The roles of the Duke and Isabella have been discussed in detail in Chapters 2 and 4 of this study, but a section devoted to the portrayal of the Church in *Measure for Measure* would be incomplete without a brief reappraisal of the pseudo-Franciscan and the novice Clarisse.

445

least, that is the justification that he gives to his confessor, Friar Thomas:

> And to behold [Angelo's] sway,
> I will, as 'twere a brother of your order,
> Visit both prince and people. [I, iii, 43–5]

This expressed intention, however, is almost as suspect as the persona that the Duke is assuming. Friar Lodowick will never observe Angelo's 'sway' (that is, his rule) by '[v]isit[ing]' the 'prince' (that is, Angelo, who wields the authority of a prince). Until the final judgement-scene, Friar Lodowick and Angelo will never be on stage together, and there is no textual reference to any other meeting between them. Although the Duke, in disguise as Friar Lodowick, will claim to be 'confessor to Angelo' (III, i, 165), this assertion is as unbelievable to the audience as his further contention, in the same speech, that Angelo intended his assault on Isabella as a mere 'assay of her virtue' (III, i, 161–62).

In his guise as Friar Lodowick, the Duke transforms into a Machiavellian. He can indulge in a range of highly dubious practices while concealed from others to preserve his reputation: his alias enables him to 'strike home, / And yet my nature never in the fight / To do in slander' (I, iii, 41–3). Of the seven sacraments of the Catholic Church, he presumptuously intrudes on all but three. Although a true friar might be fully authorised to administer the sacraments, the Duke has taken no solemn vow. In assuming the garb of a friar, he is abusing the sacrament of holy orders. At the end of the play (when he no longer has the need to deceive as he has cast off his hooded disguise), he claims with reference to Mariana, 'I have confess'd her, and I know her virtue' (V, i, 524). Certainly, he appears to offer the same sacrament of reconciliation (i.e. confession) to Julietta in the prison (II, iii, 19–39). He also undertakes to prepare Claudio for death the night before his scheduled execution (III, i, 1–43), and attempts to do likewise for Barnadine (IV, iii, 47–68), intruding on the *viaticum*, the sacrament of the last rites. In addition, he presents himself as an authority on the sacrament of marriage when he persuades Mariana that "'tis no sin' to take Isabella's place in Angelo's bed as 'He is your husband on a pre-contract' (IV, i, 72–3). Vincentio's usurpation of Catholic rites and rituals in pursuit of his own ends might have provoked antipathy among Shakespeare's Protestant contemporaries, who viewed such malpractice as characteristic of the unscrupulous rulers of southern Europe (usually, Italy) so frequently presented as scheming villains in Jacobean drama. Even a modern audience may sympathise with Escalus's condemnation of the disguised Duke in the final scene: too often, Friar Lodowick's speech and actions are 'unreverend and unhallow'd' (V, i, 303).

The Duke permits himself a further liberty in his apparel as a friar: he has licence to lie. His very appearance is the most obvious lie: here is a monarch whose expressed intent is to uncover 'seemers' in the state (I, iii, 54) and yet, to achieve this goal, he becomes a 'seemer' himself by disguising his identity. As Lucio remarks, with unintended irony, 'Cucullus non facit monachum' (V, i, 261)—that is, religious garb does not necessarily signify a devout cleric. After the dreadful confrontation between brother and sister in the prison (III, i, 53–149), Friar Lodowick lies to both. To Claudio, he claims that Angelo has revealed to him in the confessional that the assault on Isabella's virtue was merely a test (III, i, 160–6)—a lie, but one that could be justified as a means of reconciling Claudio to death. To Isabella, to avoid admitting to eavesdropping, he prevaricates about how he has learned of Angelo's intentions (III, i, 183–4). He then persuades Isabella to join him in deceiving Angelo: she is to lie that she will acquiesce to the Deputy's concupiscence (III, i, 243–51). Isabella must suffer a much more hurtful lie when Friar Lodowick falsely informs her that her brother is dead (IV, iii, 114–17). The Duke's motives now seem entirely selfish: to render Isabella emotionally vulnerable so that his ultimate revelation that he has saved Claudio from death will overwhelm her with such gratitude that she will agree to his proposal of marriage. He compounds the offence by claiming that a religious obligation will compel his absence at the time when she will appear publicly to accuse Angelo of criminality. In fact, Friar Lodowick will be present throughout, in propria persona as the Duke. Additionally, when lying or promoting lies, he tends to 'protest too much' the truth of his account, for example by claiming 'every syllable' to be a 'faithful verity' (IV, iii, 126). As the Duke is not a Friar, he should not swear by 'my holy order' (IV, iii, 147)—although, as Touchstone remarks in another of Shakespeare's comedies, 'if you swear by that that is not, you are not forsworn' (*As You Like It*, I, ii, 68–70). Such a defence of the Duke's oaths, however, would itself be worryingly Machiavellian. Certainly, the Duke appears to distance himself from his Machiavellian deviousness by ensuring that the prevarications and lies are practised by his doppelgänger, Friar Lodowick, whose hooded robe he discards at the end of the play as if some magnificent butterfly is sloughing its previous identity as a loathsome caterpillar.

This transformation from seditious friar to merciful saviour is achieved by devious psychological tricks. Friar Lodowick censures the 'absent' Duke for injustice in leaving Angelo, the accused, to preside over his own trial (V, i, 295–301); yet the Duke's justice will be vindicated when Friar Lodowick is transformed before the people into the righteous judge who deposes Angelo (V, i, 354–372). Friar Lodowick's contention that 'The Duke's unjust' (line 298) would therefore seem a way of ensuring, paradoxically, that the people of Vienna will appreciate the Duke's justice, wisdom, and omniscience all the more when his ploy to entrap Angelo is fully revealed. Between these two loci, Friar Lodowick launches a remarkable tirade against the government of Vienna:

> My business in this state
> Made me a looker-on here in Vienna,
> Where I have seen corruption boil and bubble
> Till it o'errun the stew: laws for all faults,
> But faults so countenanc'd that the strong statutes
> Stand like the forfeits in a barber's shop,
> As much in mock as mark. [V, i, 314–20]

The accusation here is not of tyranny or of excessive rigour in the application of the law, which would obviously incriminate Angelo. Rather, the opposite is alleged: that indulgent administration has led to social depravity, the word 'stew' suggesting specifically sexual corruption because of its association with brothels. Angelo's government has cracked down on such debauchery. It was the Duke himself who admitted to having neglected the 'strict statutes and most biting laws', because of which 'all decorum' has gone 'quite athwart' in Vienna (I, iii, 19–31). In raising this issue here, fifty lines before he doffs his disguise and forces a general confession of 'guiltiness' from Angelo (V, i, 365), the Duke employs his alias—Friar Lodowick—to create a scapegoat—Angelo—for his own maladministration. Friar Lodowick's accusation glances from the Duke and lights on his Deputy. The Duke's alias, Friar Lodowick, has done Vincentio's lying and usurpation of the sacraments for him; now Angelo has apparently been obliged to shoulder responsibility for the Duke's earlier maladministration of Vienna. So it is that Duke Vincentio, having purged himself of his various misdeeds, emerges from the Viennese privy smelling of roses. It might be assumed that the people of the city would be deceived by these Machiavellian devices, perhaps offering 'loud applause and *Aves* vehement' (I, i, 70) at the conclusion of the Duke's final speech; but an audience is likely to be left with a profound sense of disquiet. If, in addition, the Duke wins the hand of Isabella whom he, as Friar Lodowick, has so shamelessly manipulated and deceived, that disquiet might intensify.

Chapter 4 of this study proposed (pp. 235-236 and 244-245) that the convent is presented as a place of refuge for Isabella from the debauchery that has flourished in Vienna under the Duke's rule. The good offices of the Prioress would ensure that, in the convent, she would not be subjected to any indecent advances from morally dubious men. In withdrawing from male society and in seeking 'a more strict restraint' than even the Poor Clares—the most stringent of the female orders of nuns— could demand of her, Isabella is protecting the treasure of her body, her chastity. This is clearly implied in her speech to

Angelo beginning, 'There is a vice that most I do abhor' (II, ii, 29–33). The 'vice' that she is too distressed to name is illicit sexual intercourse (or perhaps any kind of sexual intercourse), the offence for which her brother has been arrested. The worst that she could think is that Claudio has committed fornication—although her brother stoutly maintains that it is the consummation of a 'true contract' that has confirmed Julietta as 'fast my wife' (I, ii, 134–36). Isabella nevertheless 'most desire[s]' that Claudio's offence—at worst, venial—should 'meet the blow of justice' (II, ii, 30), apparently endorsing Angelo's sentence of death on her brother. Even the Old Law does not prescribe death for Claudio's offence, which is neither adultery nor incest but merely indulgence in consensual heterosexual activity. Isabella, the postulant, shows little Christian compassion or mercy in the first half of the play. Rather, she is as ruthlessly doctrinaire as her dramatic counterpart, the puritanical Angelo.

It is true that chastity is a highly-esteemed Christian virtue, especially in the Catholic Church with its veneration of the Virgin Mary; but when pursued regardless of the cost to others (including the closest of relations), jealously guarding one's chastity may distort into a selfish quest for personal salvation. This is the accusation that Angelo directs against Isabella when he asks, 'Were you not then as cruel as the sentence / That you have slander'd so?' (II, iv, 109–10), 'the sentence' being Angelo's judgement on Claudio. Just as a vice, performed for a charitable end, can be transformed into a virtue,[17] so a virtue, pushed beyond a certain critical point, may abruptly distort into a vice. Isabella passes this point in the prison-scene with Claudio, when she violently condemns her brother to execution by torture (III, i, 135–49), Angelo's sentence should Isabella refuse his sexual advances (II, iv, 162–6). Claudio has dared to beg Isabella to save him by agreeing to the Deputy's demand for her virginity. In so doing, Claudio has been transformed, in her eyes, from a beloved brother into a 'faithless coward', a

---

[17] Compare Angelo's words at II, iv, 63–4, with Claudio's identical sentiments at III, i, 133–5.

'dishonest wretch', a 'warped slip of wilderness' (that is, a bastard) guilty of 'a kind of incest' in requesting his sister to surrender her chastity. Isabella's refusal to comply with Claudio's plea is neither restrained nor reasoned, but rather panic-stricken. Hysteria is detectable in her cruel imprecation ('Take my defiance, / Die, perish!' [III, i, 142–3]), her malicious pledge ('I'll pray a thousand prayers for thy death; / No word to save thee' [III, i, 145–6]), and her callous conclusion ('"Tis best that thou diest quickly' [III, i, 150]). Compassion and forgiveness have been eclipsed by the terror of contemplating the deed that 'I abhor to name' (III, i, 101).

In fact, it is questionable whether Isabella shows any signs of such indispensable Christian virtues as compassion and forgiveness before the final scene of the play—and then not until she (grudgingly?) kneels to repay her debt to Mariana by pleading for Angelo's life to be spared. Even before Claudio's entreaty for her to sacrifice her virginity to save his life, she had shown little sympathy for her brother's predicament in her exchanges with Lucio, with Angelo, and even with Claudio himself—and certainly no inclination to offer him forgiveness, even when pleading for his sentence to be commuted. When she believes that Angelo has executed her brother, her immediate instinct is not Christian forbearance but bloody revenge on the Deputy: she 'will to him and pluck out his eyes' (IV, iii, 119). Her responses are entirely human, but scarcely virtuous.

Isabella's words do not suggest that she has unstintingly devoted herself to the demands of the religious life. Religion seems a protective garb to Isabella rather than a vocation founded on spiritual devotion. Although she is a postulant proposing entry to a nunnery, references to God, the Church, and the Christian faith are surprisingly infrequent in her conversation.[18] Her second interview with Angelo contains

---

[18] In her first interview with Angelo, she cites God and heaven (II, ii, 74–7 and 86–8), but the references are ephemeral, and she quickly switches to a classical deity, Jove and his thunderbolts (II, ii, 111–18). She does seem to believe in the efficacy of 'true prayers' when she

references to the soul, but they are always references to *her* soul (II, iv, 56 and 65) that she is not willing to jeopardise when it is inextricably associated with her virginity:

> Better it were a brother died at once,
> Than that a sister, by redeeming him,
> Should die for ever. [II, iv,106–8]

Isabella seeks refuge in the authority of such complacent maxims whenever her chastity is threatened, as confirmed in her one soliloquy when she utters the glib couplet,

> Then, Isabel live chaste, and brother, die:
> More than our brother is our chastity. [II, iv, 183–4]

No comfort here for Claudio, then, but plenty for Isabella. Religion is providing her with the pretext for preserving her virginity at the expense of her brother's life.

However, when religion provides her with the pretext for offering another woman's virginity to save her brother's life, the 'vice that most I do abhor' (II, ii, 29) is miraculously transformed into an 'image' that 'gives me content' (III, i, 260). The Duke (in the guise of Friar Lodowick and therefore apparently a figure of religious authority to whom Isabella may defer) has devised the 'bed-trick'. This will enable Mariana in disguise—rather than Isabella herself—to yield to Angelo's sexual desires. Isabella can endorse such a plan because *her* virginity will no longer be under threat. Much more than passive acquiescence is required from Isabella, however: she is to be employed to persuade Mariana to undertake what Isabella now euphemistically calls 'the enterprise' (IV, i, 66), as if sexual activity with Angelo has become some noble quest

---

promises that she and the sisterhood will intercede to heaven were Angelo to show mercy (II, ii, 152–6; and later at II, iv, 69–73); but the act of pious supplication is distorted into a malicious threat when she exclaims to her brother, 'I'll pray a thousand prayers for thy death; / No word to save thee' (III, i, 145–6).

rather than the squalid transaction that he demanded. An audience might even conclude that Isabella's persuasive powers, first endorsed by her brother (I, ii, 174–6) and then witnessed in her great debates with Angelo (II, ii and II, iv), would be heightened by this later context when Isabella, in pleading with another woman to take her place (IV, i, 51–70), is securing her own virginity.[19]

Even in the final scene, when she appears before the newly-returned Duke, Isabella's veracity and piety are called into question. Previously, she expressed a reluctance to 'speak so indirectly' (IV, vi, 1) but, having been reassured that her equivocations have the endorsement of a friar (IV, vi, 3–4), she proves to be as adept with weasel words as Friar Lodowick himself when she presents her case against Angelo (V, i, 20–128). Subsequently, despite her debt of gratitude to Mariana, she remains unresponsive while Mariana pleads desperately for Isabella to join the petition to save Angelo's life (V, i, 428–30, 434–6, and 440). Although compassion and forgiveness do not come easily to this novice nun, eventually she takes Mariana's part. Her speech, however, suggests that her moral perspicacity is distorted by self-interest. In seeking to distinguish between Angelo and her brother whom she believes executed for fornication, she claims that Claudio 'did the thing for which he died' (V, i, 447), whereas Angelo can be spared as 'His act did not o'ertake his bad intent' (V, i, 450). In fact, Angelo's 'act' was identical to Claudio's: both took a woman's virginity in potential defiance of the law; however, as in Angelo's case it was Mariana's and not Isabella's virginity that was taken, Isabella conveniently seems able entirely to overlook the matter.

---

[19] Granted, the fact that Isabella is a novice nun is insufficient to persuade Mariana that the proposed exchange has the authority of the Church. It is Friar Lodowick who must provide the religious sanction: 'She'll take the enterprise upon her, father, / If *you* endorse it' (IV, i, 66–7; italics added).

Finally, the novice has a choice to make: bride of Christ or bride of the Duke. Although the Duke proposes to her twice (V, i, 489–91 and 531–34), she remains silent. Her silence may indicate any response in the range between eager acceptance and shocked refusal. Certainly, the Duke's half-line 'but fitter time for that' with which his first proposal concludes (V, i, 491) suggests that he has encountered an initial rebuttal; but the 'old' Duke then confirms an important affinity with the young novice. Vincentio is prepared to forgive Lucio his 'slanders . . . and therewithal / Remit [his] other forfeits' (V, i, 517–18), provided that he make restitution by marrying Mistress Kate Keep-down, the mother of his illegitimate child (V, i, 516). In addition, Claudio must 'restore' her whom he 'wrong'd', by formally marrying Julietta, the mother of his child whose legitimacy is disputed (V, i, 522); while Angelo must 'love' Mariana whom he had once cruelly slandered and deserted but whom he has now married (V, i, 523–4). The Duke is regulating the sexual behaviour of culpable males in Vienna by the imposition of marriage. This was precisely the remedy that Isabella, on her first appearance, had spontaneously proposed to redeem her brother from his penalty under the statutes against fornication: 'O, let him marry her!' (I, iv, 49). As the Duke and the novice are now seen to be fully in agreement that what legitimises sexual activity is marriage—and as her vocation for the cloister has never seemed entirely convincing—there is at least the possibility that Isabella could accept Vincentio's proffered hand without creating a gross dramatic implausibility. The mendacious mendicant and the prudish postulant might become man and wife with a reasonable prospect of future concord if Vincentio and Isabella were able to discard, with their religious identity, those distasteful qualities that previously might have rendered them inimical.

Law and Order

Consideration of the Duke's dubious moral status leads us inevitably to scrutinize the territory of government. He is not the only representative of law and order in *Measure for Measure* who is seriously flawed. The fallibility of the agents of secular authority, however, does not necessarily invalidate the legal system that they serve:

> The jury passing on the prisoner's life
> May in the sworn twelve have a thief, or two,
> Guiltier than him they try. What's open made to justice,
> That justice seizes. What knows the laws
> That thieves do pass on thieves? [II, i, 19–23]

The argument is undeniable, even though it is spoken by Angelo (before his 'fall' clouded his judgement). In his exchanges with Isabella, he also defends his policy of sentencing offenders to the full extent of the law. It is, paradoxically, an act of pity:

> I show [pity] most of all when I show justice;
> For then I pity those I do not know,
> Which a dismiss'd offence would after gall,
> And do him right that, answering one foul wrong,
> Lives not to act another. [II, ii, 101–5]

Were legitimate punishment to be 'dismiss'd', that leniency would encourage the 'offence' to be repeated, motivating new criminals and creating new victims. Furthermore, when removed from society by the law, the criminal cannot reoffend. The conundrum of law and order in *Measure for Measure* is cleverly conveyed when these incontrovertible observations about enforcing the law are expressed by a magistrate who offends against the very laws that he is enforcing.

Other than the Duke and Angelo, whose conduct in government is discussed in the second and third chapters of this study, the officials of the state comprise seven speaking roles: a servant, a messenger, an anonymous Justice, Escalus, the Provost, Elbow, and Abhorson. The first three of these dramatis personae may be dealt with summarily, as each is a functionary who makes the briefest of contributions. Angelo's servant addresses the Provost at the beginning of Act II, scene ii, later reappearing twice to announce the arrival of Isabella to discuss

Angelo's verdict on her brother (II, ii, 18–19 and II, iv,18). The messenger (who may be this same servant, as he is described as 'his lordship's man' at IV, ii, 98) delivers to the Provost Angelo's note confirming Claudio's death-sentence, with a stern warning that the stipulations must be followed to the letter (IV, ii, 100–4). The Justice is a silent observer of the hearing involving Elbow, Pompey, and Froth. He speaks a mere ten words at the end of the scene, graciously accepting Escalus's invitation to dine and—as if to ingratiate himself with Escalus—commenting adversely on Angelo's sentence on Claudio (II, i, 279). His function is to elicit from Escalus an acknowledgement that Angelo's severity is 'needful' as a deterrent.

Of the other roles, Escalus and the Provost are comparable, as both sympathise with the plight of Claudio. They contrast with Angelo, who remains obdurately committed to executing the prisoner. In addition, Escalus and the Provost generally show integrity and efficiency in their pursuit of justice. In this respect, they contrast with Elbow and Abhorson, grotesque characters who, as minor officers of the law, invite ridicule rather than respect.

The Integrity of Escalus

In several important respects, Escalus resembles Polonius in *Hamlet*. It is tempting to postulate that Shakespeare wrote the two roles for the same actor. Both Escalus and Polonius are trusted, aged, senior courtiers, well-versed in affairs of state and esteemed by their sovereigns. Like Polonius, Escalus enjoys displaying his verbal wit: both persist with their puns and word-play even when it is apparent that they may be either inappropriate or unappreciated by those to whom they are directed. Unlike Polonius, however, Escalus is not a perpetual object of ridicule for being prolix, sententious, sycophantic, devious, meddling, or absent-minded. Until the final scene of *Measure for Measure*, 'Old Escalus' (I, i, 45) is associated with moderation, wisdom, and scrupulousness in his administration of the law. His name, E*scal*us may even incorporate a pun to suggest that he is an embodiment of the *scal*es of justice. In the final scene of the play, however, his dramatic purpose changes, perhaps at the expense of some consistency in his characterisation.

The Duke introduces Escalus to the audience as the epitome of good government:

> Of government the properties to unfold
> Would seem in me t'affect speech and discourse,
> Since I am put to know that your own science
> Exceeds, in that, the lists of all advice
> My strength can give you. Then no more remains
> But that, to your sufficiency, as your worth is able,
> And let them work. The nature of our people,
> Our city's institutions, and the terms
> For common justice, y'are as pregnant in
> As art and practice hath enriched any
> That we remember. [I, i, 3–13]

This speech, the Duke's elaborate compliment to his senior courtier, explains that it would be pretentious for Vincentio to lecture Escalus on the 'properties' of 'government' as the Duke's 'advice', however detailed and wide-ranging, could not match the extent of Escalus's knowledge (lines 3–7). Although Vincentio's next comment is cryptic (almost certainly, the text is corrupt), the general sense appears to be that the Duke's commission, giving Escalus new powers, should work for the benefit of Vienna when combined with the talents that Escalus has already displayed (lines 7–9). Finally, the Duke acknowledges Escalus's skills and experience in dealing with Vienna's society, civil establishments, and legal system: in the theory and practice of such matters, Vincentio can recall no predecessor at court who has surpassed Escalus.

Escalus receives his commission and is instructed to follow it meticulously (I, i, 13–14); but, before he can study its content, the Duke imparts two pieces of information, either or both of which might apparently come to Escalus as a profound

457

shock. He learns that the sovereign who so appreciates his talents is to quit the court, and that, despite all the praise that has been lavished upon him, he is to be subordinate to Angelo, another courtier, during the Duke's absence (lines 14–21). There may be a suspicion that Escalus's obedience and patience, in addition to his judgement of Angelo's character, are being tested here: having announced his plan, the Duke asks for Escalus's opinion—'What think you of it?' (line 21)—as if closely observing his courtier's response. Escalus's reply is a masterpiece of concision and tact, entirely appropriate to a courtier of his formidable experience:

> If any in Vienna be of worth
> To undergo such ample grace and honour,
> It is Lord Angelo. [I, i, 22–4]

Escalus does not overtly question the Duke's decision here and seems to endorse the choice of Angelo as the Duke's worthy Deputy. There is no obvious evidence in the words either of disappointment or of disapproval on Escalus's part; and yet the conditional clause with which his response begins suggests a sub-text of doubt in the wisdom of the Duke's strategy, subtly raising the question of whether '*any* in Vienna' could indeed be worthy to assume the 'grace and honour' that the Duke proposes to bestow on Angelo. General approval of Angelo does not presuppose specific approval of the Duke's strategy to quit Vienna while appointing Angelo in his place. On that latter issue, Escalus remains diplomatically silent.

In his initial dealings with Angelo, Escalus is both professional and respectful. Addressing Angelo as 'your honour' and obediently pledging to 'wait upon' him, Escalus requests an audience with the newly-appointed Deputy to establish his own duties and responsibilities under Angelo's forthcoming regime (I, i, 76–83). In response, Angelo modestly treats Escalus with the respect due to an equal partner:

> Let us withdraw together,
> And we may soon our satisfaction have

Touching that point. [I, i, 81–3]

At the end of this first scene, all seems equality and concord between the two magistrates; however, the new hierarchy, with Angelo in the ascendant, will have been firmly established by the time that they reappear at the start of Act II.

From that point until the end of the play, the two courtiers will be the dramatic means by which Shakespeare develops the debate on government and law that is fundamental to *Measure for Measure*. Angelo, who argues for severity and uncompromising justice, will be the advocate of 'zero tolerance'; while Escalus, generally the voice of pragmatism and moderation, will be the proponent of mercy. For Angelo, the law must be rigorously and consistently enforced if it is to be an effective deterrent (II, i, 1–4). For Escalus, the law should be used as a precise surgical instrument to remove what causes offence, rather than as a blunt, heavy weapon to be employed indiscriminately:

> Let us be keen, and rather cut a little,
> Than f[e]ll, and bruise to death. [II, i, 5–6]

The two doctrines being incompatible, Angelo's prevails in the debate, as his commission from the Duke gives him greater power than that bestowed on Escalus.

The specific issue that most clearly divides the two justices is the sentence of death imposed on Claudio. Although Escalus pleads mitigating circumstances, Angelo refuses any compromise on sentencing under the statutes regulating sexual activity. Escalus, however, in proposing a hypothetical situation in which Angelo himself might have succumbed to temptation, prophesies accurately that Angelo's severe judgement on others' vice may ultimately condemn Angelo himself:

> Let but your honour know—
> Whom I believe to be most straight in virtue—
> That in the working of your own affections,

Had time coher'd with place, or place with wishing,
Or that the resolute acting of your blood
Could have attain'd th'effect of your own purpose,
Whether you had not sometime in your life
Err'd in this point, which now you censure him,
And pull'd the law upon you. [II, i, 8–16]

At this juncture, an audience may recall the Duke's praise for Escalus's knowledge of the 'nature of our people' (I, i, 9): Escalus, a shrewd judge of human behaviour, here dramatically anticipates Angelo's nemesis. When 'time' and 'place' correspond with Angelo's 'wishing', and when his 'affections' incite 'the resolute acting of [his] blood', Angelo will indeed '[e]rr' in the same 'point' for which he now 'censure[s]' Claudio. With proleptic irony, this speech from Escalus leads Angelo to condemn himself in advance of his offence:

When I that censure [Claudio] do so offend,
Let mine own judgement pattern out my death,
And nothing come in partial. [II, i, 29–31]

Although inferior to Angelo in power, Escalus proves shrewder than his superior in foresight.

Escalus as Magistrate

In dealing with the everyday administration of the law, Escalus is also shown to be more practical and patient than Angelo. Escalus's sense of humour proves important when he is dealing with a tedious case, incompetently presented by Elbow. His ironic chuckle to Angelo—'This comes off well: here's a wise officer'—is greeted with a stony 'Go to' from the humourless Deputy (II, i, 56–7), while his later, light-hearted attempt to incite amusement in his sour colleague—'Do you hear how he misplaces?'—passes coldly unacknowledged by Angelo (line 87). In fact, Angelo appears to have fallen into a petulant silence in which he relies on Escalus to conduct the enquiry, unassisted, for over seventy lines. Angelo's patience finally snaps when he storms off stage, 'Hoping you'll find good cause to whip them all' (II, i, 136). Fortunately for Froth and Pompey, however, Escalus is more good-natured and imperturbable than his fellow justice, and certainly less likely to give an ill-founded sentence based on a premature verdict.

This is not to say that Escalus is presented as a lenient magistrate in this first trial-scene (II, i, 41–253). He proves sharp with Pompey when the pimp is obviously prevaricating (e.g. lines 95 and 115–17) and appears somewhat exasperated when Elbow, the constable, proves less comprehensible than those whom he has arrested (II, i, 169). Unlike Angelo, however, Escalus can maintain amiability and a sense of humour in his dealings. While Elbow's malapropisms, Pompey's innuendos, and Froth's inanities are the principal sources of comic humour in this scene, Escalus contributes with witticism further to lighten proceedings. When Elbow confuses his legal terms, threatening Pompey's slanders with an 'action of battery', Escalus promptly quips, 'If he took you a box o'th'ear, you might have your action of slander too' (lines 176–8). Irony, though, is sometimes too refined a weapon, and the audience may laugh less at Escalus's witticism here than at Elbow's inappropriately grateful response (line 179): the constable is blissfully unaware of Escalus's sarcasm at his expense. In response to Pompey's persistent innuendos, Escalus adopts coarser humour when dealing with the pimp's name: 'Troth, and your bum is the greatest thing about you; so that, in the beastliest sense, you are Pompey the Great' (lines 214–16). There is certainly no subtlety here, even though there is an attempt to redeem the crude comment with an erudite reference. Again, the remark may be lost on the recipient, as Pompey does not acknowledge the jibe.

Although he shows some sparks that are like wit, Escalus's success as a comedian is in doubt: there is no evidence that his humour, either frivolous or erudite, provokes so much as a smile from anyone else on stage in this scene. The only indication that one of his witticisms has been acknowledged is when it is echoed by Froth. Escalus's final warning to Froth is avuncular in tone, balancing levity with severity:

461

Come hither to me, Master Froth. Master Froth, I would not have you acquainted with tapsters; they will draw you, Master Froth, and you will hang them. Get you gone, and let me hear no more of you. [II, i, 200–4]

The darker humour in this address lies in the word 'draw': while playing on 'drawer', another name for a tapster, it combines with 'hang' to allude to a particularly brutal form of capital punishment. Froth has been warned: if he persists in his current course, he could force the law to exact an extreme penalty from him and his associates. Froth, however, is a simpleton, and the dire warning seems ineffectual as, when he departs, he merely parrots Escalus's pun (II, i, 205–7).

Escalus's tone is more peremptory but still generally restrained when he dismisses Pompey:

. . . hark you: I advise you, let me not find you before me again upon any complaint whatsoever; no, not for dwelling where you do. If I do, Pompey, I shall beat you to your tent, and prove a shrewd Caesar to you: in plain dealing, Pompey, I shall have you whipped. So, for this time, Pompey, fare you well. [II, i, 242–8]

The erudite wit returns in the reference to Julius Caesar's defeat of Pompey the Great at the Battle of Pharsalus (48 BC), but here it does little to ameliorate the threat of punishment: 'I shall have you whipped' remains both stern and specific. The prospect of what was a standard punishment in Jacobean England for lewd conduct has, however, no deterrent effect on Pompey, who shrugs off the threat (II, i, 250–3). Escalus has been moderate and just in his dealings with the two offenders, Froth and Pompey, but it seems that his warnings will go unheeded by both. Their last words before departure suggest that each will quickly re-offend, confirmed when Pompey is imprisoned in the next act (III, ii, 1ff.). Although the circumstances may suggest that Angelo's impatient advice to 'whip them all' (II, i, 136) might have proved a more effective deterrent than Escalus's avuncular warnings, summary punishment of Froth and Pompey would not have been just when the guilt of the accused pair could not be proven. Paradoxically, Escalus seems to respect the letter of the law more than his uncompromising superior has done.

Even when contemplating the case of Claudio, Escalus grudgingly acknowledges that leniency, if offered too freely, merely encourages malefactors to persist in their ways. When the anonymous justice comments that 'Lord Angelo is severe' in Claudio's case, implicitly expecting agreement, Escalus promptly responds, 'It is but needful' (II, i, 279). He clarifies his meaning with a gnomic couplet:

> Mercy is not itself, that oft looks so;
> Pardon is still the nurse of second woe. [II, i, 280–1]

Although Escalus wishes to save Claudio from his sentence, he recognises that mercy in Claudio's case might create a precedent, encouraging similar offences in others. The couplet establishes a consensus between Escalus and Angelo: strict punishment deters crime; excessive clemency promotes crime.[20] Both justices recognise punishment as a purgative for the vices of society, but only Escalus feels compassion for those who must suffer unduly as a result: 'But yet, poor Claudio!' (II, i, 282).

Escalus's genial and tactful approach does seem to bring success in the case of Elbow, however. As the constable's ineptitude clearly obstructs justice, Escalus cannot allow his employment by the parish to continue. Out of regard for

---

[20] In the next scene, Angelo will argue to Isabella that '[t]hose many' who now offend would not have done so 'If the first that did th'edict infringe / Had answer'd for his deed' (II, ii, 92–94). Duke Vincentio concurs: having ignored the 'strict' statutes' for 'fourteen years', he appears to have learned that 'the rod / Becomes more mock'd than fear'd' if employed merely 'For terror, not to use', resulting in a society where 'quite athwart / Goes all decorum' (I, iii, 20–31).

Elbow's good intentions and simplicity, however, Escalus does not summarily dismiss him from service, but rather flatters him that he has served so loyally for so long that he is now being exploited by those who continue to employ him:

> I thought, by the readiness in the office, you had continued in it some time.—You say seven years together? . . . Alas, it has been great pains to you: they do you wrong to put you so oft upon't. Are there not men in your ward sufficient to serve it? . . . Look you bring me in the names of some six or seven, the most sufficient of your parish. . . . To my house. Fare you well. [II, i, 258–72]

Escalus thus diplomatically engages Elbow to be the instrument of his own discharge from service. In another context and involving a different victim, such a strategy might have aroused misgivings in the audience about Escalus's conduct; but here, Elbow's eager compliance and obvious incompetence make the situation merely comic. Escalus's subtlety has succeeded where the blunter approach associated with Angelo might have caused distress to the hapless constable.[21]

Act II is entirely devoted to issues of clemency and stringency. Each of the four scenes is dominated by one of the three principal characters responsible for administering law and government (Escalus, Angelo, and the Duke). The standard is set in the first scene, where Escalus's interpretation of the law is characterised by moderation and conscientiousness: he tempers severity with urbanity and good humour. In stark contrast, in the second scene, Angelo appears ruthless and dour in his application of the statutes to condemn Claudio. In the third scene, the Duke's first attempt as Friar Lodowick to hear confession seems unduly pedantic and unsympathetic towards Julietta. Finally, Angelo's interpretation of the law is discredited by association in the fourth scene when he perverts justice in attempting to satisfy his sexual desire. Of the three

---

[21] Cf. II, ii, 13–14, where Angelo coldly threatens the Provost with dismissal.

principal arbiters of the law who are presented in Act II, the audience is likely to recognise Escalus as the most benign and judicious.

Escalus, who appears in one scene in each of the next two acts, remains conscientious in his judgement and stable in a crisis. He condemns Mistress Overdone to prison only after 'Double and treble admonition', declaring that her persistent offending would 'make mercy swear and play the tyrant' (III, ii, 187–8).[22] His earlier recognition that 'Pardon is still the nurse of second woe' (II, i, 281) is here confirmed, as previously lenient treatment under the law has not dissuaded her from practising as a 'bawd of eleven years' continuance' (III, ii, 190). Her desperate attempts to transfer blame to Lucio and to flatter Escalus by referring to his reputation for tolerance— 'Your honour is accounted a merciful man' (lines 185–6)—are bluntly rebuffed: 'That fellow is a fellow of much licence. Let him be called before us. Away with her to prison.—Go to, no more words' (lines 198–200). Escalus's verdict is composed and decisive.

When questioned by Friar Lodowick about the Duke's reputation, Escalus characterises Vincentio as seeking self-knowledge and practising restraint, 'A gentleman of all temperance' (III, ii, 231). It is tempting to regard Escalus's description of the Duke's virtues in the same way as Lucio's slanders against the Duke: that their accounts reveal rather more about themselves than they do about Vincentio. As Lucio's portrait of the Duke as 'One of all luxury, an ass, a madman' (V, i, 499) more obviously defines Lucio himself than Vincentio, so Escalus's praise for the Duke's conscientious self-scrutiny, altruism, and moderation celebrates the qualities most apparent in Escalus himself:

---

[22] Ironically, this is the very effect that friar Lodowick's 'slander to the state' will have on Escalus in the final scene of the play: Escalus will abandon mercy and 'play the tyrant' in condemning the 'unreverend and unhallow'd friar' to the rack.

One that, above all other strifes, contended especially to know himself. . . . Rather rejoicing to see another merry, than merry at anything which professed to make him rejoice. A gentleman of all temperance. [III, ii, 226–30]

In addition, Escalus's support for Claudio's cause never wavers. Unlike Angelo, Escalus can distinguish morally and legally between the offences of 'A bawd of eleven years' continuance' and a young man in a faithful and loving relationship. When he meets Friar Lodowick, Escalus is eager to know 'how you find Claudio prepared' (III, ii, 233–4) as he is apparently concerned with the state of the prisoner's soul on the eve of his execution. On learning that Claudio is penitent and has been reconciled to death by Friar Lodowick, Escalus responds,

You have paid the heavens your function, and the prisoner the very debt of your calling. I have laboured for the poor gentleman to the extremest shore of my modesty, but my brother-justice have I found so severe that he hath forced me to tell him he is indeed Justice. . . . I am going to visit the prisoner; fare you well. [III, ii, 243–52]

This is quintessential Escalus: quick to praise virtuous conduct; courageous in the defence of justice; compassionate towards the oppressed; and courteous, even to apparent social inferiors such as a begging-friar. He has persistently petitioned Angelo on Claudio's behalf, but to no avail. If he cannot save Claudio's life in this world, he will labour to save his soul in the afterlife—hence his gratitude for Friar Lodowick's good offices and his own resolve to comfort Claudio with a prison-visit.

When news of the Duke's imminent return breaks, the responses of Angelo and Escalus are clearly contrasted. Both are puzzled by the Duke's contradictory messages, but it is Angelo who appears threatened by the instructions to hand over authority in public and to invite any who have suffered injustice to publish their petitions in the street (IV, iv, 1–9). Escalus remains calm while explaining to the anxious Angelo that the Duke has conveyed his motives in his letters:

> He shows his reasons for that: to have a dispatch of complaints, and to deliver us from devices hereafter, which shall then have no power to stand against us. [IV, iv, 10–12]

Shakespeare is illustrating the confusion that stems from guilt, presenting Angelo as fearful of Isabella's threat at their last meeting: 'I will proclaim thee, Angelo, look for't' (II, iv, 150). By contrast, Escalus, with a clear conscience, does not question the Duke's instructions. The actor portraying Escalus might, however, look quizzically at Angelo as he utters the speech above, for Escalus is stating the obvious to a man previously 'so learned and so wise' (V, i, 468) in affairs of state. On Escalus's departure, Angelo must acknowledge that his crimes against Isabella and her brother have rendered him 'unpregnant / And dull to all proceedings' (IV, iv, 18–19). Escalus proves his moral and professional superiority by retaining his equanimity and perspicacity under pressure.

Escalus's Aberration

There is, however, a problematical change in the presentation of Escalus in the final scene. On the Duke's return, the courtier who has been so conscientious in challenging authority where appropriate, tactfully speaking truth to power throughout the play, seems to suffer a lapse of judgement and to lose his composure in a crisis when dealing with the affair of Friar Lodowick. If we presuppose coherent characterisation from Shakespeare, we might ascribe this change in Escalus partly to his appointed role as prosecutor and partly to his loyalty and deference to the Duke, who has seemingly already condemned the friar and his associates. A plausible alternative, however, is that Escalus's transformation should be attributed to a change in his dramatic purpose. Before Act V, scene i, Escalus's primary function was to present a moderate alternative to Angelo's severity in administering the law. As the Duke is to take over that function in this final scene of *Measure for Measure*, Escalus must vacate the position, unless he is to diminish Vincentio's dramatic status on the Duke's resumption of supreme power in Vienna. It is the Duke who must restore composure, order, and justice after Escalus's incensed and arbitrary condemnation of Friar Peter, Isabella, Mariana, and (particularly) Friar Lodowick.

At the beginning of the final scene, both justices—Angelo and Escalus—are greeted warmly and offered 'public thanks' (V, i, 7) by the Duke on his return. Escalus, the Duke's 'old and faithful friend' (line 2), is invited to take the Duke's hand (lines 14–18): he and Angelo receive the honour of acting as 'good supporters' (line 19) for the Duke's triumphant return to Vienna. Escalus, however, must defer to the two senior justices throughout the appeals of Isabella, Friar Peter, and Mariana, remaining silent while the Duke occupies the judgement-seat and Angelo becomes the defendant (lines 20–244).

When the Duke announces his intention to withdraw, however, Escalus again becomes active. As Angelo now sits as judge in his own case, Escalus assumes the role of prosecuting counsel at the Duke's behest:

> You, Lord Escalus,
> Sit with my cousin; lend him your kind pains
> To find out this abuse, whence 'tis derived. [V, i, 244–6]

The Duke, however, appears already to have passed judgement on the complainants against Angelo: the court should 'punish' the 'foolish friar' (Friar Peter) and the 'pernicious woman' (Mariana) who is '[c]ompact with her that's gone' (Isabella), as they have been 'set . . . on' by 'another friar' (Friar Lodowick) to practise 'this abuse' (lines 239–47). The previously scrupulous Escalus seemingly adopts the Duke's judgement and presupposes the guilt of Angelo's accusers, particularly Friar Lodowick—but then, as prosecutor, it would be his function in court to denounce the accused rather than to plead on their behalf. Accordingly, the usually astute Escalus appears to be deceived by Lucio's slanders, expecting Friar Lodowick to prove 'a notable fellow' (lines 265–6), that is, a rogue. It may also be to Escalus's discredit that he becomes a stooge for Lucio's bawdy innuendos when he speaks of how he will 'handle' Isabella in interrogation (line 271) and when he proposes to 'go darkly to work with her' (line 277)—both remarks prompting smutty puns from Lucio, ever alert to double entendres.

On confronting an impenitent and forthright Friar Lodowick, Escalus appears oblivious to their previous meeting (III, ii, 206–53), when he treated this same friar with gratitude and praise. In this final scene, Escalus first appears shocked by the friar's lack of respect for the court (line 289), then authoritative when threatening to unleash the Duke's power (lines 293–94), and finally incensed by the Friar's accusations against the Duke and his Deputy:

> Why, thou unreverend and unhallow'd friar!
> Is't not enough thou hast suborn'd these women
> To accuse this worthy man, but in foul mouth,
> And in the witness of his proper ear,
> To call him villain? And then to glance from him
> To th'Duke himself, to tax him with injustice?
> Take him hence! To th'rack with him!—We'll touse you
> Joint by joint, but we will know his purpose.
> What! Unjust! [V, i, 304–11]

In his moral outrage as prosecuting counsel, Escalus appears to have lost his self-control, as is shown by the staccato exclamations; but with it, he would seem to have lost so many of the admirable qualities previously portrayed in him, including his moderation and his good judgement. Although Shakespeare's contemporaries, more accustomed to the brutal exigencies of the law, might have found Escalus's threat to impose dire torture on Friar Lodowick less disquieting than a modern audience is likely to do, Escalus seems to have pre-judged the vital issues that are being tried before the court. According to Escalus, Friar Lodowick has 'suborn'd' Isabella and Mariana (that is, induced them to perjure themselves) to accuse the 'worthy man', Angelo, of being a 'villain'. Moreover, to Escalus's indignation, Friar Lodowick has censured the Duke himself for the 'injustice' of allowing the accused to preside at his own trial.

When Escalus employs Lucio to interrogate the friar, Lucio rather than the friar is believed, even though Lucio merely continues to attribute his own slanders of the Duke to Friar Lodowick. The friar's denials lead to Escalus's final outburst:

> Such a fellow is not to be talked withal. Away with him to prison! Where is the Provost? Away with him to prison! Lay bolts enough upon him: let him speak no more. Away with those giglets too, and with the other confederate companion!
>
> [V, i, 342–6]

Well-nigh inarticulate with rage, Escalus appears to have lost all restraint, discrimination, and sense of justice. Four righteous accusers (the 'giglets' are Isabella and Mariana) are to be thrown into prison while the bearer of false witness (Lucio) prevails and the guilty defendant (Angelo) remains unpunished, his reputation untarnished. Escalus has abandoned the role of impartial arbiter just as surely as the Duke will almost immediately assume it—once he has cast off his mendicant garb seven lines later. Although the Duke's restoration of order and justice will be dramatically satisfying to the audience, it seems to be achieved at the expense of consistency in the characterisation of Escalus, who has entirely abandoned his previously diplomatic, restrained manner, degenerating into ranting in which he out-Herods Herod.

Escalus's tirade is, however, thematically consistent: *Measure for Measure* is a play which illustrates that the assertions of those in authority, when set against the testimonies of lesser mortals, will always be believed. The Duke has condemned Friar Lodowick in advance of his appearance before the court. Angelo has alleged a conspiracy against him, masterminded by 'some more mightier member' such as this same Friar Lodowick. Escalus might plausibly be predisposed, because of his belief in the veracity of his two senior colleagues in law, to condemn the friar. Like Angelo, Escalus encounters, during legal proceedings, a situation that transforms his former personality. Escalus's misjudgement illustrates the force of Angelo's sneer when Isabella threatened to testify against him: 'Who will believe thee, Isabel?' (II, iv, 153). As Angelo perceived in his second soliloquy,

> O place, O form,
> How often dost thou with thy case, thy habit,
> . . . tie the wiser souls
> To thy false seeming! [II, iv, 12–15]

Even Escalus, prominent among the 'wiser souls' of Vienna, appears to have been swayed by rank ('place'), dignity ('form'), and the plausibility of those in authority who practise 'seeming' under the guise of dignified outward appearance and dress ('case' and 'habit'). Such is the power of prejudice.

The Duke, however, promptly absolves Escalus from blame for the harsh condemnation of Friar Lodowick and his associates:

> What you have spoke, I pardon: sit you down. [V, i, 360]

Having served his immediate purpose of acting as an enraged foil to offset the Duke's equanimity, Escalus can now revert to his former measured, judicious language as he ruefully comments to the Duke on Angelo's downfall (V, i, 378–9). With his percipience restored, Escalus passes judgement on the former Deputy:

> I am sorry one so learned and so wise
> As you, Lord Angelo, have still appear'd,
> Should slip so grossly, both in heat of blood
> And lack of temper'd judgement afterwards.
>
> [V, i, 468–71]

Ironically, Escalus's judgement of Angelo reflects on Escalus himself (as was the case with his earlier judgement of the Duke). Like Angelo, Escalus is one who has 'still' (always) seemed 'so learned and so wise', but whose 'temper'd judgement' suffered through 'heat of blood' in his angry confrontation with Friar Lodowick. It is, nevertheless, entirely appropriate that Escalus's last speech in the play should conclude with a reference to 'temper'd judgement', the core quality in Escalus's previous portrayal. His former character has been re-established. The Duke can therefore reward him, not as the ranting tyrant briefly witnessed in the immediately preceding trial-scene, but as the conscientious, judicious courtier and magistrate consistently presented in his every previous appearance:

> Thanks, good friend Escalus, for thy much goodness;
> There's more behind that is more gratulate. [V, i, 525–6]

With this promise of future recompense, Escalus leaves the stage with his dignity restored, as part of the Duke's triumphal procession to 'our palace' (line 535).

A Gentle Provost

The Provost resembles Escalus in that he conscientiously tempers justice with compassion. Unlike Escalus, however, he remains a consistent character throughout the play: there will be no aberration for dramatic expediency, as there is in Escalus's final scene. He further differs from Escalus in that he is never named, but identified solely by his professional function as keeper of Vienna's prison. This creates an irony, as those responsible for running Shakespeare's contemporary gaols were notoriously corrupt and brutal,[23] as suggested when the Duke observes the Provost's character in one of his customary gnomic couplets:

---

[23] Numerous examples are offered by Gamini Salgado, *The Elizabethan Underworld* (London: Dent, 1977; repr. Stroud: Alan Sutton, 1992); for example, pp. 174, 195–6, and 201.

This is a gentle provost; seldom when
The steeled gaoler is the friend of men. [IV, ii, 84–5]

The expectation is that a jailer should be cold, hard, and inflexible ('steeled' like chains, weapons, or instruments of torture), and brutal in his manners; but this Provost is 'gentle' (noble and kindly), sympathetic towards his charges.

When the Provost is first presented to the audience, Shakespeare is quick to exonerate him from any blame for the public humiliation of the unhappy lovers whom he is supervising. Questioned by Claudio, the Provost explains that this pageant to mortify the prisoners derives not from any 'evil disposition' on his part, but from the orders of Lord Angelo (I, ii, 110–11). He also offers a kindly concession to Claudio, allowing him to converse with Lucio for a further fifty lines when duty would compel the Provost to move the prisoner along (see I, ii, 130). Claudio appears to recognise the Provost as a potential ally, addressing him as 'good friend' (I, ii, 131), an indication that the Provost is expected to be sympathetic to the request for 'one word' with Lucio, Claudio's potential saviour. During the exchanges between Claudio and Lucio, the Provost remains close enough to the two friends to overhear their plan to recruit Isabella to plead for Claudio. This would explain how, on his next appearance (with Angelo), the Provost is able to identify Isabella as 'a very virtuous maid; / And to be shortly of a sisterhood, / If not already' (II, ii, 20–2): he is presented as recalling Claudio's description of his sister to Lucio. This is characteristic of a Provost who takes a personal interest in the well-being of his charges.

In the first half of Act II of *Measure for Measure*, the great debate takes place between leniency and severity in the administration of justice: just as Escalus argued against Angelo in the first scene, so the Provost takes over Escalus's role at the start of the second scene. Like Escalus, the Provost believes that Claudio's capital sentence is disproportionate. He goes as far as to risk his own position by petitioning Angelo on the matter. Shakespeare furnishes him with a brief soliloquy or aside immediately before his interview with Angelo, to make the Provost's benevolent motivation clear:

> I'll know
> His pleasure, may be he will relent. Alas,
> He hath but as offended in a dream;
> All sects, all ages smack of this vice, and he
> To die for't! [II, ii, 2–6]

The rough-hewn verse, with irregular rhythm and caesurae, suggests the Provost's anguish as he vainly hopes that Angelo will mollify the capital sentence. He defends Claudio on the grounds that his offence, which was inadvertent ('as . . . in a dream'), is common to all classes and generations.

Like Escalus, the Provost shows tact and caution in broaching to Angelo the subject of a reprieve:

> Is it your will Claudio shall die tomorrow? [II, ii, 7]

There is no overt challenge to Angelo's authority in this line; only a diplomatic questioning of the Deputy's wishes. On encountering Angelo's peremptory response, the Provost is obliged to explain why he is raising the issue of the death-sentence:

> Lest I might be too rash.
> Under your good correction, I have seen
> When, after execution, judgement hath
> Repented o'er his doom. [II, ii, 9–12]

Again, there is no explicit accusation of harshness directed against Angelo's 'good correction'. First, the Provost deflects any potential blame for rashness (in the proposed speedy execution of Claudio) from Angelo to himself: he fears 'I [not 'you'] might be too rash'. Delicately, the Provost suggests that it may be to Angelo's advantage to reconsider his verdict on Claudio, as the Deputy might come to regret the sentence after the execution. Angelo, however, appearing to believe that his authority is being challenged, rounds on the Provost:

> Go to; let that be mine;
> Do you your office, or give up your place,
> And you shall well be spar'd. [II, ii, 12–14]

The sharp contrast here between the Provost's tactful compassion and Angelo's peevish aggression should attract from the audience particular sympathy for the Provost's position. He is not merely threatened with dismissal for his conscientious attempt to reprieve Claudio; Angelo's final line ('you shall well be spar'd') shocks us by indicating that the new Deputy would regret the dismissal of this 'gentle provost' no more than he will regret the execution of 'the most gentle Claudio' (IV, ii, 70). Angelo shows no appreciation of the Provost's good offices.

Recognizing from Angelo's complacent bluntness that his appeal for Claudio cannot succeed, the Provost respectfully redirects his petition:

> I crave your honour's pardon.
> What shall be done, sir, with the groaning Juliet?
> She's very near her hour. [II, ii, 14–16]

Again, the Provost is motivated by concern for the welfare of his charges. The disparity between him and Angelo is marked, as the Deputy grudgingly concedes that 'the fornicatress', whom he refuses to grace even with her name, should be offered 'needful, but not lavish means' (II, ii, 23–4). His mean-spirited response accentuates, by contrast, the Provost's charitable concern for Julietta. When 'the groaning Juliet' re-appears in the next scene, the Provost is quickly able to offer her words of support:

> I have provided for you; stay a while
> And you shall be conducted. [II, iii, 17–18]

Regardless of whether his application to Angelo has succeeded, the Provost has ensured that special provision has been made for Julietta's greater comfort and safety. This conscientious intervention is characteristic of the Provost's zealous concern for the two lovers in his charge.

He is not, however, indiscriminate in seeking clemency for all those in the prison. He can distinguish between a prisoner worthy of sympathy and one deserving harsh punishment:

> Call hither Barnadine and Claudio.
> Th'one has my pity; not a jot the other,
> Being a murderer, though he were my brother.
>
> [IV, ii, 58–60]

Both prisoners have been sentenced to death by Angelo, but the Provost would not strive to save Barnadine, the murderer. His support for Claudio, however, never wavers: when invited to observe the whole of the first interview between Isabella and Angelo (see II, ii, 26), the Provost offers choric comments as asides, expressing his wish that Isabella might persuade Angelo to spare Claudio: 'Heaven give thee moving graces!' (II, ii, 36) and 'Pray heaven she win him' (II, ii, 126). Similarly, when Friar Lodowick arrives at the prison the night before Claudio's scheduled execution, the Provost hopes that he brings 'some pardon or reprieve / For the most gentle Claudio' (IV, ii, 69–70). Furthermore, the Provost's first question to the friar is, 'What comfort is for Claudio?' (IV, ii, 75). On learning that the sentence has not been remitted, the Provost condemns Angelo as 'a bitter deputy' (IV, ii, 76). In all these contexts, the Provost acts as a moral arbiter for the benefit of the audience, his compassion for Claudio thrown into sharper relief by his condemnation of Barnadine and Angelo.

The Provost as Functionary

It is easy to overlook the many minor functions performed by the Provost in the course of the play. Although his is not one of the major roles in respect of the number of words that he speaks, he is on stage for a substantial part of any performance, often as a silent but benign presence, observing and moderating the behaviour of others. He monitors the whole of the conversation in which Claudio recruits Lucio to assist him (I, ii, 108–84), witnessing Claudio's noble acceptance of his arrest and learning of Isabella whom (as already indicated) he will later characterise to Angelo as the epitome of female piety. He is apparently present throughout the hearing involving Pompey and Froth in Act II, scene i.[24] Certainly, he is invited to observe the whole of the Deputy's first interview with Isabella, where his presence as chaperon might plausibly inhibit Angelo from expressing any illicit passion for the novice until their later, private conference in Act II, scene iv. In addition, he witnesses the Duke's confession of Julietta (in Act II, scene iii), the Duke's spiritual preparation of Claudio for execution (in Act III, scene i), and the harrowing exchanges between Claudio and Isabella (also in Act III, scene i), all of which occur in the prison.

Although the Provost is presented as a trusted witness to legal and spiritual proceedings, his primary responsibility is for the supervision of the prison, a charge that he performs with efficiency and conscientiousness, as well as compassion. He saves Pompey from a whipping by appointing him as the apprentice of Abhorson, the hangman, after which he instructs the two in preparation for the imminent executions (IV, ii, 1–29 and 46–58). He encourages Claudio to reconcile himself to death (IV, ii, 61–7). He receives Angelo's written confirmation that Claudio is to be executed, reading out the 'private message' (V, i, 458) to disabuse the disguised Duke, who was complacently expecting a pardon from Angelo (IV, ii, 83–125). Thereafter, he briefs Friar Lodowick (the Duke's alias) on the background and character of the murderer, Barnadine (IV, ii, 126–51), information that the Duke will use to formulate the 'head-trick'.

---

[24] The Provost's entry is noted at line 31 but no stage-direction thereafter indicates his exit. This issue and its ramifications are discussed by Lever, pp. xvii–xviii.

477

The Provost's moral judgement is consistently sound, as he discriminates clearly between those worthy of praise and those worthy of blame. Having been present while the disguised Duke prepared Claudio for execution (III, i, 1–43), he can recommend Friar Lodowick to Escalus as 'this friar' who 'advised [Claudio] for th'entertainment of death' (III, ii, 206–7). In addition, the Provost's testimony against Mistress Overdone, whom he identifies as 'A bawd of eleven years' continuance' (III, ii, 190), confirms the justice of Escalus's imprisonment of her.

In most productions, he is on-stage almost continuously throughout the great trial-scene with which the play concludes.[25] Under instruction from the Duke, he contributes substantially to the 'stage-management' of this final scene. It is the Provost who introduces the disguised Duke to the court over which Angelo is presiding, in preparation for the coup de théâtre when Friar Lodowick will transform into Vincentio at the drop of a hood. He is dispatched by the Duke as a witness to the marriage of Angelo and Mariana conducted by Friar Peter (V, i, 375–7). Thereafter, he introduces two 'muffl'd' prisoners, one of whom, in a second coup de théâtre, will be revealed as the miraculously-preserved Claudio. From such evidence, the audience will recognise the Provost as a law-officer of 'honesty and constancy' (the Duke: IV, ii, 153), supervising and legitimising procedures by his mere presence. Hence, when the Duke promises him promotion at the end of the play (V, i, 527–8), an audience should recognise that, in a play entitled *Measure for Measure*, one who has so conscientiously performed his duties to the state should rise in Vienna's justice-

---

[25] Lever maintains (pp. 136–7n.) that the Provost's entry should be reserved until V, i, 276 rather than being part of the general procession on to the stage at the very start of this final scene. Braunmuller and Watson demur (p. 324n.), arguing that the Provost should be on-stage for the whole of Act V (except for his brief exit to fetch the 'muffled' figures of Claudio and Barnadine).

system in proportion to the fall of one who has so offended against the system: Angelo.

The Duke's *Free Dependant*

The Provost's general integrity and his passionate concern for the welfare of Claudio and Julietta win the confidence of the Duke, disguised as Friar Lodowick. It is the Provost who graciously welcomes Friar Lodowick to the prison on learning that the friar intends to 'minister' to 'the afflicted spirits' (II, iii, 4–9), and who immediately introduces him to Julietta as a prisoner in need of such sympathetic support as the friar can offer:

> Look, here comes one: a gentlewoman of mine,
> Who, falling in the flaws of her own youth,
> Hath blister'd her report. She is with child,
> And he that got it, sentenc'd: a young man
> More fit to do another such offence,
> Than die for this. [II, iii, 10–15]

The Provost's speech confirms his unwavering support for the lovers. His description of Julietta as 'a gentlewoman of mine' not only suggests his respect for her social status but also hints – in the words 'of mine' – that he might feel a paternalistic concern for her case. His speech maintains that her offence was not a deliberate criminal act but rather an unfortunate accident ('falling in the flaws' suggesting that she has merely stumbled in a storm) that has injured her reputation ('blister'd her report'). Similarly, when he refocuses on Claudio, he is loath to condemn what Claudio has done ('More fit to do another such offence'), showing dismay at the capital sentence. Immediately afterwards, he comforts Julietta with the reassurance that provision has been made for the birth of her child (II, iii, 17–18; already quoted). In so doing, the Provost singles himself out as a potential ally to the disguised Duke, who will labour for the rest of the play to redeem the lovers from Angelo's sentence on them.

479

As the play progresses, the Provost is increasingly involved in the plans to save Claudio. Although he does not recognise Friar Lodowick as the Duke in disguise, the Provost provides every assistance that the friar entreats. Having graciously welcomed Isabella's prison-visit (III, i, 45 and 49), he complies with Friar Lodowick's wish to be allowed, unseen, to overhear the conversation between Isabella and Claudio. After the painful conclusion of that interview, the Provost grants Friar Lodowick's request to be left alone to consult with Isabella (III, i, 172–8). Already, he is expediting the Duke's plans, if only by compliance with Friar Lodowick's requests.

The Provost quickly establishes himself as the necessary instrument to save Claudio's life. Once it becomes clear that Angelo will not relent on the issue of Claudio's execution, even after the successful conclusion of the 'bed-trick', the Provost is taken into Friar Lodowick's confidence:

> There is written in your brow, Provost, honesty and constancy. . . . [I]n the boldness of my cunning, I will lay myself in hazard. . . . I crave but four days' respite: for the which, you are to do me both a present and a dangerous courtesy . . . [i]n the delaying death. [IV, ii, 152–63]

Although his admirable qualities have been acknowledged by the mysterious friar, the Provost is understandably reluctant to undertake the deception that the friar suggests: it might cost him his life to disobey 'an express command' (IV, ii, 164–7); the substitution of Barnadine's head for Claudio's would not deceive Angelo (IV, ii, 172–3); and such complicity in saving a condemned man 'is against my oath'. (IV, ii, 181). These responses to Friar Lodowick portray the Provost as one whose integrity is tempered by a strong practical sense. Although Friar Lodowick seeks to allay the Provost's misgivings, only the supreme authority of the Duke is sufficient to sway the Provost to disobey the Deputy's command:

> . . . I will go further than I meant. . . . Look you, sir, here is the hand and seal of the Duke. . . . The contents of this is the

return of the Duke: you shall anon over-read it at your pleasure, where you shall find within these two days he will be here. . . . Call up your executioner, and off with Barnadine's head. . . . Yet you are amazed; but this shall absolutely resolve you. [IV, ii, 189–209]

With these words from the disguised Duke, the Provost is recruited to participate in the 'head-trick'. Without the Provost's compliance, no such deception could have been practised on Angelo to save Claudio's life.

Like Isabella when enlisted to the 'bed-trick', the Provost quickly becomes proactive in the deception once convinced not only that it is morally justifiable but also that it has a good prospect of success. The plot to substitute Barnadine's head for Claudio's was always suspect, as the Provost had indicated: 'Angelo hath seen them both, and will discover the favour' (that is, Angelo will recognise Barnadine's face; IV, ii, 172–3). When Barnadine refuses to comply with the executioners, seemingly thwarting the disguised Duke's plan, it is the Provost who saves the day:

> Here in the prison, father,
> There died this morning of a cruel fever
> One Ragozine, a most notorious pirate,
> A man of Claudio's years; his beard and head
> Just of his colour. What if we do omit
> This reprobate till he were well inclin'd,
> And satisfy the deputy with the visage
> Of Ragozine, more like to Claudio? [IV, iii, 68–75]

So soon after being recruited to the Duke's plot, the Provost has seized the initiative and resolved a seemingly intractable problem. Ragozine's head is a much more suitable substitute than Barnadine's: because of Ragozine's close facial similarity to Claudio, the trick to deceive Angelo is more likely to succeed. Having accepted the friar's command to sever Ragozine's head and to send it to Angelo as Claudio's, the ever-cautious Provost foresees further possible obstacles. If it

481

were discovered that Claudio and Barnadine had been spared, the Provost's own life would be in danger for failing to carry out Angelo's command to execute them both (IV, iii, 81–5). The disguised Duke suggests confining the two surviving prisoners 'in secret holds' for two days until the Duke's return, reassuring the Provost 'you shall find / Your safety manifested' (IV, iii, 86–90). In response, the Provost declares, 'I am your free dependant' (IV, iii, 90), suggesting not only that he is friar Lodowick's 'willing servant' but also, in the ambiguity of the word 'free', that he feels no guilt for a deception that is morally justifiable.

The Provost now becomes the Duke's agent and messenger. He is to be dispatched with letters announcing the Duke's imminent return to Vienna (see IV, iii, 92–6). When the disguised Duke recruits Friar Peter's assistance for the final trial-scene, he reassures him that 'The Provost knows our purpose and our plot' (IV, v, 2). The implication is that the Provost, although presumably still unaware of the Duke's disguise, has otherwise been taken fully into his confidence. The Provost will be dispatched half way through the trial to summons Friar Lodowick to appear before the court (V, i, 251),[26] and will then be commanded by Escalus to arrest him forcibly (V, i, 343–6) after the friar has testified.

Even after the Duke's disguise has been cast aside, the web of deception devised by the erstwhile Friar Lodowick persists, and the Provost must continue to play his pre-determined role. The two men, both of whom know Claudio to be alive, perform an interlude in which the Duke appears to dismiss the Provost from his post for executing Claudio without a 'special warrant' (V, i, 454–9). The Provost can now impart that the life has been spared of one of the men condemned by Angelo:

---

[26] Although the exchange at V, i, 251–2 clearly suggests that the Duke dispatches the Provost to fetch Friar Lodowick, Lever prefers to attribute the errand to 'an Attendant', delaying the first entrance of the Provost until line 276.

> Pardon me, noble lord;
> I thought it was a fault, but knew it not;
> Yet did repent me after more advice.
> For testimony whereof, one in the prison
> That should by private order else have died,
> I have reserv'd alive. . . . His name is Barnadine.
>
> [V, i, 460–5]

This is all a dramatic ploy to provide an opportunity for the introduction of not one but *two* prisoners before the court (V, i, 467ff.), so that Vincentio can demonstrate his power and mercy. The Provost first identifies Barnadine, whom the Duke duly pardons, with provision that the prisoner should accept religious instruction from Friar Peter. Contributing further to the web of disguise and deception planned by the erstwhile Friar Lodowick, the Provost equivocates as a prelude to revealing the identity of the second prisoner:

> This is another prisoner that I sav'd,
> Who should have died when Claudio lost his head;
> As like almost to Claudio as himself. [V, I, 485–7]

In so doing, the Provost complements the Duke's plan to emerge 'like power divine' from his disguise as Friar Lodowick: a prisoner unjustly executed under Angelo's regime is miraculously restored to life on Vincentio's return to power. Vincentio reaps the glory, but the Provost manages the trick.

The Provost has spoken his last line, but there remains the need for Vincentio to recompense him for his good offices. The Duke does not merely acknowledge his gratitude, but pledges promotion to the Provost:

> Thanks, Provost, for thy care and secrecy;
> We shall employ thee in a worthier place. [V, i, 527–8]

The audience enjoys the satisfaction of witnessing merit rewarded. It would be easy to overlook the full significance of

Vincentio's next words, however, which also refer to the Provost:

> Forgive him, Angelo, that brought you home
> The head of Ragozine for Claudio's. . . . [V, i, 529–30]

As the title of the play is *Measure for Measure*, echoing the Sermon on the Mount, Angelo's pardon from the Duke must appear conditional: the Deputy's trespasses can be forgiven only if he can forgive those who trespass against him. In pardoning the Provost for his deception, Angelo is showing himself worthy of pardon. The Provost is therefore instrumental in saving both Claudio *and* his persecutor, Angelo, from the extreme penalty that might otherwise have been exacted. If Duke Vincentio is 'like power divine', then the Provost is a principal agent in redeeming sinners.

Elbow

We move from the sublime to the ridiculous, from the Provost, a scrupulously honest officer of the law, to Elbow, an idiotic constable. Elbow is apparently well-intentioned but, of the characters in the play who provoke laughter, he is the one who most obviously is laughed *at*, rather than laughed *with* (his only rival being Froth). He is the stock constable of Shakespearian comedy, in his stupidity and his verbal clumsiness indistinguishable from Dogberry in *Much Ado About Nothing*,[27] and generally similar to Dull in *Love's Labour's Lost*. He appears in only two scenes (II, i and III, ii), in both of which he is set against Pompey, whom he has arrested.

Even when introducing himself to Angelo and Escalus, Elbow illustrates his propensity for mangling the language:

---

[27] According to John Aubrey (1626–97), Dogberry was drawn from the life: see Salgādo, p. 168. Dogberry and Elbow are twin portraits of the archetypal English parochial constable.

I am the poor Duke's constable. . . . and do bring in here before your good honour two notorious benefactors. [II, i, 47–50]

Shakespeare is recycling malapropisms from *Much Ado About Nothing*, where Dogberry also, with intended modesty, claimed to be one of 'the poor duke's officers' (by which he meant 'the duke's poor officers') and, in addition, where he confused 'malefactors' with 'benefactors'.[28] Elbow's offences against the English language persist as he confuses 'piety' with 'profanation' (line 55), 'protest' with 'detest' (lines 68 and 74; repeating Mistress Quickly's error from *Merry Wives of Windsor*: I, iv, 135), and 'carnally' with 'cardinally' (line 79). The errors culminate when he (without any apparent impudence or irony) refers to Angelo and Escalus as 'varlets' and to Pompey as an 'honourable man' (lines 85–6).

As details about his wife and his relationship with her emerge, Elbow invites further ridicule. Although it is difficult to be certain, because his language is so confused, Elbow has apparently brought Pompey and Froth before the justices to accuse them of attempting a sexual assault on his wife. Unfortunately for him, his allegations raise the suspicion that his wife has been frequenting Mistress Overdone's brothel in search of sexual satisfaction:

. . . this house, if it be not a bawd's house, it is pity of her life, for it is a naughty house. . . . [M]y wife, . . if she had been a woman cardinally [*sic*, for 'carnally'] given, might have been accused in fornication, adultery, and all uncleanliness there. [II, i, 75–80]

When thwarted by Pompey's tedious testimony for the defence, Elbow attempts to condemn brothel, pimp, and bawd—but, unfortunately for him, confuses 'respected' and 'suspected':

---

[28] *Much Ado About Nothing*: III, v, 19 and IV, ii, 4–5.

First, and it like you, the house is a respected house; next, this is a respected fellow; and his mistress is a respected woman. [II, i, 159–61]

Pompey's riposte—'his wife is a more respected person than any of us all' (lines162–3)—redeploys Elbow's malapropism to imply that the constable is a cuckold (that ultimate humiliation for an Elizabethan or Jacobean male). Worse follows when Pompey continues the jest by alleging that Elbow and his wife were 'respected' of consummating their relationship before they married (lines 167–8). If so, then the couple were guilty of a similar offence to that for which Claudio and Julietta have been condemned under Vienna's statutes.

Elbow's confusion over words proves merely a symptom of general stupidity. While indignantly but ineptly defending himself against Pompey's charge of fornication, Elbow threatens to bring an 'action of battery' (by which he may be presumed to mean 'slander') against Pompey (lines 171–6). When Escalus mocks Elbow's ignorance of these legal terms (lines 177–8), the joke falls on deaf ears: Elbow, mistaking trenchant irony for good advice, thanks Escalus sincerely (line 179). Finally, when Escalus acquits Pompey on the grounds of insufficient evidence, Elbow seems to think that he has achieved a victory rather than experienced a humiliation:

Marry, I thank your worship for it.—Thou seest, thou wicked varlet now, what's come upon thee. Thou art to continue now, thou varlet, thou art to continue. [II, i, 186–9]

As Elbow has proved so impercipient that he frequently fails to recognise when he has suffered a personal injury, it is relatively easy for Escalus to persuade the constable to participate in his own removal from office. With a combination of sympathy and flattery, Escalus encourages Elbow to believe that he has been exploited by his parishioners who have relied on his services for too long. Elbow's vanity is apparent when he proudly refers to his record as parish constable for '[s]even year and a half' (line 257), and implies that he is superior to the 'men in [his] ward' who lack 'any wit in such matters' (lines 263–5). When he agrees to nominate 'some six or seven, the most sufficient of [his] parish' (lines 269–70) as a short-list of replacements for him in his role of constable, he appears not to appreciate that this will cost him 'some piece of money' that he earns in pay (line 267). Any sympathy that an audience might feel for Elbow's loss of livelihood is mitigated by amusement at his ridiculous vanity, ineptitude, and folly.

When Elbow re-appears, however, he is triumphant rather than chastened, because his previous nemesis, Pompey, has incriminated himself:

Marry, sir, he hath offended the law; and, sir, we take him to be a thief too, sir: for we have found upon him, sir, a strange pick-lock, which we have sent to the deputy. [III, ii, 14–17]

Regardless of whether the 'pick-lock' is a tool for burglary or, as the editorial tradition has suggested, a covert reference to a device for unfastening chastity-belts, it appears to be the incriminating evidence that was lacking when Escalus was previously obliged to release Pompey from custody. Elbow is delighted that Pompey will now be brought before Angelo, a less indulgent justice than Escalus:

He must before the deputy, sir; he has given him warning. The deputy cannot abide a whoremaster. If he be a whoremonger and comes before him, he were as good go a mile on his errand. [III, ii, 33–6]

Of course, the irony would be lost on Elbow that Angelo is proving as sexually corrupt as any Viennese 'whoremaster' likely to be prosecuted by him. Elbow is presented as relishing the idea that Pompey's sentence from Angelo is likely to be as severe as that imposed on Claudio:

His neck will come to your waist—a cord, sir. [III, ii, 39]

As a Franciscan friar, a Cordelier, the Duke will wear the order's distinctive knotted rope around his waist, an attachment comparable with that likely to stretch Pompey's neck. Although it may briefly appear to Elbow that Pompey could escape justice if bailed by a friend, Lucio defies Pompey's expectations of support and so Elbow is able to drive his victim off to jail with 'Come your ways, sir, come' (III, ii, 77 and 81). Elbow's vengeance is complete on the man who, he believes, sought to corrupt his wife and who blackened his reputation before Escalus. Regardless of whether he is soon to be replaced as constable, his final appearance in the play is a comic triumph for him.

Abhorson

What are we to make of the name of the second incompetent functionary of the law: Abhorson? It seems to be a fusion of 'abhor' and 'whoreson', with a hint of 'abortion' thrown in for good measure. It suggests a character as revolting in manner and appearance as in his occupation of hanging, drawing, and quartering malefactors, and chopping off heads.

Yet, like his counterpart outside the prison, Elbow, he is inordinately proud of his function. When instructed by the Provost to train Pompey as his assistant, Abhorson displays ridiculous vanity in his objection:

A bawd, sir? Fie upon him, he will discredit our mystery.
[IV, ii, 26–7]

Abhorson considers his occupation as equivalent to that of a guildsman, a member of a skilled trade or 'mystery', the secrets of which must be guarded from access by the uninitiated and the unworthy. The audience has already been made aware, by Pompey's deliberate irony, of how debased the occupation of hangman is:

Sir, I have been an unlawful bawd time out of mind, but yet I will be content to be a lawful hangman. [IV, ii, 14–16]

The only social distinction between bawd and hangman is, it would seem, that the former is 'unlawful' and the latter 'lawful'; but (implicitly) neither deserves any esteem. Challenged by Pompey to prove that the hangman's calling merits the title of a 'mystery', Abhorson proves as confused as Elbow when attempting to articulate an argument:

> Every true man's apparel fits your thief. If it be too little for your thief, your true man thinks it big enough. If it be too big for your thief, your thief thinks it little enough. So every true man's apparel fits your thief. [IV, ii, 41–5]

Most editors regard the text as corrupt here, but surely it is intended not make complete sense.[29] Abhorson does not even mention the hangman's trade directly (although the hangman would expect to receive the clothes of those whom he executed as part of his remuneration). The use of 'So' at the opening of the final sentence of Abhorson's argument would seem to indicate that he believes that he has proved his case, when rather he has proved the intellectual superiority of Pompey, who previously had wittily presented the sex-trade as a 'mystery' on the grounds that whores are adept at 'painting', a guildsman's skill (IV, ii, 34–8). Although he reluctantly agrees to accept Pompey as his understudy, Abhorson remains ridiculously disdainful in his manner: he refers to Pompey with distaste as 'bawd' (IV, ii, 52), using the condescending second-person pronoun 'thee' (IV, ii, 52) and the scornful vocative 'Sirrah' (IV, iii, 21); and he issues blunt imperatives gruffly when compelling Pompey to extricate the dangerous Barnadine from his cell (e.g. IV, iii, 21, 30, and 33).

Abhorson's final function is to confront Barnadine with the news of his imminent execution. This is done without subtlety:

---

[29] Braunmuller and Watson nevertheless find Abhorson's 'chop-logic roughly coherent' (p. 269n.).

Truly, sir, I would desire you to clap into your prayers; for look you, the warrant's come. [IV, iii, 39–40]

The expression 'clap into' would seem more appropriate to some hurried chore than to spiritual preparation for the afterlife, while 'the warrant's come' makes the ominous arrival of an official document imposing the death-sentence sound strangely routine and inconsequential. In response, Barnadine does not seem to take the threat of Abhorson's words seriously. The executioner must therefore provide further evidence of his ominous intent:

Look you, sir, here comes your ghostly father. Do we jest now, think you? [IV, iii, 47–8]

Friar Lodowick has arrived to prepare Barnadine for death, but the prisoner is no more impressed by the words of the disguised Duke than he was by those of the incompetent executioner, who pursues Barnadine offstage to 'bring him to the block' (IV, iii, 64). Barnadine, however, will be one of the recipients of the Duke's general amnesty at the end of the play and so, with no further function to perform, Abhorson the executioner disappears permanently from the stage.

Divine Justice

It is not the secular law that reasserts its authority in the Duke's final judgement in *Measure for Measure*. There will be no call for the services of the constable, the executioner, or his assistant, nor for the good offices of those honourable functionaries, Escalus and the Provost. Rather, the Duke's preferred agent is Friar Peter; and the instruments by which the Duke ensures reform are the institutions of the Church.

The sacrament of marriage is the chief means by which justice is secured at the end of *Measure for Measure*. At first, this may seem a perfunctory or unsatisfactory resolution to the complex moral challenges posed by the play; but further reflection offers some persuasive arguments to the contrary. Claudio, Julietta, and Mariana—lovers who, by enduring prolonged anguish, have passed the test of fidelity and (implicitly) thereby purged any impure desire—receive marriage as a divine blessing on their union. By contrast, marriage will be an ideal punishment for Lucio, the penalty for his promiscuity being the derision that he will suffer as a cuckold, the husband of (allegedly) a promiscuous woman. For Angelo, if he accepts the Duke's injunction to 'love' Mariana (V, i, 523), marriage will be a reward; whereas, should he resent Mariana—as Lucio might resent Mistress Kate Keep-down, for forcing him reluctantly into marriage—the sacrament will transform into a humiliating disparagement. As for the morally-ambiguous Duke and Isabella, marriage, if mutually accepted, would appear to an audience a positive affirmation of their characters; if rejected, a condemnation. No 'sentence' under the laws of Vienna could perform this equitable function of being simultaneously an incentive or a disincentive, a reward or a punishment, a blessing or a curse, depending on the moral and spiritual status of the recipient.

There is, however, one character who benefits from the general amnesty whose case cannot be resolved by the sacrament of marriage: Barnadine, the murderer. His 'stubborn soul / That apprehends no further than this world' (V, i, 478–9) is impervious to correction by the state. The Duke's response is to 'quit' him of his 'earthly faults' (V, i, 481)—that is, to repeal the death-sentence on him—while placing him under the jurisdiction of the Church. The state can do no more than to pardon Barnadine in this world, but the Duke is implicitly warning that this self-confessed murderer will face a higher judgement; hence the Duke's injunction to 'take this mercy to provide / For better times to come' (V, i, 482–3). It is for Friar Peter, who performed Angelo's marriage-ceremony, to take upon him the care of Barnadine's soul (V, i, 483–4). All malefactors in the play must ultimately submit to divinely-ordained justice.

491

The title of the play, *Measure for Measure*, refers to that section of the Sermon on the Mount that warns against the dangers of judgement in this world. It is entirely fitting, therefore, that, in the final scene of the play, divine mercy, grace, and judgement should transcend the powers of earthly authority. Although presented as a monarch anointed to administer God's justice on Earth, 'like power divine' (V, i, 367), Duke Vincentio implicitly recognises the deficiencies of secular justice.[30] His own previous leniency and Angelo's more recent stringency in earthly government have both been weighed in the balance and found wanting. Other characters have similarly noted the limitations of man-made statutes. Escalus has recognised the contradiction of his own position: when he pleads for the law to spare Claudio's life even though 'Pardon is still the nurse of second woe' (II, i, 281), he is acknowledging that, when human law is merciful, it encourages re-offending. Pompey cheekily remarks that being a bawd is an offence only because the statutes of Vienna choose to make it so, implying that the human laws are partial (II, i, 224). Angelo observes at the close of his final soliloquy that, without divine guidance, even a jurist as experienced as he cannot resolve dilemmas relating to crime and punishment:

> Alack, when once our grace we have forgot,
> Nothing goes right; we would, and we would not.
>
> [IV, iv, 31–2]

Angelo's implication is that contradictions resulting from human imperfection can be resolved only if we strive to recover 'grace', that is, the Grace of God.

Implicitly, the Duke appears ultimately to accept that the only possible resolution to the social ills of Vienna is to defer to the higher authority of God. God has provided the seven sacraments to redeem sinners on this Earth; and, on Doomsday,

---

[30] Vincentio's rueful admission of his own mismanagement of the state at I, iii, 19–39 and his condemnation of corruption in Vienna at V, i, 314–20 suggest no less.

God will sit in final Judgement on all souls. Even the knowledge, understanding, and experience that Vincentio has accrued while 'a looker-on here in Vienna' (V, i, 315) cannot compare with the omniscience, omnipotence, and omnipresence of God. The sacrament of marriage is chosen to regulate unruly sexual desire on Earth, while arbitration on other human sins will be deferred until the Last Judgement. The marital union of the Duke and Isabella, both of whom have spent much of the play in religious garb, might even symbolise the successful conquest of earthly desires by spiritual aspirations—although their dubious behaviour when associated with religious orders and the uncertainty of Isabella's acceptance of the Duke's proposal of marriage make this interpretation tentative, at best. What is more certain is that, although the 'enrolled penalties' of Vienna may have condemned Claudio to death, the law of God proves more merciful. By marrying, Claudio is at one and the same time purging his sexual offence, vindicating his relationship with his betrothed, and legitimising his child. In addition, marriage offers Angelo the opportunity to make amends to the woman whom he wronged, to regulate the sexual desire that threatened to transform him into a rapist and murderer, and to alleviate the self-disgust so apparent in his three soliloquies. Secular and canon law may be dispensed by one ruler in Vienna, but justice ultimately resides in the realms of the Divine. Shakespeare's play—even though it is no straightforward moral interlude—offers this profoundly Christian resolution.

Chapter 8

A Play Defined in Performance

The First Folio of 1623 admits of only three categories of plays on its title-page: *Mr. William Shakespeares Comedies, Histories, & Tragedies.* Shakespeare's associates, John Heminges and Henry Condell, who assembled the volume, included *Measure for Measure* as the fourth of the comedies. It was as a comedy, then, that *Measure for Measure* first appeared in print—although not until seven years after Shakespeare's death, and nineteen years after the play's first recorded performance.

Those who would re-classify *Measure for Measure* argue that it does not sit comfortably amongst the comedies of the First Folio. There is some truth in this. The main plot of most of Shakespeare's most popular comedies—among them *The Two Gentlemen of Verona, The Taming of the Shrew, A Midsummer Night's Dream, Much Ado About Nothing, As You Like It* and *Twelfth Night*—could be summarised by the maxim, 'The course of true love never did run smooth' (*A Midsummer Night's Dream*: I, i, 134). Generally, in these comedies, pre-marital love is tested by trials and tribulations from which the lovers ultimately emerge triumphant, with marriage as their reward. The implication is that, having successfully overcome all obstacles to their matrimony, and having grown in mutual understanding, the lovers (or most of the couples, at least) will live happily ever after. All other considerations in the plot are subservient to this reassuring outcome. Not so in *Measure for Measure*. Although the pairs of lovers—Claudio and Julietta, and Angelo and Mariana—are reunited, and their spousals confirmed at the end of the play, the theme of love has been secondary in a plot concerned primarily with government and justice.

Although amusing interludes may be encountered in performances of *Measure for Measure*, sinister 'open' silences in the final scene call into question whether happiness is ultimately unalloyed. Laughter is not an indispensable component of comedy—anyone reading Dante's *Divine Comedy* in search of hilarity or even light humour will be disappointed—but a happy ending is a prerequisite. However, no joyous words pass between Isabella and Claudio after the latter is unmasked, and their last speeches to each other (in Act III, scene i) were a frighteningly bitter exchange that might disfigure any future reconciliation. In addition, Angelo offers no verbal confirmation that a happy ending will result from his enforced marriage to Mariana: he is silent as to whether he will obey Vincentio's command to 'love her' (V, i, 523). The most disturbing intimation of a potentially 'unhappy' ending, however, is encountered in the final exchanges of the play, when Isabella's acquiescence to the Duke's overtures of marriage is by no means certain. She offers no verbal response to either of his two proposals (V, i, 489–91 and 531–4). Rather than concluding with the joyous celebrations expected of comedy, *Measure for Measure* closes with (potentially) more sombre events.

Although there are sound reasons, then, for questioning whether *Measure for Measure* is a comedy in the customary Shakespearian sense, it remained classified as such for nearly three centuries. During the Victorian era, however, the prevailing piety, concern for public morality, and sexual repression apparent in polite society rendered particularly shocking a play about a powerful magistrate who sexually propositions a novice nun. The bardolatry established in the previous century nevertheless persisted: Shakespeare was still proudly regarded as the greatest poet, dramatist, and genius of this or of any other nation. How, then, could this universally-revered writer of transcendent human understanding have produced such a morally questionable work? A solution offered itself when F. S. Boas, towards the close of Victoria's reign, proposed the segregation from the Shakespearian canon not only of *Measure for Measure* but also of certain other works considered morally problematical. Henceforward, these were to be classified as the Bard's 'problem plays'.

We should question whether there is any justification for our continuing use of this generic title. To modern audiences and readers, 'problem play' inevitably carries with it the implication of, at best, an aberration on Shakespeare's part or, at worst, a serious error of judgement. Nevertheless, as certain plays written in the late Nineteenth and early Twentieth Century were also called 'problem plays', this reclassification of *Measure for Measure* might be vindicated if close affinities could be identified between these later works and the Shakespearian 'problem plays' nominated by successive critics. Alternatively, if it could be established that *Measure for Measure* displays certain major textual 'problems' which are not apparent in the mainstream of his works, then accommodating this and similar works into a Shakespearian sub-genre of 'problem play' might be defensible. In either case, if *Measure for Measure* and certain other Shakespearian plays are to be reclassified as 'problem plays', then it should be possible to offer a universally-acceptable definition of the new Shakespearian genre.

There was bound to be a reaction to the view that *Measure for Measure* was a 'problem play', and it came in 1930 when G. Wilson Knight offered a diametrically opposite opinion: far from being morally controversial, the play was a parable fully congruent with the teachings of the Gospels. The three protagonists—Vincentio, Angelo, and Isabella—were to be regarded as moral types, reinforcing the didactic message of the text. The inevitable conclusion was that *Measure for Measure* should be considered as a late example of a morality play.

More recently, there has been considerable critical support for the view that *Measure for Measure* is a tragicomedy.

Although such a composite genre is not recognised in the threefold division of Shakespeare's dramatic works in the First Folio, it does conflate two of the categories encountered there. This reclassification is therefore less contentious than either the 'problem play' or the 'morality play' label.

The history of *Measure for Measure* on stage offers some support for each of these reclassifications. Criticism of the play affected the way that it was performed, and performances of the play affected the attitude of the critics: there was a symbiotic relationship between the two. As we shall see, however, this relationship was sometimes achieved by emending the text of *Measure for Measure*, which resulted in a play significantly different from that attributed to Shakespeare in the First Folio.

A Problem Play?

Measure for Measure paid a heavy penalty for defying orthodox nineteenth-century notions of propriety. In 1827, Samuel Taylor Coleridge dismissed the play as 'a hateful work': he considered the comic exchanges 'disgusting' and the tragic passages 'horrible'.[1] Similarly, Joseph Hunter condemned *Measure for Measure* as 'improbable and disgusting' in 1845.[2] At the height of the Victorian age, in 1889, Arthur Symons complained of 'something base and sordid in the villainy' of the characters.[3] Four years later, William Archer observed, in reviewing a heavily-cut performance by the Shakespeare Reading Society, that 'there is no other play of Shakespeare's in which so much of the dialogue is absolutely unspeakable before a modern audience. Therefore, large cuts were inevitable. . . .'[4] It was in the context

---

[1] Geckle, p. 80.
[2] Geckle, p. 96.
[3] Geckle, p. 202.
[4] Alexandra Jones, 'Audience Reactions to *Measure for Measure*', 2004, accessed 13 November 2019, http://www2.cedarcrest.edu/academic/eng/lfletcher/measure/Ajones.htm.

of this moral distaste expressed by his contemporaries and their forerunners that F. S. Boas first proposed (in 1896) that *Measure for Measure* was a 'problem play'.[5]

By labelling certain of Shakespeare's works as 'problem plays', however, Boas was inviting comparisons between them and the problem plays that had originated in France in the 1850s and had spread throughout Europe, particularly under the influence of Henrik Ibsen between the 1870s and 1890s. George Bernard Shaw was the most prominent exponent of the problem play in the UK at the turn of the century. The problem plays of the late Nineteenth and early Twentieth Century addressed contemporary moral preoccupations; but they tended to focus on a single, potentially ephemeral, issue. If the specific social, political, moral, or economic problem that each addressed had lost its novelty and power to shock—or if the issue had been successfully resolved—then the play would no longer warrant public attention. For example, Shaw's three *Plays Unpleasant* (the collective title is indicative of the prejudice that 'problem plays' face) were controversial when they were first published in the 1890s, because they presented issues that scandalised Shaw's contemporaries: the presence in polite circles of exploitative slum landlords, sexually promiscuous socialites, and wealthy former prostitutes. Such topics would be less likely to cause shock and outrage if addressed in performance today, which may explain why such problem plays (with the notable exception of Ibsen's works) are relatively neglected in the theatre in the Twenty-First Century. In short, 'modern' problem plays tended to have a short shelf-life because each scrutinised one controversial question that, even if not swiftly resolved, would gradually lose its contentious edge.[6]

---

[5] *Shakspere and his Predecessors* (London: John Murray, 1896).

[6] Shaw himself recognized the problem, observing that 'a drama with a social question for the motive cannot outlive the solution of that question.' ['Should social problems be freely dealt with in the drama?', *The Humanitarian*, 6 (May 1895), quoted by Robert W.

Measure for Measure, by contrast, sustains interest, remaining fresh and relevant, as the multiple issues that the play addresses are of enduring and universal relevance. Shakespeare raises contentious issues concerning government, justice, human relationships, and morality—especially sexual mores—while offering no conclusive resolutions to those issues; hence, the perceived 'problem'. In this respect, *Measure for Measure* resembles *Hamlet*, *Troilus and Cressida*, and *All's Well that Ends Well*, which are also usually attributed to the period 1600–1604 and which have also intermittently been labelled as 'problem plays' since Boas first grouped them together in the 1890s. According to George Bernard Shaw, however, problem plays result from the writer's moral indignation and desire to correct profound social injustice:

> When we succeed in adjusting our social structure in such a way as to enable us to solve social questions as fast as they become really pressing, they will no longer force their way into the theatre. . . . If people are rotting and starving in all directions, and nobody else has the heart or brains to make a disturbance about it, the great writers must.[7]

It could not be argued convincingly that *Measure for Measure* is the result of such radical fervour: Shaw was prepared to mount a soap-box to tell his audience what to think; Shakespeare preferred impartially to dramatize contentious issues, implicitly inviting his audience to arbitrate. The absence of an unambiguous didactic purpose distinguishes Shakespeare's plays written between 1600 and 1604 from those problem plays of the Nineteenth and Twentieth Centuries which were fashioned to effect political or social reform.

Corrigan, ed., *The Modern Theatre* (London and New York: Macmillan, 19640), p. 973]
[7] 'The Problem Play', in *The Cry for Justice: An Anthology of the Literature of Social Protest*, ed. Upton Sinclair (Philadelphia: Winston, 1915), Bartleby, accessed 4 January 2020, https://www.bartleby.com/71/1528.html.

Each of Shakespeare's so-called 'problem plays' is likely to leave an audience puzzled as to the appropriate reaction to dramatic situations and characters. Not only is it probable that individual members of the same audience will differ in their responses, but even a single theatregoer may feel an unsettling ambivalence in his or her reactions. Those intent on fathoming authorial intention or establishing a single 'correct' response to the play may, then, face a 'problem'; but their quandary is dubious justification for associating *Measure for Measure* and certain other Shakespearian texts from the opening years of the 1600s with a dramatic genre that emerged over 250 years later with an emphatic agenda of social and/or political reform.

The problem plays of the late Nineteenth and Twentieth Century, however, are sometimes called 'plays of ideas', and *Measure for Measure* certainly abounds in ideas. As a strongly philosophical play, it scrutinizes and comments trenchantly on aspects of government, law, religion, and society. The communication of these ideas is not restricted to the protagonists alone: profound and often contradictory viewpoints are expressed by a whole gamut of characters, from nobles to knaves. Shakespeare invites his audience to consider such conflicting ideas throughout *Measure for Measure*, producing a comedy that demands intellectual engagement from its audience. Opposing philosophical opinions are carefully counterpoised, although some may appear either more or less attractive because of their consequences as ultimately revealed by the plot, or because of their close association with the moral status of the characters who express them. Nevertheless, there is ultimately no definitive resolution to this intellectual conflict between opposing theories concerning politics, ethics, and legislation. Tom Stoppard, the modern English playwright most closely associated with 'dramatizing ideas', once remarked, 'I write plays because writing dialogue is the only respectable way of contradicting myself.'[8] Shakespeare might well have agreed.

Writing some fifty years after Boas first associated *Measure for Measure* with the word 'problem', E. M. W. Tillyard observed that the play is 'radically schizophrenic', as the two halves are dramatically mismatched.[9] The earlier scenes, principally poetical and firmly rooted in the political realism of Shakespeare's histories and tragedies, sit uneasily beside the later scenes, which are predominantly prosaic, abound in folk-tale improbabilities (such as the 'bed-trick' and the 'head-trick'), and conclude with the multiple-marriage convention beloved of Shakespeare's 'happy' comedies. Tillyard observed that the transition between these two halves is startlingly abrupt: the re-emergence of the Duke at Act III, scene i, line 151. The social and political situations explored so realistically up to this point in the play are entirely within the province of the histories and tragedies. The remainder of the play, by contrast, delights in the conventions of romantic fiction, the familiar territory of the comedies.

Even if we agree with Tillyard that the two halves of the play are divided by a conspicuous fault-line, we might still observe that they exemplify Shakespeare's best tragic and comic writing. The first half contains outstanding examples of dramatic poetry. For example, Angelo's first soliloquy ranks with Hamlet's 'O, what a rogue and peasant slave am I!' (*Hamlet*: II, ii, 543–601) and Macbeth's 'If it were done when 'tis done' (*Macbeth*: I, vii, 1–28) in its scathing self-examination. In addition, the Duke's speech to Claudio encouraging contempt for life, and Claudio's contrasting speech to Isabella concerning the terrors of death, share the same thematic balance and eschatological concerns encountered in the most famous speech in world literature: Hamlet's soliloquy,

---

[8] 'Tom Stoppard', British Council: Literature, Accessed 1 February 2019, https://literature.britishcouncil.org/writer/tom-stoppard.
[9] *Shakespeare's Problem Plays* (London: Chatto & Windus, 1950; repr. Harmondsworth: Penguin, 1970), p. 10.

'To be, or not to be' (*Hamlet*: III, i, 56–88). The second half of *Measure for Measure* skilfully concludes a plot of intriguing complexity. This success is achieved while deploying a wide range of characters whose personalities, circumstances, and relationships continue deeply to engage the audience across both halves of the play. When we experience the full extent of *Measure for Measure*'s dramatic and poetic achievements in performance, Tillyard's 'problem' seems rather to be a skilfully-achieved equilibrium between disparate elements.[10]

What further 'problems' does *Measure for Measure* pose, and are they of sufficient significance to justify the unappealing soubriquet of 'problem play'? Primarily, there is the issue of the explicit treatment of disturbing sexual themes to consider. As we have seen, *Measure for Measure* seemed particularly scandalous to nineteenth-century editors, audiences, and readers because the corruptive influence of lust is a conspicuous theme of the play. It should not, however, have shocked Shakespeare's contemporary audience so easily because (as illustrated in Chapter 6 of this study) early seventeenth-century London bore such a close resemblance in its depravity and misrule to the Vienna of *Measure for Measure*; nor should it shock a twenty-first-century audience encountering explicit sexual references daily on television, in newspapers, in modern literature, and via the internet. The sexual themes which, during certain periods in the critical tradition, were met with dismay and distaste, now seem particularly topical, with the media abounding in stories (true and false) of the powerful and influential exploiting for their sexual gratification the weaker or more vulnerable. *Measure for Measure* explores erotic desire in such a convincing, thought-provoking manner that it fully engages

---

[10] After the intellectual and dramatic sophistication of the first half of the play, the contrived denouement will be familiar (and perhaps, therefore, more readily acceptable) to twenty-first century audiences: contemporary film and television crime-thrillers, including modern courtroom dramas (of which *Measure for Measure* is an eminent precursor), habitually permit a decline in plausibility to resolve a convoluted plot.

audiences dramatically whilst rewarding prudent—rather than prurient—consideration of those very issues that offended so many nineteenth-century commentators.

Further to justify the opinion that *Measure for Measure* is a Shakespearian 'problem play', textual issues have been cited, specifically missing lines, questionable phrasing, and confusions over chronology. Were these anomalies to prove a major distraction to the more alert (or more pedantic) members of an audience, they might constitute a defining 'problem'. As early as 1662, a certain 'Johnson' had written of *Measure for Measure*, 'There is, perhaps, not one of Shakespeare's plays more darkened than this, by the peculiarities of the author, and the unskillfulness of its editors, by distortions of phrase, or negligence of transcription.'[11] Modern textual scholarship, however, has tended to disagree. Oversights and inconsistencies in the text are not disproportionately frequent or problematical in *Measure for Measure* when compared with other texts in Shakespeare's First Folio. Although the loss of a line or two of the Duke's first major speech may cause momentary puzzlement (at I, i, 7–9), his gist remains reasonably clear. Similarly, an audience is unlikely to be excessively troubled by issues that might concern an editor: that a couplet is probably missing between lines 267 and 268 of the Duke's sententious review at the end of Act III scene ii; and that the Duke's aside, while Isabella is persuading Mariana to undertake the 'bed trick' (IV, i, 60–5), is too brief and extraneous to be convincing. Similar textual anomalies to those encountered here and elsewhere in *Measure for Measure* recur in Shakespearian works that have never suffered from the prejudicial title of 'problem play'. As the aforementioned 'Johnson' had continued his critique of the play by confirming that 'the light or comic part is very natural and pleasing', it is clear that even he had no objection to the appellation 'comedy' being applied to *Measure for Measure*.

---

[11] Alexandra Jones, quoting from F. E. Halliday, *Shakespeare and his Critics*, (London: Duckworth, 1958), p. 238.

As for the chronological inconsistencies, Shakespeare often shows scant regard for such considerations in other plays (for example, in *Othello*, with its supposed 'dual time-scheme'). A well-paced and well-performed production of *Measure for Measure* should give an audience little leisure to ponder such discrepancies lurking in the text. For example, when did Mistress Overdone first learn of Claudio's sentence in Act I? What, specifically, is the proposed day and hour of Claudio's execution in Acts II–IV? Is it morning or evening when the Duke is in the presence of Isabella and Lucio in Act IV?[12] In each of these cases, there is conflicting textual evidence. It is doubtful, though, whether these minor aberrations, of a kind encountered so frequently elsewhere in Shakespeare's works, justify segregating *Measure for Measure* as a 'problem play'.

To recognise that Shakespeare's *Measure for Measure* raises problematical issues is not to concede that it is a 'problem play'. We have no satisfactory, universally-recognised definition of 'problem play'; nor any consensus as to which *are* 'Shakespeare's problem plays'. Even the most influential critics cannot agree which plays fit into the genre. Boas categorised *Measure for Measure*, *All's Well that Ends Well*, and *Troilus and Cressida* as Shakespeare's problem plays, with a nod towards *Hamlet* as a link to the tragedies. W. W. Lawrence included a section on *Cymbeline* in his 1931 study.[13] In 1963, Ernest Schanzer excluded all of the previous 'problem' canon except *Measure for Measure*, importing in their stead *Julius Caesar* and *Antony and Cleopatra*.[14] Other critics have variously proposed that *The Merchant of Venice*, *Timon of Athens*, and/or *The Winter's Tale* should be regarded as 'Shakespeare's problem plays'. The fact that *Measure for Measure* is the one play consistently included by Shakespearian critics in the 'problem' canon—perhaps the one from which the

---

[12] For a fuller discussion of these anomalies, see Lever, pp. xiv–xvii, and Appendix 1 of this study, pp. 567–576.

[13] *Shakespeare's Problem Comedies* (London: Macmillan, 1931; revised Harmondsworth: Penguin, 1969).

[14] *The Problem Plays of Shakespeare* (New York: Schocken, 1963).

critics take their individual bearings—would seem to confirm that the play is sui generis rather than part of a sub-genre.

Without a fixed and generally-accepted definition, we cannot determine how many of Shakespeare's plays—if any—belong to the 'problem' genre. Critics have tended to formulate their definition of 'problem play' according to their individual predisposition. For example, W. W. Lawrence conceded, 'The "problem" is not like one in mathematics, to which there is a single true solution, but is one of conduct, as to which there are no fixed and immutable laws. Often, it cannot be reduced to any formula. . . .'[15] If 'it' (presumably, the 'problem') cannot be reduced to any formula, then how can we establish a defining principle for the genre? If we suspect that certain of Shakespeare's ripe theatrical plums are unsuitable for general consumption, we should not expect to make them either more appetizing or more digestible by throwing more and more of them into a separately-labelled paper bag from which the bottom has dropped out.

Modern theatregoers and readers, many of whom consider Shakespeare's language challenging, will be discouraged from viewing or reading a Shakespearian 'problem play' for fear that any text presenting eminent academics with a 'problem' will prove impenetrable to them. By contrast, to call *Measure for Measure* a Shakespearian comedy should not deter audiences. Let's stick with 'comedy', then, with the prospect of enjoyment that 'comedy' promises. Better to find a comedy surprisingly dark than to disregard the play altogether because it is described, unenticingly, as a 'problem'.

A Morality Play?

In his seminal work on Shakespeare, *The Wheel of Fire* (1930), G. Wilson Knight proposed that *Measure for Measure*

---

[15] *Shakespeare's Problem Comedies*, p. 21.

'tends towards allegory or symbolism'.[16] He called the play 'this masterpiece of ethical drama', insisting, 'The play must be read, not as a picture of normal human affairs, but as a parable, like the parables of Jesus.'[17] When he defined the dramatic function of the three protagonists, Wilson Knight offered further insight into his allegorical interpretation:

> Thus Isabella stands for sainted purity, Angelo for Pharasaical righteousness, the Duke for a psychologically sound and enlightened ethic. . . . The Duke's sense of human responsibility is delightful throughout: he is like a kindly father, and all the rest are his children. . . . As the play progresses and his plot on Angelo works he assumes an ever-increasing mysterious dignity, his original purpose seems to become more and more profound in human insight.[18]

Ten years later, the influential critic, F. R. Leavis, endorsed Wilson Knight's reading of the play as 'the only adequate account' of *Measure for Measure*, confirming the Duke as 'a kind of Providence directing the action from above'.[19] Thus, in well under half a century, Shakespeare's scurrilous 'problem play' had been miraculously transformed into Shakespeare's ethical 'morality play', without a word of the text being changed.

Although Shakespeare and his contemporary audience would not have recognised 'problem plays' as a dramatic genre, they were entirely familiar with morality plays. Known to their contemporaries as 'moral interludes' or 'moralities', morality plays were popular throughout the Fifteenth and Sixteenth

---

[16] The relevant chapter is reprinted as '*Measure for Measure* and the Gospels', in *Shakespeare*: Measure for Measure: *A Casebook*, ed. C. K. Stead (London: Macmillan, 1971), pp. 91–121. The quotation may be found on p. 91.

[17] Stead, p. 120.

[18] Conflating Stead, pp. 92 and 98.

[19] Quoted by Stead, p. 18.

Centuries. They resembled dramatized sermons or spiritual fables, their didactic purpose being manifest. They brought moral instruction to a predominantly illiterate audience, the plot often illustrating the wisdom and benevolence of God or of God's agents. Angels and devils came and went freely. The dramatis personae comprised types—often personified abstractions such as Death, Knowledge, or Good Deeds—whilst protagonists such as Everyman, Mankind, or Youth represented humanity in general rather than clearly-individualised human beings. Should the protagonists be threatened with damnation or other dire punishment, the expectation was that they should be directed towards salvation by divine intervention or by justice tempered with mercy.

Parallels between characters and situations in the later morality plays and in *Measure for Measure* are readily recognisable. In the interlude known as *Respublica*, probably written by Nicholas Udall and performed in the first year of Queen Mary's reign (1553–4), Justice is envisaged as an earthly judge—'I, Justice, from heaven am come youe to visytte' (V, v, 1407)[20]—rather than as God sitting in judgement on high, as in earlier morality plays. When the Duke, 'like power divine', miraculously appears to deal justice in the final scene of *Measure for Measure*, he resembles his counterpart in Udall's play. In *The Contention between Liberalitie and Prodigalitie* (1567), we learn that Justice has left the country, to be replaced by Equity, who sits in his judgement-chair, just as Duke Vincentio in *Measure for Measure* apparently leaves Vienna, appointing Angelo to take his place—although Angelo's justice scarcely proves equitable. There is evidence that *The Contention between Liberality and Prodigality* was performed before Elizabeth I as late as 1600–1. Its appearance on stage and in print at the very opening of the Seventeenth Century

---

[20] '*Respublica*, A.D. 1553: A Play on the Social Condition of England at the Accession of Queen Mary', Internet Archive, accessed 20 July 2020, https://archive.org/stream/respublicaadapl00magngoog/respublicaada pl00magngoog_djvu.txt.

suggests that it may have been known to Shakespeare sufficiently to shape his conception of subject-matter and genre as he was working on *Measure for Measure*, affecting his portrayal both of the Duke and of Angelo. On the title-page of the 1602 edition, however, *The Contention between Liberality and Prodigality* is *not* described as a moral interlude (as its dramatis personae comprising vocations and personified abstractions might have suggested), but rather as 'a pleasant comedie'.[21] Such evidence suggests that the morality tradition was being subsumed into the comic genre during this period.

Angelo is the character in *Measure for Measure* who most clearly displays the conventions of the morality play adapted for the purposes of a comedy. Although convincingly portrayed as a hypocritical Puritan, Angelo is also a dramatic construct in the morality-tradition. In Tudor moral interludes such as *Youth*, *Mankind*, *The Castle of Perseverance*, and *Everyman*, mercy and divine grace were illustrated when sinful indulgence by the protagonists was followed ultimately by repentance and absolution. So it is with Angelo.

Shakespeare would certainly have been familiar with Christopher Marlowe's play, *Dr. Faustus,* in which this morality-play convention of the sinner ultimately saved by penitence and absolution was radically altered. First staged around 1592–3 and drawing extensively on the morality-play tradition, *Dr. Faustus* became the most frequently-performed play in the final decade of the Sixteenth Century, when Shakespeare was establishing his reputation as a playwright in London. The influence of Marlowe's Faustus on Shakespeare's Angelo is implicit. Both characters are admired intellectuals. Both are guilty of overweening pride (*hubris*) that leads them wilfully to sin. Both, while aspiring to transcend their human limitations, paradoxically become sub-human and depraved. Faustus laments in his first scene that he is 'but Faustus, and a

---

[21] 'A Pleasant Comedie, Shewing the contention between *Liberalitie and Prodigalitie*' (London, 1602), Internet Archive, accessed 20 July 2020, https://archive.org/details/cu31924013324185/, p. 9.

man' (line 23), aspiring to superhuman powers but ultimately sinking to bestial depths in which he envies creatures without a soul that can escape eternal punishment; Angelo, striving for superhuman perfection by refusing to acknowledge his human appetites, ultimately comes to detest himself as a rapist and a murderer.

Angelo, however, experiences a very different nemesis from Faustus. Although neither thinks himself worthy of forgiveness, Faustus is publicly celebrated but ultimately damned, whereas Angelo is publicly humiliated but ultimately redeemed. Faustus's despair, his inability to believe that the many crimes that he has committed against God can be forgiven, results in his body being torn apart by devils and his soul being dragged to hell for eternal torments. Angelo, craving death as the just penalty for crimes that he believed that he had committed but which he has unwittingly avoided through the intervention of Vincentio, receives the Duke's amnesty. In this vital detail of the sinner saved by last-minute providential intervention, Shakespeare follows the morality-play tradition rather than the Marlovian tragic innovation.

Unlike *Dr. Faustus*, *Measure for Measure* does not overtly incorporate the paraphernalia of the morality plays that preceded it. Marlowe adopted personified abstractions—the masque of the Seven Deadly Sins—for his play. No personified abstractions are presented on stage in Shakespeare's play.[22] In keeping with the morality tradition, great emphasis was placed on exploring eschatological issues in *Dr. Faustus*: do devils suffer? what torments are encountered by the damned in Hell? can the sinner who has rejected God ever be accepted into

---

[22] The nearest that we approach such personified abstractions in the play is during Pompey's speech at the beginning of IV, iii, where he lists the prisoners with whom he is acquainted in Vienna's jail, e.g. 'Master Deep-vow', 'young Drop-heir', and 'wild Half-can'. This is, however, the only context in the play where those named are no more than types of the kind encountered in morality plays. Furthermore, none of those mentioned in Pompey's speech is presented on stage.

Heaven? By contrast, Shakespeare dispenses with much of this conventional morality-play apparatus, as the fate of the soul after death is not an overriding preoccupation in *Measure for Measure*.[23] Marlowe frequently deployed both devils and angels on stage, theatrical devices that he borrowed from the moral interludes. Devils do not appear on stage in *Measure for Measure*, although much mention is made of Satan and his works, particularly in references to (and by) Angelo. Divine agents are also absent from the stage: there is no attempt in *Measure for Measure* directly to represent either God or the angels, although they had been frequently embodied in the earlier moralities. Claudio may talk of civil authority as 'the demi-god' (I, ii, 112); the Duke may claim that the death of Ragozine is 'an accident that heaven provides' (IV, iii, 76); and Angelo may associate Vincentio with 'power divine' in the final scene (V, i, 367); but these are pious references of a kind that might be expected in any Elizabethan or Jacobean drama, rather than proof of a close affinity with the morality plays.

If *Measure for Measure* were a morality play, we should expect it to draw a clear distinction between virtue and vice. Instead, Shakespeare's play seems deliberately to blur the boundaries. Although a simplistic view of *Measure for Measure* might regard the Duke and Isabella as the principal 'good' characters, counterpoised by Angelo as the 'villain' of the piece, neither side of this equation bears closer scrutiny. Angelo and Isabella seem, paradoxically, to be corrupted by virtue, while the Duke seems intent on disguising malpractice under the integument of piety. William Empson, not the first to recognise 'the unpleasantness of the two good characters' (the

---

[23] Among the few contexts in which this issue is considered in *Measure for Measure* are Isabella's riposte to Angelo at II, iv, 106–8; Claudio's appeal to Isabella beginning 'Ay, but to die' (III, i, 117–31); and the Duke's refusal to execute the unshriven Barnadine for fear of imperilling both their souls (IV, iii, 66–8). By contrast, in Shakespeare's *Hamlet*, as in Marlowe's *Dr. Faustus*, there is persistent deliberation over what will happen to both body and soul after death.

Duke and Isabella), concluded that Shakespeare 'found he did not like his saints when he had got them'.[24] It might be safer to say that Shakespeare recognised that the extremes of both good and evil are qualified by human limitations.

Measure for Measure defies consideration as a parable or as an allegory because its protagonists—the Duke, Angelo, and Isabella—cannot be regarded simply as clear embodiments of the distinctions between good and bad. Rather, the play illustrates how readily the virtues of a 'good' character can distort into vice. In the Duke's case, the pursuit of an apparently worthy goal is achieved only through dubious conduct that causes much needless suffering. Angelo's impartial rigour in the administration of justice, seemingly righteous practice, marks the beginning of his degeneration into tyranny when he fails to distinguish between inadvertent wrongdoers and hardened criminals. Isabella so jealously guards her personal virtue that it disfigures into a callous, selfish obsession that threatens to destroy her relationship with her wretched brother. Each of these protagonists might aspire to virtuous principles, but each, under the pretext of behaving scrupulously, is betrayed by self-interest into the maltreatment of others.

Just as dubious means are not necessarily vindicated by virtuous ends, so pious intentions do not invariably secure praiseworthy outcomes. For example, the Duke's seemingly laudable attempt to offer greater civil liberty to his subjects leads to social disorder (see I, iii, 19–31 and V, i, 314–20). Later, when disguised as Friar Lodowick, the Duke strives to save Claudio from execution and to bring Angelo to justice, both virtuous ends; but, in so doing, he causes extreme and unjustifiable anguish to Julietta (II, iii, 37–42), to Claudio (III, i, 1–172), and particularly to Isabella (IV, iii, 114–22). Vincentio may achieve his worthy objectives, in that Claudio is

---

[24] 'Sense in *Measure for Measure*' in Stead, pp. 206–8. Stead adds, 'The problem [for critics] arose . . . with Isabella and the Duke, characters who, it was felt, were meant to be admirable but who were not . . .' (p. 13).

granted full amnesty while Angelo is exposed as a hypocritical tyrant; but an audience may recognise that the Duke's deceit, false oaths, and abuse of the sacraments of the Church were not indispensable in securing those successes. Vincentio's proposal of marriage to Isabella at the end of the play raises the question of whether his motives could ever be regarded as altruistic: should they not, rather, be recognised as elaborate ploys to disguise the selfish pursuit of his amatory ambitions? Or are such considerations futile because the inconsistencies of the Duke's character and actions, born of the comic tradition, defy such moral scrutiny?

A judge who insists on the imposition of justice, rejecting compromise and partiality, might seem the moral ideal; but *Measure for Measure* demonstrates how inflexibility in the administration of the law may stem from unworthy motives and evolve into tyranny. There are clues that Angelo's judicial severity is rooted in his obsession with his reputation: Claudio believes that the death-sentence imposed on him reflects Angelo's concern 'for a name' (I, ii, 158 and 160); while Angelo himself admits in soliloquy his jealous desire to preserve his 'gravity, / Wherein . . . I take pride' (II, iv, 9–10). The new Deputy appears eager for the respect and fear that a severe judge instils in those over whom he wields power. When Angelo pontificates about the law, he does so to justify the extreme penalties that he imposes on Claudio and Julietta,[25] prosecuted for a marriage that they believed to be a 'true contract' (I, ii, 134). In so doing, Angelo fails to distinguish between an inadvertent offence on the part of two faithful lovers and, for example, the deliberate flouting of the statutes against sexual misconduct by those frequenting Mistress Overdone's 'house of resort'. As a result, Angelo's strict enforcement of the law, a seeming virtue, is not unambiguously endorsed by *any* other character in the play, but rather

---

[25] For example, at II, i, 1–4 and 17–31; at II, ii, 37–106; and at II, iv, 42–9.

condemned, even by his fellow officers of state.[26] Even before Angelo's first encounter with Isabella, whose presence will deform his zeal into lust, Shakespeare does not encourage us to admire the inflexible judge.

In Angelo's sexual obsession with Isabella, we witness how he can 'Corrupt with virtuous season' (II, ii, 168). The expression is deliberately ambiguous: Angelo not only attempts to corrupt virtue in another when he encounters it, but also becomes corrupted himself when he encounters virtue. Angelo has never been sexually aroused by 'the strumpet / With all her double vigour, art and nature' (II, ii, 183–4). An alluring, provocatively-adorned prostitute—that is, vice which presents itself as vice—holds no attraction for him. Rather, piety and purity, in the form of Isabella, overwhelm Angelo's resistance: 'this virtuous maid / Subdues me quite' (II, ii, 185–6). As Angelo believes that love of virtue is corrupting him in the person of Isabella (II, ii, 181–3), he concludes that the 'cunning enemy' (i.e. Satan) deploys 'saints' such as Isabella to ensnare a 'saint' such as he believes himself to be (II, ii, 180–1); but even this recognition that the Devil is seeking to destroy him does not empower him to resist the temptation. Angelo, who witnesses the supreme virtue to which he aspires embodied in Isabella, can contemplate no way to encompass it but by perverting it.

Isabella's case, like Angelo's, suggests that the uncompromising pursuit of virtue may reach a tipping-point at which it abruptly transforms into a vice. She is presented in the early part of the play as 'a very virtuous maid' (II, ii, 20) who dearly prizes her chastity and abhors licentiousness in others. Such sentiments, admirable in a novice nun, might justify why she should place the preservation of her virginity before the preservation of her brother's life. What is deplorable, however, is the cruel tirade that she unleashes on her brother for begging her to save him. His irresolution on the brink of execution is

---

[26] For example, by Escalus at II, i, 4–40 and III, ii, 244–8; by the Provost at II, ii, 2–12; and by the anonymous Justice at II, i, 279.

deserving of understanding and compassion, but her imprecations against him smack not of moral righteousness but rather of hysteria, egotism, or vindictiveness. Rather than showing sympathy for a brother threatened with torture and death, she berates him as a coward and a degenerate worthy of execution, one for whose death she will pray persistently without offering the least plea to redeem him (III, i, 135–49). Her apparently virtuous resolve to preserve her virginity has abruptly distorted into a selfish and cruel denunciation of an already tormented victim.

At crucial times, each of the three protagonists in *Measure for Measure*—the Duke, Angelo, and Isabella—suffers from a lack of 'charity', the Christian love of humankind that embraces compassion, mercy, and forgiveness. In his First Epistle to the Corinthians, Chapter 13, Saint Paul asserts the supremacy of charity, dismissing all other Christian virtues and pursuits as worthless if charity is lacking. In his exploitation of others to achieve his ends, the Duke neglects such charity, causing widespread distress. There is little charity in Angelo's prosecution of those who contravene the laws against sexual misconduct, and none at all in his attempt to pervert Isabella in defiance of those same laws. Finally, and most emphatically, charity is entirely lacking from Isabella's condemnation of her imprisoned brother; she shows scant charity in her dealings with others until, ultimately, she deigns to intercede for Angelo at the end of the play.

Although *Measure for Measure* was clearly influenced by the morality-tradition, it is not a dramatized sermon, as no overarching moral or spiritual message is manifest. Its multifaceted characters defy categorization as simple embodiments of moral abstractions, just as the complexities of its plot resist classification as simple spiritual lessons. Rather than following the Catholic tradition—as morality plays do—of unambiguous doctrinal instruction deriving from the authority of the Church, *Measure for Measure* adopts a more 'Protestant' course, inviting the individual to seek the path to salvation through conscientious personal reflection.

Because *Measure for Measure* is not overtly didactic, stubbornly refusing to promulgate any clear doctrine concerning correct human behaviour, it is distinct both from the morality plays that preceded it and from the problem plays that succeeded it. Shakespeare's play raises a plethora of questions while avoiding simplistic answers, implicitly inviting his audiences to think for themselves. This is no weakness of *Measure for Measure*, but rather its strength, in engaging the intellectual and moral judgement of its audiences. As there is no unequivocal spiritual message, however, it is disqualified as a morality play, just as surely as it is disqualified as a problem play because there is no unequivocal socio-political message. Although it may not seem an orthodox comedy, *Measure for Measure* achieves a more-or-less happy ending in spite of the disturbing issues that it dramatizes. There is, then, little point in reclassifying *Measure for Measure* under the designation of 'problem play' or 'moral interlude' when it corresponds less to the distinguishing features of these genres than it does to those of the genre with which it has been associated since first it was printed. A comedy, then, let it remain for the time being—although a comedy sui generis.

A Tragicomedy?

Rather than anatomizing love, as Shakespeare's comedies tend to do, *Measure for Measure* seeks 'Of government the properties to unfold', as the Duke announces in the first full line of the play. Like Shakespeare's great tragedies, most of which also stem from the first decade of the Seventeenth Century, and like his histories from the previous decade, *Measure for Measure* is an intensely political play, investigating issues of governance and justice. Unlike all the tragedies in the First Folio, however, no-one in *Measure for Measure* is murdered, executed, slain in battle, driven to suicide, or otherwise subjected to a premature demise: death, the sine qua non of

Shakespearian tragedy, is entirely absent from the stage.[27] *Measure for Measure* may treat of themes explored in the great tragedies—for example, tyranny, corruption, injustice, and suffering— but the expectation of a tragic denouement created by the early Acts of the play remains unfulfilled. Neither can *Measure for Measure* be regarded as a history play, the only genre other than comedy or tragedy admitted in the First Folio of 1623. Although one major facet of its plot may be loosely based on documented fact—an account of the tyranny of a lascivious Spanish dignitary[28]—there is no attempt in *Measure for Measure* to present any historical event or personage with any degree of verisimilitude. Just as Mariana insists that she is 'neither maid, widow, nor wife', the only three types of woman endorsed by the Duke (V, i, 178–9), so *Measure for Measure* might seem to challenge categorisation as either comedy, tragedy, or history, the only three types of play ratified by Shakespeare's compilers, Heminges and Condell.

It is tempting, however, to recall Polonius's reference to a 'tragical-comical-historical-pastoral' genre (*Hamlet*: II, ii, 395). Although the line might be dismissed as characteristic of Polonius's pedantic prolixity, the context confirms that Shakespeare and his contemporaries recognised that distinct genres such as comedy and tragedy could be fused to form a new, composite dramatic variety. To call *Measure for Measure* a tragicomedy might not, then, be an anachronism.

However, the definition and practice of tragicomedy in the decade in which Shakespeare wrote *Measure for Measure* call into question whether the play *would* have been regarded as a tragicomedy at the opening of the Seventeenth Century.

---

[27] The only death occurring during the play is the fortuitous demise from a fever of Ragozine, a pirate who never appears on stage and whose single function is to supply a head that Angelo might mistake for Claudio's.

[28] The widespread influence of a letter recording the injustice practised by this Spanish count is discussed in Chapter 1, 'Sources of the Plot', p. 21.

Giambattista Guarini, in *Il Compendio della Poesia Tragicomica* (1601), asserted that

> He who composes tragicomedy takes from tragedy its great persons but not its great action, its verisimilar plot but not its true one, its movement of the feelings but not its disturbance of them, its pleasure but not its sadness, its danger but not its death; from comedy, it takes laughter that is not excessive, modest amusement, feigned difficulty, happy reversal, and above all the comic order. . . .[29]

This contemporary Italian definition of the genre seems remote from Shakespeare's achievement in *Measure for Measure*. 'Happy reversal' and the restoration of 'comic order' may be encountered at the end of the play; but 'great action', 'disturbance of . . . feelings' and 'sadness' are scarcely absent, while 'amusement' is scarcely 'modest'.

What, though, was the contemporary English conception of tragicomedy? Five years after the first recorded performance of *Measure for Measure*, John Fletcher defined his play, *The Faithful Shepherdess*, as 'a pastorall Tragie-commedie', adding that

> A tragie-comedie is not so called in respect of mirth and killing but in respect it wants deaths, which is inough to make it no tragedie, yet brings some neer it, which is inough to make it no comedie. . . .[30]

Measure for Measure undeniably complies with this definition, but the definition itself is too vague to be of much value. The

---

[29] Quoted by George L. Geckle, ed., *Twentieth Century Interpretations of* Measure for Measure: *A Collection of Critical Essays* (Englewood Cliffs, NJ: Prentice-Hall, 1970), p. 12.

[30] *A Digital Anthology of Early Modern English Drama*, Folger Shakespeare Library, accessed 20 July 2020, https://emed.folger.edu/sites/default/files/folger_encodings/pdf/EMED-FS-orig-2.pdf, p. 8. See also Braunmuller and Watson, p. 2.

question is whether Shakespeare's play corresponds with the Jacobean *practice* of tragicomedy. Braunmuller and Watson (pp. 2–3) think not: '*Measure for Measure* seems markedly different from tragicomic practice in Shakespeare's time, which was far more romantic from its opening premises to its final scene.'

Even in his so-called 'middle-period happy comedies' immediately preceding *Measure for Measure*, Shakespeare was testing how close to the squally seas of tragedy he could steer a plot when navigating the generally balmier waters of comedy. For example, in *Much Ado About Nothing* (1598–9), that intimate moment when two lovers finally confess their reciprocal adoration is transformed abruptly to horror when Beatrice announces the price that Benedick must pay for her love: to kill his best friend, Claudio (IV, i, 287). Similarly, the tormenting of Malvolio and his concluding curse, 'I'll be reveng'd on the whole pack of you' (V, i, 364), infuse a measure of bitterness into the sweetness of the multiple marriages at the end of *Twelfth Night* (1601–2). Neither of these two comedies, where darker veins permeate the lighter mood of the main plot, is usually regarded as a tragicomedy; but the juxtaposition of the tragic and the comic is more conspicuous in *Measure for Measure*. Certainly, the conventions of Shakespearian comedy—the restoration of order, multiple marriages, and a generally happy denouement—predominate at the end of *Measure for Measure* as surely as they do at the end of *Much Ado*, *Twelfth Night*, or any of the other 'happy comedies'; but, in the case of *Measure for Measure*, not before the grim depths of tragedy have been sounded in the preceding scenes.

If the social and political world of Shakespeare's great tragedies is to be dramatically convincing, then so must the protagonists be who inhabit that world. Shakespeare's tragedies create an entirely reasonable expectation in their audiences that protagonists should be judged according to 'realistic' standards of conduct. Those characters may alter abruptly or evolve gradually, but not without dramatic justification. Hamlet is wildly erratic in his behaviour, but the multiple facets of his character coalesce into an overall coherency. Isabella's fluctuations between incapacitating self-doubt and violent moral indignation bear comparison here: she too is convincingly characterised, despite her vicissitudes. In a further tragedy, more closely contemporary to *Measure for Measure*, Othello degenerates from an authoritative, self-possessed ruler to a soul ensnared by a 'devil', corrupted by sexual obsession. In this respect, his similarity to Angelo is striking. Like the protagonists of the tragedies, Angelo and Isabella remain psychologically convincing, even when their behaviour may seem inconsistent. In addition, the relationship between Angelo and Isabella, corrupt ruler and victim of oppression respectively, displays particularly strong affinities with *Richard III*, *Hamlet*, *Macbeth*, and *King Lear*, four Shakespearean plays classified as 'tragedy' (or 'history') that present dramatically the suffering of victims seeking justice from tyrants who pervert the law for their own evil purposes.

The Duke's province, by contrast with that of Angelo and Isabella, lies in the world of the comedies. Because of the different expectation created by unrealistic settings and improbable circumstances, comedies rely much less than the tragedies and histories on credible characterisation. The Duke does not appear in five of the opening eight scenes of the play—the tragic exposition and its development—and is entirely absent from the four longest scenes in Acts I and II (I, ii; II, i; II, ii; and II, iv). Conversely, Isabella and Angelo dominate Act II, that part of the play most obviously concerned with the law and government, the province of the tragedies and histories. From the beginning of Act III, the Duke appears in all but two of the remaining nine scenes as the second half of *Measure for Measure* works towards its comic denouement. The two scenes in which he does not appear are relatively insignificant, totalling under fifty lines between them. In the final scene of the play, when all the major characters and many of the lesser characters are on stage, the Duke speaks almost half of the total number of lines, and very nearly seventy percent of the lines in the coda between his unhooding and the

519

final curtain. In short, the two 'tragic' protagonists predominate in the tragic induction to *Measure for Measure*, while the sole 'comic' protagonist predominates in the comic denouement.

The behaviour of protagonists in the comedies can be as inconsistent and implausible as dramatic circumstances require. For example, in two Shakespearian comedies that immediately precede *Measure for Measure*, dramatic circumstances at the end of the play dictate sudden and implausible changes in the characters and attitudes of the three dukes presented on stage. Throughout *Twelfth Night* (probably first performed in 1602), Duke Orsino declares the constancy of his passion for the Lady Olivia and is entirely preoccupied with soliciting her love, despite long and persistent rejection; yet he abruptly and improbably redirects his affections to Viola as soon as he learns of Olivia's marriage. In *As You Like It* (probably first performed in 1603), the usurping Duke Frederick rages tyrannically, confirming his murderous propensities when he embarks on a fratricidal mission; but, after a chance encounter with 'an old religious man' late in the play, he is suddenly and miraculously 'converted . . . from the world' to a life of pious devotion. His elder brother, the exiled Duke Senior, having scorned the court and declared his preference for the pastoral paradise of the Forest of Arden throughout his exile, resumes his courtly privileges with unashamed alacrity when offered the opportunity by his brother's abdication. Such abrupt and implausible changes of character, motivation, and attitude are not incongruous in the comedies, as these inconsistencies are entirely appropriate to the folk-tales with which these plays have such close affinity. Duke Vincentio in *Measure for Measure* belongs to the same fantasy-world inhabited by Duke Orsino, Duke Frederick, and Duke Senior in Shakespeare's immediately-preceding comedies. Early in the play, he scorns those who 'stage' themselves to the 'eyes' of 'the people' (I, i, 167–72) and declares that he is proof against 'the dribbling dart of love' (I, iii, 1–3); but, in the final scene, this same Duke Vincentio courts the 'loud applause and *Aves* vehement' (I, i, 70) of Vienna's citizens, and requests the hand of Isabella in marriage. These inconsistencies, though implausible, are comparable with those of the dukes who were his immediate predecessors in Shakespeare's 'romantic' comedies.

By contrast with Duke Vincentio, Isabella and Angelo seem alien to such improbable realms of fiction. This may produce a dissonance between 'tragic' and 'comic' events and characters, a challenge to *Measure for Measure* in performance. For example, when the Duke proposes marriage at the end of the play, his folk-tale origins would suggest that his offer should be gratefully accepted to ensure the happy ending proper to a comedy; but when Isabella receives the Duke's marriage-proposal, the fact that this 'tragic' character has so cherished her virginity (while never indicating interest in any future other than as a nun) might render her acceptance improbable. The deciding factor may be that, since early in Act III, when (as E. M. W. Tillyard noted) the tide of tragedy turned, *Measure for Measure* has complied with the Shakespearian comic tradition, the plot working towards multiple marriages at its conclusion. Having strayed from her earlier tragic province into the territory of comedy, Isabella may well be obliged dramatically to yield to fictional conventions by accepting the Duke's proposal. In this way, the tragic and the comic become 'married' at the end of a play in which all such conflicts and divisions are ultimately reconciled.

Like the Duke throwing off his disguise as Friar Lodowick to reveal his true status, so *Measure for Measure* shrugs off its earlier appearance as a tragedy to resolve itself in its latter scenes into a comedy. If we feel the need to challenge the classification of *Measure for Measure* as pure comedy, and if we recognise the dangers of re-classifying it as a either a problem play or as a moral interlude, then we might venture to regard it as a kind of tragicomedy. Alternatively, we could side with Simon McBurney, who directed the play at the National Theatre in 2004 and 2006: according to him, *Measure for Measure* 'resists ultimate definition'.[31] In the final analysis, however, recognising that *Measure for Measure* is a comedy

---

[31] *The Independent*, 23 May 2004, pp. 14–15.

521

but, by Shakespearian standards, potentially a particularly *dark* comedy, remains the least controversial and most satisfactory conclusion.

Measure for Measure in Performance: The First 350 Years

At the start of the second act of *Measure for Measure*, Escalus offers advice to Angelo about the dangers of extremism:

Let us be keen, and rather cut a little
Than f[e]ll, and bruise to death. [II, i, 5–6]

The sense of these lines is that it is better to be restrained and precise when removing what offends, rather than to unleash a savage assault that could prove fatal. Escalus is referring to sentencing under the law, but his aphorism might equally be applied to the process of editing the text of a Shakespearian play for the stage. The wisdom of Escalus's counsel, however, went largely unheeded for over three hundred years of stage-performances of *Measure for Measure*, many of which, rather than restricting themselves to judicious cutting, radically disfigured Shakespeare's text—often without achieving any great popular acclaim.

Performances of *Measure for Measure* in England—relatively infrequent until the Twentieth Century—generally aimed to endorse contemporary tastes, attitudes, and mores. In addition, some productions sought to exploit the unusual capacity of *Measure for Measure* to reflect political events affecting the country. To achieve these objectives, *Measure for Measure* was often heavily cut, extensively interpolated, and even conflated with other performance-texts to cater for the tastes of prospective audiences and to reflect topical issues in a non-controversial manner. It might be suspected that the presentation, in unabridged form, of a play concerning the corruptive influence of power and sexual desire in high places was at certain times considered too inflammatory to be staged with impunity. For example, we know of no performance of *Measure for Measure* between that attended by the newly-crowned King in December 1604 and the closure of the theatres under the Puritans in 1642. This period of neglect might suggest simply that the play did not appeal to playgoers during the reigns of James I and Charles I. Alternatively, the portrayal on stage of sexual scandal at court, and of seditious elements in society challenging the rule of law, might have cut rather too close to the bone later in the Jacobean era.

Between the Restoration in 1660 and the end of the Seventeenth Century, the text of *Measure for Measure* was twice treated by playwrights as a repository of lines, characters, and incidents that could be freely abridged, augmented with new lines, and blended with other texts. The aim was to produce a play more in keeping with contemporary preferences and attitudes. Not surprisingly, in these two Restoration adaptations of *Measure for Measure*, voices of dissent and complaints against the injustices of government were suppressed: the bloody civil war was too fresh in the public memory for political controversy to be explored on stage. The underworld characters were excised, together with their bawdy banter, while Isabella's lines were mollified to present her as more submissive and 'feminine'. Similar redactions, suppressing the comic roles and accentuating Isabella's modest compliance (with the Duke, but not, of course, with Angelo) persisted in productions over the ensuing two centuries.[32] These productions interacted with prevailing trends in Restoration criticism to present Isabella as an icon of female virtue, piety, and gentleness rather than as the zealot fiercely defending her conceptions of morality and justice who emerges from the unedited Shakespearian text.

---

[32] Rachod Nusen, 'English Productions of *Measure for Measure* on Stage and Screen: The Play's Indeterminacy and the Authority of Performance' (PhD thesis) Lancaster University, 6 May 2016, https://eprints.lancs.ac.uk/id/eprint/79345/1/2016rachodphd.pdf, pp. 98 and 107.

The first of the two extensive Restoration revisions arrived on stage in 1662. Sir William Davenant's *The Law Against Lovers*, without any acknowledgement to Shakespeare, grafted characters from *Much Ado About Nothing* (including the lovers, Beatrice and Benedick) on to *Measure for Measure*, to produce a play that more closely resembled a romantic comedy. Any sequences likely to cause moral or political disquiet were adapted or expunged: underworld interludes were deleted, Angelo's proposition to Isabella became a test of her virtue rather than an attempted seduction, and any strife in the prison between sister and brother was removed. Davenant's version encouraged a Royalist interpretation of the Duke and his Deputy: Vincentio's mercy was accentuated to present him (and, by implication, Charles II) as 'like power divine'; while Angelo's rule was portrayed as more overtly repressive, implicitly to discredit the recently defunct puritan Commonwealth under Cromwell. Davenant even bestowed Cromwell's title of 'Lord Protector' on Angelo, to make the association between the two incontrovertible. Vincentio's return in Act V to depose Angelo from the judgement seat was thus a dramatic representation of what had occurred in England just two years before: the triumphant restoration of the monarch. Not surprisingly, in this version, Isabella was given a final speech confirming her dutiful acceptance of the Duke's proposal of marriage. Who could resist such an offer from the merry—and merciful—monarch on his return?

Thirty-seven years later, as the Seventeenth Century drew to its close, Charles Gildon used Davenant's play as a basis for his 'new' drama: *Measure for Measure* or *Beauty the Best Advocate*. This version, performed towards the end of the reign of William III, dispensed with Davenant's characters imported from *Much Ado about Nothing*, preferring to conflate *Measure for Measure* with Purcell's opera, *Dido and Aeneas*, which was performed as part of Angelo's birthday celebrations.[33] Gildon's play was partly shaped by the concerns and tastes of a rapidly

---

[33] When the play was revived in 1706, Motteux's *Acis and Galatea* replaced the Purcell opera.

expanding bourgeoisie, a significant contingent of its intended audience. In the interests of moral and political orthodoxy (but also to comply more closely with Aristotle's unity of time), it elided the whole of Act I, together with any reference that might condone illicit sexual activity.[34] Gildon's Isabella is to become a nun because of economic necessity: she has no fortune. Angelo, risen to prominence from obscurity, is now a bourgeois who 'values money more highly than honour or love'.[35] For example, he had planned to marry Mariana for her dowry, to improve his financial circumstances. Even his proposition to Isabella subliminally suggests a business-transaction: her acquiescence to his sexual request will render him 'rich' while making her no 'poorer' (IV, i, 60). Presenting Angelo's corruption in this manner might implicitly advocate to the commercial classes the need for probity in economic and amatory affairs, while simultaneously appealing to the sense of moral superiority of the higher-class members of the audience.[36]

The dismissive remark of Charles II's Poet Laureate should be seen in the context of these significant changes in theatrical audiences and their dramatic tastes. John Dryden, writing in 1672, condemned *Measure for Measure* as 'grounded on impossibilities, or at least so meanly written, that the comedy

---

[34] Gildon's version has the lovers already fully married. Claudio and Julietta are waiting for the priest who married them to return from France. Angelo is concealing his marriage to Mariana. In addition, Claudio does not plead with Isabella to sacrifice her virginity to save him. These major changes to Shakespeare's text, summarized by Braunmuller and Watson (pp. 125–6), radically simplify the moral complexity of the play.

[35] Nusen, p. 104.

[36] The suspicion that Gildon's version of *Measure for Measure* was written in response to the tastes of the increasingly significant commercial classes receives support from J. Douglas Canfield's general assertion that 'by the end of the seventeenth century, aristocratic tragicomedy is becoming moribund and its form is already being appropriated to bourgeois ideology.' 'The Ideology of Restoration Tragicomedy', *ELH* 51 (1984), pp. 461–462.

neither caused your mirth, nor the serious part your concernment.'[37] If a Shakespeare play is generally considered implausible, inferior to the dramatic standard of the day, or alien to the interests, experiences, or predilections of contemporary audiences, then 'improving' it by whatever means seem appropriate can be justified on artistic grounds, as well as on pragmatic, commercial grounds.

It was, paradoxically, because of the growing reverence for Shakespeare in the Eighteenth Century that the scripts used for productions of *Measure for Measure* remained heavily elided. Anything likely to be considered vulgar or subversive was suppressed to further Shakespeare's growing reputation for moral propriety and impeccable discernment. Unfortunately, removing such 'vulgar' and 'subversive' elements from *Measure for Measure* was likely to render the play considerably less amusing and compelling in performance.

Eighteenth-century performances of *Measure for Measure*, although relatively infrequent,[38] were based on scripts considerably closer to the original in Shakespeare's First Folio than either Davenant's or Gildon's performing-texts had been. Many lines, nevertheless, were still redacted, and others were added to prompt-copies. When the play was revived by John Rich at London's Lincoln's Inn Fields in 1720, it was 'perhaps an approximation to Shakespeare's text'.[39] This acting-edition was, nevertheless, heavily cut and eight lines were added at the end. The general intention was to make the play more morally wholesome while avoiding any implicit criticism of either the

---

[37] 'Dramatic Poetry of the Last Age', quoted by Stead, p. 12.
[38] *Measure for Measure* was acted 133 times in London in the Eighteenth Century: see C. B. Hogan, *Shakespeare in the Theatre, 1701–1800*, 2 vols (Oxford: Clarendon Press, 1952–57), I, pp. 301–308, and II, pp. 400–411 and 718. There were further performances at Bath, Liverpool, Salisbury, and York. In addition, the play was performed thirty-one times in Dublin between 1738 and 1837.
[39] F. E. Halliday, *A Shakespeare Companion* (London: Duckworth, 1952; revised Harmondsworth: Penguin, 1964), p. 310.

recently-established Hanoverian monarchy or the increasing political power of Robert Walpole.[40]

After an apparently successful 1738 production at the Drury Lane Theatre, London,[41] the play returned to the London stage at Covent Garden in the 1770s. From the notes on this production supplied by the contemporary critic, Francis Gentleman, we know that he thoroughly approved of the extensive cuts to 'ribaldry' and to other 'unworthy' aspects and 'indecent' details encountered in Shakespeare's text. The speeches of Lucio's two gentleman-associates, reference to Claudio's offence, the vulgar trial at the start of the second act, and the character Barnadine, were all considered worthy of the censor's pen. A concluding interpolation ensured that the ending of the play loyally supported the notion of a benevolent monarchy; but the political ambiguities apparent even in this heavily-edited text, and the 'haughty' performance of Mrs. Yates as Isabella, prevented this production from being either a critical or a popular success.[42]

It was for Sarah Siddons to establish, between 1783 and 1811, her epoch-making portrayal of Isabella as 'a thing enskied and sainted' (Lucio: I, iv, 34). Her interpretation could be accomplished, however, only by cutting words that might undermine Isabella's presentation as modest and compassionate: for example, her line, 'More than our brother is our chastity' (II, iv, 184), was elided, presumably because it implies pride, complacency, and a lack of human sympathy. From 1794, she was joined on stage by her brother, John Philip

---

[40] Nusen, pp. 205–206. According to Angela Stock's Introduction to the second edition of *Measure for Measure*, ed. Brian Gibbons, (Cambridge: CUP, 2006), p. 52, James Quin, who played the Duke in this production, repeated his role every year until 1734, and again in 1737.

[41] Amnon Kabatchnik, *Blood on the Stage, 1600–1800: Milestone Plays of Murder, Mystery and Mayhem* (Lanham, Maryland: Rowman and Littlefield, 2017), p. 55.

[42] Nusen, p. 207–212.

Kemble, as the Duke. Their performances encouraged, among theatregoers and writers, those prevailing nineteenth-century critical opinions of Isabella as ideally pious and virtuous, and of the Duke as worthy and dignified.[43]

To counterbalance the presentation of Isabella and the Duke as so unambiguously admirable, Kemble's acting-edition simplified Angelo into a monochrome villain, deleting his two great soliloquies in Act II.[44] This elision would inevitably have dehumanised Angelo, depriving the audience of the opportunity to empathise with him as he struggles with temptation. The potential for tragedy would therefore have diminished, as Angelo was not a conscientious man succumbing to sin, but rather in a wilful degenerate intent on evading punishment. The moral complexity of Shakespeare's play would have been replaced by the simple opposition between good (Isabella and the Duke) and bad (Angelo), more appropriate to a moral interlude.

Among the additions to Kemble's acting-edition were a reconciliation between Isabella and Claudio, and a conclusion confirming Isabella's acceptance of the Duke's offers of marriage. These interpolations glossed over the two (potentially) darkest silences in the play. Other excisions and embellishments to the prompt-copy of these productions suggest a staunchly monarchist agenda, vital in supporting public order and morale during a long period of international crisis: at the time of the 1794 Drury Lane production, the Terror that was sweeping France had led, in the previous year, to the execution of King Louis XVI; and, during the 1803 Covent Garden production, preparations to repel the expected invasion of England by Napoleon were at their height.

Measure for Measure had been performed infrequently in the Eighteenth Century until it entered the repertoire of Siddons and Kemble. There were, therefore, many for whom the play

---

[43] Nusen, pp. 212–214.
[44] Stock, p. 52, n. 3.

remained better known either through acquaintance with Shakespeare's edited text or through knowledge of contemporary critical comments, rather than through viewing the play in performance. When William Robson praised John Emery's portrayal of Barnadine in 1811, he confessed how seeing *Measure for Measure* on stage transformed his appreciation of a minor character and amplified his admiration for the playwright:

> I had read the play often, and the character was familiar to me as that of a depraved, abandoned wretch; but here was a real, sombre splendour thrown upon it by the power of genius, and, with an oppressed chest, I sighed, 'Oh, nature! Oh, Shakespeare! Who shall ever know the end or depth of your beauties?'[45]

The corollary of Robson's comment is that full appreciation of *Measure for Measure* might be precluded—and prejudicial judgements nurtured—during periods when stage-performances were unavailable to reveal the play's potential.

Further evidence of enthusiasm for the play in performance came five years later in the *European Magazine*, in response to the 1816 revival of *Measure for Measure* at the Covent Garden Theatre, London:

> The infinity of Shakespeare's genius is no where more comprehensive than in the machinery of this play. He fathoms the depths of the human heart, not as an inquisitor; but by combining those secret sympathies which invest distinct degrees and attributes in society with the eloquence of truth. . . . We conclude by insisting that with all its *delicate* imperfections, 'Measure for Measure' is a very fine play, and we exult at its re-introduction to the stage[46]

---

[45] Gamini Salgado, *Eyewitnesses of Shakespeare: First Hand Accounts of Performances 1590–1890* (New York: Harper and Row, 1975), p. 218.
[46] Salgado, p. 217–18.

Such effusive praise of Shakespeare was characteristic of the age (bardolatry having firmly established itself in England during the latter half of the Eighteenth Century). What is exceptional here is the anonymous critic's assertion that no other play illustrates Shakespeare's extraordinary talents more completely than *Measure for Measure*, and that its performance on stage should be celebrated.

Affirmative comments like these would soon become scarce in a century when the text of *Measure for Measure* was increasingly regarded as an affront to public decency. Severe expurgation was necessary before the play was deemed suitable for public consumption, for fear of condoning political dissent by staging a potentially subversive play and, more particularly, for fear of offending audiences with a coarse, bawdy comedy. The scarcity of opportunities to see *Measure for Measure* in performance allowed critical opinion to harden against the play. The adverse effect of such criticism on public attitudes made productions of *Measure for Measure* more commercially risky and therefore even less likely to be staged. It was a vicious circle.

The publication in 1818 of *The Family Shakespeare* by Dr. Thomas Bowdler is indicative of prevailing opinion: it was considered necessary to suppress elements in all of Shakespeare's dramatic works to prevent them from offending or corrupting those of a susceptible nature. With bowdlerization the order of the day, *Measure for Measure* was always likely to be a prime target for the censor's pen. Bowdler himself employed the Siddons/Kemble version of the text that drew a veil of modesty over Shakespeare's bawdy original.[47] As the Nineteenth Century advanced, prevailing moral attitudes were increasingly hostile to anything that might promote scurrility or sedition. As a result, there was only one (1829) performance of

---

[47] Braunmuller and Watson, p. 126.

Measure for Measure in London between Macready's performance as the Duke in 1824 and Phelps's in 1846.[48]

When Samuel Phelps launched his new production of *Measure for Measure* at Sadler's Wells (in 1846; revived, intermittently, until 1857) he was so cautious as to make further extensive alterations to Kemble's already heavily edited text of the play—especially to any aspect that might offend the public sense of decency.[49] He did, however, retain Kemble's concluding interpolation which, with all the other changes to Shakespeare's text, was likely to ensure an anodyne entertainment in which a wise Duke and a saintly Isabella happily contemplated wedlock in a morally whitewashed Vienna. When Phelps revived the production in 1850, however, it seemed to be in response to public outrage at the presumption of Pius IX's 'Popish Aggression' in declaring Cardinal Nicholas Wiseman to be 'Archbishop of Westminster'. To present a less favourable view of Catholicism in the play, Phelps stepped down from performing Vincentio as a 'good Duke' (Isabella: III, i, 190), re-casting George Bennett (who had previously played Angelo) to portray Vincentio in a less favourable light. After all, Friar Lodowick, the Duke's *alter ego*, claims to be 'late come from the See / In special business from his Holiness' (III, ii, 213–14), and emissaries of the Pope were now likely to receive a harsher welcome from the majority in Phelps's London. Once again, *Measure for Measure* was being staged to reflect contemporary political issues.

---

[48] During this period when *Measure for Measure* was absent from the London stage, we encounter the accusations of indecency levelled against the play by Coleridge in 1827 and Hunter in 1845. However, the growing prejudice against the play in England does not appear to have deterred the young Richard Wagner in Magdeburg, who freely adapted *Measure for Measure* as the libretto for his comic opera *Das Liebesverbot* ('The Ban on Love') in 1836: *Das Liebesverbot*, Wikipedia, accessed 21 July 2020, https://en.wikipedia.org/wiki/Das_Liebesverbot.

[49] Nusen, pp. 222–234.

During the latter half of the Nineteenth Century, opportunities to view *Measure for Measure* on stage continued to be rare, because of misgivings about its scurrility and subversiveness, as attested by this review of a performance in 1876:

> That the play is no longer popular upon the boards is also explained by the facts that the poetic beauties in which it so richly abounds can hardly be separated in representation from the alloy which the incidents cast upon them. The story, though of absorbing interest, is not altogether pleasant to modern ears.[50]

There was an average of only one production in London every twenty years, each production averaging a run of only five performances.[51] Even when the play was staged early in the Twentieth Century, *Measure for Measure* was still being bowdlerized for fear of giving offence. *The Times* of 23 February 1906 reported that the Oxford University Dramatic Society (OUDS) had found it necessary to cut parts of the text when performing *Measure for Measure*, apparently to avoid the public offence caused when the popular actress, Adelaide Neilson, had performed the role of Isabella in the 1870s.[52] This same heavily-edited OUDS text was staged at the Adelphi Theatre the following month. Yet William Poel had successfully produced a relatively 'uncut' version of the text in 1893 at the Royalty Theatre in London and would retain this text when revisiting his performance as Angelo at the Gaiety Theatre in Manchester in 1908.

---

[50] Anonymous review of 'Haymarket Theatre', *Morning Post*, 3 April, 1876, quoted by Nusen, p. 235.

[51] Janice Norwood, 'A Reference Guide to Performances of Shakespeare's Plays in Nineteenth-Century London', in *Shakespeare in the Nineteenth Century, edited by G. Marshall* (Cambridge: CUP, 2012), pp. 351–415.

[52] *Measure for Measure*, Wikipedia, accessed 20 July 2020, https://en.wikipedia.org/wiki/Measure_for_Measure.

Poel used a much more authentic version of Shakespeare's text than either Kemble or Phelps had done (although he still altered or elided words with even mild sexual associations, to avoid giving offence).[53] The greatest service that Poel did for *Measure for Measure*, however, was to insist that Shakespeare's plays should be performed according to Poel's conception of how they were staged in Elizabethan and Jacobean times: in a small, intimate theatre with minimal sets, rather than on a huge, ornate stage where actors would seem remote and their speech declamatory. *Measure for Measure*, particularly during the duologues in the first half of the play, greatly benefits when the audience can understand character and motivation better by observing facial expressions and gestures at close quarters, and by responding to subtle modulations of the voice. By this means, it was possible to convey greater psychological realism in the performances of characters such as Angelo, Isabella, and Claudio. When Poel's revived production was invited down from Manchester for the Stratford-upon-Avon Shakespeare Festival in 1908, it proved a critical and popular success, an uncommon event among productions of *Measure for Measure* during previous centuries. Now that the play had been rescued from heavy censorship in performances conducive to establishing a closer relationship between audiences and actors, the extent of Shakespeare's achievement in *Measure for Measure* could be more generally appreciated.

Tyrone Guthrie championed *Measure for Measure* for over thirty years. He directed a celebrated performance with Charles Laughton (Angelo), Flora Robson (Isabella), and James Mason (Claudio) for the Vic-Wells Shakespeare repertory group in 1933.[54] Guthrie directed the play again at the Old Vic (London) in 1937 and at the Bristol Old Vic in 1966. He was also involved in the establishment of the Stratford Festival of Canada where, in its second season (1954), *Measure for*

---

[53] Details of Poel's pioneering work involving *Measure for Measure* are offered by Nusen, pp. 150–160.
[54] Kabatchnik, p. 55.

Measure was one of two Shakespeare plays staged in a nine-week run.[55]

As the Twentieth Century advanced, the frequency of productions of *Measure for Measure* in England increased, with Stratford-upon-Avon as the focal point. There had been no new production of *Measure for Measure* at the Shakespeare Memorial Theatre between its first performance of the text in 1884 (revived in 1885) and the production staged to coincide with Shakespeare's birthday in 1923.[56] Once the New Shakespeare Memorial Theatre (opened in 1932) had established momentum, however, *Measure for Measure* was generally produced every five years or so, for example in 1940, 1946, 1950, and 1956. The influence of *The Wheel of Fire* (published in 1930) on Stratford performances was evident during this period. Wilson Knight's 'morality play' reading of *Measure for Measure* immediately affected the William Bridges-Adams production at Stratford in 1931, and Dukes 'like power divine' recurred on stage in those subsequent Stratford productions by Frank McMullan (1946), Peter Brook (1950), and Anthony Quayle (1956).[57]

During the first 350 years of its stage-history, *Measure for Measure* was dogged by the assumed unfitness for public consumption of two indispensable aspects of its plot. First, the comedic sections were considered darkly scurrilous rather than frivolously amusing. Second, it was feared that the political sections were disquietingly subversive rather than staunchly pro-establishment. Successive productions addressed these problems by altering Shakespeare's text, often in radical ways. Certain lines, sections, and characters were cut, while others were added to transform *Measure for Measure* into a play that endorsed the contemporary political situation in England and validated (rather than challenged) prevailing public attitudes.

---

[55] 'Stratford Festival', Wikipedia, accessed 20 July 2020, https://en.wikipedia.org/wiki/Stratford_Festival.

[56] Nusen, pp. 236–238.

[57] Nusen, pp. 239–49 and 254–256.

Well-intentioned and dutiful as these productions may have been, they usually proved incapable of conveying to an audience the challenging complexity and the remarkable dramatic power of Shakespeare's original drama.

In the years after the Second World War, however, fundamental changes in public attitudes to morality and authority rendered obsolete any accusation that the full text of Shakespeare's *Measure for Measure* was too lewd or seditious to stage. With the advent of public subsidies that reduced the dependency of theatres and studios on commercial success, productions of the play were liberated from the constraints of orthodoxy. The potential of *Measure for Measure* to challenge the establishment (as opposed to endorsing it) could now be explored much more fully and frequently, both on stage and on screen.

Performances in More Recent Years[58]

Since the Second World War, *Measure for Measure* has established itself as a kind of dramatic chameleon, a play that, seemingly magically, adapts itself to the colours of its immediate environment—that is, to prevailing aspects of the contemporary society in which it is performed. Its mood can be buoyantly amusing or gloomily oppressive, according to how it is presented. In addition, the play has proved capable of addressing contentious issues concerning gender, sexuality, and race. Most remarkably, after 350 years of productions that consistently *endorsed* the status quo, the play has more recently proved versatile as a topical satire against political hypocrisy, and as a critique of contemporary social injustice. It is now considered not merely acceptable but even desirable to emphasise the vulgar humour and/or the subversiveness of *Measure for Measure* in performance when, within living

---

[58] I have limited my comments to productions staged in England. A short history of modern performances in the USA is offered by Kabatchnik, pp. 57–61.

memory, such a policy would have been considered distasteful and irresponsible.

The prospect of vulgar humour liberally interlarded with downright obscenity (long the justification for bowdlerizing or suppressing *Measure for Measure*) has recently become an inducement to swell audiences: witness the theatre-company that confidently advertised the play as 'Shakespeare's filthiest comedy'.[59] Although England took centuries to accommodate the 'indecency' of Shakespeare's text, as early as the 1940 production at the Shakespeare Memorial Theatre in Stratford-upon-Avon, the comic roles had been not merely reinstated but also treated sympathetically.[60] Once the underworld characters with their scurrility and lewd banter had been fully restored to performance-texts of *Measure for Measure*, the comedic aspects of the play could more readily be exploited by directors for the entertainment of audiences.

Shakespeare's Globe, opened in London in 1997, is an ideal stage on which to release the full comic potential of *Measure for Measure*, as it offers excellent opportunities for intimate interaction between actors and audiences. In John Dove's 2004 Globe production, the comic characters were given free rein to address the audience directly and to intermingle with those in the pit, creating a rapport that invited seditious complicity. On his return in the final Act, the Duke (Mark Rylance) descended from the stage warmly to greet the groundlings, instantly transforming playgoers into citizens of Vienna welcoming him home. This was a production that presented *Measure for Measure* as an optimistic, hilarious comedy. In the course of the dance with which the production ended, all was warmth and

---

[59] The Frog and Peach Theatre Company, New York, on flyers for its 2013 production (Kabatchnik, p. 60). The Company also advertised *Measure for Measure* as 'Shakespeare's most shocking comedy', presupposing that a modern audience, unlike its nineteenth-century precursors, would welcome the prospect of being scandalised.
[60] Nusen plausibly suggests (p. 238) that this may have been expedient in time of war, when social unity was vital in the struggle for victory.

forgiveness, with Angelo and the Duke shaking hands, and Claudio and Isabella embracing. Throughout the performance, the stage-business, to complement Shakespeare's dialogue, was decidedly risqué, thoroughly amusing the audience. Although this caused disquiet among some journalists and reviewers, who feared that lewd behaviour on stage might seem to condone sexist abuse,[61] others thought this 'the most harmless and cheerful rendering of the play',[62] recognising that 'the core Globe audience wants a traditional and light-hearted production with lots of bawdy laughs.'[63]

More recently, the potential of *Measure for Measure* for licentious hilarity was emphasized in the Globe's 2015 production, directed by Dominic Dromgoole. The tone was set even before the Duke's opening lines: Mistress Overdone and her crowd of pimps, whores, and clients were down in the pit, mixing freely with the audience and performing exaggerated sexual acts in makeshift 'houses of resort'. Among the most memorable parts of this performance, in which Dean Nolan's Constable Elbow figured prominently, were slapstick interludes and 'Keystone Cops' pursuits as Angelo's officers-of-the-law attempted to arrest the full complement of Vienna's 'knaves' and 'drabs' on and around the stage. These incidents predominated in the first part of the play, the 'tragic' exposition that might otherwise have been too dark to allow for an entirely 'happy' comedy.[64]

---

[61] Two examples are offered by Nusen, pp. 172–173.

[62] Michael Dobson, 'Shakespeare Performances in England', *SS* 58 (2005), p. 277.

[63] Robert Tanitch, 'Rylance Gets Laughs at the Globe', *Morning Star*, 8 July 2004, p. 9.

[64] Sleeve-notes to the DVD recording of this production boast that 'audiences are treated to the lighter side of depravity in a "riotously enjoyable" (*The Independent*) "crowd-pleasing saucy romp" (*Evening Standard*) . . . [in] Dominic Dromgoole's "buoyant production" (*Guardian*)' (William Shakespeare's *Measure for Measure*, Globe on Screen [London: Royal Opera House Enterprises Ltd., 2016]).

Roxana Silbert had similarly chosen to highlight the potential of the text to amuse when she directed the play in the intimate environment of The Swan at Stratford in 2011. Both Raymond Coulthard's Duke and Joseph Kloska's Pompey interacted mischievously with theatregoers. The former played frivolous conjuring-tricks while casting ironic, knowing glances towards the audience; the latter adapted some lines and improvised others to involve individual playgoers in the action.[65] Isabella's ready acceptance of the Duke's concluding proposal of marriage, the exception rather than the rule in twenty-first-century performances, was restored, to ensure a harmonious ending.[66] In each of these productions, the sombre side of *Measure for Measure* was underplayed to allow its lighter elements to be emphasized.

By contrast, Peter Brook's 1950 production of *Measure for Measure* at the Shakespeare Memorial Theatre, Stratford-upon-Avon, was remarkable for the 'darkness' of its scenography.[67] Sets were shadowy and sinister, with instruments of torture prominent in the prison scenes. Sombre-suited figures of authority, moving among filthy, groaning criminals and crowds of shabby, brazen prostitutes, faced the imminent threat of insurrection from the oppressed. In this production, cruelty and suffering seemed ubiquitous in Angelo's Vienna.[68] Nicholas Hytner's 1987 RSC version was similarly 'dark'. Pompey oversaw a rent-boy operation based in a men's toilet, a sordid reflection of underworld reality in *Measure for Measure*; while '[t]he spectre of mass incarceration loomed over Hytner's production,' as if reflective of authoritarian government in contemporary Britain under Margaret Thatcher.[69]

---

[65] Trevor Fox's Pompey similarly employed this approach in Dromgoole's 2015 production for the Globe.

[66] Nusen, pp. 315–321.

[67] Brook acknowledged the influence of Antonin Artaud's 'Theatre of Cruelty' on his work, an influence that extended to subsequent 'dark' productions of *Measure for Measure*.

[68] Nusen, pp. 249–254.

[69] Braunmuller and Watson, pp. 133 and 134.

Modern directors have recognized the opportunity to darken the tone of *Measure for Measure* by exploiting the open silences prevalent in the final scene, particularly the silence between the Duke and Isabella. Famously, in his 1970 production for the RSC, John Barton directed Estelle Kohler's Isabella to reject the offers of marriage from Sebastian Shaw's Duke.[70] As Kohler was thirty and Shaw sixty-five, the mismatch was all too apparent to the audience. Barton's radical decision nevertheless attracted adverse comments from contemporary reviewers because such a grim conclusion to the play defied the stage-tradition of a happy ending. Gradually, however, this 'dark' innovation gained currency among his fellow directors. As soon afterwards as 1973, in his touring-production for the National Theatre, Jonathan Miller also interpreted Isabella's open silence at the end of the play as her rejection of the Duke.[71] Rejection—or irresolution, at least—is now encountered more frequently than acceptance. For example, when Gregory Doran directed for the RSC in 2019, the play concluded with Lucy Phelps's Isabella in a baffled stand-off with Antony Byrne's Vincentio.

One of the darkest readings of *Measure for Measure* came from Charles Marowitz, but it could be achieved only by extensive cutting of the text and reallocation of lines. Marowitz staged his version of the play in 1975, at The Open Space Theatre in London. The first half of the performance, although abridged, remained mostly true to Shakespeare's original, but the second half was radically shortened and altered. Isabella was raped. Claudio was executed. Angelo was exonerated— because the Duke found it politically expedient. Finally, Vincentio, in a drunken and vulgar spectacle, celebrated his deputy's escape from justice with Escalus and Angelo, whose lines were a collage of snippets deriving from the speech of

---

[70] Kabatchnik, p. 56.
[71] Nusen, pp. 268–274.

comic characters excluded from Marowitz's performing-text.[72] This conclusion profoundly challenged the audience's preconceptions about characters and outcomes.[73]

More recent productions have confirmed that *Measure for Measure* can be successfully 'divorced' from a conventional happy ending by exploiting the open silences rather than by resorting to radical alterations of Shakespeare's text, such as those undertaken by Marowitz. For example, in Nicholas Hytner's RSC production in 1987, the expectation of forgiveness and reconciliation in the concluding scene was challenged when the hapless Duke was apparently *intimidated* into pardoning Barnadine, after which his proposal of marriage received no response from Isabella.[74] Nine years later, in Sean Holmes's 2003 production for the RSC, Angelo (Daniel Evans) was an obviously reluctant participant in his marriage to Mariana, and when Isabella (Emma Fielding) led the Duke (Paul Higgins) from the stage at the final curtain, it seemed more likely that her purpose was to remonstrate rather than to acquiesce.[75]

The treatment of Isabella has been presented in particularly 'dark' ways, suggesting a feminist agenda to expose how women can be oppressed by abusive male power. Keith Hack's 1974 RSC *Measure for Measure*, strongly influenced by Brechtian stage-techniques, is a good early example. When a

---

[72] The full text of this version of the play is available in Charles Marowitz, *The Marowitz Shakespeare* (London: Marion Boyars, 1978). The final scene is reprinted in *Measure for Measure* ed. Jane Coles and Rex Gibson (Cambridge: CUP, 1992), p. 178.

[73] Later, in 1990, Marowitz would stage an even more shocking version which ended with the Duke, Angelo, Lucio, and Claudio advancing on Isabella with murderous or rapacious intent (D. K. Holm, 'Variations on "Measure for Measure"', *Portland Mercury*, 12 October 2000, https://www.portlandmercury.com/theater/variations-on-measure--for-measure/Content?oid=23108; and Braunmuller and Watson, p. 129).

[74] Nusen, p. 293.

[75] Nusen, pp. 203–211.

decidedly devious and manipulative Duke (Barrie Ingram) went to embrace Isabella (Francesca Annis) in the final scene, he enveloped her, Dracula-like, in the same ornate cloak of office that he had stripped from Angelo shortly before. This imaginative deployment of an item of costume, used to signify the subjugation of Isabella and the obliteration of her will, suggested to the audience that the Duke's carnal intentions were as morally obnoxious as Angelo's.[76]

The sexual humiliation of Isabella was still more apparent when Simon McBurney directed *Measure for Measure* at the National Theatre in 2004. During the first interview between Angelo (Paul Rhys) and Isabella (Naomi Frederick), Toby Jones's Lucio not only physically prevented her from leaving (at II, ii, 42–7), but also unbuttoned her upper garment to make her more sexually alluring, before propelling her back towards the Deputy.[77] In her second interview (II, iv), Angelo's rapacious intentions were made clear not merely by his brutal words but also by his efforts to remove Isabella's clothing, and to force her to touch him intimately. In the final moments of the play, when David Troughton's elderly, hobbling Duke proposed marriage to Isabella, the backdrop was lifted to reveal a bloodstained bed.[78] Horrified, she turned away, as if to appeal to the audience. Immediately, the sound of a heavy door slamming, accompanied by an abrupt blackout, left the shocked audience to contemplate the implications.[79] Was the bloody bed a projection of Isabella's fear of sexual activity, or evidence of the Duke's dark past? Was the slamming door, that threat of

---

[76] Nusen, pp. 274–278.

[77] Nusen, p. 327.

[78] In McBurney's 2006 Complicité version, what was on the bed apparently changed from performance to performance: a bloodstain; a red rose; a sex-aid. Each was likely to elicit a different audience-response. See Braunmuller and Watson, p. 46.

[79] Nusen, p. 329, and Alan Bird, '*Measure for Measure*—National Theatre 2004', *London Theatre*, 28 May 2004, https://www.londontheatre.co.uk/reviews/measure-for-measure-national-theatre-2004.

'perpetual durance'(III, i, 66), the actual or the imagined penalty for refusing the Duke's proposal; or did it signify Isabella's conception of the ordeal of marriage to a decrepit autocrat?[80] It is difficult to conceive a darker conclusion to the play than McBurney's, or a production more disturbing in portraying Isabella as the victim of sexual exploitation by powerful, unscrupulous, older men.

Experimental productions of *Measure for Measure* have also engaged with issues of sexual politics. The film *M4M: Measure for Measure*, directed by Gabriel Manwaring and released in 2015, explored LBGT issues by changing the gender of Isabella from female to male. As a result, the illicit desires encountered in the text were transformed from heterosexual to homosexual.[81]

The relationship between power and gender was central when Josie Rourke directed the play at the Donmar Warehouse, London, in the autumn of 2018. She abridged *Measure for Measure* into a seventy-minute, one-act drama which, after an interval, was performed a second time—but with significant changes—to the same audience. In the initial staging, in Jacobean costume and retaining the original gender-relationships, Hayley Atwell's Isabella had to endure the sexual advances of Jack Lowden's Angelo before screaming at Nicholas Burns's shifty, disreputable Duke to signify her refusal of his offer of marriage. In the second performance, in modern costume, the roles of Isabella and Angelo were

---

[80] Naomi Frederick was twenty-seven when she played the role of Isabella. David Troughton, in the role of the Duke, was fifty-four, twice her age, and certainly old enough to be her father. A similarly disquieting age-difference between duke and novice was apparent in John Barton's 1970 production and Nicholas Hytner's 1987 production (both for the RSC), and in Trevor Nunn's 1991 touring version for The Other Place in Stratford.

[81] See *Measure for Measure*, 'Adaptations and cultural references: Film adaptations', Wikipedia, accessed 19 July 2020; and the anonymous IMDb review, 17 July 2015, https://www.imdb.com/title/tt2708382/.

reversed. Now Isabella was the Duke's female deputy (speaking Angelo's lines), and Angelo was a member of a chaste male religious order, pleading for the life of his brother. This provocative gender-switch invited a feminist reading of the Deputy's fate: when the Duke of a patriarchal society delegates power to a woman in the confident expectation that she will fail, the moral balance of the play lurches disturbingly. During her period in power, Isabella's government was persistently undermined by the disapproval of her male colleagues, accompanied by behind-hand mockery. The 'bed-trick' was transformed into a chauvinist conspiracy, as it was devised and executed by three men (rather than by one man and two women, as in the original text). The Angelo-substitute in Isabella's bed enjoyed non-consensual sexual congress while recording her orgasmic cries which could later be used to coerce her into acquiescence (a disturbing intimation of 'revenge porn'). Finally, Isabella was forced by Vincentio to marry the sexual partner who had deceived and coerced her. Isabella, as deputy, may have been corrupted by power and sexual desire, but ultimately the greater corruptive power of the patriarchy prevailed. In both her roles (as a chaste nun in the '1604' version and as a corrupt deputy in the '2018' version), Isabella was the victim of male oppression.[82]

Some modern productions of *Measure for Measure*, influenced by post-colonial theory, have addressed issues of race and imperialism. When Michael Rudman directed the play in 1981 for the National Theatre, it was set on an indeterminate Caribbean island where the underclasses, far from seeming degenerate, celebrated their culture in a glorious carnival romp.

---

[82] Alex Woods, *WhatsOnStage*, 12 October 2018, https://www.whatsonstage.com/london-theatre/reviews/measure-for-measure-donmar-hayley-atwell-lowden_47790.html; Michael Billington, *The Guardian*, 12 October 2018, https://www.theguardian.com/stage/2018/oct/12/measure-for-measure-review-sex-power-and-shock-atwell-lowden-donmar; and Natasha Tripney, *The Stage*, 12 October 2018, https://www.thestage.co.uk/reviews/2018/measure-for-measure-hayley-atwell-review-at-donmar-warehouse-london/.

Only two roles were played by white actors: Escalus and the Provost were perhaps intended to embody the legacy of colonial government when the remainder of the cast was black.[83] This was a bold, politically-motivated decision at a time when black actors were relatively rarely seen on the national stage, and when serious race-riots were affecting several cities in England.[84] When the production was revived for the New York Shakespeare Festival two years later, the Duke was re-cast as white, perhaps implying—in a play in which a white governor leaves a black deputy in power—that the contagion of corruption may persist in a colony, even after the withdrawal of the imperialist power. At a more modest level, in Nicholas Hytner's 1987 production for the RSC, the roles of Claudio and Isabella were played by black actors to signify oppression by white authorities.[85]

The post-colonial agenda was resumed in 2002, when Phil Willmott's *Measure for Measure Malaya* was staged at the Riverside Studios in Hammersmith. Willmott's approach was strikingly similar to Davenant's, 340 years earlier. Both presented their perspective on recent political history by extensively redacting and supplementing Shakespeare's text. Willmott, by presenting those with power as the white imperialists and those without power as the indigenous Malay population, transformed *Measure for Measure* into a play about

---

[83] Kabatchnik, p. 56. In Gregory Doran's 2019 production for the RSC, these same two characters (Escalus and the Provost) were cast as women. As Escalus is passed over in favour of Angelo in the first scene, and as both Escalus and the Provost are snubbed by Angelo when discussing the law and sentencing early in Act II, this cross-gender casting might appear to accentuate the sexist attitudes of the patriarchy of Vienna.
[84] 'From April to July 1981, England suffered serious riots across many major cities. . . . the Brixton riots in London, the Toxteth riots in Liverpool, the Handsworth riots in Birmingham, the Chapeltown riots in Leeds, and the Moss Side riots in Manchester.' ['1981 England Riots', Wikipedia, accessed 20 July 2020, https://en.wikipedia.org/wiki/1981_England_riots]
[85] Braunmuller and Watson, p. 130.

racism and colonial oppression. This process involved no major changes to the main plot, but considerable liberties were taken with the text to ensure the production's political agenda was manifest. Although the critics were unimpressed by this 'distortion',[86] it opened up new possibilities in interpreting key events in the play. As Claudio was played by a male of colour whereas a white woman was cast as Julietta, their offence was implicitly compounded by miscegenation: interracial intercourse might offend the governing classes. Additionally, Anglo-Saxon Angelo's inability to recognise the difference between the Eurasian bodies of Isabella and Mariana might imply that colonialists are unaware of the individuality of those whom they subjugate: to the complacent imperialist, the natives all look the same!

Rudman and Wilmot are not alone in choosing *Measure for Measure* to explore a political agenda, although usually that agenda is closer to home than a Caribbean island or Malaya, and more immediate than the colonial past. For example, in a BBC production broadcast on 5 November 1994, David Thacker elided all references to Vienna from his performing text, setting the play in a modern British police state. His objective was recognised as a thinly-veiled critique of Home Secretary Michael Howard's Criminal Justice and Public Order Act, given royal assent only two days earlier. Howard's measure was the legislative embodiment of John Major's 1993 'Back to Basics' speech at the Conservative Party Conference in Blackpool, in which the Prime Minister expressed his determination to pursue 'respect for the family and respect for the law'.[87] Thacker recognised the potential of the speech to instigate, in the UK, a moral crusade comparable with Angelo's determination to criminalise unauthorised sexual activity in renaissance Vienna. The production presented a shady political system dependent on surveillance and mass media: it opened with the Duke observing social disorder, crime, and public

---

[86] Examples are quoted by Nusen, pp. 116–117.

[87] 'Back to Basics (campaign)', Wikipedia, accessed 20 July 2020, https://en.wikipedia.org/wiki/Back_to_Basics_(campaign).

lewdness through multiple CCTV images projected on to a huge screen, and closed with the Duke televising his return to power and his deposition of Angelo. Mistress Overdone's fear that all 'houses of resort' were to be 'pulled down' (I, ii, 88–9) was vividly realised when riot police broke through her door, causing widespread panic and destruction. The police used similar brute force to arrest Claudio while he was enjoying an intimate dinner with Julietta in a restaurant. Soon afterwards, in the prison like a subterranean labour-camp, Claudio was subjected to a humiliating internal examination by a prison-officer, in full view of all those passing the window of the detention-room. Claudio's question, 'Fellow, why dost thou show me thus to th'world?' (I, ii, 108) now had a grim new context. The gaoler's reply, 'I do it not in evil disposition / But from Lord Angelo by special charge' (I, ii, 110–11) suggested the brutality of an administration bent on crushing any moral aberration. Thacker's production, after judicious pruning of Shakespeare's text, but with no lines added, projected this dystopian vision of the social oppression that might result from the Government's new bill.

Other directors have similarly recognised how readily *Measure for Measure* can offer a critique of the prevailing political situation, not merely in the UK but as far afield as America and Russia. Only a year before Marowitz's 1975 production, US President Gerald Ford granted his predecessor, Richard Nixon, a pardon that precluded any prosecution for crimes committed during Nixon's presidency. This was the justification for the Duke, in Marowitz's production, to exonerate Angelo. Marowitz confirmed that his agenda in making radical alterations to Shakespeare's text was to reflect recent political abuse in the USA:

What concerns me is the traditional morality of *Measure for Measure* tested in a contemporary society where Watergate-styled corruptions are often the rule and not the exception. I wanted the audience to be angry with the Duke, Escalus, and

Angelo in a way that Shakespeare's narrative would never permit.[88]

Social repression and state exploitation of 'shame' were emphasised in Declan Donnellan's production of *Measure for Measure* (staged in Moscow and London between 2013 and 2017).[89] The director's choices invited the audience to recognise the parallels between Shakespeare's play and the political situation in contemporary Russia: the play was performed in the Russian language, with a Russian setting and modern costumes. Inevitably, Angelo's brief period of government between the Duke's departure and return now seemed to represent Dmitri Medvedev's 2008–12 presidency, sandwiched between the two presidencies of the more powerful Vladimir Putin. Isabella's reference to 'man, proud man, / Dress'd in *a little brief authority*' (Isabella: II, ii, 118–19; italics added) would have assumed a particular relevance to Medvedev's situation. Like Russian history in the second decade of the Twenty-First Century, *Measure for Measure* confirms that, even during an apparent interregnum, supreme power resides not with the deputy but with the dominant oligarch.

As in America and Russia, so in the UK. Concern over British involvement in the Iraq War and apprehension at the state's intrusion into personal privacy were both issues that were addressed in Simon McBurney's 2004 production of *Measure for Measure* at the National Theatre. Vincentio's Vienna abounded in CCTV cameras, by means of which the Duke spied on his citizens without their knowledge or consent. An image of US President George Bush was flashed on screen at Lucio's mention of the 'sanctimonious pirate' (I, ii, 7), to alert an amused audience to the political subtext. Prisoners in the Provost's gaol were clad in orange jumpsuits, like those

---

[88] Marowitz, p. 21, quoted by Nusen, p. 112.
[89] *Measure for Measure*, Wikipedia, accessed 20 July 2020.

worn by US political detainees at Guantanamo Bay.[90] This production was an uncomfortable reminder that surveillance societies and unjust detentions are not merely the stuff of fictional drama.

Bob Komar had a similar political objective when he set his 2006 film of *Measure for Measure* in the British Army. This was a time when widespread concern over the behaviour of armed forces (particularly the mistreatment of prisoners during and after the Iraq War) could be represented by the injustices and sexual offences encountered in Shakespeare's play. The troops in the film were involved in drunkenness, drug abuse, debauchery, and extreme violence. Even their commander (i.e. the Duke) indulged in sexual misconduct from the outset. As the comic scenes were cut, there was no respite from this grim depiction of how corruption can be rife among those very agents tasked with maintaining law and order.[91]

However, when a production deliberately grafts a contemporary socio-political agenda on to a Shakespearian play, that policy is not without risk. Audiences may find the performance gimmicky; critics may dismiss it as perverse. Additionally, the socio-political agenda (like that of fin de siècle problem plays) can prove ephemeral and parochial. As stage-productions, by their very nature, are usually limited to a specific time and place, this last objection may be irrelevant in the theatre; but for on-screen productions, which may be

---

[90] Michael Billington, '*Measure for Measure*: National, London', *The Guardian*, 28 May 2004, https://www.theguardian.com/stage/2004/may/28/theatre1; and Lisa Hunt, '*Measure for Measure* @ National Theatre, London', *MusicOHM*, 1 February 2006, https://www.musicomh.com/theatre/measure-for-measure-national-theatre-london.

[91] Anonymous review, 'Modernized *Measure for Measure*', 27 April 2011, http://reviewmodernizedmeasureformeasure.blogspot.com/; and 'KJ', 'Modernized *Measure for Measure*' *Bardfilm*, 17 September 2009, http://bardfilm.blogspot.com/2009/09/modernized-measure-for-measure.html.

viewed many years after they were filmed, and in countries with very different cultures from the one in which the production was made, socio-political 'spin' can prove a defect rather than an asset.

In its 'traditional' scenography, costume-design, and direction (by Desmond Davis), the BBC Television Shakespeare *Measure for Measure*, broadcast in 1979, employed a full text and presented an orthodox reading of the play. The opening credits were superimposed over a 'historical' watercolour of Vienna and accompanied by renaissance lute-music, evoking central Europe in the Seventeenth Century. The 'traditional' happy ending was retained: Kenneth Colley's Duke, rather than appearing enigmatic or devious, seemed wise and benevolent in his final judgements; Tim Pigott-Smith's Angelo, stricken with self-loathing, was suitably thankful to be redeemed by his union with Mariana; and Kate Nelligan's Isabella, dignified and restrained throughout her performance, graciously accepted the Duke's concluding marriage-proposal. Desmond Davis's *Measure for Measure* endorsed producer Cedric Messina's stated aims for the whole of the BBC Television Shakespeare Series (screened in the UK between 1978 and 1985): to avoid being 'experimental' and to offer 'definitive' productions.[92]

The BBC Television Shakespeare *Measure for Measure* was part of a commercially-successful series exported to well over

---

[92] Nusen, p. 124. However, the early screenings (of which *Measure for Measure* was one of the most satisfying) did not always meet with critical approval: 'So awed, so reverential, so safe have these . . . productions been that the BBC appears in danger of embalming, not offering Shakespeare for the delight of the wider public.' [Christopher Nicholson, 'A Precious Stone Called Culture' (*Daily Mail*: 11 December, 1978), p. 23]. Even John Wilders, literary consultant to the series, recognized this shortcoming: '. . . the worst fault of the television Shakespeare is that they tended to be cautious and rather too safe and unambitious and lacking in originality.' [quoted by Ace G. Pilkington, *Screening Shakespeare from* Richard II *to* Henry V (Newark: University of Delaware Press, 1991), p. 27]

fifty countries.[93] It was therefore seen by far more people than any other production in the play's history, before or since. Despite so many adventurous and imaginative interpretations on stage, film, and television, this was therefore the most influential production of *Measure for Measure*; yet it allowed no obvious contemporary agenda to be superimposed on Shakespeare's text. Had it attempted to do so, by reflecting preoccupations prevalent in Britain or America in the late 1970s, it might have proved less relevant, accessible, or comprehensible in most of those other countries in which it was screened. Cedric Messina's production allowed the play to speak for itself, leaving individual viewers free to identify the relevance of *Measure for Measure* to their own experience. Without the assistance of superimposed 'colour', it was easier for Shakespeare's 'chameleon' play to assimilate itself into a wide range of different surroundings.

Performances of *Measure for Measure*, although relatively infrequent for over 300 years of its history, included those that sought to be topical by emphasizing issues that reflected the concerns of their contemporary audiences. To this end, what Shakespeare originally wrote was subjected to extensive alteration, initially to suit the tastes of prospective audiences, but more recently to stimulate popular interest by controversial or even sensational means. When well-established theatres began to receive state subsidies as national institutions, productions of *Measure for Measure* dared to become more subversive, to challenge rather than to endorse both prevailing

---

[93] According to Susan Willis, the series was screened in Australia, Austria, the Bahamas, Bahrain, Barbados, Belgium, Bhutan, Bulgaria, Canada, Chile, China, Colombia, Czechoslovakia, Dubai, Egypt, France, Greece, Honduras, Hong Kong, Hungary, India, Iraq, Ireland, Italy, Jamaica, Japan, Jordan, Kenya, Korea, Lebanon, Malaysia, Mexico, Netherlands, New Zealand, Panama, Peru, the Philippines, Poland, Portugal, Puerto Rico, Qatar, Romania, Saudi Arabia, Singapore, Spain, Sri Lanka, Taiwan, Thailand, Trinidad and Tobago, Turkey, UK, USA, Venezuela, West Germany and Yugoslavia (*The BBC Shakespeare Plays: Making the Televised Canon* [Chapel Hill, NC: University of North Carolina Press, 1991], p. 333, n. 60.

public opinion and the established political system. As this exciting potential was more widely recognised, performances of the play proliferated; for example, in the summer of 2015, a theatregoer could have chosen between no fewer than three different productions of *Measure for Measure* without leaving London.[94] With imaginative design, creative direction, and usually no more than discreet editing, certain memorable productions have invited audiences to recognise that Shakespeare's play is fully relevant to their own world—that it offers a significant reflection of contemporary attitudes and events. These can be the most satisfying of all productions, confirming that, in any age, *Measure for Measure* can be enjoyed as 'a play for today'.

A Play for Today

Shakespeare drew to an unusual extent on topical materials when writing *Measure for Measure*; yet so many of the events, personalities, and texts prominent today reflect, to a startling extent, aspects of the themes, characters, and plot of this play dating back to 1604. By the time that these words are read, any overly specific examples that might be offered to illustrate the contemporary relevance of the play will have become outdated. The instances retained here are therefore limited to issues recently drawn to public attention that are likely to have enduring ramifications.

Among the central concerns of *Measure for Measure* is whether the handfasting that binds Claudio to Julietta and Angelo to Mariana is legitimate marriage. Angelo refuses to regard it as such, condemning Claudio and Julietta under the statutes against fornication, and breaking his own vows to Mariana, destroying her reputation to justify his decision. The lovers, as illustrated in Chapter 5 of this study, are innocent

---

[94] Mark Lawson, 'The power of shame: why Measure for Measure is more relevant than ever', The Guardian, 27 October 2015, https://www.theguardian.com/stage/2015/oct/27/measure-for-measure-shakespeare-young-vic-globe.

victims of intransigent law. It might seem inconceivable that such victims could be encountered in modern British society; but, on 19 November 2017, a *Sunday Times* headline declared, 'Six in 10 Muslim wives not legally married.'[95] It transpired that the traditional Islamic wedding (*nikah*) is not recognised in England's family courts until it has been complemented by a separate civil ceremony. This means that, in the event of a marital breakdown, many Muslim wives cannot expect, as a matter of course, to receive an equal portion of the family's wealth and possessions. If the woman has not participated in a civil marriage-ceremony, she must pursue her case for compensation before a civil court. *Nikah* may be a 'true contract' but, like the nuptial of Claudio and Julietta, it appears to lack the necessary 'denunciation . . . / Of outward order' (I, ii, 134–8) for it to be recognised in England.[96]

Angelo's indecent proposal to Isabella is the most enduring memory left by any production of *Measure for Measure*. An authority-figure seeks sexual satisfaction from a reluctant victim who knows that the consequences of refusal would be dire. Such abuse of power for sexual gratification could not be more topical or enduring, with the media abounding in such stories, particularly from the worlds of politics, entertainment, and high society. Although accused men have claimed in their defence that their sexual activities with women were always consensual, could the women propositioned by such powerful men have refused consent without jeopardising their futures? The parallels between these cases and Isabella's relationship

[95] Two days later (21 November 2017), on UK television, Channel 4 broadcast its documentary on Muslim marriages not recognised by family courts in England.

[96] A more well-known example of a 'marriage' that was deemed invalid by the courts was that of the celebrities Mick Jagger and Jerry Hall in Bali in 1990. After they separated in 1999, the High Court in London refused to recognise the nuptial on the grounds that the couple had failed at the time to register their marriage with the Indonesian authorities. Again, there was inadequate 'denunciation . . . / Of outward order'.

with both Angelo and the Duke invite recognition and consideration.

Once Angelo has proposed his offensive bargain—her virginity in exchange for her brother's life—he commands Isabella to

Fit thy consent to my sharp appetite. [II, iv, 160–8]

The verb 'fit' is particularly well-chosen by Shakespeare. It is an imperious command, a monosyllable comprising a short vowel and hard concluding consonant for brutal impact. Moreover, semantically, 'fit' implicitly contradicts its grammatical object, 'consent': 'fit' suggests manipulation, if necessary by using force to achieve its objective; whereas 'consent' presupposes free acquiescence. The two concepts cannot reasonably co-exist. Furthermore, 'sharp appetite' creates the image of a menacing weapon being brandished, as well as functioning as a phallic symbol. 'Consent', offered voluntarily, should not be secured by means of an intimidating imperative from one wielding such a pointed threat. In short, Angelo's words here, a subliminal description of the sexual act, confirm his intention to rape Isabella.

Recognition that consent ceases to be consent when it is coerced also applies to the ending of *Measure for Measure*, where the Duke twice proposes marriage to Isabella in the concluding fifty lines, only to be met with silence. That silence could well denote acquiescence and, in performance, was consistently presented as such until the latter years of the Twentieth Century; but when an aristocrat proposes to a commoner in circumstances as deviously engineered as those by which Vincentio has sought to win Isabella's consent, there is likely to be the suspicion of insidious compulsion.

A distinction should, nevertheless, be drawn between the Angelo/Isabella relationship explored in *Measure for Measure* and the modern trend in popular entertainment (novels, drama, and film) to present women as helpless or passive victims of predatory but sexually attractive males.[97] A reader or viewer may suspect something morbidly prurient—or even dangerous—in some recent texts in which the male abuser of women remains darkly mysterious but strangely alluring.[98] Angelo, by contrast, grows increasingly abhorrent without ever seeming attractive. His potential victims emerge triumphant, as he does not succeed either in rejecting Mariana by means of false insinuations or in compelling Isabella to submit to his sexual demands. Although Shakespeare may allow the audience to understand (and perhaps even to empathise with) Angelo's self-destructive passion, *Measure for Measure* offers no incentive, explicit or implicit, to relish or to condone his behaviour. Shakespeare subtly modulates the audience's response to Angelo through the medium of his three soliloquies and his concluding penitent speeches; whereas the motivation of the male protagonists in comparable recent fiction has tended, at best, to be sketchily portrayed or, at worst, to remain entirely undisclosed.[99]

We are told that we live in a post-truth era: 'fake news' achieved increasing prominence in association with the Brexit referendum in the summer of 2016 and with the US presidential

---

[97] I refer less to Heathcliff in *Wuthering Heights* (1847) than to the modern successors of Stanley Kowalski in *A Streetcar Named Desire* (1947; more specifically, after Marlon Brando's erotically-charged performance as Stanley in the 1951 film): most recently, Christian Gray in the *Fifty Shades* series of erotic novels (2011–17), and the numerous characters in contemporary film and television who seem embodiments of dangerously destructive male allure.

[98] Coleridge's description of his opium-fuelled nightmares prefigures, with uncanny accuracy, the reactions provoked by such recent fiction: 'Desire with loathing strangely mixed / On wild or hateful objects fixed ('The Pains of Sleep', 23–4). When the object of 'loathing' and the object of 'desire' are fused into one and the same male protagonist, moral discrimination becomes confused. Shakespeare's portrayal of Angelo avoids such moral confusion.

[99] It would, however, be more difficult to make the same distinctions between the conventions of modern fiction and the Duke's behaviour towards Isabella in the final scene.

elections later that same year. An illegitimate offspring, 'alternative facts', was spawned very soon afterwards, in January 2017. The deliberate dissemination of malicious rumours and deceptions posing as truths was prevalent in the claims and counter-claims of the political parties throughout these democratic processes, and subsequently in the 2019 General Election in the UK. If John Keats was correct and 'beauty is truth', then we live in an ugly age politically. Yet *Measure for Measure* prefigures this ugliness: the fact that disinformation is also a frequent and disturbing presence in *Measure for Measure* may lead us to wonder whether there was ever an age in which the truth was inviolate.

The Duke is the primary source of 'fake news' in the play. To disguise his true intent to observe, incognito, his people, his court, and his deputy, he feigns a diplomatic mission to Poland (I, iii, 14–16), deliberately disseminating disinformation in pursuit of his political purposes. According to Lucio, the Duke's disappearance from Vienna has led to public speculation about the Duke's whereabouts and activities:

> Some say he is with the Emperor of Russia; other some, he is in Rome. [III, ii, 85–6]

The rumours are mistaken, but they suggest that the 'fake news' published by the Duke may not have convinced the people of Vienna, who have responded by inventing plausible alternatives. Fake news thus begets fake news in the play, as it does in contemporary society.

Lucio rightly accuses the Duke of deliberate deception:

> The Duke is very strangely gone from hence;
> Bore many gentlemen—myself being one—
> In hand, and hope of action: but we do learn,
> By those that know the very nerves of state,
> His giving out were of an infinite distance
> From his true-meant design. [I, iv, 50–5]

Lucio's words should usually be treated with a measure of scepticism, as his assertions are often fanciful; but here, his general gist is accurate (whether intentionally or not). The Duke indeed 'Bore many gentlemen . . . / In hand' (that is, deceived them): he has already confessed to Friar Thomas (in Act I, scene iii) that his 'giving out' was far from his 'true-meant design'.

In his disguise as Friar Lodowick, Duke Vincentio uses disinformation, ostensibly to bring both Claudio and Isabella to mortification, although it is questionable whether his actions are spiritually beneficial. Rather, he seems to take delight in manipulating the feelings of others by calculated recourse to lies.[100] To Claudio, he claims that, as Angelo's confessor, he knows it to be true that Angelo's proposition to Isabella was a trial of her virtue (III, i, 160–67). The audience, having witnessed the encounters between Angelo and Isabella in Act II, and having heard two soliloquies from Angelo, knows full well that the Deputy's attempted bargain with Isabella was no innocent 'assay of her virtue' but, rather, a criminal attempt to compel her sexual compliance. Alleging that the report derives from a confidant with access to classified information—here, the disguised Duke's claim to be Angelo's confessor—is a characteristic ploy that enables purveyors of 'fake news' and 'alternative facts' to give greater plausibility to invented accounts.[101]

Later, the Duke will lie to Isabella that her brother is dead: 'His head is off, and sent to Angelo' (IV, iii, 115). The Duke's justification, offered in an aside, is that his fabricated

---

[100] Again, this issue is uncomfortably topical, with the general public increasingly aware of (usually domestic) abuse involving a person employing devious psychological means to create dependency by breaking the will of his/her partner.

[101] Perversely, the lies seem to run counter to the Duke's purpose: having convinced Claudio, with these words, that he is about to die, Vincentio will then labour for the remainder of the play to save Claudio from execution.

information will ultimately 'make her heavenly comforts of despair / When it is least expected' (IV, iii, 109–10); but this sounds like special pleading. The obvious immediate effect is to reduce the usually decorous Isabella to tearful threats, laments, and imprecations. Like so many purveyors of 'fake news' and 'alternative facts', the Duke may be suspected of finding gratification in the distress or disruption caused by the disinformation that he disseminates.

The Duke must, however, pay a price for spreading 'fake news'. As he cannot reveal his identity to his interlocutors when he is disguised as Friar Lodowick, he must endure the slanderous 'alternative facts' that Lucio utters about him. Only when he re-emerges as the Duke in the final scene can he express his exasperation at the damaging accounts that Lucio has given of his character:

> And yet here's one in place I cannot pardon.
> You, sirrah, that knew me for a fool, a coward,
> One of all luxury, an ass, a madman:
> Wherein have I so deserv'd of you
> That you extol me thus? [V, I, 497–501]

The Duke's concluding question here is disingenuous as, under the anonymity of disguise, he has lied so extensively to others, for example allowing Lucio to believe that his friend, Claudio, has been executed. In being slandered by Lucio, the Duke has experienced 'measure for measure', in that the disseminator of 'fake news' has become its victim.

As a source of 'fake news' and 'alternative facts', Lucio may appear as guilty as the Duke—but Lucio's slanders are, until the final scene, less calculated and less harmful. Most of Lucio's allegations concerning Angelo are too fanciful to be taken seriously (III, ii, 99–107). Who could believe that Angelo is the spawn of a mermaid (line 104), or the product of copulation between two codfish hung out to dry (line 105)? Yet this—according to Lucio, at least—is the popular report (the 'social media' of the day). Lucio personally testifies to the truth of an obviously whimsical contention: that Angelo is so sexually frigid that his urine emerges as a frozen stream (lines 106–7). The allegation here appears capricious rather than malicious. Although his subsequent descriptions of Angelo as 'ungenerative' (III, ii, 108) and 'ungenitured' (III, ii, 167–8) are potentially more slanderous as they portray the Deputy as sterile or a eunuch, these slurs on Angelo's frigidity seem to be a spontaneous insult or sneer, rather than premeditated disinformation.[102]

As so many of his allegations against Angelo are incontrovertibly fabrications, Lucio's accompanying allegations against the Duke are tainted by association. Nevertheless, they seem more personal than Lucio's assertions about Angelo, because they are more plausible. To contrast with Angelo, the sexless, ascetic intellectual, Lucio represents the Duke as an inveterate lecher, a sot, and a fool (III, ii, 110–36). The sexual allegations are the most extensive and the most insidious. Lucio takes the opportunity to present the Duke's apparently virtuous actions as evidence of his concealed vices: Vincentio's tolerant regime and his charitable support of the poor and needy are distorted into proof of his sympathy for lechers, his begetting of numerous illegitimate children, and his indiscriminate lasciviousness. Lucio will echo some of these allegations in a later scene, calling Vincentio a 'duke of dark corners' (IV, iii, 156) and a 'woodman' (IV, iii, 161), both veiled accusations of carnal promiscuity. In addition, Lucio seeks to give his charges of sexual indulgence validity by claiming intimate acquaintance with Vincentio: 'Sir, I was an inward of his . . . well known to the Duke' (III, ii, 127 and 155). Like so many purveyors of 'fake news' and 'alternative facts', he invents plausible authority to support his fictions.

---

[102] Lucio's allegations, plausibly the result of his exasperation at Angelo's ruthless prosecution of sexual indulgence, should strike an audience as ironic after witnessing Angelo's sexual awakening in the previous Act.

Thus far, however, there is no evidence that Lucio's 'alternative facts' about the Duke have been publicly aired; rather, they seem to have been invented spontaneously, to shock or to embarrass the presumably pious Friar Lodowick, whom Lucio (despite his claim to be an 'inward' of the Duke) has not recognised as Vincentio in disguise.[103] There could be no damage to the Duke's reputation were the allegations to be disseminated no further. In the final scene of the play, however, Lucio's fanciful claims become undeniably malicious allegations—the most damaging kind of 'fake news'. Friar Lodowick, who had threatened to report Lucio's defamations to the Duke (III, ii, 150–62), is now suspected of leading a conspiracy against Lord Angelo. Lucio therefore seeks to attribute to Friar Lodowick his own slanders of the Duke (V, i, 260–2). On the entry of the friar, Lucio seizes the opportunity to exonerate himself from just accusation by bearing false witness against the man who has pledged to testify against him:

Come hither, goodman Baldpate, do you know me? . . . And do you remember what you said of the Duke? . . . And was the Duke a fleshmonger, a fool, and a coward, as you then reported him to be? [V, i, 324–33]

This is Lucio's most damning piece of disinformation, as it is spoken before the court and the assembled people of Vienna. Friar Lodowick, arrested for conspiracy and sedition, becomes a convenient scapegoat as the alleged source of slanders against the Duke—slanders that Lucio himself had devised. Once Friar Lodowick's true identity has been revealed, Lucio's readiness to disseminate 'fake news' and 'alternative facts' will cost him his liberty and his reputation: he will be obliged to marry a woman whom he had dismissed as a whore. As with the Duke, his 'post-truth' performance recoils on him.

---

[103] For a discussion of Nevill Coghill's contention that Lucio sees through Vincentio's disguise, see Chapter 6, 'Lucio the Social Commentator', p. 383n.

As the Duke experiences in his dealings with Lucio, false allegations of sexual impropriety can be particularly damaging. In March 2016, Operation Midland, investigating an alleged VIP paedophile ring in Britain, was concluded without any charges being brought against those investigated, and with profuse apologies and damages to those whose lives had been publicly exposed to scandal by the enquiry. The leading informant to the Midland team, the fantasist Carl Beech, was convicted in July 2019 of perverting the course of justice (together with other offences). Like Carl Beech's accusations against prominent men, Lucio's most lurid and damaging allegations are of a sexual nature. The Duke, accused of being indiscriminately promiscuous in his sexual habits, philosophically observes,

> Nor might nor greatness in mortality
> Can censure 'scape. Back-wounding calumny
> The whitest virtue strikes. What king so strong
> Can tie the gall up in the slanderous tongue?
> [III, ii, 179–82]

Measure for Measure, like the experience of the Operation Midland team, teaches us to be wary of accepting unsubstantiated allegations as categorical truths. Fake allegations, like fake news, destroy reputations and lives.

There is also the case of Angelo to consider in relation to the modern practice of so-called 'revenge porn', whereby a sexual malcontent publishes an incriminating image that humiliates and destroys the reputation of the former partner. This was what Angelo did to Mariana by 'pretending in her discoveries of dishonour' (III, i, 226–7). The penalty that she was obliged to pay was social ostracism for five years, apparently at a refuge for fallen women at 'Saint Luke's; there at the moated grange' (III, i, 265). The victims of modern 'revenge porn' may have willingly participated in an immodest act that they now regret; but Mariana participated in no such shameful pursuit: she is the victim of 'fake news' disseminated by Angelo. By these contemptible means, Angelo sought to justify his mercenary rejection of Mariana, discounting their formal exchange of marriage-vows.

Angelo uses a similar device against Isabella, when she threatens to proclaim his corruption to the people of Vienna. He responds that no-one will believe her because his reputation, his ascetic life, his authority, and his testimony

> Will so your accusation overweigh,
> That you shall stifle in your own report,
> And smell of calumny. [II, iv, 156–8]

According to this complex, powerful imagery, the scales of the law will be so loaded against any just charges that Isabella might bring against Angelo that she will be suffocated by any (vain) attempt to publish her grievances, acquiring the noisome reputation of a slanderer.[104] Again, female 'honour' is threatened by the tyrant Angelo: Isabella faces the dilemma of sacrificing either her reputation (were she to pursue her accusations against Angelo) or her chastity (were she to yield to his demand for her virginity).

It is entirely appropriate dramatically that Angelo, destroyer of the reputation of virtuous women, should ultimately be punished by the destruction of his own reputation for virtue when he is publicly exposed. Under the rule of measure for measure that governs the play, all perpetrators of 'fake news' and 'alternative facts' must pay a proportionate penalty for their misdemeanours.

Isabella is the archetypal victim of male sexual abuse, isolated and seemingly powerless to pursue redress. After Angelo has proposed his perverse exchange to Isabella—her virginity in return for her brother's life—she contemplates her circumstances in her only soliloquy in the play, beginning,

---

[104] The reference to 'smell', suggesting the stench of decomposition, may remind the audience of the corruptive effect of the 'carrion' with which Angelo identified himself in his first soliloquy (II, ii, 165–8).

561

To whom should I complain? Did I tell this,
Who would believe me? [II, iv, 170–1]

Her rhetorical questions presuppose negative answers. She can complain to no-one, because Angelo is 'the voice of the recorded law' (II, iv, 61): in the Duke's absence, there is no higher authority in Vienna. Furthermore, if she were to complain publicly, no-one would believe her because of Angelo's 'unsoil'd name, th'austereness of [his] life, / [His] vouch against [her], and [his] place i'th'state' (II, iv, 154–5).

Just as Isabella fears that she will not be believed when making her accusations against Angelo, so modern society, for too long, has made it difficult for victims of 'invisible' crimes (such as sexual abuse) to obtain justice. When the powerful and privileged commit offences behind closed doors, their weaker, disadvantaged victims may face myriad difficulties and dangers in bringing their ordeals to public notice. Recently, however, abused women world-wide have sought strength through fellowship in sharing their experiences via #MeToo. Measure for Measure foreshadows this twenty-first-century development when Isabella and Mariana offer each other mutual belief and support in their efforts to call their abuser, Angelo, to account.

These two victims of Angelo's injustice work in close conjunction in the final Acts of the play, each offering encouragement or assistance to the other when she might falter or fail. Although it is the disguised Duke who formulates the 'bed trick' whereby Mariana (instead of Isabella) will accept Angelo's embraces, it is Isabella who undertakes to persuade Mariana to participate. In exchanges that are represented as taking place off-stage (between lines 60 and 65 of Act IV scene i), Isabella must inform Mariana of Angelo's indecent proposal to her, and secure Mariana's agreement to take Isabella's place in Angelo's bed, to repeal the death-sentence on Isabella's brother. As both women have fallen victim to the duplicity of Angelo, each would be thought more likely to believe the other's account, in spite of Angelo's reputation for asceticism and virtue.

Subsequent to their first meeting in the play, the two ill-treated women remain mutually supportive, their joint evidence establishing the case against Angelo. Immediately before the final trial-scene, when Isabella expresses doubts about her instructions 'To speak so indirectly . . . / . . . to veil full purpose' (IV, vi, 1–4), it is Mariana who persuades her to comply with the simple advice, 'Be rul'd by him' (IV, vi, 4), where 'him' is the friar who has briefed them both on how to address the court. Ultimately, during the trial, the two women employ apparently conflicting accounts of Angelo's conduct to confuse the Deputy prior to his final exposure as a common criminal. They are shown to gain confidence and power from working together to bring to justice the man who has abused them both.

Finally, with Angelo publicly discredited and condemned, Isabella and Mariana combine to secure Angelo's reprieve. Although Mariana has suffered five years of grief, shame, and loneliness because of Angelo's maltreatment, she remains faithful to him: 'I crave no other, nor no better man' (V, i, 424). When the Duke appears to reject Mariana's appeal to save Angelo, Mariana turns to Isabella to intercede on behalf of her and of her newly-wedded husband. Isabella responds with a substantial plea for leniency, even though she has been the victim of Angelo's sexual blackmail, and believes her brother executed by the very man for whose life she is pleading (V, i, 441–52). Ultimately, the combined strength of the two appeals achieves its objective. As Lucio observed early in the play,

> . . . when maidens sue,
> Men give like gods; but when they weep and kneel,
> All their petitions are as freely theirs
> As they themselves would owe them. [I, iv, 80–3]

The two female victims, wronged by the same powerful man, ultimately achieve justice by believing in each other's causes, combining their efforts, and increasing their strength through unity, until they triumph over their oppressor. They have the grace to show mercy when the balance of power eventually tips in their favour, even though their former oppressor showed no mercy to them when he held sway. It may be too much to hope that *#MeToo* can lead to such reconciliation between abusers and abused, but *Measure for Measure* offers a compellingly idealistic vision of the virtues of compassion and forgiveness in such circumstances.

Looking Back

Measure for Measure has suffered from prejudice for most of its life. The Seventeenth Century, convinced that the play had been born ugly, strove to obscure its perceived deformities, either by concealing it entirely from public view, or by over-dressing it in borrowed clothes. In the Eighteenth Century, any putative blemishes detected on William Shakespeare's offspring were assiduously removed from sight, for fear of adversely affecting the reputation of the revered parent. In the ethically-obsessed Nineteenth Century, *Measure for Measure* was stigmatised as a problem child corrupting others with foul language, lewd conduct, and an obstinate refusal to endorse orthodox moral behaviour. Critical reports were filed for many years before this alleged delinquent was ultimately identified as a member of a subversive gang that included *All's Well that Ends Well* and *Troilus and Cressida*. It was proposed that these problematical siblings should suffer exclusion, for fear that the reputation of the moral majority of Shakespeare's other progeny would be tainted by association. In the second quarter of the Twentieth Century, however, probation was granted when the capacity of *Measure for Measure* to promulgate Christian doctrine caused excitement. Since then, this previously much-maligned member of Shakespeare's abundant dramatic family has frequently been recruited as a political agent, a powerful voice capable of swaying opinion on a wide range of social issues. Most importantly, after more than 350 years of stigmatisation, the virtues of the former pariah are now (more or less universally) recognised and acknowledged.

Particular credit for the rehabilitation of *Measure for Measure* should be given to William Poel. At the end of the Nineteenth Century, he established that the play works best as Shakespeare wrote it, in a performing-space where the audience, by observing the actors closely, can develop a more sympathetic understanding of the characters. Since then, performances on apron stages, in the round, and on screen have explored the potential of a play in which too much psychological detail is lost when it is heavily edited or adapted, when theatregoers are too remote from performers to distinguish subtleties, and when actors are obliged to revert to a declamatory style. The BBC television-productions of 1979 and 1994 confirmed that *Measure for Measure* is particularly well suited to performance on the small screen. The soliloquies from Angelo and Isabella, the Duke's frequent choric monologues, and the unusual frequency of sustained duologues in this play[105] are opportunities for the camera to establish an air of intimacy while scrutinising gesture, facial expression, and vocal nuance for shades of meaning. Similarly, in theatres with audiences in close proximity to performers, there is every opportunity for actors to suggest the full psychological complexity of the characters whom they are portraying. Such performances encourage an audience to empathise with the characters and their circumstances, rather than merely to condemn their faults from a critical distance. The humanity of Shakespeare's creations, and the intensity of their dilemmas, have been fully revealed in recent years by these more 'intimate' full-text productions of *Measure for Measure* on stage and screen.

We encounter an unusually wide range of Shakespeare's dramatic art in *Measure for Measure*. The play has the power to challenge and to amuse, to distress and to delight, both on the

---

[105] For example, those between Lucio and Claudio (II, i), the Duke and Friar Thomas (I, iii), Isabella and Lucio (I, iv), Isabella and Angelo (II, ii and II, iv), the Duke and Claudio (III, i), Isabella and Claudio (III, i), the Duke and Isabella (III, i and IV, iii), and the Duke and Lucio (III, ii and IV, iii).

page and on the stage. While artfully balancing tragic and comic elements, it explores many of the complex social, legal, political, and moral issues that embrace both Shakespeare's world and our contemporary society. *Measure for Measure* weighs anarchy against authority, indulgence against abstinence. Criminal excess is ultimately moderated by merciful judgement. Sexual licence is ultimately moderated by marriage. Although the play may have begun its dramatic life in response to the interest created by the political writings of a new monarch, James I, it continues to hold up a mirror to society over 400 years later, when James Stuart's opinions no longer concern or affect the day-to-day workings of the contemporary world. Such is the enduring power of Shakespeare's dramatic writing in *Measure for Measure*: it is a complex, fascinating, and relevant play that richly rewards thoughtful study, imaginative staging, and frequent viewing.

Appendix 1

Measuring the Time-Scheme

Let's postulate that two critics are discussing the time-scheme of *Measure for Measure*. Critic A argues that the play is chronologically compressed, representing no more than the passage of four days between the opening and closing curtains. Critic B demurs, maintaining that the play is expansive, representing the passage of months, or even years, within the scope of its five Acts. What are the possibilities? That A is correct? That B is correct? That both are wrong? Surely, both cannot be right! Yet both can cite apparently irrefutable evidence in support of their opinions. Here is a further illustration of why, as implied in the title *Measure for Measure*, we need to weigh evidence thoroughly and impartially before reaching our conclusions.

Support for Critic B's expansive time-scheme might begin with certain specific chronological references in *Measure for Measure*. Mariana was betrothed to Angelo 'five years since' (V, i, 216), during which period she has become acquainted with Friar Lodowick, the alias that the Duke assumed only *after* relinquishing government. Mariana can speak of the friar as 'a man of comfort, whose advice / Hath *often* still'd my brawling discontent' (IV, i, 10–11; italics added). Her words suggest a protracted period of intimate contact between them, an impression reinforced when she confirms her confidence in Lodowick: 'Good friar, I know you do [respect me], and so have found it' (IV, i, 54). Barnadine has been a prisoner for 'nine years', but it is only since the Duke's departure that compelling evidence has emerged to convict him as a murderer (IV, ii, 129–37), since when he has been tried and sentenced by Angelo. As for the duration of the Duke's government, there is seemingly contradictory evidence. According to Claudio, 'nineteen zodiacs have gone round' since the 'drowsy and

567

neglected act' against fornication was enforced (I, ii, 157–9); whereas the Duke himself maintains that he mitigated the 'strict statutes and most biting laws' for a mere 'fourteen years' (I, iv, 19–21).[1] The general sense of each of these two apparently contradictory claims is, however, congruent: for many years, the laws of Vienna have been applied with a light touch by the Duke (and, possibly, by his imagined predecessor), only for Angelo, on his appointment, to release the full force of Vienna's forgotten legislation on a shocked populace. Logically, such a transformation in the government of the city would require a considerable lapse of time between Vincentio's departure (in I, i) and the earliest evidence that the policies introduced by Angelo are biting (in I, ii). During this hiatus, Claudio and Julietta have been tried and 'Condemn'd upon the act of fornication' (V, i, 73); while a proclamation has been issued that 'all . . . houses of resort [i.e. brothels] in the suburbs' must be 'pulled down' (I, ii, 86–94). Since Angelo was appointed Deputy, the administration of the law in Vienna has been radicalised. Such a transformation presupposes the passage of weeks or months, rather than days or hours, between Act I scene i (the Duke's departure) and Act I scene ii (the earliest evidence of Angelo's new, stringent regime).

The scene that follows, however, would seem to support Critic A's position that the time-scheme is rigorously compressed. In Act I scene iii, the Duke appears in the friary as if fresh from his retreat from the Viennese court. He explains in the future tense (rather than the present) his plans to test whether Angelo's 'power' will 'change' his 'purpose': 'Hence *shall* we see' (I, iii, 53–4; italics added). He has yet to put his strategy into action, confirmed when he announces his intention to disguise himself as a mendicant and asks for appropriate instruction (lines 43–8). His words suggest that, chronologically, this scene should immediately follow Act I, scene i, with Vincentio arriving in the friary on the day of his

---

[1] Such an error could be attributed to the difficulty faced by a First Folio scribe or compositor in distinguishing between the Roman numerals xix and xiv.

departure from the Viennese court.[2] Such evidence implies a lapse of (at most) hours, rather than days, weeks, or months, between Act I, scene i, and Act I, scene iii.

By Act II, scene i, Elbow can refer to Mistress Overdone as one 'whose house . . . was . . . plucked down in the suburbs; and now she professes a hot-house; which I think is a very ill house too' (II, i, 63–6). The tavern/brothel in the suburbs having been demolished, Mistress Overdone has now established a new bath-house/brothel, presumably, in the city (see I, ii, 88–92), where she has already built up her custom and incurred the interest of Constable Elbow. Such a process would again require weeks or months, rather than days or hours, which provides plausible support for Critic B's position.

Yet, according to a series of references to time in the text, Mistress Overdone had first learned of the imminent demolition of her old brothel only a few hours, at most, before Elbow's condemnation of her new brothel. The chain of evidence begins in Act I, scene ii. Lucio, dispatched from Mistress Overdone's (pre-demolition) tavern/brothel in the suburbs to intercept Claudio on his way to prison, promises the condemned man that he will secure the assistance of Isabella '[w]ithin two hours' (I, ii, 183). On meeting Lucio, Isabella pledges to petition Angelo that same day, so that she can send her brother 'soon at night' news of her 'success' (I, iv, 88–9). Haste is necessary as Claudio is to be executed 'by nine tomorrow morning' (II, i, 34). This would mean that Isabella has her first meeting with

---

[2] In performance, scenes ii and iii of Act I might be transposed in the interests of logical chronology. Vincentio departs from his court nine lines before the end of scene i, sufficient hiatus to allow for an audience to accept his relocation to the friary after the scene-change. The scene involving Mistress Overdone, Pompey, Lucio, and Claudio might then occur an indefinite time afterwards. Although, in its current position, scene iii (in the friary) might appear as a 'flashback' to modern audiences familiar with such cinematographic devices, the evidence of other Elizabethan and Jacobean plays suggests that Shakespeare's audience expected a stricter chronological sequence of events.

Angelo (II, ii) on the day that Claudio urged Lucio to enlist his sister's help. It follows that Mistress Overdone's first appearance in Act I, scene ii, and Elbow's testimony against her in Act II, scene i, must occur on this same day (Critic A's Day 1); and yet, in that implausibly brief time, she has apparently transformed her place of residence, the ostensible nature of her business, and her clientele, a chronology which Critic B would dismiss as impossible.

The precise schedule for the execution of Claudio is one of the more contentious issues in the play. When his name is first mentioned by Mistress Overdone, she informs us that he is to be executed 'within these three days' (I, ii, 62–3). This time-scheme might suggest a gap of at least a day between Act I, scene ii, and Act II, scene i, where Angelo instructs the Provost,

> See that Claudio
> Be executed by nine tomorrow morning. . . . [II, i, 33–4]

This schedule for the execution is first confirmed and then contradicted in the very next scene. Initially, Angelo insists both to the Provost (II, ii, 7–14) and to Isabella (twice: II, ii, 82 and 106) that Claudio must die 'tomorrow'. After hearing Isabella's plea for her brother's life, however, Angelo instructs her to continue her petition 'tomorrow . . . / At any time 'fore noon' (II, ii, 156–61). Logically, any plea entered between 9.00 a.m. and noon on that day would be vain, as Isabella's brother's life would already have been forfeited. It must be assumed that Claudio has secured a day's reprieve, even though there is no direct reference in the text to any command to delay his execution for twenty-four hours (that is, until the morning of Critic A's Day 3).

It follows that the Duke's confession of Julietta in Act II scene iii occurs early on Critic A's Day 2 (following Isabella's first interview with Angelo towards the end of Day 1). The Provost now informs the Duke/friar that Claudio is to be executed 'tomorrow' (line 16), news that the Duke repeats to Julietta—'Your partner, as I hear, must die tomorrow'—and that Julietta echoes in desperation (lines 37–40). These repeated references to Claudio's imminent execution (supporting Critic A's reading of the time-scheme) heighten the dramatic tension.[3]

On this same morning, Isabella returns to Angelo as instructed, only to be solicited by him for her sexual favours. He demands of her, 'Answer me tomorrow' (II, iv, 166), at which she immediately flies to the prison to confer with her brother. It follows that the whole of Act III must take place on the same day as Act II scene iv (Critic A's Day 2), when Claudio was originally scheduled for execution 'by nine' in the 'morning'. Isabella now informs Claudio that 'Tomorrow you set on' (III, i, 60) and that 'thou diest tomorrow' (III, i, 102), apparently privy to the assumed stay of execution until Day 3. The Duke, disguised as Friar Lodowick, also informs Claudio that 'tomorrow you must die' (III, i, 167). These references sustain the tension, confirming that Claudio's execution remains imminent, even though they presuppose knowledge on the part of both speakers that the condemned man has secured the twenty-four-hour reprieve.

Very soon after her encounter with her brother (in performance, a few minutes of unbroken dialogue), Isabella is dispatched by Friar Lodowick back to Angelo, with the instruction, 'if *for this night* he entreat you to his bed, give him promise of satisfaction' (III, i, 263–4; italics added). The bed-trick, then, is to take place on the night of Angelo's ultimatum to Isabella (Day 2), as Vincentio confirms at the end of the Act: 'With Angelo *tonight* shall lie / His old betrothed, but despised' (III, ii, 271–2; italics added).[4]

---

[3] Braunmuller and Watson (p. 222n.) record that the word 'tomorrow' occurs twenty-five times in *Measure for Measure*, more than in any other play by Shakespeare, and most often in relation to the proposed schedule for Claudio's execution. At times in the text, statements that Claudio's execution will be 'tomorrow' seem to be repeated out of habit, rather than to supply a plausible chronology.

[4] With reference to Mariana's accusation against Angelo—'But Tuesday night last gone, in's garden house, / He knew me as a wife'

571

It follows that the first scene of Act IV must occur on the evening of Day 2, with Mariana agreeing to the bed-trick as '[t]he vaporous night approaches' (line 58). In this scene, as we have already noted, Mariana twice speaks of her long familiarity with, and trust of, the friar—as if in support of Critic B's extended time-scheme. The specific references to time in the preceding scenes, however, indicate that this is the same day on which Vincentio first appeared as Friar Lodowick at the prison (II, iii), having assumed the guise of a friar (at most) the day before, on Critic A's Day 1. Such a tight schedule would offer insufficient time for Vincentio to have comforted Mariana 'often', or to have won her trust entirely by frequent instances of his esteem for her.

In the next scene, set in the prison, it is approaching 'dead midnight' (IV, ii, 62) on Critic A's Day 2, that same 'heavy middle of the night' (IV, i, 34) at which time Isabella has pledged to satisfy Angelo's sexual demands. After the midnight tryst, Angelo's perfidious message to the Provost advances the execution by four hours (IV, ii, 118–20), increasing the suspense by making a strategy to save Claudio still more urgently required. By the end of the scene, 'it is almost clear dawn' (IV, ii, 209) on Day 3, and Claudio's execution expected at any moment. To save Claudio's life, Friar Lodowick promises the Provost that the Duke will return to government 'within these two days' (IV, ii, 197), a reference that determines the schedule for the remaining action in the play: all will be completed before the end of Critic A's Day 4.

There is no time-lapse between this scene and the next (Act IV, scene iii), as Pompey and Abhorson attempt to bring Barnadine to the block to supply the severed head required 'by five' (IV, ii, 121) on the morning of Day 3. Subsequently in this scene, the Duke reassures the Provost that 'Ere twice the sun hath made his journal greeting' (IV, iii, 88) he will be safe from

---

(V, i, 228-9)—Critic A might argue that the four-day time-scheme of the play runs from Monday to Thursday.

any consequences of deceiving Angelo. His words confirm Vincentio's intention to return to government on Day 4. Immediately afterwards, Vincentio informs Isabella that 'The Duke comes home tomorrow' (IV, iii, 127). This third day concludes with Angelo's 'Good night' to Escalus in the ensuing scene (IV, iv, 17), after they have read the Duke's letters announcing his return the following day.

It follows that the two concluding scenes of Act IV take place on the fourth and last day, the morning of Vincentio's return. The Duke indicates that he is meeting with courtiers 'anon' (IV, v, 13)—that is, 'immediately' (or 'soon', at least)—before his progress into the city. This pageant is under way by the time that Friar Peter meets Isabella and Mariana in Act IV, scene vi. The grand finale of Act V follows immediately, one continuous scene which represent dramatically that same period of time that it occupies in performance.

Critic A would make the case for a chronologically compressed time-scheme by insisting that, according to Shakespeare's explicit textual signposts, commencing in Act I, scene ii, Claudio is first introduced to the audience on Day 1, with his execution scheduled for Day 2. Implicitly, his sentence is then delayed until Day 3, to allow time for Isabella's second meeting with Angelo. Claudio is freed on Day 4, when the Duke returns to government. Critic A, in arguing that plausibility must be sacrificed in response to the need for dramatic impetus, would maintain that Angelo's appointment as deputy (I, i), Claudio's public humiliation on the streets of Vienna (I, ii), Vincentio's conference with Friar Thomas (I, iii), Isabella's first meeting with Lucio (I, iv), the trial of Pompey and Froth (II, i), and Angelo's first interview with Isabella (II, ii) all occur during the course of a single day: Day 1.

Set against Critic A's contracted time scheme, we have Critic B's protracted time-scheme concerned with broader contexts than Claudio's execution. Critic B's evidence is generally implicit rather than explicit. For example, on his first appearance after quitting his court, Vincentio announces that

573

Angelo 'supposes me travelled to Poland' (I, iii, 14)—a journey of several hundred kilometres that might take weeks, rather than mere hours. Subsequently, the possibility is expressed that Vincentio is 'with the Emperor of Russia' or 'in Rome' (III, ii, 85–6). Had the Duke completed any of these substantial journeys, that might plausibly have allowed Angelo a sufficient period to redirect the ship of state. Mistress Overdone's remark, 'in the Duke's time' (III, i, 458), is a further suggestion that the Duke has been long absent. Such an extended period would bridge the interval between the first and second scenes of the play. In that case, the third scene could be (rather unconvincingly) explained as implying that Vincentio, who has 'ever lov'd the life remov'd' (I, iii, 8), withdrew to a cloister where he waited for an indefinite but protracted period before announcing to Friar Thomas his proposal to disguise himself as a friar. Meanwhile, Mistress Overdone and Pompey, evicted from their demolished tavern/brothel in the suburbs, have set up a bath house/brothel elsewhere in the city, attracting new clientele. During this period, the Duke, in the guise of Friar Lodowick, has become confessor to Mariana, frequently comforting her and gradually gaining her confidence. These circumstances logically require weeks, months, or even years to have lapsed during the course of Act I.

It would seem, then, that Critic A and Critic B have both observed the play conscientiously, but that their observations need to be combined to provide even a moderately satisfactory overview. Conflicting dramatic demands in *Measure for Measure* require that some references that suggest a considerable passage of time should be set against other references that compress the main action of the plot into a much shorter period, perhaps merely four days. Audiences subconsciously register that the plot requires sufficient time for a duke to conduct a putative overseas embassy whilst actually practising the functions of a friar, for that friar to form a close relationship, based on trust, with an abandoned woman, for a deputy to introduce and to enforce substantial governmental reforms, and for a brothel-keeper to transfer her business from suburb to city. Nevertheless, to sustain dramatic tension, the

574

beheading of the condemned man, anticipated early in the play, must constantly appear so imminent that the event is likely to occur within hours, or even minutes. A degree of inconsistency—both in the time-scheme and in the characterisation—proves dramatically expedient in ensuring the successful resolution of the plot. This reading proposes that a kind of dramatic equilibrium should be observed between Critic A's compressed time-scheme and Critic B's expanded time-scheme.

Unfortunately, as we have already seen, no such neat formula can fully resolve all the contradictions in the text between specific references to time. This is particularly true of two consecutive scenes in Act IV. Examination of scenes ii and iii suggests that certain problematical chronological references are simply errors, rather than an ingenious dramatic ploy to run two conflicting time-schemes simultaneously. In proposing the 'head-trick' as a remedy, the Duke first requests of the Provost 'four days' respite' (IV, ii, 159–60) before Angelo is removed from authority, but almost immediately produces evidence of the Duke's return to government 'within these two days' (IV, ii, 197). As, on the same day, the Duke/friar confirms to Isabella that 'The Duke comes home tomorrow' (IV, iii, 127), the extra days initially requested from the Provost simply disappear from consideration. At line 51, the Provost has instructed Abhorson to provide his axe by 'tomorrow, four o'clock' even though, under a dozen lines later, the Provost informs Claudio that his execution is scheduled for 'eight tomorrow' (line 62). It is not until line 119 that the Provost receives Angelo's command for Claudio's execution to be advanced by four hours to 'four of the clock', the time that he had earlier conveyed to Abhorson as if by clairvoyance. The inconsistency, presumably the result of an error in the text, may cause confusion to an audience. Similarly, it is at 'dead midnight' (line 62) that Claudio is told that he will be 'made immortal . . . by eight tomorrow', that is, he will be executed in eight hours' time; yet, at line 91, it is still 'tomorrow' that 'he must die', although it is 'near the dawning' at this moment (line 92), 'almost day' by line 104, and 'almost clear dawn' at line 209. Another day has been added to the schedule for Claudio's execution: he was originally to die on Day 2; then his appointment with death was implicitly rescheduled for Day 3; but now it seems that the execution will take place on Day 4. A further discrepancy occurs in scene iii, when the Duke greets Isabella with 'Good morning' at line 111, but Lucio greets the Duke with 'Good even' at line 148. On this evidence, Act IV, scene iii would seem to encompass Day 3 (from dawn to dusk) in under forty lines, with no obvious lapse in the intervening dialogue to account for such a substantial passage of time. These inconsistencies in chronology suggest mistakes rather than any inscrutable dramatic motive.

Although we cannot be certain to what extent Shakespeare deliberately or inadvertently incorporated all the conflicting references to time into the text of *Measure for Measure,* we can at least assess their general dramatic effect. The impact of a so-called 'dual time scheme' in *Othello,* another Shakespearian play first performed soon after the reopening of the Southwark theatres in April 1604, has been much discussed since the discrepancy first drew critical attention in the Seventeenth Century. More recently, it has been suggested that a comparable dual time-scheme functions in *Measure for Measure.* The 'short measure' of time identified by Critic A and the 'long measure' deduced by Critic B coexist in one and the same play. As the plot of *Measure for Measure* unfolds, reference may be offered to whichever time-scheme is appropriate or expedient to the particular context, thereby ensuring the audience's understanding of, and engagement with, the immediate dramatic situation. Even if the resultant contradictions were to be noticed, they should not significantly impair enjoyment of the play. When an injection of pace or tension is demanded, explicit reference to Critic A's 'short measure' can be relied upon to deliver the necessary excitement; but when plausibility is paramount, implicit reference to Critic B's 'long measure' will offer a convincingly expansive time-perspective. Most members of an audience, borne along by the pace of the performance, would not pause to consider the discrepancies between the two 'measures'.